THE ROUTLEDGE COMPANION TO PERFORMANCE PHILOSOPHY

The Routledge Companion to Performance Philosophy is a volume of especially commissioned critical essays, conversations, and collaborative, creative and performative writing mapping the key contexts, debates, methods, discourses and practices in this developing field.

Firstly, the collection offers new insights on the fundamental question of how thinking happens: where, when, how and by whom philosophy is performed. Secondly, it provides a plurality of new accounts of performance and performativity – as the production of ideas, bodies and knowledges – in the arts and beyond. Comprising texts written by international artists, philosophers and scholars from multiple disciplines, the essays engage with questions of how performance thinks and how thought is performed in a wide range of philosophies and performances, from the ancient to the contemporary. Concepts and practices from diverse geographical regions and cultural traditions are analysed to draw conclusions about how performance operates across art, philosophy and everyday life.

The collection both contributes to and critiques the philosophy *of* music, dance, theatre and performance, exploring the idea of a philosophy *from* the arts. It is crucial reading material for those interested in the hierarchy of the relationship between philosophy and the arts, advancing debates on philosophical method, and the relation between Performance and Philosophy more broadly.

Laura Cull Ó Maoilearca is Professor and Head of DAS Graduate School at the Academy of Theatre and Dance, Amsterdam.

Alice Lagaay is Professor of Cultural Philosophy and Aesthetics in the Design Department at Hamburg University of Applied Sciences, Germany.

ROUTLEDGE THEATRE AND PERFORMANCE COMPANIONS

THE ROUTLEDGE COMPANION TO THEATRE, PERFORMANCE AND COGNITIVE SCIENCE
Edited by Rick Kemp and Bruce McConachie

THE ROUTLEDGE COMPANION TO AFRICAN AMERICAN THEATRE AND PERFORMANCE
Edited by Kathy A. Perkins, Sandra L. Richards, Renée Alexander Craft, and Thomas F. DeFrantz

THE ROUTLEDGE COMPANION TO THEATRE OF THE OPPRESSED
Edited by Kelly Howe, Julian Boal, and José Soeiro

THE ROUTLEDGE COMPANION TO THEATRE AND POLITICS
Edited by Peter Eckersall and Helena Grehan

THE ROUTLEDGE COMPANION TO DANCE STUDIES
Edited by Helen Thomas and Stacey Prickett

THE ROUTLEDGE COMPANION TO PERFORMANCE PRACTITIONERS
Edited by Franc Chamberlain and Bernadette Sweeney

THE ROUTLEDGE COMPANION TO PERFORMANCE PHILOSOPHY
Edited by Laura Cull Ó Maoilearca and Alice Lagaay

THE ROUTLEDGE COMPANION TO THEATRE AND PERFORMANCE HISTORIOGRAPHY
Edited by Tracy C. Davis and Peter W. Marx

For more information about this series, please visit: https://www.routledge.com/handbooks/products/SCAR30

THE ROUTLEDGE COMPANION TO PERFORMANCE PHILOSOPHY

Edited by Laura Cull Ó Maoilearca and Alice Lagaay

LONDON AND NEW YORK

First published 2020
by Routledge
2 Park Square, Milton Park, Abingdon, Oxon OX14 4RN

and by Routledge
52 Vanderbilt Avenue, New York, NY 10017

Routledge is an imprint of the Taylor & Francis Group, an informa business

© 2020 selection and editorial matter, Laura Cull Ó Maoilearca and
Alice Lagaay; individual chapters, the contributors

The right of Laura Cull Ó Maoilearca and Alice Lagaay to be identified
as the authors of the editorial material, and of the authors for their
individual chapters, has been asserted in accordance with sections 77 and
78 of the Copyright, Designs and Patents Act 1988.

All rights reserved. No part of this book may be reprinted or reproduced
or utilised in any form or by any electronic, mechanical, or other
means, now known or hereafter invented, including photocopying and
recording, or in any information storage or retrieval system, without
permission in writing from the publishers.

Trademark notice: Product or corporate names may be trademarks
or registered trademarks, and are used only for identification and
explanation without intent to infringe.

British Library Cataloguing-in-Publication Data
A catalogue record for this book is available from the British Library

Library of Congress Cataloging-in-Publication Data
Names: Cull, Laura, editor. | Lagaay, Alice, editor.
Title: The Routledge companion to performance philosophy /
edited by Laura Cull Ó Maoilearca and Alice Lagaay.
Description: Abingdon, Oxon; New York, NY: Routledge, 2020. |
Series: Routledge companions; 18 |
Includes bibliographical references and index.
Identifiers: LCCN 2020000649 | ISBN 9781138495623 (hardback) |
ISBN 9781003035312 (ebook)
Subjects: LCSH: Performing arts—Philosophy.
Classification: LCC PN1584 .R59 2020 | DDC 791.01—dc23
LC record available at https://lccn.loc.gov/2020000649

ISBN: 978-1-138-49562-3 (hbk)
ISBN: 978-1-003-03531-2 (ebk)

Typeset in Bembo
by codeMantra

For Ren Stephen Zerdy Daddario

CONTENTS

List of illustrations *xii*
List of contributors *xv*

Introduction 1
Laura Cull Ó Maoilearca and Alice Lagaay

PART I
Genealogies, contexts and traditions 19

1 Performances of philosophy in Ancient Greece and in modernity: suddenly a philosopher enters the stage 21
Ira Avneri and Freddie Rokem

2 Theravādin Buddhist philosophy and practice in relation to performance 34
Jerri Daboo

3 Performance philosophy and spirituality: the way of *tasawwuf* 42
Michael Ellison and Hannah McClure

4 Whose *Tempest*? Performance philosophy and/as decolonial cacophony 53
Andrés Fabián Henao Castro

5 The playwright as thinker: modern drama and performance philosophy 61
David Kornhaber

6 Performance Philosophy seen through Nishida's 'acting intuition' 69
   Mayuko Uehara and Elisabeth L. Belgrano

7 Performance in Anglo-American philosophy 77
   Anna Pakes and David Davies

8 Performance Philosophy in Latin America: how to perform a Utopia called America? 88
   Luciana da Costa Dias

9 Diminishing returns: on the performativity of musical sound 97
   Anthony Gritten

10 Performance Philosophy and the philosophy of mediality 109
   Jörg Sternagel, Elisabeth Schäfer and Volkmar Mühleis

11 The theatre of research 117
   Anke Haarmann

PART II
Questions and debates 125

12 Opening the circle, towards a radical equality: performance philosophy and animals 127
   Laura Cull Ó Maoilearca

13 Performance Philosophy as inter-philosophical dialogue 140
   Cosimo Zene

14 Decolonizing performance philosophies 153
   Melissa Blanco Borelli, Anamaría Tamayo Duque and Cristina Fernandes Rosa

15 Theatre-thinking: philosophy from the stage 166
   Flore Garcin-Marrou

16 Philosophy and theatre: incestuous beginnings, looking daggers and other dangerous liaisons – a dialogue 174
   Emmanuel Alloa and Sophie-Thérèse Krempl

17 Aesthetics of [the] invisible: presence in Indian performance theory 182
   Sreenath Nair

PART III
Methods, techniques, genres and forms   193

18 Performing phenomenological methodology   195
    Maxine Sheets-Johnstone

19 Daring to transform academic routines: cultures of knowledge and
    their performances   204
    Jörg Holkenbrink and Anna Seitz

20 Resonance of two   213
    Karen Christopher

21 *Lying Fallow:* anonymity and collectivity   223
    Rajni Shah

22 Play in performance philosophy   245
    Alice Koubová

23 Landscape performance   253
    Tess Denman-Cleaver

24 Re-telling the self: the lived experience of modern
    yoga practice   262
    Theodora Wildcroft

25 The think tank: institution as performance   272
    Sonya Dyer

26 Touch   280
    Naomi Woo

27 In-between: a methodology of Performative Philosophy:
    thoughts on embodiment and the public (with Helmuth Plessner)
    reflecting the philosophy-performance-festival [soundcheck
    philosophie]   288
    Eva Maria Gauss and Katrin Felgenhauer

28 Africanist choreography as cultural citizenship: Thomas 'Talawa'
    Prestø's philosophy of Africana dance   299
    'Funmi Adewole

PART IV
Figures   **311**

29 Rūmī   313
   Will Daddario

30 Adrian Piper   317
   Lauren Fournier

31 Diogenes   322
   Yunus Tuncel

32 A dice thrower   326
   Mischa Twitchin

33 Open text – open performance: Hélène Cixous and Ariane Mnouchkine   330
   Elisabeth Schäfer, Esther Hutfless and Gertrude Postl

34 Roger Federer   335
   Einav Katan-Schmid

35 26 Mesostics Re and not Re John Cage   339
   Anthony Gritten

36 Confucius   347
   Mi You

37 Rudolf Laban   351
   Juliet Chambers-Coe

PART V
Performance as Philosophy and Philosophy as Performance   **363**

38 Theater as if theory   365
   Esther Neff and Yelena Gluzman

39 Dance as embodied ethics   379
   Aili Bresnahan, Einav Katan-Schmid and Sara Houston

40 Philosophy on Stage   387
   Arno Böhler and Susanne Valerie [Granzer]

41	Pas de Deux: Écriture Féminine Performative *Tina Chanter and Tawny Andersen*	397
42	Onanism, handjobs, smut: performances of self-valorization *Fumi Okiji*	405
43	Explosions of 'creative indifference'. Salomo Friedlaender, Sun Ra, serendipity and the idea of a 'heliocentre' *Alice Lagaay in conversation with Hartmut Geerken*	415
44	In the making – an incomplete consideration of the first decade of *Every house has a door* 2008 to 2018 as performance philosophy *Will Daddario, Matthew Goulish and Lin Hixson*	424
45	Blackout: thinking with darkness *Tru Paraha and Theron Schmidt*	437
Index		447

ILLUSTRATIONS

Figures

3.1	A sema gathering in Konya at Şeb-i Arus celebration time. Photo credit: Güvenç Özgür	48
6.1	Elisabeth L. Belgrano, *Frozen Moment 2* (2019). Elisabeth L. Belgrano	72
11.1	Alexander von Humboldt and Aimé Bonpland in the Amazon Jungle. Painting by Eduard Ender, 1850	118
11.2	*Critical Art Ensemble Target Deception. Video Stills.* Critical Art Ensemble http://critical-art.net/target-deception-2007/	122
12.1	A photograph of the author, age 17, just before leaving to go to art school. Authors own	128
12.2	*Sheep Pig Goat*, Wellcome Collection and Fevered Sleep. Image by Ben Gilbert for Wellcome	133
12.3	*Sheep Pig Goat*, Wellcome Collection and Fevered Sleep. Image by Ben Gilbert for Wellcome	135
12.4	*Sheep Pig Goat*, Wellcome Collection and Fevered Sleep. Image by Ben Gilbert for Wellcome	136
12.5	*Sheep Pig Goat*, Wellcome Collection and Fevered Sleep. Image by Ben Gilbert for Wellcome	137
12.6	*Sheep Pig Goat*, Wellcome Collection and Fevered Sleep. Image by Ben Gilbert for Wellcome	137
14.1	Image from Rafael Palacios' Sankofa Danzafro, *Fecha Límite* (2017). Sergio Gonzáles Álvarez	158
20.1	Sophie Grodin (left) and Karen Christopher (right) in *Control Signal* (2013). Jemima Yong	216
20.2	Sophie Grodin (left) and Karen Christopher (right) in *Control Signal* (2013). Jemima Yong	216
20.3	Sophie Grodin (left) and Karen Christopher (right) in *Control Signal* (2013). Jemima Yong	219
20.4	Sophie Grodin (left) and Karen Christopher (right) in *Control Signal* (2013). Jemima Yong	219

20.5	Karen Christopher (left) and Sophie Grodin (right) in *Control Signal* (2013). Jemima Yong	221
28.1	Thomas Prestø, *I:Object* (2018). Tale Hendnes/Tabanka dance ensemble and Dansens Hus, Norway	303
28.2	Thomas Prestø, *I:Object* (2018). Tale Hendnes/Tabanka dance ensemble and Dansens Hus, Norway	306
37.1	Circles in the dimensional planes by Sylvia Bodmer, 1959. N/C/PE/1/66 from the University of Surrey Archive, University of Surrey	353
37.2	A figure in an icosahedron by Rudolf Laban, 1938–40. L/C/5/83 from the University of Surrey Archive, University of Surrey	354
37.3	Three figures around edges of an icosahedron by Rudolf Laban, 1938–40. L/C/6/89 from the University of Surrey Archive, University of Surrey	354
37.4	Figure in a tetrahedron by Rudolf Laban, 1938–40. L/C/1/77 from the University of Surrey Archive, University of Surrey	355
37.5	Two figures in tetrahedrons, and a shape made by interlocking tetrahedrons by Rudolf Laban, 1938–40. L/C/5/77 from the University of Surrey Archive, University of Surrey	356
37.6	Three figures by Rudolf Laban, 1938–40. L/C/6/80 from the University of Surrey Archive, University of Surrey	356
37.7	Figures within spiralling lines by Rudolf Laban 1938–40. L/C/3/47 from the University of Surrey Archive, University of Surrey.	357
37.8	Two figures by Rudolf Laban, 1938–40. L/C/5/87 from the University of Surrey Archive, University of Surrey	358
37.9	Impressions of figures by Rudolf Laban, 1938–40. L/C/3/12 from the University of Surrey Archive, University of Surrey	358
37.10	Rudolf Laban directing a movement choir at a Summer Course at Moreton Hall, 1942. F/(L)/2/60 from the Rudolf Laban Archive, University of Surrey	359
38.1	An approximately 400-word description of *Theorems, Proofs, Rebuttals and Propositions: A Conference of Theoretical Theatre*, written by Esther Neff and Yelena Gluzman to document the conference as a performance work, and published in *Emergency Index: An Annual Document of Performance Practice* (2013). The facing page (not shown here) included names of plenarists, date and venue information, along with an image from the conference. Four plenary performances were presented at the conference: *Plato's Symposium*, by the Finnish performance group Reality Research Center (Maria Oiva, Jani-Petteri Olkkonen, Tuomas Laitinen, Wisa Knuuttila, in collaboration with performance and culinary artist Carmen C. Wong); *REVOLUTION*, by Peruvian media artist Amapola Prada; *IDEA MACHINE*, by US theater and media artist Mike Taylor; and *Poultry Paradise and its Discontents: Nightshifts*, by Japanese-American performance theorist Kikuko Tanaka. Names and extant contributions and responses of conference participants are available at https://theatreastheory.wordpress.com/. Page image courtesy of Ugly Duckling Presse	366
38.2	Reality Research Center, *Plato's Symposium* (2013). Meal designed and prepared by Carmen C. Wong. Natalya Dikhanov	367

38.3	Mike Taylor, *IDEA MACHINE* (2013), workshop at the Collapsable Hole, with project cast and conference participants. Hilary Sand	373
38.4	Installation view of Amapola Prada's *REVOLUTION* (2013) at Glasshouse Projects. Hilary Sand	375
39.1	Demetrius Burns laid on the ground while playing the part of Tamir Rice during an interpretive dance at the Black Lives Matter rally at the TD Garden [Boston]. CRAIG F. WALKER/GLOBE STAFF	382
44.1	Bumper sticker design by Jordan Williams	431

Tables

44.1	424

CONTRIBUTORS

Aili Bresnahan is Associate Professor of Philosophy at the University of Dayton in the US. Her research specialty is in the philosophy of art, particularly in the philosophy of dance, improvisation, and performance, and she is the founder and moderator of the DancePhilosophers Google group. Her professional website is www.artistsmatter.com.

Alice Koubová is a senior researcher at the Philosophy Institute of the Czech Academy of Sciences and lecturer at the Academy of Performing Arts in Prague. She has published *Self-Identity and Powerlessness* (Brill), *To Think from the Secondary Position. Towards the Question of Performance Philosophy* (NAMU, in Czech) and other books and articles on performance philosophy, post-phenomenology and ethics. She examines the performative aspects of thinking and reflective components of the theatre – both theoretically and in practice.

Alice Lagaay is Professor of Aesthetics and Cultural Philosophy in the Design Department at Hamburg University of Applied Sciences. She is a founding core convener of the Performance Philosophy international research network and joint editor of the Performance Philosophy book series at Rowman & Littlefield. Inspired by how theory can feed on and enrich one's experience of life, she seeks innovative formats for the communication of philosophical content. Her current research explores the concept of "creative indifference" in the works of 20th-century philosopher Salomo Friedlaender/Mynona.

Anamaría Tamayo Duque is Assistant Professor in the Performing Arts Department at the Universidad de Antioquia, Colombia. She has a BA in Anthropology and a PhD in Critical Dance Studies from UCR. Her research areas are popular dance, national dances, dance and the screen and embodiments of gender/race in Latin America; decolonial philosophy, dance and political citizenship in Colombia.

Andrés Fabián Henao Castro is Assistant Professor of Political Science at the University of Massachusetts Boston. Before joining UMB, he was the Karl Lowenstein Fellow at Amherst College, and currently holds a Post-Doctoral Fellowship at the Academy of Global Humanities and Critical Theory at the University of Bologna. His research deals with the relationships between ancient and contemporary political theory, via the prisms of decolonial theory, psychoanalysis, critical theory and poststructuralism. His current book manuscript, *Antigone in the Americas: Democracy, Sexuality and Death in the Settler Colonial Present*, criticizes the theoretical reception of Sophocles' tragedy, *Antigone*, in democratic theory, queer theory and the theory of biopolitics by foregrounding the settler colonial logics of capitalist accumulation by which subject-positions are aesthetically distributed in the play and its theoretical reception.

Anke Haarmann is Professor of Design Theory and Design Research at Hamburg University of Applied Sciences. She works as a conceptual artist, curator and theorist of visual culture, with a focus on artistic research, theory of the self, and public space.

Anna Pakes is Reader in Dance Studies and director of the Centre for Dance Research at University of Roehampton, London. She was educated at Balliol College, Oxford, the *Centre National de la Danse Contemporaine* in Angers (France) and Laban Centre London. Anna's research and teaching now focuses on philosophies of dance, with a particular interest in analytic aesthetics. She has published on a range of philosophical themes as they relate to dance, including the mind-body problem, Husserlian phenomenology, the epistemology of practice as research, dance historiography and performance re-enactment. She co-edited the volume *Thinking through Dance: the philosophy of dance performance and practices* (published by Dance Books, 2013) with Jenny Bunker and Bonnie Rowell. Her translation of Frédéric Pouillaude's book *Unworking Choreography* was published by Oxford University Press in 2017. Her own monograph on the ontology of dance works is forthcoming also with OUP.

Anna Seitz is a trained philosopher and dramaturg who teaches at the Centre for Performance Studies at the University of Bremen and works closely with the Theater of Assemblage (*Theater der Versammlung*) – one of the very first research theatres in Germany.

Anthony Gritten is Head of Undergraduate Programmes at the Royal Academy of Music in London. He has published on Cage, Debussy, Delius and Stravinsky, written for visual artists' catalogues and philosophy dictionaries, and on numerous issues in Performance Studies, including artistic research, collaboration, distraction, empathy, ensemble interaction, ergonomics, listening, problem solving, recording and timbre.

Arno Böhler teaches at the University of Vienna, Department of Philosophy (faculty member) and at the University of Applied Arts Vienna. He is founder of the philosophy performance festival *Philosophy On Stage* and head of the residency program for arts-based philosophy and artistic research in South-India (*baseCollective*).

Cosimo Zene is Professor Emeritus in the Study of Religions and World Philosophies at SOAS (School of Oriental and African Studies), University of London, in the Department of Religions and Philosophies, where he also acted as Head of Department between 2011 and 2014. During this period he set up the new BA World Philosophies Programme, which was successfully launched in 2016–17.

Cristina Fernandes Rosa is a Senior Lecturer in Dance at the University of Roehampton and author of the book *Brazilian Bodies and Their Choreographies of Identification* (2015). She was a research fellow at Freie Universität Berlin's International Research Centre "Interweaving Performance Cultures" (Germany, 2012–2013) and earned her PhD from the University of California, Los Angeles. Rosa's area of interest includes dance in the Americas and the African diaspora, as well as colonial and postcolonial issues in dance.

David Davies is Professor of Philosophy at McGill University in Canada, where he has taught since 1987. His books include *Philosophy of The Performing Arts* (Oxford: Blackwell, 2011); *Aesthetics and Literature* (London: Continuum, 2007); and *Art as Performance* (Oxford: Blackwell, 2004). He has a PhD in Philosophy from the University of Western Ontario (1987), following a BA in Politics, Philosophy and Economics (Wadham College, Oxford, 1970) and an MA in Philosophy (Manitoba 1979). For the past 20 years his research has focused mainly on metaphysical and epistemological issues in the Philosophy of Art, where he has also published widely on topics relating to literature, film, photography, music, dance, performance and the visual arts.

David Kornhaber is Associate Professor of English and Comparative Literature at the University of Texas at Austin, USA. He is an affiliated faculty member with the Department of French and Italian and the Centre for European Studies. He is the co-editor of the journal *Modern Drama* and the author of *Theatre & Knowledge* (Palgrave, 2019) and *The Birth of Theater from the Spirit of Philosophy: Nietzsche and the Modern Drama* (Northwestern University Press, 2016).

Einav Katan-Schmid, PhD, is researcher, dance maker and a dramaturge based in Berlin. She has published on dance practice from the perspectives of embodied philosophies of perception, pragmatist aesthetics and hermeneutics. Her book *Embodied Philosophy in Dance – Gaga and Ohad Naharin's Movement Research* (2016) was published by Palgrave Macmillan in the Performance Philosophy series.

Elisabeth L. Belgrano is a singer/researcher focusing on 17th-century vocal performance practice as part of contemporary performative settings. She is currently researching the practice of 17th-century vocal ornamentation as a method for communicating and creating trust applicable to multiple scales. In 2005 she received the prestigious Noah Greenberg Award from the American Musicological Society "for distinguished contribution to the study and performance of early music". She was awarded a PhD in Performance in Theatre and Music Drama in 2011 and has been holding an adjunct position at the University of Gothenburg.

Elisabeth Schäfer is a philosopher. She teaches philosophy, queer and feminist theory at the University of Vienna. Her main research areas include deconstruction, queer-feminist philosophy, performance philosophy, artistic research.

Emmanuel Alloa is Full Professor in Aesthetics in the Philosophy Department at the University of Fribourg (Switzerland). He led the Philosophy Dialogues series at the *Scène nationale de Gennevilliers* in Paris (2010–2016) and has occasionally been involved as a performer in theatre and art projects. Although academic work now absorbs most of his time, he does not want to give up exploring new venues for thinking, especially in their embodied and experimental form.

Esther Hutfless is a philosopher and psychoanalyst in private practice in Vienna, Austria. She teaches philosophy, psychoanalysis, feminist and queer theory at the University of Vienna. Her main research areas include deconstruction, psychoanalysis, feminist philosophy, écriture féminine, queer theory.

Esther Neff is the founder of Panoply Performance Laboratory (PPL), a thinktank and collaborative entity generating performances-as-art, situations, performance of and as theory, social research projects and discursive social situations such as conferences, thinktanks, symposia, meetings, festivals, exhibitions, workshops and tours. PPL operates as work by Neff and collaborators and was a public lab site in Brooklyn, NY, 2012–2018. Neff is also a theorist and researcher whose texts have appeared in journals, handbooks and essay collections. They/she is/are the co-founder of MARSH (Materializing & Activating Radical Social Habitus) in St. Louis, organizer of PERFORMANCY FORUM, and instigator of Brooklyn International Performance Art Foundation.

Eva Maria Gauss is currently working on a PhD thesis "Concepts of the Body in Actor's Voice training" at the University of Marburg. She holds a master's degree in Philosophy and Theatre Studies and a degree in Speech Communication and Voice Studies. She is a co-founder of the Philosophy-Performance Festival [soundcheck philosophie], and carries out practical and theoretical research in lecture performances and similar formats, sometimes under the name Petra Lum.

Flore Garcin-Marrou is Lecturer in Theatre and Performance Studies at the University of Toulouse (France) and holds a PhD in French Literature from the Sorbonne, entitled "Gilles Deleuze, Félix Guattari: Between Theatre and Philosophy". Her current research essentially focuses on the relation between French contemporary philosophy and contemporary theatre.

Freddie Rokem is Professor (Emeritus) in the Department of Theatre at Tel Aviv University and is currently the Wiegeland Visiting Professor of Theater & Performance Studies (TAPS) at the University of Chicago. He is the author of *Philosophers and Thespians: Thinking Performance* (2010) and the prize-winning *Performing History: Theatrical Representations of the Past in Contemporary Theatre* (2000).

Fumi Okiji is an assistant professor in Women, Gender, Sexuality Studies at the University of Massachusetts Amherst, USA, whose work crosses music and critical theory, black feminist thought and performance studies. Her research and teaching looks to black music for ways to understand modern and contemporary life, exploring the potential such representation holds for social criticism. Okiji's book *Jazz as Critique: Adorno and Black Expression Revisited* was recently published by Stanford University Press.

'Funmi Adewole is a dance practitioner with a background in African dance drama, improvised dance and movement research. She is presently a lecturer in the dance department at De Montfort University, Leicester. Her research interests include dance and cultural politics and choreography and dance of Africa and the Diaspora. She continues to perform and also works as a dance dramaturge, mainly with choreographers who draw from social dance forms or work in a cross disciplinary context. She received a lifetime Achievement Award in Dance of the African Diaspora in Britain in 2019 from the UK's national body for dance One Dance UK.

Gertrude Postl is Professor of Philosophy and Women's and Gender Studies at Suffolk County Community College, Selden, NY, USA. Research focus: feminist philosophy, deconstruction (reading/writing, author, text), aesthetics and political thought; key figures: Hélène Cixous, Julia Kristeva, Luce Irigaray, Roland Barthes, Jacques Derrida.

Contributors

Hannah McClure, PhD, is a movement specialist and a registered and certified healer/bodywork therapist. Her background in professional performance spans fifteen years and includes the production of ten seasons of work with various companies, including Open Air Dance and The Prisms Project. Her study of Sufism is a natural outcome of her practice-based research into ritual and performance. Broad areas of interest include ritual and religion, Sufism, shamanism, somatic awareness, ways of knowing (practice-research, embodiment, trance), processes of transformation and heart-centred sustainability.

Hartmut Geerken, born in 1939, is a free-jazz musician, composer, writer, publisher, author of radio plays, filmmaker, collector of gongs and a joyful practitioner of 'creative indifference'. He has spent the last fifty years collecting, transcribing and publishing the writings of Salomo Friedlaender/Mynona.

Ira Avneri teaches at Tel Aviv University, Israel. He integrates *his creative work as* a director and dramaturge *with his theoretical research of* spatial and bodily aspects of philosophizing. His stage works focus on adaptations of canonical Western drama.

Jerri Daboo is Professor of Performance at the University of Exeter, UK. She worked professionally as a performer and director for fifteen years, before taking up the position of Lecturer in Exeter in 2004 after completing her doctorate on Buddhism and performance. Her practical and theoretical research areas take an intercultural and interdisciplinary approach to examining actor and dancer training and performance, particularly through Buddhist philosophy and practice; the work of Michael Chekhov; ritual performance, with a focus on the Southern Italian ritual of tarantism; and the connection between culture, place and identity, with particular reference to the British South Asian communities.

Jörg Holkenbrink (1955–2020) was the Director of the Center for Performance Studies at the University of Bremen and the Artistic Director of Theater of Assemblage (*Theater der Versammlung*). His work focuses on performative research and performance in research, cultures of knowledge in dialogue, and productions on the interface between academia and art.

Jörg Sternagel is currently interim Associate Professor in Media Theory at the Department of Art and Design at the University of Applied Sciences Europe, Campus Berlin. Since 2016, he has been a Postdoc Researcher at the Institute for Critical Theory at the Zurich University of the Arts. His work focuses on theories of alterity and the performative, imagery and mediality, philosophy of existence. His latest publications include the monograph *Pathos des Leibes. Phänomenologie ästhetischer Praxis* (Zürich/Berlin 2016) and the co-edited collection *Gegenstände unserer Kindheit. Denkerinnen und Denker über ihr liebstes Objekt* (Paderborn 2019). Further information: www.joerg-sternagel.de

Juliet Chambers-Coe is a GL-Certified Movement Analyst and a PhD candidate at the Guildford School of Acting at the University of Surrey. Juliet trained as an actress (GSA) and for over a decade worked in theatre, TV, film and radio. Since gaining a master's degree in Somatic Studies and Labananalysis from the University of Surrey in 2005, she has applied Laban Movement Analysis to theatre and actor training both as a Movement Director and as a teacher. Juliet teaches Laban and movement studies at Drama Studio London and Rose Bruford College. She is also the creator of the *Labanarium*: a resource and network centre for the movement community.

Contributors

Karen Christopher is a collaborative performance maker, performer, and teacher. Her company, Haranczak/Navarre Performance Projects, is currently engaged in creating a series of duet performances. She was a member of Chicago-based Goat Island performance group for 20 years until the group disbanded in 2009. She works at South House – her new studio in Faversham, Kent – where she, continues to define her practice in collaborative performance making. Karen is an Honorary Fellow of University College Falmouth and an Artist Research Fellow in the Department of Drama at Queen Mary, University of London.

Katrin Felgenhauer (University of Hildesheim) is currently working on her PhD thesis on the systematics of the performative in the field of social philosophy. She is a member of the association Expedition Philosophie and co-organizer of the Philosophy-Performance Festival [soundcheck philosophie].

Laura Cull Ó Maoilearca is Professor and Head of DAS Graduate School at the Academy of Theatre and Dance, Amsterdam. Her books include *Theatres of Immanence: Deleuze and the Ethics of Performance* (2012); *Encounters in Performance Philosophy* (2014), co-edited with Alice Lagaay; *Manifesto Now! Instructions for Performance, Philosophy, Politics* (2013), co-edited with Will Daddario and *Deleuze and Performance* (2009). She is a founding core convener of the international research network, Performance Philosophy, joint series editor of the Performance Philosophy book series with Rowman & Littlefield and an editor of the Performance Philosophy journal.

Lauren Fournier is a writer, independent curator, video artist, filmmaker, sometimes performer and maker of sound and experimental music. Her work brings together artistic practice, theory and philosophy, exhibition-making, critical and creative writing, teaching and collaboration. She currently teaches critical theory, aesthetics, social practice and art history in the School of Image Arts at Ryerson University. She is a SSHRC Postdoctoral Fellow in Visual Studies at the University of Toronto, where she is working on a series of moving image and text work that extends her doctoral research in autotheory to issues of land, settler-colonialisms, intergenerational trauma and class. She is the director of *Fermenting Feminism*: an ongoing, site-responsive curatorial experiment that engages fermentation, or microbial transformation, as a metaphor and material practice through which to engage historical and present-day feminisms.

Lin Hixson co-founded *Every house has a door* in 2008, the Chicago-based performance company that she directs. She was director of the performance group Goat Island (1987–2009). She was awarded the United States Artists Ziporyn Fellowship in 2009, and a Foundation for Contemporary Arts fellowship in 2014, and received an honorary doctorate from Dartington College of Arts, University of Plymouth in 2007 (all awards shared with her collaborator Matthew Goulish). She has received fellowships from The National Endowment for the Arts, The Illinois Arts Council, and the Chicago Dancemakers' Forum. Her writing has been published in the journals Poetry, Performance Research, and Parallax, as well as the anthologies *Imagined Theatres: Writing for a Theoretical Stage* (2017) and *The Creative Critic – Writing as/about Practice* (2018). She is Full Professor of Performance at The School of the Art Institute of Chicago.

Luciana da Costa Dias is core founder of the Performing Arts Graduate Program at the Federal University of Ouro Preto (PPGAC/ UFOP), in Brazil, working at UFOP as

Associate Professor of Aesthetic and Theatre Theory since 2011. She is also a founder member of the Brazilian research group: "APORIA: Philosophy and Theatre Studies" since 2014 and a core convener of Performance Philosophy. Luciana's research activities are focused on a hermeneutic-phenomenological approach to art and modernity. She is particularly interested in the crisis of modernity (as a metaphysical crisis and its possible overcoming through art) through the works of Nietzsche and Artaud, as well as in a transversal perspective on art/performance – as an immediacy of presence – and how this might affect theatre and performance studies.

Matthew Goulish co-founded *Every house has a door* in 2008 with Lin Hixson. He is dramaturg, writer and sometimes performer for the company. His books include *39 microlectures – in proximity of performance* (Routledge, 2001) and *The Brightest Thing in the World – 3 Lectures from the Institute of Failure* (Green Lantern Press, 2012). His essays have appeared most recently in *Richard Rezac Address* (University of Chicago Press, 2018) and *Propositions in the Making – Experiments in a Whiteheadian Laboratory* (Rowman & Littlefield, 2020). He teaches in the Writing Program of The School of the Art Institute of Chicago.

In her first life, **Maxine Sheets-Johnstone** was a dancer/choreographer, professor of dance/dance scholar. In her second and ongoing life, she is an interdisciplinary scholar affiliated with the Department of Philosophy, University of Oregon, where she taught periodically in the 1990s and where she now holds an ongoing Courtesy Professor appointment. She has published 10 Books and over 90 articles in science, humanities and art journals.

Mayuko Uehara 上原麻有子 has been professor of Japanese philosophy at Kyoto University since 2013, prior to which she held the post of Associate Professor at Meisei University in Tokyo for six years. She obtained her PhD from the École des Hautes Études en Sciences Sociales in Paris. She currently serves as editor-in-chief of the *Journal of Japanese Philosophy* (SUNY Press). Her recent writings include "Nishida Kitarō as Buddhist Philosopher: Self-Cultivation, a Theory of the Body, and the Religious Worldview" (Springer, 2019), "Trends and Prospects in Japanese Philosophy After 1945: The Contemporary Philosophy of Hiromatsu Wataru: From Marxist Philosophy to the Theory of Facial Expression" (Rowman & Littlefield International, 2019), *Philosopher la traduction / Philosophizing Translation* (edited by Uehara, Nanzan Institute for Religion and Culture/Chisokudō Publications, 2017), "Name and Existence — A Reflection on the Philosophy of Kuki Shūzō" (Department of Japanese Philosophy Graduate School of Letters Kyoto University, 2017), "The Nishida Philosophy and the Conceptualization of the First Person" (The Kyoto Philosophical Society, 2016), "A Reinterpretation of Nishida's Philosophy: Facial Expression Considered from The Viewpoint of Intuition-Action"(Iwanami shoten, 2015).

Melissa Blanco Borelli is Associate Professor in Theatre, Dance and Performance Studies at the University of Maryland. She is the author of *She Is Cuba: A Genealogy of the Mulata Body*, which won the Society of Dance History Scholars' 2016 de la Torre Bueno Prize for best book in Dance Studies. She has been faculty at MIT, University of Surrey, UK and Royal Holloway, University of London, where she remains affiliated as a Reader in Dance Theory and Performance. Her research interests include identity and corporeality; blackness in Latin America; dance on screen; film studies; feminist historiography and performance/auto-ethnography; cultural memory; digital humanities; decolonial aesthetics; and thinking beyond "the human." A recipient of a UK Arts and Humanities Research Council grant, she is the Principal Investigator on a project that co-creates digital performance archives with Afro-Colombian and indigenous communities affected by the armed conflict. She is the current President of the Dance Studies Association.

Mi You is a curator and research associate at the Academy of Media Arts Cologne. She curated performative programs at Asian Culture Center (Gwangju) and the inaugural Ulaanbaatar International Media Art Festival (2016) taking the silk road as a figuration for deep-time, de-centralized and nomadic imageries. Her academic interests are in performance philosophy, science and technology studies, and the philosophy of immanence in Eastern and Western traditions. Her writings have appeared in Performance Research, PARSE, MaHKUscript: Journal of Fine Art Research, LEAP, Yishu, among others.

Michael Ellison completed his music education at New England Conservatory (BM) Tufts (MA) and the University of California Santa Barbara (PhD). Professor of Composition at the University of Bristol, Ellison has been commissioned by BBC Symphony Orchestra, Acht Brücken Festival, Radio France, Aspects des musiques d'aujourd'hui, Grenoble Festival, New York Youth Symphony, Siemens Foundation, Nova Chamber Music Series, amongst many others. He is Principal Investigator on the five-year, Bristol-based European Research Council project *Beyond East and West: Developing and Documenting an Evolving Transcultural Musical Practice* (2015–2020) and has co-directed Istanbul's Hezarfen Ensemble since its founding in 2010.

Mischa Twitchin is a lecturer in the Theatre and Performance Department at Goldsmiths, University of London. His book *The Theatre of Death – the Uncanny in Mimesis: Tadeusz Kantor, Aby Warburg and an Iconology of the Actor* is published by Palgrave Macmillan in their Performance Philosophy series, and examples of his performance- and essay-films can be seen on Vimeo: http://vimeo.com/user13124826/videos.

Naomi Woo is a Canadian pianist and conductor. She currently holds the position of Assistant Conductor of the Winnipeg Symphony Orchestra, and completed a PhD in Music at the University of Cambridge as a Gates Cambridge Scholar.

Since 1999, **Rajni Shah** has worked independently and with other artists to create the conditions for performances, publications, conversations and gatherings on and off-stage. At the time of publication key performance works include *hold each as we fall* (1999), *The Awkward Position* (2003–4), *Mr Quiver* (2005–8), *small gifts* (2006–8), *Dinner with America* (2007–9), *Glorious* (2010–12), *Experiments in Listening* (2014–15), *Lying Fallow* (2014–15), *Song* (2016) and *Ropewalk* (2019).

Sara Houston is Deputy Head of Dance at University of Roehampton. She won the BUPA Foundation Prize for her research work in dance and Parkinson's and she was awarded a National Teaching Fellowship in 2014. Her book *Dancing with Parkinson's* is published by Intellect Books.

Sonya Dyer is an artist and writer from London. Dyer's practice is concerned with how the future is constructed within the contemporary imagination. She runs the *…And Beyond Institute for Future Research*, a peripatetic think tank creating possible futures. Recent projects include Rewriting the Future, Site Gallery, (2019), Another World is Possible, CAMP, Copenhagen (2018) and The Claudia Jones Space Station (BALTIC Centre for Contemporary Art and The NewBridge Project, Newcastle, 2017).

Sophie-Thérèse Krempl is a Berlin-based philosopher, social scientist, theatre dramaturge and author.

Sreenath Nair is a Senior Lecturer at the Lincoln School of Performing Arts, University of Lincoln, UK, and Editor-in-Chief of *Indian Theatre Journal* published by Intellect. His publications include *Restoration of Breath: Consciousness & Performance* (Rodopi, 2007); *The Natyasastra and the Body in Performance* (McFarland, 2015); *Manikin Plays* (Cambridge Scholars Press, 2013); *Evocative Body: Technique as Knowledge in Indian Performance*, co-authored with Ralph Yarrow (Routledge, forthcoming).

Susanne Valerie [Granzer] is an actress and Emeritus Professor at the renowned Max Reinhardt Seminar, University of Music and Performing Arts Vienna. Parallel to her career in acting, she was awarded a PhD in philosophy by the University of Vienna in 1995. Her research focuses on the actor on stage, artistic research and Performance Philosophy. Together with Arno Boehler she directs the residency program for arts-based philosophy and artistic research in South India (*baseCollective*). Further information: https://www.susannegranzer.at/

Tawny Andersen is a performance theorist and a performing artist. She is currently a SSHRC-funded postdoctoral fellow working under the supervision of Dr. Laura Cull Ó Maoilearca at the Centre for Performance Philosophy at the University of Surrey. She holds a PhD from the Department of Art History and Communication Studies at McGill University, and an MA in performance studies from the Université Libre de Bruxelles. Tawny's academic research is nourished by her extensive performing career with renowned European directors such as Jan Fabre, Meg Stuart and Kris Verdonck.

Tess Denman-Cleaver is an artist whose work spans performance, writing, workshops and installation. Her projects and commissions have been presented at Tate Britain, Hatton Gallery (Newcastle), Turner Contemporary, Tate St Ives, M_HKA Gallery (Antwerp), Paul Melon Centre (London), Audiograft Festival (Oxford) and Wilkinson Gallery (London), Middlesbrough Art Weekender, Globe Gallery (Newcastle) and for English Heritage. Tess was 2018–19 Artist in Residence at the Sonic Arts Research Unit (Oxford). She was the Artistic Director of Tender Buttons theatre and performance company between 2010 and 2018 and a programmer at The Northern Charter (Newcastle) between 2015 and 2018. Tess has a PhD on landscape and performance philosophy and works as Producer of Artists' Moving Image at Tyneside Cinema.

Theodora Wildcroft, PhD, is a researcher investigating the democratization and evolution of physical practice as it moves beyond both traditional and early modern frameworks of relationship. Her PhD was a significant advance in the analysis of contemporary yoga pedagogies. She is a Visiting Fellow at the Open University, UK, and a writer, teacher and independent scholar, respected by students, scholars and practitioners.

Theron Schmidt is a writer, teacher, and artist, currently living and working on unceded Gadigal land. He has published widely on contemporary theatre and performance, participatory art practices and politically engaged performance. He is a founding co-convener of the international Performance Philosophy network, co-editor of the journal *Performance Philosophy* and associate editor for *Performance Research*.

Tina Chanter is Professor of Philosophy at Newcastle University. She has published on contemporary French philosophy, drawing inspiration from a range of sources, including feminist theory, race theory, psychoanalysis, art, politics, film and tragedy. Her most recent books are *Whose Antigone? The Tragic Marginalisation of Slavery*, and *Art, Politics and Rancière: Broken Perceptions*. She taught in the US, most recently in Chicago, before returning to the UK, where she worked and taught in Bristol and London before her recent move to Newcastle University.

Tru Paraha received her PhD in artistic research from the University of Auckland, and works as a research fellow at the Faculty of Arts. Her current research unravels black holes and their implications for speculative choreography, performance and creative writing.

Volkmar Mühleis is a philosopher at LUCA School of Arts in Brussels and Ghent. His recent publications include *Girl with Dead Bird - Intercultural Observations* (2018) by Cornell University Press/Leuven University Press.

Will Daddario is the author of *Baroque, Venice, Theatre, Philosophy* and numerous articles on theatre historiography. He is co-editor of the Performance Philosophy Book Series and the *Performance Philosophy* journal. He is passionate about thinking beyond the constraints of academic disciplinary boundaries. He is a teacher, scholar, grief worker, and itinerant philosopher who currently resides in Asheville, NC. Within academic circles, he is most active in the Performance Philosophy research network where he functions as a curator of ideas and co-editor of the Book Series and Online Journal. In the realm of grief work, he and his wife are building Inviting Abundance, a consulting business that promotes the cultivation of a creative grief practice. As a philosopher, he is deeply committed to learning about the world in which we live. His most recent projects dive into the poetry and philosophy of Jay Wright.

Yelena Gluzman is an experimental theater director, researcher and communication scholar, whose scholarly work engages with performance studies, cognitive science, ethnomethodology, and science & technology studies. In her current doctoral work at UC San Diego, she stages, analyzes and considers methods of interdisciplinary translation and collaboration, particularly focusing on the cognitive sciences and their laboratory-based methods for evoking and studying mind. Her own research uses layers of methods (performance ethnography, ethnomethodological approaches, discourse analysis, ethnography, reenactment) and media (texts, theater, performance, video) to conduct experimental, collaborative research in which seemingly incommensurable disciplines can become visible, actionable, and theoretically viable to each other. She is the founding editor of "Emergency Index: An Annual Compendium of Performance Practice" and the Emergency Playscripts series for Ugly Duckling Presse, and recently co-embarked on a new project called Feminist Theory Theater.

Yunus Tuncel teaches Philosophy at The New School, New York, USA and in New York University's Liberal Studies Program. He is a member of the International Association for the

Contributors

Philosophy of Sport (IAPS) and is co-founder of the Nietzsche Circle, serving on its Board of Directors and the Editorial Board of its electronic journal, The Agonist. In addition to Nietzsche and history of philosophy, he is interested in 20th-century French thought and recent artistic, philosophical and cultural movements, including postmodernity and 'post-humanism. His primary areas of research are art, dance, experiences of the body in general, culture, music, myth, sports and spectacle. He is interested in the fusion of art, sport and philosophy in various cultural formations.

INTRODUCTION

Laura Cull Ó Maoilearca and Alice Lagaay

Performance philosophy is an emerging interdisciplinary and international field of thought, creative practice and scholarship open to all researchers concerned with the relationship between performance and philosophy, broadly construed.[1] That is, although the development of the field might be traced back to the identification of a 'philosophical turn' within Theatre and Performance Studies (in around 2008–2009) – in which researchers in that field seemed to be taking an increasing amount of interest in philosophy and engaging with it with a new-found depth and focus – it later became clear that the growth of interest in the performance–philosophy relationship was a broader *inter- and transdisciplinary* phenomenon, coming from Philosophy and other disciplines including Dance, Music and Visual Art, as much as from Theatre and Performance.

Since it first emerged in around 2011–2012, the term and field of 'performance philosophy' has accrued a degree of recognition – both institutional and more widely communal – as an area of research. Writing in 2015, our North American colleagues and fellow conveners Wade Hollinghaus and Will Daddario described performance philosophy as 'still coming into its own as a discipline, trying to determine what it is and what it can do' (2015, p. 51), whilst in 2017, contributor Andrés Fabián Henao Castro called it 'a discipline in its first becomings' (Henao Castro 2017, p. 190). However, despite its infancy, the field already has a professional association with over 3,000 members from more than 56 different countries, a journal, book series and biennial conference. As such, recent work has described performance philosophy as a field that is gaining 'momentum throughout Europe and North America' and in which 'an increasing number of scholars are bringing their perspectives to bear upon innovative approaches to performance and thinking practices' (Street, Alliot & Pauker 2017, p. 5). For his part, Alex Pittman has noted the ways in which performance philosophy now operates as a contemporary category related to a community of 'those who identify their work under that heading' (Pittman 2016, p. 166). Whether or not they have been framed as such by their authors, we are now seeing some books being described as works of 'performance philosophy' (Goulish 2014; Pittman 2016[2]). Though there are also references to the idea of performance philosophy as a retrospective label – that might also be used to describe and reconsider historical figures or practices '*avant la lettre*' (Lagaay 2015).

| ***Field:*** Throughout this introduction, and indeed the book as a whole, there is mention of performance philosophy as an emerging or recently emerged interdisciplinary "field". To the extent that the notion of a "field" might be understood to imply that its boundaries are clearly distinguishable from other fields, this description of performance philosophy as a field is somewhat misleading. One would have to imagine a landscape with overlapping fields and with chunks of earth from one field parasitically invading or hopscotching between different fields. To relativize the appropriateness of the notion of field here is not, however, to suggest that performance philosophy might not have clear boundaries *per se*. The point, rather, is to underline the importance of the fact that some characteristics of certain instances of performance philosophy – in particular, **methodological self-reflexivity** and a **sensitivity to form in relation to content** – can occur in other "fields" too. Whenever this happens, one could argue that it constitutes an instance of performance philosophy – even when the discipline or context might be seemingly far removed from the more common realms (in the arts and humanities) that people who do performance philosophy generally come from. If an element of the expertise of those engaging in performance philosophy has to do with developing a certain *dramaturgical sensitivity* (with regard both to the generation of knowledge and to the potential of its communicability), then it is important that this not be limited to the realm of performance philosophy, but that it be applicable or transferable to and transformable within other disciplines too. One could imagine, for instance, that a mathematician or a biologist or an information technologist (or someone from any other at first sight not primarily artistic or performance-related realm) could discover or provide insights that would be relevant for the performance philosophy "field".

In 2012, we were among a group of 11 people who founded the research network, also called Performance Philosophy, partly in recognition of the fact that the last 15 years had seen this unprecedented surge of international and interdisciplinary interest in the performance–philosophy relationship.[3] But at the same time, the launch of Performance Philosophy was also a kind of performative act in itself, insofar as it simultaneously sought to bring a new field into existence through the act of naming it as such.

| ***Simultaneously***. The multi-tasked aspect or double nature evoked here is characteristic of a lot of work that falls into the realm of performance philosophy. The simultaneity may occur on multiple levels, but it refers most significantly to the manner in which instances of performance philosophy do not just think, philosophize or perform *upon* or *about* a given subject or theme; they simultaneously reflect their own performativity, both in the sense of exposing their own performance as constituting an act of showing addressed to a particular audience, and in the more politically salient performative sense of *bringing about* a reality, i.e., of being engaged in changing an aspect of the world (or bringing into being new worlds within "*this* one" which is not one), through and *in* the very doing of their work. Reception, or the "reading" of this simultaneity may be challenging, as it calls for a form of double vision that can be a strain, or even seemingly impossible: focusing on one dimension or process tends to rule out seeing the other(s) – at least at one and the same moment. Thus, reading simultaneity involves training one's awareness that multiple dimensions and forces (e.g. the locutionary, illocutionary and perlocutionary to use J. L. Austin's terms here) are at play at one and the same time, without the focus on one resulting in a loss of sight of the other(s). There are multiple

simultaneous processes at work now in the writing of this text. The linearity of text does its best to mask them. Engaging in performance philosophy is learning to attend to this simultaneity.

Introducing the emerging field of performance philosophy is a complex task – not least because it is, and has been from the beginning, a collective enterprise. As our colleague Theron Schmidt has noted, it would certainly be a mistake to think that any *one* voice could encapsulate or speak for the field *per se*. As such, this introduction (itself multivocal, attempting simultaneously to state, show, set the stage, perform and bring about) should only be read as one introduction amongst others: a partial account best considered alongside those that might perceive and articulate the field – its concerns, contexts, insights and limitations – in notably differing ways and through divergent vocabularies. Whilst perhaps it goes without saying, it still seems important to explicitly acknowledge and reiterate that our own account of, or perspective on, performance philosophy is by no means representative or exhaustive; it is not intended to be definitive and should not be taken to hold any more authority than alternative accounts existing elsewhere or yet to come.[4] Indeed, we hold strongly to the view that the great vitality of the realm lies in its very multiplicity, polyphony, mutability and openness to ongoing collaborative authorship, including in the form of a co-production that seeks to hold together disagreement and mutually exclusive positions.

| ***What is a Companion?*** Although now obsolete, the English language used to include the verb: to companion, meaning 'to make equal'. The very idea of equality as a verb rather than a noun – of an equalizing act – speaks to performance philosophy, as we understand it. Less an authoritative guide, then – or a comprehensive overview produced from a totalizing 'view from nowhere' (Nagel 1986) – this book seeks to practise a kind of equalizing or companioning in terms of the relationships between performance and philosophy that it stages, the different registers and voices, hesitations and interruptions it displays, and with you, its readers.

| ***Equalizing act.*** What might it mean to equalize the relationship between performance and philosophy? To see philosophy as a kind of performance and performance as a kind of philosophy? A reminder here that the word 'kind', meaning "class, sort, variety," comes from the Old English *cynn*, meaning "family", and is related to the Proto-Indo-European root gene meaning "to give birth, beget". So, thinking performance as a kind of philosophy and philosophy as a kind of performance means thinking how one gives birth to the other, how the two are related through familial ties, and how they might play together – child-like, as it were (*Kind* = child in German) (cf. Chapter 22 by Koubová in this book). That performance philosophy might also be invested in *being kind*, as in, considerate and hospitable, is another dimension of its ethico-affective practice.

We are grateful to Routledge for the invitation to produce the Companion at this particular moment in time: when it feels as though the principal organization and research network for the field, Performance Philosophy, is going through an important period of change and critical self-reflection.

| ***Critical self-reflection***: The convenors of the Performance Philosophy network have been deliberating for some time now the pros and cons of becoming a more formal

organisation (with an agreed charter and a democratic governance structure). So far, the decision *not* to pursue that route has been driven by the strong desire to affirm and protect the wildness of the non-structured, fundamentally open nature of performance philosophy as an approach to thinking and creating that is not, for instance, bound by any agreed body of methods. Among the potential downsides of that openness are a) the challenge to establish transparent criteria to evaluate the *quality* of instances of performance philosophy, and b) the difficulty of achieving visibility, especially from potential institutions that only support other entities with similar legal and formal structures. So, just as we find ourselves in an uneasy embrace with the textual format of the Companion – here – there has been an ongoing ambivalence as to the extent to which the Performance Philosophy network needs to "get itself organized" (and if so, how). Anarchy can require a lot of organization, it turns out.

And indeed, this writing also comes at a time when the field itself has perhaps reached a certain degree of maturity – such that we might even allow ourselves to drop the notion of the field as 'emerging' rather than 'emerged', were it not for the value for many in continuing to consider it as somehow perpetually emergent, in process or unfinished (as has also been argued with Performance Studies and other areas). In this context, the reader may sense multiple impulses at work in our approach to the editing of this book and the selection of contributors. On the one hand, we are grateful for the input of those authors who have had a long-standing engagement with the field to support us in a process of consolidating some of our developing understanding of its myriad international contexts and historic lineages. On the other, we have used the editorial work as a chance to meet and engage with the thought of new authors who may not have been involved in performance philosophy prior to their contribution to this volume. The aim of this is not appropriative or imperialist – albeit we recognize the risk it might appear (or even, despite itself, function) as such. Rather, the motivation behind the gesture is to locate and support transnational and transdisciplinary conversations and solidarities – under the broad(ening) church that is 'Performance Philosophy' – whilst respecting the contextual specificity and uniqueness of these practices (which might go by many names, in multiple languages: performative philosophy, 'philo-performance', philosophy on stage and so forth).

| ***Interdisciplinarity***: Thinking in an interdisciplinary way is more complex and challenging than simply adding one discipline to another as if it were a case of just combining, and therefore quantitively multiplying, knowledge by drawing together various methods and results of research from different realms. The process itself can sometimes involve a sort of *unlearning* so as to see things outside of one's habitual perspective, perhaps behaving for a while as if one really were someone else, in order to allow for a new perspective, a new source of insight or creativity. Working in an interdisciplinary manner means venturing into a kind of no-man's-land. One might begin by taking along certain familiar principles, habits and assumptions with one on this journey into unfamiliar territory, but after a while the limitation of those habits will invariably become apparent – they do not necessarily apply in the new, now hybrid, world. New habits and methods will need to be acquired. Venturing out of one's comfort zone, as any migrant knows, ultimately involves embarking on a process of radical questioning of those principles and habits once taken for granted (although always initially acquired). One never just integrates a new culture without both changing it and also letting go of what one thought one was to begin with. Perhaps all performance

Introduction

philosophers are hybrid, transdisciplinary thinkers carrying the experience of various cultures of knowledge and research, stemming from patchwork families – necessarily relativists.

A note on terminology and translation. Readers will notice that this book includes texts that speak of "performative philosophy", alongside "performance philosophy" and "philosophy performance". These terms are not entirely synonymous, but their usages constitute their own concepts and carry different associative shades of meaning which we have sought to retain both in terms of our approach to translation and editing (rather than imposing a homogenizing "consistency"). We have also actively ensured that this book includes multiple texts translated from other languages as well as several contributions by people for whom English is not their first language. In working with these authors and their texts, we have consciously tried to strike a balance between rendering the texts accessible to, and as readerly as possible for, an international English-speaking audience and at times allowing a significant sense of otherness, something of an untranslatability to shine through, which stems from the particular cultural contexts of their provenance.

| ***(Un) translatability.*** The invitation here is to consider and take seriously the fact that there are a multitude of different contexts and registers of thinking and speaking, of performing, creating and *translating* at play (and quite a few in this book too) – and that there is *no single* language (no single 'English' in this case) into which each text is translated. This very realization: that the problem of translation is in fact pertinent *to all performances*, even the ones that appear to occur in the same grammatical language as the language (assumed to be) spoken by the audience to whom the performance is addressed, could in itself be considered part of the performance philosophy "project". To ponder upon this realisation is to question the assumption of a universal(izably) "clear" academic language, which nevertheless is very often implied. What does it mean, and what does it take to really understand one another? *Who is speaking (for) the foreign?*

It is a well-known fact (theorized by Walter Benjamin and others) that questions of linguistic register and style, of vocabulary and grammar, are never "just" questions of language. Behind each and every chapter of this book lies a very particular context, built up of collective and individual assumptions and cultural habits. Where a particular context is closer to one's own familiarity, one tends to be quicker to orient oneself in it, or one might even overlook it as a particular context and assume it to be universalizable – familiarity renders blind. Where one might stumble over a particular register, format or style of language (or even question its layout on the page), where it perhaps seems a little awkward, strange or off-beat, the tendency might be to dismiss it as a "bad" style, intentionally obscure or as an imperfect or failed translation. Our hope, however, is that the reader will recognize in those potential moments of disturbance the opportunity to consider the possibility of a different, unfamiliar world that the text might be a messenger from. Some chapters also include references to actual terms or concepts in the original language, such as, amongst others, German in Böhler/Granzer and Gauss/Felgenhauer; Japanese in Uehara; Pali in Daboo; Sanskrit in Nair; and Arabic in Daddario.

| ***Haptesthai (to touch)***, hybristês, periagein (revolving apparatus), keiner (no-one), anattā (non-self), anicca (impermanence), dukkha (suffering), sunyata (emptiness),

tasawwuf (purity), wafiza, makam, geophilosophy, mestizaje, rasa, alambana, uddipana, anubhava, bhava, 主体 [*shutai*], ta'wil, haqiqah', urafā, Leiblichkeit, Mitwelt (being-with-world and vice versa), **Unverfügbarkeit** (ungraspability).

Defining performance philosophy. There are multiple overlapping usages of the term 'performance philosophy'. That is, performance philosophy might refer to the field, to a method, practice or mode of thought (doing performance philosophy), or to an object (a book described as a work of performance philosophy). The term is used in the context of thinking towards a 'performance philosophy' rather than a philosophy *of* performance; researchers have begun to consider what it might mean for them to inhabit the role of the 'performance philosopher' alongside the potentially comparable positions of philosopher of performance and the philosophically minded performance maker, but also alongside the dramaturg, life-coach, pedagogue, sportsperson, ethnographer, activist and mystic. A performance by a company like contributors *Every house has a door* could be called a piece of 'performance philosophy'; however, the process through which that performance was created could equally be described as such, as could the work that others might seek to do alongside it as collaborating researchers. There were, of course, prior uses of the term 'performance philosophy' before the inauguration of the network in 2012. Scholars discussing the enactment of philosophy as a way of life, and particularly the acts of the Cynic, Diogenes of Sinope – who appears in our Figures section – have also used the term 'performance philosophy' (Bosman 2006; Papazian 2009). Here though, the term often seems to retain traces of the anti-theatrical prejudice that Western philosophy has often shown, insofar as 'performance philosophy' is equated with mere showmanship.

> | ***Multiple overlapping usages***. This 'Companion to Performance Philosophy' brings into a collective choreography various voices and approaches to writing that do not all stem primarily from academic *or* scholarly disciplines but evoke a variety of discourses, practices, approaches to and experiments in the field from various realms of life. Some texts constitute reflections about the authors' artistic/performance practice, others are more explicitly instances of that practice itself. Our hope is that by including and placing side by side – on equal terms – these different registers of discourse and thinking, the book will a) draw attention to the staged aspect of academic discourse itself – *thereby helping to render debatable and negotiable the often unquestioned formats in which scholarly knowledge is generated and transmitted*; b) push the boundaries of what the term "interdisciplinary" can mean – by explicitly going beyond the usual confines of academia; c) avoid repeating the gesture by which the 'artist' or any instance of 'practice' is consciously or unconsciously reduced to an *application* of (higher) theory. Performance philosophy seeks to explore the knowledge and theory-generating potential of *all* performance practices – including (as just one instance thereof) the explicitly philosophical or academic.

Again, without any pretence of being exhaustive, we might also suggest that among its principle concerns, researchers in the field of Performance Philosophy investigate a diverse range of issues, including how ideas and practices from the fields of performance and philosophy can be productively brought together in ways that are invigorating and potentially transformative for both. They seek to question our existing ideas of what counts as 'performance' and 'philosophy' – considering, for instance, the idea of philosophy as an embodied, performative practice. There are interests in working to extend or expand qualitatively the concepts of philosophy and performance, rather than necessarily seeking to encompass one within the other or to erase the differences between the two. There are efforts to revisit questions of the relationship between performance, thought and knowledge, alongside related fields such as 'artistic research', by considering the ways in which performance operates as a way of thinking, mode of enquiry and potentially as a kind of 'philosophy'. There are explorations that probe the academic confines in which theory (as an always embodied, lived practice) is conventionally elaborated and negotiated, seeking to identify and expand gaps in the professional fence that keeps theory bound to a certain exclusive language – and to let experienced life seep in through those holes. And there are multiple collaborative endeavours by which people from different professional backgrounds, or with complementary expertise come together to integrate or invent new terms and develop playing fields for new questions always placing themselves on the cuff of something unthought or unknown, exposing themselves to the 'impossible' (Koubová & Lagaay 2014) out of which live acting-thinking emerges. Common to many or all of these lines of flight is an attentiveness to the performativity of the academy particularly in terms of pedagogical practices but also wider behaviours. There has been a long-standing understanding – in the German context especially (cf. Chapter 19 by Holkenbrink & Seitz) – of the potential value of using techniques and approaches from theatre and performance to interrogate this performativity. And yet – at least in our experience – the notion of academic exchange as 'mere transfer', rather than the production of knowledge, remains dominant in many contexts.

> | *Performance & Philosophy.* Do the terms mean anything outside particular instances thereof? Is it possible to generalize the notion or phenomenon of performance, or the practice of philosophy? Of course, there have been attempts. Take, for instance, the idea that a central characteristic of performance is its live, unrepeatable quality (cf. chapter 17 by Nair). And that philosophy, as the word itself states, conveys or stems from a love of wisdom. Would performance philosophy then be the *live* love of wisdom? I close my eyes for a moment and try to imagine, projected onto the screen of my inner eyelid, a depiction of wisdom unfolding in the now. I add to that an image of wisdom being loved in the continuous present… (pause for dramatic effect)… if we could capture this in music, what a fine intro sequence that would make!
> | *The live love of wisdom.* She is less fearful than I. But why do I fear live thought? It is, I suppose, the worry that "the live" will somehow be less careful, less precise than its pre-prepared counterpart. "Here's one I made earlier". But as in the arts – live thought can, of course, be rehearsed too – a live performance is always rehearsed to some degree. Live thought emerges as the movement of difference and repetition; as the repetition of difference. As improvisation – for instance – live thought can be built on specific techniques and structures; the result of training and expertise rather than some kind of free for all or imaginary spontaneity. Preparation turns down the volume on fear as the affect that has the potential to restrict my capacity to act: to enact live thought, to live thought.

Amongst these myriad concerns, performance philosophy has taken a particular interest in the relationships between form, content and medium with respect to philosophy, theory and thought. As Anna Street has noted, 'the question of medium persistently takes centre stage in the development of this venture called Performance Philosophy' (Street 2017, p. 97) – along with a desire to revisit what remain in many contexts the unquestioned standard forms for how thought is shared, from the academic conference to the book. In this respect, Performance Philosophy as an organization has tended to share with groupings like the SenseLab in Canada (see Manning and Massumi 2014, pp. 90–98), a resistance to the 'communicational model' of thought in favour of a performative one – for instance, through an embrace of 'No-paper formats'[5]. This question of how philosophy is performed, including the forms of 'Theory' in the age of smart media, has been particularly foregrounded by Jon McKenzie, who asks:

> How will we perform or *do* theory in the twenty-first century? What role might Performance Philosophy play? And *must one do philosophy by (means of) the book?* Can it—and theory—survive their incorporation by graphe, by plasticity, by transmediation? How might they live on?
>
> *(McKenzie in Street et al. 2017, p. 84 – emphasis added)*

And yet, mainstream academic presses, in the UK and North America at least, seem to be dragging their feet over rethinking the possibilities of publication in the digital era:[6] experimentation seemingly stifled by the pressure to locate ways to monetize the realms of the online and open access.

> | ***Publishers.*** Conducting a peer review of a book proposal, a reviewer was asked to comment on the "timeliness and likely shelf-life of the research" proposed. A performance philosopher, the reviewer responded: "FIRST QUESTION – BERGSON RESEARCH AND PERFORMANCE PHILOSOPHY ARE INCREASINGLY TIMELY (NO PUN). SECOND QUESTION IS SOMEWHAT SILLY (GREAT RESEARCH IS POTENTIALLY ETERNAL OR AT LEAST INDEFINITE – THOUGH I BELIEVE THAT ARISTOTELIANISM WENT THROUGH A LESS POPULAR PERIOD IN 300–600AD)".

Beyond – or besides – linearity. Since one of the methodological principles of performance philosophy is a dramaturgical sensitivity to the relationship between content and form, it follows that for many of the contributors to this volume, the written word in its most habitualized or conventional academic, neutrally voiced linear form has not been the chosen mode in which to present or perform their work.

> | ***Alternative formats.*** The reader will find in this volume multiple chapters that experiment with various form and formats, designs and layouts. There are dialogues and multivocal choreographed conversations, co-authored texts, texts that make use of columns and blanks, or employ various fonts, diagrams and images in more than one standard way. Accommodating the needs of writers/performance philosophers, for whom not just the medium but the format and layout of that medium is often intrinsic to the content of their work, presents a challenge for most academic publishers whose production processes are increasingly streamlined, involving the use of strict non-negotiable templates. Our attempt to stretch the boundaries of what a template can allow is not an affected attitude, not a gimmick, but an essential consequence of the dramaturgical sensitivity, caring for the relation between form and content, that is integral to many instances of performance philosophy. There is certainly a potentially subversive element at play here. But questions of 'design' in this context are not to be dismissed as trivial or superficial; they harbour and speak from an ethical and indeed political concern for the possibilities of what *and how* thinking or performing theory can be and do.

Introduction

One difficulty with making use of alternative formats (in terms of vocal modality, the rendering visible of markings of collaboration, design and layout) is that the rules of how to approach, read or navigate a given medium have to be established anew each and every time, in this instance for each chapter – and they have to be established virtually at the same time (another instance of simultaneity) as the performance/chapter is being carried out. This requires an attentiveness on the part of the audience or reader that is probably uncharacteristic and more challenging than is the case in other more normatively defined disciplinary fields. However, a valuable and somewhat unexpected result of this seemingly experimental approach is that once one is accustomed to the idea that each instance of performance philosophy calls for a conscious reflection and establishment of what is the appropriate format in which to present and perform itself, there is, in a sense, no going back: the deliberateness and staged dimension of *all* performances (be they standard or non-standard, conventionally academic or not) become undeniably evident. Even the most normatively conformist academic presentation is thus revealed in its staged performativity – and, moreover, a dramaturgical bar is introduced, with which to measure whether or not the performance succeeds.

In dominant approaches to Philosophy, at least in the Anglo-European sphere, there has been little consideration of questions of form. As Plato expert, MM McCabe has recently observed, for instance, Plato scholarship tends to focus on the supposed 'content' of the dialogues more so than on their dramatic form (McCabe 2019). In turn, as Martin Puchner has emphasized, this lack of attention to form has enabled the continuing stereotype of Plato as a simply 'anti-theatrical' figure despite his sustained commitment to the exploration of ideas in a theatrical form (Puchner 2010). The field of performance philosophy, by contrast, has been one site in which researchers seeking to investigate the relationship between philosophical form and content have begun to congregate. Colleagues in Germany, Austria and the Czech Republic have perhaps particularly advanced our understanding of these questions: through projects like *Philosophy on Stage* in Vienna and [*soundcheck philosophie*] in Halle & Leipzig – discussed in Chapter 40 (Böhler & Granzer) and Chapter 27 (Gauss & Felgenhauer), respectively. In many cases, this is a question of researchers coming from Philosophy or based in academic Philosophy departments looking to question how philosophy is practised, taught, disseminated and so forth. These considerations have also been prominent in the biennial events hosted by the Performance Philosophy network since 2013, with a first climax brought about in the manifesto for the Prague conference in 2017, "How does Performance Philosophy Act? Ethos, Ethics, Ethnography".[7] Originally referred to as a biennial 'conference', these events have become increasingly concerned with matters of form, format and structure – seeking to approach the 'conference' itself as performance: that which performatively produces events of thinking (rather than representing thinking already done elsewhere), and as a site of experiment for how thought might be performed beyond conventional academic settings. The call here is not to reject the standard academic conference paper as somehow necessarily rendering passive or being authoritarian – but it is a call for greater attention to the form suggested by particular modes of thought to consider formats like the 'paper' as the one amongst others rather than the unquestioned default.

| We invite submissions for contributions in the following formats:[8]

1. Conference papers – 20 mins.
2. "No paper" presentations – 15 mins. or 90 mins. panels
3. "Doing together…watching in the midst of doing" workshop proposals – 90 mins.

4   Performance lectures – 20 mins.
5   Re-enactment lectures – 15 mins.
6   Audio essays – 10 mins.
7   Children & parent dialogues – 15 mins.
8   Brief interventions – 2 mins.

Beyond 'application'. The methodological issue of 'application' has been a matter of recurring concern and debate within performance philosophy from the outset – echoing a wider discussion in related fields such as Film Philosophy. It has been a core theme of initial articulations of the field in terms of the distinction between performance philosophy and the philosophy of performance (Cull 2012, 2014; Cull Ó Maoilearca 2018). It was also the defining question of a symposium held at the Centre for Performance Philosophy at the University of Surrey in 2017. The *Beyond Application* symposium sought to

> explore the question of how philosophy and the arts might encounter one another in ways that challenge the tendency towards application – for instance, when the arts are treated as illustrative of extant, transcendent philosophical ideas rather than as generating their own, new philosophy immanently (CFP).[9]

By 'application', we might mean: a tendency within the philosophy of art or in related fields such as art theory to use the work of art more as a means to illustrate a pre-existing set of ideas, than to generate new ones; to privilege a given idea of philosophical thinking over one of artistic thinking, rather than allowing the arts to expand our understanding of philosophy and of thought, perhaps. When we think of application, we may also think of a rather one-way relationship between philosophy and the arts in which a concept is understood to change how we perceive the arts, but in which little attention is paid to the reciprocal capacity of the arts to change how we understand a concept.

> | **Against "default" systems**. When the model of knowledge transfer (as opposed to its collaborative generation) is critiqued, binaries of active and passive states of reception are often simplistically applied to learning behaviours, where the former is supposedly *automatically* created by the use of new scenographic elements (swivelling chairs for students) and the latter guaranteed to be reinforced by old architectures (the turn against the tiered lecture hall as *necessarily* hierarchical and passive-making). Whilst Performance Philosophy's affirmation of the 'no paper' format for some of its biennial events might be seen to endorse this binarizing view, the call is – in fact – not for any one form to be outlawed unilaterally, so much as for form to be taken into greater consideration and pluralised according to the needs and concerns of specific contexts. The objection is more to the standard conference paper as *default* than it is to the form *per se* (which can have its own performative force in the context of particular events). Performance philosophy seeks to counter any form of lazy or default "application" by striving to remain *attentive*. The form of attention implied is one that resonates with that which in the context of his vision of education, Tim Ingold has recently described as a form of 'longing' – the stretching of a life along a line that involves actively listening, caring, being present, and attentively accompanying others (cf. Ingold 2018, pp. 20–21). Attention/attentiveness means precisely countering default, system thinking by dramaturgical, sensory awareness. It carries ethical and political consequences.

Introduction

In turn, we might want to acknowledge that the kind of parasitism that application seems to risk goes both ways insofar as artists might use philosophy to add conceptual weight to their practice, or adopt an illustrative approach to a practice which places little faith in the creative process, form or event itself to generate unexpected thinking. Or again, as Esa Kirkkopelto (2015) has discussed, even if philosophy remains a very useful resource for artists to support the articulation of the performance – including, specifically, the very notion of performance as research, as a way of thinking, as a mode of inquiry or even as a kind of philosophy in itself – it can be that philosophy continues to serve as a legitimizing authority in such discourses. As Kirkkopelto puts it:

> Artists turning to philosophy and philosophers inherently risk remaining unilateral: such thinkers tend to be used as ultimate authorities, whose role in the discourse is to frame the area of questioning and to define its basic orientation. There is no question of criticizing or challenging Deleuze, Merleau-Ponty, Foucault, Dewey or Wittgenstein through one's own humble practice! From the point of view of the artist, however, this kind of preliminary delimitation is deeply compromising. From the philosophical point of view, in turn, the relation itself remains *unphilosophical*. When, then, do artist-researchers really think philosophically?' … What is more important is to recognize the genuine nature, in other words the *philosophical bearing*, of the questions practitioners present to their artistic and academic communities as well as to a wider society.
>
> *(Kirkkopelto 2015, p. 6)*

In this respect, any renewed engagement with performance by philosophers might not be received as a cause for celebration in and of itself; what matters (for performance practitioners and scholars) is *how* such an engagement takes place. More emphatically, there is a growing movement amongst researchers concerned with the relationship between philosophy and the arts that scholars must find alternatives to the mutual instrumentalization and disciplinary inequalities that arise from the application paradigm, or philosophy *of* the arts approach, that has historically dominated approaches to aesthetics and arts theory. Whether in relation to Music (Bowie 2007), Film (Mullarkey 2009; Sinnerbrink 2011), Dance (Cvejić 2015) or interdisciplinary arts practices (Manning & Massumi 2014), contemporary philosophers and theorists are increasingly calling for a philosophy *from* rather than *about* the arts, insofar as the latter tends to reproduce the hierarchies between philosophy and the arts as modes of knowledge. At the heart of this call, for many, is the view that the arts themselves are philosophical, can do philosophy or can make an independent contribution to philosophy, above and beyond their capacity to serve as applications or illustrations of pre-existing philosophical ideas or examples used to justify ontological claims.

> | **Modes of knowledge**. And have we even begun to problematize sufficiently the various possible declensions of this word 'knowledge' in relation to our own craft? As performers of performance philosophy – on the theatrical stage, at conferences, in lecture halls, seminar rooms, on the page, faced with the screen, in the meeting room, in our studies, during lunchtime contemplations, or siestas, during dinner conversations, weekend walks, or in the water – *how do we bring about what we know*? How much patience, waiting, marinating, rehearsing, regurgitating, how much trying to get on top of this knowledge, how much *giving up* of control, of the illusion of sovereign ego is required? When the introductions are over and the spotlight comes on… how much

trust in the urgency of the live moment is required such that when the voice speaks it is mine thinking live, now, speaking to you, the audience, keeping your eyes alert, your mind attentive with my unfolding questions – which are never just mine (otherwise they would be of no interest).

Expanding the canon – decolonizing Performance Philosophy. Whilst clearly canonical figures do appear here, the Companion does attempt to contribute to the questioning and insistent expansion of cultural canons that has been ongoing since at least the 1960s, informed by feminism, the civil rights movement, Marxism, postcolonial and queer studies. In particular, we hope that we have made at least some gestures towards the critique of the ongoing Eurocentrism of academic Philosophy, which remains dominated by Western and specifically Anglo-European thought at the expense of – for example – African, Chinese, Indian, Japanese, and, Latin American philosophies. Inspired by the call for an inter-philosophical dialogue by decolonial thinkers like Enrique Dussel, and the institutional innovation of people like contributor Cosimo Zene (who led the foundation of the BA World Philosophies programme at SOAS in London), this Companion is part of a modest first effort to decolonize performance philosophy. The question of how, specifically, this decolonization might be practised is taken up across a range of chapters – but particularly in Chapter 4 by Andrés Fabián Henao Castro; Chapter 8 by Luciana Dias; Chapter 13 by Cosimo Zene; and Chapter 14 by Melissa Blanco Borelli, Anamaría Tamayo-Duque and Cristina Fernandes Rosa. As ever, the call is not for a mere increase of racial and cultural 'diversity' within a system of representation that remains fundamentally structured according to Eurocentric, colonial values, but a qualitative change to the system itself.

> | **Its critical reflection of form** is, in a sense, an extension of the concern to *decolonize performance philosophy*. It is understood that every instance of performance philosophy (including the chapters in this book) must find and establish its own way of communicating within itself the rules by which it is to be "read" – as opposed to presuming that every proposal, text or instance of performance philosophy counts towards reaffirming a universalizable standard by which it can be measured.

In this particular instance, the point is clearly not to "prove" that non-Western forms of knowledge and modes of thought can be patronizingly recognized as "(proper) Philosophy" according to criteria that continue to be determined by Western gatekeepers. Rather, one benefit of understanding the identity of Philosophy itself as performative is that it draws our attention to the tension between its lived plurality (creative production of new and multiple philosophies) and the imposition or reiteration of norms of what counts as 'true' philosophy in a given context. Performance philosophy has always invited the consideration of how dominant ideas of what philosophy is and how it is practised might be expanded and changed in contact with the performing arts and with performative activity in a wider sense. Increasingly, we hope that it will also turn its attention to the possibilities of reciprocal transformation among forms of thought and knowledge emerging from the plurality of lived geographical and cultural contexts and the geopolitical inequalities that structure such encounters.

Indeed, one of the most important criticisms of performance philosophy as it has emerged thus far has been to note the ways in which it has participated in the 'epistemological erasure of the global south' in terms of the performances and philosophies it foregrounds (Henao Castro 2017, pp. 193–194). For instance, in a very fair and balanced review of our earlier edited collection, *Encounters in Performance Philosophy* (2014), Andrés Fabián Henao Castro notes how, in primarily citing European continental philosophy and Euro-USA performances, 'philosophy, performance, and their encounter, remain dominantly circumscribed in the geography of the global north, without such circumscription provoking much self-critique or methodological reflexivity' (ibid.).[10] And with respect to much of the early work in the field, Henao Castro is right to suggest that 'the effort to undo the inequalities that organize the encounter' between performance and philosophy as *disciplines* was largely being done 'at the expense of rethinking all the other inequalities pervasive in their histories' (Henao Castro 2017, pp. 193–194).

This Eurocentric perspective is embedded in the very narrative of the relationship between philosophy and performance too – which, most frequently, is cited as beginning with the 'ancient quarrel' between philosophers and thespians in the Republic. Likewise, the universalizing tendencies of Western philosophy have already been a cause for concern for performance scholars focused on particular bodies and the operations of social difference that (in)form their experience (DeFrantz 2007, p. 189).[11] Clearly, there can be no simple opposition of Philosophy and Performance Studies in this regard, given critics like Rustom Bharucha's analysis of Schechner's ethnocentrism in the context of his intercultural theatre practice (Bharucha 1984). Indeed, Bharucha suggests that Schechner's broad-spectrum is itself a universalizing gesture that fails to take the cultural difference of varying performance traditions into account: a homogenizing gesture of application in other words, rather than a qualitative extension or actual change to the idea of performance as determined by Western theatrical norms (Bharucha 1984, p. 12).[12] And certainly, the relationship between identity and difference, repetition and novelty remains philosophically unresolved in Schechner's model.

The issues raised by both Henao Castro (and elsewhere, differently, by Pittman) do not simply amount to 'the liberal complaint that this emergent field must strive to be more inclusive and diverse' (Pittman 2016, p. 168) in the inconsequential and ultimately still exclusionary ways that critics locate in the diversity strategies of many institutions. In these models, different groups are ostensibly included, but only by dint of leaving precisely that which differentiates at the door. This is not about simply reinforcing the liberal humanist idea of philosophy as that which supports the 'ever-expanding enfranchisement of the marginalised into liberating (intellectual) activity' according to the recognition of some supposed 'commonality' (Ó Maoilearca 2019). Rather, such critiques suggest that one role for performance philosophy, alongside the many overlapping fields with which it shares concerns, is to consider how it will actively support an actual and ongoing *pluralization* of thinking and *equalization* of knowledges; how it will practise an ethics in thought built not on resemblance but difference, not quantitative expansion but qualitative mutation.

> | ***Your companion.*** It is intriguing to imagine who might be reading this book now, what brought them to it (or it to them) and how they might use it. Was it to find friends working in similar ways? To seek a way out of bewilderment and isolation in their academic endeavours? Fact is, as hybrids of a kind, people working in the realm of performance philosophy are fairly likely to be living professionally precarious lives. I mean, there aren't many jobs in this realm are there? Is this something that should be mentioned or somehow addressed here? Does the very fact that there is now this "Routledge Companion to…" provide some hope that one's existence as an in-between thinker may be gaining academic acknowledgement? It would be nice to think that it brings a dash of optimism where prospects might otherwise (particularly in this year 2020) seem quite bleak.

The structure of this book. The Companion is structured into five sections.

| **Five sections.** As ever, there are places where the distinctions between parts are somewhat arbitrary – and essays that appear in one place could easily have appeared in another. The very notion of 'performance as philosophy' – for instance – is clearly a matter for 'Debates', a question of 'Methods' and among the 'Contexts' for Performance Philosophy.

Part I: Genealogies, contexts and traditions aims to explore a range of genealogies, both historical and contemporary entry points, by which performance philosophy can be contextualized in relation to different discourses and practices. Again, the content here should not be considered exhaustive in any way, but should invite one to consider a multitude of pathways in order to gain an understanding of the reach of performance philosophy as a field and/or method of working from a multitude of disciplines, various geopolitical locations and throughout different ages.

Part II: Questions and debates – as the title suggests, it means to foreground both long-standing and some newer areas of debate within performance philosophy, including ongoing conversations surrounding methodology – particularly in terms of the application paradigm we have referenced here; surrounding key ideas in performance such as the notion of presence and its interaction with visibility and representation; the critique of anthropocentrism and the role of the nonhuman; and the need for decolonial approaches to knowledge.

Part III: Methods, techniques, genres and forms draws together contributions that shed light on the particular nature, setting, function and consequence of the embodied act(ion)s involved in various forms of phenomenology-based philosophy and performances. The chapters here offer a glimpse *behind the scenes*, as it were, of the dramaturgical apparatus always at work in the generation and communication of the knowledge of one's craft, be it in an artistic, academic, educational or social media context. We glance before, after and in-between the unfolding of modes of performance philosophy as these take the form of dialogue and duet, play, rhythm and touch, or with special attention given to the identity building (and dissolving), transformational role of landscape and lying fallow.

Part IV: Figures is constituted by a collection of brief entries exemplifying individuals whose life-work might advance and multiply our thinking on what it is to practise performance philosophy. Whilst the volume as a whole resists the very possibility of 'comprehensiveness', this is particularly the case in this section which presents a consciously arbitrary and modest selection of individuals whose working lives might be productively considered in the context of Performance Philosophy. This is not a 'representative sample' that stands for the whole of how performance philosophy might be lived and by whom – but a real part of an indefinite whole without limit.

| *'Figures' of performance philosophy*: It is regrettable, for instance, that all the 'figures' in this section are human. We would have liked to have had an entry on Koko the Gorilla. Or Noc the Beluga. Or Carolee Schneeman's cat. We might also have included organic figures from the plant world...(The Major Oak of Sherwood Forest, the Avenue of Baobabs in Madagascar....) or even the performance philosophy potential of inanimate figures...(*Ponte dei Sospiri* – The Bridge of Sighs – in Venice...)?

Part V: Performance as philosophy and philosophy as performance showcases various examples which, depending on one's chosen perspective, might be regarded as performances taking the shape of philosophy or, inversely, as philosophies that emphasize their performative element. In fact, as has been underlined time and again in this introduction, both perspectives – performance as philosophy and philosophy as performance – tend to co-exist simultaneously and it is a question of developing a stereophonic attentiveness in order to appreciate both at the same time – and how they intermingle. Given centre stage in this context is the proximity between theory and theatre, in the broadest of senses of both terms – where making something palpable and witnessable (not necessarily visible or spectacular) is the guiding principle in a dialectic that tends to oscillate between active volition (in the sense of consciously attending to and preparing the conditions for something to be brought about in the event) and active–passive acquiescence – being open to luck, the possibility of failure and the serendipity of the given.

We are enormously grateful to all those without whom this book, as the collective endeavour that it is, would not have made it into existence: to Ben Piggott, our extremely helpful and patient editor at Routledge, for his positive support throughout the process; to John Barrett, Steven Lindberg and Niels Barmeyer, for their translation work; to Jules Bradbury, Emma Freeman and June Graff for copyediting; to designer Paul Jackel for his work on the cover image. To our colleague conveners of the Performance Philosophy network and the organizers of the most recent biennials, conversations and collaborations with whom have informed so much of this volume. We would like to thank all of our contributors for their creative and conceptual labours and their patience with our (at times) eccentric editorial process – including those who were invited to contribute but whose writing has sadly not made its way to this final volume for a range of reasons.

As ever, Laura would like to acknowledge the unseen but unwavering support of her husband, John Ó Maoilearca, without whom nothing would get done and whose care has made it possible to survive the very difficult couple of years during which this book has been produced. Alice, in turn, thanks all her family and friends for their continuous encouragement, generosity and forbearance – and especially her closest, Lula, Eliza and Max, for keeping the rhythm and staying cool, rockin' it and being rocks, while she juggles innumerable balls.

We dedicate the book to baby Ren Stephen Zerdy Daddario born during the final stages of the writing of this introduction.

Notes

1. For this opening definition, we have amalgamated various existing definitions of performance philosophy as given in the introduction to the Performance Philosophy book series (https://www.palgrave.com/gp/series/14558), the Performance Philosophy journal (http://www.performancephilosophy.org/journal) and the Performance Philosophy network (http://performancephilosophy.ning.com).
2. For example, Pittman says of Fred Moten and Stefano Harney's *The Undercommons* (2013): 'With its insurgent, cacophonous modes of thinking that so strain against the common sense of the present that I do not know what else to call it than "performance philosophy"' (Pittman 2016, p. 168).
3. In addition to the authors, the other founding conveners were: Will Daddario, Kélina Gotman, Karoline Gritzner, Eve Katsouraki, Esa Kirkkopelto, John Ó Maoilearca, Freddie Rokem, Theron Schmidt and Dan Watt.
4. For other introductions to the field, interested readers might look to *Inter Views in Performance Philosophy: Crossings and Conversations* (2017) edited by Anna Street, Julien Alliot, and Magnolia Pauker.
5. For example, for the SenseLab's first event Dancing the Virtual in 2005:

    A ban was set in place as regards presenting already-completed work of whatever kind. This was not meant to imply that participants would enter as blank slates. On the contrary, they were encouraged to bring everything but completed work. They were encouraged to come with all their passions, skills, methods, and, most of all, their techniques, but without a predetermined idea of how these would enter into the Dancing the Virtual event.

    (Manning and Massumi 2014, p. 97)

6 As McKenzie explains:

> Smart media are emerging scholarly genres that include video essays, theory comix, TED talks, and dozens of other media forms. These genres supplement the traditional scholarly genres of books and articles, and are emerging from popular culture, business, and academic contexts. In general, working in smart media involves thinking in interactive multimedia, presenting in new venues, and engaging new audiences… At a deeper level, smart media entail a massive redesign of our experience of knowledge, and a restructuring of its underlying architecture, for smart media open a new space for thought.
>
> *(McKenzie 2017, p. 86)*

7 http://web.flu.cas.cz/ppprague2017/manifest.html (1.9.2019). See also Chapter 22 in this book (Koubová) for an account of this conference and its manifesto.

8 Quoted from the Call for Contributions for the 2019 Performance Philosophy conference held in Amsterdam (*Between Institution and Intoxication: How does Performance Philosophy Intervene?*) https://performancephilosophy-amsterdam.nl/Call-for-Contributions

9 From this perspective, performance philosophy might be construed to have a particular but by no means exclusive affiliation to philosophies of immanence – as marked in the work of members of the Performance Philosophy community such as Arno Böhler and Susanne Granzer, Tero Nauha and John Ó Maoilearca. This is particularly foregrounded by the special issue of the Performance Philosophy journal on immanence, which arose from the Vienna-based research project, *Philosophy on Stage*, led by Böhler.

10

> *Encounters in Performance Philosophy* emphasizes European continental philosophy – Merleau-Ponty, Deleuze, Derrida, Laruelle, Lacoue-Labarthe and Nancy are, with Plato, Nietzsche and Heidegger, the most often cited philosophers – and Euro-USA performances, problematically inscribing performance philosophy in the continuous epistemological erasure of the global south, which reproduces a different, yet related geopolitical hierarchy of knowledge. Exceptions to this tendency are Arno Böhler's chapter, which not only draws from European philosophy but also from Asian philosophers such as the Yoga-Sutra of Patañjali, and Alan Read's chapter, which includes a discussion of the eighth-century Iraqi literary scholar Al-Jahiz. Philosophy, performance and their encounter, however, remain dominantly circumscribed in the geography of the global north, without such circumscription provoking much self-critique or methodological reflexivity… It is not unfair to claim that the political (dis)encounter between performance and philosophy, the one that performance philosophy seeks to confront through the immanence of an as that thinks alongside, denies a proper along to the other side of the globe, buried beneath the text in the depths of the cavernous south from which the philosopher and thespian of the north have emerged into the light. Encounters in Performance Philosophy inaugurate a discussion of the futurity of the nascent field that it contributes to forming, the one Cull hopes will become something else than the mere application of "extant philosophy to performance" (15). I harbor another hope: that the effort to undo the inequalities that organize the encounter between these two disciplines will not be done at the expense of rethinking all the other inequalities pervasive in their histories
>
> *(Henao Castro 2017, pp. 193–194).*

11 Thomas DeFrantz (2007) has criticized dominant tendencies in Western philosophy for neglecting the difference of bodies, from the perspective of dance:

> What can philosophy do for dance? In broad strokes, Western philosophy seeks to universalize experience, to encourage rumination from one author's perspective that might offer insights of use to many. Dance, though, hopes to explore the particular gesture, the particular release of energy, the particular moment of possibility without desire for broad appeal. Odd bedfellows, philosophy and dance have spawned a tiny literature concerned with aspects of Western theatrical dance, explored in large part by men (Sparshott 1988 and 1995; Fancher and Myers 1981) and phenomenological approaches to body knowledge, largely offered up by women (Foster et al. 2005; Fraleigh 1996 and 2004; Sheets-Johnston 1966). Although a palpable line of gender divides the discussion, this constant emerges: Philosophy tends to push conversations around dance away from physical movement toward a space of contemplation, where bodies can become interchangeable, and, in many ways, irrelevant.
>
> *(DeFrantz 2007 p. 189)*

12 As Bharucha puts it:

> Underlying Schechner's method in applying theoretical models to differing performance traditions is his faith in "universals." In *Drama, Script, Theatre, and Performance*, he emphatically states: "It is my belief that performance and theatre are universal, but that drama is not" (Schechner 1977, 60).
>
> *(Bharucha 1984, p. 12)*

References

Bharucha, Rustom. 1984. 'A Collision of Cultures: Some Western Interpretations of the Indian Theatre', *Asian Theatre Journal,* Hawaii, v. 1, n. 1, pp. 1–20.

Bosman, Philip. 2006. 'Selling Cynicism: The Pragmatics of Diogenes' Comic Performances', *The Classical Quarterly,* v. 56, n. 1, pp. 93–104. doi:10.1017/S0009838806000085

Bowie, Andrew. 2007. *Music, Philosophy, and Modernity.* Cambridge: Cambridge University Press.

Cull, Laura. 2012, February. 'Performance as Philosophy: Responding to the Problem of "Application"', *Theatre Research International,* v. 37, n. 1, pp. 20–27.

Cull, Laura. 2014. 'Performance Philosophy: Staging a New Field', in Laura Cull and Alice Lagaay (eds.), *Encounters in Performance Philosophy.* London & New York: Palgrave, pp. 15–38.

Cull Ó Maoilearca, Laura. 2018. "Notes toward the Philosophy of Theatre", in David Kornhaber and Martin Middeke (eds.), 'Drama, Theatre, and Philosophy'. Special issue of *Anglia. Journal of English Philology,* v. 136, n. 1 (March 2018), pp. 11–42.

Cull, Laura and Lagaay, Alice (eds.). 2014. *Encounters in Performance Philosophy.* London & New York: Palgrave.

Cvejić, Bojana. 2015. 'From Odd Encounters to a Prospective Confluence: Dance-Philosophy', *Performance Philosophy,* v. 1, n. 1, pp. 7–23. Available at: <http://dx.doi.org/10.21476/PP.2015.1129>. Accessed on: May 3, 2019.

DeFrantz, Thomas. 2007. 'Exhausting Dance: Performance and the Politics of Movement (review)', *TDR: The Drama Review,* v. 51, n. 3, New York, pp. 189–191. Available at: <https://muse.jhu.edu/>. Accessed on: May 3, 2019.

Goulish, Matthew. 2014. Endorsement, in Alan Read (ed.), *Theatre in the Expanded Field: Seven Approaches to Performance.* London & New York: Bloomsbury, backcover.

Henao Castro, Andrés Fabián. 2017. 'Review of Cull, Laura and Alice Lagaay (eds.). Encounters in Performance Philosophy and Chow, Broderick and Alex Mangold (eds.). Žižek and Performance', *Journal of Contemporary Drama in English,* v. 5, n. 1, pp. 189–197.

Hollinghaus, Wade and Daddario, Will. 2015, March. 'Performance Philosophy: Arrived Just in Time?', *Theatre Topics,* v. 25, n. 1, pp. 51–56.

Ingold, Tim. 2018. *Anthropology and/as Education.* London & New York: Routledge.

Kirkkopelto, Esa. 2015. 'For What Do We Need Performance Philosophy?' *Performance Philosophy,* v. 1, pp. 4–6. Available at <http://dx.doi.org/10.21476/PP.2015.117>. Accessed: May 3, 2019.

Koubová, Alice and Lagaay, Alice. 2014. "Performing the Impossible in Philosophy", in Laura Cull and Alice Lagaay (eds.), *Encounters in Performance Philosophy: Theatre, Performativity and the Practice of Theory.* London & New York: Palgrave Macmillan, pp. 39–62.

Lagaay, Alice. 2015, April. 'Minding the Gap – Of Indifference: Approaching 'Performance Philosophy' with Salomo Friedlaender (1871–1946)', *Performance Philosophy,* v. 1, pp. 65–73. Available at: <http://www.performancephilosophy.org/journal/article/view/27/81>. Accessed on: May 3, 2019.

Manning, Erin and Massumi, Brian. 2014. *Thought in the Act: Passages in the Ecology of Experience.* Minneapolis: University of Minnesota Press.

McCabe, M.M. 2019. Unpublished remarks, presented as part of 'On Dialogue: A Performance Philosophy Workshop', King's College London, April 3, 2019.

McKenzie, Jon. 2017. "Philosophical Interruptions and Post-Ideational Genres: Thinking Beyond Literacy", in Anna Street, Julien Alliot and Magnolia Pauker (eds.), *Inter Views in Performance Philosophy: Crossings and Conversations.* London: Palgrave Macmillan, pp. 117–124.

Mullarkey, John. 2009. *Refractions of Reality: Philosophy and the Moving Image.* Basingstoke: Palgrave Macmillan.

Nagel, Thomas. 1986. *The View from Nowhere.* Oxford: Oxford University Press.

Ó Maoilearca, John. 2019. "When the Twain Shall Meet: On the Divide between Analytic and Continental Film Philosophy", in N. Carroll, L. Di Summa and S. Loht (eds.), *The Palgrave Handbook of the Philosophy of Film and Motion Pictures*. London: Palgrave Macmillan, pp. 259–284.

Papazian, Michael. 2009. "Democracy and Philosophy as a Way of Life", in Elizabeth Kaufer Busch and Peter Augustine Lawler (eds.), *Democracy Reconsidered*. New York: Lexington Books, pp. 79–86.

Pittman Alex. 2016. 'Encounters in Performance Philosophy ed. by Laura Cull and Alice Lagaay and: Adorno and Performance ed. by Will Daddario and Karoline Gritzner (review)', *TDR: The Drama Review*, v. 60, n. 2, New York, pp. 166–169.

Puchner, Martin. 2010. *The Drama of Ideas: Platonic Provocations in Theater and Philosophy*. Oxford: Oxford University Press.

Sinnerbrink, Robert. 2011. *New Philosophies of Film: Thinking Images*. London & New York: Continuum.

Street, Anna, Alliot, Julien and Pauker, Magnolia (eds.) 2017. *Inter Views in Performance Philosophy: Crossings and Conversations*. London: Palgrave Macmillan.

PART I

Genealogies, contexts and traditions

1
PERFORMANCES OF PHILOSOPHY IN ANCIENT GREECE AND IN MODERNITY
Suddenly a philosopher enters the stage

Ira Avneri and Freddie Rokem

The context

The basic facts are well known: Ancient Greece was the 'birthplace' of the discursive practices of both theater and philosophy. The more or less simultaneous composition of a large body of dramatic works and the emergence (with Socrates and Plato) of mature philosophical thought is a unique phenomenon. Developing through an intense dialogue, the two discursive practices were, however, also frequently in competition, at times even regarding each other with scorn and suspicion, initiating what is famously known as the 'ancient quarrel between philosophy and (dramatic) poetry'. Through their multi-leveled interactions, each discursive practice also integrated features of the other, either drawing attention to the philosophical aspects of dramatic writing and theater performances or to the dramaturgical and performative dimensions of philosophy.

We will begin with a brief presentation of two paradigmatic cases of such 'transgressions', with Oedipus as a philosophical dramatic character and Socrates as a performative philosopher. Then, we will examine in detail Socrates' performative philosophizing as depicted in his delayed entrance to Agathon's house in Plato's *Symposium*. And in closing, we will briefly discuss how certain aspects of the Socratic/Platonic legacy of philosophical performativity have reappeared in the work and thinking of Walter Benjamin and Bertolt Brecht.

Sophocles' *Oedipus Tyrannus* (dated around 429 BCE) plays a double role in this context. First, it features a dramatic character who triumphantly takes on the role of the philosopher when solving the riddle of the Sphinx to define what a human being is.[1] Second, around 335 BCE, almost a century after it was written, the play served as the bedrock for Aristotle's *Poetics*. Composed at a time when the arts of playwriting and theatrical performances had deteriorated, the *Poetics* was the first philosophical text *about* drama/tragedy, rather than a philosophical drama of the kind that Plato had marvelously sketched in his dialogues.

It is important to note that *Oedipus Tyrannus* repeatedly emphasizes that Oedipus had solved the riddle of the Sphinx using his own intelligence, without any supernatural intervention. This riddle defines the human as a creature with *many* shifting legs (i.e. multiplicity and transformation) and a *single* voice (i.e. unity and sameness). In Platonic terms, this interaction between one and many is echoed in the dialectics between the eternal, pure Forms and their many transient manifestations. In Aristotelian terms, however, the riddle of the Sphinx seems to violate one of the basic principles of logical thinking, the Principle of Non-contradiction, which later became the basis for the Law of Identity. As Aristotle claims in his *Metaphysics*, "the *same* attribute cannot at the *same* time belong and not belong to the *same* subject in the *same* respect" (1005b; our emphasis. Aristotle, 1984, p. 1588). However, in Sophocles' *Oedipus Tyrannus*, as Charles Segal has noted, "noncontradiction gives way to a fantastic, irrational 'logic' of paradoxes in which opposites can in fact be equal and 'one' can simultaneously be 'many'" (Segal 1999, p. 216. See also Rokem 2010, 2016).

As a 'prize' for solving this paradoxical riddle, Oedipus marries the widow-queen, his mother, thus becoming the ruler of Thebes and unwittingly fulfilling the second part of the Delphic prophecy. This alone is not sufficient to abolish the plague in Thebes. The plague, it is said, will only cease when the person who killed King Laius is found. The murderer turns out to be Oedipus himself, who, whilst knowing the universal identity of humans, fails to know his own identity as a singular subject, the *gnōthi seautón* ('know thyself') commanded by the Oracle.

The second paradigmatic case is Socrates, whose manner of philosophizing was often seen as theatrical – even in the eyes of Plato, his most ardent pupil. Socrates' philosophical mission was also directly related to the Delphic Oracle. As he himself argues in his defense-speech (in 399 BCE, as transmitted in Plato's *Apology*), the Oracle had disclosed to his longtime friend Chaerephon that there was no man wiser than Socrates. Upon hearing of it from Chaerephon, the perplexed Socrates, who until then had believed that he possessed no wisdom, began wandering about Athens to check its veracity by seeking someone who is wiser than him – in order, finally, to confirm that the Oracle is irrefutable (22a), a 'Popperian'-like logic of verification of a given assumption on the basis of unsuccessful attempts to refute it (*Apology*, 21e–22e).[2]

Socrates' response to the 'riddle' of the Oracle (as he terms it; 21b)[3] signaled his Oedipus-like insistence that the traditional methods of oracular interpretation must give way to rational inquiry, testing the veracity of divine pronouncements. But, as he began to question people who had made claims to wisdom, Socrates found out that he himself is indeed the wisest, for he is the only one who knows that he *does not know* (22d–23b), which – like the Cretan who claims that all Cretans are liars – is in itself paradoxical. As he tells it, he was unable to find even a single person who could grasp the notion of wisdom as knowledge of ignorance. While his interlocutors perceived themselves as knowledgeable when in fact they knew nothing, he himself was aware of his own ignorance and did not pretend to know anything apart from that (21c–d).

The *Symposium* – Plato's only dialogue named after the occasion for its plot – is the earliest known record of a philosopher engaging with the practices of theater. It presents a detailed report of the private banquet held in honor of Agathon's victory in the annual tragedy festival of *Lênaea*, presumably in 416 BCE. Arriving at the exclusive party with his admirer Aristodemus, Socrates eventually joins the group of prominent Athenian citizens, including the playwright Aristophanes whose comedy the *Clouds* (performed in 423 BCE; the earliest known text to mention Socrates) features a satiric, somewhat malicious depiction of Socrates' philosophical performance, which, according to Plato, has nourished the charges against Socrates (*Apology*, 18c–d, 19c). Gathered in the intimate setting of Agathon's house, they celebrate the playwright's victory in the tragedy competition by staging another competition, a playful contest (*agôn*) of speeches in praise of Eros – the divine, mythological personification of the human *erôs*.

However, this competition begins only after Socrates finally makes his entrance, concluding a long standstill outside the house (*Symposium*, 174d–175c). Through the interruptions, first caused by his absence and the delay of his entrance and then by his presence and indoor actions, Socrates transforms the house of the dramatist into a stage (or 'home') for performing philosophy. When Alcibiades makes a sudden 'drunken' entrance, just after Socrates has completed his speech on Eros (based on Diotima's teachings – a sophisticated way of defending his own claim of ignorance), the discussion takes on new forms of theatricality, turning into a fierce and much less playful *agôn* between these two ex-lovers (212c ff.). Finally, at dawn, before leaving Agathon's house to spend the day in the baths and the market place, Socrates lectures the two playwrights – who are too tired to hear his arguments and fall asleep – that the same man could possess the knowledge required for composing both tragedies and comedies and that the man who can compose tragedies should be able to compose comedies as well (223c–d).

At a certain point, Aristodemus also falls asleep and misses most of the discussion epitomizing the *agôn* between the discursive practices of philosophy and dramatic poetry. As Aristodemus had realized in real-time and later told Apollodorus, the narrator of the dialogue, he had only heard the key points of Socrates' argument but could not remember most of what was said (223c–d). One possible interpretation of Socrates' early morning 'lecture' is that philosophy encompasses both dramatic genres, while the playwrights, who either compose tragedy or comedy but not both,[4] are incomplete, like the split two-legged humans searching for their missing half, according to the myth presented in Aristophanes' speech on Eros.

While Oedipus' employment of logical reasoning (which Aristotle regarded as the foundation for philosophy as well as for dramatic narratives) leads to the destruction of himself and his family, Socrates' performance of philosophy eventually serves as evidence in the trial that results in his death-sentence. Athens, Plato suggests, cannot be a home for Socratic philosophy. The philosophical performances of Oedipus and Socrates are thus the paradoxical expressions of a uniquely tragic spirit, combining triumph and downfall, which was cultivated during a short period in Classical Athens when the discursive practices of philosophy and performance were in competitive yet fruitful dialogue with each other.

Socrates' standstill

In Plato's works, Socrates' odd behavior is often denoted by the word *atopos*, or *atopia*, and its variants. Formed by the combination of the Alpha privative and the Greek word *topos* (meaning 'place', 'location', and sometimes also 'topic'), *atopia* is often translated as 'outlandishness' or 'strangeness'; yet literally, it signifies a quality of 'placelessness', an absence of 'normal' location, something that eludes categorization or a specified context (cf. Schlosser 2014, pp. 12, 142).[5] Socrates' *atopia* implies his unique stance in Athens as an outsider inside: he is a stranger to the traditional patterns of thought and behavior as well as to the common manner of expression; yet, he is no foreigner. His presence embodies the dialectics of familiarity and strangeness discussed in the Allegory of the Cave. "It's a strange image (*atopon eikona*) you're describing, and strange prisoners (*desmôtas atopous*)", Glaucon reacts to the account of the state of affairs inside the cave, to which Socrates replies: "They're like us" (*Republic*, 515a. Plato 1997, pp. 1132–1133).

The term *atopia* can define almost any philosophical model, since philosophy is, in Maurice Merleau-Ponty's words, "never entirely within the world, yet never outside the world" (cf. Hadot 2002, p. 36). Still, there seems to be no philosopher more suitable to this term than Socrates. He is considered atopic not just in terms of his appearance and manners, but also in terms of his mode of thinking, his way of philosophizing, and his public practice of a private spatio-temporal logic that challenges the Athenian conventions of space and time.

The initial movement intrinsic to Socrates' atopic philosophizing is his idle wanderings, *systematically* examining people while strolling around in search of someone wiser than him. As he interprets the Oracle's reply, he is given a divine mission to examine himself and others (*Apology*, 28e–29a, 33c), in order to show the Athenians their ignorance through his knowledge of his own ignorance (29d–30a). Socrates' claim that the Oracle's reply is what has produced his philosophical quest identifies the beginning of philosophizing with wandering. Like the excursions of Walter Benjamin's *flâneur*, these wanderings are confined to, and associated with, a specific spatio-temporal urban environment: fifth-century BCE Athens in the case of Socrates, and nineteenth-century CE Paris in the case of the *flâneur*. Still, to Socrates, the city is above all its inhabitants: in his wanderings, he 'collected' *people* for the sake of conversation, and not the kind of crystallized experiences, neglected memories, and miniature objects that the *flâneur* collects in his excursions to flea-markets and half-hidden arcades.

As Silvia Montiglio has rightly pointed out, there is no philosophizing without wandering, the movement that activates the quest for wisdom, but the more advanced and even ideal Platonic posture for contemplation is a *static* one (Montiglio 2005, pp. 178–179). Wandering marks the initial shock experienced by the soul when 'falling' into the body; yet, the philosopher yearns for what is beyond movement, since according to Plato the ability to grasp the truth is limited to a stable position. From the *Phaedo*, we learn that when the soul detaches itself from the senses to inquire by itself, it sights the Invisible and the Intelligible (83a–b) and ascends to the realm of the Eternal. There, imitating the pure Forms, it ceases to move and remains stable. This condition of the soul is called 'wisdom' (79c–d).

Marking a movement toward transcendence, the vertical axis was part of the way Greek cosmology treated the space of the *polis*, a model whereby the human sphere (the horizontal axis) is located between the upper-world of the Olympus and the under-world of Hades (Wiles 1997, pp. 175–176). In Greek drama, the vertical is often related to an improper attempt to transcend the boundaries of the human sphere (and its tragic consequences), as exhibited in *Oedipus Tyrannus*. For Plato, however, it denotes the notion of ascent as the proper philosophical path, as exhibited in the movement up the Ladder of Love in the *Symposium* (as well as up and out of the cave in the *Republic*). Socrates employs a terminology of ascent to explain that through such movement, the philosophical lover frees himself from the contingency of mortal beauty in favor of a gaze at the pure form of Beauty (211a–b). While Aristophanes suggests that *erôs* moves the lovers on the horizontal axis, *toward each other*, Socrates suggests that *erôs* directs the (philosophical) lover *upward and beyond*, from pursuing the beauty of one particular body to a gaze at the Beautiful in itself – the pure, godlike Form of Beauty (Vernant 1990, pp. 470–473. See also Bloom, 1993, p. 484).

While the *Apology* depicts the initial stage of Socrates' philosophizing, acted out through his conversations with others as he wanders around on the horizontal axis, the *Symposium* depicts an advanced stage of that quest, acted out through Socrates' conversations with himself while standing still in solitude,[6] his body fixed immovably to one spot as his mind runs free, as if moving vertically up the Ladder of Love.[7] The first instance of this gesture, beginning while Socrates is on his way to Agathon's house, occurs in a neighbor's doorway (front porch). The narrative itself moves into the house, and the 'offstage' act is made present 'onstage' through Agathon's servant's report (175a–c).

The second instance, reported later in the dialogue by Alcibiades (220c–d), is said to have occurred about sixteen years earlier, when Socrates stood motionless for more than 24 hours during the Athenian expedition to Potidaea. Even if we know from other sources that long standstills were habitual for Socrates (e.g. in Aulus Gellius, *Noctes Atticae*, 2:1:1–3), the only instances of this gesture in the entire corpus of Plato's works are those in the *Symposium*.

In the broader context of Plato's philosophy, standstill is identified with the retreat of the soul to the Intelligible (e.g. *Phaedrus*, 247b–c). Hence, it is fitting that this image is introduced (only) in the *Symposium*, a dialogue in which the retreat is manifested as a journey up the Ladder of Love, an inner movement in a static position, with Socrates himself as the philosopher engaged in this ascent (Montiglio 2005, p. 176).

The scenes in which he stands still in solitude, immersed in thoughts whose content is not reported to us, characterize Socrates as a perfect *erôtikos*, the lover of Wisdom and pure Beauty, who is essentially alone at the top of the Ladder of Love. Standstill – the metaphorical posture for temporarily withdrawing from the stream of life (*Republic*, 496d–e) – is a mark of physical, mental, and intellectual stamina, as well as of stepping out of time, coinciding with the image of the Platonic philosopher as gazing upon Eternity, e.g. in the *Symposium* (210a–212a) and the *Republic* (484b). Indeed, Socrates' most intense reflections occur when he performs this odd act, with his body held tight while his thoughts run free (Montiglio 2005, pp. 172–173).

In the *Symposium*, the drama that precedes the eulogies to Eros is designed as a theater of interruptions, exhibiting Socrates' *atopia*, and not by chance: Eros, like Socrates, is out-of-place. Although the door to Agathon's house stands open, awaiting the guests, and although the banquet has already begun (174d–e), Socrates refrains from entering, forcing his companion Aristodemus to enter alone in a party to which he was not invited in the first place. Socrates himself stands immobile in a neighbor's doorway. As the narrative reveals, this outdoor act steals the focus from the indoor event. The cause of the disturbance is not Socrates' presence but rather his absence, or more precisely, his atopic presence-through-absence. This dialectics of presence and absence is not just characteristic of Eros, oscillating between poverty and plenty, but can also be seen as structuring the phenomenology of desire itself (Halperin 1992, p. 101).

Unlike the Ionian soldiers at Potidaea, who do not try to interrupt Socrates' standstill and even take their bedding outside to get a better view of this spectacle, Agathon obsessively attempts to interfere with the standstill that occurs outside his house. He asks Aristodemus twice about Socrates' whereabouts (174e); orders his servant to go look for Socrates and bring him in (175a); and when he hears that Socrates is standing still nearby, ignoring requests to come inside, he tells his servant: "How odd (*atopon*). […] Call him again and keep on calling him" (175a. Plato 2008, p. 5). At that point, Aristodemus interferes and urges Agathon to leave Socrates alone: "This is one of his habits. Sometimes he turns aside and stands still wherever he happens to be. He will come in very soon, I think. Don't disturb (*kineite*, 'move') him" (175a–b, ibid.). Aristodemus may not know for certain that Socrates will enter, but he does know that Socrates must be allowed to enter in his own time, of his own free will – which indeed Socrates does, without any explanation, when the dinner is already halfway through (175c. Blondell 2006, pp. 149–151).

Writing about entrances and exits in Greek theater – a stage device which advances or arrests the dramatic action by regulating the presence and absence of characters – Oliver Taplin notes that in a good play, "each entrance and exit does not happen at random; it is put into a dramatic context in order to further artistic purposes which could not be served in any other way" (Taplin 1977, p. 67). Conforming to this theatrical logic, in Plato's dialogues, each entrance – especially Socrates' – furthers not just the drama but also the philosophical themes explored in them. The *Symposium* is a good example of this spatial dramaturgy, since Socrates' entrance into Agathon's house is preceded by an atopic display of his commitment to philosophy, evident both in the contemplative standstill itself and in his refusal to enter before concluding it. Performing this standstill in a neighbor's doorway – the typical place of the lover, according to Pausanias (183a), as well as of Eros himself, according to Diotima (203c–d) – Socrates is determined to enter only in his own time.

Socrates' entrance

Socrates' late entrance into Agathon's house is succeeded by two entrances which manifest a transition from 'high' philosophical *erôs* to 'low' bodily *erôs*: Alcibiades' entrance, immediately after Socrates' speech, when Aristophanes wants to protest against something that Socrates has said (212c); and the invasion by some revelers who take over and impose their own drinking rules on the diners, thereby bringing to the gradual dissolution of the party (223b). Here we will discuss only Socrates' entrance, foreshadowing Benjamin's discussion of the entrance as a form of philosophical interruption, as embodied in the image of the sudden appearance of a stranger – personifying philosophy – at a house-door (coinciding with the Greek conception of the stranger, *xênos*, as a *thuraios*, 'the one at/connected with the door'). In the *Symposium*, the notion of the 'sudden' (*exaiphnês*) is used to depict the other two entrances, but the ultimate strangers are Socrates and Diotima, his 'teacher' in the dialectics of *erôs*.[8] By initially refraining from entering Agathon's house in favor of a display of philosophizing; by sending Aristodemus to enter before him; by his own late entrance while the banquet-dinner is already halfway through; and finally by making Diotima enter the discussion through a reenactment of their conversations in his eulogy of Eros, Socrates initiates the transformation of the dramatist's house into a temporary home for performing philosophy. In the *Symposium*, this phrasing encompasses the two meanings of 'to perform': Socrates is both *doing* philosophy and *presenting a display* of philosophy.

The entrance of philosophy into the non-philosophical space of Agathon's house is already evident in the initial exchange between Socrates and the host, when the theme of ignorance vs. knowledge is introduced. When Socrates enters, Agathon invites him to his couch, adding in jest that through the bodily contact derived from lying one beside the other, he himself may acquire the piece of wisdom (*sophia*) that came into Socrates' mind in his standstill (175c–d). Socrates accepts the invitation, joining Agathon, yet dismisses the latter's playful-erotic remark by claiming – also in jest – that if wisdom were something that could flow through mere contact, from the one who is full to the one who is empty, he would value having the place beside Agathon so that his own inferior wisdom could be filled with Agathon's abundant wisdom, brilliantly displayed at the theater in front of more than thirty-thousand spectators (175d–e).

This is Socrates' third demonstrative rejection of Agathon. The first was his absence from the public celebration in honor of Agathon on the day before the private banquet, disclosing his tendency to avoid events that are, literally speaking, crowded (174a). The second was Socrates' behavior when arriving at the banquet, culminating in his self-absorbed yet publicly visible standstill. The fact that Socrates would stop somewhere to think is not something rare; yet, he challenged Agathon, both as a host and as a dramatist, by doing it in the theatrical way that he did, just outside the banquet (Rhodes 2003, pp. 199–202). Socrates' third rejection – that wisdom can flow from one person to another – is, however, not in total jest. In fact, a serious issue is at stake here: the transmission of knowledge and wisdom. *Haptesthai*, Agathon's verb for his proposal to touch Socrates, is the same verb later used by Diotima to denote the ability to grasp truth at the top of the Ladder of Love (212a).

As Andrea Wilson Nightingale has pointed out, a Platonic philosopher would necessarily reject such a proposal, since wisdom is not a good that resides in the bodily sphere of exchange, just as education is not an exchange of commodities (Nightingale 1995, pp. 47–48, 50). Plato's Socrates regards learning as a process of recollection, elicited from within with the help of a guide rather than imparted from the outside by a teacher. Perhaps exposing his own implicit critique of Socrates, Plato makes Agathon interpret these rejections as provocations on Socrates' part. When Socrates claims that Agathon's wisdom is superior to his own, Agathon suspects him of *pretending* ignorance and accuses him of being *hybristês* (175e). Derived from the same root as *hybris*, *hybristês* is often translated as 'being sarcastic'; yet, it also denotes an outrageous and even violent behavior. Later, this charge is picked up by Alcibiades, who had not yet been present when Agathon voiced it. Like Agathon albeit from a different stance, Alcibiades stresses Socrates' false pretenses of being ignorant (216d–e) and of being a lover (222a–b). Both of them consider these pretenses to be an indication of hubris and Socrates' praise of others to express an ironical disguise for contempt. As Chris Emlyn-Jones rightly claims, in the *Symposium*, "the boundaries of the Socratic and the theatrical are presented at their most ambivalent" (Emlyn-Jones 2004, p. 403).

Probably both favoring and denouncing Socrates, Plato's description of his philosophical hero's performative behavior before and after entering Agathon's house suggests that Socrates plays to an audience no less than the playwrights do. This is evident first and foremost in his unusual apparel – bathed, shod, and fancily dressed (174a). To dress up like that is to prepare for a performance, because as Socrates tells Ion, rhapsodes are expected to be dressed up and to look as beautiful as possible for their contests (*Ion*, 530b). Suiting himself to the specific occasion and to the beauty of the host, Socrates has carefully planned his appearance in the *Symposium*. However, unlike Agathon's external, audience-dependent theatricality, Socrates' theatricality creates the impression of being directed inward, only indirectly aimed at an external audience. Nevertheless, his overall attitude bears the quality of a display. In the end, Socrates' *agôn* with Agathon is a contest between two skilled performers.

Benjamin and the aesthetics of thinking

Almost immediately after Benjamin and Brecht had become close friends in 1929 (cf. Wizisla 2009), Benjamin began theorizing the principles of Brecht's work. The first version of his essay "What is Epic Theatre?" was written in 1931 but was withheld, apparently for political reasons, after it had been accepted for publication in the *Frankfurter Zeitung*, remaining unpublished during his lifetime (though a second, much shorter version, was published anonymously in 1939, about a year before he took his own life). In this text, Benjamin draws attention to one of the central features of Brecht's theater: the interruption (*Die Unterbrechung*), which "does not reproduce conditions but, rather, reveals them. This uncovering of conditions (*Entdeckung der Zustände*) is brought about through processes being interrupted" (Benjamin 1973, pp. 4–5).

What Benjamin terms the "very crude (*primitivste*) example" of an interruption is the sudden appearance of a stranger at a domestic scene of potential violence:

> The mother is just about to pick up a pillow [in the second version of the essay, a 'bronze statue'; I.A. and F.R.] to hurl at the daughter, the father is opening a window to call a policeman. At this moment a stranger appears at the door. 'Tableau', as they used to say around 1900 (*um 1900*).

Through such a *tableau*, Benjamin explains, "the stranger is suddenly confronted with certain conditions: rumpled bedclothes, an open window, a devastated interior"; not an unusual situation, he adds, because there are many bourgeois scenes that look exactly like this. According to Benjamin, the greater the devastations of the social order, "the more marked must be the distance between the stranger and the events portrayed" (ibid., p. 5).[9] This, he argues, intensifies the interruption:

> The thing that is revealed as though by lightning in the 'condition' represented on the stage – as a copy of human gestures, actions and words – is an immanently dialectical attitude. The condition which epic theatre reveals is the dialectic at a standstill.
> *(Ibid., p. 12 with minor adjustments)*

This principle will also serve Benjamin to theorize our understanding of history. In the N-convolute ("On the Theory of Knowledge, Theory of Progress") of the *Arcades Project* (*Das Passagen-Werk*), he expands the concept of dialectic at a standstill: "The dialectical image is an image that emerges suddenly, in a flash. What has been is to be held fast – as an image flashing up in the now of its recognizability" (N9, 7. Benjamin 1999b, p. 473). The dialectical image, he explains, "is that wherein what has been comes together in a flash with the now to form a constellation. In other words: image is dialectics at a standstill" (N3, 1. Ibid., p. 463).

In Benjamin's eyes, the interruption of the sequence of time is in fact what makes history truly historical – in keeping with the idea of a "present which is not a transition, but in which time takes a stand and has come to a standstill".[10] As in Plato's design of the atopic scenes in which Socrates stands immobile for an unspecified period of time, leisurely privatizing the public space, Benjamin's dialectics at a standstill crystallizes the arrest of an 'objective' flow, an image flashing up in the now of its 'recognizability' (in German, the word is *Erkennbarkeit*, which can also be translated as 'knowability'). It is a caesura in and of the spatio-temporal order; a gesture of interruption not just *in* time and *of* time but also *in* space and *of* space; or, in Benjamin's own words, discussing Brecht's theater, a "damming of the stream of real life (*Die Stauung im realen Lebensfluß*)" (Benjamin 1973, p. 13).[11] When the stream of life is brought to a sudden halt, the image is frozen under a lightning flash of truth. What was thought to be known appears as new in its strangeness: the familiar appears as unfamiliar, even *Unheimlich*, viewed through a demystified illumination and open to re-examination – in and through a constellation, where the situation becomes transformed into an image at a standstill.

Alongside this convergence, there is also a crucial difference between the two models. Socrates' dialectical standstills mark a tension *between* his body and his mind. As we have seen, his moments of external motionlessness are also his most intense moments of internal motion on the Ladder of Love. In his standstills, Socrates establishes his own 'private theatre' on the stage of the 'theatre of the world'. In the end, though, this 'theatre' and the performance of thinking staged in it are the cause and effect of each other, because Socrates' gesture of interrupting the stream is what sets the stage for a Socratic philosophy of interrupting the stream. In this process, the standstill is both a precondition and a result; it is the stage both for and of its own philosophical appearance.

Benjamin's Dialectics at a Standstill, however, marks a dialectics of motion and stasis *in the same thing*. This tension can appear in the realm of a body, as in the case of the angel of history (*Angelus Novus*) who is blown into the future by a storm we call 'progress', coming from Paradise, while he is fixedly contemplating the "one single catastrophe, which keeps piling wreckage upon wreckage and hurls it at his feet" (Benjamin 2003, p. 392).[12] But it can also appear in the realm of the mind, as evident in Benjamin's claim that thinking involves not only the flow of thoughts but their arrest (*Stillstellung*) as well (Benjamin 2003, p. 396). This transformation of the activity of thinking into a performative expression is even more explicit in the *Arcades Project*, in Benjamin's claim that "where thinking comes to a standstill in a constellation saturated with tensions – there the dialectical image appears. It is the caesura in the movement of thought" (Benjamin 1999b, Convolute N10a, 3, p. 475).

The opening sentence of *The Origin of German Tragic Drama* (published in 1928) provides such a caesura, exemplifying the dialectics of the image itself: "It is characteristic of philosophical writing that it must continually confront the question of representation (*Es ist dem philosophischen Schrifttum eigen, mit jeder Wendung von neuem vor der Frage der Darstellung zu stehen*)" (Benjamin 1998, p. 27). This sentence can even be seen as a self-reflexive staging of such a caesura in the medium of language, where 'philosophical writing' – which is the outcome of philosophical thinking – must 'with every turn' (*mit jeder Wendung*) literally 'face' the question of *Darstellung*. The word *Wendung* means both a bodily 'turn' in a certain direction, personifying the writing as a physical movement, through a *Wendung* of language, which also means its use of idioms and expressions.

This choreography (the 'bodily writing') of thought, enabling the philosopher to 'turn' toward *Darstellung* through language and contemplation, recalls Plato's Allegory of the Cave, where turning around is an image for philosophical pedagogy. The prisoners in the cave are chained so that they can see nothing but the flickering shadows of illusions on the wall in front of them and are prevented from turning their heads. But at a certain point one of them is mysteriously released from his chains; someone or something *compels* him to stand up, turn around, and walk toward the fire that burns far above and behind them (*Republic*, 514a–515c). The first step of the ascent from the cave is an act of turning around (*periagein*), exemplifying a dialectics of compulsion and freedom.[13]

In Benjamin's model, however, we are free from the outset to turn in every direction, to face *Darstellung* – a term which can be translated both as 'presentation' and 'representation' (and is actually positioned between them) – evoking a state for showing as well as making something visible in the liminal space where philosophy and performance overlap and interact. Benjamin's thesis on the German Mourning Play, which opens with the above-mentioned reflection, staging the caesura of thinking itself, is based on the assumption that "as essences, truth and idea acquire that supreme metaphysical significance expressly attributed to them in the Platonic system". And this, Benjamin adds in the "Epistemo-Critical Prologue" of his book,

> is evident above all in the *Symposium*, which contains two pronouncements of decisive importance […]. It presents truth – the realm of ideas – as the essential content of beauty. It declares truth to be beautiful. An understanding of the Platonic view of truth and beauty is not just a primary aim in every investigation into the philosophy of art, but it is indispensable to the definition of truth itself.
>
> (Benjamin 1998, p. 30)

Brecht and the appearance of the thinking man

During the years 1929 to 1933, before Benjamin and Brecht were forced to leave Germany after the Nazi takeover of power, Brecht explored new forms of artistic expression in a broad range of *Lehrstücke*, 'Learning Plays'. Reflecting Brecht's Marxist-materialist approach, the *Lehrstücke* expose sharp ideological conflicts through fundamental social, economic, and legal paradoxes and injustices, simultaneously using a wide range of meta-performative devices, as well as more direct forms of audience participation. And perhaps most strikingly in this context, Brecht included a broad range of figures defined as thinkers or philosophers who enter, like Herr Keuner (often referred to as Herr K., as in two of Kafka's novels which abound in interrupting strangers) as well as in the short dramatic fragment "Nothing comes from Nothing" (*Aus Nichts wird Nichts*) and the much more extensive *Fatzer* materials.

Herr Keuner, Brecht's 'thinking man', is a trickster-figure reacting cynically to seemingly simple everyday situations: "'What are you working on?' Herr K. was asked. Herr K. replied: 'I'm having a hard time; I'm preparing my next mistake'" (Brecht 2001, p. 7). Treating Keuner as the prototype for the suddenly appearing stranger-philosopher, Benjamin suggests that the name *Keuner* combines two 'etymologies' rooted in the Ancient world. The first is

> based on the Greek root *koinós* – the universal, that which concerns all, belongs to all. And in fact, Herr Keuner is the man who concerns all, belongs to all, for he is the leader. But in quite a different sense from the one we usually understand by the word. [...] His main preoccupations lie light-years away from what people nowadays understand to be those of a 'leader'. The fact is that Herr Keuner is a thinker.[14]

Benjamin's second 'etymology' from "What is Epic Theatre? [First Version]" sees *Keuner* as a Swabian *outis*, a metamorphosis of Ulysses. Just as Ulysses is "the Greek 'Nobody' who visits one-eyed Polyphemus in his cave", Keuner challenges the monster called 'class-society'. This 'Nobody' is actually a Swabian stranger, since in Brecht's home-dialect, the German word for nobody – *keiner* – is pronounced as *keuner*. To this, Benjamin adds that unlike Ulysses,

> Keuner never leaves the threshold of his house at all. He likes the trees which he sees in the yard when he comes out of his fourth-floor tenement flat. 'Why don't you ever go into the woods,' ask his friends, 'if you like trees so much?' 'Did I not tell you,' replies Herr Keuner, 'that I like the trees in my yard?' To move this thinking man, Herr Keuner (who, Brecht once suggested, should be carried on stage lying down, so little is he drawn thither), to move him to existence upon the stage – that is the aim of this new theatre.
>
> *(Benjamin 1973, p. 5 with minor adjustments)*

During the years of exile as well as after his return to Berlin at the end of World War II, Brecht was periodically also working on the *Messingkauf Dialogues*, depicting the conversations of a philosopher who "has come to a large theatre after the performance has finished, to talk with the theatre people. He has been invited by an actress" (Brecht 2014, p. 11). In these dialogues, which were never completed during Brecht's lifetime, the philosopher arrives at the theater – the 'home' of performance for many generations. His discussions with the dramaturg, an actor, an actress, and a backstage worker (variously referred to in the text as the lighting technician, the stage hand or the worker) are going to take place on the stage itself, during four nights, after the evening's show, in the form of a Socratic dialogue.

In these fragments, Brecht touches on a number of topics relating to how the philosopher conceives the theater, and in particular, as the latter says:

> The fact that you apply your art and your whole apparatus to imitating incidents that occur between people, making your spectators feel as though they're watching real life. Because I'm interested in the way people live together (*das Zusammenleben der Menschen*), I'm interested in your imitations of it too.
>
> *(Ibid., p. 13)*

The philosopher is barely interested in the art of theater in itself – he does not value it much, and is unfamiliar with its vocabulary (e.g. 'the fourth wall') – yet, he does have a basic sense of what he is looking for, comparing himself "to a man who, let's say, deals in scrap metal, and goes to see a brass band wanting to buy not a trumpet or any other instrument, but simply brass" (ibid., p. 17). Just like the scrap-metal dealer wants to buy the musical instruments not because of their artistic value but because of their commercial value as metal, so the philosopher is interested in the possibility of 'melting down' the apparatus of the theater (the musical instruments) and 'molding' it, as raw-metal (the brass), for his own 'scientific' purposes:

> I am approaching you in my search for incidents between people - which you do imitate here in some way. […] I've heard that you manufacture such imitations; and now I'm hoping to find out whether they are the kind of imitations I can use.
>
> *(Ibid.)*

Brecht's philosopher explores the materiality of the theater – what it is made of – with those who work there. His disruptive quality seems to be embodied less in his way of turning the theatre stage into a site for philosophical reflection, and more with the kind of materialist philosophy he advances. At the same time as this is an interruption of the practitioners habitual modes of working – which they clearly resist – it also opens up possibilities for restructuring their work for a theater of the future, a philosophical theater, which the philosopher proposes to call *Thaëter*. As Brecht claimed, on another occasion, "the future of the theatre is a philosophical one".[15]

In Benjamin's diary entry from July 24, 1934, during his first visit to Brecht's exilic home in Svendborg on the island of Fyn in Denmark, he remarks that on a horizontal beam in Brecht's study, there is a painted inscription 'saying' that "The truth is concrete (*Die Wahrheit ist konkret*)". Facing the beam, standing on the window ledge, is a wooden donkey that can nod its head; and "Brecht has hung a little notice round its neck with the words: 'I, too, must understand it (*Auch ich muss es verstehen*)".[16] The domestic performance that Brecht has staged in his study presents an ongoing dialogue between two inscriptions facing each other, one about the concreteness of truth (its materiality as opposed to an abstract, universal truth), on the beam, and the other, the donkey's agreement, on the note hanging around its neck. This performance consists of two inscriptions which are activated every time Brecht and Benjamin enter the study, witnessing the silent interaction between the beam and the donkey, interrupting the frozen communication which transforms the study into a home for both philosophy and performance, unified in an image at a standstill – a *tableau*, as we still sometimes say…

Notes

1 The full text of the riddle, and the answer:

> <u>Riddle</u>: There is on earth a creature with two legs, four legs and one voice, three legs too. Alone it changes in form of creatures who exist on earth, in air, on sea. But when it goes resting on more feet then the strength of its limbs is weaker.
> <u>Answer</u>: Listen, like it or not, ill winged songstress of death to my voice, which will end your folly. You mean a human, who crawling on the ground at first is four footed, a babe from the womb then in old age leans on a stick as third foot, with a burden on back, bent double in old age.
> *(Quoted from: Euripides 1988, p. 61)*

2 Namely, after Karl R. Popper's famous model of verification, as presented in the essay "Science: Conjectures and Refutations" (in Popper 1963, pp. 43–86). The question as to what extent in searching for someone who is wiser than himself the challenge to the Oracle is disrespectful to the gods (in this case Apollo) would call for further discussion.
3 Socrates treats the Oracle's reply as a riddle (*ainigma*) presented by the god, intertwining two questions: 'Who is Socrates?' and 'What is wisdom?' See Howland 2006, pp. 66–67.

4 According to Oliver Taplin, "[…] though we know of well over 100 fifth-century [BCE] playwrights, we do not know of a single one who produced both tragedy and comedy"; Taplin 1986, p. 163.
5 As Jacques Lacan writes, "*atopos* refers to a case that is unclassifiable or unsuitable. *Atopia*, you cannot put it anywhere"; Lacan 2015, p. 103.
6 In Plato's works, one's private thoughts are depicted as a conversation of one's soul with itself (e.g. in the *Sophist*, 263e–264b; *Theaetetus*, 189e–190a). See Denyer 2008, p. 79.
7 The Ladder of Love is a vertical image, but the ascent to its top is not an absolutely vertical journey. At least on two of the six rungs, the lover's movement partially involves a horizontal dimension as well, understood in terms of generalization. Ruby Blondell suggests that instead of a ladder, we should think here of a *staircase*; Blondell 2006, pp. 147n2, 151.
8 Diotima, just like Socrates (and Eros), is an outsider: (1) she 'speaks' at a banquet at which she herself is not present; (2) she is introduced as a female voice into the men's space; and (3) she is regarded as a stranger in Athens even after helping to delay the plague for about a decade (201d–e).
9 There is curiously no example of such a scene, neither in Brecht's plays, nor – it seems – in any contemporary dramatic work. Judith Butler notes that it is "apparently drawn not from a play, but from a daydream, perhaps"; Butler 2015, p. 39.
10 Quoted from Benjamins' essay "On the Concept of History" (often referred to as "Theses on the Philosophy of History"), in Benjamin 2003, p. 396.
11 As Rebecca Comay puts it, "time here undergoes its own peculiar shattering: a fissure erupts within the continuum of experience"; Comay 2005, p. 95.
12 In the context of the difference between Socrates' and the angel's dialectics of motion and stasis, one can recall Giorgio Agamben's comment that those who see the angel of history as a melancholic figure (e.g. Gershom Scholem) "would therefore most likely be horrified to witness what would happen if the angel, instead of being driven forward by the winds of progress, paused to accomplish his work"; Agamben 1999, p. 154.
13 "The logic at work here is this: to be freed is to be compelled to turn", A.J. Bartlett writes, alluding to Jean-Jacques Rousseau's claim that the 'general will' forces us to be free; Bartlett 2011, p. 119.
14 As Benjamin suggested in a radio-talk about Brecht, broadcast in the *Frankfurter Rundfunk* in June 1930. Quoted from Benjamin 1999a, p. 367.
15 This is a quote from "Latest Stage: Oedipus", the newspaper review Brecht wrote of Leopold Jessner's production of *Oedipus Tyrannus* and *Oedipus at Colonnus*, which premiered at the Berlin Staatstheater in January 1925. Brecht's future wife, Helene Weigel, played Jocasta's maid in this production. Quoted from Brecht 2015, p. 43.
16 Quoted from Benjamin's "Notes from Svendborg: Summer 1934", in Benjamin 1999a, p. 785.

References

Agamben, Giorgio. 1999. *Potentialities: Collected Essays in Philosophy*, edited and translated by Daniel Heller-Roazen, Stanford, CA: Stanford University Press.
Aristotle. 1984. "Metaphysics", translated by W.D. Ross, in: *The Complete Works of Aristotle*, edited by Jonathan Barnes, Princeton, NJ: Princeton University Press, Vol. 2, pp. 1552–1728.
Bartlett, A. J. 2011. *Badiou and Plato: An Education by Truths*, Edinburgh: Edinburgh University Press.
Benjamin, Walter. 1973. "What Is Epic Theatre? [First Version]", in: *Understanding Brecht*, translated by Anna Bostock, London: Verso, pp. 1–13.
Benjamin, Walter. 1998 (1977). *The Origin of German Tragic Drama*, translated by John Osborne, London and New York: Verso.
Benjamin, Walter. 1999a. *Selected Writings, Vol. 2: 1927–1934,* edited by Michael W. Jennings et al., Cambridge, MA and London: Harvard University Press.
Benjamin, Walter. 1999b. *The Arcades Project*, translated by Howard Eiland and Kevin McLaughlin, Cambridge, MA and London: Harvard University Press.
Benjamin, Walter. 2003. *Selected Writings, Vol. 4: 1938–1940*, edited by Howard Eiland and Michael W. Jennings, Cambridge, MA and London: Harvard University Press.
Blondell, Ruby. 2006. "Where Is Socrates on the 'Ladder of Love'?", in: *Plato's* Symposium: *Issues in Interpretation and Reception (Hellenic Studies 22)*, edited by James H. Lesher et al., Cambridge, MA: Harvard University Press, pp. 147–178.
Bloom, Allan. 1993. "The Ladder of Love", in: Allan Bloom: *Love and Friendship*, New York: Simon & Schuster, pp. 429–546.

Brecht, Bertolt. 2001. *Stories of Mr. Keuner*, translated by Martin Chalmers, San Francisco, CA: City Lights Books.
Brecht, Bertolt. 2014. *Brecht on Performance: Messingkauf and Modelbooks*, edited by Tom Kuhn, Steve Giles, and Marc Silberman, London: Bloomsbury.
Brecht, Bertolt. 2015. *Brecht on Theatre*, edited by Marc Silberman et al., London: Bloomsbury.
Butler, Judith. 2015. "Theatrical Machines", *Differences: A Journal of Feminist Cultural Studies*, Vol. 26, No. 3, pp. 23–42.
Comay, Rebecca. 2005. "The Sickness of Tradition: Between Melancholia and Fetishism," in: *Walter Benjamin and History*, edited by Andrew Benjamin, London and New York: Continuum, pp. 88–101.
Denyer, Nicholas (ed.). 2008. *Plato: Protagoras*, Cambridge: Cambridge University Press.
Emlyn-Jones, Chris. 2004. "The Dramatic Poet and His Audience: Agathon and Socrates in Plato's *Symposium*", in: *Hermes: Zeitschrift für klassische Philologie*, 132. Jahrgang, Heft 4, pp. 389–405.
Euripides. 1988. *Phoenician Women*, translated by Elizabeth Craik, Wiltshire: Aris and Phillips.
Hadot, Pierre. 2002. *What Is Ancient Philosophy?* translated by Michael Chase, Cambridge, MA and London: Harvard University Press.
Halperin, David M. 1992. "Plato and the Erotics of Narrativity," in: *Methods of Interpreting Plato and His Dialogues* (Oxford Studies in Ancient Philosophy, Supplementary Volume), edited by James C. Klagge, Nicholas D. Smith, pp. 93–129.
Howland, Jacob. 2006. *Kierkegaard and Socrates: A Study in Philosophy and Faith*, Cambridge: Cambridge University Press.
Lacan, Jacques. 2015. *Transference (The Seminars of Jacques Lacan, Book VIII)*, translated by Bruce Fink, Cambridge and Malden, MA: Polity Press.
Montiglio, Silvia. 2005. *Wandering in Ancient Greek Culture*, Chicago and London: The University of Chicago Press.
Nightingale, Andrea Wilson. 1995. *Genres in Dialogue: Plato and the Construct of Philosophy*, Cambridge: Cambridge University Press.
Plato. 1997. "Republic", translated by G.M.A. Grube (and revised by C.D.C. Reeve), in: *Complete Works*, edited by John M. Cooper, Indianapolis, IN: Hackett Publishing, pp. 971–1223.
Plato. 2008. *The Symposium*, translated by M.C. Howatson, Cambridge and New York: Cambridge University Press.
Popper, Karl. 1963. *Conjectures and Refutations: The Growth of Scientific Knowledge*, London: Routledge and Kegan Paul.
Rhodes, James M. 2003. *Eros, Wisdom, and Silence: Plato's Erotic Dialogues*, Columbia: University of Missouri Press.
Rokem, Freddie. 2010. *Philosophers and Thespians: Thinking Performance*, Stanford, CA: Stanford University Press.
Rokem, Freddie. 2016. "The Ludic Logic of Tragedy", *Performance Research*, Vol. 21, Issue 4, pp. 26–33.
Schlosser, Joel Alden. 2014. *What Would Socrates Do? Self-Examination, Civic Engagement, and the Politics of Philosophy*, New York: Cambridge University Press.
Segal, Charles. 1999. *Tragedy and Civilization: An Interpretation of Sophocles*, Norman: University of Oklahoma Press.
Taplin, Oliver. 1977. *The Stagecraft of Aeschylus: The Dramatic Use of Exits and Entrances in the Greek Drama*, Oxford: Clarendon Press.
Taplin, Oliver. 1986, November. "Fifth-Century Tragedy and Comedy: A *Synkrisis*", *Journal of Hellenic Studies*, Vol. 106, pp. 163–174.
Vernant, Jean-Pierre. 1990. "One... Two... Three: *Erôs*", in: *Before Sexuality: The Construction of Erotic Experience in the Ancient Greek World*, edited by David M. Halperin et al., Princeton, NJ: Princeton University Press, pp. 465–478.
Wiles, David. 1997. *Tragedy in Athens: Performance Space and Theatrical Meaning*, Cambridge: Cambridge University Press.
Wizisla, Erdmut. 2009. *Walter Benjamin and Bertolt Brecht – The Story of a Friendship*, translated by Christine Shuttleworth, New Haven, CT: Yale University Press.

2
THERAVĀDIN BUDDHIST PHILOSOPHY AND PRACTICE IN RELATION TO PERFORMANCE

Jerri Daboo

Aspects of Buddhist philosophy and practice can offer much in the way of considering the nature of the experience of performance and performing. This is a vast subject, so this chapter will examine a few of the main concepts from Theravādin Buddhism,[1] particularly the idea of *anattā* and parts of the *Mahāsatipattāna Sutta*.[2] This leads to an understanding of two key points that relate philosophy to performance: the idea of non-self or emptiness of both performance and performer; and a deeper understanding of the embodied practice of mindfulness/insight, both of which can help the actor to a new way of understanding and creating a 'character', which is 'neither the same nor another', a phrase that will be explained later in the chapter.

Aldo Tassi states the following about philosophy in relationship to theatre:

> ...it is an activity that seeks to transport us to the place where boundaries are established so that we may 'see' how things come to be. Like the theatrical stage, the theatre of the mind is a place for seeing, and it is philosophy's task to bring light and allow us to see what usually remains obscure or hidden in our perceptual dealings with things. Both philosophy and theatre, then, originally arose as activities to take us beyond the empirical level to involve us in the pursuit of truth as an unconcealment process.
>
> *(Krasner & Saltz 2006, p. 3)*

Taking this definition as a starting point, Buddhism is particularly useful when considering the connection of philosophy to theatre, as it engages with practice and reflection that is based in removing obstacles to seeing reality. Through this, there can be an understanding that 'reality', as we usually see it, is, in fact, as much an illusion and imagining as what we see in theatre. Buddhism is an embodied philosophy, as it is through lived practice and direct experience of the teachings that the philosophy is realised in the bodymind.[3] As such, we become our own philosophical experiments, and are both object and subject of study, the observer and the observed. Through a highly systematic process of practice and observation, what can be realised and understood is that the idea of 'self' is constructed. The ways in which we construct this idea of 'self' can be seen by following the practice laid out in the teaching (*dhamma*), and this can lead to a liberation (*nibbāna*) from the continual cycle of conditioned existence (*samsāra*). Whilst Buddhist philosophy draws on aspects of older forms of philosophy and practice from India, the focus on direct lived experience also makes it distinctive, as Analayo explains:

> The philosophical setting of ancient India was influenced by three main approaches to the acquisition of knowledge. The Brahmins relied mainly on ancient sayings, handed down by oral transmission, as authoritative sources of knowledge; while in the Upaniṣads one finds philosophical reasoning used as a central tool for developing knowledge. In addition to these two, a substantial number of the wandering ascetics and contemplatives of that time considered extrasensory perception and intuitive knowledge, gained through meditative experiences, as important means for the acquisition of knowledge. [...] When questioned on his own epistemological position, the Buddha placed himself in the third category, i.e. among those who emphasized the development of direct, personal knowledge. Although he did not completely reject oral tradition or logical reasoning as ways of acquiring knowledge, he was keenly aware of their limitations.
>
> *(Analayo 2003, p. 780)*

Thus, Buddhism can be seen as a form of practice-based research, comparable to the ways in which a performance practitioner needs to conduct experimentation and body-based work in order to create a performance that examines a set of questions and themes which are played out in different ways in the studio. In Buddhism, what can be understood through the practice are the Three Characteristics of Existence: *anattā* (non-self), *anicca* (impermanence), and *dukkha* (suffering). Buddhist philosophy believes that there is no singular, fixed 'self' which continues unchanged from moment to moment. What can be realised instead is rather a constantly changing or impermanent pattern of reactions happening within the bodymind. In other words, what I label as 'me' in this moment is different from the 'me' of the preceding or following moments. The third Characteristic of suffering, or *dukkha*, occurs when we try to hold on to the idea of 'I', 'me', or 'mine' as being real and permanent, instead of realising that the sense of 'my self' is a conceptual label rather than a fact. 'Suffering' is really a mistranslation of *'dukkha'*, which literally means 'bad formations', and has tended to imply to westerners that Buddhism is about suffering, particularly as the first of the Four Noble Truths, a core part of the Buddha's teaching, is usually translated as 'Suffering exists' (*Dukkha-ariyasacca*). However, *dukkha* refers to any kind of formation of experience that we hold onto in order to create the illusion of a continuous, singular, permanent 'me', which can include feelings of joy, love, pleasure, and sensuality. Buddhist practice leads to the insight that these feelings are constructed in response to conditionings, and that the understanding of the reality of 'non-self' can lead to knowing that these formations are in fact 'empty' (*sunyatā*), in the way that the 'self' is emptiness, or a construct that is not real.[4]

The practice that can lead to this realisation is that of awareness or mindfulness *(sati)* into the entire processes of the bodymind in each moment in order to understand this at an organic level, rather than as an intellectual idea. As G.P. Malalasekera explains, "an individual is a being, something that is, but in the Buddha's teaching, the individual's being is, in fact, a becoming, a coming-to-be, something that happens, an event, a process" (George 2000, p. 53). There is a constant movement or stream of ever-changing patterns from which we create or imagine a sense of continuity, which we label as our-'self', and believe it to be the same 'self' that exists across each moment. Walpola Rahula states that instead of being a fixed object, the "series is, really speaking, nothing but movement. It is like a flame that burns through the night: it is not the same flame nor is it another" (Rahula 1959, p. 34) (in Pali: *naca so naca anno* – 'neither the same nor another'). To explain this another way, if I were to look at a photograph of myself from when I was ten years old, I am clearly not the same person as I was then, and yet I am not a completely different person either. This paradox of being 'neither the same nor another' can also be applied to the experience of the actor in creating a character, which they both are-and-are-not. This will be discussed later in relation to the work of Michael Chekhov.

In a similar way to this idea of non-self, the nature of performance itself can also be understood as being an event or process, something that comes-to-be in a moment, and is then gone. In this way, it is also an act or creation of the imagination, an illusion that is constructed. If, as Tassi suggests, the theatre is a place for us to 'see' truth, as is a Buddhist practice, it is also a place of emptiness (*sunyatā*) due to its impermanence. The experience of the repetition of a theatrical performance can also be seen as being *naca so naca anno*, in that it is the same play that is performed night after night, and yet its performance is different on each occasion. It is both neither the same, nor another. This reality of 'self' and performance is encapsulated in a line from the opening verse of the major Buddhist text, the *Dhammapada*, which states that, "Our life is the creation of our minds". This indicates that the way that we tend to perceive the world and ourselves as being permanent and singular is being created by the 'self' that wants to hold onto this idea for its own preservation, rather than seeing the reality outlined in the Three Characteristics of Experience. In this way, both our selves and theatre are imaginative constructions and illusions. Whilst this may be challenging for some Western philosophies, David George points out that "Buddhists have less of a problem than those brought up in a Western philosophical tradition in seeing all 'realities' as somehow partly imaginative" (George 2000, p. 55). The final verse of the beautiful *Vajracchedikā*, the Diamond or Diamond-Cutter *sutra*, shows the very insubstantiality and emptiness of 'self', performance, and the world, and connects it with the imagination:

> Thus shall you think [perceive] of all this fleeting world:
> A star at dawn, a bubble in a stream;
> A flash of lightening in a summer cloud,
> A flickering lamp, a phantom and a dream.
> (Price & Wong 2003)

One of the main forms of practice that the Buddha taught, in order to study and understand these ideas of the reality of 'non-self', is found in the *Mahāsatipatthāna-Sutta*. This is "[t]he most important discourse ever given by the Buddha on mental development" (Rahula 1959, p. 69), and is still very popular in homes and monasteries in Theravādin countries, as it has been since the earliest times of the Buddhist tradition. A copy of the *sutta* is often kept in homes, and regularly chanted to the dying. It is an extraordinary text in that it not only outlines the philosophy in a way which can be studied, but it is above all a training manual for the bodymind, listing detailed exercises in a systemised manner to guide the practitioner through the entire process of mindfulness and insight from beginning point through to liberation. The practice is what the Buddha described as the Sole or Only Way (*ekayānomaggo*), and the *sutta* states that it need only be followed completely for seven days in order to be free from the realm of *samsāra*. The *sutta* is found twice in the Pali Canon, once in the Middle-Length and then in the Long Discourses. The second version is slightly longer, and so has the prefix *'Maha'*, meaning 'great', in the sense of length. The word *sati* (*smrti* in Sanskrit) is usually translated as 'mindfulness'. It "had originally the meaning of 'memory' or 'remembrance'" (Thera 1988, p. 9). One of the practices associated with it was to remember back through every moment of one's life starting with the present moment, and on reaching the point of birth, to carry on back through all past lives. This was to be able to observe the repeating patterns and habitual tendencies existing in the being through all the changes of form. It also implies 'body memory', in that habitual reactions become established as bodymind patterns, and so mindfulness – observation of these patterns – is also a process of remembering and being aware of the whole organism, including its history.

The concept and practice of 'mindfulness' has taken on a particular currency in Western cultures in recent years and is used very freely to relate to ideas of relaxation and wellbeing. However, this is often separated from the actual rigorous practice found in Buddhism, which is undertaken in order to lead to an insight (*vipassanā*) that establishes the realisation of non-self, and observes the habitual patterns of conditioning in the bodymind that form the illusion of a singular and permanent 'self' that is held onto as being 'real'. The first stage of mindfulness practice is that of *samatha*, or deep concentration that calms and focuses the mind. This is often the stage that contemporary approaches to 'mindfulness' tend to reach, and leave it there. However, this is actually only the first stage to be undertaken in order to create a calm mind, that can then lead to the insight (*vipassanā*) practices that are very challenging to the 'self' that wants to cling on to the belief in its own existence as a fixed identity. The calm must be established first through *samatha*, and then the *vipassanā* wakes up the bodymind to the insight of understanding and realisation of the realities of existence as a continual movement.

In order to show the nature of this embodied philosophy, I will examine aspects of the first exercise in the *sutta*, which is *ānāpānasati*, or Mindfulness of Breathing. This is part of the first of the four sections in the *sutta* known as *Kāyānupassanā,* or Mindfulness of Body. The entire practice starts first with the physical base of the body. In this form of *ānāpānasati*, the passage of the breath is observed as it moves through the body in terms of whether it is long, short, deep, or shallow. Whilst this practice in itself will produce a calming of the bodymind, this is just observed, rather than being an intentional result. Indeed, this form of observation is specifically one of 'non-interference': it is just noting what is happening. This differs from the yogic breathing exercise of *pranayama*, which controls the breath to produce particular results in the bodymind. In *satipatthāna*, breathing is "representative of the bodily functions (*kaya-sankhara*)" (Thera 1988, p. 63). Through following the breath as it arises and falls in the body, there can be an awareness of *anicca,* the impermanence of breath and body, and hence *anattā*. The breath is seen as being the embodied manifestation of the Wind or Air element – *vayo-dhatu*, and so has no fixed, abiding existence in itself.

At the end of the section on *ānāpānsati*, as it does at the end of every listed exercise, the *sutta* states that through doing the exercise, the practitioner will be both arising and passing away and observing the body *in* the body as arising and passing away. In this way, there can be an embodied understanding of impermanence and non-self through the mindfulness of the body in and by the body itself. This leads to the phrase in the *sutta,* also repeated at the end of each section:

"Atthi kāyo" ti vā panassa sati paccupatthitā hoti. Yāvadeva nānamattā yapatissatimattāya anissito ca viharati, na ca kinci loke upādiyati.

('Now his awareness is established: "This is body!" Thus he develops his awareness to such an extent that there is mere understanding along with mere awareness')

(Vipassanā Research Institute 1998, pp. 6–7)

The phrase '*Atthi kāyo*' ('This is body!'), exclaimed in this way, "indicates that the meditator at this stage clearly understands experientially, at the level of sensations, 'body' in its true nature: its characteristic of arising and passing away ... [and has no] attachment towards 'I', 'me', or 'mine'" (Vipassanā Research Institute 1998, p. 89). Mindfulness of breathing is such an important practice because it leads directly to experiencing the body, which means feeling sensations in the body. The sensations may be related to the breath, the oxygen flowing in the blood, etc., but those details are not important. The body-in-body experience is not imagined or contemplated but felt throughout the body. [...] By equating the observation of the breath with experiencing sensations, the Buddha is pointing to the critical importance of the body and sensations in the proper practice of meditation. It is the awareness of these sensations by direct experience throughout the body, while maintaining equanimity with the understanding of impermanence that perfects the four *satipatthānas* (Vipassanā Research Institute 1998, p. 86–87).

The practice should lead to an engaged, embodied, and active awareness that is "performed with *paccanubhoti* (direct experience), which is *yathābhūtanāna-dassana* (experiential knowledge of the reality as it is)" (Vipassanā Research Institute 1998, p.xiv). This is the direct seeing of reality that cuts through illusions and obstacles, just as Tassi had suggested that theatre can also do, offering a place where engagement with performing or watching allows for the embodied philosophical manifestation of *yathābūtam*, or seeing things as they really are.

This brief examination of the first part of the *Mahāsatipattāna Sutta* has shown that Buddhism is an embodied philosophy that leads the practitioner to the insight of the reality of 'non-self' and impermanence. As discussed previously, this can be applied to an understanding of theatre and performance as also being empty and impermanent constructs of the imagination. The practice can also help the actor in considering how they create a 'character' on stage which they both are-and-are-not. To offer an initial way to approach this, I draw on the ideas and exercises of Russian practitioner Michael Chekhov (1891–1955), whose work with actors is based in a psychophysical approach of embodied imagination to help the actor create a character through concentration and playfulness. I use the term 'embodied imagination' to indicate that this is not a matter of just visualisation, but rather the way that an image is experienced and fills all the senses and the entire bodymind, and thus can create a change within it. If the practice of *satipatthāna* can result in an understanding of the way that 'self' is created through the bodymind, then it is possible to use this understanding to create another 'self', that of the character, in the moment of the play. This avoids an over-identification with the psychology of the character which could be harmful for the actor, or result in a weaker performance which lacks a deeper awareness of the body and embodiment. As Chekhov said, "We see so many actors today who stand with their hands in their pockets and say 'I love you' – No relation between words and movement. Your body must say the words" (Chekhov 1937). The awareness of body and an understanding of how to construct 'self' though the embodied imagination offer a way into a performance experience of concentration and ease, where the performer is aware that both they and the character are 'neither the same nor another'.

Chekhov's acting exercises are aimed at helping the actor access their creativity. As I have written elsewhere (Daboo 2007, 2015), his exercises stress the importance of a strong concentration for the actor, particularly in relation to the processes of imagination and visualisation. In the statement below, the 'object' can refer to the image of a character, or a colour, shape, smell, or physical object:

> [W]e must move our whole being towards the object. [...] So by our will we must move inwardly towards the object of our concentration. The physical body remains quiet but something moves towards this object. When you are *with* the object, the physical body must remain free and relaxed. Then you will feel that your looking and seeing is of

secondary importance. [...] The last step is to "take" the object and keep it - to such an extent that you will not know whether the object has you, or you have the object - you have become one with it. And when you become one, a miracle happens - you know exactly how heavy it is, what shape it is, what noise it makes, what shape it is from all sides at the same time. With our eyes we see the surface. When we approach the object with our physical body we know it somehow vaguely, when we "take" it, we know it better, and when we are "taken" by it, all the qualities of the thing we know and experience. [...] This process of concentration, of "merging" together, is the only way to really *know* things.

(Chekhov 1985, p. 44)

This resonates with the discourse and practice of *samatha* in Buddhism, where the focus of the mind on an object leads to a state of inner stillness, merging with the object that is the centre of focus, which in the case of *ānāpānasati* is the flow of breath. The word *samatha* comes from *sama*, meaning 'inner stillness', where the bodymind is calm and at ease, as the first stage in the process. The focused concentration required for this is described as *citekaggatā*, meaning 'one-pointedness of mind'. It is this total, engaged focus and concentration, of merging with the object of visualisation, that leads to a forgetting of the 'self', and a realisation of non-self. For the actor, this can also occur in the experience of being engaged with a physical exercise or series of movements, where the absorption in and with the action leads to a sense of non-self through total engagement with the action. This idea of 'forgetting the self' comes from the process of exploration of the 'self' through the exercises, leading to the state of non-self. In Buddhist terms, this can be seen in the *Genjo Koan* by the 13th-century Zen master Dōgen, who wrote:

> To study Buddhism is to study the self.
> To study the self is to know the self.
> To know the self is to forget the self.
> To forget the self is to become one with all things of the world.
>
> (Nisker 2000, p. 191)

The process of studying the self through examination of how the 'self' is constructed through habitual patterns and conditionings, seen in Chekhov's exercises as well as Buddhism, leads to a knowing of the 'self', which is a forgetting of the 'self', or non-self. This forgetting can then allow for a freedom and new possibilities of the bodymind, which in the case of the actor, can mean a potential for creating a character through body and voice that is carefully constructed to suit the needs of the moment of the play. Chekhov's exercises such as the Imaginary Body and Psychological Gesture allow for a playful and creative use of the embodied imagination, where a concentrated and easeful bodymind explores the possibilities of the character to find an embodiment that is suitable, but also knowingly constructed, and therefore 'not-me'. However, it is also 'not-not-me', in that it is still the bodymind of the actor that is manifesting the character on stage. If the 'me' of the 'self' is removed, then it leads to the paradox of 'neither the same nor another' – the character is not the actor, but also not a completely other person on stage. As Rahula explains, in relation to the understanding of the construction, and therefore emptiness of 'self':

> There is no unmoving mover behind the movement. It is only movement. ... [T]here is no thinker behind the thought. Thought itself is the thinker. If you remove the thought, there is no thinker to be found.
>
> (Rahula 1959, p. 26)

The character is a construct created by the actor, therefore imagined, not real, an illusion, and empty. Similarly, the 'self' of the actor is also imagined and constructed, which is realised in the experience of forgetting the self through engaging with the process of the psychophysical engagement in a performance. Buddhist philosophy can help in understanding this paradox of non-self that leads to being 'neither the same nor another' as the reality of existence.

At the start of this chapter, Tassi suggested that the created and imaginary world of theatre can help to reveal truth, and that philosophy also has this ability to reveal what has been obscured in a process of 'unconcealment'. In Buddhist terms, there are two types of truth: *paramattha-sacca*, often translated as 'ultimate' or 'absolute' truth, and *sammuti-sacca*, usually translated as 'relative' or 'conventional' truth. These translations are problematic in themselves, as the original terms do not refer to absolutism or relativism as seen in Western philosophy. Put simply, *paramatha-sacca* is the experience of 'things as they really are', a non-conceptualised understanding of non-self and emptiness. It is knowing, rather than knowing about, and is not found in the realm of language, which is a description of the experience, rather than the experience itself. However, Buddhism recognises the need for language and an 'everyday' understanding relating to the phenomenal world in order for us to be able to operate in the world and communicate with others. This is *sammuti-sacca*, which is seeing people, objects, etc., as having coherence of self, and using language in comparative terms to express it. *Sammuti-sacca* literally means 'covered' or 'concealed' truth (Varela et al. 1999, p. 226), in that it is covering or hiding the reality of *paramattha-sacca*. If the concepts, words, and metaphors are removed, then the truth of non-self and impermanence will be revealed. It is this process of revealing or 'unconcealment' through the embodied philosophy of Buddhism that may also be seen in theatre, which creates an imaginary world that can uncover the reality of our lives.

Notes

1. There are three main Schools of Buddhism. Theravādin is the earliest of these, with the word meaning 'Teaching of the Elders'. Texts from the Theravādin school are mainly in Pali, so terms in this chapter will be in their Pali form, unless indicated.
2. A sutta (or sutra in Sanskrit) is a teaching or discourse, usually in the form of a written text.
3. I use the term 'bodymind' in this chapter to indicate a psychophysical unity of body and mind, which is also at the heart of Buddhist philosophy and practice. Later in the chapter, I also use the terms 'body' and 'mind' separately when discussing specific exercises in the *sutta*, which is due to the particular focus of these exercises. However, the aim is to realise the psychophysical unity through the exercises.
4. For further elaboration on these and other aspects of Theravādin Buddhist philosophy, see Thera (1988) and Rahula (1959).

References

Analayo, B. 2003. *Satipatthana: The Direct Path to Realization,* Cambridge: Windhorse Publications.
Chekhov, M. 1937. *Art Is Higher Activity than Life*, June–July 1937, Chekhov Dartington Archives, DWE 18 B.
Chekhov, M. 1985. *Lessons for the Professional Actor,* New York: Performing Arts Journal Publications.
Daboo, J. 2007. 'Michael Chekhov and the Embodied Imagination: Higher Self and Non-self', *Studies in Theatre and Performance*, 27(3), pp. 261–273.
Daboo, J. 2015. '"As the Shadow Follows the Body": Examining Chekhov's Creation of Character through "Eastern" Practices', in Autant-Mathieu M. (ed.) *The Routledge Companion to Michael Chekhov*, New York: Routledge, pp. 282–296.

George, D. 2000. *Buddhism as/in Performance,* New Delhi: D.K. Printworld (P) Ltd.
Krasner, D. & Saltz, D. 2006. 'Introduction', in Krasner, D. & Saltz, D. (eds.) *Staging Philosophy: Intersections of Theater, Performance and Philosophy.* Ann Arbor: University of Michigan Press, pp. 1–18.
Nisker, W. 2000. *Buddha Nature,* New York: Bantum Books.
Price, A. F. & Wong, M.-L. (trans), *The Diamond Sutra,* ed. FaHui [Online], Available at http://naplesmindfulness.org/Sutra/THE%20DIAMOND%20SUTRA.pdf, Accessed 12th April 2003.
Rahula, W. 1959. *What the Buddha Taught,* Oxford: Oneworld Publications.
Thera, N. 1988. *The Heart of Buddhist Meditation,* Maine: Samuel Weiser Inc.
Varela, F., Thompson, E. & Rosch, E. (eds.) 1991. *The Embodied Mind: Cognitive Science and Human Experience,* Cambridge, MA and London: MIT Press.
Vipassana Research Institute. 1998. *Mahāsatipatthāna Sutta: The Great Discourse on the Establishing of Awareness* Igatpuri, India: Vipassana Research Institute. (Pali text, English translation and commentary).

3

PERFORMANCE PHILOSOPHY AND SPIRITUALITY

The way of *tasawwuf*

Michael Ellison and Hannah McClure

It is commonly taught and accepted in the analytic and continental traditions that philosophy began and extended from a Greco-Roman heritage. Socrates, Plato and Aristotle are lauded as philosopher-scientists who birthed the reign of rational thought. However, prior to the Greco-Roman emergence of rationalism, extensive philosophical, scientific and artistic bodies of knowledge were cultivated in Africa (such as The Maxims of Ptohhotep in Egypt, 25th Century BCE), Asia (Taoism in 5th Century BCE and The Vedic Period in 2nd Millennium BCE) and the Middle East (in the Sufi oral tradition). Sufism, while related to Islam in contemporary structures, is considered by its adherents to be the heart or root of religious and philosophical thought. For them, Sufism is born of a universal truth: that the heart itself is the key to all knowledge and transcendence. The heart is the ground upon which immanence occurs within the human soul. Without a single progenitor or figurehead, Sufism has been revealed in various forms and languages across time. Its central forms of communication rely on music, movement, poetry, natural sciences and fine arts (Burckhardt 2004; Blann 2005). Foundational to both early and later Sufi philosophy is the concept of *tasawwuf* or purity. The brothers and sisters of purity were known in pre-Islamic times as the *hannifya*, *Ekuanul Safa* and later the *Sahabi Safa* (Khan 2014). Their specific, devotional practices grew out of the oral and early traditions which grouped philosophy, science, art and spirituality together into complete 'life-ways'. For example, in Sufism, the fields of healing and medicine are related deeply to music, with a vast knowledge of tonalities and scales which remedy specific illnesses. Likewise, Sufism connects the sciences of astronomy and geology to music, insofar as the placement of stars and planets in relation to land forms creates known magnetic fields, where music and whirling have spontaneously occurred.

For the purposes of this paper, we will be focusing on tasawwuf as lived philosophy and embodied Sufi thought. Through particular focus on makam structures and whirling process, issues of practice and transculturalism are raised in relation to the spiritual purpose of tasawwuf, which is foundational to the perception and realisation of Sufi philosophies. As performance philosophers who seek to move beyond not only body–mind dualities but all manner of binaries, and who seek to articulate knowledges perceived and expressed in domains other than linear thought, the essay proposes that there is much we can take from the integrative, reciprocal principles of Sufism in our approach. This essay does not seek to define 'original Islam' as a philosophy, for that has already been done by countless Islamic scholars. Rather, it seeks to highlight the modes of knowing by experience and doing which are central to Sufism, and therefore the foundation or centre of later religious thought and philosophy. As knowing through doing remains central to advances in Performance Philosophy, we seek to foreground the idea that knowing by doing may contain the sacred within it and that by the inclusion of the sacred within the precepts of Performance Philosophy, wider dimensions of critique are enabled which allow 'South and East' knowledges of the more subtle aspects of ontology a place within the Western critical canon.

Sufi philosophy

In the view of perennialist scholarship,[1] the Enlightenment was not a harbinger of reason, progress and harmony but rather the beginning of a period during which the sacred and the feminine as the interior mystical dimension of the sacred were systematically stripped out of thought, policy making and governance (Nasr 2008; Latifa 2014). However, the older ways of life which honoured the feminine (mystical) principle and tended to value life and its interdependent balance remain in living memory among Sufis across Central Asia and Anatolia. From the time of agriculture, a shift took place which has arguably led to the progressive emergence of a global mindset characterised by force and dominance (Guénon in Herlihy 2009). At our current juncture, contemplation of the sacred, the soul and the feminine is essential to our conversation, and here Sufism and Islam as a nested set of knowledges have much to offer.

The sacred – understood as anything pertaining to the creator and therefore all things – is foundational not only to tasawwuf but to all of original Islam. Here, we differentiate 'original Islam' from the natural proliferation of varieties over time in order to allow for a discussion of that which birthed tasawwuf and to which early Sufis – and the practices that evolved with them – aligned themselves. While many practitioners of religion in general (and Islam is no exception) have come to rely on rule for its own sake, it must be remembered that within Sufism, doctrine is considered an outgrowth of the sacred heart within religion, and a means by which to remind ourselves of this heart. The directive of religious action is unification with the divine, which in Islam is Allah. The Sufi perspective on Islam regards human life as an opportunity to grow ourselves in the image of Allah, who is understood as universal consciousness and love, and that to which, upon our deaths, we must return (Quran, Sura Tin 95:4 and Bakara 2:30). According to oral and written tradition, each person shapes the condition of the soul – and similar to Hinduism, Buddhism and Judaism – it is the fire of earth with its paradox and duality by which we initiate our free will and draw ourselves near to that ultimate sacredness. The exoteric rules and doctrine of Islam have one purpose: to facilitate a whole society which lives in rhythms and decisions which allow individuals to align themselves to God as divine/unity consciousness (Schuon 1983).

Seyed Hossein Nasr (1997), a prolific scholar in the perennialist school, writes of the urgent need for contemporary human life-ways to (re-)connect to the sacred and (re-)form our ideals of social structures towards harmonious reciprocity. His thought stems from early critiques of Western philosophy and earlier writings in perennialist thought such as René Guénon, Frithjof Schuon, Martin Lings, Jean-Louis Michon and Marco Pallis, among others. In perennialist thought, the concept of a living tradition underpins discourses in order to highlight the mechanisms by which thought is produced through the entirety of a civilisation. From a critical approach where tradition is at the centre, rather than excluded, differences between East and West, North and South become heightened. The problem of Eurogenetic philosophy and its self-centric European gaze is that a hierarchy is produced whereby the rational and reductive positions of post-Enlightenment thought are raised to a superiority over the inclusive, holistic structures which position the interior modes of knowing as equal to the rational.

Perennialist scholar, Titus Burckhardt (2008), positions the tendency of the Western mind towards classification on the opposite end of a spectrum from Sufism, where there is a natural integration and coherence between body and mind. This is related to the concept of 'an intellect of the heart' aligned with the intellect of the mind. Equally, Sufism, while rooted in Islam, has at its base the older, oral aspect of living tradition which views expressions of religion as a ripening of forms consistent with phases of human existence (Blann 2005). In this manner, the heart – which is central to tasawwuf (or purity) – has been brought forward as the 'seat of the soul' (Nasr 2002) and the organ of perception upon which divine union and resulting knowledges take place. Here, the heart is understood both a physical organ in the body and the metaphysical organ of alchemy (Burckhardt 2008).

As the later parts of this essay will go on to discuss in more depth, it is the manner of access to the heart which is unique to tasawwuf. For us, tasawwuf is a form of knowing, a lived philosophy and a spiritual practice at once. The insights of tasawwuf can only be known by experience, or regular practice. Practitioners speak to the knowledges obtained through practice via symbolism and with words; however, these are never enough to fully transmit the knowledges themselves. Words simply act as a guide for those who would wish to seek the knowledge themselves. As a philosophy of purity, it is a lived philosophy, with practices grounded and seasoned in tradition.

Knowledges stemming from Sufism (esoteric experience) and Islam (exoteric regulation) are established and fulfilled within a living tradition composed of lived dimensions of practice. The living aspect speaks to continuity over time, not to a rigid set of rules but one where evolution and development occur through people's lives, experiences and bodies both personal and collective. As a philosopher, William Chittick writes:

> the erudite European is led to see borrowings by one tradition from another where in fact there is only a coincidence of spiritual vision, and fundamental divergences where it is only a question of differences in perspective or in mode of expression. It is inevitable that such confusions should arise since a university training and bookish knowledge are in the West deemed sufficient authority for concerning oneself with things which in the East remain naturally reserved to those who are endowed with spiritual intuition and who devote themselves to the study of these things in virtue of a true affinity under the guidance of those who are the heirs of a living tradition.
>
> *(Chittick in Burckhardt 2008, p. xiv)*

Thus, tasawwuf is related to a long, broad view of philosophy. The purpose of Sufi arts, which are tools for tasawwuf, is to bring the *murid* or student into direct experience of Allah and thus open doors of perception and knowing which are understood as accessible only through a deep, personal reciprocity with divine intelligence (Schuon 1984; Burckhardt 2004, 2008).

Tasawwuf

Tasawwuf and Sufism are one and the same.[2] Both consider that, by way of experience, we come to perceive the intellect of the heart, as nuanced, self-articulated and creative of our very existence. In Sufism, transformation of the heart via the means of tasawwuf results in a purification and enlivening of the 'subtle bodies' of the human: first, the emotional and mental bodies, but then also – and most importantly – purification of the soul.³ There are many layers of teachings about the heart in Sufism which we cannot address in depth here. However, it should be noted that tasawwuf without the heart at its centre would be devoid of purpose for Sufi practitioners. Where performance as such may share in matters of intentionality, generation of presences and experiences of transcendence (Fischer-Lichte 2007), it is the heart at the centre which is exceptional to Sufism. As such, the tradition cannot be divorced from its philosophy purely for study, the practice cannot be divorced from the knowledges it generates and expresses, and nor can the heart be divorced from the foundations of tasawwuf. 'The most intimate centre of the heart is called the mystery, *sirr*, and this is the inapprehensible point in which the creature meets God' (Burckhardt 2008, p. 86).

Tasawwuf, rather than being purely performative, is also generative in nature, which means that it produces the states it is intended to create within the student by a mutual actioning of practice and surrender. As Burckhardt writes, 'The inner nature of the Sufi is not receptivity but pure act' (2008, p. 11): the act of prayer, the act of fasting, the act of care, the act of *dhikr* and the act of whirling. The act here is a putting in motion of universal principles, not to be confused with outward acts but rather an intentionality in attitude that allows space for divine presence to emerge from the action. Even so, Sufi teachings suggest that all experiences of divine presence are gifts inasmuch as they come when they come. The Sufi *murid* releases themselves from expectation within the action.

Sufi practices such as dhikr, fasting, prayer, music and whirling seek to generate knowledges and intelligences of the heart in the subtle layers of the self. As Khan proposes:

> When a mystic speaks of self-knowledge this does not mean knowing how old one is, or how good one is or how bad, or how right or how wrong; it means knowing the other part of one's being, that deeper, subtler aspect. It is upon the knowledge of that being that the fulfilment of life depends…One might ask, "How can one get closer to it?" The way that has been found by those who searched after the truth, those who sought after God, those who wished to analyze themselves, those who wished to sympathize with life in one single way, and that is the way of vibrations… The Hindus have called it *mantra yoga*; the Sufis have termed it *wafiza*. It is the power of the word that works upon each atom of the body….
>
> (Khan 1983, pp. 43–44)

For Sufis, vibration is the basis and essence of rhythm. From rhythm comes movement, and it is the vibration which communicates and moves between inner and outer worlds. Rhythm is then the root of manifestation; it is how thought comes into being and how matter comes into form. Again Khan writes:

> The philosophy of form may be understood by the study of the process by which the unseen life manifests into the seen… the unseen, incomprehensible, and imperceptible life becomes gradually known, by becoming first audible and then visible; and this is the origin and only source of all form.
>
> (1983, p. 32)

The philosophies of *tasawwuf*, based in rhythm as the foundational matrix of all life, are written in geometries, weavings and patterns, calligraphies, bodily movement, daily activity, notes and modes as well as thought. As such, thought is both at the beginning of expression – as perception of process, and at the end – as explicit oral or written language. We thus see a continuum from direct experience to expression in philosophical terms such as words.

The tools of tasawwuf, which shift vibration through breath, movement and sound, have been utilised across traditions and across time in various ways. Tasawwuf, as a Sufi set of modalities, shifts the vibration of the physical and subtle bodies towards remembrance of the divine. It is called remembrance as union with the divine is considered our natural state of being: one which we tend to forget but practice enables us to remember. The tools of tasawwuf differ in two ways from other performance practices which shift breath, movement and sound. First, their intention towards purification and union foregrounds the action; and second, the actions are held within a living tradition which guides and protects the *murid*, and which furthers the results of the action towards ever more subtle states. Tasawuuf is thus differentiated from performance upon the stage or mise-en-scene, where the states generated are for the benefit of an audience. The actions of tasawwuf are for the experience of the *murid*. The actions of tasawwuf are also aiming or pointing at a set of specifically spiritual experiences which are known, seasoned and passed across time through the living continuity of the tradition.

In the next sections, music and whirling will be discussed – both as practices specific to the lived experiences of the authors and as tools of *tasawuuf* utilised within performance contexts.

Performance philosophy in makam

Another embodiment of performance philosophy within tasawwuf appears in the musical world of *makam*. Makam is a modal musical language extending from Western China as far as Morocco and the Balkans. The musical language of makam (Arabic: *maqam*; *mugam* in Central Asia) grew alongside Sufism across the same geographies and covers a similar time period historically. Makam music's history in Anatolia is inextricably woven with that of *tasawwuf,* especially with the Mevlevi order formed after Mevlâna Jelaluddin Rūmī's death (1273), which had substantial influence in both the Selçuk and Ottoman courts, up to the 20th century. At the beginning of Rūmī's masterpiece, the *Mesnevi,* the human being is compared to an end-blown reed flute – *the ney* – which produces music of most exquisite beauty only when empty (of ego or lower self), waiting to be filled with divine breath (Rūmī 1995). Mevlâna states that the *ney* cries because it has been cut from its source, and longs to go back. Makam's rhythmic counterpart, *usul*, comprises patterns combining 'Dum', 'tek', 'kyâ' and 'hek', which are in Ottoman manuscripts not represented linearly, but in circular form. For some Mevlevi *Ayıns*,[4] the 'Dum' beginning each cycle is compared to Allah's command at the beginning of the universe: 'Be!' (Baysal 2018). Usul cycles, which range from two beats to 128, show a philosophy of time as circular and spiralling in nature, unclosed and regenerative (i.e. eternal), mirroring the motions of the dervish in Mevlevi ritual, an utterly different perception to linear thought as described in the introduction.

As Denise Gill describes in *Melancholic Modalities* (Gill 2017), after the banning of *tarikats* such as the Mevlevis in Republican Turkey in 1925, the spirituality reflected in makam music largely went underground. However, Gill's extensive interviews with makam music practitioners make clear that the intentions being embodied even in instrumental expressions include longing for a mystical, ultimate source; for death, for wedding with the *Beloved*, as well as nostalgia for a time when spirituality could exist more openly. Many aspects of makam are thus reflections of Sufi practice and philosophy.

Besides its cyclical nature and its longing for a divine source, another key reason *makam* retains a spiritual core is because its tuning remains closer to nature – to the overtone series and the pure 5ths and 3rds derived from this. Makam tuning has, especially in Turkey, remained closer to systems proposed millennia ago by Pythagoras, Ptolemy and al-Farabi – than the more recent, now seldom-questioned Western Equal Temperament tuning, which does away with pure overtonal intervals. Analogous to the layers of heart and intellect, and levels of self and Self described in Rumī (Chittick 1983), tuning in Turkish makam features three functioning levels: (1) resonant pure 5ths (Pythagorean), which provide frames for the tetrachords and pentachords constituting all makams; (2) one-koma alterations of Pythagorean degrees, which allows in the resonant pure 3rds of just intonation to create an exquisite, 'softer' embodiment of harmony, especially in makams such as *Rast, Segâh, Hicaz* and *Hüzzam*; (3) the movable 'zones' *(bölge)* of extremely expressive, variable and unstable pitch areas of the *Uşşak* family.[5] This third layer bends, pulsates, slides and cries, enriching makam's expressive universe to give it one of its most characteristic sounds, recalling the 'burnt' metaphor for spiritual maturation in sufism: 'Hamdim, pistim, yandim. (I was raw, I cooked, and I burnt)' (Mevlâna Rumī in Gill 2017). In makam music, it is especially these *bölge* that create this feeling of 'burntness'. How exactly one sings or plays these highly culturally specific nuances is a subject of endless debate, and ultimately a matter of choice and aesthetic – indeed, divergences on interpretation of these *bölge* are often key components for distinguishing one musical style or school from another (Bayley and Reigle forthcoming 2020).

Another essential, yet rarely analysed element of makam music is its multi-dimensional timbral palette. The influence of Qu'ranic recitation, with its 'rules' for relative syllable length, including elongation of soft consonants such as 'l' and 'n' in the nasal cavity and similar nuances, helps create multi-dimensional timbral palettes within a single vocal line, or even between sustained vowels and 'soft consonants' (l, for example) of a single word (Nelson 2001). Makam music instrumentalists such as Tanburi Cemil Bey were profoundly influenced by Qu'ranic reciters. The sound palette of makam music thus directly relates back to recitation, and is therefore the stuff of revelation: the Qu'ran is an essentially orally transmitted document (ibid.), whose content *must* be recited (sung) in order to have its full meaning comprehended. Recitation of the Qu'ran, is, then, a form of philosophy which *must* be embodied in sound to be understood, again bringing philosophy into practice.

Descriptions of makam music as 'monophonic', therefore, miss the inherent depth inherent in both its tuning and timbral soundscape, and depth of performative meaning. Instead, we can hear in makam a fluid, multi-dimensional sound aesthetic, shaped by pitch, subtlety of nuance and subtle timbral modulation. All of these are central to makam's ability to convey spiritual states, and together with *seyir* (melodic shape) combine to manifest the *hal* (states of being), transmitted from one generation of musicians to the next, and to their listeners. It is thus evident that none of this transmission of the profoundest truths of the interrelated cultures of Qu'ranic recitation, tasawwuf, or makam would be possible without performance.

Movement and whirling

Like music, movement is intrinsic to the way of tasawwuf. We can see this in the sway and pulse of *dhikr* and the bodily movements of the breath as well as in the whirling *sema*. Vibration in this way speaks, shows and expresses the truth of the heart. Such conversations may be obfuscated at the level of language and yet they are intricate, palpable and profound in their own circular, moving mode of expression. Whirling can only be known as an embodied form, for it is not just movement but a living breathing philosophy which must be encountered repeatedly and over time for its processes to become perceptible.

Whirling as a practice was utilised across the ancient world, by Zoroastrians, shamans of Central Asia, and is still currently a part of the Tibetan Five Times Rites. *Dhikr*, fasting and prayer, as methods of getting into contact with the subtle bodies and dimensions, have been part of the cultural landscape of Central Asia and Anatolia since before the times of

Figure 3.1 A sema gathering in Konya at Şeb-i Arus celebration time.⁶ Photo credit: Güvenç Özgür

Islam (Sultanova 2011). Whirling itself came into popularity on a larger scale with Mevlana Jalulddin Rūmī, father of the Mevlevi Order of Sufis. Specific ceremonies for whirling, called *sema*, are enacted by the Mevlevi, Naqshabandi, Cerrahi, Qadiri and Bektashi orders as well as by the Alevi. The Ruhaniat Order from America also utilises whirling, as do many 'New Age' spiritual developments such as the work created and expounded by Osho.⁷

Whirling is a movement of rotation (like usul). It is both ancient and achievable by everybody as there is no fixed form which dictates that one must whirl fast or slow, with arms raised or low. The spheres of the planet rotate around the sun. Whorls of water and wind move life through the planet. Our blood rotates as it runs in spirals through our arteries and veins. It is the turning around of bones, muscles and intention upon an *axis mundae*. The term *axis mundae* has been used to denote that the physical axis of the human, the spine, is also representative and functionally in service to the axes of the material and spiritual worlds (McClure 2015). The actual movement of the whirling can be done in a number of ways: with two feet, with one foot that pushes, to the left and to the right, with arms raised and with arms in rest. What is central to all forms of whirling across the many diverse Sufi orders is the humbleness of the approach. For while all things spin, whirling is more than spinning. For Sufis, whirling is the heart cracking open. It is a meeting of the divine and the personal within a moment of time. Whirling is vulnerability grounded by trust. It is a moment where visual dominance fades and the senses reorganise to face inwards. Finally, whirling is a vibration which expresses fully in our bodies when a tenderness of heart is allowed and manifest. From the juxtaposition of action and surrender, effort and vulnerability, power and tenderness, the dynamic and transformative philosophies of tasawwuf arise.

Sefik Can, sheik of the Mevlevi Order in Turkey, writes:

> Whirling (sema) means listening to music, moving with the excitement induced by the music, and entering into ecstasy…whirling has different effects on people's spirits. It enhances one's love of God and produces many spiritual states. These states clean the vices in the heart and finally open the eye of the heart […] This whirling is not the mere turning of the body. This whirling is turning with the heart, spirit, love, faith and with all one's physical and spiritual existence.
>
> *(2011, pp. 204 and 205)*

Can continues, 'That whirling and that harmony take you from yourself, and you also go to the beyond. When you feel all this outside the whirling, what would you have felt if you had participated in the whirling?' (2011, p. 205). This highlights for us the necessity of embodied experience.

The *semazen,* one who dances the *sema,* is known as the one who stands at the door between worlds. This stance is a generative matrix, a humbling and submissive act, a process made manifest through physical and mental effort. Can such a stance be an art? Is there possibility for a spiritual basis to emerge in collective thought, for an articulation of esoteric philosophies in multifaceted expressions? It has been said by some that in the future, the whirling *sema* may be recognised as a form of art, a high art with a special purpose that is known and respected by many (Celebi 2009). It is precisely this sort of intercultural possibility where we find fruitful intersections between performance, philosophy and world philosophies and a valuable contribution to the canon of performance philosophy as a field.

Transcultural performance philosophy in 21st-century music and makam today

Today, a new performance philosophy is emerging that takes makam as one of its central elements onto a broader world stage: transcultural music. Transcultural musical practices create new music that draws with integrity from the idioms of *more than one established tradition* in their creation. Such practices often implicitly address, whether purely in more abstract 'musical' terms, or more openly, the host of questions and possibilities brought forth by the 21st-century phenomena of globalisation, cultures colliding, rapidly changing societal demographics, climate change and proximity of peoples to 'others' unlike themselves in most parts of the globe today. Conflicts between forms of modernism and 'tradition' may also be a part of this, as divisions between 'high' and 'low', commercial and non-commercial and so on. Many transculturally active musicians' intentions relate to mitigating or healing the still-present effects of colonialism in post-colonial societies. Others may have no intention except a strong desire to 'bridge' across divides or demystify the 'other' (Brinner 2009). Far from being geographically or ethnically defined, transcultural (sometimes called 'transtraditional') music may even be attempted by musicians who have grown up in the same city, but live entirely different musical lives when not collaborating.[8] The impetus itself may spring from a desire directly of musicians, or may be at the request of producers, festival directors or composers.

Makam music has become an integral part of such 'inter-' or 'transcultural'[9] experiments within contemporary music, especially since around 2003. Ensembles such as Kudsi Erguner (France), Hezarfen Ensemble (Turkey), Atlas (Netherlands), Omnibus (Uzbekistan), along with composers such as Onur Türkmen, Michael Ellison, Artyom Kim and Jakhongir Shukur today have in common the desire to draw on makam as a major world tradition while spinning out new musical idioms that draw from multiple sources, commissioning and producing influential new works in the process. The aforementioned ensembles diversify the sounds and musical culture composers can draw on, give glimpses of new sonic worlds and combinations to be discovered, and are finding enthusiastic audiences in this 'in between' time excited by new aesthetic possibilities emerging from sometimes integrating, sometimes colliding performance philosophies. At stake is not only the evolving status of makam music worldwide, clearly enhanced by such efforts, but also the very definition of what 'contemporary music' means in the *present* time. This encompasses a vision that composers and practitioners of music around the world increasingly will have the experience and tools to create works inclusive of multiple traditions, drawn on as equally respected sources and practices.

In such a new and diverse area of activity (there is not one style but rather a multiplicity of possibilities), it is unknown before even a single project how the value or artistic results will be defined; indeed, it is questionable whether the 'old' standards of criticism and valuation even apply. Transcultural performance also raises a host of questions – who is its audience, are there multiple perspectives for appreciating such art – how can such creations achieve satisfactory unity or integrity; by whose standards are success or failure defined? Whatever the answers, it is clear that transcultural music opens a host of new, stimulating, aesthetic possibilities directly related to our time. What is also evident is that inter- and transcultural 'free play of the imagination' within the arts can begin to address wider societal issues of shifting identities where words often fail, sometimes seriously, often playfully. A transcultural performance philosophy which includes makam in relation to other contemporary music opens doors for not only aforementioned structural enrichments and *hal,* but also increased capacity for transcending the hegemonic monoculturalism that too often exists in ignorance of others equally valid still today, and reconnection to the heart.

Conclusion

Tasawwuf, rooted in Islam but also bigger than Islam and inclusive of many truths from other mystical schools of thought and practice, has its own philosophies that are of vital importance to the intercultural and worlding projects of our era. In putting tasawwuf, Islam and performance philosophy in conversation with each other, it is hoped that openings may emerge not only in thought, but in practice through and with the arts. We remind the reader that transcultural efforts, which move beyond appropriation and through desire, offer a pathway where art and the divine might meet once again, as they have done in previous civilisations. The dimensions of knowledge opened by the particular study of tasawwuf find specific relevance to debates of both foundation and application, as practical means of engagement where intellect and knowledge move beyond classification into possibilities rich in difference, connectivity and divine inspiration. The care and respect which are necessary in encountering tasawwuf have been highlighted throughout this paper. Here, we remind the reader that encounters with the sacred are necessarily experiential. When the heart and mind come into reciprocity and resonance with each other, the synergistic intelligence which emerges is poignantly Sufi in nature and it is this poignancy of thought and experience which we offer to the field of performance philosophy as another way of knowing, of doing and of being in the world.

Tasawwuf is in itself a living, breathing philosophy. While its practices may be shared upon the performance stage, their true intent and direction are for the *murid's* life. In opening the practices of tasawuuf to performance, the *murid* who is also a performer may grow in new directions and the fruits of their practice shared with a welcoming public. This is a crossover where performance and spiritual practice meet in the life of the *murid*, for the benefit of all. Thus, performance philosophy can embrace tasawwuf as a mode of knowing, a lived philosophy and a spiritual endeavour at once. This embrace is transcultural; it opens new thresholds and directions to philosophies of the West through discourse, practice and, where possible, sincere engagement.

Notes

1 The perennialist school of thought studies spirituality and religion from various world traditions, with a specific emphasis on Sufism by many of its proponents. Looking to the foundational truths across religions and systems, discourses embrace that which is universal in nature and specific in culture. The authors of this paper are from the traditionalist arm of perennialist thought.

2. While Sufism may encompass the beliefs, practices and dimensions of multiple religions, Tasawwuf is generally related to the Islamic expression of Sufism. In this regard, Sufism and Tasawwuf are one and the same, and hold the same truths; however, Sufism may extend itself into additional cultural manifestations.
3. The term 'subtle body' is used to denote aspects of the self which extend beyond the skin: the magnetic fields which extend through the emotional and mental fields into and across space, the spiritual body and aspects of the self known as the spirit and soul.
4. The suite of compositions comprising the musical accompaniment for Mevlevi Whirling.
5. Uşşak, Hüseyni, Hüzzam, Saba, Karcığar – the makam structures most distinctive to music of this geography (Necdet Yaşar, in Signell 1976).
6. Şeb-i Arus is the yearly celebration of the passing of Mevlana Jalaluddin Rūmī, founder of the Mevlevi Order of Sufis. Sufis from around the world gather in Konya, Turkey, and wherever they are locally, to hold sema (whirling ceremony). The image shows the author, McClure, and her companions in *sema* in the style of Oruç Güvenc, with several different orders practising together.
7. The author, Hannah McClure, trained with a Mevlevi Order in London and later connected to the work and legacy of Rhami Oruç Güvenç in Turkey. Güvenç's work brought together the whirling forms, music and practices of many different Sufi orders to create an inclusive whirling sema which welcomes *murids* from every religion and part of the world.
8. For example, a ney player from the makam tradition, and a cello player from the Western orchestral tradition, who have both grown up in Istanbul.
9. A distinction is also to be made between intercultural or transcultural musicking, based on Ric Knowles' (Knowles 2010) Theatre & Interculturalism, addressing a host of other adjectives applicable for any art form drawing more than one culture into its creative orbit. In brief, intercultural interaction involves the serious learning and apprehension of the forms, aesthetics and performance practices of some 'other' tradition or culture. Transcultural, as defined by the present author (Ellison 2016), means to draw extensively from more than one artistic tradition freely to create something new, using concretely recognisable performance elements (i.e. instruments, performance practices) of more than one culture in these new creations.

References

Bayley A. and Reigle R. (ed.) Forthcoming 2020. *Makam Instruments and Voices in Contemporary Music*. Bristol: ERC.

Baysal, O. 2018. "Zaman Makam Analiz Modeli" ["Time Makam Analysis Model"]. *IX. International Hisarlı Ahmet Symposium Proceedings*. Editor: Çaghan Adar. Matbaa-I Bekâ. Afyonkarahisar. pp. 298–313.

Blann, G. 2005. *The Garden of Mystic Love: Sufism and the Turkish Tradition*. Nashville: Four Worlds Publishing.

Brinner, B. 2009. *Playing across a Divide: Israeli-Palestinian Musical Encounters*. Oxford: Oxford University Press.

Burckhardt, T. 2004. *The Essential Titus Burckhardt: Reflections on Sacred Arts, Faiths and Civilizations*. Edited by Stoddardt, W. Perennial Philosophy Series. Bloomington: World Wisdom.

Burckhardt, T. 2008. *Introduction to Sufi Doctrine*, translated from the 1959 original, Matheson, D.M. & Lahore, M.A. (eds.) Bloomington: World Wisdom.

Can, S. 2011. *Fundamentals of Rūmī's Thought: A Mevlevi Sufi Perspective*. edited and translated by Saritoprak, Z., Clifton: Tughra Books.

Celebi, E. 2009. Interview. Digital Recording. 18th Dec. Konya.

Chittick, W. 1983. *The Sufi Path of Love: The Spiritual Teachings of Rūmī*. Albany: State University of New York Press.

Ellison, M. (2016) "Gesture in poetry, movement and music: Approaching the total artwork through Sufism in Say I am You and Deniz Küstü (The Sea-Crossed Fisherman)", *Dance, Movement & Spiritualities*, Volume 3, Number 3, 1 September 2016, pp. 217–241

Fischer-Lichte, E. 2007. *Theatre, Sacrifice, Ritual*. London/New York: Routledge.

Gill, D. 2017. *Melancholic Modalities: Affect, Islam & Turkish Classical Musicians*. New York: Oxford University Press.

Herlihy, J. 2009. *The Essential René Guénon*. Bloomington: World Wisdom.

Khan, H.I. 1983. *The Music of Life: The Inner Nature and Effects of Sound*. New Lebanon: Omega Publications.

Khan, H. I. 2014. "On the Origins of Sufism". https://sufiway.org/about-us/the-origins-of-sufism. [Accessed 30/–09/–18].

Knowles, R. 2010. *Theatre and Interculturalism*. Basingstoke: Palgrave MacMillan.

Latifa, D. 2014. "On Our Religious Subconscious, the Problem of Petro-Islam and the Disappearance of Mysticism", in J.Y. Atals (ed.) *Halal Monk: A Christian on a Journey through Islam*. Yunus Publishing, pp. 119–134.

McClure, H. 2015. "Actualising the Contents of the Heart: The Journey of a Female Mevlevi Semazen". PhD thesis: The University of East London.

Nasr, S.H. 1997. *Man and Nature: The Spiritual Crisis of Modern Man*. Chicago: ABC International.

Nasr, S.H. 2002. "The Heart of the Faithful Is the Throne of the All-Merciful", in J. Custinger (ed.) *Paths to the Heart: Sufism and the Christian East*. Bloomington: World Wisdom, pp. 32–47.

Nasr, S.H. 2008. *The Garden of Truth: The Vision and Promise of Sufism, Islam's Mystical Tradition*. New York: HarperCollins.

Nelson, K. 2001. *The Art of Reciting the Qu'ran*. Cairo: American University in Cairo Press.

Quran. Religious text.

Rūmī. 1995. *The Essential Rumi*. Translated by Coleman Barks. New York: HarperCollins.

Schuon, Frithjof. 1983. "Islam and Consciousness of the Absolute", in *Studies in Comparative Religion*, Vol. 15, Nos. 1 and 2 (Winter-Spring). [online] www.studiesincomparativereligion.com. Accessed 06/08/19.

Schuon, Frithjof. 1984. *The Transcendent Unity of Religions*. Wheaton: Quest Books.

Signell, K.L. 1976. *Makam: Modal Practice In Turkish Art Music*. Seattle: Asian Music Publications.

Sultanova, Razia. 2011. *From Shamanism to Sufism: Women, Islam and Culture in Central Asia*. London: I. B. Taurus.

4
WHOSE *TEMPEST*? PERFORMANCE PHILOSOPHY AND/AS DECOLONIAL CACOPHONY

Andrés Fabián Henao Castro

Introduction

In this chapter, I offer three settler colonial logics of accumulation – elimination, exclusion, and fungibility – as a theoretical model by which to better understand the various ways in which modern capitalism holds the bodies that it racializes and genders ontologically captive to different positions of abjection.[1] I trace these logics in Shakespeare's *The Tempest* and its various rewritings, partially by moving beyond the Prospero/Caliban dichotomy that still dominates decolonial/postcolonial interpretations of the play (Vaughan & Vaughan 1991; Henry 2000; Wynter 2003). *The Tempest*, I claim, is a play saturated with various forms of captivity, related yet irreducible to the one that Caliban suffers, and better explained by the three settler colonial logics of accumulation that I offer as a decolonial way of doing performance philosophy.

As Laura Cull (2014) argues, performance philosophy does not merely bring two separate disciplines together; their encounter actually changes our understanding of them both. On the one hand, performance is no longer conceived as merely illustrative of philosophical ideas, but as "partaking in the experience of thought" (Cull 2014, p. 24). On the other hand, philosophy no longer places itself outside of the object that it examines, and recognizes in that non-philosophical outside, as Gilles Deleuze and Félix Guattari (1994, p. 41) famously articulated, something "closer to philosophy than philosophy itself". Philosophy and performance have, nevertheless, historically participated in the displacement of the differentially located colonized subjects to the site of the unthought, as the objects of someone else's knowledge that never become thinking subjects themselves. Thus, in 'geophilosophy', Deleuze and Guattari (1994, p. 93) both acknowledge that there is Chinese, Hindu, Jewish, or Islamic philosophy, to name only a few, only to claim, a few lines later, that "nevertheless, philosophy was something Greek – although brought by immigrants". Notwithstanding their anti-capitalist critique, rather than abstract (de)territorializations of thought – innocently 'brought by immigrants' – I prefer to situate the (re)production of thought, and its performance, in variable colonial logics of capitalist accumulation, logics that seek to hold some captive, in order to endow others with the exclusive capacity to think and act.

Ontological captivity

Captivity is central to *The Tempest*.[2] Prospero, the former Duke of Milan and main character of Shakespeare's play, explicitly regards his life on the Island as an imprisonment, as he was forced into exile there by his treacherous brother, Antonio, and King Alonso of Naples. Even before Prospero's imprisonment, however, we find the state-sanctioned exile of the Algerian witch Sycorax. She was abandoned on the Island while pregnant with Caliban as an alternative punishment to the death penalty 'for one thing she did' – though what that 'one thing' is, the play never reveals (Act 1, Sc. 2, p. 266).[3] Prior to Prospero's forced settlement on the island, Sycorax confines the spirit Ariel, indigenous to the territory, into a cloven pine. Ariel is confined for twelve years, and Prospero only releases him in order to hold him captive again. Prospero also enslaves Caliban (Shakespeare's anagram for 'cannibal', based on a misreading of Montaigne's 1580 essay, 'Of Cannibals'), for supposedly having tried 'to violate the honor' of his daughter, Miranda (Act 1, Sc. 2, p. 416). Miranda herself is also in exile, having been banished with her father when she was only three years old.

Though all of these characters face some form of confinement, we should not equate the conditions of their captivity. Unlike Prospero and Sycorax, Ariel and Caliban are not only confined to the island but also to Prospero's will. Their captivity, however, also differs considerably. Unlike the labor of Ariel, who flies and rides on the curled clouds in order to produce tempests for Prospero, the enslaved Caliban provides free manual labor for the master, "[making their] fire, [fetching their] wood, and [serving] in offices that profit [them]" (Act 1, Sc. 2, p. 373). The division of labor between Ariel and Caliban translates, in turn, into the different conditions of their confinement. Not only is Ariel allowed more mobility than Caliban, who is held captive in a hard rock and kept from the rest of the island (Act 1, Sc. 2, p. 410), Prospero deploys a gratuitous use of violence against Caliban, in order to break his rebelliousness.

There are more captives, still, in this play. When Ariel's tempest successfully reroutes the European ship carrying Prospero's enemies to the Island, Prospero holds them captive as well. The captivity of his enemies is, compared to that of the other characters, considerably limited; it lasts only long enough for Prospero to expose the treachery of Antonio and Sebastian, and arrange a marriage for his daughter. We should note here the ways in which, under the hetero-patriarchal conditions of European colonialism, Miranda's marriage might also be considered a continuation of her captivity, moving from the control of her father to that of her new husband, Ferdinand (this also happens to Claribel, forced to marry the King of Tunis).

Temporality is not the only difference between the captivity of European men in the play and the endless confinement that Sycorax, Caliban, Ariel, Miranda, and Claribel suffer, even if such endlessness does seek to ontologize their captivity, as it is their racially and sexually marked bodies that are politically signified, as if 'naturalizing' their abjection. Held ontologically captive, their confinements are by no means equivalent. As the hero of Shakespeare's romance, Prospero represents what Sylvia Wynter (2003, pp. 289–290) calls the "overrepresentation of the human by Man$_1$", making 'humanity' rest on the dehumanization of the indigenous spirit, Ariel, the exploited laborer, Caliban, and the witch, Sycorax. She is perhaps the most dehumanized of all, called the 'swine-raven', not only depicted in monstrous form, but also made responsible for the reproduction of monstrosity (Caliban is 'hagseed').[4] Although by no means dehumanized like Ariel, Caliban, and Sycorax, the humanity of Miranda and Claribel is, unlike that of Prospero and all the other men in the play, severely constrained by their sexual objectification. They are both moved without consent from natal to arranged conjugal families. They are thus made ontologically unfree, distinguished in these ways from the unfreedom that characterizes other European men in the play, like Stephano and Trinculo. Nonetheless, it would be wrong to conflate the specific shape of their patriarchal confinement and the enslavement experienced by Caliban and Ariel or the ceaseless degradation experienced by Sycorax. Violently expropriated from her control over her own body, the 'virtuosity' that oppresses Miranda places her in a colonially constructed 'womanhood' that remains inaccessible to Sycorax, confined to the sub-human order of the monster.[5] Hence, unlike Ariel's humming, Caliban's cursing, and the radical silence into which Sycorax is buried, Miranda's speech is intelligible and even capable of reproducing the injurious language of the master, as she does when she refers to Caliban as an 'abhorred slave', whose race she declares 'vile' (Act 1, Sc. 2, pp. 421 and 430). Her speech, however, remains ultimately subordinated to her sexually reproductive labor; thus, she can look down on Caliban but must look up to Ferdinand, who she names 'a thing divine' (Act 1, Sc. 2, p. 500).

Decolonial cacophony

Decolonial aesthetics radically challenged some of the ontological modes of captivity evident in Shakespeare's play, through the Antillean reinvention of Caliban in the late 1960s. The publication of Aimé Césaire's play, *Une tempête* (1969), Edward Kamau Brathwaite's collection of poems, *Islands* (1969), and Roberto Fernández Retamar's essay, 'Cuba until Fidel' (1969), inverted one hierarchy: heroizing Caliban, instead of Prospero, as the character who embodied the material and spiritual struggle for freedom. Though perhaps the best known, the Antillean Caliban was not the first character through which authors challenged the valorization of Prospero. Uruguayan essayist José Enrique Rodó had tried to do so unsuccessfully through *Ariel* (1900), in a text that confusingly argued against the hemispheric hegemony of the United States in Latin America through a naïve romanticization of the Greek origins of European cosmopolitanism. More problematically, Rodó's *Ariel* praised Latin American *mestizaje* as both an anti-black and an anti-indigenous idealization of Europe. He thus praised Latin America as a 'great ethnic tradition', with 'a sacred place in the pages of history', that could only 'ascend in the movement of life' by overcoming the rebelliousness of Caliban, appropriating to itself Ariel's indigeneity to the territory, and responding 'with agility to Prospero's call' (Rodó 1988, pp. 73, 98 and 99).

The inability to address Ariel's indigeneity explains the otherwise problematic representation of Ariel as a mulatto slave, and Caliban as a black one, in Césaire's ultimate embrace of the latter as the real liberatory force. It also explains Retamar's (1989, p. 39) characterization of Ariel as an intellectual that could "choose between serving Prospero (…) or allying himself with Caliban in his struggle for true freedom". But in doing so, as Jodi Byrd (2011, p. 59) argues, indigeneity is detached, "from the original inhabitants of the Americas and relocate[d] (…) on settlers and arrivants themselves".[6] The foregrounding of the Prospero–Caliban master/slave dialectic, she claims, "draws upon the settler effacement of the indigenous", and "serves the larger function of indigenizing arrival to the Americas and rendering indigenous peoples absent and foreign in their own lands" (Byrd 2011, pp. 59–60). Rather than recentering the play's narrative on the Prospero–Ariel settler/native dialectic, I would argue that we need a triangulated schema that better accommodates the different logics of accumulation structuring the positionalities of these characters. Here, I find Byrd's (2011, pp. 65–66) notion of cacophony, as a reading practice "aimed at dismantling the ontological prior of the colonization of indigenous peoples that is always already deferred when claims to Caliban are made", as a useful decolonial tool by which to reorient performance philosophy toward the interruption, rather than reproduction, of the ongoing logics of accumulation.

The philosophical work that Shakespeare's *Tempest* performs, as a performative text that thinks, is ideologically complicit with the colonial fungibility of aliens and elimination of natives, both of which the settler colonial order regards as entirely deprived of thought. Decolonial cacophony, thus, offers performance philosophy a politics by which to navigate the gap that sustains its encounter, a way of situating the conceptual characters that performance philosophy (re)invents, against the settler colonial history of capitalist accumulation by which some of them are rendered sensible, on the conditions that others are not (to echo Jacques Rancière's terms).

Settler colonial logics of capitalist accumulation

Settler colonial critique traces different structures of racialization in relation to the specific forms of colonial capitalism and territorial occupation embedded in a society's history. According to Patrick Wolfe (2006), franchise colonies like British India, or French Algeria, differ from settler colonies like the occupation of indigenous territories by the US, or Palestine by Israel, in the particular ways in which they mix the expropriation of land with the exploitation of labor. Wolfe thus argues that settler colonialism is unique in its combination between two forms of racialized violence: a *logic of elimination* that names an overriding structural tendency toward indigenous genocide, and a *logic of exclusion* that structures the exploitation between the colonizer and the racialized, coerced laborers who are brought to work the land in the place of native people.

These coerced, exploited, racialized workers have various names in settler colonial studies. Byrd (2011) refers to them as 'arrivants', and Iyko Day (2016) as 'aliens'. Like Byrd's 'arrivant', Day's 'alien' names a position originally occupied by enslaved Africans during the European colonization of indigenous territories in the Western Hemisphere. Day's concept is, however, more capacious than Byrd's, as she also understands the ongoing reproduction of the 'alien' to refer to Asians and other non-indigenous people of color in North America, who, though differently from the history of chattel slavery, are still exploited by the settler class.

While Day does in her analysis differentiate between anti-Asian and anti-black racism, ultimately these differences are underthematized by the dualistic logic she inherits from Wolfe. Thus, I propose an additional settler colonial logic of fungibility. Fungibility is Afro-pessimism's way of naming the hyper-alienation constituted when capitalism profits not from the exploitation of one's surplus labor-time, but from the entire appropriation of the subject's existence, when slavery transmogrifies black people into a thing to be sold in the market. As Frank Wilderson (2010) further develops, the worker, albeit exploited, belongs to civil society and is socially recognized and endowed with the capacity to perform and thus to appropriate, even if in the minimal and always alienated form of self-ownership. The slave, by contrast, lies outside of civil society, and is produced, as both Hartman and Wilderson (2003, p. 188) claim, as "[a] body that you can do what you want with". Entirely expulsed from the social order of the human, fungibility specifies the radical and particular form of social death engendered by settler colonial capitalist anti-blackness.[7] The territorial form of alienation that the Middle Passage produced distinguishes anti-blackness from other forms of alien labor and, I argue, makes it possible for the first time to implement a logic of elimination within a logic of exclusion. Thus, as Hartman (2008, p. 79) reconstructs, after consulting a Dutch historian, the death rate of the slave trade reached "70% before the survivors were adjusted to life in the Western Hemisphere". In short, counted as property, rather than as persons, the settler colonial order exploits socially dead, rather than living labor, when it doubles the exclusion of the black alien by means of a territorial alienation. This means, first, that the white master owns what the enslaved black body both produces and sexually reproduces, given that all claims to kin could be arbitrarily invaded by property relations, eliminating, as Hortense Spillers (2003, p. 218) argues, "all the customary aspects of sexuality, including 'reproduction', 'motherhood', 'pleasure', and 'desire'". Territorial alienation also made it possible for masters to own the performance (dance, music, etc.) of the slave, but also "the slave's own enjoyment of her/ his performance: that too belongs to white people" (Hartman & Wilderson 2003, p. 188). The logic of fungibility thus names a unique positionality within settler colonization.

This positionality is further complicated by the fact that, when turned into cargo, as Spillers (2003, p. 220) says, "one is neither female, nor male". This does not mean, as some Afro-pessimist theorists have claimed, contra intersectionality, that racial differences have ontological priority over sexual differences (Wilderson 2010, p. 24; Warren 2017, p. 394). Rather, it means that one needs to interrogate a paradoxical mode of doing gender through its abject undoing, within variable logics of fungibility and elimination. To borrow from Judith Butler's (1990, p. 31) performative theory of gender, we could say that black and indigenous women are to white women "*not* as copy is to original but, rather, as copy is to copy". The difference is that I situate the performatively enacted signification that sediments this differential copying of gender in a settler colonial history: one that destroys indigenous and African people's different ways of signifying the members of their communities, in order to compel hetero-patriarchal reproduction as exclusively intelligible for white settlers.

Settler colonial logics of accumulation in *The Tempest*

Reading *The Tempest* in its decolonial cacophony reveals Prospero to inhabit the position of the European settler, Ariel as the native, and Caliban and Sycorax as fungible aliens. In the triangulated system that I offer, the relationship between Prospero and Ariel is one of elimination, that between Prospero and Caliban/ Sycorax one of sexually differentiated fungibility, and that between Prospero and Miranda one of intra-settler sexual oppression. And if Ariel is not eliminated but given his freedom by the end of *The Tempest*, it is because, unlike the real story of English colonialism in Barbados, Prospero returns to Naples via his instrumentalization of Miranda's marriage to Ferdinand, a return that no longer forces Miranda to reproduce the settler, if one that does extend the captivity of Caliban.[8]

The real story of settler colonialism is better represented in Marina Warner's rewriting of *The Tempest* in her wonderful novel, *Indigo* (1992), where Prospero does not leave, Ariel is not freed, and Caliban is publicly executed to set a precedent. Warner, thus, decolonially performs philosophy when her novel displaces the 'original' by narrating the story not only from the perspective of the settler, but also from that of the native and the fungible alien. Sycorax is no longer silent in Warner's novel, only because she no longer occupies the radical position of abjection she was forced to represent in Shakespeare's original. No longer dehumanized in Warner's version, Sycorax is endowed with even greater symbolic power than Miranda, as she has the capacity to name others: in Warner's novel, Sycorax names the child that she adopts after saving him from the womb of his dead mother, who was drowned while shackled. We should read here the haunting memory of all those who died similarly during the Middle Passage, when "the slavers tossed out any among their load who were failing, if one in three survived the journey, the trade still worked out as a cheap method of acquiring labor" (Warner 1992, p. 97). She names the child Dulé, meaning grief, years before he becomes known to settlers as Caliban. But Dulé's birth mother, like Shakespeare's Sycorax, is buried in an infinite silence from which Dulé can only recover the horrible details of her death and speculations of her past. Because Warner's Sycorax no longer occupies the position of Shakespeare's Sycorax, she can name and even educate, like Prospero. In Warner's version, the greatest beneficiary of Sycorax's transmission of knowledge is an Arawak native, named Ariel, she also adopts and loves with great affection (Warner 1992, p. 114).[9]

Everything changes on the island with the arrival of Kit Everard in 1618, Warner's Prospero. Having become rich in the otherwise insecure English settlement in Surinam, Everard heads to the island. And, unlike other unsuccessful European attempts to settle in it, he succeeds by holding Sycorax and Ariel hostage. In Warner's novel, thus, the colonization of the island is predicated on this sexually differentiated aspect of colonial power and violence: Everard rapes Ariel, and produces a son, Roukoubé, whom he immediately disowns (Warner 1992, pp. 172–173). This 'monstrous intimacy', as Christina Sharpe (2010) would call it, is what allows the settlers to strengthen their position in the island, learn how to survive conditions other settlers could not, and make the future plantation more lucrative by cultivating indigo. We also see the colonial expropriation of female-transmitted knowledge in Warner's story, with the colonizers using the knowledge of indigo that Sycorax had shared with Ariel.

In Warner's version, Miranda does not marry Ferdinand, and Prospero does not return to Naples, after setting Ariel free and acknowledging Caliban as his own.[10] Rather, Everard stays, publicly executes Dulé, never looks for Roukoubé, and brings his fiancée, Rebecca, to the indigenous land that he has expropriated, in a heterosexual ritual that marks reproductive futurism as the prerogative of the settler. It is through these ongoing logics of elimination, exclusion, and fungibility that settler colonialism links time to being, while regulating that which differently racialized women are forced or forbidden to pass on.

Decolonizing performance philosophy

The various forms of ontological captivity dispossessing the sexually differentiated settler, native and fungible alien, can only be challenged through the active contestation of the ongoing logics of elimination, exclusion, and fungibility that characterize settler colonial capitalist accumulation. It is Prospero who enunciates *The Tempest's* last form of confinement, when he pleads to the audience, "As you from crimes would pardoned be, Let your indulgence set me free". If never just a metaphor, as Eve Tuck and Wayne Yang (2012) rightly argue, the texts to which performance philosophy also traces its origins need to be freed, not by aesthetic indulgence but through decolonial critique. Decolonial cacophony offers a way of unsettling the logics of accumulation by which bodies and capacities are distributed in the aesthetic landscape of this emerging field, so that the gap that sustains the encounter of performance and philosophy no longer participates in the eliminations, exclusions, and fungibilities that reproduce the coloniality of knowledge, power, and being.

To decolonize performance philosophy means to desediment the positions that have been colonially constructed as aesthetically sensible, if only by rendering others nonsensible. This form of desedimentation, decolonial cacophony adds, requires the plural voicing of that which is refused from construction, by retelling the story from the perspective of the sexually differentiated native, alien, and reluctant settler. In those stories survives a subversive form of resignification that performance philosophy can amplify, if this field joins them in mobilizing the signs by which the colonial order seeks to hold them ontologically captive, against their racist and sexist capitalist usages and toward empowerment and liberation.

Notes

1 Fungibility is a concept developed by Afro-pessimist theory, in order to distinguish the temporally bounded exploitation of the worker from the temporally endless accumulation of the slave. Saidiya Hartman (1997, p. 21) first conceptualized fungibility as the making of the captive body into "an abstract and empty vessel vulnerable to the projection of others' feelings, ideas, desires, and values". Accumulation, thus, refers not only to the material appropriation of the slave's labor, but also to their libidinal exploitation, as not only their labor but their entire existence, and that of their kin – equally transmogrified into property – the masters appropriate.
2 Despite the many shortcomings of Margaret Atwood's (2017) retelling of Shakespeare's play in her novel, *Hag-seed*, her contemporization of the story in the Fletcher Correctional does capture the racialized form of ontological captivity that traces a historical continuity between the turning of the Caribbean island into a state of exception via plantation slavery and today's prison-industrial complex. For a genealogical tracing of these forms of confinement to modern slavery and colonial racialization, see Browne (2015).
3 All citations are from the Folger Library version. See Shakespeare ([1612] 2015).
4 For one of the best analyses of the representational monstrification of Sycorax, see Warner (2000, pp. 97–113): for one of the first decolonial challenges to the silencing of Sycorax, see Wynter (1994). For a more contemporary contestation of Sycorax's silencing through the genre of horror, see Brooks (2018).
5 On the role that the European witch-hunt played for the forms of gender expropriation characteristic of early modern capitalism, see Federici (2004). As intersectional feminists have argued, the modern/colonial construction of 'woman' as passive, virtuous, and submissive excluded black and indigenous women otherwise cast as overtly sexual; see Davis (1983, pp. 222–244) and Lugones (2007, pp. 188–199).
6 'Arrivant' is a term Byrd (2011, p. xix) borrows from the Afro-Caribbean poet Edward Kamau Brathwaite to signify "those people forced into the Americas through the violence of European and Anglo-American colonialism and imperialism around the globe".
7 On the concept of social death as "the permanent, violent domination of natally alienated and generally dishonored persons", see Patterson (1982, p. 13).
8 The 1609 tempest that wrecked the *Sea Venture* close to the Island of Bermuda – renamed as such in 1505 by the Spanish conquistador Juan de Bermúdez – is the event that, according to most historically inclined interpretations of Shakespeare, inspired *The Tempest*, written in 1612.
9 Of all of the characters in Shakespeare's *The Tempest,* Ariel continues to be the more gender fluid, represented as male, female, and even non-human in an arguably unintentional acknowledgment that, as Lugones (2007, p. 196) claims, indigenous peoples "recognized more than two genders, recognized 'third' gendering and homosexuality positively, and understood gender in egalitarian terms rather than in the terms of subordination that Eurocentered capitalism imposed on them".
10 In Atwood's (2017, p. 273) version, a group of prisoners suggest an alternative interpretation of that acknowledgment, claiming Prospero to be Caliban's father.

References

Atwood, M. 2017. *Hag-seed*, New York: Hogarth.
Brathwaite, E. K. 1969. *Islands*, London: Oxford University Press.
Brooks, B. 2018. *Searching for Sycorax: Black Women's Hauntings of Contemporary Horror*, New Brunswick: Rutgers University Press.
Browne, S. 2015. *Dark Matters: On the Surveillance of Blackness*, Durham: Duke University Press.
Butler, J. 1990. *Gender Trouble: Feminism and the Subversion of Identity*, New York: Routledge.
Byrd, J. 2011. *The Transit of Empire: Indigenous Critiques of Colonialism*, Minneapolis: University of Minnesota Press.
Césaire, A. [1969] 2002. *A Tempest*, New York: Theater Communications Group.
Cull, L. 2014. 'Performance Philosophy — Staging a New Field', in L. Cull and A. Lagaay (ed.) *Encounters in Performance Philosophy*, Basingstoke: Palgrave Macmillan, pp.15–38.
Davis, A. 1983. *Women, Race, Class*, New York: Vintage.
Day, I. 2016. *Alien Capital: Asian Racialization and the Logic of Settler Colonial Capitalism*, Durham: Duke University Press.

Deleuze, G. & Guattari, F. 1994. *What Is Philosophy?*, New York: Columbia University Press.
Federici, S. 2004. *Caliban and the Witch: Women, the Body, and Primitive Accumulation*, New York: Autonomedia.
Hartman, S. 1997. *Scenes of Subjection: Terror, Slavery and Self-Making in Nineteenth Century America*, Oxford: Oxford University Press.
Hartman, S. 2008. *Lose Your Mother: A Journey along the Atlantic Slaver Route*, New York: Farrar, Straus and Giroux.
Hartman, S. & Wilderson, F. 2003. 'The Position of the Unthought', *Qui Parle*, 13 (2), 183–201.
Henry, P. 2000. *Caliban's Reason: Introducing Afro-Caribbean Philosophy*, New York: Routledge.
Lugones, M. 2007. 'Heterosexualism and the Colonial/Modern Gender System', *Hypatia*, 22 (1), 186–209.
Patterson, O. 1982. *Slavery and Social Death: A Comparative Study*, Cambridge: Harvard University Press.
Retamar, R.F. 1969. 'Cuba until Fidel', *Bohemia,* 19 September, 85–97.
Retamar, R. F. 1989. *Caliban and Other Essays*, Minneapolis: University of Minnesota Press.
Rodó, J. E. [1900] 1988. *Ariel*, Austin: University of Texas Press.
Shakespeare, W. [1612] 2015. *The Tempest*, New York: The Folger Shakespeare Library.
Sharpe, C. 2010. *Monstrous Intimacies: Making Post-Slavery Subjects*, Durham: Duke University Press.
Spillers, H. 2003. *Black, White, and in Color*, Chicago: Chicago University Press.
Tuck, E. & Yang, K. W. 2012. 'Decolonization Is Not a Metaphor', *Decolonization, Indigeneity, Education & Society*, 1 (1), 1–40.
Vaughan, A.T. & Vaughan, V.M. 1991. *Shakespeare's Caliban: A Cultural History*, Cambridge: Cambridge University Press.
Warner, M. 1992. *Indigo*, New York: Simon Schuster.
Warner, M. 2000. '"The Foul Witch" and Her "Freckled Whelp": Circean Mutations in the New World', in P. Hulme and W. Sherman (ed.) *The Tempest and Its Travels*, London: Reaktion Books, pp. 97–115.
Warren, C. 2017. 'Afro-Pessimism, G̶a̶y̶ Nigger #1, and Surplus Violence', *GLQ*, 23 (3), 391–418.
Wilderson, F. 2010. *Red, White & Black*, Durham: Duke University Press.
Wolfe, P. 2006. 'Settler Colonialism and the Elimination of the Native', *Journal of Genocide Research*, 8 (4), 387–409.
Wynter, S. 1994. 'Beyond Miranda's Meanings: Un/Silencing the "Demonic Ground" of Caliban's "Woman"', in C. B. Davies and E. S. Fido (ed.), *Out of the Kumbla: Caribbean Women and Literature*, Trenton: African World Press, pp. 355–372.
Wynter, S. 2003. 'Unsettling the Coloniality of Being/Power/Truth/Freedom: Towards the Human, After Man, Its Overrepresentation – An Argument', *The New Centennial Review*, 3 (3), 257–337.

5

THE PLAYWRIGHT AS THINKER
Modern drama and performance philosophy

David Kornhaber

In April of 1896, George Bernard Shaw interrupted his Easter vacation in Hertfordshire to file an urgent report in *The Saturday Review*: not a statement on socialist politics or a polemic about the London stage but a book review – a lengthy account of the inaugural volume in the first English translation of Friedrich Nietzsche's collected works. Shaw knew that most of his readers had probably never heard of the then obscure German thinker, so he opened his review with a tongue-in-cheek explanation and comparison. "I may as well explain that Nietzsche is a philosopher", he writes. "That is to say, something unintelligible to an Englishman. To make my readers realize what a philosopher is, I can only say that *I* am a philosopher" (Tyson 1991, p. 188, emphasis in original). It would not be the only instance in which Shaw described himself as a philosopher, nor the only one where he declared himself Nietzsche's equal. "The artist-philosophers are the only sort of artists I take quite seriously", he famously declared in the Epistle Dedicatory to *Man and Superman*, explaining that the difference between the two occupations "is merely formal" (Shaw 1965, p. 164). And to his German translator, Siegfried Trebitsch, he once wrote that, "I want the Germans to know me as a philosopher, as an English (or Irish) Nietzsche (only ten times cleverer)" (Laurence 1985, p. 298). For Shaw, the boundary between theater and philosophy was a fluid one. While not every playwright of the era deserved to be counted as a philosopher (in Shaw's estimation, most of his peers would most certainly not make the cut), there was nothing in his mind to make the writing of plays necessarily any different than the writing of philosophical tracts. More and more, he believed, the theater would be seen as the equal of the university classroom or the scholarly society as a powerful forum for intellectual inquiry. "There is, flatly, no future now for any drama … except the drama of thought", he predicted (Shaw 1965, p. 45).

Shaw's opinions on the alignment between philosophy and theater echo and amplify those of many others connected to the movement known as modern drama. As I have previously argued, the emergence of modern drama between the late nineteenth and mid-twentieth centuries, both as a mode of theatrical practice and as an object of academic study, should be regarded as an important development in what I have called the "pre-history of performance philosophy" (Kornhaber 2015, pp. 24–35). Much of the groundwork for contemporary approaches to the interrelationship of performance and philosophy – most especially a belief in the capacity of the former to actually manifest the latter – begins in the way that figures associated with the modern drama either as practitioners or critics started to think about the connections between drama, theater, and philosophy during this period. It is not that the era of modern drama represents any sort of origin point for such thoughts. In the European tradition, the acknowledgment of a special relationship between theater and philosophy goes at least as far back as Sir Philip Sidney's *Defense of Poesy* from 1583, where he argues that the playwright aids the philosopher, whose "knowledge standeth so upon the abstract and general", by making it so that audiences "may understand him" and "can apply what he doth understand" (Cook 1890, p. 15). This is to say nothing about the shared origins and ongoing entanglement of philosophy and theater in the classical era. Rather, the particular way in which the relationship between philosophy and theater starts to be conceived during the period of modern drama, and the increasing frequency with which dramatists considered and spoke of the art of playwriting as an explicitly philosophical act during this epoch, presages important aspects of what has become known as performance philosophy. To be sure, many of the artistic assumptions of the period run against contemporary approaches to performance practice – most obviously the privileging of literary authorship in the figure of the playwright and the idea of theatrical performance as an orchestrated, iterable enactment and instantiation of literary texts. But behind and alongside these ideas ran a powerful sense that the theater itself was a place where philosophical meaning might not just be communicated, but *actively constructed* – not just a more entertaining version of a lecture hall but what Shaw potently called an actual "factory of thought" (Adams 1991, p. 74).

To trace the origin and development of this idea within the era of modern drama, it is important first to disentangle the various meanings and sometimes conflicting temporalities of modern drama itself. In the broadest sense, modern drama is sometimes taken to encompass nearly the whole of European and North American playwriting since the later nineteenth century, with its origins often tied to the work of Henrik Ibsen (and with Georg Büchner acknowledged as an untimely precursor) and its legacy continuing into the present day.[1] A more circumspect definition confines the period only to the first half of this expanse, from Ibsen's plays of the 1860s to Samuel Beckett's plays of the 1950s, or roughly from *Brand* (1865) to *Endgame* (1957) – an approach that has the benefit of linking the epoch of modern drama to that of the European modernist movement which it prefigured, paralleled, and briefly survived.[2] In some ways, this is a constructed tradition, one fashioned as much out of later critical accounts as announced by the dramatists themselves. Works like Eric Bentley's seminal *The Playwright as Thinker*, from 1946, and Robert Brustein's later update in *The Theatre of Revolt*, from 1961, played an important role in establishing the movement as such and fashioning its official canon, drawing connections among playwrights from across Europe and North America who in many cases never met or interacted with one another, who sometimes agreed on very little of substance artistically (and even less politically), and who in some cases worked nearly a century apart from one another.[3]

Yet in creating the modern idea of "modern drama", critics like Bentley and Brustein were nevertheless drawing on or expanding connections that the artists themselves had first put forward. From Ibsen onward, most of the dramatists who were later connected to the movement understood themselves to be participating in a common revolution of dramatic form, and the term "modern drama" appeared in many of their own writings as well as contemporaneous critical accounts of the period. What that term actually meant often differed substantially from one playwright to the next. For August Strindberg, it was supposed to invoke the short, naturalist dramas on offer at Paris' Théâtre Libre during the 1880s and 1890s; for Shaw at the turn of the century, it pointed toward his "play of ideas"; for Eugene O'Neill during the 1920s and early 1930s, it evoked the formal experimentation that he had adapted from the German expressionist theater.⁴ None of these add up to an internally coherent artistic movement, but they do share an impulse toward the revision and reform of what they see as a moribund theatrical culture, one that the authors variously locate in the Parisian boulevard theater, West End drawing room plays, or conservative Broadway fare. As Toril Moi has argued, the modern drama, like other forms of what she calls early modernisms, may best be understood as manifesting a common spirit of critique rather than expounding any sort of shared artistic program: what these plays "have in common is not what they *are*, but what they are *against*", she writes (Moi 2008, p. 3). Even more than being a theater of revolt, as Brustein framed it, the modern drama was perhaps most obviously a theater *in revolt*, vigorously and sometimes violently searching for new dramatic forms capable of accommodating new viewpoints and communicating new meanings.

From this perspective, it is hardly surprising that one of the few common denominators across the global and temporal expanse of the modern drama is the idea that the new drama being expounded, whatever its specifics might be, stood in some new and important relationship to the realm of philosophy – not in the vein of morals and ethics, with which the theater had long been saddled when attempting to prove its secular worth, but rather in the mode of originating, testing, demonstrating, or criticizing ideas themselves. In fact, this perspective was often articulated with surprising specificity – a matter not of the drama's broad inheritance from the domain of philosophy, but of particular debts supposedly owed to specific philosophers and philosophical systems. This dynamic can be traced back to the movement's very origins. Few figures are more connected to the genesis of modern drama than the Danish scholar and literary critic Georg Brandes, who was personal friends with both Ibsen and Strindberg and played a pivotal role in bringing critical attention to their work. For Brandes, both playwrights were inextricably connected to the philosophers whose views he felt they espoused. With Ibsen, the main philosophical interlocutor that Brandes recognized within his dramaturgy was Søren Kierkegaard. "It actually seems as though Ibsen had aspired to the honor of being called Kierkegaard's poet", he claimed (Gosse 1907, p. 224). With Strindberg, it was Nietzsche – an unknown figure at the time whom Brandes was also instrumental in popularizing. "Well, Strindberg, as someone who hates 'the small', you'll surely take to Nietzsche", Brandes told him during an encounter in Copenhagen (Robinson 1992, pp. 328–329). Brandes even made an introduction between the two, who exchanged a number of enthusiastic letters, shortly before Nietzsche's descent into madness in 1889.

Yet, the linkage of playwright and philosopher in the tradition of modern drama goes far beyond the individual sensibilities and critical appraisals of Brandes alone. Beyond Strindberg himself, Shaw, O'Neill, W.B. Yeats, and later Antonin Artaud, all professed a profound influence from Nietzsche. For Brustein, Nietzsche was "the most seminal philosophical influence on the theater of revolt, the intellect against which almost every modern dramatist must measure his own" (Brustein 1964, p. 8). But he was hardly the only such influence. In Italy, Luigi Pirandello held a special affinity for Arthur Schopenhauer (less so for Nietzsche himself), as well as for Henri Bergson, and he found himself in an ongoing and contentious dialogue with Benedetto Croce, who publicly dismissed the playwright's philosophical aspirations.⁵ In Russia, Lev Shestov claimed his contemporary, Chekhov, as his own, describing the latter's dramaturgy as a form of "creation from nothing" in line with his own existentialist philosophy.⁶ In Germany, Bertolt Brecht dedicated his work to the communication of Karl Marx's ideas, describing his theater as "an affair for philosophers, but only for such philosophers as wished not just to explain the world but also to change it" – a reference to Marx's famous concluding dictum in his *Theses On Feuerbach* (Willett 1964, pp. 69–76). In France, Samuel Beckett saw early commentators link him closely to the existentialist philosophy of Jean-Paul Sartre, as in Martin Esslin's comments in *The Theatre of the Absurd* that Beckett's works, alongside other plays in the absurdist mode, should be considered "an expression of the *philosophy* of Sartre and Camus – in artistic, as distinct from philosophic, terms" (Esslin 1961, p. 24; emphasis in original). From the very beginnings of the modern drama, there had persisted the idea that the modern stage exists for the communication of ideas, not just in a general sense but also in a series of very specific intellectual transmissions.

This is not, it is important to stress, the position of contemporary performance philosophy, nor can it properly be considered a precursor to that position, which holds that the theater is capable of not just disseminating pre-existing philosophical ideas, but of generating and exploring such ideas in the act of performance, itself. Yet, the history of modern drama's relationship to philosophy remains an important part of the genealogy of performance philosophy nonetheless – not because of the stance that most of the movement's early critics and explicators took toward the relationship between drama and philosophy, but instead because of the persistent resistance that the movement's dramatists, themselves, put forward against these views. In other words, the internecine debates that frequently manifested between the leading modern dramatists of the era and the critics seeking to define and explain their works contemporaneously begin to demonstrate important aspects of the stance that would be adopted in the later emergence of performance philosophy.

One sees this explicitly even in the brief statement of identity with which Shaw jokingly opens his review of Nietzsche's works. To state unequivocally "*I* am a philosopher", as Shaw does, is to demand the status of an equal, and to thereby argue that the dramatist need not only commit to communicating and explaining the philosopher. If anything, Shaw views the relationship between philosophical drama and philosophical prose as reversed – his plays being the origin point of his ideas and the genesis of his extensive body of prose writings. All those famous prefaces, prologues, and afterwords that mark Shaw's career actually constitute an apparatus of explication that he erected only *after* a play's performance run had finished. For Shaw, performance both predates and predicates publication, meaning that the flow of ideas between philosophy and drama is essentially inverted.

Shaw's stance is similar to that of many other modern dramatists who found themselves pegged as being artistic explicators for another's ideas. Ibsen, for one, always resisted Brandes' assertions of his connections to Kierkegaard. As Edmund Gosse argues in an early biography from 1907, Ibsen "could not bring himself to read the prose of the professional thinkers" (Gosse 1907, p. 224). His philosophy originated from within the realm of the arts, not without. "For academic philosophy and systems of philosophic thought he had a great impatience… if he read at all, it was poetry", Gosse writes (Gosse 1907, p. 223). Strindberg would likewise come to protest the association with Nietzsche originally suggested by Brandes. Though the playwright was for a time infatuated with Nietzsche's philosophy and described himself as being 'intellectually impregnated' by his ideas, he would come to distance himself from that early obsession, and to harshly criticize those who saw Nietzsche's stamp too prominently within his works (Robinson 1992, pp. 282–283). "One must pass through … Nietzsche and then purge oneself of him", he ultimately declared (Robinson 1992, p. 328). Again and again across the history of modern drama, playwrights, who had been critically coupled to a particular philosophical view or pre-established school of thought, sought in their own descriptions of their work to uncouple, complicate, or dismantle those relationships. "I never read philosophers… I never understand anything they write", Beckett famously averred in describing his reading habits, echoing Ibsen's reaction to Brandes' zealous statements regarding his own links to philosophy a century before (Graver and Federman 1997, p. 217).

On one level, this may seem like little more than a manifestation of Harold Bloom's "anxiety of influence", but it is important to remember that the playwrights who so strongly objected to an overemphatic coupling with academic philosophy were not merely clearing a space for their own intellectual invention; they were also declaring the potential for the drama, itself, to do philosophical work (Bloom 1973). Their argument is not that of Sir Philip Sidney, wherein theater translates the work of the philosopher so that the masses "may understand him". Nor is it that of Friedrich Schiller, who argues in "The Stage as a Moral Institution", from 1784, that the theater might be a "handmaid" to philosophy by helping it to "diffuse the light of wisdom over the masses" (Dole 1903, pp. 53–61). In other words, theirs is not an argument about the role of the stage in disseminating philosophical views, as had long been one of the established modes of thinking about the relationship between the theater and the philosophical thought. Rather, it is an argument about the capacity of the stage to build philosophical systems *on its own*: to propose, posit, and test ideas originating within the realm of the theater itself. This is a major shift in the way that the relationship between theater and philosophy had been conceptualized in the European tradition – an argument for the equal status of the playwright in the hierarchy of thinkers who populate the history of ideas and a gateway for acknowledging the philosophical potential of the stage itself, of performance itself.

It is in this sense that one of the most flamboyant and famous acts of revolt within the history of the modern drama – the quintessential revolt within the theater of revolt – is not so much a rupture but a culmination. When Antonin Artaud declared in 1938 that there should be "no more masterpieces", he was not so much dismantling the arc of the modern drama's development as it came before him, as he was expressing its fulfillment (Artaud 1958, p. 74). Artaud's revolt against discursive drama seems total on its face. He rejects psychology, language, dialogue, and discourse. He specifically identifies pillars of the long European theatrical tradition within his polemic, singling out figures like Sophocles and Shakespeare in his attack, but he might just as easily have included Ibsen, Shaw, O'Neill, or any number of other landmark figures of the Bentley–Brustein canon. Instead, he wants imagery, sensation, and feeling to become the primary modes of theatrical expression. Yet insofar as Artaud still sees a philosophical purpose in the theater, his break is less than total. "The true theatre", he writes, "is born out of a kind of organized anarchy after philosophical battles", not representing philosophy as such but rather "the materialization of the idea" (Artaud 1958, p. 51). What he demands is a philosophical theater that speaks only in the language of the theater, that borrows nothing from beyond the stage, and that is unashamed of its own tools and sees them as sufficient. As far apart as their dramaturgies may be, as different as their worldviews and politics and aesthetics might seem, there is an echo here of Shaw's insistent demand that, as a playwright, "*I* am a philosopher".

In a sense, the trajectory of the modern drama can be traced along the axis of its growing commitment to insisting on its own inherent philosophical potential. Early instances of protest against a reductionist view of the drama's philosophical capacity argue primarily over the origination point of a play's ideas, debating whether they came from an outside philosophical figure or from the playwright alone. Later instances of this debate begin to change the terms and to question what an idea even is, positing that the theater may in fact have its own ways of thinking. Hence Artaud's demand that the theater be grounded not in the logos of academic philosophy but in what he calls "the physical knowledge of images" (Artaud 1958, p. 80). Even a figure as different in outlook and aesthetics from Artaud as Brecht puts forward his own version of this claim. As committed as Brecht remained throughout his middle and later career to conveying

Marxist ideas through his plays, he also maintained that the theater must do so *on its own terms*, which are unlike those of any other form of philosophical thought. This is one of the main points of his famous *Messingkauf Dialogues*, wherein he likens the philosopher who attempts to understand the theater to the "man who deals in scrap metal" and who sees in a trumpet not a musical instrument but only "its value as brass, as so-and-so many pounds of brass" (Kuhn et al. 2014, p. 25). Philosophers are figures who see the parts, but do not understand the whole, and who apply the wrong measure of value to what they find. The means by which the theater builds ideas is simply different from other philosophical or polemical forms, Brecht insists. Its truths are achieved "by means of hypnosis", one wherein the actors "go into a trance and take the audience with them", as he writes in "A Dialogue about Acting", sounding as much like Artaud as like himself (Willett 1964, pp. 26–28).

If there is a culmination to this trajectory and a bridge to the later views of performance philosophy itself, it arguably appears most vividly in Beckett's early plays, especially in *Waiting for Godot*. As many have argued before, *Godot* is a deeply metatheatrical play. It is, as Elinor Fuchs argues, as much about the nature of dramatic construction as it is about anything else – its "Aristotle in negative" form being a necessary component of "the play's very 'soul'" (Fuchs 2007, pp. 532–544). In a similar vein, the play can also be read as enacting a culminating statement on the contentious relationship between theater and philosophy that had been at issue throughout the modern drama's development. Vladimir and Estragon spend the duration of the play waiting in vain for the arrival of a meaning that exists outside of their own present condition: an order, a command, a *thought* of some sort, to break them out of the endless present tense of their predicament and orient them toward some future, outside goal. That it never arrives does not deprive their situation of meaning so much as it illuminates the perspective that the meaning might already be present, that it might be internal to their situation, and that it might be constituted between them within each moment that they pass on stage. The arrival of outside communications need not be a transformative necessity; the play exists without it. The ideas of the play exist without it. They exist within the constitution of the play itself. When Vladimir warns Estragon in the play's second act that "we're in no danger of ever thinking anymore", the line carries a pointed double meaning – referring on the one hand to the deeply dulling experience and encroaching mental breakdown of Beckett's long-waiting, long-suffering protagonists, while also evoking the degree to which the burden of intellectual meaning no longer rests on the statements and expositions of such characters (Beckett 1954, p. 64). Instead, as Theodor Adorno writes of Beckett's work, "thought transforms itself into a kind of material of a second degree" (O'Connor 2000, pp. 319–352). Thought need not be transferred to the stage; it resides there inherently, with its own shape and its own form. "When applied to drama, the word 'meaning' is multivalent", Adorno observes (O'Connor 2000, p. 321). It is not that the playwright has *not* become a figure of great intellectual capacity in the era of the modern drama. It is that the idea of the dramatist gaining that philosophical gravitas from some outside source largely misses the point. As Beckett's work helps make clear, consolidating the position of so many other modern dramatists before him, the playwright, *pace* Bentley, has always already been a thinker.

That Beckett's early works mark one of the traditionally demarcated endpoints of the movement known as modern drama even as they only begin to anticipate the contours of his own long career, which continued for decades past the end of the modern drama itself, speaks to the idea that something was finished in those early works and that something else began anew after them. What seems to be completed here is the idea that performance and philosophy might stand at some remove from one another, however closely related their aims may be. A play like *Waiting for Godot* thus becomes the last masterpiece in Artaud's call for "No More Masterpieces", a discursive drama committed to deconstructing the idea of discursive drama, gesturing toward the intellectual possibilities that lie beyond discourse. Beckett's work thereafter would be more and more an instantiation of philosophy than an explication of the same. From the algorithmic movements of *Quad* to the vast abstraction of *Not I*, his plays would continue to fulfill Adorno's prediction that "thought transforms itself into a kind of material".

In this transformation, we see a passage into the contemporary ideation of performance philosophy and its insistence that performance be regarded as a form of philosophical activity. The modern drama did not begin from or ever directly articulate this exact position, but it played a vital role in making such a stance intellectually and artistically available. If, as has long been observed, the modern drama marked a distinct moment where the theater moved decidedly closer to philosophy, it also constituted a reverse motion away from a particular hierarchical version of that relationship. Drawn to philosophy but wary of being made a mere mouthpiece of any individual philosopher's ideas, given to expressions of philosophical capacity while also advocating for the intellectual potency of its own natural tools, the modern drama was a pivotal site of negotiation between the previously separated realms of performance and philosophy. The modern dramatist – the vaunted playwright as a thinker – stood at the heart of these negotiations. In ultimately claiming a philosophical role for themselves, such dramatists also claimed one for the performances upon which their work relied. That is how their philosophy would be read, not within a book but upon a stage. Performance had been transformed into a tool of philosophy; it would only be a matter of time before it became a means of philosophy as well, a mode of philosophy, even a form of philosophy unto itself. If the playwright could be regarded as a thinker, as so many modern dramatists argued, eventually performance itself would come to be recognized for what it always was: a form of thought.

Notes

1 For fully elaborated versions of this expansionist view, see David Krasner, *A History of Modern Drama*, 2 vols. (Hoboken: Wiley-Blackwell, 2011 and 2016), or Kirsten Shepherd-Barr, *Modern Drama: A Very Short Introduction* (New York: Oxford, 2016). On the difficulties of defining modern drama as a movement, see, in particular, Ric Knowles, Joanne Tompkins, and W.B. Worthen, eds., *Modern Drama: Defining the Field* (Toronto: University of Toronto Press, 2003).
2 On the fraught relationship between modern drama and modernism proper, see especially Martin Puchner, *Stage Fright: Modernism, Anti-Theatricality, and Drama* (Baltimore: Johns Hopkins, 2012).
3 Eric Bentley, *The Playwright as Thinker: A Study of Drama in Modern Times* (1946; Minneapolis: University of Minnesota Press, 2010); and Robert Brustein, *The Theatre of Revolt: An Approach to the Modern Drama* (1961; Boston: Little, 1964).
4 See, for instance, August Strindberg, "On Modern Drama and Modern Theatre", *Selected Essays*, trans. and ed. Michael Robinson (Cambridge: Cambridge University Press, 1996), 73–86; George Bernard Shaw, "The Play of Ideas", *The New Statesman and Nation* 39 (6 May 1950); Eugene O'Neill, "Memoranda on Masks", *The American Spectator* (November 1932).
5 See, in particular, Lisa Sarti and Michael Subialka, *Pirandello's Visual Philosophy: Imagination and Thought across Media* (Lanham: Rowman & Littlefield, 2017). For an earlier account focused especially on Bergson, see also Adriano Tilgher, "Life versus Form", *Pirandello: A Collection of Critical Essays*, ed. Glauco Cambon (Englewood Cliffs: Prentice-Hall, 1967), 19–34.
6 See Lev Shestov, "Creation from Nothing: On Anton Chekhov", *A Shestov Anthology*, ed. Bernard Martin (Athens: Ohio University Press, 1971), 93. See also Olga Tabachnikova, *Anton Chekhov through the Eyes of Russian Thinkers: Vasilii Rozanov, Dmitrii Merezhkovskii, and Lev Shestov* (London: Anthem, 2012).

References

Adams, E.B. (ed.) 1991. "Terrence Rattigan, 'Concerning the Play of Ideas'", in *Critical Essays on George Bernard Shaw*, New York: G.K. Hall & Co, pp. 74–77.

Artaud, A. 1958. *The Theatre and Its Double*, trans. Mary Caroline Richards, New York: Grove Press.

Beckett, S. 1954/1982. *Waiting for Godot*, New York: Grove.

Bloom, H, 1973. *The Anxiety of Influence: A Theory of Poetry*, Oxford: Oxford University Press.

Brustein, R. 1964. *The Theatre of Revolt: An Approach to the Modern Drama*, Boston: Little, Brown.

Cook, A.S. (ed.) 1890. *Sir Philip Sidney, The Defense of Poesy (1583)*, Boston: Ginn & Co.

Dole, N.H. (transl.) 1903. *Friedrich Schiller, "The Stage as a Moral Institution", Aesthetic and Philosophical Essays*, vol. 8, Boston: FA Niccolls and Company.

Esslin, M. 1961. *The Theatre of the Absurd*, New York: Vintage.

Fuchs, E. 2007. "Waiting for Recognition: An Aristotle for a 'Non-Aristotelian' Drama", *Modern Drama* 50.4, pp. 532–544.

Gosse, E. 1907. *Ibsen*, London: Hodder & Stoughton.

Graver, L. & Federman, R. (eds.) 1997. "Interview with Gabriel d'Aubarède", in *Samuel Beckett: The Critical Heritage*, London: Routledge and Kegan, pp. 215–216.

Kornhaber, D. 2015. "Every Text Is a Performance: A Pre-History of Performance Philosophy", *Performance Philosophy* 1.1, pp. 24–35. doi:10.21476/PP.2015.1125

Kuhn, T. et al. (ed.) 2014. "Bertolt Brecht, Messingkauf, or Buying Brass", in *Brecht on Performance*, trans. Charlotte Ryland et al., London: Bloomsbury, pp. 1–142.

Laurence, D. (ed.) 1985. "'To Siegfried Trebitsch' 26 December 1902", in *Bernard Shaw Collected Letters 1898–1910*, New York: Viking, pp. 297–298.

Moi, T. 2008. *Henrik Ibsen and the Birth of Modernism: Art, Theater, Philosophy*, Oxford: Oxford University Press.

O'Connor, B. (ed.) 2000. "Trying to Understand Endgame", in *The Adorno Reader*, trans. Michael Jones, Oxford: Blackwell, pp. 319–352.

Robinson, M. (transl. & ed.) 1992. *Strindberg's Letters, vol. 1: 1862–1892*, London: The Athlone Press.

Shaw, G.B. 1965.*The Complete Bernard Shaw Prefaces,* London: Paul Hamlyn Ltd.

Tyson, B. (ed.) 1991. *Bernard Shaw's Book Reviews*, vol. II, University Park: The Pennsylvania State University Press.

Willett, J. (ed. & transl.) 1964. *Brecht on Theatre: The Development of an Aesthetic*, New York: Hill and Wang.

6

PERFORMANCE PHILOSOPHY SEEN THROUGH NISHIDA'S 'ACTING INTUITION'

Mayuko Uehara and Elisabeth L. Belgrano

Part I – Mayuko Uehara

Nishida Kitarō (1870–1945) is a particularly important philosopher in the modern history of Japanese thought. He created the intellectual foundations of the so-called "Kyoto School" of philosophy, and indeed, it could be said that his thinking acted as a primary source from which philosophy in Japan developed. At the beginning of the twentieth century, Nishida created a new paradigm of thinking which attempted to go beyond the modern Western dualism of subject and object. His philosophy of the body and action, which he developed at practically the same time as Husserl, and which I shall briefly introduce here, was based upon this paradigm.

The formative and creative character of 'acting intuition'

I want to begin this examination by first looking at the foundational logic of 'acting intuition', since this directly concerns performance philosophy. By 'acting intuition', Nishida means a logic which accounts for the formation of the world of historical reality. It is also referred to as a 'logic of production', or a 'logic of creation'. In the real world, the world in which we live, we may find acts of formation, production or creation.

Nishida defines 'acting intuition' as "seeing things through action, with the thing determining me, at the same time I determine the thing" (Nishida [1948] 1979, p. 131). At the basis of the logic of 'acting intuition' is a perspective on the body, whereby the mental and the physical are taken as constituting two sides of a whole. This outlook does not correspond to a dualistic subject–object schema, whereby "I", as the privileged subject, stands opposed to the thing, and constitutes it. Rather, according to Nishida, subjects and things reciprocally form and create each other. Furthermore, the creation of things *requires* the action of the body. What Nishida wishes to stress here is the expressive creativity of the body, which moves as an organic element of historical reality.

But what exactly does this 'action' mean, for Nishida? We know that it has a close relation to creation, or production, by the body. Yet beyond that, what else can we say? There is a helpful paragraph on this concept in the 1937 text, "Acting Intuition":

> While the world is determined through and through as a historical present, at the same time it also incorporates within itself a self-negation. Where the self transcends itself,

passing from present to present, here we find action taking place. Action is therefore concrete practice, action is production.

(Nishida [1948] 1979, p. 543)

In the 1920s, Nishida had initially understood 'action' as a form of conscious subjectivity. However, while in the 1930s the 'action' of this quotation, which he locates within the historical world, does maintain some aspect of a function of consciousness, it has also been enlarged. It now includes the so-called 'external' actions, such that, as a spectrum, it extends "from the instinctual functions of animals to the actions of human beings" (Nishida [1948] 1979, p. 545). Furthermore, there is clearly a stronger emphasis on that aspect which we would identify in the creative action of the human being.

However, Nishida also writes that: "Our bodies are not only something which works, but also something which sees" (Nishida [1948] 1979, p. 345). With the body functioning as a medium, 'action' and 'intuition' are shown to be two sides of a whole. This conception is used by Nishida to support his own theory of the "dialectical movement of history" (ibid., p. 546). The interconnected nature of these two features – action and intuition – follows from Nishida's perspective on the body as being equivocal. From the decade following 1910, Nishida takes the following stance with respect to the body: "The will is the body of the world of spirit, and the body is the will of the physical world" (Nishida [1950] 1978, p. 239). As we can see here, Nishida conceives the body as that which straddles both the intelligible world and the physical world at the same time.

What, then, is the relationship between intuition and action? Nishida states that, put concretely, intuition is "the bodily grasping of things" (Nishida [1948] 1979, p. 549). That is to say, when we take the body as a boundary, and look at the so-called 'internal' or 'external' worlds, intuition is that which we grasp from the internal side. Conversely, things are what we grasp from the external side. This is the nature of the 'two sides of the same coin' relation between 'action' and 'intuition' when viewed from the perspective of the body in Nishida's thinking.

To repeat, Nishida's definition of 'acting intuition' is that of "seeing things through action, with the thing determining me, at the same time [as] I determine the thing" (ibid., p. 131). The relation between 'thing' and 'I' here should not be understood as taking place abstractly, on the level of intellect. Although it appears as though it is the 'I' which is in a position to grasp the 'thing', in fact the I is also *led* by the thing, and, at the same time, gives the thing its form. This is the thing as created not biologically, but socially and historically. Nishida understands the thing as the 'historical thing' (ibid., p. 549). The 'things' of the historical world are not only seen within the perceptual world, but rather are seen by way of the body, which, as Nishida puts it, "is formed as the self-determination of the world of sensibility". When the "perceptual body" becomes the 'historical body', it is capable not only of 'understanding' and 'thinking'; it is also the body which 'wills' and 'acts' (ibid., p. 169, p. 171). Nishida also provides the following explanation of 'acting intuition':

> To look at things actively-intuitively, means to be able to look at them as that which ought to be negated. The subject主体 [*shutai*] is formed through the self-negation…. our body is also that which makes, and also that which is made, at the same time. It is that which looks, and at the same time is that which is seen.
>
> *(Ibid., p. 547)*

What Nishida means here is that when 'the made' – in other words, the thing which has already been given some kind of form – is seen or intuited by the 'subject', 'I' is negated at the same time. 'Negation' is a key term in Nishida's writing. According to my interpretation, it means that the simply given is 'determined' or 'articulated'. At the same time, 'the maker' or the 'subject', while negating itself, creates the 'thing' which is to be 'the made'. In other words, the 'maker' is simultaneously determining or articulating itself. Therefore, with both the maker and the made, we see a form of negation occurring: where what is given is not simply kept as it is, but is *created* or turned into something new.

This is why Nishida states that "within the world of historical development, the made is made in order to make the maker". That is, within the world of reality, we have a movement which is the reciprocal workings of the subject 主体 [*shutai*] and the object 客体 [*kyakutai*],[1] the reciprocity of "from the made to the making", and "from the making to the made". We can see historical development as arising out of this reciprocal movement.

Since the body is necessarily drawn into considerations of intersubjectivity, I would now like to examine how we can use this movement of acting intuition to consider the question of expression.

From Nishida's theory of the body toward the problem of bodily expression

According to the logic of acting intuition, "the made" is made "outside the body", as an "extension of bodily movement" (Nishida [1948] 1979, p. 551). And yet, Nishida does not give sufficient consideration to how the body itself is also that which is made. He emphasizes expressiveness in the making of things, but did not examine the question of bodily expression within the purview of acting intuition. Fortunately, we can find just such an account in the theory of corporeality provided by Nishida's disciple, Kimura Motomori (1895–1946). Kimura goes beyond Nishida in explicitly taking up the importance of the material and physical aspects of the body, viewing the body as essentially a "formative-expressive-existence".

"In our daily lives, it is on the basis of the body that we take our internal movements and attitudes, and vitally grasp them, or express them, through concrete clarity. We do this, because, as human beings, we are essentially spiritual and, at the same time, an expressive, physical existence. It is also because, in the physical, the internal appears as its concrete form. Eyes often 'speak as much as mouths', as they say. The whole human body vitally expresses the interior. In this manner, interior life expresses itself directly and bodily by way of the body. Here, we see how the first level of the expressive life appears" (Kimura 2000, pp. 200–201).

To summarize, Kimura divides the 'formative-expressive-existence' of the body into three stages. He recognizes and gives weight to the fact that the interior is directly expressed in each part of the body. Kimura sees it as the first level of expressive life, which he refers to as the "self in itself". There is a second level which is the "self for itself" (ibid., p. 201). This is the phase of the formative nature of the body. This so-called 'formative nature' refers to expressive acts such as winking, which do not simply reveal a mind, but are a form of technique. According to Kimura, this second phase is more important than the first. Furthermore, these phases of expressive life – of the "self in itself" at the same time as the "self for itself" – come together as a formative whole in a third and final stage: a "dialectical exchange of internal and external". Here, we have a higher level "self-aware creative activity" (ibid., p. 202). We can understand this as a different way of describing Nishida's logic of acting intuition: that is, the creative process of historical things.

This formative-expressive theory of Kimura is well suited to explain the expressions of the face. As research into the body frequently points out, there are conscious and unconscious expressions. Kimura's "self in itself" fits with such unconscious, unmediated expressions. Meanwhile, his "self for itself" corresponds to conscious, intended expressions. In

Figure 6.1 Elisabeth L. Belgrano, *Frozen Moment* 2 (2019). Elisabeth L. Belgrano

turn, in reality, conscious and unconscious expressions are frequently layered on top of each other, appearing as a single expression. Here, we have Kimura's "expressive life as both in itself at the same time also for itself".

Part II – Elisabeth L. Belgrano
Acting intuitively – a performance (research) meditation

Fingers and eyes keep reading the text on the screen.[2] Circling words and sentences. Searching for wisdom in the written words, but also in the non-written words that keep appearing while reading. Encountering Mayuko Uehara's interpretation of Nishida's theory of the body and his concept of 'acting intuition'. As a somatic vocal performance philosopher, searching for wisdom involves filtering philosophical theories through one's own lived psycho-physical experiences which incorporate the body/mind as an undivided tool for making sense of the process of living, learning and knowing. The arrival in Japan and in Kyoto is part of an urge to further investigate the concept of Nothingness.[3]

This research method always begins with a reading of a musical source: a manuscript from the seventeenth century. This was a period in European history when debates on the concept of Nothingness led to an intense discourse between Venetian and Parisian academics. Nothingness was also one of the central keywords behind the productions of the first operatic performances in Venice around 1640 (Belgrano 2011). After years of curious encounters through performance research, Nothingness is now encountered at the Kyoto School of Philosophy, and in dialogue with Uehara.

Reading moves into thinking, recalling the past. As a silent (research) meditation. Remembering. While traveling. By train. Looking through the window. Trying to catch the intuitive meaning of what can be seen outside. Externally. Taking out a phone from a bag. Starting to take pictures without any specific goal, other than catching the moment while in motion. Every photographic moment is blurred. Transformed into abstract horizontal lines tightly knit together. Self-negation is consciously present. Landscape has transformed through the motion of the train. Karen Barad's words emerge along with the blurred landscape. Contemplating on reciprocal 'acting-intuition', while observing the colors beautifully entangling with one another.

> To be entangled is not simply to be intertwined with another, as in joining of separate entities, but to lack an independent, self-contained existence. Existence is not an individual affair. Individuals do not preexist their interactions; rather, individuals emerge through and as part of their entangled intra-relating. Which is not to say that emergence happens once and for all, as an event or as a process that takes place according to external measure of space and time, but rather that time and space, like matter and meaning, come into existence, are iteratively reconfigured through each intra-action, thereby, making it impossible to differentiate in any absolute sense between creation and renewal, beginning and returning, continuity and discontinuity, here and there, past and future.[4]
>
> (Barad 2007, p. ix)

The body/mind mediates a materialized entanglement of Nishida's and Barad's theories. The psycho-physical experience of their theories allows for the body/mind to grow, to expand and to express. Every thought appears internally within the body/mind as a frozen moment. As a black stroke of a brush on a paper. Moving along with the experience of being determined, while reciprocally determining the situation where one finds oneself moving. Voice along with thoughts carefully keeps forming into sound, words, sentences and full texts:

> Seeing and acting is a unity of opposites. Forming is seeing, and from seeing comes acting. We see things, acting-reflecting, and we form because we see.
>
> (Nishida [1958] 2015, p. 186)

The issue of dealing with primary or secondary sources becomes irrelevant when consciously entering into 'acting intuition' as a body/mind practice. There is no conscious intention to compare one part with another, but rather to place oneself right in the middle of the 'formative-expressive-existence': to use Kimura's term. Seeing the self within the world of historical development. Within the world of reality.

Performing 'acting intuition': from a (different) bodily perspective

They had spoken about *frozen moments*, herself and Uehara, when they visited the archives of Nishida's calligraphies. The term had become part of daily acts and thinking. *Frozen moments*. She kept saying the words to herself over and over. The calligraphies had also made a significant impression on her way of thinking. Like experiencing the blurred abstract pictures, now part of her camera. Or the dialogue itself with Uehara. Or like the musical score in her bag. A copy of a manuscript, written by hand in seventeenth-century Paris. A *frozen moment* from four hundred years ago. Somehow, all these *frozen moments* had come together through her action, and were now part of her train journey through Japan. They determined her as she determined them. They made her body shiver. Embodying the unity of opposites was a sensation that was somehow easier to perform than to describe.

While thinking through her vocal performance philosophy, more questions kept coming to her: What was this logical 'acting intuitive' production, in her ways of producing vocal sound; in her ways of creating a vocal ornament; in her ways of listening beyond the seventeenth-century handwritten lines in the score; in her ways of tuning into imaginations that kept feeding her movements while singing? Could the art of imagining be considered part of a logic of 'acting intuitive' production? She tried to come to terms with her vocal practice from different perspectives. In practice, sound would never come out of her body if she didn't allow her body to be filled with air. And since body and mind acted reciprocally as body/mind, mind had no less importance in the way air found space inside her body. She would give herself silent reminders as she had learned in her Alexander Technique lessons: to allow the neck to lengthen, the back to be long and wide, the arms to grow longer in all their joints. Her thinking would produce a psycho-physical transformation internally as well as externally.

She recalled the words of Nishida cited by Uehara: "Seeing things through action, with the thing determining me, at the same time I determine the thing". She translated seeing to sensing. Any sensuous impression had an impact on her own production of sound. The bird singing outside the window caused her to attune to a unique quality of sound. How it differed in quality from another singing bird. Or the sound of the train moving through the landscape. Voicings of other people around her. She tuned into all these other sounds. They determined her at the same time as she determined them. She was never afraid of listening even further. She was open and curious. Not afraid of taking risks. Anything became a source in her imaginative production of sound. Any encounter created an impression for her body/mind and voice to act back on. Her hands, eyes and face would search to caress her findings: to hold them, to tune into their existence, to search for any unwritten meaning.

And here – in this very intimate moment of tuning into the thing she encountered – she found herself becoming Nothing. She moved through Nishida's term 'self-negation' and thought; when the self moves through a sensation, the self is somehow left behind. Or, the self is so intimately related to the memories imagined internally that she herself as a body/mind becomes part of something new that is been born in that very moment. The sound that came out of her body was the result of this self-negating logical process. It had nothing at all to do with comparing or projecting herself into the thing she observed, but instead it was about being diffracted[5] through the encounter itself. This self-negating experience could only happen if the body/mind was allowed to see without making any direct judgments. Also, the body/mind had to let go of habits and follow the unexpected movements. All together it was a sensuous way of reasoning, including a profound *will* to tune into imagined states of becoming. In this process, judgments were created in the form of negated and expressed meaning-makings. New vocal sounds became *frozen moments* through her performance philosophizing. Voice became a 'formative-expressive-existence'.

The landscape kept passing her window. She closed her eyes for a moment. Words kept passing her body/mind. Negated words. Negated thoughts.

With closed eyes, she kept thinking of Uehara's interpretation of Nishida's and Kimura's theories on bodily expression. She had to take all these thoughts with her back into her own embodied experiences of producing vocal expression. With eyes closed, she wandered into her memories of vocal encounters. One such encounter still echoed within her whole body/mind. Eyes looking close into hers while they both sang. Eyes following her voice. She remembered. The song surrounded them on all sides. It filled the room, the house, the island, the earth, and the universe. She recalled her own thoughts: eyes gave light and freedom; every joint in her body grew wider and wider. Air filled her lungs and her spine was extending in all directions. Wonder. The only word to be remembered. His memory had left an emptiness in his life. His story was sad. But in the moment their eyes met and she started to sing, he could sing despite his earlier complaints of not having any voice left in his body. He didn't actually sing very much, but it was not important. Because she could hear his voice in a way she had never heard it before. Still if he wasn't sounding at all, she could hear him. She smiled and opened her eyes. She was still sitting in her chair – a window seat.

She looked at the score in front of her at the table. Singing, to her, meant *humbly* entangling with both internal and external vocal expressions. If voicing can be understood as 'formative-expressive-existence', then reading another human's facial expression can be translated into the experience of reading a vocal manuscript, while at the same time entangling with the notions of performing 'a non-self-evident body' as the 'Self in itself'; moving 'from the made to the making' or the 'self for the other'; producing vocal sound as a 'dialectical exchange of internal and external'.

The train stopped. She stood up and took her luggage. A text had been written. Vocal performance philosophizing on 'acting-intuitively' through vocal expression- as-a-'formative-expressive-existence' had become a sort of *frozen moment*. A silent vocal performance in words.

She stepped off the train. Waiting for her connection. She put her right hand into the pocket of her coat. Her fingers found a tiny paper. Folded. She took it out. Read the words. It was a citation she had been careful not to forget. She read it again.

> In the historical world, there is nothing that is merely 'given'. 'Given' is something 'formed' which, negating itself, forms the forming. The formed has passed away, and has entered Nothingness.
>
> *(Nishida [1958] 2015, p. 177)*

Notes

1. The terms "*shukan*" and the "*kyakkan*" are not used here from the epistemological, but the bodily perspective. The sonogram "*tai*" [体] means "body".
2. The author would like to thank the following for their support of this research: Royal Academy of Music, Kungliga Vetenskapsoch Vitterhetssamhället i Göteborg, Sven och Dagmar Saléns Stiftelse, Helge Axson Johnssons Stiftelse, Gertrude och Ivar Philipsons Stiftelse and Japanstiftelsen.
3. See Belgrano 2011, 2016. For the past thirteen years, my focus has been to investigate the embodiment of vocal Nothingness. Along the road, philosophers of Nothingness have joined the pilgrimage, such as Luigi Manzini, Dominique Bouhours, Vladimir Jankélévitch, Karen Barad and now Nishida Kitarō.
4. The terms entanglement and intra-action are central in Barad's theory. The term intra-action differs from the usual term inter-action which assumes preexistence of an entity, prior to actions made by one upon another. According to Barad's agential-realist ontology "'individuals' do not preexist as such but rather materialize through intra-action" (Kleinman 2012, p. 11). This chapter allows for a very first attempt to start reconfiguring an entangled understanding of Barad's concept of intra-action and her theory of 'agential realism' with Nishida's concept of 'acting intuition', considering both philosophers' attempts to overcome binary perspectives in relation to Nothingness. This discourse will be developed further on another occasion.
5. Diffractive methodology is applied in an intra-active encounter. See Barad 2014.

References

Barad, K. 2007. *Meeting the Universe Halfway. Quantum Physics and the Entanglement of Matter and Meaning*. Durham & London: Duke University Press.

Barad, K. 2014. "Diffracting Diffraction: Cutting Together-Apart", *Parallax*, 20, 3: 168–187.

Belgrano, E. 2011. *"Lasciatemi Morire" o farò "La Finta Pazza". Embodying vocal NOTHINGNESS on stage in Italian and French 17th century operatic LAMENTS and MAD SCENES*, ArtMonitor Ph.D. dissertation. No 25, University of Gothenburg.

Belgrano, E. 2016. "Vocalizing Nothingness: (Re)configuring Vocality Inside the Spacetime of Ottavia", *Journal of Interdisciplinary Voice Studies*, 1, 2: 183–195.

Kimura, M. [1938] 2000. "Body and Mind". In *Selected Works of Kyoto Philosophy,* Vol. 7, Praxis of the Beauty, Toei sha.

Kleinman, A. 2012. "Intra-actions– Interview of Karen Barad by Adam Kleinmann". *Mousse* magazine # 34. pp. 76–81, available at https://www.academia.edu/1857617/_Intra-actions_Interview_of_Karen_Barad_by_Adam_Kleinmann_

Nishida, K. Z. [1948] 1979. *NKZ/Œuvres Completes de Nishida Kitarō*. Vol. 8, Tokyo: Iwanami Shoten.

Nishida, K. Z. [1950] 1978. *NKZ/Œuvres Completes de Nishida Kitarō*, Vol. 2, Tokyo: Iwanami Shoten.

Nishida, K. Z. [1958] 2015. *Intelligibility and the Philosophy of Nothingness.* London: Forgotten books.

7
PERFORMANCE IN ANGLO-AMERICAN PHILOSOPHY

Anna Pakes and David Davies

Theorising performance in the Anglo-American tradition

Anglo-American philosophy, like continental philosophy, is best thought of as a philosophical tradition that provides thinkers with resources upon which they can draw in their own individual philosophical inquiries. In the Anglo-American (or 'analytic') tradition, issues in the philosophy of language have played a central role, and this has tended to focus the attention of philosophers on linguistic issues in their respective fields. In the philosophy of art, this was exemplified in the very influential idea that the philosopher's task was to analyse the language used in art criticism (Beardsley 1958). The so-called linguistic turn, often seen as central to contemporary work in Anglo-American philosophy (Rorty 1967), involved a commitment to address metaphysical, epistemological and axiological questions in a linguistically inflected way. Central figures in this tradition include Frege, Russell, Moore, Wittgenstein, Quine, Davidson and Kripke. To philosophically address a question within this tradition is to bring to bear the broad range of philosophical resources that these philosophers and their successors have developed. As we shall see, these resources can be, and have been, brought to bear in various ways on the issues of concern to performance philosophy. Exploring these engagements will provide the basis for a constructive critique of assumptions embedded in some articulations of performance philosophy's rationale.

Neither artistic performance nor the performing arts received much attention in Anglo-American philosophy of art prior to 1968. A principal focus of attention was the perceived error in traditional philosophical attempts to 'define' art. 'Ordinary language' philosophers, such as John Passmore (1951), Morris Weitz (1956) and William Kennick (1958), bemoaned the "dreariness" of aesthetics and argued, by appeal to the later views of Ludwig Wittgenstein (1953), that attempts to provide a definition of 'art' rested on a misunderstanding of the linguistic roles played by this and other related terms.

This Wittgensteinian challenge to aesthetics as a serious philosophical field elicited two kinds of response. First, some philosophers transposed the definitional project into an 'institutional' key. The defining conditions of artworks, it was claimed, are not manifest properties of objects or events, but the institutional frameworks within which certain objects and events are generated and received. Second, some philosophers renounced the definitional project in favour of a seemingly more modest task – that of clarifying the nature of the entities in particular art forms, through which the artistic contents of works in those art forms are articulated. While adherents of the first approach occasionally made very abstract claims about the social practices in the performing arts (Dickie 1974), it was in the context of the second approach that philosophical interest in the performing arts developed and, especially in the case of music, flourished, coming to rival or even surpass more traditional interests in painting and literature. Two books published in 1968 led the way.

First, in *Languages of Art*, Nelson Goodman looked at how differences in our artistic practices could be understood as reflections of differences between the symbol systems to which the entities that served as the vehicles of artworks belonged. For example, Goodman argues that musical and literary works differ from paintings, in that the former, unlike the latter, can be fully appreciated through an engagement with different instances of a work. This is possible because the properties required in well-formed instances of musical and literary works can be divorced from their histories of making through the use of a notational system, whereas this is not the case for paintings. The distinctive properties of musical notation played a central role in Goodman's account. In trying to explain the relationship between musical works and performances, Goodman argued that the role of the score is to preserve the identity of the musical work from performance to performance. This required that the scores definitive of particular musical works could be unambiguously retrieved from individual performances. For this to be possible, only those features of works that can be captured in musical notation can be constitutive of those works. This excludes other devices used by composers such as verbal indications of mood, tempo and dynamics, and led Goodman to further conclusions that struck many of those involved in actual musical practice as outrageous. For example, he claimed that no verbal markings on the score of a musical work can constrain correct performance of that work, and that any performance of a musical work that departs in the slightest way from what is formally notated in the score is not a performance of that work. Interestingly, some critics of treatments of the performing arts in Anglo-American philosophy wrongly take Goodman's very counterintuitive claims to exemplify the latter (Taruskin 2010; Bowie 2015), even though nearly all subsequent work in Anglo-American philosophy of music has repudiated these claims. It is also worth noting that Goodman's assumption that performable works can be retrieved from individual performances overlooks issues central to contemporary debates about dance reconstruction and our ability to access past dance works through notational transcriptions or videos of performance events (Conroy 2009, McFee 2011, Pakes 2017).

The project of the second book published in 1968, Richard Wollheim's *Art and its Objects*, was to understand the nature of the things that serve as the vehicles of works in the different arts, and to explain how such things can possess the appreciable properties rightly ascribable to those works. Starting with the provisional hypothesis that all artworks are physical objects, he addressed the obvious objection that this could not hold for literary and musical works. We take the latter to be distinct from the particular physical objects or events – copies of novels and performances of musical works – through which they are appreciated. Wollheim maintained that musical and literary works are 'types' of which their performances are 'tokens'.[1] The refinement of this suggestion has been a central thread in Anglo-American philosophy of music.

Two generalisations are broadly true of Anglo-American philosophy of performance following the publication of Goodman's and Wollheim's books. First, the focus of philosophical attention was, for a long time, the musical arts. The assumption was that the model held to accurately represent matters in Western classical music would also apply *mutatis mutandis* to other kinds of music, and to theatre and dance. This model, which might be termed the 'classical paradigm' (Davies 2011), holds that a performance in the performing arts is generally *of* something else – what we can call a performable work – and plays a necessary part in the appreciation of the latter. Performable works prescribe certain things to performers, and are appreciated for the qualities realisable in performances that satisfy these prescriptions. The salient question, then, is what performable works must be if they allow for different performative interpretations and are appreciable through those interpretations. Alternative answers to this question have taken performable works to be: (1) abstract objects that exist eternally and are discovered by their 'creators' (Kivy 1983; Dodd 2007); (2) abstract objects *as picked out* by one or more individual in a particular art-historical context (Levinson 1980); (3) higher order but non-abstract objects somehow dependent upon, or constituted by, certain concrete objects and events – scores, particular performances, etc. (Rohrbaugh 2003; Caplan and Matheson 2006; Davies 2012); or (4) fictional entities that we posit to help us in our practice (Kania 2012). Second, while a relation to performances partly defines what it is to be a performable work, the interest of Anglo-American philosophers in performances was for a long time parasitical upon their interest in the things performed. The only salient exception, reflecting developments in performance practice, was an interest in the nature and significance of *authenticity* in musical performance (Kivy 1995). Both of these features of analytic treatments of performance are apparent in what, until recently, was the only general philosophical treatment of artistic performance in the forty years following the publication of Goodman's and Wollheim's books, Paul Thom's *For an Audience* (1993).

Over the past twenty years or so, however, matters have been changing. First, whereas failings in Goodman's treatment of the performing arts might be seen as resulting from the attempt to impose a simple philosophical model upon a complex set of practices, Anglo-American philosophy of performance, and of art more generally, has come increasingly to define its task pragmatically, as one of providing a philosophical framework that does justice to our practices and furthers their self-understanding. This tendency is characterised in David Davies' 'pragmatic constraint', which purports to capture a methodological assumption taken to be implicit or explicit in earlier work by figures such as Arthur Danto (1981), Jerrold Levinson (1980) and Gregory Currie (1989). According to the 'pragmatic constraint':

> Artworks must be entities that can bear the sorts of properties rightly ascribed to what are termed "works" in our reflective critical and appreciative practice; that are individuated in the way such "works" are or would be individuated, and that have the modal properties that are reasonably ascribed to "works", in that practice.
>
> *(Davies 2004, p. 18)*

Two consequences of this 'pragmatic' shift in Anglo-American philosophy of the performing arts are salient in the present context:

1. There has been increasing sensitivity to the diversity of our practices in the performing arts, and a consequent awareness of the need for a plurality of philosophical models for the performing arts. Philosophers have argued for the limited applicability of the 'classical paradigm' not only in theatre and dance, but also in music itself. While some have striven to accommodate the diversity of our practices through drawing more subtle distinctions within the general framework of the classical paradigm (Davies 2001), others have rejected that framework altogether for particular fields of performance practice. James Hamilton, for example, has repudiated entirely the application of

the 'classical paradigm' to theatre, proposing instead that we view a theatrical script as merely one among a number of 'ingredients' upon which a theatrical company can draw in working out a production or an individual performance through collective rehearsal (2007). Andrew Kania has argued that a philosophical model of jazz performance should eschew the idea of performed works – jazz, as he nicely puts it, is all play and no work (2011). Kania (2006) has also followed Theodore Gracyk (1996) in defending the idea that works of rock music are recorded 'tracks' to be distinguished from much thinner 'songs' that are freely interpreted in rock performances. While some work on dance still takes the classical paradigm as a model (McFee 1992), other work looks much more closely at 'non-classical' aspects of dance practice (Carroll and Banes 1982; Conroy 2009; Pakes 2017). As noted earlier, work on dance has also raised theoretical concerns about the idea that dance practice has access to, and works with, a tradition of performable works. Dance studies are one of the growth areas in this burgeoning Anglo-American interest in performance practice. Relatedly, whereas philosophical attention to artistic performance in the Anglo-American tradition was for a long time dominated by work in the philosophy of music – which was felt to be both representative of artistic performance in general (through the 'classical paradigm') and more tractable to philosophical inquiry using the resources of the tradition – increasing attention has been paid not only to dance and theatre (as cited), but also to performance art (Davies 2011).

2   Whilst philosophical interest in performance on the part of Anglo-American philosophers was derivative upon their interest in the performed works taken to be appreciable through such performances, there has been a growing interest in performance for its own sake. Although this originated in an interest on the part of philosophers of music in the improvisatory performances characteristic of jazz, other aspects of performance practice have drawn increasing attention. In the first systematic analytic study of the performing arts since Thom's book (Davies 2011), for example, there are lengthy discussions not only of improvisation but also of rehearsal, the relationship of the performer to the audience and the embodied nature of the performer.

Performance as philosophical medium

Clearly, then, performance has been an *object* of philosophical enquiry in the Anglo-American tradition. Is it also acknowledged as a *medium* of philosophical investigation? Certainly, there are various arguments for dance and theatre as *thinking* practices, even as distinct forms of thought, and arguments that see the performing arts as ways of *knowing*, even ways of generating *new* knowledge. To show that performance thinks is not yet to show that it does philosophy: thinking takes many forms, not all of them plausibly construed as philosophical. And knowledge can be practical, scientific, anthropological and so on, rather than (or without necessarily also being) philosophical. Nonetheless, these arguments have the potential to support a performance-as-philosophy thesis, and assist in elaborating its most convincing versions. They can be summarised in terms of three broad categories.

Firstly, some arguments seek to demonstrate the sophisticated thinking intrinsic to performing or performance-making, either as part of a general account of expertise and its conditions (Montero 2016) or as part of an effort to draw out the educational value of a particular performance practice such as dance (Carr 1978, 1984, 1999). Some of these arguments emerge from a more general interest in philosophy of mind in forms of enacted and embodied cognition, some from a concern in philosophy of education, philosophy of action and ethics with forms of practical reasoning, whilst some also connect with efforts to articulate the epistemological basis and value of performance practice as a form of academic research (Pakes 2003, 2004, 2018 [2009]). It is argued that performing and making – over an extended period of apprenticeship – develop distinctively practical kinds of thinking and reasoning in the agent, generating 'knowledge *how*', rather than 'knowledge *that*', in Gilbert Ryle's terms (Ryle 1963 [1949]). Such knowledge does not derive from prior theoretical understanding, but is an intelligence or rationality intrinsic to the developed practice as such. Rather than moving from general laws to empirical facts (or vice versa), practical reasoning puts the agent's purposes in relation with the particular circumstances in play, concluding in appropriate action. Such reasoning, it is argued, underpins intentional action generally, including the intentional action involved in artistic making and performing.

Carr's later work acknowledges that the model of practical reasoning accounts well for "the acquisition of fairly routine or habitual techniques – staying well clear of the less predictable creative and imaginative aspects of dance practice" (Carr 1999, p. 126). He suggests conceptualising creative dance knowledge as a form of *phronesis* (or practical wisdom) in Aristotle's sense: that is, not in terms of technical command of processes standing apart from the agent herself, but rather as a creative sensitivity to circumstances as they present themselves to the agent in the midst of making, a kind of "attunement to the particularities of situations and experiences" (Pakes 2018, p. 19). The self is implicated, unfolded and cultivated, not set aside in cool objectivism, and the process of performance-making thereby also becomes a process of self-knowledge. Does this mean that such practical wisdom remains locked into the person of the artist-researcher, or can it also be disseminated or generalised in some way? It might be disseminated via collaborative studio practice and workshops. But it is not obvious that such wisdom is shared through any dance or performance product (where there is one), since the audience member's relationship to this work is qualitatively different to the artist's. Also, this kind of knowledge seems largely internal to performance practice: it has no object beyond performance itself, although potentially it results in the agent's heightened reflection upon her encounters with others and thereby on social relations and the nature of collectivity.

This links to a second category of arguments about performance thinking: arguments that dance – and, perhaps, physical theatre or other kinds of performance which emphasise their bodily aspect – enhance understanding of human embodiment more generally. Eric Mullis (2016), for example, suggests that engagement as a dancer with certain kinds of improvisational practice (specifically, Gaga technique and Contact Improvisation) is a way to foster new somaesthetic experiences and explore new realms of embodied sensation. Provided we move away from a narrow conception of philosophy as advancing arguments, he suggests, this somaesthetic process is philosophical insofar as it prompts self-reflection on the characteristics of those experiences, and contemplation of the nature and social significance of embodiment more generally. In experiencing different modes of corporeality, I become aware of a range of alternatives which relativises my everyday, social habitus. This "opens the door to intelligent self-fashioning" and to the pursuit of "increasingly rich somaesthetic experience" through different body practices (Mullis 2016, p. 62). But it also enables understanding of how embodiment structures experience on individual and social levels. Moreover, those practices like Contact Improvisation, that involve embodied interaction at a deep level, make possible an encounter with otherness that teaches me how to accommodate difference and work collaboratively regardless of my partner's gender, ethnicity, sexuality or political ideology. This constitutes an "embodied ethic" which furthers both understanding and ability to act in a morally and aesthetically sensitive way (Mullis 2016, p. 69). Mullis's elaboration of this dance-as-philosophy thesis draws significantly on Richard Shusterman's somaesthetics and its pragmatist inheritance (Shusterman 2008, 2012), but also links (like arguments in the first category) with the much older Socratic philosophical project of self-knowledge.

Still, though, it seems that the thinking, knowing or putative philosophising of such practices is confined to the performer or performance-maker. It remains unclear how it gets shared (or, indeed, tested) more widely. A third category of arguments, however, suggests that the *audience member*'s act of engaging with the performing arts fosters cognitive skills and offers a form of emotional education. In David Best's formulation (1978, 1985), the arts make possible the expression of a conception of "life issues" or "life situations": they offer a new perspective on human predicaments and concerns, refining the concepts under which our feelings about these are experienced, enabling "finer shades of feeling" to emerge (McFee 1992, p. 168). Engagements with artworks, then, enable existential insight in affective terms. The "life issues" thesis concerns art generally, not the performing arts specifically. But if "*what* is said about life in a work is *inseparable* from that particular work" (Best 2004 [1982], p. 168), then distinct experiences of performance will offer similarly unique emotional refinements. So performance is no mere vehicle for messages or ideas that could be communicated otherwise: experiencing a particular performance is the *only* way to engage in the reconceptualisation and refinement of feeling that it makes possible. In this respect, there are affinities with more recent claims about performance practice itself doing philosophy by expressing problems (Cvejić 2015).

'Performance thinking': some examples

We noted earlier Mullis's claim that the somaesthetic process characteristic of certain kinds of dance experiences is philosophical, insofar as it prompts self-reflection on the characteristics of those experiences, as well as more general contemplation of the nature and social significance of embodiment. But if this is to support the idea that artistic performance can be a way of doing philosophy, we need to counter the analogue of an objection raised by Paisley Livingston (2006) against the idea that 'film' can do philosophy. Livingston's argument can be re-expressed in the following terms. If film experience is to count as a kind of philosophising, two conditions must be met. First, the purported advancement in philosophical understanding through film experience must depend upon *distinctively cinematic* features of that experience, and not, for example, on features of the cinematically presented narrative that it might share with a literary work. What a film can *share* with a literary work are features of its narrative that can be characterised linguistically in purely propositional terms – its narrating certain events involving certain individuals. If the philosophical value of a film lies *only* in its narrative so construed, it adds nothing of philosophical interest not already there in the literary text. Both literary work and film may indeed have such philosophical value, but in neither case will it have anything to do with the distinctly artistic values of these works – values residing in the different ways in which they present the shared narrative. If there is an interesting sense in which *a cinematic work* can do philosophy, the philosophical value of that work must at least in part depend upon the use of cinematic means.

The second of Livingston's conditions, meanwhile, is that the advancement in philosophical understanding must occur in the experiential engagement with the film, rather than in later reflection, where something extracted from that engagement is verbally transcribed and introduced into a propositionally articulated philosophical problematic. If we take the thesis of 'performance as philosophy' to be subject to parallel requirements, the worry about Mullis' claim is that it may not meet the second requirement. Even if we think that the self-reflection and insight identified by Mullis requires the somaesthetic processes generated in dance experience, is it not *later* reflection upon such experience that yields these kinds of insights? The same problem arises for the spectatorial reconceptualisation and refinement of feeling, identified by Best and Cvejić.

In countering such scepticism, it is helpful to draw upon Robert Sinnerbrink's notion of 'cinematic thinking' which is intended to counter Livingston's argument as it relates to film. Sinnerbrink maintains that we should focus upon the ways in which cinema can do philosophical work in virtue of its *aesthetic dimensions* – "the multifarious sensuous and affective ways in which film can provoke altered states of mind, body, and thought" (Sinnerbrink 2011, p. 52). "Works of cinematic art", he argues,

> do not generally make abstract universal claims in theoretical or argumentative terms. Rather, they aesthetically (that is to say, cinematically) disclose novel aspects of experience, question given elements of our practices or normative frameworks, challenge established ways of seeing, and open up new paths for thinking.
>
> *(Sinnerbrink 2011, p. 141)*

'Cinematic thinking', in Sinnerbrink's sense, is internal to our experiential engagement with a film, rather than occurring subsequent to that experience. What is of philosophical value, then, occurs in a dialogical process involving our experiential engagement with the 'aesthetic dimensions' of the film and the reflections prompted thereby. While we may have recourse to language to describe the cinematic thinking elicited in us by a film, the philosophising is intrinsic to the cinematic thinking, not something that occurs when we export content from the film. Sinnerbrink's account speaks to Livingston's argument in that (1) it makes the doing of philosophy internal to the watching of a film and (2) it also makes it essentially cinematic, dependent not on the narrative, per se, but upon the "aesthetic dimensions" of the film where intrinsically cinematic means are used to produce affect. Philosophy here is "an accompaniment to the film…, elaborating and translating the uniquely cinematic aesthetic experience into a register that opens up a transformative encounter with philosophical reflection" (Sinnerbrink 2011, p. 181).

In the case of performance as philosophy, the analogue to cinematic thinking would be "performance thinking": the stage action or image produces, in performer or viewer, an affective experience that hinges on the specifically theatrical or performative means employed, and which itself generates philosophical reflection as an intrinsic part of that experience. One example would be the thinking provoked through Jérôme Bel's *Disabled Theater* (2014), a work made with members of the Swiss group Theater Hora, all of whom are professional actors with learning disabilities. At the start of the work, each performer walks to the front of the stage to stand for a minute in silence, looking directly at members of the audience. Their action raises a number of questions that frame the unfolding work: what do we, as viewers, expect of/from the performers? How are the actors' identities related to their stage personae and our reactions? (How) does the fact of the performers' disabilities affect the audience's approach to watching? Crucially, the embodied presence of the viewer in the auditorium and the durational quality of these "introductions" push their effect beyond simply raising these questions about the nature of performance, and towards a lived negotiation of its ethics: each minute feels long, and the discomfort increases cumulatively as audience members have to decide how to meet the gaze of the performers across the black box divide. As the work develops, selected performers present dances of their own devising, but also talk about the choreographer's choice of material, with those dancers whose solos were not selected voicing disgruntlement about Bel's aesthetic judgements. The announcer (who sits at the side of the stage throughout, detailing the instructions given by Bel to the performers) then explains how the choreographer, in the face of the dancers' complaints, decided that the solos he initially left out should be shown after all. And so the last section of the performance is devoted to presenting these "rejected" dances, raising a plethora of questions about choreographic craft, authorship, performance virtuosity, the basis of aesthetic preference and what grounds our judgements of others' actions. The work wears on its sleeve its own strategies of construction, explicitly undoing itself as a composition and provoking philosophical reflection through the self-conscious experience of watching. And it is this experience, not the show's verbal content or post-performance interpretation, which does the philosophical work.

Another instance of performance thinking is evident in the ending of Patrick Marber's adaptation of Eugene Ionesco's *Exit the King* [*Le roi se meurt*] for the National Theatre in London in 2018. The play is "an attempt at an apprenticeship in dying" (Ionesco and Bonnefoy 1970), examining with brutal honesty and humour the difficulty of understanding and coming to terms with the fact of one's end. "Your Majesty, you're going to die in 68 minutes", announces Queen Marguerite (Indira Varma), checking her watch impatiently, soon after the grand entrance of the chief protagonist, King Bérenger (Rhys Ifans). These kinds of self-conscious references to the theatrical frame draw attention to the stage action as microcosm of the human predicament, with the King passing through various stages of denial, anger, despair and depression as the stage time elapses. The action is surreal: Bérenger is a 500-year-old tyrant whose kingdom (the auditorium to which the actors frequently gesture) is crumbling in parallel with his physical and psychological selves. Ifans, by turns, rants melodramatically and quivers pathetically, as his five companions observe, advise, berate, comfort and scorn him. But it is the final extraordinary *coup de théâtre* of the production that enables the most vivid and profound philosophical exploration of what it might be to die.

In Marber's production, ten minutes from the end, all but Queen Marguerite have disappeared. As she begins to intone her long final monologue, verbally stripping away the different layers of existential attachment, the façade of the castle wall splits apart, gradually revealing a narrow red walkway, receding – with the king's throne – into the dark depths of the stage space. Ifans, back to the audience, begins to walk hesitantly along this pathway as it extends further and further, impossibly far, into the distance, like the King himself gradually dwindling to the point of vanishing. The visual effect is astonishing, offering a "haunting image of extinction" (Hemming 2018) that "sears itself into your retinas" (Cavendish 2018). As it develops over ten minutes, the action embodies a philosophical reflection on what it means for consciousness to dwindle and eventually evaporate, a reflection which depends, crucially, on the physical presence of the audience in the theatre, their embodied relation to the illusion of impossible depth and the durational quality of the scene. We grasp the unfolding implications of disappearing consciousness because of the growing spatial gulf between our physical presence as spectators, the dwindling Ifans and the receding end-point of his walk, and because we are forced to play out the gradual effacement of the persona who has been the work's empathetic centre. The existential predicament physicalised here is not something that the stage directions prescribe, but a feature of this particular theatrical production: it is an effect of the staging as such, and not of the narrative content or of verbal reflection after the fact of the performance.

Value(s) of philosophy of performance

We hope to have demonstrated ways in which performance thinking operates in some works of dance and theatre, with the audiences' affective experience of those works embodying philosophical reflection. This essay has also highlighted how various conceptualisations of performance as philosophy connect with – or derive from – a wider body of Anglo-American philosophical literature about performance. Our account challenges the idea that analytic philosophy often adopts a transcendent approach or an "application" model that posits performance as mere illustration of preconceived ideas rather than as itself a source of philosophical insight (Cull 2014, p. 24; Cull Ó Maoilearca 2018).

In closing, however, we also want to reassert the value of philosophies *of* dance, theatre and performance, alongside performance philosophy in its various modes. Some performance philosophy writing urges us to "move beyond application in our approach to the use of philosophy with respect to the arts; that we stop thinking in terms of producing philosophies *of* performance" (Cull 2014, p. 17). The worry is that philosophy *of* performance dominates the stage with its authoritarian gestures, assuming the power to define what counts as/in performance and thinking. As suggested in this essay, however, we might rather think of philosophies of dance, theatre and performance as addressing philosophical problems or puzzling issues that already arise in these practices. What is it for a work to express? How is artistic or aesthetic engagement with something either different or similar to other kinds of engagement? What are the ethics of representing violence? What kind of thing is a dance work, as distinct from a performance event? Is a dance work a thing at all? These are questions raised *through* the making, performing and reception of art, which might be addressed by various means – further performing, making or writing – more or less well suited to the task, depending on the particular question. A range of resources or strategies might be employed in the process: for example, developing or testing arguments; exploring and interpreting images; attempting to clarify the concepts implied by the practice and its discourse. Other practitioners, philosophers and/or philosophical traditions might be invoked either to support a particular way of thinking about the problem or to identify critically how and where such thinking goes wrong. But unless the authority of these voices goes unquestioned, this is not a case of pre-existing philosophy being applied uncritically to practice, nor of practice (ab)used to illustrate that philosophy for purely extra-artistic aims. The philosophical problems in question are immanent in the art. The elaboration of those problems may be immanent too. But equally there may be some things we want to say about these problems that cannot be said via the means of the performance itself, so other resources come into play. That does not inevitably imply transcendence, nor application as an impoverished or impoverishing practice. It might be both enriching and liberating. And if so, this does not seem to be the kind of application that we want to move beyond. Thus, even if there are plausible senses in which performance does philosophy, this does not obviate the value and interest of philosophy *of* dance, theatre and performance, for which what it is to do philosophy through performance remains an enduringly important question.

Note

1 The type/token distinction is one that should be familiar from more everyday contexts, even if the terminology is new. Consider the question, 'how many letters are there in the word "sheep"?'. If we count the number of occurrences of individual letters, the correct answer is five: 's', 'h', 'e', 'e', 'p'. If, however, we count the number of different kinds of letters that occur, the correct answer is four: 's', 'h', 'e', 'p'. In the terminology of interest to us here, we might explain this difference as follows: the word-type 'sheep' contains two tokens of the letter-type 'e'. In the case of literature and music, works might be identified with *structure*-types – verbal or sonic – and tokens of those works would be individual objects or events exemplifying those structure-types. While the dominant view of the nature of types themselves is that they are abstract entities of some sort, this is a matter of some current dispute.

References

Beardsley, M. C. 1958. *Aesthetics: Problems in the Philosophy of Criticism*, New York: Harcourt Brace.
Best, D. 1978. *Philosophy and Human Movement*, London: George Allen and Unwin.
Best, D. 1985. *Feeling and Reason in the Arts*, London: George Allen and Unwin.
Best, D. 2004 [1982]. 'Aesthetic and Artistic; Two Separate Concepts: The Dangers of "Aesthetic Education"', *Research in Dance Education*, 5:2, 159–175.
Bowie, A. 2015. 'The 'Philosophy of Performance' and the Performance of Philosophy', *Performance Philosophy*, 1, 51–58.
Caplan, B. & Matheson, C. 2006. 'Defending Musical Perdurantism', *British Journal of Aesthetics*, 46:1, 59–69.
Carr, D. 1978. 'Practical Reasoning and Knowing How', *Journal of Human Movement Studies*, 4, 3–20.
Carr, D. 1984. 'Dance Education, Skill and Behavioural Objectives', *Journal of Aesthetic Education*, 18:4, 67–76.
Carr, D. 1999. 'Further Reflections on Practical Knowledge and Dance a Decade On', in G. McFee (ed.) *Dance, Education and Philosophy*, Oxford: Meyer and Meyer Sport, 123–141.
Carroll, N. & Banes, S. 1982. 'Working and Dancing', *Dance Research Journal*, 15:1, 37–42.
Cavendish, D. 2018. 'Exit the King Review, National Theatre: Rhys Ifans Drives This Chilling Memento Mori', *The Telegraph*, 25th July [Online], Available at: https://www.telegraph.co.uk/theatre/what-to-see/exit-king-review-national-theatre-rhys-ifans-drives-chilling/, Accessed 15th November 2018.
Conroy, R. 2009. *The Art of Re-making Dances: A Philosophical Analysis of Dancework Reconstruction*, Unpublished PhD Thesis, University of Washington.
Cull, L. 2014. 'Performance Philosophy: Staging a New Field', in L. Cull and A. Lagaay (eds.) *Encounters in Performance Philosophy*, Basingstoke: Palgrave Macmillan, 15–38.
Cull Ó Maoilearca, L. 2018. 'Notes towards the Philosophy of Theatre', *Anglia: Journal of English Philology*, 136:1, 11–42.
Currie, G. 1989. *An Ontology of Art*, New York: St Martin's Press.
Cvejić, B. 2015. *Choreographing Problems: Expressive Concepts in European Contemporary Dance and Performance*, Basingstoke: Palgrave Macmillan.
Danto, A. 1981. *Transfiguration of the Commonplace*, Cambridge, MA: Harvard University Press.
Davies, D. 2004. *Art as Performance*, Oxford: Blackwell.
Davies, D. 2011. *Philosophy of the Performing Arts*, Oxford: Wiley-Blackwell.
Davies, D. 2012. 'Enigmatic Variations', *The Monist*, 95:4, 644–663.
Davies, S. 2001. *Musical Works and Performances*, Oxford: Oxford University Press.
Dickie. G. 1974. *Art and the Aesthetic: An Institutional Analysis*, Ithaca, NY: Cornell University Press.
Dodd, J. 2007. *Works of Music*, Oxford: Oxford University Press.
Goodman, N. 1968. *Languages of Art*, Indianapolis, IN: Bobbs-Merrill.
Gracyk, T. 1996. *Rhythm and Noise: An Aesthetics of Rock*, Durham, NC: Duke University Press.
Hamilton, J. 2007. *The Art of Theatre*, Oxford: Wiley-Blackwell.
Hemming, S. 2018. 'Exit the King, National Theatre, London - Stylish but Laborious', *Financial Times*, 26th July [Online], Available online at https://www.ft.com/content/1faf1022-90ca-11e8-bb8f-a6a2f7bca546, Accessed 15th November 2018.
Ionesco, E. & Bonnefoy, C. 1970. *Conversations with Ionesco*, London: Faber and Faber.
Kania, A. 2006. 'Making Tracks: The Ontology of Rock Music', *Journal of Aesthetics and Art Criticism*, 64:4, 402–414.
Kania, A. 2011. 'All Play and No Work: An Ontology of Jazz', *Journal of Aesthetics and Art Criticism*, 69:4, 391–403.
Kania, A. 2012. 'Platonism vs. Nominalism in Contemporary Musical Ontology', in C. Mag Uidhir (ed.) *Art and Abstract Objects*, Oxford: Oxford University Press, 197–212.
Kennick, W. 1958. 'Does Traditional Aesthetics Rest on a Mistake?', *Mind*, 67:267, 317–334.
Kivy, P. 1983. 'Platonism in Music: A Kind of Defense', *Grazer Philsophische Studien*, 19, 109–129.
Kivy, P. 1995. *Authenticities*, Ithaca, NY: Cornell University Press.
Levinson, J. 1980. 'What a Musical Work Is', *Journal of Philosophy*, 77, 5–28.
Livingston, P. 2006. 'Theses on Cinema as Philosophy', *Journal of Aesthetics and Art Criticism*, 64:1, 11–18.
McFee, G. 1992. *Understanding Dance*, London: Routledge.

McFee, G. 2011. *The Philosophical Aesthetics of Dance: Identity, Performance and Understanding*. Binsted, UK: Dance Books.

Montero, B. 2016. *Thought in Action: Expertise and the Conscious Mind*, Oxford: Oxford University Press.

Mullis, E. 2016. 'Dance, Philosophy and Somaesthetics', *Performance Philosophy*, 2:1, 60–71.

Pakes, A. 2003. 'Original Embodied Knowledge: The Epistemology of the New in Practice as Research', *Research in Dance Education*, 4:2, 127–149.

Pakes, A. 2004. 'Art as Action or Art as Object? The Embodiment of Knowledge in Practice as Research', *Working Papers in Art and Design*, 3, available online at: https://www.herts.ac.uk/_data/assets/pdf_file/0015/12363/WPIADD_vol3_pakes.pdf.

Pakes, A. 2017. 'Reenactment, Dance Identity and Historical Fictions', in M. Franko (ed.) *The Oxford Handbook of Dance and Reenactment*, New York: Oxford University Press, 79–100.

Pakes, A. 2018 [2009]. 'Knowing through Dance-Making: Choreography, Practical Knowledge and Practice-as-Research', in J. Butterworth and L. Wildschut (eds.) *Contemporary Choreography: A Critical Reader*, 2nd edn, London: Routledge, 11–24.

Passmore, J. 1951. 'The Dreariness of Aesthetics', *Mind*, 60:239, 318–335.

Rohrbaugh, G. 2003. 'Artworks as Historical Individuals', *European Journal of Philosophy*, 11:2, 177–205.

Rorty, R. 1967. *The Linguistic Turn: Recent Essays in Philosophical Method*, Chicago: University of Chicago Press.

Ryle, G. 1963 [1949]. *The Concept of Mind*, 2nd edn, Harmondsworth: Penguin.

Shusterman, R. 2008. *Body Consciousness: A Theory of Mindfulness and Somaesthetics*, Cambridge: Cambridge University Press.

Shusterman, R. 2012. *Thinking through the Body: Essays in Somaesthetics*, Cambridge: Cambridge University Press.

Sinnerbrink, R. 2011. *New Philosophies of Film: Thinking Images*, London: Continuum.

Taruskin, R. 2010. 'Setting Limits', in *The Danger of Music and Other Anti-Utopian Essays*, Oakland: University of California Press, 447–466.

Thom, P. 1993. *For an Audience: A Philosophy of the Performing Arts*, Philadelphia, PA: Temple University Press.

Weitz, M. 1956. 'The Role of Theory in Aesthetics', *Journal of Aesthetics and Art Criticism*, 15:1, 27–35.

Wittgenstein, L. 1953. *Philosophical Investigations*, Oxford: Basil Blackwell.

Wollheim, R., 1968. *Art and Its Objects*, Cambridge: Cambridge University Press.

8
PERFORMANCE PHILOSOPHY IN LATIN AMERICA
How to perform a Utopia called America?

Luciana da Costa Dias

How does Performance Philosophy act in Latin America?

Performance Philosophy is a new transdisciplinary field, but with old resonances.[1] Both component fields – Performance and Philosophy – are now repositioned (into the established friction zone). Within this, how are we to understand Latin America? The continent's problems go beyond a structural crisis of modernity and its disciplinary boundaries, even though we all suffer the effects of such a crisis. Furthermore, we are dealing with issues originating from a so-called deficient political and socioeconomic modernisation (Schwarz 1992), deeply marked by our past as colonies and victims of slavery, in counterpoint to our Amerindian heritage. The question of how Performance Philosophy acts in Latin America transcends the construction of the field, as it needs to get "dirty" and mix with different colours and problems. The issue widens: What features could Performance Philosophy display in places with strong colonial heritage and enormous political and economic problems, such as Latin America? Can Performance Philosophy also embody local questions, and affect, or be affected by, local problems? Can the field of performance philosophy open into a less colonial perspective, and into a thinking beyond borders or territories, that also encompasses a thinking from the "Global South"?

In this chapter, comprising two movements – *Thinking from outside* and *Performing from within* – I will attempt to address the issue of how Performance Philosophy might be embodied in Latin America. However, as a Latin American and a Brazilian researcher, I am compelled to note that this is not a simple question. It addresses a complexity – and a Utopia – named (Latin) America, struck by multiple perspectives, crossed by divergent lines of flight, and unsolved problems. This task is also surrounded by the risk of generalisation. Thus, to avoid such a risk, I will shift back and forth between "macro" and "micro" approaches throughout this chapter. By doing so, I hope to offer some perspectives that can be of help to future researchers.

Thinking from outside: a Utopia named America

"A Utopia named America" refers to the multiplicities and incongruences that surround America's representations in the Western world's imaginary, which motivated, for instance, Chilean artist, Alfredo Jaar, to billboard '*This is not America*' in Times Square, New York

City, as a geopolitical version of the surrealist René Magritte's pipe. This work, named "*A Logo for America*", was billboarded at Times Square in New York for the first time in 1987, and then again in 2014. It also flashed above London's Piccadilly Circus in 2016, as part of "*Under the same Sun*", a contemporary Latin American art exhibition organised by the South London Gallery. There is a whole American continent beyond the anglophone portion, and more; America is not univocal. There is a Hispanic America and a Portuguese America, partially differentiated by language but brought together as 'Latin America' by their historical struggles, colonial past, and economic problems. We could state that there are "Americas"; not one, but many: a multiplicity of countries and experiences. In addition, as 'Américas', in Portuguese, or 'Las Americas', in Spanish, America is gendered as female. For us, Latin Americans, the whole continent is seen as a huge, feminine body. Like Lucio Agra (2016), I consider that the continent, in itself, has a performative character, and "she" performs in a very specific way.

Since its "discovery", the American continent has generally been approached as "raw material" – open to exploitation and speculation. From *Of Cannibals* (1580), an essay by Michel de Montaigne that describes the ceremonies of the Tupi-nambás, an Amerindian tribe from Brazil, to Hegel's *Philosophy of History* (1837) and his famous assumption that America is 'the land of future', European thinking has attempted to understand and absorb what the discovery of a "new world" meant. A series of representations were developed, built up over the centuries, portraying America as "exotic" and "non-western" – a series of variations that ranges from something to be conquered, a new ground to be broken, to the Utopian dream of a new beginning or a "promised land".

America, to modern thinking, was a shadow zone, and, in this regard, Ortega y Gasset wrote "The case of Hegel clearly reveals the error that consists in equating what is historical with the past" (Ortega y Gasset 1966, p. 15) – not any past, but with a linearly, logically, and progressively constructed single ("universal") narrative of the past. He argued that if America does not belong to a linear progression of the spirit from Ancient Greece to the Modern State of the nineteenth century, "it is certainly something future" (Hegel 1991). Thus, 'a Utopia named America' also refers to a kind of paradox: "America" as a different order of things; something before, but also beyond modern times.

Naturally, the Tupi-nambás tribes would have told a different narrative than Montaigne or Hegel. In colonial times, most indigenous people were "assimilated" (by forced marriage, forced Christianisation, and, ultimately, by death). The few that survived now live in poverty, often caught in violent conflicts over land rights. Mignolo, in his book *The Idea of Latin America* (2005), explains that there should be various and plural narratives regarding the history of colonisation in the Americas, but that, instead, they were unified under a totalising global/universal narrative. Today, on the contrary, such a "diversity of silent, but living, historical forces" must be exposed in what he calls "the project of decolonizing knowledge" – a project that insists that coloniality was the other face of modernity, the "dark side of the renaissance" (Clavo 2016).

Attempting to think beyond such an embedded modern conception of history, *Post-History* (2013), by Czech-Brazilian philosopher Vilém Flusser, criticises the Western world and contemporary culture from the point of view of a crisis in values which has led to this current technical, fragmentary age – an age that is marked by both the end of grand narratives and the fragmentation of modern subjectivity. Flusser is a thinker who literally lived the American Utopia. He came to America to flee Nazism and lived in Brazil for over three decades, a time considered by many scholars as decisive for his work. If his earlier work was marked by the influence of existentialism and phenomenology, his later work would change, thanks to his experience as an immigrant. So, in 1974, he wrote a (the?) fundamental book for Brazilian Studies, *Phenomenology of the Brazilian*, which he based on his "non-historic experience of reality" (Flusser 1998).

Flusser thinks of Brazil as neither a better nor a worse complement to the European self, but as something else. From a European/Western point of view, Brazil is unimaginable, absurd, sometimes abject. For him, all modern categories and concepts (including history, alienation, progress, and development) are inappropriate for thinking about Brazil, as they conceal the profound alterity within the country. The only way to think of the novelty that a place such as Brazil represented within the modern world-view was to engage in truly "becoming Brazilian". His "philosophical autobiography", written at the end of his life, would be named *Bodenlos* (2007), a German word that literally indicates that the floor or ground (*boden*) has fallen away – the abyssal experience in which someone has lost ground or is "groundless". In Flusser's experience, this work refers not only to the loss of all existing models of experience, knowledge, and judgement, but also to the loss of structure (the "world-view", in a hermeneutic-phenomenological perspective) that had connected these models (Flusser 2007).

Flusser's exile experience can be expanded to a macro perspective, since he saw this groundless experience as a result of the modern crisis in values (reason, subject, freedom, and so on) as well as, at the same time, a real Brazilian experience. He realised that modern values have always been "in crisis" in Latin America, and he was not the first. An intellectual debate had already taken place in 1968–1969, between Mexican philosopher Leopoldo Zea Aguilar and Peruvian philosopher Augusto Salazar Bondy, who debated the possibility of the existence of a Latin American philosophy.

To Salazar Bondy, a thinking unique to Latin America would have the task to establish 'a philosophical identity', and thereby also the necessary 'philosophical difference' with what was Western/European thinking. He considered that any Latin American philosophy that fails in such a task would be only an 'imitated thought' or a colonised thought (Salazar Bondy 2004). However, Zea Aguilar considered the nexus between Latin American and European culture with respect to the Latin American identity problematic, because America (as a Utopia) has always been addressed as a product of the European imaginary. This has led Latin Americans to constantly feel inferior because, in assuming this European idea of America, such huge expectations could never be fulfilled (Zea Aguilar 1986).

Another figure to embrace the American Utopia, but in a totally different way, was Antonin Artaud (1896–1948), the well-known French writer and actor whose work is considered revolutionary and paradigmatic to theatre and performance studies in general. However, the impact that his trip to Mexico – and the alteration of his conceptions and misconceptions of its native culture – had on his work is not so well-known. Mexico was the object of Artaud's theatrical fantasy long before he even visited the country. His *Second Manifesto* even describes a play called *The Conquest of Mexico* in order to exemplify his ideas concerning the physicality of his 'new theatre' (Artaud 2013).

Artaud would arrive in Mexico in February 1936 and remain until late October. He first went to Ciudad del Mexico, where he gave three public lectures at the Universidad Nacional Autónoma del México. As a former associate of the Surrealist movement, Artaud would partially share the surrealistic vision of the failure of the Western world. He also believed that the Western world had lost something. This "something" was what he went looking for outside Europe, and what made him leave Mexico City behind and go in search of the Rarumari, a native tribe from Sierra Tarahumara, later pictured in his book *The Peyote Dance* (1945) and other writings (Artaud 1976).

Nevertheless, if primitivism was a tendency within twentieth-century modernism, it is interesting to note that Artaud rarely used the word "primitive" in his texts, except sarcastically. Rather, he employed terms such as 'ancient cultures' (Artaud 1984) and he genuinely believed that this ancient non-Western Amerindian culture could get the Western world (and his own damaged self) back on track. Of course, America could not fulfil Artaud's great expectations (his own Utopia), and he went back to France just before his final breakdown. Nonetheless, his travel to Mexico ignited one of the most relevant aspects of Theatre and Performance Studies today: the ethno-anthropological turn, an approach later developed by Victor Turner and Richard Schechner, as well as practitioners such as Eugenio Barba, Jerzy Grotowski, and others.

Artaud's experience was that of a 'foreigner' in search of his own Utopia. Would it be the same to someone born and raised in Latin America? It would be far worse. If we return to the idea of a *Bodenlos*/groundless experience, another point stands out as central: instead of Latin Americans having absorbed a "ground" similar to Europeans (since we lost most of a pre-Columbian world-view with colonisation and adopted – mainly by force – modern European values, whilst, at the same time, we rarely see ourselves only as children of the African diaspora), we had never felt that modern values or European culture have truly or totally been our own. Two historical traumas were never truly overcome: (1) the Portuguese/Spanish invasion, which almost eradicated indigenous populations; and (2) forced colonisation of the continent through African slavery (c.1501–1866). If the size of the indigenous population in 1492 is a controversial subject, there is no controversy about the fact that America was not discovered, but instead, invaded: staging a systematic genocide of the indigenous inhabitants. However, the African slave trade is the largest diaspora in modern history. Brazil received almost four million Africans, and was the last country in the Western world to abolish slavery. The African presence in Brazil is vast and polyphonic, deeply embodied through music and culture, although prejudice still persists. We all feel "*Bodenlos*", in one sense or another.

Performing from within: America, 'Thy name is woman'

Latin America is huge. In 2016, its population was estimated at more than 639 million people. It is ethnically and economically diverse, presenting a wide gap between the richest and the poorest. Not by coincidence, such an economic gap falls roughly along racial and political lines, with indigenous or African descendants being mostly on the poorer side of the divide. In the case of Brazil, modernisation was a top-down process carried out by authoritarian regimes in the 1930s and 1960s/1970s. Thus, it preserved and recreated the social, economic, and cultural divisions between the elite and the rest of society. As Roberto Schwarz argues, dominant classes have embraced the project of modernity and, by doing so, have preserved their own niche of privilege (Schwarz 1992). In this context, archaic power relations, paternalistic regimes, and artisanal forms of production coexist with political and economic modernities, such as democracy, citizenship, industrial production, and high technology. Latin America assimilated modernity (and democracy) after its own fashion. Indeed, to understand the sinuosity of Latin American misplacement in the twentieth century, it is necessary to follow the current overlaying of a semi-oligarchic dominant order, a semi-industrialised capitalist economy, and a semi-transformative social movement (Canclini 1995). Maybe this is one of the reasons why Levi-Strauss, in his book, *Tristes Tropiques* (1961), considers that America went "from barbary to decadence".

Néstor Canclini spearheaded a debate on Latin American modernity, regarding the disparities between "deficient" political and socioeconomic modernisation on the one hand,

and "exuberant" cultural modernity on the other. He states that such a disjuncture is a dynamic element performed within national culture (Canclini 1995). Structural violence had always permeated Latin America, and it is still performed within social, political, and economic relationships today. So, it is no surprise that the same violence is now seen under the guise of a (neo-)fascist wave. For instance, Brazilian cultural and artistic "exuberance", alongside the violence still performed within our power structures, is the country's strongest paradox.

It would be an impossible task, within the limits of one chapter, to trace a broad panorama of Latin American performance. As Lucio Agra states, "…books on the subject are still being written" (Agra 2016, p. 136). Although the rapidly expanding literature is still fragmentary in the face of such a monumental subject (at the same time, general and regional), gaps remain, accentuated by differences and approximated by the similarities of a "political spectrum of terrible shapes that push forward the body into the centre of action" (Agra 2016). For example, Brazilian art in the regime years (1964–1985) bloomed, through artists that, in one way or another, were connected to conceptual art and other art forms that valued the body as a plastic-ideological object, including Hélio Oiticica, Lygia Clark, Artur Barrio, among others.

Most Latin American countries were under the shadow of military dictatorships at some point between the late 1950s and early 1980s. Nevertheless, those years were thought-provoking, with growing conceptual art, happenings, and performance art as actions against oppression. If, from a political point of view, Latin American states and their National Projects may seem immature, the same cannot be said about Latin American art and performance, which became extremely rich during the twentieth century (Alcázar and Fuentes 2005; Taylor and Townsend 2008). It is necessary to understand that as the avant-garde movements in Latin America made evident, no well-established artistic canon was present to confront; they faced quite the opposite: a complete absence of roots in the soil of any well-established artistic tradition. Our art history begins as avant-garde, and there is no longer a single Eurocentric narrative in art or in history, but rather many pluriversal and polyphonic histories are arising.

In *Rhizome* (1976), Deleuze and Guattari discuss Western thinking's secular obsession with roots, as something to be overcome by what they call a 'nomadic' form of thinking whereby passive roots are replaced by active rhizomes. Could the *Bodenlos* experience now be the experience of an age, with the contemporary age as an age that is looking for new forms of grounding? Are we all now refugees or exiled in our own lands? However, hybridisation as a main characteristic of post-modern and contemporary thinking brings us to the perception that, currently, all cultures are border cultures, permeated by others and always acting in relation to others. Latin America has been hybrid and multicultural since the beginning. As Latin Americans, we are learning not to bemoan the absence of roots, but instead to celebrate them. This is one of the reasons why Lucio Agra considers that Latin America is "performative" in itself (Agra 2016); it had embodied certain artistic language features even before it was systematised by practice and as a field (in other words, even before the formal advent of Performance Studies (Schechner 2002)).

For instance, in 1928, *The Anthropophagic Manifesto* was published by poet Oswald de Andrade in Brazil (de Andrade 1991), giving birth to Anthropophagy as a concept that embodied the Brazilian way of thinking. The translation of *Antropófago* as cannibal is not entirely accurate. Cannibals would eat human flesh as part of their normal diet, while an Anthropophagus only does so ritualistically, as an act of revenge in order to absorb an enemy's strength. This is a calculated act of survival and resistance. According to Duchet, the synonymy between cannibals and anthropophagus becomes common worldwide precisely after Montaigne's essay, which conflated the two terms. However, their difference remained in Latin America, mainly in Brazilian representations (Duchet 1971). De Andrade considered cannibalism as a very distinctive and primordial Brazilian trait, present in some travel narratives from as far back as the sixteenth century. These early writings on Brazil shaped the representation of this southern part of the "new land". Perhaps it could still be our strategy to survive and overcome our traumas, devouring everything in order to embody a *thinking from outside* and then becoming able *to perform it from within*. The most iconic and famous *Manifesto* line affirms its plurivocal and hybrid character, being written not in Portuguese, but in English, "Tupi or not Tupi, that is the question".

This is the question, the challenge that all Latin America faces in a post-colonial world. This is a delicious word play that is, simultaneously, a celebration of the Tupi tribes (once major in Brazilian south-eastern regions – today practically extinct) as one root of Brazilian identity; and the exacerbation of a metaphorical instance of cannibalism as the other, very distinct, Brazilian cultural feature. De Andrade "devoured" Shakespeare as an anthropophagic ritual, and, thus, Shakespeare is now part of him and can be "swallowed" into his manifest. Since then, the concept of anthropophagy has become one of the richest categories associated with Brazilian identity, challenging and deconstructing several dualities, such as civilisation/barbarism, modern/primitive, and colonial/post-colonial.

Anthropophagy as an epistemological tool can be related to Performance Philosophy as a manner of radical embodiment, and a way for philosophical questions to be absorbed and become "flesh and blood" in Latin America, radically assuming local identities. If Anthropophagy is "the only original Brazilian philosophy and, in some ways, the most radical of the artistic movements we produced" (de Campos 1976), it is because it proposes a radical way to incorporate thinking. Anthropophagy originates from multiple sources with multiple meanings. It may sound primitivist, but it can also be deconstructivist. It can sound pre-modern, but it is also post-modern. It can be related to Brazilian "pre-history", but it is also deeply "post-historic". It is one of the many worldwide by-products of the European avant-garde, but it is also as groundless (or rootless) as it is Brazilian. As raw philosophy, it nurtures an anthropophagic reason that also aims to deconstruct Western logocentrism, as we digest and (re-)think it (Birnbaum and Olsson 2009).

Oswald sought out elements mainly repressed in the past which could help explain our present. With such an approach, deeply influenced by Nietzsche and Freud, he was capable of "producing" (in the sense of the Greek word *poiesis*) Brazil as "difference" (and maybe Latin America, in a broader sense), i.e. a country that culturally performs alterity in its own fashion, as a thinking of difference. The use of cannibalism as a metaphor is far from Eurocentric. It tends to (proto-)deconstruct categories from the European tradition. In *The rule of anthropophagy: Europe under the sign of devoration* (1986), written by the Brazilian Concrete Poet and essayist, Haroldo de Campos, such metaphor takes centre stage, expanding and absorbing a variety of foreign influences, including Derrida's deconstruction. Indeed, Derrida and Haroldo de Campos met in Paris in the 1960s and remained friends for life, exchanging letters and writings.

> Anthropophagy (...) is the thought of critical devoration of the universal heritage, formulated not from the insipid, resigned perspective of the 'noble savage' (idealized within the model of European virtues) but from [the insolent] point of view of the 'evil savage', [white-men eaters – the anthropophagus]. The latter view does not involve a

submission (an indoctrination), but a transculturation, or better, a 'transvalorization': a critical view of history as a negative function (in Nietzsche's sense of term), capable of appropriation and of expropriation, de-hierarchization, deconstruction. (...) The great and unclassified Machado [de Assis] gives us the metaphor of the head as a 'ruminator's stomach'.

(de Campos and Wolff 1986, pp. 44–45)

In an expanded sense, anthropophagy can be considered as an 'epistemology of the South', using the terms of Boaventura de Sousa Santos (de Sousa Santos 2015). Since Richard Schechner and the advent of Performance Studies "...performance is a lens to understand the world", and, within the scope of Performance Philosophy, performance has grown into a radical philosophy, as embodied through a deep connection between anthropophagy and Performance Philosophy. Or, in a playful provocation, I could just claim that Performance Philosophy is also something to be devoured, absorbed in order to become part of us, as well. After all, anthropophagy is both a way of thinking, a philosophy, even an aesthetic movement, a manifesto; much more than an epistemological tool to understand how this part of the globe performs in a visceral anti-colonial, anti-authoritarian attitude, anthropophagy turns into our manner of radical embodiment, a sense of being alive and savagely surviving – *an act of what I call "raw philosophy"*.

However, if Latin America is performative in itself, as stated previously, how does it perform? We could think about a "cultural performance", a concept coined in the 1950s by anthropologist Milton Singer (Singer 1972), which describes how a culture formulates its self-understanding and self-image through different kinds of performances. We will not fully develop this idea within the limits of this chapter, but, inside such a scope, music could be considered as the most widely known trace of Latin American cultural performance: Tango, Samba,[2] Bossa-nova, and Tropicalia, among others. What we devour becomes part of ourselves – of our hybrid self, a stronger self even when we exhibit our scars and open wounds through our cultural performance. Because we are not a Utopia, we are flesh and blood. And we bleed.

Yet, there is a second aspect of the Latin American performative self to consider, and that is how it can incorporate the questions and problems that arise within the continent through performance art. Many Latin American (mainly female) performers, such as Tania Bruguera, Regina Galindo, and Beatriz Santiago Muñoz, could be discussed here, but I will highlight only one: Ana Mendieta, a Cuban-born artist, who devoured the "mixed spiritual legacy of Spanish-colonial Catholicism, Afro-Cuban religious practices like *Santeria* and the indigenous nature worship of the Caribbean" (Heartney 2004), activating a potent dialogue among different artistic languages inside a deep sense of respect for the American continent and her hybrid ancestry. She is best known for her *Silueta Series*, in which her body silhouette was inscribed (through paint, blood, fire, and other natural elements) on various materials, in outdoor and indoor landscapes, recorded through photography and film. The *Silueta Series* presents a strong gesture, connecting her own female body with the wounded Latin American body – devouring and embodying through the *Series* (our) traumas and themes, such as violence, displacement, and cultural, spiritual, racial and gender identities. As in an act of raw philosophy, Mendieta's work, through the deep destratification of her own body (Deleuze and Guattari 1987), can catalyse the deterritorialisation of *Las Americas*: her solitude is deeply embodied in Mendieta's *Silueta Series*.

In this essay, I aimed to draft some general aspects of the relationship between performance and philosophy in Latin America: a relationship as fragmentary as the continent itself. I attempted, through philosophical interrogation, to rearticulate questions concerning the performativity of (and on) the American continent. Returning to the original question: How does Performance Philosophy act in Latin America? This cannot be completely answered at this moment. If Latin America is multiple, divergent, and far from any simple categorisation, Performance Philosophy, as a developing field, makes us free to unearth new approaches for our ground-to-be. To develop together, at a global level, an identity and a way of thinking beyond Western tradition remains an ongoing task.

Notes

1 This chapter was mainly written during my sabbatical year as a Visiting Research Fellow at the Centre for Performance Philosophy, at the University of Surrey (UK), granted by the Federal University of Ouro Preto (Brazil), where I work as an Associate Professor.
2 I suggest the album 'Mulher do Fim do Mundo' ("*Woman from the end of the world*"), from Elza Soares, named *Brazilian singer of the Millennium* by BBC Radio in 1999, whose style could be called "dirty samba" (or "samba sujo"), given it is samba hybridised with dissonant sonorities – from punk rock to jazz. Her music and her life are inseparable. Soares' husky voice bears the weight of her own hard experience that, as so many Latin American lives, embodies exile, poverty, violence, and the death of her children. And yet, she sings, celebrating life until the very end.

References

Agra, L. 2016. 'Fora do Mapa, o Mapa: Performance na América Latina em dez anotações', *ARS Journal*, São Paulo, v.14, n.27, pp. 135–148.
Alcázar, J. & Fuentes, F. 2005. *Performance y arte-acciónen America Latina*, México, ExTeresa.
Artaud, A. 1976. *The Peyote Dance*, New York, Farrar, Straus & Giroux.
Artaud, A. 1984. *México y Viaje al País de los Tarahumaras*, México, Fondo de Cultura Económica.
Artaud, A. 2013. *The Theatre and Its Double*, Richmond, Alma Classics.
Birnbaum, D. & Olsson, A. 2009. 'An Interview with Jacques Derrida on the Limits of Digestion'. *E-flux journal*, No. 2. [Online] https://www.e-flux.com/journal/02/68495/an-interview-with-jacques-derrida-on-the-limits-of-digestion/ Accessed 9 October 2019.
Canclini, N.G. 1995. *Hybrid Cultures: Strategies for Entering and Leaving Modernity*, Minneapolis, University of Minnesota Press.
Clavo, M.I. 2016. 'Modernity vs. Epistemodiversity'. *E-flux Journal*, No. 73 [Online] https://www.e-flux.com/journal/73/60475/modernity-vs-epistemodiversity/ Accessed 9 October 2019.
de Andrade, O. 1991. 'Cannibalistic Manifesto', *Latin American Literary Review*, v.19, n.38, pp. 38–47.
de Campos, H. 1976. 'Revistas re-vistas: os antropófagos', *Revista de Antropofagia*, São Paulo, CLY.
de Campos, H. & Wolff, M.T. 1986. 'The Rule of Anthropophagy: Europe under the Sign of Devoration', *Latin American Literary Review*, v.14, n.27. pp. 42–60.
de Sousa Santos, B. 2015. *Epistemologies of the South*, London, Routledge.
Deleuze, G. & Guattari, F. 1976. *Rhizome*, Paris, Les Éditions de Minuit.
Deleuze, G. & Guattari, F. 1987. *A Thousand Plateaus: Capitalism and Schizophrenia*, New York, Continuum.
Duchet, M. 1971. *Anthropotogie et Histoire au Siècle des Lumières*, Paris, Flammarion.
Flusser, V. 1998. *Fenomenologia do brasileiro: Em busca de um novo homem,* Rio de Janeiro, EdUERJ.
Flusser, V. 2007. *Bodenlos*, São Paulo, Annablume.
Flusser, V. 2013. *Post-History*, New York, Univocal Publishing.
Heartney, E. 2004. 'Rediscovering Ana Mendieta', *Art in America Magazine*, v.92, n.10, pp. 139–143.
Hegel, G.W.F. 1991. *The Philosophy of History*, Buffalo, Prometheus Books.
Levi-Strauss, C. 1961. *Tristes Tropiques*, New York, Criterion.
Mignolo, W. 2005. *The Idea of Latin America*, Oxford, Blackwell Publishing.

Ortega y Gasset, J. 1966. 'Hegel y América', *El Espectador*, vols. VII–VIII, Madrid, Espasa Calpa.
Salazar Bondy, A. 2004. 'The Meaning and Problem of Hispanic American Philosophic Thought'. In *Latin American Philosophy in the Twentieth Century*, edited by J.E. Garcia, Amherst, NY, Prometheus Books, pp. 233–244.
Schechner, R. 2002. *Performance Studies: An Introduction*, London, Routledge.
Schwarz, R. 1992. *Misplaced Ideas: Essays on Brazilian Culture*, Routledge, Chapman & Hall.
Singer, M. 1972. *When a Great Tradition Modernizes: An Anthropological Approach to Modern Civilization*, London, Praeger Publishers.
Taylor, D. & Townsend, S.J. 2008. *Stages of Conflict: A Critical Anthology of Latin American Theater and Performance*, Ann Arbor, Michigan Press University.
Zea Aguilar, L. 1986. 'The Actual Function of Philosophy in Latin America'. In *Latin American Philosophy in the Twentieth Century*, edited by J.E. Garcia. Amherst, NY, Prometheus Books, pp. 219–225.

9
DIMINISHING RETURNS
On the performativity of musical sound

Anthony Gritten

Introduction: a special relationship

There is a special relationship between music and philosophy. A long tradition of thinkers like Adorno, Lacoue-Labarthe, and Nietzsche, and in their wake, writers like Andrew Bowie, Daniel Chua, and Michael Spitzer, to name only a few men, have argued that the historical imbrication of music and philosophy symbolises or hides a deeper unity between the two modes of world-making (c.f. e.g. Adorno 1998; Bowie 2009; Chua 2017; Lacoue-Labarthe 1995; Nietzsche 2000; Spitzer 2006). Lacoue-Labarthe, for example, has probed the autobiographical operation of music, using psychoanalytical tools to unpack the 'echo of the subject', while Chua has used Levinas to explore possible conjunctions between Beethoven and ethics. And there are, of course, a huge number of studies examining music quite straightforwardly with the help of philosophical tools.

In this essay, I bracket this type of study. I focus instead on what it is within musical sound that lends itself to the types of relationship that such writers have claimed. Put interrogatively: what is the performativity of musical sound such that it can have this kind of relationship with philosophy? Musical Performance Philosophy provides me with a case study of the special relationship between music and philosophy. I start by examining the operation of performativity within Performance Philosophy, unpacking Performance Philosophy's "opening to [the] reciprocal (in)determination or mutual transformation" (Cull O'Maoilearca 2014, p. 23) of performance and philosophy. Considering the prospect of a specifically *musical* Performance Philosophy, and arguing that what characterises it is that the event is not just staged theatrically but sounded, I go on to propose that "(in)determination" is a particular type of indeterminacy related to the manner of energetic expenditure in sound events, and requires a different phenomenological approach towards the practitioner's body both to what usually suffices for Performance alone or Philosophy alone and to what might suffice for other modes of Performance Philosophy. With respect to music as a cultural practice, music's special relationship with philosophy comes from its empirical being-towards-death, which I constitute in terms of entropy. Despite the potentially huge scale of this claim, my aim is merely to establish the centrality of entropy to accounts of musical sound *qua* humanly significant practice, and to start the process of investigating how this impacts upon Performance Philosophy and its practitioner.

Methodology

Before the main body of the argument, I mention three methodological issues. These issues concern the characteristics of a specifically musical Performance Philosophy, as opposed to, say, a theatrical, filmic, or dance Performance Philosophy (although this assumption about genre differences is rather Platonic and should itself be problematised).

First issue. The question of performativity raises its head both in the domain of content and in the domain of form: "What does Performance Philosophy do?" and "How does Performance Philosophy intervene?" to cite the titles of the second and fourth Performance Philosophy conferences held in Chicago and Amsterdam, respectively. Performativity *qua* content is addressed below in the main argument of this essay. In terms of performativity *qua* form, there are two registers, one epistemic and one epistemological. In terms of the epistemic register, it may be that Performance Philosophy is *itself* performative, i.e. more complex than merely some linear additive connection between Performance and Philosophy. Certainly, the global disciplinary movement within Higher Education that self-identifies with this name has expended much energy not just investigating but experimenting materially with multiple notions of which multimedia events might be identified (though not necessarily defined) as examples of Performance Philosophy. In terms of the epistemological register, it may be that Performance Philosophy is (simply!) the *study of* performativity, and is not itself meaningfully performative. In this case, when it comes to the prospect of a specifically musical Performance Philosophy, it is centrally sound (and thence music) that needs to be investigated in terms of its performativity. These two registers of performativity *qua* form may coexist, of course, and the matter does not require resolution here, although in my opinion this essay itself is *about* performativity, and only minimally performative in how it wants you to think.

Second issue. In order to investigate the prospect of a specifically musical performativity, I need to know what is meant by performativity in general. However, there is no single definition encompassing enough of the discourses of practice and theory to claim an acceptable centre ground. Although there are good surveys of the term (Krämer 2014; Loxley 2006), there remains a massive diversity in how the term is used. Gender theorists use it to phrase the normativity of utterances (c.f. Butler 1990, 1993). Anthropologists, operating with speech act theory (after Searle after Austin), insist on getting to the bottom of the context of an utterance. Derrideans, acknowledging the concept of iterability, would rather admit that context and act are necessarily split from the beginning (c.f. Hall 1999). Behavioural economists and sociologists read socio-political behaviour performatively, taking human activity as, in addition to merely achieving its immediate goal, instantiating a position vis-à-vis identity and ideology. Film makers assume that their film is performative in several registers, operating as they do both artistically and commercially. And so on. I shall avoid registering here a working definition of performativity, cobbled together from an admixture of the various theories on offer, most of which are from domains other than sound. This is because my aim is to approach the issue of how the performativity of sound is constituted and to argue that it requires a different approach to those represented earlier, all of which take the concept onwards from its origins in Austin's theory of how verbal utterances do things. In contrast, my object is not an object: it is the transient phenomenon of musical sound, which is constituted phenomenologically with both a virtual register (sounds heard as tones) and an empirical register (sounds heard as sound waves). My emphasis in this essay is more towards the latter, which is as much constituted *by* time as *in* time.

Third issue. My larger context is music, and I introduced the issues in the opening paragraph with reference to this term. In what follows, though, I use the term sound or musical sound in order to avoid some of the cultural baggage that has accumulated around the term music.

The learning community

In order to situate my constitution of musical performativity, I begin by considering the mode of self-presentation or "(in)determination" that Performance Philosophy might claim to embody within the academic community: how it situates itself as a mode of academic discourse and articulates itself with respect to its various interlocutors. I do this by means of a brief discussion of how argumentation and reasoning operate within the university.

In an elegant discourse upon what he terms 'The Learning Community', Martin Parker Dixon (2018) argues that in the contemporary university,

> we *ought* to reacquaint ourselves with the techniques of rigorous argumentation; namely, with the *arts* of positing theses, explaining them, defending them from objections and counter-theses; with the arts of defining our terms, of using evidence, of evaluating other people's arguments, of producing novel ideas or 'theories' and examining the consequences.
>
> *(Parker Dixon 2018, §1)*

These arts are unpacked and explained in some detail, with an eye for (re-)positioning the university study of music (back) where it belongs alongside the rest of the humanities and indeed on a par with STEM disciplines, since it is Parker Dixon's claim that all disciplines should share their core mode of reasoning. For Parker Dixon, music is "*an object of serious intellectual enquiry*", but this claim is only plausible if it is acknowledged axiomatically that "Scholars have an *obligation to make available* to the university community their understanding of a particular subject" (Parker Dixon 2018, §§ 1 & 2, respectively). The majority of Parker Dixon's energy is expended discussing the ways in which communally agreed processes of "making available" should operate within the context of university discourse. His argument presents a neat defence of an older – and he would probably claim wiser – constitution of the university: before neo-liberalism had its way and the decline set in (funding cuts, competitive benchmarking, students as consumers). Parker Dixon's value judgements about the contemporary university (as if there is such a generic thing as "the" university: every university is a singular and unrepeatable entity with its own idiosyncratic successes and failures) need to be debated properly elsewhere; Parker Dixon himself concludes optimistically that "Reasoned, dialogical thinking is *worked through*, it can hold its own, and it can make a genuine difference to the way we think and what we do" (Parker Dixon 2018, § 9).

Here, I take the liberty of using Parker Dixon's position on the manner in which musicians "participate in a language game of reasonable and dialogic elaboration on the aspects of the art of music that interest them" (idem) as a way of affording my argument a meta-disciplinary framework. I sidestep much of his nuanced discussion in order to consider the demographic that comes last in his pecking order, perhaps understandably so given the priorities of the contemporary university: performers (idem § 8). Ignoring the distinction between universities and conservatoires, which is more cultural than financial, and on the back of Parker Dixon's claim that performers do in fact have an important role to play in the university, that their operation has a certain performative force within academic discourse,

I wish to consider what place might be given over to Performance Philosophy (which lies beyond Parker Dixon's remit), and to musical Performance Philosophy in particular.

Consider briefly one of Parker Dixon's central case studies: Byrd's motet *Circumdederunt me*. Parker Dixon discusses this piece, or, more accurately, Joseph Kerman's extended description of it, in order to unpack the mechanisms of "authoritative judgement". He writes: "We can add that the truth of such judgements (in the sense of it 'really being the case that' *Circumdederunt me* is mournful and great), if treated as a standalone characteristic, or indeed a verdict, is something of a distraction. What matters is going through the transitions and phases of a process of reasoning, weighing up evidence, and considering the consequences of various assertions" (idem § 6.4). This is the claim that university discourse operates in such a manner that one feels obliged, having followed the reasoning, to assent to Kerman's claim about Byrd and become a member of the Kantian *sensus communis*, even if it feels as if the actual judgement itself about *Circumdederunt me* is a "distraction" from the argumentation that generated it (at least for the scholar constructing the argument). Put another way, using Austin's later terminology, the statement has illocutionary force and aims both to state something with a certain truth value and to force a movement of consciousness in a particular direction: perhaps to make the reader desire to go away and sing or listen to the motet.

How does Performance Philosophy compare to this type of university discourse (hardly a flattering term)? For a start, Performance Philosophy includes within its remit events that are primarily non-linguistic and mixed mode alongside conventional written artefacts designed for reading. Indeed, much of the force of Performance Philosophy comes from its multiple media, multiple modes, multiple registers, and multiple voices. More fundamentally, and in addition to these very multiplicities, I claim that one of the primary characteristics of Performance Philosophy lies at a tangent to the inferentialist approach to judgement. To wit: insofar as Performance Philosophy is a discourse, it desires to embody processes analogous to "reasoning, weighing up [and] considering" in events that themselves (1) have an aesthetic value and (2) produce affects and effects upon those exposed to them: in short, Performance Philosophy's mixed multimedia assemblages make of everything a distraction. Thanks to Austin, "felicity" has become the criterion for evaluating such performative utterances, rather than a process of truth verification (Hatt 1999, p. 82), and Performance Philosophy makes the most of the possibilities offered by this new approach to dialogue – a happy distraction. Indeed, Performance Philosophy seeks explicitly to position itself on the "margins" of discourse, to "tympanise" and "philosophise with a hammer", as Derrida rewrites Nietzsche (Derrida 1982). Loosening up reason's machinery, it proliferates and pauses irrevocably upon the argument's component parts, thus stymying the conclusion's chances of escaping from materiality into logic and its chances of becoming-propositional. In the sense pursued below, Performance Philosophy is not merely the complexifying of argumentative discourse; arguably, so is the type of reasoning proposed by Parker Dixon, at least insofar as it drives a wedge between everyday discourse and university discourse. In addition, Performance Philosophy also celebrates reasoning – hence, it is distracting – by virtue of (1) its material embodiment as events; (2) its emphasis on the internal organs of reasoning; and (3) its deliberate evisceration and retortion of the logic behind argumentative reasoning. (Here, it is clearest that Performance Philosophy is qualitatively different from Performance alone and Philosophy alone.)

One further comparison between university discourse and Performance Philosophy lies in their respective relationships to what Parker Dixon terms "that strange place called the 'real world'". While he acknowledges the worries and tensions within the contemporary university around the issue of how to reconcile – or at least juxtapose peacefully – different language games, Performance Philosophy worries less about whether or not the world's insistence that "it is our *right* to say, believe or value as we do" (Parker Dixon 2018, § 4.7) (i.e. without university discourse intervening and slowing down everyday life) is a reasonable premise for everyday discourse. This openness of its approach to "the real world" is less directed towards what Jon McKenzie terms the "challenge" of performance (McKenzie 2001) (which, it could be argued, remains driven by an overly narrow *telos* of success: the performativity of performativity), and more drawn towards entropy (which is not the same thing as failure).

From energy to entropy

The previous section unpacked Performance Philosophy's intervention in the world (the form of its events). I now begin to unpack what Performance Philosophy does (its content). The focus moves towards musical sound and the prospect of a specifically musical Performance Philosophy, considering the performativity of sound in terms of its constitution into virtual and empirical registers.

Thus far, it is unclear how sound operates within the discourse constructed by Parker Dixon and deconstructed at a tangent by Performance Philosophy, and the extent to which it operates in a properly transformative manner within the dialogic proposing of hypotheses, providing of evidence, and deducing of conclusions. Even if, as I claimed earlier, Performance Philosophy takes university discourse and exposes it to retortion, proliferation, and distraction (repurposing it into aesthetic material and in the process making terms like hypothesis, evidence, and conclusion redundant), even if, operating in not quite the opposite direction, it takes aesthetic material and reads it philosophically (thus making its artistic value secondary), or even if energy is expended in both directions at once, then the manner in which sound's empirical matter operates across the discourse still needs consideration. Hence the following question: What changes when an event is not just *staged* theatrically, as with university discourse, which is based upon transactions within the classical public *agora*, but *sounded*, whereupon the distinction between public and private becomes redundant, and whereupon the body's relationship to space is configured differently?

In the previous section, I claimed that Performance Philosophy operates at a tangent to the university discourse constituted by Parker Dixon. This tangent is articulated well by McKenzie, who, with some brilliance, discusses the dynamics of performance and performativity in the contemporary world. His central claim is that the world has drifted from a "discipline" paradigm towards a "performance" paradigm, and he summarises this distinction by noting

> that the mechanisms of performative power are nomadic and flexible more than sedentary and rigid, that its spaces are networked and digital more than enclosed and physical, that its temporalities are polyrhythmic and non-linear and not simply sequential and linear.
>
> *(McKenzie 2001, p. 19)*

In many respects, the "global performance stratum" analysed by McKenzie is the stratum within which Performance Philosophy expends its energy as it operates across discourse at a tangent to Parker Dixon's inferentialism. McKenzie's approach to performativity – to the three modes of performance (cultural, managerial, technological) and their three modes of evaluation (efficacy, efficiency, effectiveness) – is an efficient means of analysing the rise of the performative paradigm (Perform – Or Else!), the rise of the discipline of Performance Studies (from which emerged Performance Philosophy), and the impact of these rises on everyday constructions of what performance does and how performance intervenes into human life. Indeed, his very characterisation of performance has itself become ever more familiar and normative since *Perform or Else* was published in 2001: "Across the performance stratum, hybrid, hyphenated subjects rapidly emerge and immerge, passing through a variety of subject positions and switching quickly between innumerable language games. Multi-tasking, channel-surfing, attention-deficit disorders: these portend the emergence of fractal, (n-1) dimensional subjectivities" (McKenzie 2001, p. 180).

However, I depart from McKenzie's position for a reason stemming from the empirical register of sound (which is my problem rather than McKenzie's, since his focus is neither on Performance Philosophy nor on musical sound). This is that, although musical sound does not really fit into the discipline paradigm that McKenzie critiques, and seems to be more at home within his performance paradigm, in fact there remains a major problem for sound in relation to McKenzie's theory. This is that sound is not efficacious, efficient, or effective (McKenzie's desiderata for performances henceforth). Musical sound is governed more by its own echoing, fading, and dying: by a decline and deterioration that, stronger and stranger than death, witnesses the end of sound waves' disturbances and the re-emergence of silence or background noise (it matters not for my argument). If we are to constitute the performativity of sound, then we need to acknowledge its incessant, unceasing, and "centrifugal topology of thought" (Lagaay & Koubová 2014, p. 42), and the constitution of its relentless being-towards-death. This I construct in terms of sound's entropy, which term has the advantage of recalling the sound's virtual register to its empirical register, of recalling tones to the sound waves upon which they are supervenient. This psychoacoustic axiom (that all sounds end in the same way, but each sound begins differently) is essential to the performativity of sound, to its power and force; the performativity of sound cannot be based on its presence alone, on a notion of empirical plenitude and neurological activation alone, or on a nominal sense of how listening engages sound. This, despite the prevalence of accounts of sound that fetishise its onset transients and steady-state components and that assume that, because "A sound has a beginning, a middle, and usually an end" (Casey O'Callaghan 2007, pp. 10–11), the phenomenological import of a sound's acoustic envelope must therefore be symmetrical.

In this essay, in contrast, I take the end of sound to be its phenomenological core. In the next section, I examine Casey O'Callaghan's theory of sounds, attempting to show how the later chapters of his book, described modestly as concerning "sound-related phenomena" (O'Callaghan 2007, p. 108), deal with the most fundamental aspects of sound: the ways in which sound becomes "mediated, impoverished, and illusory" (idem, p. 158). Extrapolating from his theory, I shall claim that these chapters concern the special relationship between sound and death, the ways in which sounds end after various prosthetic aids to their "perdurance" (idem, p. 27) and the memorials and archives erected by humans to pay tribute to their past.

In this section, though, let us consider further the empirical decline and deterioration of sound. The task is to confront the behaviour of sound matter. Sound is forever disturbing the environment in a gesture of simultaneous birth-death. It might be, *pace* Husserl, that time consciousness can be understood by analogy with musical melody, but for my purposes, the point is that sound *qua* temporal event has a destiny that lies outside the intentionality of sonic subjectivity, and this destiny is its perishing as the echo dies out and the energy driving the disturbance that created the sound waves dissipates outwards into the environment. So, we should consider the relationship between sound and time in terms of an essential *qualia* that is the decline of the energy coming from the sound's source. This decline is both experienced (felt) and empirical (measurable). The reason? Sound, like other forms of energy, obeys the second law of thermodynamics, i.e. the process of entropy.

Entropy is a measure of the amount of order-disorder in an event in relation to the amount of energy within the event; if there are no external disturbances, then entropy measures of the event show that it increases towards an eventual equilibrium state, while simultaneously the degree of uncertainty in the event (the inability of an observer to measure multiple dimensions at the same time) goes down. In the context of this essay on the prospect of a specifically musical Performance Philosophy, entropy is a central component of sound and thence of its performativity, and embodies the decline of argumentative reason in the face of matter's inexorable drift towards certain equilibrium. Sound, in other words, operated on by time, finds its energy being drained, dissipated, and dispersed. As such, it is a razor-sharp indicator of the death drive, and this means that constructing auditory perception as a matter of property and propriety, as if sound can be owned while being listened to, is mere hubris. Entropy is what makes human experience human, namely, risky and Sisyphean, forever listening up hill, in the knowledge that sonic subjectivity will be given the slip by sound, which will have always already slipped away before listening could grasp its essence, resisting the classical Husserlian dimensions of intentionality, *noesis* and *noema* (more on Husserl in the next section).

Therefore, if we wish to pursue the prospect of a *musical* Performance Philosophy, then this is on the basis that the performativity of musical sound is to be found in its transitory phenomenology, in its temporary presence, in its paradoxical failure to hang around and perform, in its permanent exiting from the stage of performance, and in its ghostly relationship to the public *agora*. Sound's self-absenting is its performativity. Hence, musicking is the most epistemically violent of artistic practices: it takes a certain force to keep it going, stop it sinking, and maintain its sounding presence (Barenboim 2008), against its natural tendency to fade out and absent itself from the world. It requires an external input of energy, an exercise of force.

Moreover, if the performativity of sound is to have the genuinely transformative power that is frequently attributed to it, and which has been a theme in debates about Performance Philosophy, then it needs this social efficacy to be pragmatic and non-idealistic. It is unproductive to construct models of sonic subjectivity in terms of social intervention if the sound presupposed is not what actually happens (i.e. is not what dies out). Theories of sound's possibilities are grounded in accounts of timbre, but this is itself frequently theorised in terms of its contribution to the presence of sound (as opposed to its absence: its decline and deterioration). Thus, standard measurements of timbre are snapshots based on single temporally bounded frozen slices of time (as with visual presentations of spectrograph data), and even when it is acknowledged in the measurement that timbre evolves dynamically, it is normally assumed that its evolution is connected to the continuation of sound's presence (as opposed to its encroaching absence, the silence that is to come). What happens after the timbral attack of a sound and after its steady state needs further theorising, not as an unfortunate tail-end of the sound, but as one of its central components – perhaps even as *the telos* of sound as such. To this I now turn.

The end(s) of sound(s)

In this section, I listen to a quiet register of O'Callaghan's theory that for my purposes constitutes an argument about how sonic subjectivity operates in the face of entropy. This helps me to unpack the performativity of sound, and leads towards a specifically musical Performance Philosophy in which sound becomes sonic subjectivity by virtue of its entropic performativity. O'Callaghan's claim of "sonic realism" (O'Callaghan 2007, pp. 1–12) affords me this springboard, situating his theory at a chiasmus between music and philosophy and thus returning full circle to the claims of Adorno, Bowie, and others. What follows is based upon my assumption that the end of a sound is intimately related to the end of sound; and that the manner of each individual sound's stopping and its broader human significance are intimately related.

What is O'Callaghan's position? Putting to one side his arguments against other theories of sound (largely sounds as properties and sounds as waves, O'Callaghan 2007 §§ 2.2 & 2.3, respectively), statements of his core claims are as follows. "Sounds are public objects of auditory perception". Sounds are *particular individuals*, "non-mental particulars". "Sounds do not travel"; rather, it is sound waves that travel through the medium. "A sound is not motion in the medium, but the activity of one thing's moving or disturbing another" in a periodic or wave-like manner. In short, sounds are "events constituted by the *interactions* of objects and bodies with the surrounding medium". Sound events are of a particular type of "interaction", for which O'Callaghan consistently uses the term "disturbance" (127 times, in fact). By this term, he means an event "in which mechanical energy is transferred from one medium into another" (idem, pp. 13, 17, 56, 61, 65, 70 & 112, respectively). This is a crucial link to entropy's role within sound, for it is the energy profile of a sound that determines how it is to start, continue, and end, just as, in the case of activity generally, "Our acts and experiences are themselves temporal unities which arise, persist, and perish" (Zahavi 2003, p. 85).

"Perish" is indeed the key to sonic performativity, as I now claim by extrapolating from O'Callaghan. In terms of the sonic subjectivity implied within O'Callaghan's theory, the chapters are allocated to different dimensions of sound's becoming subjectivity: thus, Chapters 2 and 5 concern the 'what' of sound, Chapters 3 and 4 concern 'where', Chapter 6 concerns 'how', and Chapters 7–10 are concerned with sound's 'when'. The last of these dimensions has the closest relationship to sound's performativity, because of the operation of entropy. How does O'Callaghan's theory construct this dimension? In what follows, I consider a few core aspects of O'Callaghan's arguments, focusing on (1) the various interference effects that he discusses under the heading of "transmission events", and (2) the issue of recorded sound (sound that sounds as if it has no body to speak of). Consider some more or less obvious facts: sounds are "events that take time" and "require time to unfold"; they "have duration", and "are events that do not outlast […] their sources". O'Callaghan fleshes out this claim by explaining that

> To be a sound as heard is to be a temporally extended particular whose identity is partly determined by a pattern of qualitative changes though time. A sound, moreover, is constitutively tied to the activities of and changes to objects and a medium. Without either sort of activity and change, there would be no sounds.

The point is that, since sounds fade away, their "temporal extension" and the "activities [and] changes" of the medium are central to the sound, particularly the end portion of the sound's acoustic envelope. As O'Callaghan notes, "Sounds hold our concern in light of their behaviour through time" (O'Callaghan 2007, pp. 59, 70, 91–92, 118, 127 & 160, respectively). What is this "behaviour"?

One of the ways in which sound behaves, in which its duration plays out, and in which its temporal extension is materially expended is by means of what O'Callaghan terms "transmission events". These are the events to which sound is subjected as its sound waves travel through the medium, including the passing from one medium into another (e.g. air into water) and the diffusion across an unevenly textured space (e.g. the different impact on sound of transmission in e.g. a square room with a wooden floor as opposed to a circular carpeted room). It is here that it is clearest how a musical Performance Philosophy requires something more than merely a staging *in* space, namely, a sounding *of* space. Transmission events sap sound of energy, absorbing and transferring energy away from its originating investment within the sound waves. Most importantly for O'Callaghan's theory, transmission events are to be distinguished from the originating "disturbances" that O'Callaghan describes in terms of "strikings and crashings", "collisions or pushings" (idem, pp. 61 & 65, respectively) – say, of vocal chords against each other, or of drum stick against drum skin. Indeed, O'Callaghan's logic requires him to drive a wedge between them and to value disturbances more highly than transmission events insofar as "the primary targets of our perceptual interest in an environment" (idem, p. 109) are concerned (fight or flight). To wit:

> Sounds furnish us with awareness of sound-generating events, which are of paramount interest for what they tell us about the world. They tell us such things as how the furniture is arranged and when it is being moved. Transmission events, however, enjoy little utility beyond what we learn through their effects on how we perceive the primary sounds they occlude; for example, when we perceive a sound as muffled, we learn that a barrier may intervene.
>
> *(Idem, p. 100)*

This relative evaluation of disturbances and transmission events – the latter supplement the former – has a logical place within O'Callaghan's theory of sounds, but phenomenologically it under-characterises the performativity of sound (to be fair, this is not O'Callaghan's focus). This is because it is precisely transmission events, and everything that they encompass, including distortion, decrescendo, and death, is central to sound's performativity. Transmission events are more than merely uninvited guests at the sonic event, more than merely redundant tail-ends to the acoustic envelope: they drive sonic performativity as an effect of entropy's energy-sapping operation, and map out the contours of the sonic world in which the disturbance sounds. O'Callaghan describes the sound-generating disturbances as "events in which mechanical energy is transferred from one medium into another" (idem, p. 65) and this is an entropic process of setting in motion and loss of motion, decline and deterioration: subjectivity's eventual "perishing", following Zahavi.

At one point in his discussion of recorded sound, O'Callaghan describes mediation as "assisted perception of objects and events in real time" (idem, p. 158), hinting at a prosthetic construction of cognition. Indeed, in its logic of mediated access to something that is not merely self-present, it is analogous to the classical Husserlian approach to temporality (for "mediator", read "retention"):

> In short, this variety of mediated perceptual awareness requires that one enjoy an experience as of the original particular, that one enjoy an experience as of the mediator, that one's awareness as of the original occurs in virtue of one's awareness of the mediator, and that one's awareness as of the original particular depends causally and in a counterfactual supporting manner upon that original particular.
>
> *(Idem, p. 153)*

The point is that mediation is what temporality and reproductive technologies share, and it is unavoidable: indeed, perception is intimately intertwined with mediation (perception without mediation is not perception). And mediation drifts towards entropy, towards the necessary diluting of presence (though "diluting" is unhelpful rhetoric: there is nothing negative about the fact that presence is mediated and thus internally sapped of its energy). This mediation, the fact that, to use O'Callaghan's example, we can hear FDR talking behind/through/within the loudspeaker, and not worry about imputing subjectivity to the sound despite the fact that FDR is long dead, is characteristic of the telegraphic distributed culture of the first world (which, for better and for worse, has relied heavily on technologies of mediation). However, if, as I have suggested, there is a strong analogy between the logic of mediation and the logic of Husserlian temporality, then it should be worked through to the following point: as such, the mediation of sound perception, and hence the performativity of sound more generally, is riven through with its own ending, fading, and entropy. It is not just temporality as some kind of extended perceptual process that deals in protention and retention; mediation, being itself a technology of sonic death, deals in the same phenomena, constructing the relationship between protention and retention entropically, which is to say, *pace* Husserl, pushing the open-ended nature of time's passing to its natural extreme. This has implications for the way in which the performativity of sound is constructed and for the prospect of a specifically musical Performance Philosophy: primarily, the proposal that sound may not have the presence that it sounds like; or, in reverse, that sonic presence may not be what it sounds like. *Contra* most theories of sound, sound may not *be* anything other than a process: "open, plural, and processual", as the editors of this volume phrased the matter in their proposal.

Conclusion: a special body

I have hung much upon O'Callaghan's excellent philosophical theory of sounds, given that he does not focus on *musical* sound; it is the topic of only one short section (O'Callaghan 2007, § 10.7). I have read Parker Dixon's Quodlibet tangentially to his direction of travel. I have bounced off McKenzie's paradigm-shifting claims with a phenomenon – musical sound – that fails to operate in a fully performative manner. And I have displaced the scientific concept of entropy far away from its home: a huge artistic misprision set in motion by the belief that it affords me a way of understanding that the success of sound is located, not within its living and sustained projection, but within its death. What might be concluded?

Understandably, philosophers get excited by the "vibration that animates the auditory apparatus" (Nancy 2007, p. 29), and by the sound that "brings to the world of being the astonishment of what, for a moment, is nothing yet – of what *is already* without yet being *something*" (Lyotard 1993, p. 151). Many others voicing similar sentiments could be cited. However, they would do well to withdraw a little and recall sound to its ending – which is also its end. For the entropy of sound, which may seem to be merely a metaphor drawn from scientific discourse, is in fact the fate of sonic performativity, both phenomenologically and empirically. Entropy is built into sound from the start.

With respect to the special relationship between music and philosophy mentioned at the start of this essay, I conclude that, as this relationship is embodied within Performance Philosophy, it concerns the relationship between the practitioner's body and her world. Performance Philosophy is not merely a practice that embodies the insights produced independently by Performance and Philosophy; as activities, they themselves are perfectly capable of such acts of material representation. And it is not a practice wherein Performance operates as a cipher for Philosophy, or vice versa. Rather, Performance Philosophy is characterised by events in which the practitioner's body operates as a body rather than merely as a vehicle: retortion, slowing down, and proliferation are its material traces. It operates as an energetic transformer in which issues of subjectivity – the subjectivity of the sound, the subjectivity of the discourse, and the subjectivity of the practitioner – are primarily constituted as materially embodied and excessive with respect to the propositions, challenges, and disturbances that construct Performance alone and Philosophy alone. Entropy is a lesson that the practitioner's body learns the hard way, sound disappearing before its time. Sonic subjectivity within musical Performance Philosophy, bound by the entropic performativity of sound, (1) is not merely an epiphenomenon contingent upon propositions properly framed within an ethic of the "consideration shown to others by *demonstrating one's working*" (Parker Dixon 2018, § 1), (2) is not merely "the truth of everything emerg[ing] through the cracked and uneven joints that bind together performatives and performances" (McKenzie 2001, p. 177), and (3) is not merely a function of "individuat[ing] sounds primarily in terms of their causal sources and their spatio-temporal boundaries" (O'Callaghan 2007, p. 62). It is the indeterminacy of sound writ large across its practitioner's body, which is unable to "demonstrate" its own mechanisms before it dies out, which is unable to "bind" matter together, and which is unable to "individuate" events apart from their own disappearance. This is unproblematic – and pragmatic.

I return, finally, to my initial claim that its "opening to reciprocal (in)determination or mutual transformation" is a fundamental component of Performance Philosophy. The indeterminacy of sound and the indeterminacy of sound's becoming sonic subjectivity are core drivers within the performativity of sound, and key to the manner of its simultaneous staging-sounding. I now close with the following somewhat schematic phrase about the prospect of a specifically musical Performance Philosophy constituted around the performativity of sound: entropy intervenes fatally into sound's indeterminate perdurance. This fatality deserves investigation – and celebration.

References

Adorno, Theodor. 1998. *Beethoven: The Philosophy of Music: Fragments and Texts*, trans. Edmund Jephcott. Cambridge: Polity Press.
Barenboim, Daniel. 2008. 'The Power of Music', in: idem. *Music Quickens Time*. London: Verso, pp. 3–110.
Bowie, Andrew. 2009. *Music, Philosophy, and Modernity*. Cambridge: Cambridge University Press.
Butler, Judith. 1990. *Gender Trouble: Feminism and the Subversion of Identity*. New York: Routledge.
Butler, Judith. 1993. *Bodies that Matter: On the Discursive Limits of 'Sex.'* New York: Routledge.
Chua, Daniel. 2017. *Beethoven and Freedom*. Oxford: Oxford University Press.
Cull Ó Maoilearca, Laura. 2014. 'Performance Philosophy: Staging a New Field', in: Laura Cull Ó Maoilearca & Alice Lagaay (eds.), *Encounters in Performance Philosophy*. London: Palgrave Macmillan, pp. 15–38.
Derrida, Jacques. 1982. 'Tympan', in: idem. *Margins of Philosophy*, trans. Alan Bass. Chicago: University of Chicago Press, pp. ix–xxix.
Hall, Kira. 1999. 'Performativity', *Journal of Linguistic Anthropology* 9/1–2 (June), pp. 184–187.
Hatt, Michael. 1999. 'Race, Ritual, and Responsibility: Performativity and the Southern Lynching', in: Amelia Jones & Andrew Stephenson (eds.), *Performing the Body / Performing the Text*. New York: Routledge, pp. 71–82.
Krämer, Sybille. 2014. 'Connecting Performance and Performativity: Does It Work?', in: Cull Ó Maoilearca & Alice Lagaay (eds.), *Encounters in Performance Philosophy*. London: Palgrave Macmillan, pp. 223–237.
Lacoue-Labarthe, Philippe. 1995. *Musica Ficta: Figures of Wagner*, trans. Felicia McCarren. Stanford: Stanford University Press.

Lagaay, Alice & Alice Koubová. 2014. 'Performing the Impossible in Philosophy', in Cull Ó Maoilearca & Alice Lagaay (eds.), *Encounters in Performance Philosophy*, London: Palgrave Macmillan, pp. 39–62.

Loxley, James. 2006. *Performativity*. New York: Routledge, 2006.

Lyotard, Jean-François. 1993. 'The Survivor', trans. Robert Harvey & Mark Roberts, in: idem. *Toward the Postmodern*. New Jersey: Humanities Press, pp. 144–163.

McKenzie, Jon. 2001. *Perform or Else: From Discipline to Performance*. New York: Routledge 2001.

Nancy, Jean-Luc. 2007. *Listening*, trans. Charlotte Mandell. New York: Fordham University Press.

Nietzsche, Friedrich. 2000. *The Birth of Tragedy from the Spirit of Music*, trans. Douglas Smith. Oxford: Oxford University Press, 2000.

O'Callaghan, Casey. 2007. *Sounds: A Philosophical Theory*. Oxford: Clarendon Press.

Parker Dixon, Martin. 2018. 'The Learning Community: A Quodlibet', in: Björn Heile, Eva Moreda Rodriguez & Jane Stanley (eds.), *Higher Education in Music in the Twenty-First Century*. New York: Routledge, pp. 30–54.

Spitzer, Michael. 2006. *Music as Philosophy: Adorno and Beethoven's Late Style*. Bloomington: Indiana University Press.

Zahavi, Dan. 2003. *Husserl's Phenomenology*. Stanford: Stanford University Press.

10
PERFORMANCE PHILOSOPHY AND THE PHILOSOPHY OF MEDIALITY

Jörg Sternagel, Elisabeth Schäfer and Volkmar Mühleis

In order to contour Performance Philosophy in terms of a philosophy of mediality, the following contribution aims to reflect the relationship between medium and mediality. It will be shown that this relationship can be revealed as a relation of affects and thinking. Thus, the question of what a medium is, is approached from three angles: in terms of its function as an in-between (meta), as poiesis or bringing forth (dia), and as affect and affectivity. The article focuses on the following three perspectives. First: creation. In this part, the text approaches the realm of the performative and the medial as the manner in which something appears *as* something *through* something. Second: the body as a medium, with references to Marina Abramović and Jean-Luc Nancy. Here, the body is addressed as the spacing of space that provides the interaction of the image and the body, matter and meaning, sense and sensing and is thus a medium in itself. Third: mediality in the objectified world, regarding the Western tradition as well as glimpsing at an intercultural horizon.

To ask what media philosophy is leads one to inspect its basic concepts and its respective structures, and to explore the relationship between medium and mediality. To ask what a medium is might first point us towards technical media like photography, video, audiotape, and computers, but it might also point us towards symbolic processes like communication, writing, and financial transactions, or further still towards material carriers like air, light, and water. Are the necessary conditions of a medium thereby located in the core of the relational and can this be called the in-betweenness of media? If so, then *medium* – meaning middle – would be taken to be the condition of possibility for all cultural practices, as the German media philosopher Dieter Mersch has suggested: 'Humans cannot but mediate [...]'.[1] This means that a medium cannot be conceived as independent from its mediation or medialization and vice versa. Therefore, one would have to argue for an etymological conceptualization of the medium in terms of both *meta* (in-between) and *dia* (poiesis or bringing forth). In asking what a medium is, one might therefore begin to understand it both in terms of *meta* (in-between) and *dia* (poiesis), as that which relates and affects bodies, materials, signs, contexts, and so on. Subsequently, one may come to understand the medium in terms of *affect*. What does this mean? Media have the potential to affect; this means that they set some-*thing* or some-*body* into motion. It is this quality that can be seen as the precondition for the instrumental and autonomous character of media. In this way, *affect* is the very property that all media share. One might also propose a specific philosophical framework for understanding mediation based on the figure of the messenger (Krämer 2008). According to this, the medium *presents* rather than *represents* something. From this perspective, in thinking the medium, the emphasis is on creation as the primary function of media rather than translation and transmission.

While one may say that each medium embodies a philosophy, a medium does not carry a medium theory in and of itself. As a perspective from the outside, the gesture of theory can generally be understood as being *about* something, while as an experience from the inside, philosophy is always already *part of* that which it attempts to say something about. In a similar way, what a medium is – its manner of revealing the world or transmitting something – already contains another medium. This means that media do not have to wait for philosophy in order to be conceptualized; they always already work on this conceptual task themselves. But how? How do they mediate? Is mediation a precondition for constituting something as a medium, or is it the other way around? One might point out that media should not be seen here as the object of analysis within media philosophy, but as the very *concept of the medium* and the *medial*. Media philosophy is concerned with classical epistemological questions such as: How is the world offered to us, given the fact that our environment is accessible to us through the use of a media-saturated set of technologies? Following Friedrich Kittler and his strong influence on the German-led field of media materialism, media are often seen as *materialities of communication* that generate the perceptual conditions which structure our specific access to the world. However, epistemological questions addressing media cannot be reduced to historical reconstructions of paradigmatic media shifts, such as those described by Kittler in, for instance, *Grammophon, Film and Typewriter* (1999). Rather, we need to shift the focus to a philosophy of mediality.

To ask what mediality is requires that one deal with an ensemble of structural concepts like materiality, format, functionality, intermediality, reflexivity, responsivity, and performativity. All of these concepts contribute to a gradual *uncovering* of the respective mediality of a medium: the structural organization that accompanies, frames, and enters every medial process without directly disclosing itself, be it in the form of a specific materiality, performance, technique, imagination, discourse, apparatus, or symbolic order. In other words, as soon as one decides to ask what *mediality* is, and as soon as one shifts the focus from what is experienced to *how* and *by what means* something is experienced, the very conditions of appearance come into view. This shift then acknowledges a close connection between concepts of the *performative* and the *medial* that are key features of thought in media philosophy, since both the performative and the medial situate attention *on* and *in* the world. To the extent that social, cultural, technical, and political transformations are derived from events and practices, human reality is not simply conveyed. It cannot be grasped exclusively by facts and numbers but must rather be acknowledged through reference to dynamic correlations in space and time, and to dimensions that are describable in terms of materiality, embodiment, performativity, and mediality. For we do not only speak *about* the world, in speaking we act *in* and *on* the world; we are never autonomous subjects enabled to carry out pure metatheory. We co-exist with others – even in producing theories – with other human and non-human beings. We act and react with and through various media: through language, voices, faces, bodies, and gestures. This gives rise to a host of *aisthetic* (i.e. sense-related) and ethical dimensions of the *performative* and the *medial* which unfold in – and enfold – research and teaching with regard to (non-) speaking and (non-) acting, intentionality and responsivity, being and alterity. Thinking the performative and the medial always already takes place in and through our bodily shared existence. This is a good reason to address performance as a philosophical activity in its own right.

Creation

Somewhere in Istanbul, the writer and translator Jessica Sequeira notes in her book *Other Paradises. Poetic Approaches to Thinking in a Technological Age*:

> … a curtain comes up and a pair of puppets slides into view. Behind the screen, men in caps and loose-fitting blouses move the figures with wood sticks, as they laugh quietly. A cloth has been pinned up with a rectangle cut from its center. Against the backlit paper, the dangling figures tell a story. At times the puppets move rhythmically, as if to a chant or tambourine beat. Other times they jerk abruptly, as when one of the male characters tries to imitate a female dancer's movements. Left and right, there the hips go quick. The crowd laughs, […]
>
> (Sequeira 2018, pp. 55–56)

With Sequeira, we enter a shadow play and are immediately within a realm of the performative and the medial in which something appears *as* something *through* something, in which the shadow of a puppet appears *as* a shadow of a puppet *through* the puppet, the figure on a stick, behind the cloth, the backlit paper, by the hands of its player – in this case the lead artist, the 'Haveli'. The play's two stock figures are named 'Karagöz' and 'Hacivat' who are played out in opposition to one another. While Karagöz is 'educated and elegant, trained at a Muslim theology school and fond of sprinkling classical Turkish literary references into his speeches', Hacivat is a 'man of the people, rude but straightforward, with wild schemes to make money that never get off the ground. The two men have much in common, and not just in their matching black beards, puffy hats and tunics in different shades of the same style. They share a rhythm of speaking, a certain sense of humor' (Sequeira 2018, p. 56). Structures of the performative and the medial successively become visible like this. Within these structures, the situation at hand is created, though Sequeira does not pause here; she adds a reflection on an apprentice – someone the Haveli will watch during an afternoon performance – where he 'will speak his lines in a deep voice behind the screen, as shadows accompany the puppet figures' (idem). While the Haveli is pleased to watch his apprentice perform in such a manner, it strikes him that something is missing – not something as apparent as a body part of a puppet – but something less tangible that is situated in the number of jokes the apprentice is telling, where 'the words consume those that preceded them, and are chased by a dissolve of raucous cackling' (idem). The sheer number of jokes kept in circulation makes the apprentice tired. He speaks, in search of the perfect joke to accompany his figures: 'Just one, to be told a single time or repeated. No more than that is necessary. The whole show that spools over a few useless hours could then take just one minute. All the jokes he hears now are simply sparks that fly off the absent joke' (idem, p. 57). The Haveli wonders if he is any closer to this joke than his apprentice and that question terrifies him. Paralyzed by fear, he asks what if he never finds the perfect one, although he seeks it. For him, his apprentice, and the other players, the absent joke becomes a constant shadow that accompanies the figures as they move across the screen. 'The opposite of Karagöz is not Hacivat. The opposite of both of their imperfection is the perfection of the ideal joke' (idem, p. 57). There is an absence then in making: 'to produce in an unproductive way makes one aware of what is missing in production – the *unpuppet*. There is a thing that one can never achieve, an absence one realizes is there during the process of creation' (idem, p. 57).

The body as a medium

Somewhere in the life of a young artist – one who was to become one of the most famous artists and performers of the contemporary Western world – the artist is meditating on a sky full of clouds through the windows of her studio and she is painting these clouds. All of a sudden, 12 military planes cross her view, painting 'on the sky' with various colours, an event one can experience during military parades. The artist wonders why she is painting clouds in her sketchbook and why she is not painting directly on the sky, like those planes. Because her father was a general in the military, she visits him in his barracks, asking for 12 planes to paint the sky. A request which had not been acceded. Also, since she had no chance to get the planes and to paint the sky, her understanding of how to make art changes. The artist is Marina Abramović and she tells this story in an interview given in the course of her show 'The Artist Is Present. The Body as Medium' at the Museum of Modern Art, New York, in 2010. She recalls that she stopped drawing and painting in the sketchbook and started performing and acting on stage, working with the body, and working with materiality as a medium. She says, 'I could never go back to the seclusion of the studio and be protected by the space there' (Abramović 2010).

In the Western tradition, we are used to *speaking about* the body rather than taking into account that with every speech act *about the body*, the *body itself* speaks, too. This is apparent not only when the body is the topic of our philosophical, scientific, and even artistic endeavours, we are often used to speaking *about*. *Speaking about* seems to be the dominant gesture of Western thought. We speak and think *about* the body, forgetting that in that very process, the body is present. The body even has to disappear. Yet at the same time, we are in a fundamental need of the body, of its materiality, of the senses of the body, while we are speaking and thinking and making art, and so on. Isn't it just as much the *body's* thinking and speaking and making art and the like, while we declare ourselves (our relation to the world of ideas, of the intelligible) to be the originators?

The body does not seem to be ejected completely within the framework of Western philosophy and culture, not because someone is speaking *about* the body, but because bodies are constantly uttering: themselves, something, sense/senses. Bodies *matter* (Butler 2011).

The French philosopher Jean-Luc Nancy, whose conception not to write *about* bodies but rather to let bodies write – *exscribe* themselves – becomes crucial here and evokes the planes Marina Abramović wanted to draw with. The corporal constitution of our being-in-the-world can be revealed to us as an 'ex-position' (Nancy 2008, pp. 32–35), as Nancy puts it, similar to Abramović, who wanted to leave the protected space of her studio in order to be exposed to making art. Nancy's thinking of bodies turns around the tender spot of touch, touch as the crucial trope that comes to stand in his philosophy as the side-marker of the most fundamental limits which shape and form our thinking of, and our interactions with, the world. Nancy's thinking oscillates between subject and object, inside and outside, matter and meaning, soul and body, and mind. In his text 'Corpus', he presents a contemporary and continuative interpretation of the Aristotelian position of thinking the body. As general determinations of a natural body, Aristotle specified that it is limited by its surface (Physics, III.5, 204b), it is somewhere and has a special place (ibid., III.5, 205a), it is capable of movement and has a tendency to move to its proper place (ibid., IV.1, 208b), it contains a certain space (which coincides with the body itself), and it is itself contained in another surrounding body, which is being touched by it at the place of its boundary. It is limited in its extension, as there can't be a body with limitless extension; yet, it can be divided – at least potentially – ad infinitum (ibid., III.5, 208a). To Nancy, the body is not a space within boundaries, not a mass limited by its surface. The body is rather a place of existence. The body is taking place at the limit, being exposed to an outside: "Bodies aren't some kind of fullness or filled space [...]: they are open space, [...], a space that could also be called a place. [...] Bodies are places of existence. The body makes room for existence. More precisely, it makes room for the fact that the essence of existence is to be without any essence. [...] The body is the being of existence" (Nancy 2008, p. 15). And Nancy continues: "As being existence, the body is the being exposed of the being" (ibid., p. 35). "A body is being exposed. And to be exposed, it has to be extended" (ibid., p. 124). For Nancy, bodies are both open and infinite. He writes: "As being exposed to an outside, they are open to touch and being touched. Bodies delight in touching and being touched. [...] [B]eing touched, spacing / being spaced make here the essence of the being" (ibid., p. 119). The body exposes not only the essence of being, but is also a breakthrough of sense.

In writing, at the edge of articulated language, the body touches sense and thus creates the body of sense. Sense, as the intelligible, the beginning, and the end, is floating at the limit, which is the body. "The body is the architectonics of sense" (ibid., p. 25). Nancy never gets tired of emphasizing that there is no soul apart from the body, no subject except the body itself. He quotes Freud's late note: "*Psyche ist ausgedehnt; weiß nichts davon*". / "The psyche's extended: knows nothing about it". The 'psyche', in other words, is body, and this is precisely what escapes it, and its process of escape is what constitutes it as "psyche", in a dimension of not (being able/wanting) to know itself (cf. Ibid., p. 21). So, for Nancy, the soul doesn't represent anything other than the body, but rather the body outside itself (cf. Ibid., p. 126). What has been thought under the name of soul is nothing other than the experience of the body. This experience of the body is an act of "self sensing", of touching upon the self (cf. Ibid., p. 134f.). A body touches on the outside, but at the same time, it touches itself as outside. A body accedes to itself as outside (cf. Ibid., p. 128). The soul is the being outside of a body, and it is in this being outside that it is its inside (cf. Ibid., p. 129). In other words, the soul is the difference from itself that makes the body, which Nancy equates with the Aristotelian definition of the soul as the form of a living body (cf. Ibid., p. 126). Nancy insists that we should not think of a body as taking up space. Bodies are not full. Bodies are not filled. They are actually open. Open spaces. Bodies are spaces which open space: 'It is the very plasticity of expansion, of extension according to which existences take place' (idem, p. 57). Nancy's conception of the body exists at the limits, or more precisely: Nancy's conception of the body exists *as the limit*. A limit is the side-marker between spheres. The very limit of the body or the body as the very limit recurs between sign and signification, matter and meaning, and so intelligible and sensual dimensions get in touch with each other. A transfer happens, a transfer of sense to the senses. The limit of the body recurs in the tender spot of touch. For Nancy, bodies sense themselves, which means they are only insofar as each touches upon the other and this touching is in itself the limit that marks the spacing of existence (cf. idem p. 34). It provides an opening space. Space provides transfer, transformation, translation, and transposition. An open space occurs as a fragmented space. In this space, there is space: *as a medium*, the body as the spacing of space provides, transfers, transforms, translates, and touches the interaction of the image and the body, matter and meaning, sense and sensing. It's touching. That's what it is – as a medium.

Mediality in the objectified world

Performance philosophy focuses on the relation of affects and thinking. This relationship is generated via differences between a medium and mediality. The example of Sequeira accentuated the performative, medial side of this relation, while our reflection on Nancy emphasized the medium. There is no hierarchy in this corresponding contrast. Nonetheless, there is a switch in focus between a performance with tacit philosophical connotations that Sequeira analysed, and an explicit philosophical writing, articulating certain ideas in their contexts. Philosophically, we might think of the difference between tacit, bodily knowledge – as stated by Michael Polanyi in his study *The Tacit Dimension* – and rationalized knowledge. How does performance relate to both these aspects of knowledge? And to other elements that nurture and influence knowledge such as longings, feelings, intuitions, ideas? Traditionally in philosophy, we have two positions in this respect. From the position of Socrates, we could define the theoretical knowledge of an instrument (a medium) by the practical proof of this knowledge, demonstrated by knowing how to play or to use it; in this way, the practice (the performance) is the criterion. From the position of Aristotle, we could separate practice and theory in favour of an indirect relation, regarding the question to which extent knowledge can go beyond our human dimensions, towards ontological structures. It is not necessary that both sides contradict each other, even if there are not many examples following the Socratic option of performative, practical proof if you compare it with the scholarly tradition coming from the Aristotelian one.

Beyond Socrates and Aristotle, the performative is more than a proof of knowledge and the philosophical is never separated from the human condition. Performance philosophy *shakes* both sides in the relation of the medium and mediality. Our body is already a medium, as Nancy shows, provoked by an absence – just think of the 'unpuppet' from the example of Sequeira – that stimulates a longing for a response to this provocation. The differentiation via the body (that I cannot leave, therefore I am) is mediality: the balancing of what I have to respond to, with my senses, my imagination, my thinking. We cannot live without the organ of our skin (unlike the loss of our eyes); touch is the only sense that shapes our body as a sensitive identity. Therefore, Nancy has a point in accentuating touch – but again, there is no hierarchy between the senses; this was made clear by phenomenology and Gestalt Psychology, by Maurice Merleau-Ponty (see his study *The Structure of Behavior*) and, most prominently today, by Bernhard Waldenfels (in *Phenomenology of the Alien*). So, the first field of performative and medial research in philosophy is one of affects in relation to thoughts and thinking, at all times a bodily relation, one of medialities contrasting its medium – *corpus*. At the same time, a body is not generated by itself; it is interwoven with time and space, nature and culture, the ontological horizons that Aristotle pointed at and that shifted from metaphysical belief to contemporary physics. The development of homo sapiens – the form of our head, our skeleton – went hand in hand with the way we started to walk, to orientate ourselves to the frontal view, to use not just our hands as objects, but also things as instruments, media. André Leroi-Gourhan documented this profoundly in *Gesture and Speech*. In combining phenomenological and paleontological insights, Bernard Stiegler described the mediality contrasting its medium with regard to the path of evolution (in *Technics and Time*); that with the handling of given objects, we orientated ourselves towards the world and therefore towards ourselves, and so externalizing *stimulated* internalizing. Accordingly, the question is now: to which degree do we feed our bodily mediality via an objectified world; and to which extent can we accentuate external dimensions of the body as well as internal, imaginative, thinkable perspectives? Every landscape – structured in phenomenological terms by the horizons of our awareness – is a media landscape, and is part of this orientating and resonating. Every object/source can be a sign of orientation, codification, and communication: *archi-writing*, as Jacques Derrida calls it in *Of Grammatology* (Derrida 1997, p. 178). This means that external objects can become carriers for meaning, symbolically and technically – media as fine art or media as databases, for example. The second field of performative and medial research in philosophy can be identified as this kind of 'media landscape'.

All of this may sound familiar from a Western viewpoint, but we need to be careful: there is a generalization of typically Western concepts to make anthropological statements. Nancy talked about 'existence', 'exposure', 'extension'; with Stiegler, we mentioned 'externalization', and so on. All of these terms start with the prefix 'ex-', linguistically linked to the concept of immanence versus transcendence. Then, we focused on the notion of the object. Again, this is bound by the linguistic difference between subject and object and all the thinking that begins with such a difference, even with *difference* as such, the very premise of difference being the nexus of Western, Greek-based thinking. These axioms that carry our thinking, principal ideas grounded in Greek and Latin, are the media of our own articulation in the so-called 'media landscape'. We have to be aware that our conceptions are limited: limited by the emphasis of epistemic concepts – knowledge – when compared with other possible preferences – *living*, like in the Taoist tradition that François Jullien explores with his philosophical writings (for example, in *Detour and Access*). In this tradition, our 'media landscape' is not what it seems. With this recognition, we discern a third field of performative and medial research in philosophy: the intercultural, within the large horizons of human evolution and anthropology, embedded in what is beyond us. Can we lose the notion of the object, to think of a house as a practice, for example? That the house is about change and the foundation about regulation? What is the process of making an object out of something? To draw a line, to make a distinction? What does a line *do* – in intercultural terms, what does it mean? Why did Western people design instruments, such as pencils and ball pens, appropriate for writing in the form of lines rather than use brushes, for example? How do lines affect (the content of) one's thoughts? And likewise what would be (or have been) the impact of using brushes? Following and contradicting Socrates, one might suggest that the premise of *not* knowing has to be rediscovered, shown, and explored in the practical performance of handling instruments, of handling media. That *I cannot play* is the starting point of intercultural try-outs. I cannot play, and I do not know. Please, show me. How I can *think this*?

Note

1 '*Denn der Mensch kann nicht anders als zu vermitteln*, [...]' (Mersch 2010, p. 186) translated by E. S.

References

Abramović, Marina. '*The Artist Is Present. The Body as Medium*' 14 March–31 May, 2010, online: https://www.youtube.com/watch?v=OUrwdqwzqMU, last accessed 13 February 2019.
Aristotle. 1991. *Physics,* Princeton, NJ: Princeton University Press.
Butler, Judith. 2011. *Bodies that Matter*, New York: Routledge.
Derrida, Jacques. 1997. *Of Grammatology*, Baltimore, MD: John Hopkins University Press.
Jullien, François. 2000. *Detour and Access – Strategies of Meaning in China and Greece*, Cambridge, MA: MIT Press.
Kittler, Friedrich A. 1999. *Grammophon, Film, Typewriter*, Stanford, CA: Stanford University Press.
Krämer, Sybille. 2008. *Medium, Bote, Übertragung. Kleine Metaphysik der Medialität*, Frankfurt am Main: Suhrkamp.
Leroi-Gourhan, André. 1993. *Gesture and Speech*, Cambridge, MA: MIT Press.
Merleau-Ponty, Maurice. 1968. *The Visible and the Invisible*, Evanston, IL: Northwestern University Press.
Merleau-Ponty, Maurice. 1983. *The Structure of Behavior*, Pittsburgh, PA: Duquesne University.

Mersch, Dieter. 2010. 'Meta/Dia. Zwei unterschiedliche Zugänge zum Medialen.' In: *ZMK Zeitschrift für Medien- und Kulturforschung*, 1/2: Medienphilosophie, pp. 186–210.

Nancy, Jean-Luc. 2008. *Corpus*, New York: Fordham University Press.

Polanyi, Michael. 2009. *The Tacit Dimension*, Chicago, IL: University of Chicago Press.

Sequeira, Jessica. 2018. *Other Paradises. Poetic Approaches to Thinking in a Technological Age*, Winchester/Washington, DC: Zero Books.

Stiegler, Bernard. 1998. *Technics and Time, 1 – The Fault of Epimetheus*, Stanford, CA: Stanford University Press.

Waldenfels, Bernhard. 2011. *Phenomenology of the Alien – Basic Concepts*, Evanston, IL: Northwestern University Press.

11
THE THEATRE OF RESEARCH

Anke Haarmann

In the *Berlin-Brandenburgische Akademie der Wissenschaften*, there is a picture by Eduard Ender dated 1850 and entitled "Alexander von Humboldt and Aimé Bonpland in the Amazon Jungle". It depicts the two men surrounded by their fieldwork instruments. There are measuring instruments, specimen containers and various botanic species awaiting analysis; there is a straw hat under the table, a woven basket leaning against a wooden chest, a belt with watches attached to it and other instruments on the ground by the explorers' feet; there are various boxes, bowls and magnifying glasses, and several books and papers piled up on the table. Alexander von Humboldt himself is leaning against the table, with one arm on a pile of papers, his foot on a satchel and a document (perhaps a map?) on his knee. He gazes as if into the lens of this painted snapshot, while Aimé Bonpland stands behind him on the other side of the table, looking across at his colleague; he has a plant specimen in his hand. The hut is a half-open shelter, looking out onto a bright tropical landscape with palm trees and, far off in the distance, karst rock faces, while inside the hut, the explorers lounge in the shade. An unreal ray of light falls upon Humboldt, bringing him into the spotlight; it is a theatre of research and exploration that is depicted here.

This article engages with the staged quality, the insight-generating performativity of exploration or research.[1] At first glance, therefore, it is not performative philosophy as such that is my focus here, but an understanding of the exploration of nature as a performative practice. However, this understanding of natural science as a performative practice suggests an inspiring relationship with both performative philosophy and artistic research. For the stage set of natural science allows for the notion that research in general takes place as a practice by way of the active aesthetic staging of explorers, objects and modes of understanding. It is this aesthetic-performative practice that turns the exploration of nature into an artistic practice. That is to say that artistic practice and the practice of research or exploration merge at the node of epistemic staging. This aesthetic-performative practice of natural science suggests that scientific research as a whole, as well as philosophy, can be considered in terms of a performative exploration of thinking.

In order to open up this horizon of an aesthetic-performative practice of research, I would like to return for a moment to the forefather of modern-day fieldwork portrayed in the painting, illuminated by an imaginary spotlight and surrounded by the various props of his jungle laboratory. Addressing his virtual audience, Humboldt presents the spectacle

Figure 11.1 Alexander von Humboldt and Aimé Bonpland in the Amazon Jungle. Painting by Eduard Ender, 1850

of exploration with himself as the central protagonist surrounded by an artful composition of his explorer's objects: a carefully staged snapshot of both his active engagement with the diversity of nature, and a certain dignified aloofness from the jungle of tropical truths.

The paintings depicting Humboldt and Bonpland on their journey through South America were created at a later date in Europe on the basis of their travel reports and surely embellished by the painter's imagination. The scene that is shown here, however, is especially noteworthy from an epistemological perspective. The jumble of fruits, leaves, sextants and documents depicted in the painting does not so much evoke the orderly analysis of nature but present, rather, a complex mixture of utensils, artefacts, documents and explorers. The illustrator of this scene obviously wanted to portray fieldwork as an active practice, a staged enactment that emphasizes the aesthetic-performative signature of research or exploration.

The empirical exploration of nature – the painting speaks to us thus – is both a productive and an aesthetic practice, one in which the skilful arrangements of butterfly nets, microscopes, sextants, as well as herbariums, pens and pencils play just as eminent a role on the path to knowledge as do the human assistants and beasts of burden involved in such fieldwork. Inspired by this insight, one could open up the horizon of all research and suggest that the conceptual research at work in theoretical argument is also both a productive and an aesthetic practice within which the arrangement of books, writing implements, gestures of explanation and authority in speech are just as relevant to research in terms of epistemology as its rhetoric or pure argument. Considered in this way, both empirical and conceptual research would share this aesthetic-performative signature in their respective spheres of action.

The insight into the performative and aesthetic process of nature exploration as creative action is also apparent in many other works of art that focus on research situations. Perhaps art is especially suited not only for portraying the aesthetic-performative character of research and exploration but for recognizing this quality in the first place, since aesthetic-performative arrangements are in the specific domain of art, and it therefore sees its own reflection in the aesthetic-performative action of exploration. Indeed, perhaps we need art in order to identify the practical-aesthetic character of exploration and to provide us with a suitable instrument of insight into research as practice.

The installation works of the artist Mark Dion also focus on the orchestrated staged actions of fieldwork. Dion has built his spatial installations as scenarios that appear as three-dimensional still lives on the theme of modern-day expeditions. His depiction of the arena of the natural sciences suggests the explorer's imminent entrance. Dion's installation sets are snapshots that are at the same time frozen and arranged – as in the unloading of scientific utensils from a ship onto the land to be explored, or in the construction of a research station by the riverside in the jungle. The patina of the objects that make up the installation evokes fantasies of concrete density: trunks, barrels, ropes, baskets, used for mobile stockpiling and the handling of transportation point to the travelling situation the explorers are in. The rigour of scientific research is conveyed by designated instruments, nets, flasks with specimens in formaldehyde or notepads, all of which serve the purpose of collecting, observing, recording and conserving. The stage set of fieldwork is complemented by traces of everyday life, by which the contingency of the research situation is set in scene. Any notion that pure and unadulterated research results are developed from scientific facts alone is undermined by the metonymical juxtaposition of commonplace items of everyday use, such as pieces of clothing, shaving utensils, spectacle cases, items of travel and objects of science. In observing this scene, one imagines the sweaty cloth of linen as integral to the specimen; one understands the desire for clean water as integral to the butterfly hunt. As an artistic installation, the objects in the arrangement expose the situational truth of any research mission as a mix-up. Mixed in with the research subject are objects, patina, scientific claims, ways of life, as well as the technology of the instruments. Research – this is the message of this artistic installation – is never intellectually pure but always physically imbued within its surroundings. Datasets and thought alone are not the sources of knowledge but, rather, personal involvement with the matter and the staged presentation of the act of exploration.

In this work by Mark Dion, the arrangement of objects conveys an artistic claim about research as practice. It suggests that the research situation early explorers found themselves in was indeed quite a muddle. But Dion's artistic work does not assert this by conceptual means. It is by rendering visible the dense sequence of semantically rich objects involved in the process that he shows how explorative fieldwork has always involved the journeying of living human beings and that like the unthought variables in an equation, these factors – the journey factor and the human factor – have a considerable impact on the results of the research by the simple fact that they exist. Dion's installations "exemplify" – as the theoretician of symbols, Nelson Goodman, would call this manner of symbolic referencing – the existence of the many objects in a situation of plenty as the ineluctable reality of all research situations. By way of their presentation mode, Dion's installations thus claim that the dissected specimens under the microscope certainly do not represent the whole story.

The success of Dion's installations in the world of art rather than, say, in the sociology of science corresponds to the charming antiquity of his scenarios and the historicizing romanticism it evokes. See against the backdrop of our 21st-century expectations, his installations, with their brittle leather trunks, dented metal tubes for optical instruments and damaged butterfly nets, Dion's installations have something of the same effect on us as the delightful images of children in the shaky super 8 movies of bygone days. Is it only the early days of fieldwork that can be viewed as aesthetically staged in the manner described? Are performative perspectives only to be found in the practices of such explorers, and is, therefore, the idea that the general practice of research is both productive and aesthetic but a remnant of an outdated romanticism?

Dion, I believe, forfeits some of the epistemological poignancy that his artistic work could have because he diminishes the relevance of the research practice he articulates by situating it in a long-gone era and drawing on the patina of past centuries. Indeed, his artistic installations do not disturb the disembodied claim of scientific research. The notion that 18th- and 19th-century explorers were not in a position to conduct their work in a neat and objective manner because science was still in its infancy does nothing to trouble, as it were, the methodical character of fieldwork as such. The objects in his installations hail from the modern beginnings of scientific exploration and nothing in the works themselves points to the fact that purity of research is indeed a systematic myth or that its imperfections are not limited to a historical interim that with the refinement of instruments could evaporate not only transform.

The observation of a Dion installation can be likened to a visit to an antique shop for romantically inclined fans of Alexander von Humboldt; it would primarily seem to be about the decorative, artisanal and haptic aspects of the exhibits.

However, in a series of performative excavation projects, Dion tackles the theme of fieldwork in a manner that is focused on action rather than installation. Of particular relevance in this regard is his *Raiding Neptune's Vault: A Voyage to the Bottom of the Canals and Lagoon of Venice*, which was created in the context of the 1997 Venice Biennale. As the name suggests, this performative piece centres on the excavation of mud sediment from the canals and the lagoon of Venice. The mud was filled into containers and then explored for all manner of objects by the artist Dion, clad in a white apron and wearing gloves. He collected algae, crustacae and worms, as well as bits of plastic, ceramic shards and pieces of metal. Whether it was a historically significant cultural artefact, or a cheap plastic trinket, an object of culture or a product of nature, dead or alive – anything distinguishable as something apart from the mud was transferred to the *laboratory*, a small room where all objects were cleaned and categorized according to a variety of criteria. Some of the objects were eventually presented in the *treasure cabinet*, but the *laboratory* was also part of the Venice exhibition, showing the objects the artist had found at the various stages of cleansing, collecting, sorting and presentation. By its performative design, the "raiding of Neptune's vault" presents itself as a procedure or treatment, as a sequence of actions or a form of processing. The performance represents a handling in the course of which utensils regurgitated and shaped by the amorphous mud of the lagoon are distilled and transformed into objects of display. In Venice, Dion staged a metamorphosis in which not only the objects of archaeological desire become visible, but the very work of handling these objects presents itself, *performs* itself, in action, work that is necessary so that the transformation of primordial mud into a select item of research can occur. Two central aspects in the set of actions by which archaeological objects are transformed are (i) the process of cleaning, i.e. of identifying and separating that which belongs to the object from that which is superfluous, and (ii) the allocating of value to individual objects by way of their categorization. A certain hierarchy of value is made evident as a procedure of decision-making in the transition from *laboratory* to *treasure cabinet*. Archaeological research is thus a performative-productive process; such is the insightful result conveyed by this work of art, which lifts this very process of the refinement of things from dirty to clean, from chaos to order, onto the performative stage, thereby bringing it into full view.

Like a chemist in a laboratory situation, Dion reproduces an assumed or imagined procedure and thereby demonstrates its existence. The activity of research thus really exists; not as an activity that merely discovers facts, but as a process that in working on these facts establishes them, and brings them into existence, as relevant. The excavation performance shows how the value of epistemic facts is in fact created. As with the value of an object of art, the value of scientific things is determined by the symbolic character they take on as findings or artefacts in a collection. As collectors' items – *pars pro toto* – they represent an abstract whole, of which they are the trace or imprint, and indeed the value of which can be understood *because* of them. No scientific thing created from an active scientific process stands for itself alone or for its own singular profane materiality. It points to a wider system of references and meanings – it becomes abstract by its incorporation into a family of scientific findings and objects of study. The patterned piece of porcelain thus refers to porcelain culture as a whole and to the artisanal developmental level of an entire epoch. The condensed fragment of sediment therefore also points to the climatic situation at the time of its creation. These objects have become referential symbols as a result of the action of research. Research is quite obviously a performative practice dedicated to the creation of symbols and values. Its action works on a similar terrain as that of art. By the performative repetition of the research practice, art is therefore able to paradigmatically enact this practical, performative and symbol-producing dimension of *research as art*. The actively selective, dramaturgical and performative-aesthetic process of understanding the world is thus made visible by means of the artistic re-enactment of research activity. Art turns this process, which has perhaps so far been overlooked or taken for granted, into an exclamation mark. Artistic performance ostensibly refers to the performative-aesthetic practice by which research takes place. As an aesthetic-performative practice, the practice of research is obviously also an artistic practice and the process of scientific research comes together with the artistic process in the realm of the aesthetic. This raises the question of the epistemic dimensions of this process. The formative, dramaturgical and performative-aesthetic quality of scientific research also leads to a second question, which is whether there are perhaps actively formative, dramaturgical and performative dimensions to *any* understanding of the world.

If this is the case, then even theoretical thought can be seen as a method, as a presentational sequence of actions, that is, as creative processing. In the laboratory of the study or library, at the scholar's writing desk, theoretical thought thus draws out figures from the amorphous metaphorical mud, the white noise of cultural discourse, distilling lines of argument and transforming them into clear reasons. These, too, are then *presented*, not in display cabinets but in respected publications and at prestigious conferences. And so, here too, along with the cleansing of thoughts from discursive contamination as a process of separating what belongs from what is superfluous to it, the essential factor of this method of producing clean figures of argumentation by thought is the valorization of any assertions by means of classification.

Philosophers are surely masters in the active creation of categories and the formation of concepts in which thoughts can be placed and kept as if in a treasure cabinet. The thinking exploration of the cultural pool of concepts becomes understandable too in its affinity with artistic action against the backdrop of this aesthetically active signature of its own practice – just as, in reverse, artistic action can explain the aesthetic-performative dimension of empirical and conceptual research.

In a final examination of empirical, conceptual and artistic research, I propose to return to the study of another work of art. This time, the focus is on the political dimension of the performative aspects of research. The rendering visible and the recognition of aesthetic-performative action do indeed imply a politics of the epistemic as well as a politics of power strategy.

Like Mark Dion, Critical Art Ensemble engages in an artistic exploration of scientific research. This group of artists analyses the research practices of the natural sciences by way of artistic imitation. Their performances and installations involve the public display of experimental arrangements. They usually address those research contexts that are particularly controversial with regard to politics, especially the politics of power, those that would seem to require the scrutiny of the wider public. Their project *Target Deception* is about military research into biological weapons.

During the performance of *Target Deception* in Leipzig in 2007,[2] Steve Kurtz, a member of Critical Art Ensemble, stated in front of a camera that he was rather pleased with the bacteria experiment that his group had just put on display. He added that while the experiment had made the impression of being successful in terms of performance, if held to account by scientific criteria, it would probably be deemed a failure. As Kurtz spoke, a marching band was playing in the public square in front of the Leipzig town hall, lined up next to a row of human testees. The performance exemplified the dramaturgical character of scientific experiments. In contrast to science institute researchers, the artists had put the experimental research setup on public display, thereby revealing to the viewers the spectacular aspects of experiments, which would otherwise normally take place behind closed doors or in secret locations. The aesthetic, performative, dramaturgical and active aspects of research all regularly take place in hidden locations, and are then obscured by the cleansed lines of argument in the science journals in which the findings are officially published against the backdrop of a claim to scientific objectivity.

Critical Art Ensemble radicalizes this theme by publicly re-enacting military experiments. At first glance, these experiments concern an analysis of the spread of bacteria. How do bacteria cultures act when sprayed into the air space? How do they spread in an urban cityscape? These questions are not only relevant for basic research but also for the effective military use of biological weapons. The artistic setting for the Leipzig performance envisaged that bacteria cultures would be deliberately sprayed from the medieval spire of the Leipzig town hall by members of the artist collective. In this operation, Critical Art Ensemble took

Figure 11.2 Critical Art Ensemble Target Deception. Video Stills. Critical Art Ensemble http://critical-art.net/target-deception-2007/

on the role of the scientific lab managers, and its members were accordingly dressed in white lab coats. The picturesque town hall spire was to symbolize that political power whose hegemony finances, organizes and implements scientific experiments. To epitomize the military interest of experimenting with bacteria in urban space, a dressed-up military band played in marching formation. The testees were all students who assumed the bacteria to be harmless specimens of their kind. They were key to studying the precipitation and spread of the microorganisms. After the release of the bacteria, their clothing was scanned. In the artistic setup, however, no bacteria were detected on the testees; whatever had been sprayed had basically vanished into thin air. Finding micro cultures on the testees' clothing would have been a success in terms of the scientific problem and military interests. In that case, the release and the subsequent detection of the cultures would have been in a verifiable and viable context. The Leipzig wind, however, had blown the bacteria away, so there was no sign of a controlled contamination of the urban air space – just as there would have been in a real experiment, says Steve Kurtz from Critical Art Ensemble. The ambivalence between a pretty performance and the defective experiment addressed by the artist constitutes, in fact, the success of the artistic research and an essential aspect of that event. Even without the deliberate undermining of the scientific experiment by the artists, their performative presentation was all about making the deficient test results visible. Even though the scientific setup of the experiment was accurately re-enacted in all its formal elements, the experiment still failed, albeit in a scientifically correct manner, just as in a scientific institution where experiments regularly fail because of nature's unpredictability but without tainting anyone's belief in the objectivity of science.

Of course, in the sciences in general, error rates are neither sufficiently presented nor as openly communicated as they are in this work of art, whose purpose is to explore the practices of research in a performative light. The people who happened to be present (willingly to see the art piece or by chance) in the urban space of Leipzig at the time warranted a public scrutiny that is simply not there in cases of military research which are carried out in secret. Those present were able to consider whether scientific experiments are successful when they are conducted under real-life conditions and when there is a clearly recognizable interest guiding the research setup. By way of its re-enactment study of the theatrical character of research, the artist collective reveals the insight that the creation of knowledge is an orchestration guided by interests. But that insight, made perceptible in the urban space, should not unsettle us; such is the ironically cheerful message of the artist collective to the critical audience. For the practical use of supposedly objective research, results would have failed anyway due to the chaotic system of reality.

The artistic reasoning of Critical Art Ensemble employs the two classic tools of persuasion found in the arsenal of natural science, both of which are also artistic methods: an experimental setting and testimony. Scientific research results are generated on the stage of the laboratory and in the context of precisely arranged setups which then obtain their validity through collective observation by an audience of witnesses. These results have to be comprehensible for the collective. During a real military weapons research project, the collective of witnesses would involve a minimum number of observers, who would all be obliged to keep whatever they observed secret. In the civil sciences, similarly, the witness stand usually consists of a select circle of experts. While the regular scientific lab stage can thus be likened to a chamber play, Critical Art Ensemble expands this closed circle by staging the experiment for the general public. They exhibit a scientific experimental setup as an art installation and performance. The scrutinizing public can thus not only follow, validate or reject the spectacle of staging the experiment, but they can also behold the theatrical character of research itself. Content and form of experimentation are put on display and checked for plausibility during the show. Employing the mimicking practices of artistic dramatization and scenic installation, research itself is systematically explored as a performative practice and shown to an expanded critical audience of witnesses. With its themes and its artistic methods, Critical Art Ensemble confirms in an exemplary manner these assertions regarding the performativity of knowledge. Beyond the performative-aesthetic signature of research methods, this work of art also shows clearly the scientific process of cleansing, by which the dramaturgical, the actively formative, the performatively active and the selectively chosen aspects of research are clearly separated from the research results. Furthermore, this process not only ignores the performativity of research but also obscures its politics. The intentionality and situatedness, which the performative not only contains but also actively displays, are blanked out by a cleansed understanding of empirical or conceptual knowledge. This not only contradicts the facticity of the performative, which has been mapped out with artistic references here, but also what we expect from research: that there be no pretence that it is not a show.

Translated from the German by Niels Barmeyer and Alice Lagaay

Notes

1. It is perhaps noteworthy that the German term "Forschung" is very much infused by the scientific claim to discover something. This differentiates it from the English or French terms "research" and "recherche", which tend to denote a more preliminary and therefore less ambitious quest. The term is here therefore sometimes translated as "exploration", e.g. when it refers to scientific endeavours that include aspects of fieldwork, and as "research" when a more general scientific practice is intended.
2. See http://critical-art.net/target-deception-2007/

PART II

Questions and debates

12

OPENING THE CIRCLE, TOWARDS A RADICAL EQUALITY
Performance philosophy and animals

Laura Cull Ó Maoilearca

Prelude: In Circles

What if, I begin at the end?
 What if, I put the cart before the horse?
 Then we might begin here: in circles.

Consider philosophy an expanding circle.

Consider performance an expanding circle.

The etymology of the English word centre (n.) comes from the Latin *centrum*, originally the fixed point of the two points of a drafting compass, and from the Greek *kentron* meaning "sharp point, goad, sting of a wasp".

The centre is a middle point of a circle: the point around which something revolves. But the centre is also pointed and sharp – that which goads moving bodies in a particular direction.

The goad is a traditional farming implement: a spiked stick used to spur or guide livestock, for instance, to round up cattle. The elephant goad or bullhook is a tool employed in the training of elephants. It consists of a metal hook attached to a handle.

The Greeks, we are told, used the phrase "kicking against the goad" as a proverb to teach us about the foolishness of resistance against a powerful authority: those who place themselves at the centre.

Consider attention as the interval between the two points of a compass.

> My present, at this moment, is the sentence I am pronouncing. But it is so because I want to limit the field of my attention to my sentence. This attention is something that can be made longer or shorter, like the interval between two points of a compass … an attention which could be extended indefinitely would embrace, along with the preceding sentence, all the anterior phrases of the lecture and the events which preceded the lecture, and as large a portion of what we call our past as desired. The distinction we make between our present and past is therefore, if not arbitrary, at least relative to the extent of the field which our attention to life can embrace.
>
> *(Bergson 2014, p. 320)*

Figure 12.1 A photograph of the author, age 17, just before leaving to go to art school. Authors own

Extending the compass, when I left school, I remember being called to the headmistress' office, where she asked: "Are you sure you want to go to art school? Wouldn't it be better to go and study English or History first, and then do art later?". Then, when I arrived at art school, the head of the painting department told me that I was 'over-intellectualizing' my practice. Now, I see that these are 'the little machinations and less explicit forms of denigration' that have rendered artists stupid – presenting themselves under the guise of helping us to get our priorities right, or even under the noble motive of protecting the distinctiveness of art from an encroaching academicism. And so you find me, at this moment, with the sense of having come full circle in relation to my own past. I began as an artist. I tried to be an artist-researcher. I became an academic by accident. And now, I find myself learning to become a researcher-artist, or perhaps, unlearning in order to become a performance philosopher.

Introduction

In this text, I would like to consider the relationships between performance, philosophy and animals – investigating how performance might transform philosophy, and how performance might be transformed by the animal. I undertake this work in the context of the emerging field of international research and creative practice called "Performance Philosophy". Emerging from around 2012, Performance Philosophy is 'a discipline in its first becomings' (Henao-Castro 2017). Neither a sub-field of (particularly philosophically engaged) Theatre and Performance Studies, nor a marginal branch of extant Philosophy, Performance

Philosophy has cultivated itself as an independent domain and as a community not only of academics but professional practitioners working across a range of contexts, including but not limited to institutional ones. In this respect, as Street, Alliot and Pauker (2017) have argued, Performance Philosophy is not merely an interdisciplinary experiment within the confines of the academy. Rather, the expansion of the field manifests a shared sense of urgency around the need to reinvent our knowledge practices in relation to the forms of thought they tend to devalue, marginalize or exclude.

In this context, the real stakes of Performance Philosophy lie in its foregrounding of and contribution to much wider trans-disciplinary concerns to articulate and enact a new, more egalitarian paradigm for research beyond that of 'application'. There is an emerging consensus amongst researchers concerned with the relationship between philosophy and the arts that scholars must find alternatives to the mutual instrumentalization and disciplinary inequalities that arise from the application paradigm that has historically dominated approaches to aesthetics and arts theory. Whether in relation to Theatre and Performance (Cull 2012, Fisher 2015, Hollinghaus and Daddario 2015), Music (Bowie 2007), Film (Mullarkey 2009; Sinnerbrink 2011), Dance (Cvejić 2015) or interdisciplinary arts practices (Manning and Massumi 2014), contemporary philosophers and theorists are increasingly calling for a philosophy *from* rather than *about* the arts, insofar as the latter tends to reproduce the hierarchies between philosophy and the arts as modes of knowledge. At the heart of this call, for many, is the view that the arts themselves are philosophical, can do philosophy or can make an independent contribution to philosophy, above and beyond their capacity to serve as applications or illustrations of pre-existing philosophical ideas or examples used to justify ontological claims. The rise of 'artistic research' or 'practice as research' particularly foregrounds this need for a 'performance philosophy' attentive to how performance thinks, rather than a 'philosophy of performance' that asserts the authority of its way of thinking over others. Indeed, Freddie Rokem has suggested that the question of how, or in what ways, performance thinks constitutes one of 'the most urgent issues on the agenda of today's institutions of higher education' (Rokem 2010, p. 5).

My own recent research has been particularly engaged with the work of contemporary French philosopher, François Laruelle, as a key thinker of the problem of application and the equality of knowledge. Specifically, I am interested in how Laruelle's 'non-standard philosophy' (or 'non-philosophy') provides an important model for Performance Philosophy both in terms of method and ethico-political stance. As one of the most avowedly performative of any philosopher alive today – characterizing thought as a performative practice operating 'alongside' the Real rather than as a transcendent description of it – Laruelle's work holds a particular significance for Performance Philosophy. The very call for a 'performance philosophy' rather than a philosophy *of* performance is – in some respects – a direct response to Laruelle's insistence on 'an art of thought rather than a thought about art' (Laruelle 2012a, p. 5). As Tony Fisher has argued, Laruelle's notion of the equality of thought indicates 'the radical ambition of performance philosophy', even though 'the scope of that ambition has perhaps not yet been fully assayed, interrogated or understood' (Fisher 2015, p. 176). And indeed, there is much work to do to consider the crucial resources non-philosophy provides to advance the field's core concern to move "beyond application" as a dominant paradigm for the encounter between performance and philosophy by investigating both the philosophical dimensions of the performing arts, and the performative dimensions of philosophy, thought and knowledge-production.

However, my own particular concern at present is to emphasize that Laruelle's is a call for a "*radical* equality" of knowledge that obliges us to investigate how performance philosophy might operate not only as a thought beyond application, but as a thought beyond *anthropocentric* notions of equality too. That is, as Laruelle scholars (Kolozova 2010; Ó Maoilearca 2015; Smith 2015) have already begun to demonstrate, Laruelle's non-standard philosophy also has major implications for the nonhuman and animal studies. Laruelle proposes a radical equality between all forms of thought – even to the extent of no longer seeing the 'love of wisdom' (philo-sophia) as exclusive to the human or Homo sapiens (the 'wise man'). Consequently, whilst mainstream debate around equality often focuses on the idea of a universal humanity, I want to suggest that Performance Philosophy must turn its attention to the thought of nonhuman animals in order to perform a radical extension of the idea of equality itself: animals being those 'others' most like 'us' who are nonetheless not 'us'. As theatre-maker, Rajni Shah, (2018) has discussed, the etymology of the 'radical' suggests a movement of going back to the root of something. Likewise, the use of the term 'radical' in my title is not intended to imply an 'extreme' or real equality. Rather, radical equality indicates a self-referential and two-way movement: a mode of inclusion beyond application and appropriation, which introduces a mutation into the very notion of equality. As I'll expand on in what follows, I am currently in the early stages of a collaboration with the UK-based performance company Fevered Sleep on the project *Sheep Pig Goat* in which I want to explore how interspecies performance might operate as a radically equalizing process insofar as the animal is empowered to mutate our understanding of performance. According to a radical equality, performance would not be applied to the animal as the object of study; rather, it would signal that nonhuman animals are encountered as equal performers and thinkers with the capacity to change our very concepts of performance and thought. If there is a growing consensus of the need to move "beyond application", then perhaps there is also a shared sense of urgency across the field of the need to decentre the human from/in theatre and performance – to displace performance from what Una Chaudhuri calls 'the anthropocentric grammar of the "normal"' (Chaudhuri 2016, p. 1).

In the first instance, reading Laruelle has provided me with some resources to articulate my objections to recent writing about performance by philosophers and to challenge the performative subordination of the arts to philosophy enacted by so much standard philosophical aesthetics whether Anglo-American or European. To give just one recent example: according to Tzachi Zamir, the philosophy of theatre 'is not merely a description' of theatrical practice; rather, 'it undertakes to unearth the more abstract underpinnings of a practice, ones that', he suggests, 'even its best practitioners risk misrepresenting… What a philosophy of art promises […] an artist is […] a greater insight into what one does' (Zamir 2014, p. 7). Indeed, at times, Zamir even goes as far as to exclude the practice of theatrical acting from the category of thought entirely: pronouncing that while 'philosophy thinks, acting does' (ibid., p. 218). On further analysis, what becomes clear is that this gesture of authority is made possible by a reductive essentializing of thought, in its fullest sense, as essentially linguistic, and intrinsically linked to verbal language (p. 58). Whilst acting may be graciously assigned a power to touch 'what really exists', the philosopher of theatre reserves the right for his own thought to declare that acting is 'first and foremost an experience rather than a mode of knowing' (p. 218), an experience from which no thought or at best 'half-thoughts' might surface without the aid of philosophy's superior knowledge.

Part 1. The non-philosophy of François Laruelle

Consider philosophy an expanding circle and non-philosophy as one procedure through which its qualitative extension might be performed.

Laruelle's project – what he calls 'non-philosophy' or 'non-standard philosophy' – is not an anti-philosophy, nor a call for the negation of philosophy. Rather, the 'non' in non-philosophy is intended to signal the radical extension of philosophy – though not according to some rampant imperialism, or an ever-expanding application of philosophy as we know it to some new unsuspecting terrain. Instead, if non-philosophy is an extension of philosophy, it is an extension that entails a mutation or transformation of philosophy by other knowledges – including, potentially, performance. As John Ó Maoilearca suggests: 'Whereas standard philosophical approaches take their conception of what proper philosophy is and then apply it to all and sundry objects… non-philosophy is a "style of thought" that mutates with its object' (Ó Maoilearca 2015, p. 13).

Laruelle's non-philosophy seems an especially pertinent model for Performance Philosophy, in part, because of the way he characterizes non-philosophy itself: not as an abstract theory, but as an experimental practice – and specifically, in the case of his non-standard aesthetics, as an art. Experiment is key to non-philosophy as 'the manner of thinking that does not know *a priori* what it is to think' (Laruelle 2012b, p. 67) – as that which seeks to move beyond the application of thought to the Real, in favour of a practice that affirms the Real as that which produces thought performatively. An expanded concept of performance – which includes but also extends beyond the performing arts and the attendant notion of the performative, are clearly core concerns of the Laruellean project, particularly in terms of its emphasis on philosophy itself as an immanent, performative practice that operates 'according to' the Real rather than as its transcendent description of it. Indeed, Laruelle characterizes thought as 'a style, a posture' (Laruelle 2013, p. xxi), a bodily 'stance' (ibid., p. 85) and as a matter of 'comportment' (ibid., p. 23), in a manner that suggests a connection to the embodied arts of performance. As philo-fiction, for instance, non-philosophy operates as a non-representational mode of performance – a form of invention that is both immanent and real, rather than a performance or fictionalizing 'of' some prior reality. Or, as Laruelle puts it: 'To the widespread question: what is it to think?, non-philosophy responds that thinking is not "thought", but performing, and that to perform is to clone the world "in-Real"' (Laruelle 2012a, p. 233).

Laruelle's work aims to democratize or equalize the relationship that philosophy has to other forms of thought, including the arts. His non-philosophical project is an attempt to perform a qualitative extension of the category of thought without any one kind of thinking positioning itself as its exemplary form that, therefore, is in a position to police the inclusion and exclusion or relative status of other thoughts within the category. The discipline of Philosophy has often sought to play this authoritarian role, Laruelle claims. For Laruelle, standard philosophy involves the gesture wherein thought withdraws from the world in order to occupy a position of authority or power in relation to it. Or as he puts it: 'To philosophise on X is to withdraw from X; to take an essential distance from the term for which we will posit other terms' (Laruelle 2012b, p. 284). Laruelle argues that 'we must first change the very concept of thought, in its relations to philosophy and to other forms of knowledge' (p. 232). According to this democracy of thinking, the call is not 'to think without philosophy but to think without the authority of philosophy' (Laruelle 2006, np).

As Smith (2016) suggests, Laruelle's project has two main components, a critical one and a constructive one. The critical one is – to simplify – a critique of philosophical authority that includes a strong critique of the philosophy of art. Laruelle argues against philosophy functioning as explanatory commentary on works of art – suggesting that the arts 'must be delivered of its philosophical interpretations' (Laruelle 2011, p. 17). Here, Laruelle's critique is aimed not only at philosophers, but also at 'their shadows in the Humanities' (p. 51) – who claim to know art 'better than it knows itself' (p. 55). However, he is not against the possibility of producing theory in relation to art per se; rather, the constructive moment comes through his proposal for a non-standard aesthetics. Here, he promotes an approach that treats the arts as 'the equivalent of a discovery, an emergent novel' that gives rise to theory, though not as some mere 'cause' (p. 70). Standard aesthetics, Laruelle argues:

> is the claimed domination of philosophy over art by which philosophy claims to unpack its meaning, truth, and destination… In its least aggressive, least legislative form, philosophy describes art's figures, eras, its styles, the formal systems according to philosophy's own norms. Art, for its part, resists this enterprise and rebels. We propose another solution that, without excluding aesthetics, no longer grants it this domination of philosophical categories over works of art, but limits it in order to focus on its transformation.
> *(2012a, p. 1)*

For Laruelle, art is 'thought *circularly*' in standard philosophical aesthetics (Laruelle 2011, p. 142 – emphasis added). The aim of his own non-aesthetics is to think art 'outside every vicious circle' (ibid., 4), according to a radical extension of art to philosophy: 'the moment when thought in its turn becomes a form of art' (2012a, p. 2). Non-standard aesthetics involves 'the reciprocal determination of art and philosophy' (p. 1). Laruelle asks:

> Can aesthetics become a second power of art itself, can an art engender or determine its own aesthetics instead of suffering it as being philosophically imposed upon it? These formulations are not entirely precise for what we name… thought-art, which is… not a conceptual art, but a concept modeled by the art, a generic extension of art.
> *(2012a, p. 5)*

Indeed, of particular interest to this context, perhaps, are the ways in which Laruelle conceives the relationship between the roles of artist and theorist or philosopher. Let me quote him at length:

> The reciprocal autonomy of art and theory signifies that we [philosophers] are not the doubles of artists, that we also have a claim to 'creation', and that inversely, artists are not the inverted doubles of aestheticians and that they, too, without being theorists, have a claim to the power of theoretical discovery. We recognize that they have a place all the more solitary, and we receive from them the most precious gift, that we will cease to make commentaries on them and to submit them to philosophy so as finally not to 'explain' them but, on the basis of their discovery taken up as a guiding thread (or, if you like, as cause) to follow the chain of theoretical effects that it sets off in our current knowledge of art, in what is conventional and stereotypical in it, fixed in an historical or obsolete state of invention and of its spontaneous philosophy. To mark its theoretical effects in excess of all knowledge.
> *(2011, p. 71)*

But now, if Laruelle's non-philosophy is 'the manner of thinking that does not know *a priori* what it is to think' (Laruelle 2012b, p. 67), then its key interpreters are increasingly suggesting that it is also the mode of thought that does not know what the human means. While standard philosophy has constantly aimed to define the human, Laruelle suggests that, "what is needed is a reflection upon the non-separability of man and animal, and on the animal as,

Figure 12.2 *Sheep Pig Goat*, Wellcome Collection and Fevered Sleep. Image by Ben Gilbert for Wellcome

at once, model for man and clone of man" (Laruelle in Ó Maoilearca 2015, p. 188). Likewise, Laruelle is clear that: "thought is not the intrinsic property of humans that must serve to define their essence… it is a uni-versal milieu". A growing number of commentators agree that there might be a basis for animalizing Laruelle's non-philosophy – proposing that:

> alongside asking the question "how do some thoughts come to be seen as philosophical while others do not?" (the Laruellean norm, so to speak), we are behooved to ask the following: "how do some individuals come to be seen as humans while others do not?"
>
> *(Ibid., p. 188)*

In this respect, we might think of the 'non' in the term 'non-human' as operating in parallel to the non in non-philosophy: not as a negation of the human, then, but such that we might think of 'animals as nonstandard, or extended, humans' (p. 184). To see the human in the animal is what we normally call anthropomorphism. But such standard definitions assume we know the human when we see it; we must know what constitutes a human characteristic in order to project it onto the animal.

Part 2. Fevered Sleep's *Sheep Pig Goat*

Consider performance an expanding circle. In which the animal animalizes performance.

Last year, I was a research advisor on *Sheep Pig Goat* – a project by the UK-based company Fevered Sleep, commissioned by the Wellcome Collection as part of their year-long *Making Nature* programme which explored the relationship between perception and knowledge in human–animal relationships, along with all the attendant issues of mastery, anthropomorphism and anthropocentrism inevitably raised by the human production of knowledge about animals. Described by the company as a 'creative research studio', *Sheep Pig Goat* involved a week-long public presentation of 'a series of improvised encounters between human performers and animal spectators': specifically, some sheep, pigs and goats. Originally, the idea was to make a performance for an animal audience staged in the galleries at the Wellcome, a bit like Laurie Anderson's 'Concert for Dogs', perhaps. But gradually the company moved away from this towards plans for a project which would offer human visitors what director, David Harradine, describes as a space in which to 'properly, respectfully and carefully observe animals watching a performance and reflect and report back on what they've seen, whether it's the body language of a pig or a goat' (Harradine in Gardner 2017). For Harradine: 'humans do a really bad job of paying attention', and so the project was conceived as giving both the company and a wider public the opportunity to attend to animals, but also to attend to animals as themselves engaged in processes of attending, rather than as the mere objects of human observation. In particular, Harradine implies, humans have become highly selective in our perception of human–animal continuity – not least, perhaps, on account of the demanding new ethical responsibilities such a perception might raise. In this sense, as we'll see, it may be less a matter of how *much* attention we pay to animals, and more about *how* we attend (or what we mean by attention). The kind of attention that *Sheep Pig Goat* invites is not attention conventionally understood as an immobilizing gaze or a process of selection and exclusion. Rather, it is an expanded attention to animals that differs from the everyday insofar as it does not 'turn away from what it has a material interest in *not* seeing' (Bergson 2014, p. 309).

Founded in 1996 by Harradine and co-artistic director, Sam Butler, Fevered Sleep have created over 20 different projects of which *Sheep Pig Goat* is not the first to engage with animality. The performance, *An Infinite Line: Brighton* (2008), for instance, was 'an exploration of and response to the quality of natural light in Brighton', which features a white spotted stallion, Phoenix. But whilst the live horse who appeared in this early work was arguably there as a kind of 'stand-in' – a metaphor for the extraordinary indifference of the natural phenomena that the performance hoped to be 'about' – the animals in *Sheep Pig Goat* seem to move well beyond operating as mere vehicles for human expression.

The first iteration of the project took place in March 2017, in a London warehouse trying to be 'as barn-like as possible'. The animals involved – who were 'selected for their familiarity with human contact'–were transported to the site from a farm in Wales, along with their handlers, who 'advised on and supervised all aspects of the animals' participation in the project' and were present for all of the encounters with the principle function of attending to the animals' welfare. They included two female Tamworth pigs, who are kept by their handlers for breeding, and a group of four rescued goats – all adolescent males. The human performers included two dancers, a vocalist and two other musicians whom the directors described as offering them a kind of 'toolbox' for the unknown requirements of the work to come: all expert improvisers, all expert non-verbal conversationalists, valued by the directors for their heightened competencies in relational attentiveness.

It has become commonplace to define a performance practice as 'research' according to – amongst other things – the criteria of "questioning". And *Sheep Pig Goat* fits the bill here. Situated in a professional arts rather than an academic context, pre-show framing nevertheless took great care to manage audience expectation by making clear that what they were coming to see was a public staging of the research process itself – not an entertaining show or finished 'piece'. The project framed itself as a use of performance to investigate a series of questions, including: "how well do humans see animals as they really are – not as we tell ourselves they are?"; and "what do animals perceive, when they perceive us?" But even more interesting than this, I think, are the ways in which questions were a key part of how the encounters were structured. For Harradine, he and Butler's role in the project as co-directors was: "to create frameworks for the encounters, and to set tasks or targets for the performers, in an open-ended, non-directed way – through questions: *What happens if...? Can you see how...? Is there any...? Could you...?*" But then ultimately, and crucially, he suggests that: 'It is the *animals* who direct us to "direct" the performers' (Harradine 2018). In this scenario, then, it is not just the artist-researcher who might be posing the questions that guide the research. Rather, we also need to consider: what questions might the animals themselves have been posing – what questions did the sheep, pigs and goats have about the behaviour of these creatures with whom they found themselves sharing space and time? If current conventions mean that *Sheep Pig Goat* can be straightforwardly recognized as research because it asks questions, then the reason why it is research that matters is that it is also an exercise in trying to ask animals the right questions – to ask them the questions that allow them to speak, rather than the questions that silence or predetermine answers in advance, circularly (Despret 2016). Not, yes/no questions like: "Can animals perform? Can a goat dance? Are animals capable of the kinds of deliberate, conscious, chosen activity that would allow us to grant them the status of genuine performers?" But "and-and" questions like: "how can we hear the animals own questions?" and "how might animals change our very idea of questioning itself?" In this sense, we might suggest that the project is not a 'use' or application of performance to animal research, so much as a kind of animalizing of both performance and research.

So, what happened during *Sheep Pig Goat*? "Very little happened actually" – Butler says. And she is right. There was something of the self-reflexive humour of failure we find in Marcus Coates work here too – a wry smile as we catch a glimpse of our own desperation for contact with another who appears more interested in what there might be to eat, and in her fellow pig, than with anything a human might be doing. The animals in *Sheep Pig Goat* were invited to be observers of the human performers 'on their own terms': an invitation which they often appeared to take up precisely by largely ignoring them. But if from one perspective "very little happened", it is also that a lot happened. And indeed, it is because such a multiplicity of happenings took place that no single response has the power to sanction the meaning of the event as a whole. When we ask "What happened?" the response must take the form of an addition rather than a reduction. And-and.

Figure 12.3 *Sheep Pig Goat*, Wellcome Collection and Fevered Sleep. Image by Ben Gilbert for Wellcome

What happened? *Sheep Pig Goat* was a demonstration of performance's epistemic force, a project that foregrounds performance as a mode of inquiry. *But it was also* a project from which the directors emerged speaking not of a "contribution to knowledge" but of an "abyss of ignorance". It was a site of learning; *but it was also* one of unlearning. Although, perhaps, having exited the paradigm of mastery, there is no reason why research might not be defined – as Vinciane Despret suggests – as aiming to make the world *more* rather than less strange to us. From this perspective, *Sheep Pig Goat* appears as one way to respond to Despret's call 'to learn to encounter animals as if they were strangers, so as to unlearn all of the idiotic assumptions that have been made about them' (2016, p. 161). And indeed, as I sat in the encounters, I thought: If I sit here for long enough, perhaps I can unlearn the subtractive perception that allows me to see 'the identity of animals as reducible to species membership' (ibid., p. 2). Perhaps I can learn to see *this* sheep, not *a* sheep.

And I thought: Perhaps if a certain kind of scientist sat here for long enough she might unlearn to see animals 'as limited to "reactions"' – and in so doing create the possibility that animals might surprise the researcher who asks questions of them, breaking the circle of only encountering what extant knowledge has already predicted (p. xii).

What happened? There is the difference between what happened to/for the performers who were with the animals every day, unlike most of the visitors who, for the most part, only observed a single encounter. In this context, for instance, the singer described what was for her 'a moment of sheer accomplishment' – likely unnoticed by most of the visitors – when the sheep 'were comfortable enough to turn away while we were making sounds… that was so significant' (Maier 2017).

What happened? A radical indeterminacy – that functioned not just as a screen for anthropocentric projections (moving unilaterally from us to them), but as a site of a two-way movement. There were multiple knowledges projected onto the animal – at times, a given voice intervening to put an end to doubt. One of the handlers says to a dancer:

Figure 12.4 *Sheep Pig Goat*, Wellcome Collection and Fevered Sleep. Image by Ben Gilbert for Wellcome

Figure 12.5 *Sheep Pig Goat*, Wellcome Collection and Fevered Sleep. Image by Ben Gilbert for Wellcome

"The pig is making that noise, because she doesn't like you moving in between her and the other pig. She's barking because you're getting too close". But something came back in the other direction too. Such moments also felt like a kind of progress – as potential markers of appearance rather than the animals' indifference to the performers – but also as (de-romanticizing) reminders that encounters hold the possibility of conflict (Despret 2016, p. 17), such that the dance that follows becomes a choreography of negotiation. *How close is too close?*

Figure 12.6 *Sheep Pig Goat*, Wellcome Collection and Fevered Sleep. Image by Ben Gilbert for Wellcome

Coda: in circles

What if, we end at the beginning?

Then we might end here: in circles.

And by ventriloquizing Henri Bergson, himself ventriloquizing a voice of objection that declares us trapped within the very circle we seek to break:

> But this method *of creating new forms of thinking – that you call 'intuition'* has against it the most inveterate habits of the mind. It at once suggests the idea of a vicious circle. In vain, we shall be told, you claim to go beyond *philosophical thought*: how can you do that except by *philosophical thought*? All that is clear in your *argument* is *philosophical thought*. You are inside your own thought; you cannot get out of it. [...] But the same reasoning would prove also the impossibility of acquiring any new habit. It is of the essence of *philosophical* reasoning to shut us up in the circle of the given. But action [*and we shall say performance*] breaks the circle. If we had never seen a man swim, we might say that swimming is an impossible thing, inasmuch as, to learn to swim, we must begin by holding ourselves up in the water and, consequently, already know how to swim. [...] So you may *speculate* as *philosophically* as you will on the mechanism of philosophical thought; you will never, by this method, succeed in going beyond it. You may get something more complex, but not something higher nor even something different.[1]
>
> (Bergson 1911, pp. 176–177)

Performance breaks the circle. Whether it is performed by Laruelle or by the sheep, pigs and goats, this expansive gesture does not tell us what thinking is, but forces us – by kicking against the goad – to unlearn how to think.

Note

1 This is not a direct quote from Bergson; it is a hybrid passage combining text from Bergson's *Creative Evolution* and text by the author (marked in italics). The original passage is as follows:

> But this method has against it the most inveterate habits of the mind. It at once suggests the idea of a vicious circle. In vain, we shall be told, you claim to go beyond intelligence: how can you do that except by intelligence? All that is clear in your consciousness is intelligence. You are inside your own thought; you cannot get out of it. Say, if you like, that the intellect is capable of progress, that it will see more and more clearly into a greater and greater number of things; but do not speak of engendering it, for it is with your intellect itself that you would have to do the work. The objection presents itself naturally to the mind. But the same reasoning would prove also the impossibility of acquiring any new habit. It is of the essence of reasoning to shut us up in the circle of the given. But action breaks the circle ... So, in theory, there is a kind of absurdity in trying to know otherwise than by intel- ligence; but if the risk be frankly accepted, action will perhaps cut the knot that reasoning has tied and will not unloose. Besides, the risk will appear to grow less, the more our point of view is adopted. We have shown that intellect has detached itself from a vastly wider reality, but that there has never been a clean cut between the two; all around conceptual thought there remains an indistinct fringe which recalls its origin ... So you may speculate as intelligently as you will on the mechanism of intelligence; you will never, by this method, succeed in going beyond it. You may get something more complex, but not something higher nor even something different.
>
> (Bergson 1911, pp. 176–177)

References

Bergson, Henri. 1911. *Creative Evolution*, trans. Arthur Mitchell. London: Macmillan.
Bergson, Henri. 2014. *Henri Bergson: Key Writings*, edited by John Mullarkey and Keith Ansell Pearson. London: Bloomsbury Publishing.
Bowie, Andrew. 2007. *Music, Philosophy, and Modernity*. Cambridge: Cambridge University Press.
Chaudhuri, Una. 2016. *The Stage Lives of Animals: Zooësis and Performance*. London/New York: Routledge.
Cull, Laura. 2012. "Performance as Philosophy: Responding to the Problem of 'Application'." *Theatre Research International* 37(1): 20–27.
Cvejić, Bojana. 2015. *Choreographing Problems: Expressive Concepts in Contemporary Dance and Performance*, Performance Philosophy Series. London/New York: Palgrave Macmillan.
Despret, Vinciane. 2016. *What Would Animals Say If We Asked the Right Questions?* trans. Brett Buchanan. Minneapolis/London: University of Minnesota Press.
Fisher, Tony. 2015. "Thinking without Authority: Performance Philosophy as the Democracy of Thought." In Laura Cull Ó Maoilearca (ed.). *Performance Philosophy*, Vol. 1, pp.175–184.
Gardner, Lyn. 2017. 'Sheep Pig Goat: Theatre for an Audience of Animals', *The Guardian*, Theatre Blog, first published Wednesday 15 March 2017.
Harradine, David. 2018. Unpublished Correspondence with the Author. With Permission of Fevered Sleep.
Henao Castro, Andrés Fabián. 2017. 'Book Reviews: Laura Cull, and Alice Lagaay, eds. Encounters in Performance Philosophy', *Journal of Contemporary Drama in English*, 5(1): 189–197.
Hollinghaus, Wade and Daddario, Will. 2015 (March). 'Performance Philosophy: Arrived Just in Time?' *Theatre Topics* 25(1): 51–56.
Kolozova, Katerina. 2010. *The Lived Revolution: Solidarity with the Body in Pain as the New Political Universal*. Skopje: Evro-Balkan Press.
Laruelle, François. 2006. "La lettre de François Laruelle du 30 Mai 2006, 'Les effets-Levinas'." Organisation Non-Philosophique Internationale, 2006. Web. 28 April 2017. <http://www.onphi.org/lettre-laruelle----effets-levinas-12.html>
Laruelle, François. 2011. *The Concept of Non-Photography*, trans. Robin Mackay. Falmouth: Urbanomic/Sequence Press.
Laruelle, François. 2012a. *From Decision to Heresy: Experiments in Non-Standard Thought*. Edited by Robin Mackay. Falmouth: Urbanomic/Sequence Press.
Laruelle, François. 2012b. "Is Thinking Democratic?" In John Mullarkey and Anthony Paul Smith (eds.) *Laruelle and Non-Philosophy*. Edinburgh: Edinburgh University Press, 227–237.
Laruelle, François. 2013. *Anti-Badiou: The Introduction of Maoism into Philosophy*, trans. Robin Mackay. London and New York: Bloomsbury.
Maier, Sterre. 2017. Unpublished Archival Material – Interview Transcript. With Permission of Fevered Sleep.
Manning, Erin and Massumi, Brian. 2014. *Thought in the Act: Passages in the Ecology of Experience*. Minneapolis: University of Minnesota Press.
Mullarkey, John. 2009. *Refractions of Reality: Philosophy and the Moving Image*. Basingstoke: Palgrave Macmillan.
Ó Maoilearca, John. 2015. *All Thoughts Are Equal: Laruelle and Nonhuman Philosophy*. Minneapolis: University of Minnesota Press.
Rokem, Freddie. 2010. *Philosophers and Thespians: Thinking Performance*. Oxford: Oxford University Press.
Shah, Rajni. 2018. *We Are Capable of So Much More: Experiments in Listening*, PhD, Lancaster University. https://doi.org/10.17635/lancaster/thesis/234
Sinnerbrink, Robert. 2011. *New Philosophies of Film: Thinking Images*. London: Bloomsbury.
Smith, Anthony Paul. 2015. *A Non-Philosophical Theory of Nature: Ecologies of Thought*. New York: Palgrave Macmillan.
Smith, Anthony Paul. 2016. *Laruelle: A Stranger Thought*. Cambridge/Malden, MA: Polity Press.
Street, Anna, Alliot, Julien and Pauker, Magnolia. 2017. *Inter Views in Performance Philosophy: Crossings and Conversations*, Performance Philosophy Series. London/New York: Palgrave Macmillan.
Zamir, Tzachi. 2014. *Acts: Theater, Philosophy and the Performing Self*. Ann Arbor: University of Michigan Press.

13
PERFORMANCE PHILOSOPHY AS INTER-PHILOSOPHICAL DIALOGUE

Cosimo Zene

Introduction: mythos – logos – dialogue

The painstaking task of philosophising was never meant to be an individual pursuit. Indeed, from the outset, philosophy was conceived as 'a way of life', inspiring younger generations to join one of the several 'schools of philosophy' (e.g. Epicureans, Stoics, Skeptics, Pythagorians, Sophists, etc.). Dialogue, both as methodological tool and theoretical outcome, occupied a prominent place in shaping the future of philosophical enterprise. Equally, 'performance', broadly defined, implies a commitment by performers to act for *others*, in an effort to communicate, to establish a dialogue with an audience. Beyond the act of thinking which happens within silence, the 'stage' – as much as the stage of life – throws both the performer and the philosopher into the public arena, where dialogue becomes the conduit for 'being-with' or the 'being in dialogue' for a philosophy of performance.

Following a brief introduction to the idea of dialogue within Western philosophy, I will expand on this concept – with the help of Enrique Dussel and other Latin American philosophers – as relevant for a wider inter-philosophical dialogue among and between World Philosophies. I will then, in dialogue with Richard Kearney, try to outline a 'philosophy of performance' as 'thinking in action' and as part of 'philosophy as a way of life' which highlights the carnal, bodily and human dimension of both philosophy and performance. In contrast to Gramsci, who provides a profound reflection on the role of intellectuals in achieving the 'philosophy of praxis', Kearney proposes a return not to the powerful God of Christian theology, but "to the God of play, the lord of the dance, the shepherd king of the song of songs…" (Kearney & Gallagher, 2010).

When looking back at the history of Western philosophy, a predominant line of thought is evident which highlights the presence of a 'strong *logos*' characterising its trajectory. This 'Love of Wisdom', affirming itself through rational reasoning, had to compete against the paradigm of '*mythos*' – defined here, in very general terms, as a 'primitive' conception of the world and our way of relating to it – which had, until that moment in time, exemplified human endeavour in its various manifestations. There was no smooth transition from *mythos* to *logos*, and perhaps it never completely happened. In the process, however, so as to achieve supremacy, *logos* had to affirm itself with a strong will to power, in order for a reason to gain overall control.

We can date the beginning of the shift from *mythos* to *logos* to around the 6th century BCE, when the 'Presocratics' and the Sophists were active in the Greek region. This was not, however, the 'big bang' of philosophy, given that the introduction of rationalist thinking to the Western world – by way of incipient metaphysics, logic, ethics, cosmology, argumentative theology and even proto-scientific thought – was accompanied by the imagination of philosophers who still acted as mystics or shamans. With Socrates, we witness the arrival of a third element: dialogue – almost as an expansion and completion of the *mythos–logos* binary. However, even the arrival of a more rationalist philosophy with Socrates was marked in 399 BCE by him being sentenced to death. Despite the many speculations written on this verdict, there is no doubt that the beginning of Western philosophy bears the stigma of an act of violence. Was dialogue simply a methodological device so as to practise philosophy more efficiently, or did its introduction also indicate a different theoretical standing and a commitment to a philosophy of a different kind? Whatever the intentions, it seems noticeably ironic that Socrates' effort to expand the shift from *mythos* to *logos* into 'dia-logos' signalled, in fact, the weakness if not the failure of dialogue, itself. Even according to Plato and Xenophon (*Apology*), we must postulate that the struggle happening within the shift between *mythos* and *logos* was a warning of further difficulties when moving into dialogue. Was Socratic 'arrogance' solely part of a (rather poor) self-defence at the trial, or was it instead affirming a new, different and ethical manner of practising philosophy? If anything, this arrogance shows a refusal and almost a total lack of dialogue.

These piercing questions, placed at the very beginning of the Western philosophical endeavour, open up space for further questions which will probe the entity of dialogue as one of the most relevant or even indispensable tools so as to achieve philosophical success. This is not in terms of supremacy – as in winning a debate or a competition for an argument, or establishing a hierarchy – but in terms of achieving maximum results for the love of wisdom. In this sense, dialogue, even beyond the literary genre, points towards the overcoming of the (individualistic) strong *logos* resulting from the *mythos/logos* binary, in an effort to renounce the violence of *logos,* thus allowing the love of wisdom to bear its fruit. By contrast, the weakness of dialogue, anticipating dissent, points towards achieving a consensus in which differences are not eliminated, but certainly mitigated in the search for a higher and common good.

One apt metaphor to elucidate this characteristic of dialogue is the complexity of a musical score: all instruments play an individual part, but the end result is not a solo performance. As much as this can be appreciated, the ideal of dialogue is closer to a symphony in which all instruments contribute to enhance the magnificence of harmony. Even the individual contribution of the composer, as the inspirer of dialogue, and the conductor as its facilitator are geared towards a common effort, rather than an individual endeavour. This does not exclude the presence of contrast, misunderstanding, tragedy or even violence, but the main effort is, in fact, to overcome these in the name of a superior reason and for the benefit of all. In a sense, this might point towards the utopian nature of dialogue, highlighting still further its weakness as a methodological and theoretical tool for philosophising. Nonetheless and despite the weakness of utopia, "…utopias today can effectively disrupt entrenched forms of legitimation, foster new forms of political identity, and reveal new possibilities within existing institutions. Utopias are needed to understand the political choices we face today" (McKean, 2016, p. 1).

Philosophy as love of wisdom seems to remain caught in between either the temptation to make use of a strong *logos,* so as to affirm itself, or, by renouncing the violence of a strong logos, to follow the more difficult and demanding route of a weak *logos* reached through consensus, which is dictated by the wisdom of love: loving life and cherishing alterity, over and above the self-centred affirmation of the ego as the sole thinking subject. However, rather than giving into the temptation to devolve the solution of the 'crisis of the subject' to post-modernity, I see it as more pertinent to deal openly with the questions which remain unanswered by the acquired certainties of modernity, which reaffirm time and again the strong *logos* of the rational/individual thinking subject. On what grounds then, if at all, can the foundations of philosophical dialogue rest? How can we establish the validity and practice of this principle? But most of all, once we have established that it is in fact indispensable to press forward from mythos/logos into dialogue – which necessarily also involves a movement from the 'I' to the 'we' of philosophy – what are the main features which would support a true, critical philosophical dialogue and the difficulties in establishing this as a viable principle of philosophical inquiry?

While proposing to establish and sustain dialogue as a viable philosophical principle, we should not, however, take it for granted. Dialogue is not a given, but must be pursued with constant effort and commitment. Whilst past dialogic advancements will certainly favour recent interest in dialogue, they will not replace what can be achieved at present: every period must respond both to the general and contingent challenges and the difficulties faced by the practice of critical dialogical philosophy.

For instance, there seems little doubt that what we define today as ancient Greek philosophy was not solely the result of developments in that particular region, but must take account of a wider area of the Greek world, comprising at least Asia Minor, North Africa and Southern Italy. Moreover, we must also bear in mind the extended exchanges and communication taking place between Greece and surrounding civilisations, such as Egypt and North Africa, Babylon, Persia and Inner Asia. In many ways, all these cultures contributed to what in the end resulted as 'Greek philosophy'. The example of Xenophon is very revealing here: being an Athenian and one of Socrates' pupils, he was well-placed to become a prominent intellectual and a philosopher of that time. He was able to facilitate a compromise between Athens and Sparta and the different political institutions governing the two cities. He travelled widely, thus gathering different experiences and ideas, as among the Greek mercenaries at the service of Cyrus' expeditions (*Anabasis*). In turn, in his *Cyropaedia*, he celebrated Cyrus as the ideal leader and ruler, while offering one of the first examples of moral and political philosophy, but also an instance of incipient inter-philosophical dialogue.

Our own times – if we merely consider the last hundred years of our recent past – are filled with events that seem to underline a world in turmoil, in which wars, competition, confrontation and unrest appear as the most prominent activity of humankind. It would seem that more than 2,500 years of rational *logos* have been unable to dispel the thirst for violence and the intensity of aggression. And yet, during these troubled times, we have also witnessed moments in which individuals and communities have sought to propose an alternative, when reflecting on human life and experience, at times even in the midst of the most horrendous brutality.

Looking from this perspective, the history of Western philosophy runs parallel with a history of violence. More than that, and in clear contradiction to the supposed rationality of *logos*, we have gone to great lengths to justify acts of violence – wars, colonialism, slavery, racism and racial supremacy, oppression, segregation and exclusion and Eurocentrism – as perfectly 'rational' choices. The contradiction is even more poignant when, by equating the logos of reason with the Logos as 'Word of God', and as God himself, we seemingly force God into taking sides to support inhuman acts of violence (although not all theologians lend their mind to a philosophy of violence). One solution to this impasse is to open up the initial dialogue that takes place within Anglo-European philosophy to include other philosophical traditions, so as to create an inter-philosophical dialogue among and between World Philosophies.

One proponent of this line of thinking is the Argentine-Mexican philosopher Enrique Dussel who, in a recent article (2009), invites us to inaugurate, "A new age in the history of philosophy": a new age defined by the recognition of regional philosophical traditions. At the same time, as we shall see, a reflection on the concept of performance offers substantial support to the demanding task of inter-philosophical dialogue, given the widespread nature of performance as a communal human experience.

World Philosophies in dialogue

Dussel sets out his article by making a bold statement regarding the task of philosophy for a 'significant portion of the 21st century', "Our recognition and acceptance of the meaning, value and history of all regional philosophical traditions on the planet", which will be achieved through "an authentic and symmetrical dialogue", so as "to transcend the Eurocentrism of modernity" (Dussel, 2009, pp. 499–500). This dialogue must, first of all, concentrate on the 'universal core problems' posited from the very beginning by *homo sapiens*, in search of answers to fundamental, ontological questions rationally addressed. For Dussel, this also includes the 'production of myths' (*mytho-poiésis*), as symbolic narratives with universal significance, thus recovering both oral and written traditions, even through the words of Aristotle. "This is why he who *loves myth (philómythos)* is akin to he *who loves wisdom (philósophos)* (Aristotle, Metaphysics I, 2; 982 b 17–18)" (Dussel, 2009, p. 501). Dussel supports his position by quoting Levi-Strauss' work on the elaborate myths of the Tupinamba of Brazil (*Tristes Tropiques*, 1955), and Paul Ricoeur's (1964) work on ethical and mythical narrativity and the persistence of myths, as described in *The Principle of Hope*, by Ernest Bloch.

Despite the progression from the narrative of mythos to the conceptual categorisation of logos, Dussel is also mindful of preserving an awareness of the core problems addressed by speculative thought, without losing sight of the relevant communitarian role of the 'philosophers', while finding synonyms in other cultures for the 'lovers of wisdom' (the *Tlamatini* among the Atzecs, or the *Amautas* for the Mayas). Having described this movement in a number of diverse cultural settings – including Chinese and Indian (Hindu, Buddhist and Jain) – Dussel concludes that, whilst all cultures have produced 'conceptual structural categories' (albeit to different degrees), "mythical elements may contaminate even the discourses of great philosophers". For example, he suggests that we can see this in the case of Immanuel Kant's argument in favour of the 'immortality of the soul' as a way of resolving the question of 'supreme Good' (Dussel, 2009, p. 507). The error of affirming that Greek philosophy is to be taken as the prototype of philosophical discourse "arises from taking Greek philosophy as the definition of philosophy itself, rather than discovering a clear *criterion of demarcation* between mythical and philosophical categorical discourse" (Dussel, 2009, p. 505).

Most of all, Dussel underlines how it was the political and economic hegemony which provided the backbone for modern European philosophy to develop in a unique manner and to, itself, become hegemonic beyond the political and the economic, while manipulating knowledge and information coming from the periphery to the 'centre'. In this way, a 'regional' European philosophy becomes universal, or, as Dussel says, "*Philosophical Eurocentrism is, then, in essence this universality claim of a particular philosophy*, many aspects of which may still be absorbed by other traditions" (Dussel, 2009, p. 509 – emphasis added).

Dussel returns to the main issue of engaging with fundamental 'core problems' which are universal by virtue of their being ultimately *human*. As such, all philosophies located in a specific cultural context are "capable of engaging in dialogue with others through the prism of shared 'core problems' and categorical discourses of a philosophical character, which are universal to the extent that they are human" (Dussel, 2009, p. 510). It is the fact of 'being human' which marks the character of a 'philosophy of and for humanity'. In the 21st century, this inaugurates a new age of inter-philosophical dialogue, starting with the North–South dialogue, in which economic and political structures find themselves intertwined with cultural and philosophical ones. This, however, must be complemented by the South–South dialogue (Africa, Asia, Latin America, Eastern Europe, etc.), indispensable and in need of developing pertinent rules in order to tackle urgent philosophical problems, such as our inability to understand each other, and to interact peacefully.

In order to facilitate this new age of dialogue, Dussel proposes to "lay the pedagogical foundations by educating future generations in multiple philosophical traditions" (Dussel, 2009, p. 511). 'Education' in this context means to deliver taught courses at the undergraduate level on major philosophical traditions – without disregarding minor ones – since, "This is how a new generation can begin to think philosophically from within a global mindset" (Dussel, 2009, p. 511). He proposes to expand the East–West dialogue – which has occupied comparative philosophy from its inception (Kirloskar-Steinbach et al., 2014)[1] – to also include the periphery of the (philosophical) world: Africa and Latin America thus far being excluded from this dialogue. In addition to this, a "complete reformulation of the history of philosophy" is urgently needed so as to address the aforementioned exclusions (Dussel, 2009, p. 511).

As an example of inter-philosophical dialogue, Dussel proposes a reflection on the work of the Moroccan philosopher, Al-Jabri (*The Critique of Arab Reason*, 4 vols, 1984–2001; *The Arab Philosophical Legacy,* 2001). Without going into great detail, we can summarise that such a dialogue must be conducted by critical and creative philosophers who are not intent on preserving the status quo, but who would "assume the responsibility for addressing the ethical and political problems associated with the poverty, domination and exclusion of large sectors of the population, especially in the global South" (Dussel, 2009, p. 514). In Latin America, this critical philosophy has taken the name of 'philosophy of liberation'. It remains to be seen, however, how this 'liberation' can be shared, through dialogue, with other philosophies. In other words, can the Latin American philosophy of liberation also inspire other 'regional' philosophies to find a way to free themselves from their subjugation to Anglo-European philosophy, so as to establish a dialogue among equals?

Dussel is not, by any means, a solitary voice among Latin American philosophers. Among them, Walter Mignolo, Aníbal Quijano and Gabriel Soldatenko offer some useful reflections. Soldatenko, for instance, underlines that, "There is a largely neglected yet urgent need to investigate and critique the processes whereby philosophy, the universal art of questioning reality, became the province of a particular segment of humanity — the West" (Soldatenko, 2015, p. 139). Soldatenko continues:

> To be clear, the claim being made here is not that Kant and Hegel intentionally set out to create a specifically Western philosophy, but rather they serve as examples of a *common sense* that had been established outside of philosophical discourse proper that influenced the philosophical outlook of the day. This perspective took the West as the unquestioned frame of reference for civilization, and ultimately informed the modern construction of philosophy.
>
> (Soldatenko, 2015, p. 148 - emphasis added)

Equally, Quijano, bringing together the effects of political and cultural colonialism, in particular for Latin America and Africa, underlines how 'systematic repression' was accompanied by the imposition of "a mystified image of [Western] patterns of producing knowledge and meaning" by the colonisers (Quijano, 2007, p. 169). While in Asia and the Middle East, "the high cultures could never be destroyed with such intensity and profundity", in the Americas, "the cultural repression and the massive genocide together turned the previous high cultures of America into illiterate, peasant subcultures condemned to orality; that is, deprived of their own patterns of formalized, objectivised, intellectual, and plastic or visual expression" (Quijano, 2007, p. 170).[2] The effects of colonialism are still present now within 'coloniality', as an offshoot of the European paradigm of modernity and rationality, thus prompting the question of the 'production of knowledge', including the totality of this knowledge, in which the 'provincial' (or regional) has become universal. In order to solve the impasse of coloniality, we must, according to Quijano, implement an "epistemological decolonization, as decoloniality", so as to, "clear the way for new intercultural communication, for an interchange of experiences and meanings, as the basis of another rationality which may legitimately pretend to some universality" (Quijano, 2007, p. 177):

> The liberation of intercultural relations from the prison of coloniality also implies the freedom of all peoples to choose, individually or collectively, such relations: a freedom to choose between various cultural orientations, and, above all, the freedom to produce, criticize, change, and exchange culture and society.
>
> *(Quijano, 2007, p. 178)*

This very idea is expressed and expanded in similar terms by Mignolo:

> We delink from the humanitas, we become epistemically disobedient, and think and do decolonially, dwelling and thinking in the borders of local histories confronting global designs. ... Decolonial thinking can be done within existing academic structure, but is not a way of thinking that will have enthusiastic support of the administration or accumulate grants and fellowships.
>
> *(Mignolo, 2013, pp. 137–138)*

A philosophy of performance

In order to better illustrate the relationship between this discussion of World Philosophies and performance philosophy, I have chosen to take inspiration from a recent interview by Alina Feld with the philosopher Richard Kearney.[3] Most interestingly, the title of the interview-article is 'Thinking in Action', which seems very appropriate as a metaphor for performance philosophy. The concept of '*thinking in action*' returns time and again in the interview, and I must say, Kearney learned a great deal from his teacher, Ricoeur, who, in *Time and Narrative*, invites the reader to adopt a circular hermeneutics, 'from action to text and back to action', or to conceive 'translation as linguistic hospitality' (Ricoeur, 2006). But Kearney also learned from the 'applied hermeneutics' of his colleagues in Calgary: from Caputo's 'radical hermeneutics', Vattimo's 'weak hermeneutics' and Levinas' 'ethical relation with the stranger as first philosophy'. "These are people who care", says Kearney, because they are "all vitally and socially committed people" (Kearney & Feld, 2017, p. 152). Not solely thinkers, but thinkers who are able to translate their thought into action. He recalls his experience as a young student of philosophy, attending Ricoeur's lectures on Heidegger or Gadamer and the next day reading his article in *Le Monde* "discoursing on the burning issues of the day" (Kearney & Feld, 2017, p. 151).

> So I saw my teacher of philosophy operating as a man of peace and praxis, a very socially and politically committed mind. Whenever I travelled with Ricoeur to other countries he would always want to find out how people lived, how many prisons there were, what the unemployment rate was, how the schools and local councils functioned….
>
> *(Kearney & Feld, 2017, pp. 151–152)*

No wonder then, that Kearney, following these examples, has applied his own philosophy to address issues in 'conflict zones': such as the peace process in Northern Ireland, the commemoration in 2016 of WWI for the Irish (both Catholics and Protestants) or the *Guestbook Project* (2009–present), inviting people from opposing sides to recount their stories, and then to recount them again, following a dialogue exchange between the two parties. But there is also the commitment to inter-religious dialogue, which has brought an engagement between 'religion and art'. At some point, when the interviewer intervenes comparing Kearney's philosophy to Hadot's ideal of 'philosophy as a total, lived experience', Kearney prefers to clarify that there are philosophers, scholars and thinkers. *Philosophers* are "people who devote their lives to really important questioning and usually have one single world-changing idea"; *Scholars* are "brilliant academic commentators who provide detailed analysis of the great philosophical minds"; and *Thinkers* are "minds who try to apply philosophical ideas and scholarship to concrete practical matters of living and being with others". He then concludes, "If I were to place myself anywhere, it would be as a humble clerk to this kind of lived thinking, or thinking for life, thinking as healing, thinking in action" (Kearney & Feld, 2017, p. 153). Kearney's three-way distinction offers him a subtle tactic to clarify his position vis-à-vis philosophy itself which, for him, even though involving 'thinking about thinking', remains a thinking which is not separated from life and praxis. In this respect, the 'humble clerk' is reminding us of the highest vocation of a philosophy of life.

A similar taxonomy, even if less structured, is also offered by Gramsci, although, perhaps in response to the needs of his time, he used the cumulative name of 'intellectuals' to classify those who were at the forefront, as leaders, philosophers and thinkers, of the cultural and political lives of a country. He also recognised the role of 'professional philosophers' who dedicated themselves to this career and, supposedly, were to indicate to all others the right path for effective philosophising. Gramsci, however, maintained that the ability to philosophise pertained to all human beings: "Everyone is a philosopher", including the masses and common people, who would express their philosophy – as a vision of the world – through language, religion, folklore, and even what he defined as 'superstitions' (Gramsci, 1975, Q7, §1, p. 852; Q11, §12, p. 1375).[4] As a Marxist and historical materialist, Gramsci saw philosophy as intimately connected with praxis, and hence as a concrete intervention in shaping human history, or indeed as philosophy becoming politics. Hence, his 'philosophy of praxis' was to produce a political philosophy which would assist the human community – both as State and as civil society – to achieve progress in favour of the whole community, and in particular of those who were considered as 'subalterns', left 'on the margins of history' (Gramsci, 1975, Q25).

The problem, as Gramsci saw it, both in Italy and Europe, was that intellectuals in general, including professional philosophers, were totally separate from the masses ('the caste of intellectuals'), thus having little or no impact on a country as a whole. Gramsci labelled these 'traditional intellectuals', as opposed to the 'organic intellectuals' who were instead very interested in the life, history and culture of those concrete communities with which they lived (Q11, §67, p. 1505). The idea of 'organic/organicity' aims to highlight the holistic approach to a given reality, history or situation, rather than the narrow vision of a single, often obsolete, disciplinary intervention. Gramsci uses other synonyms to further qualify the philosophico-political commitment of the organic intellectual, referring to this protagonist as an 'integral historian', with the label 'integral' still referring to the totality of given circumstances (Q25, §2, p. 2284). This totality is also reflected in other similar synonyms Gramsci adopts, such as 'democratic historian' and 'democratic philosopher' (Q10, §44, p. 1332). The idea of 'democracy' here must be taken almost literally, as 'demos', meaning with and for the people. So much so that Gramsci specifies even further (particularly in Notebook 11; Gramsci, 1975), bringing the whole range of definitions to one final, revealing marker, which he dubs the 'collective thinker' (Q11, §12, p. 1392). Hence, the (real) philosopher, as 'organic intellectual', does not think individually, but collectively. Or, as he puts it, the individual achievement of a philosopher, laudable as it is, is not as relevant as an idea which has also been communicated to the people, has been understood by the masses and has motivated people's active intervention in history.[5] This is the 'end product' of a real 'philosophy of praxis': that the people, with the help of 'organic intellectuals', are able to overcome 'common sense' – which is often fragmented and inconclusive – so as to transform it into 'good common sense', thus directing it towards the 'common good'. How does this happen? Intellectuals, in contact with the masses, are able to value the 'healthy nucleus' present within common sense and bring it to a higher level of reflection, so as to transform it. This resembles very closely the hermeneutic circle – 'from action, to text, to action' – thus highlighting the unity of thought and action, or the notion of 'thinking in action', as discussed earlier. Gramsci also warns against the creation of a 'caste of intellectuals',[6] meaning that every group, especially the subalterns, if they wish to overcome subalternity, must create/provide their own intellectuals, given that every group and every category of people has its own intellectuals.

Beyond the intentionality of Gramsci's 'philosophy of praxis' – and despite the very rudimentary presentation given earlier – there is a striking similarity between the basics of a philosophy of praxis and 'performance philosophy'. What does a 'performer' do? Why is there a performance? A performer is, most of all, translating thoughts into practice in such a way that the thoughts are communicated to an audience, through this practice. Hence, there is a continuity between thought and action, and it indeed becomes 'thinking in action'. More than that, the performance also becomes an invitation to the audience to participate in the action. No performer wishes to communicate his/her thoughts to a passive audience. In the face of passivity, a performance becomes a 'provocation', so as to prompt an answer, be it a feeling or a concrete action/reaction. In this sense, the performer is also acting as an 'intellectual', using a language known to the people – starting in fact from their 'common sense' – in order to address issues shared by both the performer and the audience. At the same time, the performer wants to reach a higher level of both intellectual and life commitments, thus bringing thought and action together, once more. Of course, a whole discussion has been happening regarding 'performers' as 'artists' (or even 'artisans') – particularly in Theatre and Performance Studies – their role as intellectuals within society and their common language with artists in other societies, thus establishing a wider dialogue concomitant with World Philosophies and inter-artistic, philosophical dialogue.

However, despite many commonalities, there remains a fundamental difference between Kearney's philosophy and that put forward by Gramsci, in one particular regard: religion. Gramsci, as a historical materialist, is determined to overcome religion. For him, religion represents the 'philosophy of the masses', who need to be guided towards a higher philosophy, thus surmounting popular common sense (Q11, §12, p. 1378). Nevertheless, Gramsci placed great importance on the study of religion and its effects in society, history, culture and daily life. He was even ready to learn from religion and religious movements, especially when these favoured integration between the hierarchy of the Church and the masses of believers, thus highlighting a particular kind of effective 'intellectuals'. One clear example of this is his recovery, so to speak, of the values present in the phenomenon of the 'Reformation'. In Italy, this deep sentiment of creating 'the public spirit', a way of feeling and thinking of the masses, which touched mainly northern European regions, was completely missing. In Gramsci's view, the party ('the new Prince') was going to provide this missing 'intellectual and moral reformation' (Q13, §1, p. 1561).

For his part, Kearney is deeply concerned with religion – broadly defined – and with the 'problem of God' in contemporary thought. In a sense, he becomes a catalyst for the thoughtfulness and at times anxiety of many other thinkers/philosophers, with whom he is in dialogue. This resulted in his publication of *Reimagining the Sacred* (2015). When confronted with two extremes – either blind religious dogmatism or a total negation of the 'sacred' – Kearney prefers to adopt a third way, wishing to rediscover the sacred in a sceptical society. In other words, working on the intersection of secularism, politics and religion, he tries to locate the 'sacred' within a secular society, while putting into practice his ideal of an "existential and therapeutic model of engaged thinking", which is also translated into "the idea of thinking as a mode of catharsis and healing" (Kearney & Feld, 2017, p. 154). In this process, both "the personal work of thinking and the public work of communication – reflection and action" go hand in hand. As he puts it:

> I personally believe that for thought to be really therapeutic and transformative it also needs to be supplemented by more hands-on carnal practice of conversion and integration, including meditation, yoga, spiritual journeying, centering prayer, social action and public performance.
>
> *(Kearney & Feld, 2017, p. 154)*

Carnal Hermeneutics (2015) is another recent book edited by Kearney, in which he tries "to bring the forgotten lost body back to a Western Christian tradition, centred on the incarnation: not only the body of flesh but the spiritual body as well" (Kearney & Feld, 2017, p. 157), welcoming the re-engagement of religion and the arts, bringing together artists and scholars. All this finds inspiration in the idea of incarnation and 'transfiguration', which Kearney applies to human reality, though remaining sceptical towards a certain theodicy: "I reject the idea of a God that could justify evil or see it as still the best of possible worlds ... Radical evil does exist... But it is a human responsibility" (Kearney & Feld, 2017, p. 158). Likewise, in his work *Anatheism: Returning to God After God* (2011),[7] Kearney argues for the return of the good after the evils of the Holocaust and the World Wars of the 20th century: "Our task is to resacralize the world, make it hale, whole and healthy again. It is a choice – to re-actualise the possibility of God as love in the world. Through healing and wisdom. Catharsis and Sophia" (Kearney & Feld, 2017, p. 158).

Both Catharsis and Sophia are feminine nouns, and so is the Hebrew word *ruah*, for Spirit, which is close to the Semitic word for mercy, *reham*, meaning womb. All this invites Kearney to emphasise, "The biblical God is at root, both feminine and masculine, both Sophia and Logos" (Kearney & Feld, 2017, p. 161), contrary to what has happened in the historical experience of many religious traditions, where the 'feminine' has been eclipsed or even obliterated. Hence, this Logos is not and cannot be the 'all powerful' strong logos, the rational project found as developed within the history of Anglo-European philosophy. The resulting God, as seen by Kearney (who describes himself as "a Catholic, but a radical broken-hearted Catholic"), is not the powerful, omnipotent being of theodicy, but he is powerless, precisely because "God neither is nor is not - but may be" (Kearney, 2001). As the interviewer, Alina Feld, comments:

> [Kearney] invites us to rethink God not as actuality, but rather as possibility. Inscribing his thesis in the contemporary philosophical debates –phenomenological, hermeneutic, deconstructive – he proffers the view that God's potentiality-to-be is not a lack but *more* divine than traditional divine actuality.
>
> *(Kearney & Feld, 2017, p. 165)*

Or, as he, himself, says:

> God of desire and promise who calls out of burning bushes, makes pledges and covenants, burns with longing in the song of songs, cries in the wilderness, whispers in caves, comforts those oppressed in darkness, and prefers orphans, widows and strangers to the mighty and the proud.
>
> *(Kearney, 2001, p. 2)*

Hence, 'God as promise' means that he is only a possibility which becomes reality through our active responsibility and, I would say, through our *performance*. In Kearney's terms, the act of performance is what makes God possible, making us active participants to creation, or co-creators (Kearney & Feld, 2017, pp. 161–162).

There is one particular aspect of the 'possible God', which Kearney wishes to recover, with the help of the Jesuit Church historian, Hugo Rahner: the idea of '*God as play*' (*deus ludens*), in connection with *homo ludens*, man as play, thus also recovering various texts of the Judeo-Christian and mystical traditions concerning this concept. Eckhart picks up on the notion of the God that laughs, as does John of the Cross in his Canticles, his long poem on the Song of Songs, with its images of lovers at play. Kearney also recalls that the Sufi poetic mystical tradition was very rich in such ideas, especially Hafiz, Rumi and Halluj, and how, in Abrahamic religions, mystical movements were marginalised, neglected and often persecuted by various fundamentalisms, to conclude, "There is a battle in all Abrahamic religions to recover the God of play. I am personally hopeful about a new mysticism and new monasticism – often interreligious – where this notion of the playful God is resurfacing" (Kearney & Feld, 2017, p. 159).

Kearney exemplifies the concept of God as play still further, taking inspiration from Richard Rohr's recent book *The Divine Dance* (2016), which is a contemplative rereading of Andrei Rublev's icon of the Trinity. Early Christians applied the Greek verb for *dance* (*perichoresis*) to the mystery of the Trinity, saying whatever is going on in God is a flow – it is like a dance.

> This is all part of a new return to the God of play, the lord of the dance, the shepherd king of the song of songs. Parts of popular culture often remained close to the playful God – think of good liturgical ceremonies and Carnival, Corpus Christi processions, Christmas and Easter pageants, la Nuit de la St. Jean, Mardi Gras, All Hallows and other holy times and places of liturgical imagination.[8]

> The Christian image of the Trinity as *perichoresis* is a playful dance around the chora, circling about the core space of hospitality, the generative womb of Sarah and Mary, the Eucharistic chalice of bread and wine. Revelation of the divine is in the carnival of hospitality between the three persons opening onto the fourth – humanity. The fourth dimension involves the invitation to join the perichoretic dance – as signaled by the little mirror first inserted at the base of Andrei Rublev's Icon of the Trinity, where we see ourselves reflected in the divine play between persons: … As the old liturgical song went: "Dance, dance wherever you may be, I am the Lord of the Dance, said he".
>
> *(Kearney & Feld, 2017, p. 161)*

If dance, as *perichoresis*, has become an apt metaphor able to explain one of the biggest mysteries that has occupied the human mind when trying to make sense of the 'nature of God' as Trinity, then dance itself can represent a convincing symbol for performance philosophy. The body in movement is in unison with the mind/thoughts which give origin and motivate the dance to continue, thus highlighting the intimate bond between 'theory and praxis', or 'thinking in action' as we have been trying to emphasise in this essay. Moreover, two further points must be underscored: (i) the (mainly) communitarian aspect of dance, in which all are invited to participate; (ii) the widespread phenomenon of dance virtually in every culture and human society. The first point reminds us that, although there are intellectuals who are recognised as 'philosophers' (by profession), they do not have sole rights to this endeavour. Ideally, at least according to Gramsci, they should be 'collective thinkers', hence not thinking for-the-people but with-the-people, thus confirming his assertion that 'everyone is a philosopher' (Q11, §12, p. 1375). The second point helps us ascertain that the widespread variety of dances reflects as many ontologies – as ways of being – and epistemologies – as ways of knowing and interpreting the world. Would this be sufficient to postulate that every form of dance represents a different philosophy – a way of thinking in action? Would this connection be sufficient to then postulate a further claim that philosophies – as much as dances – can be in dialogue with each other? In other words, would dancers in a given culture understand the dance language of 'foreign' dancers and interact with them?

Conclusion

In this essay, I have sought to bring together the emerging field of Performance Philosophy and the relatively new field of World Philosophies. The contention is that Performance Philosophy lends itself to provide a suitable example of inter-philosophical dialogue, which stands both as an indispensable methodological tool and a rationale at the basis of World Philosophies. In order for World Philosophies to have a future, the first crucial operation is the recognition that Anglo-European philosophy is but one 'regional' philosophy, and that in the world, there is a great variety of epistemologies, ontologies, ethics, aesthetics, metaphysics, etc. (i.e. philosophies), which all share the values attached to the 'love of wisdom' for the simple fact of 'being human' and of belonging to humanity. As part of this process, there is the effort to recover and cherish those essential qualities which over the centuries have made philosophy meaningful for the life of the people, for all people and not solely for intellectuals and professional philosophers. We also know how often philosophy has lent itself to being an instrument of violence and oppression, thus betraying its humane vocation. For this reason, philosophy must 'decolonise' and purify itself so as to revert to being 'a way of life' in which the task of thinking becomes 'therapeutic and transformative' as Kearney's 'thinking in action' suggests.

Bringing together performance and philosophy is no real novelty, if we think of the connection between Greek tragedy and philosophy, even down to the present (Young, 2013). The novelty could perhaps lie in our ability to recognise the different places within which philosophy dwells, as, for instance, in performance philosophy – as thinking in action – or in dance, as a manifestation of performance. I have entertained in my discussion ideas such as religion and God, not with the intent of recovering something lost, but with the hope of unveiling something hidden, which has always been there: the idea of the sacred. What is sacred here is life itself, all life, human and otherwise, even when suffering and death threaten its sacredness. In many ways, performance philosophy celebrates this sacredness, by bringing it back to the whole community by way of a constant dialogue between performers and audiences in which 'thinking in action' triggers 'healing and wisdom'. This, however, does not occur in one secluded corner of our world, since the gift of performance touches everyone, and everyone is invited to participate in the infinite dance of life.

As Will Daddario (2019) points out, the open field of Performance Philosophy, which also proposes itself as an 'open question', resembles a 'living organism' whose 'generative possibilities' invite us "to think again about the presumed certainties of inherited academic knowledge" (Daddario, 2019, p. 328). Through this novel way of 'thinking',

> we do not glimpse the slow growth of vertical structures upon this open field but, rather, a horizontal flow of energies produced by moving bodies and motile thoughts. The purpose of these energies may be as yet unclear, but their vibrancy and capacity to stimulate discussion cannot be denied.
>
> *(Daddario, 2019, p. 331)*

Notes

1 "Comparative philosophy, qua philosophy, makes us aware of our own myth by introducing us to the myth of others and by this very fact changes our horizon … . Comparative philosophy does not demythologize; it transmythicizes … . It saves us from falling into the fallacy of believing that all the others live in myth except us" (Panikkar, 1988, p. 134).
2 "Henceforth, the survivors would have no other modes of intellectual and plastic or visual formalized and objectivised expressions, but through the cultural patterns of the rulers, even if subverting them in certain cases to transmit other needs of expression. *Latin America is, without doubt, the most extreme case of cultural colonization by Europe*" (Quijano, 2007, p. 170).
3 Kearney has been Professor of Philosophy at Boston College since 1999. He has published over 20 books, numerous edited books, 2 novels and a book of poetry. He completed his PhD at the Sorbonne, under the direction of Paul Ricoeur.
4 References by Gramsci are mainly taken from his Prison Notebooks, following the Italian critical edition (Gramsci, 1975), and quoted in the internationally accepted style referring to Q (followed by the notebook number), the note (§) and page number.
5 "For a mass of people to be led to think coherently and in the same coherent fashion about the real present world, is a 'philosophical' event far more important and 'original' than the discovery by some philosophical "genius" of a truth which remains the property of small groups of intellectuals" (Q11 §12, p. 1378). (On the concept of 'present', plural historical temporalities and the 'non-presence of the present', especially with reference to Louis Althusser's critique of Gramsci's 'absolute historicism', see Thomas, P. D., (2017), The Plural Temporalities of Hegemony, *Rethinking Marxism*, 29:2, 281–302).
6 At various points in the Notebooks, Gramsci refers to the 'caste of the intellectuals' so as to highlight, especially in Italy, the strong separation between intellectuals and the masses: "…because in Italy the intellectuals are far from the people, that is from the 'nation' and are instead bound to a caste tradition, which has never been broken by a strong popular or national political movement from below" (Q21, §4, p. 2116).

7 "The paradigm of anatheism is the suspense provoked by our encounter with the Stranger or Divine Other residing in the human other. Thus, anatheism is an "invitation to revisit a primary scene of religion: the encounter with a radical Stranger whom we choose or not to call God": the "event of the Stranger" is at the core of the anatheist wager" (Kearney, 2011, p. 7).

8 Here, it would be pertinent to also recall the work of Michail Bakhtin on the subversive creativity of carnival in Rabelais and Dostoevsky.

References

Bloch, E. 1995. *The Principle of Hope*, vol. 1. Translated by Neville Plaice, Stephen Plaice and Paul Knight. Cambridge: MIT Press.
Daddario, W. 2019. 'The Open Field of Performance Philosophy', *Performance Philosophy*, 4(2), pp. 325–331.
Dussel, E. 2009. 'A New Age in the History of Philosophy: The World Dialogue between Philosophical Traditions', *Philosophy & Social Criticism*, 35(5), pp. 499–516.
Gramsci, A. 1975. *Quaderni del carcere*. Edizione critica a cura di Valentino Gerratana. Torino: Einaudi.
Kearney, R. 2001. *The God Who May Be: A Hermeneutics of Religion*. Bloomington: Indiana University Press.
Kearney, R. 2011. *Anatheism: Returning to God after God*. New York: Columbia University Press.
Kearney, R., & Feld, A. N. 2017. 'Thinking in Action: An Interview with Richard Kearney', *Review of Contemporary Philosophy*, 16, pp. 150–171.
Kearney, R., & Gallagher, S. 2010. *The International Guestbook Project: Welcoming the Stranger from Hostility to Hospitality; Exchanging Stories, Changing Histories* [Online]. Available at http://guestbookproject.org/. Accessed 10 October 2019.
Kearney, R., & Treanor, B. (eds.) 2015. *Carnal Hermeneutics*. New York: Fordham University.
Kearney, R., & Zimmermann, J. (eds.) 2015. *Reimagining the Sacred: Richard Kearney Debates God*. New York: Columbia University Press.
Kirloskar-Steinbach, M., Ramana, G., & Maffie, J. 2014. 'Confluence: A Thematic Introduction', *Confluence: An Online Journal of World Philosophies*, 1, pp. 7–28.
McKean, B. L. 2016. 'What Makes a Utopia Inconvenient? On the Advantages and Disadvantages of a Realist Orientation to Politics', *American Political Science Review*, 110(4), pp. 1–13.
Mignolo, W. D. 2013. 'Geopolitics of Sensing and Knowing: On (de)coloniality, Border Thinking, and Epistemic Disobedience', *Confero*, 1(1), pp. 129–150.
Panikkar, R. 1988. "What Is Comparative Philosophy Comparing?" in G. J. Larson and E. Deutsch (eds.), *Interpreting across Boundaries: New Essays in Comparative Philosophy*. Princeton: Princeton University Press, pp. 116–136.
Quijano, A. 2007. 'Coloniality and Modernity/Rationality', *Cultural Studies*, 21(2–3), pp. 168–178.
Ricoeur, P. 2006. *On Translation*. Translated by Eileen. Brennan. With an Introduction by Richard Kearney. London and New York: Routledge.
Rohr, R. 2016. *The Divine Dance: The Trinity and Your Transformation*. New Kensington: Whitaker House.
Soldatenko, G. 2015. 'A Contribution towards the Decolonisation of Philosophy', *Comparative and Continental Philosophy*, 7(2), pp. 138–156.
Young, J. 2013. *The Philosophy of Tragedy: From Plato to Žižek*. Cambridge: Cambridge University Press.

14
DECOLONIZING PERFORMANCE PHILOSOPHIES

Melissa Blanco Borelli, Anamaría Tamayo Duque and Cristina Fernandes Rosa

In this co-authored essay, we reflect on how our respective research interests in Latin America have led us to engage with epistemologies of the global south. In your engagement with our writing, we hope you become curious about how critical theory emerges from these spaces, places, and practices. While we do not claim that the work these thinkers and practitioners do is exclusive to the significance of thinking and doing, we do contend that their work deserves the same critical attention as those thinkers and doers whose names are probably more frequently scattered throughout this volume and in standard reference works on performance and philosophy. If you have further interest in this topic, we provide a list of readings as a cursory introduction to decolonial thinking.

Sitting with Sylvia: reflections on the significance of Sylvia Wynter

There exists a well-circulated photo of Sylvia Wynter. She sits, presumably in her office, with some papers and a pen in her hand. Caught in the act of reading, editing, and perhaps even writing, Wynter turns away from the papers and looks squarely at the camera. Her hair, a gorgeous Afro crown, her glasses resting on her nose, amplifying her eyes, looking at us. Perhaps the photographer purposely caught her in *media res*. In our selfie-saturated image culture, perhaps Wynter, like many black radical intellectuals and artists, was ahead of her time. What if *she* directed the angle, the action, the image of her? Then again, given her vehement critique against Western liberalism's concepts of the "human" and by extension the "self," maybe not. Let us suppose, then, that this image is asking for *us* to have an encounter. What does it mean to encounter, and subsequently sit with, Sylvia Wynter?

Human geography scholar Katharine McKittrick poetically comments that, "any engagement with Sylvia Wynter demands openness" (McKittrick 2014, p. x). Her edited volume *Beyond Human As Praxis* (2014) invites scholars from a variety of disciplines to sit and think with Wynter and subsequently write their respective essays. Wynter's significant contributions to scholarship are far beyond the scope of this short introduction. Like McKittrick, I have been open to Wynter's effects on my own thinking since I first encountered her work as a critical dance studies graduate student. One of my professors encouraged us to think alongside Wynter and even asked us to expand on her notion of deciphering practices (1992). Developing a practice of deciphering, as per Wynter's suggestion, means to think about how particular modes of aesthetics (sound, film, performance, or any artistic 'object') develop into cultural imaginaries and the specific rules ascribed to those imaginaries. For Wynter, these rules should not, or rather, *must not,* stand in for universals; rather, they reveal the processes through which they are developed in the first place. Above all else, Wynter advocates for an abolishment of the universal, opting instead for the specificities that make respective existences in the world knowable. But the question persists: how do we know *at all*, and – for our purposes – how do we get to know Wynter in this short encounter?

This writing will not be a hagiography of Wynter. To do that would risk crystallizing her work and all that it continues to offer scholars who aspire to reframe and expand discourses about humanity,[1] aesthetics,[2] decoloniality,[3] or feminism.[4] As a poet, essayist, novelist, philosopher, and scholar, Wynter has worn many hats. She is also known as an actor, dancer, playwright, short story writer, and translator. Rightly so, she fits into the model for the performance philosopher. As a black Caribbean woman, her many roles evidence the inventiveness of black diasporic identity and the multiplicity of roles women of colour have to play in order to be valorized beyond the representational limits bestowed upon us because of coloniality and modernity. In a famous essay "No Humans Involved: An Open Letter to My Colleagues," Wynter draws from public police reports in Los Angeles that consistently use the term "N.H.I," no humans involved, to refer to the murder of black males from economically disenfranchised poor areas of the city.[5] The question concerning the humanity denied to black men (and [poor] people of colour) and the historical and philosophical rationale for this denial become the crux of this epistolary essay that moves through thinkers such as Martiniquais philosopher Frantz Fanon, Polish sociologist Zygmunt Bauman, French thinker Michel Foucault, and Eritrean anthropologist Asmarom Legesse, to name a few. This radical global, epistemological awareness enables Wynter to piece together an argument that ultimately holds us all accountable for "misrecognition in human kinship" (Wynter 1994, p. 42). Knowledge must be rewritten, she states. She advocated this to her own faculty in 1984, but it fell on deaf ears, perhaps due to her intersectional identity and the radical interdisciplinarity of her work. *Knowledge must be written.* The different places from which we know must be identified and valorized. The way we think about knowledge must mutate, shift, and we must develop tools of language, discernment, and deciphering in order to begin to understand.

Without being reductive, one of Wynter's main philosophical concerns is to undo the supremacy of the Western concept of the human. Wynter conceptualizes this in two terms – Man1 and Man2 – where Man1 emerges from the Renaissance imaginary and Man2 from the Enlightenment imaginary. These two "Men" differ in terms of historical moment and their respective developments of the concept "human," and they help explain the 'humanity' of the human (Wynter 2003). If Man1 and Man2 were ways of describing oneself to those who invented it, then these terms automatically dismiss any difference from that image on stage – to use a performative metaphor. Racism and sexism emerge as natural correlates to these constructions. To begin to think decolonially about the concept of humanity is to see the machinations of the advent of the concept. In other words, and in performative metaphoric language, we have to be willing to see that which went on (and continues to go on) backstage, namely, the development of discourses that constructed ideologies and hegemonic knowledge based on colonial and capitalist expansion. These discourses created ideas of (supposed) racial, sexual, and gendered (among other) differences, which we continue to critique and reconceptualize today.

Let us turn to Wynter's call for a deciphering practice that is

> part of the attempt to move beyond our present 'human sciences' to that of a new science of human 'forms of life' and their correlated modes of the aesthetic: to move beyond

what Adorno defined in the wake of Auschwitz as that 'evil' which still haunts human existence as the 'world's own unfreedom'.

(Wynter 1992, p. 240)

Similar to how critical dance studies asks us to think about how particular sets of choreographed choices function within a piece, a deciphering practice requires a careful inquiry into the rules that dictate a particular aesthetic practice. She explains:

> rather than seeking to 'rhetorically demystify', a deciphering turn seeks to decipher *what* the process of rhetorical mystification *does*. It seeks to identify not what the texts and their signifying practices can be interpreted to *mean* but what they can be deciphered to do, and it also seeks to evaluate the 'illocutionary force' and procedures with which they do what they do.
>
> (Wynter 1992, pp. 266–267)

This is a helpful framing, for example, for (white) performance and museum curators who often struggle to find aesthetically appropriate language for artistic work by black, brown, or indigenous artists.[6] Of course, the first port of call should be to consult with artists, philosophers, and writers familiar with or from those spaces from which the art emerges, but, as a practice, deciphering involves the long, laborious, dedicated, ethical engagement with work by another "human." Wynter's calling out of *ontocentrism*[7] necessarily returns us to shift the conversation from *what* we know, to *how* we come to know what we know. She elaborates, "the *ways* in which each culture-specific normal subject *knows* and *feels* about its social reality should in no instance be taken as any *index* of what the empirical reality of our social universe *is*" (Wynter 1992, p. 271).

Wynter's scholarship has become indispensable for those seeking to expand the important fields of critical race studies, postcolonial and decolonial studies. African American Studies scholar Alexander Weheliye was the keynote of *Genres of the Human* conference in 2018, and his concept of "humanity otherwise" relies on his own encounters with Wynter's work and his desire to expose the limitations of discourses about biopolitics (Foucault) and bare life (Agamben).[8] Weheliye's "humanity otherwise" (Weheliye 2014, p. 6) exists as stubbornly persistent forms of life whose abjection subtends the master categories of legitimate and legible humanity (white supremacist, propertied, heteropatriarchal) – but which constitute, through that very abjection, fugitive practices of alternative human being (Menzel 2016). It is these different "genres of humanity," as Wynter would call them, that offer different forms of cognition necessary for the endurance of 'humanity' today, still riddled with intersectional problems of space (e.g. forced, violent migrations, environmental catastrophes), place (e.g. social justice, (g) local economic issues, ethnic cleansing wars), and time (e.g. precarity, labour, transitional justice). Sitting with Sylvia is not necessarily a comfortable respite from a world dominated by European modernity, but it requires an acknowledgement that different contexts create different performance philosophers, who strive to expand how we think, heal, share, make performance, reconsider ontologies of thought, and effect change.

Whilst this previous section articulated a philosophical practice of 'deciphering,' this next section examines how an Afro-Colombian choreographer engages in a type of 'deciphering practice' for the marginalized indigenous and Afro-Colombian citizens of a Colombia in transition from civil war to 'post-conflict.'

Thinking, healing, and sharing: Sankofa Danzafro's *Fecha Límite*

To write this section on decoloniality and performance has been a little difficult. It seems more important to speak about what is going on in the place from where I write than about performance or decoloniality itself. Currently, there are protests from labour and student groups fighting for the right to live with dignity.[9] There are also myriad political issues that impede artists and academics from having a professional life or exercising basic rights.[10] We must look beyond the model of the Western proscenium stage and actually look at, and make connections with, the geopolitical stage itself. This is why the decolonial perspective on performance is fundamental.

In order to align decoloniality and performance philosophy, an understanding of capitalist modernity from the 15th century onwards is necessary. European modernity installed "the colonial matrix of power": integrating multiple hierarchies and classifications of superiority/inferiority, development/under-development, and civilization/barbarism (Castro-Gómez 2007b, pp. 152–172). Peruvian philosopher Aníbal Quijano situates corporeality as a decisive plane where colonial relationships of power materialize the three modalities of collegiality: being, knowledge, and power (Quijano 2000, pp. 342–386). But rather than just outlining the main ideas that constitute the core work of *the collective* modernity/coloniality/decoloniality, I want to draw attention to the spaces where a decolonial practice emerges, and to enable the body-thinkers to speak.

We dance to have a voice

This is what Colombian choreographer Rafael Palacios states when questioned about his work with his Afro-contemporary dance company, Sankofa Danzafro. Sankofa means to 'return to the root'; more than a word, it is an African philosophy from the Akan people in Ghana. This concept is part of a broader and complex system of thinking that insists on the necessity of knowing the past as a condition of understanding the present and projecting the future (Sankofa Danzafro 2018). Sankofa Danzafro enacts this exact philosophy. After twenty-one years of solid and continuous work, the company is exemplary for its pedagogic projects and its commitment to connecting Afro-Colombian communities with the past, in order to understand the present and prepare for the future (Sankofa Danzafro 2018).

Working in a country where racism and classism are as prevalent as in most of Latin America, Sankofa's artistic work intertwines resistance and re-making. It resists ways of stereotyping black Colombians, while it re-makes ways to understand contemporary dance from the topos of black diasporic memory. It offers new ways of being and feeling, especially for its Afro-Colombian dancers, and it reconfigures blackness into Colombian-ness, amidst histories of erasure and inequality, thereby re-creating new possibilities of existence.

Sankofa's most recent work, *Fecha Límite* (which can be translated as Deadline or Expiration Date), was created in 2017 in a residency at the Museo de Antioquia in Medellín. Using Afro-Colombian dance traditions from the Pacific region, this performance is a reflection on land, spirituality, and identity and the histories of dispossession and inequality experienced by Afro-Colombian and Indigenous communities.

In suit and tie, a masked dancer prowls the stage. This dragon-faced man moves around and then disappears. Dancers enter stage-left. Four men and one woman carry *bateas*[11] on their heads. Even though the style of their dresses is inspired by the ones used in traditional dances from the Colombian Pacific coast, they are not the usual colourful and celebratory ones. These are black and mournful.

Ritual, solemn, and in mourning, the movements are a play in contradictions. Using repertory of traditional celebratory dances and Afro-contemporary technique, they combine joy and sorrow, rage and power to create spaces to re-claim and re-exist. They seem to relish the joy of being together and the physical joy of being in their bodies. This is not taken for granted in communities plagued by conflict and bodies regulated by many external forces. The movements are powerful, frenetic yet contained, an aesthetic contradiction that allows a connection between the rage against belonging to a country that historically has offered little space or representation for Afro-diasporic and indigenous communities, and the choreographic power of using space to symbolize their claims for space on the land.

The dancers begin with the *bateas* on their heads, but these slowly transition from prop to an extension of their bodies, materializing those bodies from Colombia's Pacific region where the search for gold in the rivers is an everyday necessity. In their publicity material to sell the piece to foreign audiences, *Fecha Límite* is described as:

> a portrait of the daily struggle of the indigenous and Afro-Colombian communities to maintain and rebuild traditions and legacy in a society shaped by epistemicide. It is a call to action: the time of inequality is over. Now is the time for finding solutions, for rebuilding social fabric, for protecting Afro-Colombian and Indigenous communities from the rain of illegalities and injustice.[12]

This 'call to action' becomes their performance philosophy.

> *Todo el que nace se va a morir*
> *Solo un alma tengo*
> *La quiero salvar*
> *Déjalollorar*
>
> All who are born will die,
> I only have a soul,
> I want to save it.
> Let him cry.

Lyrics from a song performed on stage articulate a need to mourn. The stage design features a sky decorated with bullets as if stars, creating a sense of urgency, of emergency (using both meanings of the word): practices and subjects that emerge out of the context of violence.[13] The choreography allows its dancers and its (Afro-Colombian and/or indigenous) audiences a way to find joy and re-claim their land and identity in a context that for centuries denies the communities their citizenship (a full political, cultural, and economical citizenship). As such, *Fecha Límite* exists as an emancipatory performance practice.

The work of Rafael Palacios with Sankofa Danzafro, his mentorship of other groups such as *Jovenes Creadores del Chocó* (Young Creators from Chocó), and with other processes of dance education in many territories of the Pacific region can be understood as a diasporic epistemology, a space of enunciation that, following the *sankofa* philosophy, connects and processes the past, to understand the present and to project the future. Here, the colonial wounds enacted by patriarchy and racism (and made materially evident throughout the paramilitary crisis) are put at the forefront of his choreographic exploration.[14] Palacios highlights the cultural and personal experiences of racialized subjects, and either the witnessing of or participation in the performance allows for some processing of the pain and suffering of those oppressed by colonial legacies and systems of coloniality. Most importantly, Palacios' work

Figure 14.1 Image from Rafael Palacios' Sankofa Danzafro, *Fecha Límite* (2017). Sergio Gonzáles Álvarez

emphasizes the possibility of knowledge production from a decolonial perspective, and the creation of new possibilities of existence.

In Sankofa's *Fecha Límite,* the colonial wound and its healing process are posited in the entanglements of contemporary black subjects among the exoticizing logics and other 'epistemic traps'[15] that Western aesthetics assigns to black bodies. Sankofa's practice and pedagogy provide opportunities to open safe spaces, sites of enunciation, and self-determining practices that claim citizenship, rights, and empower participation in society. At one point in the piece, the dancers wave the Colombian flag incessantly. An almost overdetermined signification of citizenship takes on new meaning when it is an Afro-Colombian body demanding recognition and affiliation with that flag and all of its colonial, violent, and delegitimizing histories.

> *Todo el que nace se va a morir*
> *Solo un alma tengo*
> *La quiero salvar*
> *Déjalollorar*

This circling back to the words repeated in the song during the performance of *Fecha Límite* acts as a constant reminder to the audience that we have to let him/them cry, because this is a safe space where affect has political potential. And it is precisely in this safe space that the 'colonial wound' can be unveiled, made present, and experienced fully – not as something to be kept hidden, in shame or lament, but to be shared communally.[16] This sharing opens possibilities for healing though 'counter-poetics' (to use a term proposed by Wynter) that challenge hegemonic structures of being in the word through artistic form (Eudell & Allen 2001, pp. 1–7). Performance here is a tool to resist, re-create, and re-make the spaces of colonial domination from unacknowledged and unrecognized realms. In his own way, choreographer Palacios is offering up a way to begin healing the colonial wound especially for Afro-Colombian communities, but not exclusively so. His is an expansive pedagogical-performative-philosophical project whose scope aligns it to, in the case of *Fecha Límite*, the political potential of affect, especially for communities who have not been afforded the opportunity to feel or express the full potential of their subjectivity.

It was a small space inside the Museo de Antioquia where I first saw this performance. There were about sixty people present. Yet, the transfer of energy and affect was palpable. The irony of this moment rests in the fact that this particular museum has played a significant part in constructing a cultural history of the state of Antioquia as solely *mestizo* (a mix of Spanish/European and Indigenous ancestry). In effect, they have contributed to the erasure of the history of blackness as constitutive of Antioquia. Yet, there in a small corner was Sankofa Danzafro, asserting their physicality, presence, creativity, subjectivity, and power. The geopolitics of performance enables these tactical counter-poetics to counter modernity as a "machine that generates alterities in the name of reason and humanism, while at the same time excludes from its imaginary hybridity, multiplicity, ambiguity and the contingency of concrete ways of life" (Castro-Gómez 2000, pp. 145–162). Perhaps the expiration date that *Fecha Limíte* signals is a future conjunction of space and time when marginalized citizenry will be afforded equality and have their knowledge valued for its ability to generate alternative spaces for existing in the world. In the meantime, we wait for performances by artists in the global south to continue to question and undo the darker side of modernity.

Moving from the safe space generated by a Colombian choreographer for the Afro-Colombian community of his ancestry, to the conceptualizing of space by Brazilian choreographer Wagner Schwartz, who uses Brazilian geographer Milton Santos to make sense of his own place in the contemporary dance world, this last section continues the exploration of how deciphering practices establishes new geographic frontiers from which to create corporeal, spatial, and affective philosophies of performance that, in their questioning of modernity, are often censored by governments in the southern hemispheres. Ironically, the deciphering practice here turns on itself, to privilege a politics of respectability that emerged from colonial bourgeois value systems. The colonial wound is deep; yet, we must tend to it.

Geopolitics of space and censorship

In 2006, Brazilian contemporary choreographer Wagner Schwartz published a text in which he discussed the conceptualization of his performance *Wagner Ribot Pina Miranda Xavier Le Schwartz Transobjeto (2005)*, and the process of applying for a production grant, all while travelling to Europe for the first time. Schwartz came to realize that the relevance of his work, and the likelihood of receiving funding from Brazil, depended on his acknowledgement of European artists such as Xavier Le Roy, even if Le Roy might never come to know him. Schwartz wrote:

> I understood the set of relations that would make up my new project. According to Milton Santos, we live in a world that demands a discourse towards the intelligence of things and actions. Space is globalized, but it isn't *mondial* [worldly], except for in a metaphoric way. All places are worldly, but there is no worldwide space. In reality, people and places are globalized. The only worldwide dimension is the market.
>
> *(Schwartz 2006)*[17]

In this excerpt, Schwartz references the work of the Afro-Brazilian geographer Milton Santos (1926–2001), namely "1992: a redescoberta da Natureza" (1992),[18] and *Por Uma Outra Globalização: do pensamentoúnico à consciência universal* (2000).[19]

For Santos, geography is an epistemology of existence. He proposes that we consider space as an intertwined set of systems of objects and actions mediated by techniques. More importantly, his work thinks "outside the box" of Western modernity, and his culminating work on globalization offers three senses for that concept: globalization as a *fable* (the world as a constructed reality, as the globalizing agents want us to believe); as *perversity* (the world as it is and, especially, how it is felt across the global south); and as *possibility* (the world as it could be), which might emerge from "philosophies produced on the various continents, to the detriment of European rationalism" (Santos 2000, p. 60), from which I include, for example, the Amerindian concept of *buenvivir* (to live in plenitude). Above all, for Santos, the perversity of today's globalization, especially its structural organization around capital and competition, "kills the notion of solidarity, returns mankind to a primitive form of individualism and, as if we were to backslide into wild animals, reduces the notions of public and private morality to almost nothing" (Santos 2000, p. 32).

Schwartz took these three concepts, in general, and the relationship between capitalism and "primitivism/wilderness," in particular, and used them to critically reflect on his funding application, which called for a brief description and a video excerpt. It is worthwhile noting that, in Brazil, 95% of all arts and culture funding initiatives are managed by the private sector, via tax exemption laws, with the intent of advancing their brand name (Rosa 2015, p. 208–219). In his funding application, Schwartz echoed Santos and concluded that

> [g]lobalization, therefore, is first and foremost: fantasy (in this section Schwartz wrote 15 lines of text), for the transference is nothing but a promise, and perversity (in this section, Schwartz offered a five minute video recording of the work), due to the practice of competitiveness.
>
> *(Schwartz 2006)[20]*

Over time, Schwartz developed an excerpt of *Transobjeto,* based on *Bichos* (Animals/Things, circa 1960s) by counter-cultural artist Lygia Clark, into a stand-alone solo titled *La Bête* (*The Animal,* in French).

Bichos is a series of sculptures made of aluminium plates connected through hinges that evoke the idea of a backbone. Originally, it was designed to be handled and played with. In today's art market, Clark's work can cost up to two million dollars,[21] and, ironically, her "animals" are often displayed under glass cases as static objects rather than kinetic puzzles with multiple possibilities of forms and movements.[22] By contrast, Schwartz's performance seeks to restore Clark's original concept of art-making as an interactive process and, subsequently, question the commodification of the art world, which overvalues objects as investments and despises artists as disposable labour force.

La Bête begins with Schwartz laying down, naked, playing with a small replica of one of Clark's *Bichos*. After a few minutes, he asks the audience: "Do you want to try?" As a volunteer arises, the performer assumes the position of the "animal/thing" to be manipulated. Although Schwartz is present in flesh and blood, this simple gesture places him in a vulnerable position of otherness. The performer is – albeit metaphorically – dehumanized. In a review titled "La Bête and the barbarism of these dark times," dance scholar Helena Katz notes that Schwartz's choreography pushes the physicality of his body "to the edge of discomfort, imbalance and pain," hence making this vulnerability visible to the naked eye (Katz & Schwartz 2015). Resonating with Santos, Katz concludes that, "it becomes very clear that this is how things present themselves today: One can do to the other whatever one wishes. *La Bête* makes us realize that we are the ones moving barbarism forward" (Katz & Schwartz 2015).

For the past decade, Schwartz's work has gained wider recognition and, in 2017, he was invited to perform *La Bête* at the opening of the *35th Panorama da Arte Brasileira,* at the Museum of Modern Art of São Paulo (MAM). The following day, a video containing a short fragment of Schwartz's performance – depicting a moment when a mother and daughter touch his passive naked body (arms and feet, to be precise) – went viral. Whilst the opening of the exhibition was limited to invited guests and the "nudity content" of the performance was clearly signalled, Schwartz suffered a series of virtual attacks and accusations of paedophilia, with an arsenal of memes and fake news fed by socialbots. The assaults were spearheaded by alt-right organizations and political parties connected to Brazil's agro-business, the pro-gun movement, and neo-Pentecostal religions, collectively known by the anachronism BBB (meaning Beef, Bullet, and Bible). The exhibition's curator and the child's parent, choreographer Elisabete Finger, were similarly attacked and, in the following days, a furious mob invaded the museum and lashed out at its state employees.[23]

The hostile reactions against "the naked man in the museum," as the episode came to be known on social media, clearly reveal the on-going perversity of globalization – especially what Santos calls the tyranny of information, whereby "what is transmitted to the majority of humanity is, in fact, manipulated information that, instead of clarifying, confuses" (Santos 2000, p. 20). Far from being an isolated case, in 2017, alt-right groups stirred up a series of public attacks on social media against the arts and humanities, commonly associated with the Left, collectively framing them as a negative influence on civil society.[24]

Back in 1992, Santos had already noted that the most dramatic trait of our times is the role that fear and fantasy play in our quotidian life.[25] This mixture of fear and fantasy, a recipe arguably deployed in the United States military campaign in search for "weapons of mass-destruction" post-9/11, as well as the media coverage of its last election, and the Brexit vote in the UK, is consistent with alt-right tactics in Brazil. The proliferation of fake news, with its stimulation of hate and suppression of solidarity, coupled with the historical dismantling of critical thinking via cuts in basic education, has pushed disenfranchised segments of the population to support and even applaud their own oppression. In the end, the perversion of globalization in this case lies not only in the strategic manipulation of information to produce scapegoats – or a fake "axis of evil" – but also the distorted appropriation of dissident grassroots tactics, especially the democratized use of technology and means of communication such as social media, to turn the masses into decentralized agents of oppression. In March of 2018, Schwartz confessed in an interview to *Estado de São Paulo* newspaper that "[o]nce the images of 'La Bête' went viral and virtual lynching started, my body became ill. It is impossible to speak at the moment when you are tortured[26]" (Schwartz 2018). He further concludes that

> [t]he "fake news" transforms the haters' will into an image, and in the online life they experience a desire for violence, and the feeling of hatred flows through offline life, creating a sense of fear and insecurity in the public space. And, strangely enough, I felt the mourning of seeing my own body dead on the screen.
>
> *(Schwartz 2018)*[27]

The following year, Wagner Schwartz collaborated with other attacked artists on the creation of *Dominio Público* (*Public Domain*, 2018): a play that departs from the lore around Da Vinci's *Mona Lisa* to address both their freedom of expression and the political appropriation of their images. "To perform again is to return to live," Schwartz indicates.

> It is to be able to look at violence with a certain distance, that only art allows us to do. It is to leave the trauma and go to the act, to return to the spaces that produce reflection instead of confusion.
>
> *(Schwartz 2018)*[28]

Putting theory into practice, more importantly, the stories retold by each artist vivify Santos' understanding of the geopolitics of civil space as an intertwined set of systems objects (e.g. works of art) and actions (e.g. construction of discourses/narratives) mediated by techniques, especially those that decontextualize images and ascribe them new meanings. With the *Mona Lisa* in the background, the monologues problematize both the "fable" and the "perverse" sense of (globalized) modernity and its (neoliberal) reality. Meanwhile, by superimposing the stories *lived* by the artists on stage, this performative response gestures towards globalization as a *possibility*, as Santos envisioned, centred on humans rather than money, solidarity rather than competition.

These three essays were written in solidarity with one another and our commitment to highlighting people, places, and practices that theorize and articulate. In using words, bodies, movements, and aesthetics, these people, places, and practices consider the world beyond the limits of European modernity. We hope to point your attention towards this new 'ground' notably imagined by Sylvia Wynter and advocated for in her intellectual endeavours, for it is the one that will "be of a new science of human discourse, of human 'life' beyond the 'master discourse' of our governing 'privileged text' and its sub/versions" (Wynter 1990, p. 366). We remain hopeful in future intersectional explorations of epistemological differences and how, in those precious differences, alternative modes of existence can arise to rescue us all from 'the dark side of modernity.' As a field, Performance Philosophy might think about plurality, e.g. Performance Philosophies, and look across space and time for the multiplicity of ways to acknowledge, regardless of geopolitical location, how we have all been thinking and making our worlds into being.

Notes

1 See, for example: Wynter, Sylvia. "Unsettling the Coloniality of Being/Power/Truth/Freedom: Towards the Human, after Man, Its Overrepresentation: An Argument." *New Centennial Review* 3, no. 3 (2003): 257–337.
2 See, for example: Wynter, Sylvia. "Rethinking "Aesthetics": Notes towards a Deciphering Practice." in Mbye B. Cham, ed., *Ex-iles: Essays on Caribbean Cinema*. New Jersey: Africa World Press, 1992.
3 See, for example: Wynter, Sylvia. "No Humans Involved: An Open Letter to My Colleagues." *Forum NHI: Knowledge for the 21st Century* 1, no. 1 (1994): 42–71; and Wynter "Unsettling the Coloniality of Being" (2003).
4 See, for example: Wynter, Sylvia. "Afterword: "Beyond Miranda's Meanings: Un/Silencing the 'Demonic Ground' of Caliban's 'Woman'" in Carole Boyce Davies and Elaine Savory Fido, eds., *Out of the Kumbla: Caribbean Women and Literature*, 355–372. Trenton: Africa World Press, 1990.
5 This was written as a direct result of the 1991 Rodney King police brutality incident in Los Angeles and the subsequent 1992 riots after the acquittal of the police officers.
6 Here, I am thinking of the excellent curatorial work done at Berlin's Bode Museum in their exhibit *Unvergleichlich* or *Beyond Compare: Art from Africa*. Notes from the exhibit state that

> the experimental juxtaposition of works from two continents reveals possible correlations on various levels, including historic contemporaneity, iconographic and technological similarities, and artistic strategies. Despite stylistic differences, striking similarities appear in the ways works of art function in both contexts.
> *(https://www.smb.museum/en/museums-institutions/bode-museum/exhibitions/detail/beyond-compare-art-from-africa-in-the-bode-museum.html [accessed 16 April 2019])*

This type of thoughtful intervention around historical and aesthetic contexts helps reconsider how to avoid universalizing or Eurocentric claims to beauty, history, or time.
7 Ontocentrism is the idea that the human pre-exists the complex of signifying practices and discursive systems by means of which it is instituted as such a subject or mode of being (See Wynter 1992, p. 270).
8 In 2018, Wynter was honoured by her alma mater, King's College, in three ways. In June 2018, they hosted a two-day conference, "Genres of the Human: On Sylvia Wynter," the first ever conference about this influential thinker in the United Kingdom. Later, the college added her profile to their Hall of Fame, and in October 2018, ninety-year-old Wynter received an honorary

doctorate. Wynter already has the award of the Order of Jamaica in 2010 for her contribution to education, history, and culture.

9   In November 2018, there were significant student, professor, and workers' unions protests in Colombia because of newly elected President Iván Duque's neoliberal plans to de-fund public education and delegitimize unions and workers' rights with respect to ethical work conditions, fair pay, and ancestral territorial claims. There was also a demand for the state to account for the increasing number of assassinations of human rights and environmental rights activists.

10 These issues include limited access to or existence of grant funding; scarce rehearsal and performance spaces; sustainable employment opportunities as a working artist; and precarization of academic labour at both private and public universities in Colombia.

11 Shallow pan used for gold panning, a manual technique of gold mining.

12 See the Association of Performing Arts Professionals website. « https://www.apap365.org/Conference/Programs-and-Events/Special-Events/UP-NEXT/UP-NEXT-2019-Participants» Accessed 4 September 2018.

13 Since 1948's *La Violencia*, Colombia has been plagued with an over fifty-year civil war pitting conservative and liberal ideologies against one another. Exacerbated by the drug wars of the 1980s, the violence became pathological during the 1990s. A consortium of paramilitaries, guerrilla groups like the FARC, and state-funded military interventions plagued the country with mass murders, forced displacements, human rights abuses, among other collateral damages from armed conflict. In 2016, then President Juan Manuel Santos signed a Peace Agreement with the FARC technically ending the armed conflict and ushering in an era of 'post-conflict' reconciliation and peace. For more information on Colombia's 20th-century history, please consult Maria McFarland Sanchez-Moreno's *There Are No Dead Here: A Story of Murder and Denial in Colombia* (2018).

14 For further elaboration on the concept of the colonial wound, please consult Vazquez, Rolando, and Walter Mignolo. "DecolonialAestheSis: Colonial Wounds/Decolonial Healings." *Social Text Online* 15 (2013).

15 This is an expression used by Walter Mignolo in an interview by Rubén Gaztambide-Fernández. "Decolonial options and artistic/aestheSic entanglements: An interview with Walter Mignolo." *Decolonization: Indigeneity, Education & Society* 3, no. 1 (2014).

16 The term "colonial wound" first emerged in the work of Chicana feminist philosopher Gloria Anzaldua's *The Borderlands*. Walter Mignolo has taken the term and elaborated on it in his work on decolonial aesthetics.

17 Original in Portuguese:

> Entendi quais seriam as relações que iriam compor meu novo projeto. Segundo Milton Santos, vivemos em um mundo exigente de um discurso para a inteligência das coisas e das ações. O espaço se globaliza, mas não é mundial, senão como metáfora. Todos os lugares são mundiais, mas não há espaço mundial. Quem se globaliza mesmo são as pessoas e os lugares. A única dimensão mundial é o mercado.

18 See Santos, Milton "1992: A redescoberta da Natureza." *Revista Estudos Avançados* 6, no. 14 (1992): 95–106. Original in Portuguese:

> Vivemos em um mundo exigente de um discurso, necessário à inteligência das coisas e das ações. É um discurso dos objetos, indispensável ao seu uso, e um discurso das ações, indispensável à sua legitimação. Mas ambos esses discursos são, freqüentemente, tão artificiais como as coisas que explicam e tão enviesados como as ações que ensejam.

19 This book has been translated into English in 2017 as *Toward an Other Globalization: From the Single Thought to Universal Conscience.*

20 Original in Portuguese: "Globalização, portanto, é antes de tudo: fantasia (15 linhas do texto), porque a transferência não passa de uma promessa, e perversidade (5 minutos do trabalho em vídeo), pela prática da competitividade."

21 Lygia Clark's *Contra Relevo* (Objeto N. 7) (1959) sold for $2.255 million at Phillips New York in 2013. https://www.phillips.com/detail/LYGIA-CLARK/NY010513/20 (Accessed 16 April).

22 For an illustration of the range of possibilities inherent to Clark's work, please see Walker Art Center curator Peter Eleey video on Lygia Clark's Bicho and the Walker's exhibition The Quick and the Dead. Available at: https://walkerart.org/magazine/bicho-by-lygia-clark (Accessed 12 March 2019).

23 For a comprehensive list of articles regarding the political appropriation of La Bête and for an extended bibliography on the political appropriation of La Bête on the media, and its repercussion across peer-review journals, books and catalogues, see "Dossier," in Wagner Schwartz Website <<https://www.wagnerschwartz.com/dossier>>

24 Examples include a) Jo Clifford's play *O Evangelho Segundo Jesus, A Rainha do Céu* (*The Gospel According to Jesus, Queen of Heaven*, 2017), closed down for Jesus was played by Renata Carvalho, a transsexual actress; b) Santander Cultural's exhibition *Queermuseu – Cartographies of Difference in Brazilian Art* in Curitiba, closed following protests alleging promotion of paedophilia, zoophilia and blasphemy and, most ironically; c) a petition to ban the US philosopher Judith Butler from coming to Brazil and presenting at the conference *The Ends of Democracy* in São Paulo. During the event, protesters gathered in front of the venue, whereby they burned an effigy depicting Butler as the witch of "gender ideology."

25 "There have always been times of fear. But this is a time of permanent and pervasive fear. Fantasy has always populated the minds of men. But now, industrialized, it invades every moment and every corner of existence at the service of the market and of power and, together with fear, constitutes an essential part of our model of life" (Santos 1992, p. 101).

26 Original in Portuguese: "Assim que as imagens de "La Bête" foram viralizadas e o linchamento virtual teve início, meu corpo adoeceu. É impossível falar no momento em que você é torturado."

27 Original in Portuguese:

> As 'fake news' transformam a vontade dos "haters" em imagem. Elas realizam, na vida online, o desejo de violência. A sensação do ódio escorre pela vida offline, construindo a sensação de medo e de insegurança no espaço público. Eu vivi essa morte. E, estranhamente, senti o luto de ver meu próprio corpo morto na tela.

28 Original in Portuguese:

> Voltar a representar é voltar a viver. É conseguir olhar a violência com uma certa distância, essa que só a arte permite. É sair do trauma e passer ao ato, voltar a frequestar os espaços que produzem reflexão ao invés de confusão.

References

Castro-Gómez, S. 2000. "Ciencias sociales, violencia epistémica y el problema de la "invención del otro". In: E. Lander (Ed.), *La colonialidad del saber: eurocentrismo y ciencias sociales. Perspectivas Latinoamericanas*. Buenos Aires: CLACSO. 145–162.

Castro-Gómez, S. 2007b. "Michel Foucault y la Colonialidad del Poder". *En Tabula Rasa* 6: 153–172.

Castro-Gómez, S., & Martin, D. A. 2002. "The social sciences, epistemic violence, and the problem of the "invention of the other"." *Nepantla: Views from South* 3.2: 269–285.

Eudell, D., & Allen, C. 2001. "Sylvia Winter: A transculturist rethinking modernity." *Journal of West Indian Literature* 10.1/2: 1–7. JSTOR. Available at www.jstor.org/stable/23019776.

Katz, H. 2015. "'La Bête' e a barbárie destes tempos sombrios." [Online], *Estado de São Paulo*. Available at http://www.helenakatz.pro.br/midia/helenakatz11449055738.jpg, Accessed on August 12 2018.

Katz, H., & Schwartz, W. 2015. "La Bête' e a bárbarie desses tempos sombrios." Estado de São Paulo, November 30. Available at Helena Katz Website: http://www.helenakatz.pro.br/midia/helenakatz11449055738.jpg, Accessed August 30 2018.

McKittrick, K. (ed.) 2014. *Sylvia Wynter: On being human as praxis*. Durham: Duke University Press.

Menzel, A. 2016. "And the flesh shall set you free: Weheliye's Habeas Viscus." [Online], *Theory & Event* 19.1. Available at https://muse.jhu.edu/, Accessed October 7 2018.

Mignolo, W. D. 2011. "Epistemic disobedience and the decolonial option: A manifesto." *Transmodernity* 1.2, 44–66.

Mignolo, W. D., & Escobar, A. (eds.) 2013. *Globalization and the decolonial option*. New York & London: Routledge.

Quijano, A. 2000. "Colonialidad de poder y clasificación social". *Journal of World-Systems Research* 6.2, 342–386.

Sankofa Danzafro. 2018. *Sankofa Danzafro*. [Online], Available at http://sankofadanzafro.com/site/#!/sankofa/, Accessed on September 2 2018.

Santos, M. 2000. *Por Uma Outra Globalização: do pensamento único à consciência universal* [e-book]. Rio de Janeiro: Ed. Record.

Schwartz, W. 2006. "WAGNER RIBOT PINA MIRANDA XAVIER LE SCHWARTZ TRANSOBJETO."[Online], *Wagner Schwartz Website*. Available at https://www.wagnerschwartz.com/transobjeto-1, Accessed on August 12 2018.

Schwartz, W. 2018 "Senti o luto de ver meu corpo morto na tela, diz coreógrafo de 'La Bête'" *Folha de São Paulo,* March 8. Available at https://www1.folha.uol.com.br/ilustrada/2018/03/senti-o-luto-de-ver-meu-corpo-morto-na-tela-diz-coreografo-de-la-bete.shtml, Accessed on August 12 2018.

Weheliye, A. 2014. *Habeas Viscus: Racializing assemblages, biopolitics, and black feminist theories of the human.* Durham: Duke University Press.

Wynter, S. 1990. "Afterword: "Beyond Miranda's meanings: Un/silencing the 'demonic ground' of Caliban's 'woman'." In Carole Boyce Davies and Elaine Savory Fido (Eds.), *Out of the Kumbla: Caribbean women and literature*. Trenton: Africa World Press, 355–372.

Wynter, S. 1992. "Rethinking "aesthetics": Notes towards a deciphering practice." In Mbye B. Cham (Ed.), *Ex-iles: Essays on Caribbean cinema*. New Jersey: Africa World Press, 237–79.

Wynter, S. 1994. "No humans involved: An open letter to my colleagues." *Forum NHI: Knowledge for the 21st Century* 1.1: 42–71.

Wynter, S. 2003. "Unsettling the coloniality of being/power/truth/freedom: Towards the human, after man, its overrepresentation—An argument." *CR: The New Centennial Review* 3.3, 257–337.

15

THEATRE-THINKING
Philosophy from the stage

Flore Garcin-Marrou

When philosophers reflect on art, they face multiple methodological challenges due to the disparate nature and heterogeneity specific to the diverse forms and modes of art production. If they embark upon theoretical constructions based on *a concept of art*, beyond the arts in praxis, it would seem that this can only be done in a disembodied fashion by blocking out that which is *the reality of art*: namely, the arts and artists, their specific modes of production, and the audiences that come into contact with the work. And yet, the reality of art requires that we think in terms of *that which exists* and not from what generally constitutes its essence and its principles. While *thinking on art* operates vertically and makes art its subject matter, *thinking artistically* emerges from the ground from which it is produced. Thinking thereby shifts, vacating the speculative field of philosophy to survey the art's sensitive sphere. It is no longer a question of thinking of art as a finished product through the prism of imitating nature, of its relation to reality and to artifice, but rather of grasping it during its execution under the conditions in which it is created and produced, and in terms of its creative capacity – as theatre aesthetician Etienne Souriau understands the term (cf. Souriau 2015a).

This amounts to a fundamental shift in perspective that underpins the autonomy of thought in art with regard to philosophy, a shift whereby each art form can claim to be a fully fledged and unique thought-generating field. Art does not think of itself using philosophical concepts that pre-exist it. On the contrary, it is rather a question of "viewing/thinking practice as closely as possible to its internal needs" (Foucault 2001, p. 1041, trans J.B.), as a process in actuality, not as an object. Artists are better able than philosophers to determine rules and laws for the arts. The arts have no need of an authoritative external thought, like philosophy, to think of themselves.[1]

Assuming that thought in art has subjective connotations, that it is linked to an expressive medium, runs against those, who, in a Platonic tradition, consider that truth in art – despite the fact that "art in its totality is a form of thought" – can only be constantly "veiled by the dimension of appearance that is essential to it" (Rochlitz in Souriau 2015b, p. 1186, trans. J.B). Art's attachment to appearance – namely, to the realm of beings and things – is precisely its strength and the criterion for its veracity.

"Theatre-thinking" as opposed to "thinking-theatre"

In the history of philosophy, there are innumerable positions that argue against theatre insofar as it is conceived as an art of the artificial. Plato did not absolve it for being that art form in which imitation, falsehood, and equivalence triumph, contrasting it to the stability of philosophical ideas. Rousseau preferred popular festivals to theatre, fearing that the representation of mixed and paradoxically tragic feelings or other dilemmas might morally harm the youth of Geneva. Nietzsche regarded theatre as corrupt, preferring more direct forms of arts such as dance and music (cf. Badiou 2013, ch. 2). These are just three canonical examples in which theatre is deemed this or that – or rather, in the negative, as not being (enough of) this or that. The above-mentioned philosophers certainly do not find in theatre the instruments to corroborate their speculative constructions.

We cannot, however, content ourselves with relegating theatre to the status of an object or an example, allowing it to be subject to a desire for essentialisation or instrumentalisation. Theatre has no *essence* and *does not serve*. The result can only be deceptive if thus considered – and there are indeed many who are disappointed with theatre, either because they want to make it voice an opinion, or simply because they expect too much from it in relation to what it actually can convey. In effect, theatre's philosopher-enemies invariably draw on *an idea of theatre*, thus missing out on a possible reversal of perspective with respect to theatre: what if theatre were capable of thought, and capable of thinking itself?[2]

This is what distinguishes the "philosophy of theatre" from what I will call "theatre-thinking," namely – an extension of Etienne Souriau's train of thought – non-speculative thinking that expounds and thinks *from the theatre stage*. If we must reflect about/upon theatre, let us consider it from the stage's perspective and not from received ideas we have about it! Unfortunately, it is commonplace among intellectuals to theorise on theatre without feeling the necessity to specify whether they are considering it from the perspective of antique, classical, melodramatic, popular, Brechtian, post-dramatic theatre... There is no sense, however, in essentialising a chimera that we would designate as "the Theatre."

In the field of theatrical aesthetics, Henri Gouhier has already weighed up the pros and cons of two possible epistemological trajectories: thinking of theatre in terms of essence, or in terms of existence (cf. Gouhier 1943, 1952). In their recent publication *What is the Theatre?* (2019), Theatre Studies researchers Christian Biet and Christophe Triau expose the ambivalence. These are the opening lines of the Preface:

> Above all else, theatre is a spectacle, an oral genre, a fleeting performance, delivered by actors and intended for spectators. It is a work of the body, a vocal and gestural exercise addressed to an audience, most often in a specific location and with a unique décor (...) This dramatic event we call theatre relies on the delivery of that which is both promised and expected: a unique performance witnessed by an audience who have come to the site of the performance for that very reason. (...) Thus, one cannot overemphasise the complexity of this art, of its network of contradictions....
>
> *(Biet and Triau 2019, preface)*

This contemporary definition of *theatre as experience* contrasts with the more traditional definition of theatre as a place where one sees, as a place where actor and public are co-present, and where a real or imaginary world is represented, such as that can be found, for example, in the entry by André Villiers in *Vocabulaire d'esthétique* (Souriau 2015b, p. 1423).

Unquestionably, Biet's and Triau's definition emphasises theatre's peculiarity, singularity, and complexity.

It is this very singularity of theatre, its space and its time, its actual performances that Kierkegaard had already grasped and considered in his text on *Repetition* (Kierkegaard 1983), as well as in his article *The Crisis and a Crisis in the Life of an Actress* (Kierkegaard 2009). The Danish philosopher once went to the Königstädter Theatre in Berlin to see Johann Nestroy's farce-vaudeville, *Der Talisman* (1840). He appreciated the acting quality of those on stage and spotted a pretty girl in the opera-box opposite. Having spent a pleasant evening, the narrator Constantin decides to return the following day to the self-same theatre to experience a renewed pleasure. But he goes from one disappointment to the next: "No box was available for me alone, not even a seat in number five or six on the left," "the young girl was not to be found," and even Beckmann, the actor, could not make him laugh this time. After "enduring" the show for an hour and half, Constantin leaves the theatre, thinking "This is no repetition at all" (Kierkegaard 1983, p. 169). Two days later, the narrator wants to make sure, so tries going back yet again, but again, "the only repetition [is] the impossibility of repetition" (ibid., p. 170). The narrator's mistake is to have believed that repetition is a theoretical concept, possible to anticipate as soon as the decision to repeat is made. But the repetition turns out to be a non-deducible existential category which, far from being cold reasoning, is rather a concept that comes to life through the very act of live performance. Hence, it is indeed within the theatrical sphere, with all the randomness this art comprises, that the philosophical experience of repetition can – or cannot – take place. By dint of this example, Kierkegaard seems indeed to have crafted an existential "theatre-thinking" "moulded on living material" (cf. Deleuze and Guattari 1994, p. 83).

The example lifted from Kierkegaard's *Repetition* reveals to what extent philosophy can re-appraise its relation to empirical data and render fieldwork or situational inquiry a *sine qua non* for exercising thought. Here, the myth of philosophical objectivity is seriously undermined: starting from his everyday life and emotional intimacy, Kierkegaard created a situation from which he drew categories of thought. His thoughts were activated and formulated in the sphere of his relation to the stage and to theatrical performance and derived therefrom. Hence, this "theatre-thinking" is conceived as a field study, comprising an empirical grasp of the object of study in a given environment – a singular object of study, for theatre is situational, a phenomenon in action, a moving, dynamic, contradictory, dialogical reality that can only be grasped in the interaction between the phenomenon itself and its observer.

Thinking the actor's craft from the stage

Theatre-thinking is effective when it comes to considering the actor's craft. Several outstanding theatre theorists employed this approach, notably Diderot, Stanislavski, Meyerhold, and Brecht. The "learned men" of the 17th century, still harbouring Aristotle's disdainful indifference to theatrical representation, had relatively little interest in the actor's particular art. And if they did, it was invariably with Cartesian clarity and rigour. In the 18th century, Diderot ushered in a new empirical approach to theatre: his experience as a spectator enabled him to understand that theatre cannot be reduced simply to its text, but rather that it is an all-encompassing representation, and that the actor is precisely the figure who embodies theatre through the conduit of their play. Diderot's innovative aesthetic bade goodbye to an intellectualist aesthetic of the artwork related to beauty; his approach was to focus more on how to enthusiastically and emotionally fathom that which happens on stage and in its wings.

Diderot developed an in-situ-based thinking, multiplying adventures and experiments, without fear of confronting the paradoxes and contradictions of a thought in-the-making, consciously assuming a critical fragility with respect to certain and definitive positions taken on theatre (these well-known *ideas of theatre* mentioned earlier). The first mention of his experience of the stage and its coulisses can be found in the *Letter on the Deaf and Dumb* (1751) (Diderot 2010): as a spectator, Diderot experienced closing his ears during a performance and thus theorised therefrom a primary intuition on pantomime and the dramatic force of what he refers to as a *tableau* [scene]. *Conversations on the Natural Son*, published in 1757, was drawn from observations of the great figures of the Comédie-Française such as Lekain (after 1752), La Clairon, Mademoiselle Gaussin, Adrienne Lecouvreur, and Baron, but probably also the Italian actors from the New Italian Theatre, fairground performers, Marivaux performers (Silvia, Thomassin, Domenico Biancolelli), Madame Riccoboni, and Mademoiselle Jodin, as evidenced by the correspondence between Diderot and some of these actors (cf. Diderot 1994). A later publication, *Paradox of the Actor* (circa 1771–1775), was influenced by Diderot's crucial encounter with the English player Garrick in 1764 at the home of Helvétius, but also with other actors of the calibre of Lekain, La Clairon, and La Dumesnil, of which we are unsure whether Diderot experienced the anecdotes as reported.[3]

Conversations on the Natural Son is akin to ethnographic research, serving as a logbook or a field journal. The book documents notes taken on the spur of the moment, interviews, sketches, scenes, geographical diagrams, and personal reflections. The dialogues placed experimentation at the heart of theatrical work: they begin with a small cauldron of ideas where we come to realise that theatre is an entirely empirical art. Diderot himself played all the roles he observed and reproduced that which was staged by this theatrical community: a paradoxical sphere in which the work of the actor is ensnared between passion and detachment. Thus, what Diderot advocated in the *Conversations on the Natural Son* was contradicted years later in *Paradox of the Actor*: the actor's craft is considered in all its complexity, which enables field research – and it is this very complexity that underpins the method. *Paradox of the Actor* could be compared to a technical chart from Diderot's and Alembert's *Encyclopedia*, a chart that examines this enigma: "How does an actor function?" The Diderotian actor is not an "inspired" actor, but rather one who employs tools, activates his inner workings to remain "cold and still," and harnesses his emotions so as to ensure regularity in his acting, and not to exaggerate his emotional expenditure, and avoids too much physical and muscular fatigue. Thanks to this *modus operandi*, Diderot's actor can cope with the strenuous demands of the profession.

The Russian theorists of the early 20th century, Stanislavski and Meyerhold, also employed a study of the field when it came to considering the actor's craft. As is well known, Stanislavski developed a system based on the naturalistic theory (inherited from Zola, who himself practised observation techniques in his numerous notebooks, cf. Zola 1993) and on live experiments relating to his student–actors' interactions when confronted with exercises proposed by the master. In *An Actor's Work on Himself* and *An Actor's Work on a Role*, the reader is plunged into the makings of theatre, immediately invited to engage with what is being enacted on stage, avoiding any overbearing and analytical positions when in contact with a certain *idea of theatre*. This aspect of the actor's craft is emphasised by Jean Vilar in the Preface to the French edition:

> [Stanislavski] offers the actor a daily working method, the only one that has invariably been effective. One does not exercise the art of the actor, however, (…) without some confusion in one's faculties. (…) Still, it is also because the actor's odyssey is an

interminable journey into the self, a cloaked, obscure, and hermetic world, laden with folly and doubts (...).[4]

(Vilar in Stanislavski 1986, p. 9, trans. J.B.)

As with Diderot, it is not possible to establish a method or a system if the actor's approach is not empirical; that is to say, one can only fathom the actor's paradoxical and complex craft through rehearsals on a daily basis, and with a certain regularity.

Meyerhold, in his theory on the biomechanical actor, is equally concerned about the need to conceive, practise, and think the actor's art as a craft:

> Art should be utilized by the new class not only as a means of relaxation but as something organically vital to the labour pattern of the worker. *We need to change not only the forms of our art but our methods too.* (...) The work of the actor in an industrial society will be regarded as a means of production vital to the proper organization of the labour of every citizen of that society.
>
> However, apart from the correct utilization of rest periods, it is equally essential to *discover those movements in work which facilitate the maximum use of work time*. If we observe a skilled worker in action, we notice the following in his movements: 1) an absence of superfluous, unproductive movements; 2) rhythm; 3) the correct positioning of the body's centre of gravity; 4) stability. (...) This applies equally to the work of the actor of the future. In art our constant concern is the organization of raw material.
>
> *(Meyerhold 2016, pp. 243–244)*

The Meyerholdian actor exercises a craft inspired by observing a worker in action which he reactivates through gesture, according to the dynamics of the theatre stage that inspire and direct him. Meyerhold, as with Diderot and Stanislavski, developed a method he described as biomechanical, and that we still find today in multiple forms of training for actors, namely a precise physical discipline that embraces observing, reproducing, and rehearsing daily gestures. This theatrical body is not merely aesthetic: it is a political body, for it is a body that sweats, suffers, and produces.

Brecht, the last theorist we will discuss here, engaged in a "thinking-theatre": *Buying Brass*, an unfinished philosophical dialogue, begins one night in 1939. After a performance, a philosopher gets engaged in a discussion with the actress, actor, playwright, and lighting designer. This dialogue calls into question the observation as practised in the naturalistic school of theatre. The philosopher argues against Stanislavski's *modus operandi*: an artist is not a botanist who digs up a clump of fresh earth to observe it, using the theatre stage as a mirror to distort reality – moreover a partial one. The philosopher – a loudspeaker of sorts for Brecht – champions a "theatre of the scientific age" whereby treating society as a field of observation is fundamental: this theatre must "take events as seriously as possible," "using components as raw material" (Brecht 1965). But that which is observed in reality must not be directly replicated on stage. The spectator cannot be confronted with the replication of a crude reality, without commentary or perspective: the spectator cannot be in the position of Pavlov's dog that reacts to stimuli, reflexes that can skew his understanding of a situation more complex than it appears. Brecht cites an example of a small shopkeeper who watches a performance on the Paris Commune: instead of perceiving a popular revolution, he takes the revolutionaries to be enemies, who are likely to break his windows (Ibid, fragment B16). So, for Brecht, theatre grasps reality by observation, but not in any old way: scientific observation of various experiences is required, replicated by a form of theatre that makes them gain visibility. This "theatre of the scientific age" is based on a social science. The philosopher then designates that Marxism be revisited (Ibid., fragment B20). The specificities of Marxist doctrine at the service of theatre will thus be: (1) methods and criteria for observing the world; (2) judgements arising therefrom; (3) judgements leading to practical propositions; and (4) formulation and implementation in situ of a practical form of thinking, which exerts action on reality. As the philosopher points out, this has nothing to do with a philosophy that furnishes a "vision of the world," nor with a theatre that would seek to deliver "images," "illustrations," and "representations" (Ibid., fragment B21). Brecht proposed that the theatre of the scientific age employs observation, not to create illusion as in naturalism, but rather as a compositional method. Echoing Diderot's paradoxical irony, fragment [B22], which closes *Buying Brass'* first phase of writing (1939–1941), finishes with the actor's exclamation, which speaks a lot about his defeat: "That's the intellectualism that devours everything. (...) Latest fashionable attraction: quantum discontinuity! Mental acrobatics!" (Ibid, fragment B22).

What we can draw from these four theatrical theoreticians, who are all "theatre-thinkers," is that they agree that from an engagement with the stage that is theatre, one can consider: (1) that an actor operates a form of labour; (2) that theatre, by virtue of a work of investigation (*historia*), performs a gesture that is laden with (hi)story: a (hi)story – an articulation in words – that offers up the real to be thought and critiqued, from the perspective of the field of theatre. Given that they are only ever experienced, actor and theatre alike thus escape the imperialism of philosophical meaning, and assert themselves as a place and as a physical presence in which paradoxes, nonsense, and complexity are equally open to be thought and experienced.

Demanding professional recognition of the actor's role

From a contemporary perspective, what is to be gained in approaching the work of the actor through an investigation of their field? What constitutes a theatre actor today? Two visions of the actor still prevail: one mystified; the other demystified. The mystified vision draws upon a romantic ideal, on the idea of genius and divine inspiration, thus placing the actor outside the norm, beyond the realm of working society. Artists from this perspective owe their survival to favours by the powerful, to patrons who, through their gifts, protect them from the need to work in the strict sense of the term. In stark contrast to this, the demystified vision consists in portraying the artist as a worker, that is to say, as an individual who exercises his art as a profession.

Nathalie Heinich's *L'Elite artiste. Excellence et singularité en régime démocratique* [The Elite artist. Excellence and Singularity in Democratic Regimes] explores the diverse existential, social, and political positions of the artist (Heinich 2005). Heinich describes their transition from a professional to a vocational regime in the early 19th century: under a professional regime, as a craftsman, the painter works in their atelier, responding to commissions, exercising a trade. As for the vocational regime, it gained foothold in the 19th century, positioning artists among an emerging social elite, heirs to romantic ideals: vocational artists are out-of-the-ordinary, self-determined, driven by internal motivations, whose activity is based on inspirational values (and not on a work value) and on innate talents (and not on apprenticeship). Heinich thus depicts the 19th century as a time when artists were seeking singularity, rejecting that which might link them closely or remotely to work *sensu stricto*, namely to a constrained activity whose service is paid for. She cites Eugène Scribe's vaudeville show, *La Mansarde des artistes* (1821), as an example, which depicts the artist-bohemian as advocating something of a miserable existence, refusing to be gentrified, thus corresponding to a juncture when an "artistic career is no longer regarded as a job through which one earns a living (possibly from father to son), but rather as a vocation" (Heinich 2005, p. 29, trans. J.B., see also Schlanger 1997). Hence, it becomes well thought of to live *for* art, rather than to live *from* art. The legal, economic, aesthetic, and professional ramifications on the artist's status were, of course, significant: Heinich lays bare how vocational artists no longer have a social "function," but instead become a "state of mind" which becomes difficult to quantify and to remunerate. Artists thus belong to the group of "elite-artists," who are plunged into great social and economic precarity. It is something of a paradox: the artist who wants to socially single himself out, to devote himself entirely to the demands of his art, must accept to pay the price, that is, to be marginalised, poverty-stricken, or to accept an assistive mechanism upon which he depends. The artist is concurrently at the nadir and zenith of the social ladder: at once an elite, yet precarious.

In his limpid prose, Roland Barthes highlights this paradox in "The Myth of the Possessed Actor" [*Le mythe de l'acteur possédé*], a short text published in the journal *Théâtre d'aujourd'hui* in March–April 1958:

> In our society, a profession's "nobility" is routinely in inverse proportion to its profitability, in that poor or precarious trades are quite often considered heroic, which, in turn, leads to their practitioners being less well paid for their efforts. Honour replaces money in their professions, and "vocation" the motive of interest. "You, notably actors, what are you complaining about, for you are exercising a vocation?" It is unquestionably because it often pays them poorly and always chaotically that our society rewards its actors with a gratuity that costs it nothing, in the form of some sublime myths.[5]
>
> (Barthes 2002, p. 234, trans. J.B.)

For what valid reasons, we may wonder, does the theatre actor accept, under the guise of exercising a passionate profession or "vocation," to renounce financial reward for their craft? Quantifying any artistic work is challenging and this is precisely what the *Assedic* [Association for Employment in Industry and Trade] enables: to instigate a stabilised salary regime.[6] But is exercising a "vocation" necessarily incompatible with dignified remuneration? In Barthes' words: "This myth of 'being possessed' costs the actor dearly": this stage actor who believes himself only to be deserving of "the sublimated tip that society offers him hypocritically" (Barthes 2002, p. 237): "he stomachs insufficient wages, a precarious status, for he is persuaded that his vocation is at stake and that there is a kind of priceless glory to be devoured by his role" (idem). Barthes concludes: "The struggle for a better professional status is in solidarity with critical art. The actor must help himself to debunk the myths that glorify him, and which only serve to exploit him" (idem). One means available to the actor in order not to fall prey to this false *idea of the actor* who serves the interests of an economy for which culture is an expenditure is *practice in the field to consider the reality of his or her craft*.

This modus operandi that reveals the complexity of a reality and of a practice makes it possible to fight the vocational regime as defined by Heinich, which keeps putting the artist/actor in a position of self-induced precarity. Are we seriously on the right track when society implies that bankers deserve to earn more than the majority of artists because they undertake administrative tasks in a closed office with imposed schedules, unlike artists who have chosen their profession and who consequently must pay for their choice to exercise their profession by accepting economic precarity? The actor's body isn't a body destined for leisure or entertainment… but rather a body at work, political, engaged.

Translated from the French by John Barrett and Alice Lagaay.

Notes

1. The idea that it was an artist, Andy Warhol, and not a philosopher, who managed to formulate a new relation of art to reality in the 20th century can be found in Arthur Danto's analysis of pop art. "[Abstract expressionism] was metaphysical through and through, whereas pop celebrated the most ordinary things of the most ordinary lives" (Danto 1997, p. 130.) See also the introduction in Danto (1981).
2. Cf. Doganis (2012), Garcin-Marrou (2020).
3. Thanks here to Renaud Bret-Vitoz for valuable historical insights. See also: Ménil (1995).
4. Cf. also Stanislavski (1986, 2008).
5. Ibid., trans. J.B.
6. In France, the Assedic is a benefits system that allows artists who might only work at irregular intervals to receive a salary between two contracts. This allows them to stabilise their income throughout the year.

References

Badiou, Alain. 2013. *Rhapsody for the Theatre*. Edited and introduced by Bruno Bosteels. Translated by Bruno Bosteels with the Assistance of Martin Puchner. London: Verso.
Barthes, Roland. 2002. "Le Mythe de l'acteur possédé" (1958), *Œuvres complètes*, t. 1 (1942–1961). Paris: Seuil.
Biet, Christian and Triau, Christophe. 2019. *What Is the Theatre?* Translated by Jason Allen-Paisant. London/New York: Routledge.
Brecht, Bertolt. 1965. *The Messingkauf Dialogues*. London: Methuen 1965.
Danto, Arthur. 1997. *After the End of Art*. Princeton: Princeton University Press.
Danto, Arthur. 1981. *The Transfiguration of the Commonplace*. Cambridge: Harvard University Press.
Deleuze, Gilles and Guattari, Félix. 1994. *What Is Philosophy?* Translated by Hugh Tomlinson and Graham Burchell. New York: Columbia University Press.
Diderot, Denis. 1994. "Lettre à Mme Riccoboni", "Lettres à Mlle Jodin." Edited by R. Abirached. In: *Le Paradoxe sur le comédien*. Paris: Gallimard, coll. Folio.
Diderot, Denis. 2010 [1911]. *Letter on the Deaf and Dumb*. Translated by Margaret Jourdain. In: *Diderot's Early Philosophical Works*. Whitefish, Montana: Kessinger. pp. 142–218.
Doganis, Basile. 2012. *Pensées du corps. La philosophie à l'épreuve des arts gestuels japonais (danse, théâtre, arts martiaux)*, preface d'Alain Badiou, Paris, Les Belles Lettres, coll. "Japon".
Foucault, Michel. 2001. *Dits et écrits,* tome 2. Paris: Gallimard, coll. Quarto.
Garcin-Marrou, Flore. 2020. "La Pensée-théâtre", revue *Théâtre/Public*, Jan. 2020, n° 235.
Gouhier, Henri. 1943. *L'Essence du théâtre*. Paris: Vrin.
Gouhier, Henri. 1952. *Le Théâtre et l'existence*. Paris: Vrin.
Heinich, Nathalie. 2005. *L'Elite artiste. Excellence et singularité en régime démocratique*. Paris: Gallimard, coll. Bibliothèque des Sciences humaines.
Kierkegaard, Søren. 1983. *Repetition, A Venture in Experimental Psychology, by Constantin Constantius*, (1843). Edited and translated by Howard V. Hong and Edna H. Hong. Princeton: Princeton University Press.
Kierkegaard, Søren. 2009. *Kierkegaard's Writings, XVII: Christian Discourses: The Crisis and a Crisis in the Life of an Actress*. Translated by Howard V. Hong and Edna H. Hong. Princeton: Princeton University Press.
Ménil, Alain. 1995. *Diderot et le drame*, vol. I, *Le Drame,* vol. II, *L'Acteur*. Paris: Pocket.
Meyerhold, Vsevolod. 2016 [1922]: "Biomechanics." Translated and edited by Edward Braun. In: *Meyerhold on Theatre*. 4th Edition. London: Bloomsbury, pp. 243–254.
Schlanger, Judith. 1997. *La Vocation*. Paris: Seuil.
Souriau, Étienne. 2015a. *The Different Modes of Existence*. Translated by Erik Beranek and Tim Howles. Minneapolis: Univocal.
Souriau, Étienne (ed.). 2015b. *Vocabulaire d'esthétique*. Paris: P.U.F., coll. Quadrige.
Stanislavski, Constantin. 1986. *La Formation de l'acteur*, introduction de J. Vilar. Paris: Pygmalion (Stanislavski, Constantin: *An Actor Prepares*, London: Methuen 1988).
Stanislavski, Constantin 2008. *Building a Character*. London: Methuen 2008.
Zola, Emile. 1993. *Carnets d'enquêtes. Une ethnographie inédite de la France*. Paris: Plon, coll. Terre humaine.

16
PHILOSOPHY AND THEATRE
Incestuous beginnings, looking daggers and other dangerous liaisons – a dialogue

Emmanuel Alloa and Sophie-Thérèse Krempl

Emmanuel Alloa: For as long as one can remember, philosophy and theatre have entertained a passionate, yet also deeply conflict-ridden, relationship. Let's start with the present situation. Although you and I both try to keep an eye on current developments in philosophy and in theatre alike,[1] we look at them from quite different vantage points. The first question that springs to my mind is that I would like to have your opinion on what has been called "performance philosophy", and, more generally, on the "performative turn" and/or the "theatrical turn" in philosophy. For someone like me, who works in philosophy as an academic discipline, observing recent developments, I have some thoughts as to why an insistence on, say, the embodied, situated and performative side of thinking appears to be attractive for a growing number of people. I was wondering whether, from the perspective of someone who has been working in European public theatre institutions for many years, you have the impression that this tendency is mirrored by an analogous counter-tendency, a sort of "conceptual turn" in the performing arts. The reason I'm asking this is because in the visual arts some people complain that "theory" has become the grand new signifier, especially since many artists now go through more sociological and philosophical types of training, and conceptual self-fashioning might now seem to count more than the artistic quality of the works. Is there a new obsession with the "theatre of ideas", in your opinion, and is "post-dramatic" theatre equivalent to a new form of conceptualism?

Sophie-Thérèse Krempl: In theatre, as far as I can see, there is quite a backlash happening. Even if the performative approach to theatre, qualified as "post-dramatic" by Hans-Thies Lehmann in the 1990s (Lehmann 2006), also covers conceptual forms of experimenting with theatre, conceptualism conceived as a radicalization of your reading of a "theatre of ideas" had its momentum in the 1990s and early 2000s, but is now going through a phase of ideological transformation in the theatre field, while the number of conceptually working theatre directors as well as those with a performative approach is increasing. Thus, the post-dramatic, performative concept of theatre goes far beyond all those easy-to-sell ideas of conceptualism. Nevertheless, we should try to define what post-dramatic theatre encompasses, since it has indeed developed a new form of conceptualism which seeks to combine so-called performative with so-called dramatic forms, presenting not only post-dramatic but also 'post-ideological' aesthetics in theatre. But if this form of conceptualism is currently undergoing a thorough transformation, it is for a reason which should really make us nervous and worried, and not only artistically or philosophically. But I am sure we will come back to this topic later on.

In talking about theatre, the term 'theatre' itself offers manifold instances of metaphors, and makes keywords or buzzwords easily tend to work with metaphorical implementations. Theatre was never intended to be unambiguous or unequivocal, but at the same time it is possibly the most philosophical of all kinds of art. Theatre, like philosophy, engages with the human condition, but unlike philosophy, it necessarily includes the social dimension, addressing the other, in principle, as an inapprehensible being. I consider theatre to be essentially socially determined. It deals with the social conditions of human life. The moment a performance begins, it both represents a social act of communication, and results from social interaction, regardless of the number of people on stage. The audience is one of two core parts of the theatre, with or without the fourth wall. It is in fact its only stable element, which is not the case for other forms of art. Theatre is an essentially interactive event appearing in simultaneity. This basic construction of what makes an action a theatrical act – estrangement by pretending or even claiming to do something real in front of people watching – that is what we must consider when talking about theatre, performance, philosophy and performative turns, because it is important to distinguish between dramatic and performative acts, and between the philosophical and theatrical sense of representation. In understanding these distinctions, we come closer to the difference between, and the related nature of, theatre and philosophy, I suppose.

E. A.: We might wonder whether some recent developments in theatre and in philosophy point in a similar direction, or whether they stand for inverse movements. Let's take 'post-dramatic theatre' and 'performance philosophy', respectively. Some people read the turn to performance philosophy as an urge to move away from sterile scholastic nitpicking and to revert to a more Socratic situation, emphasizing the concrete situation and the 'drama of thinking', while the notion of 'post-dramatic theatre', summarizing a variety of tendencies in the avant-gardes since the 1960s, supposedly marks a move towards a more conceptual form of theatre. I would be curious to have your reading on this, and to see how this term is perceived in current cultural politics at theatre institutions. Personally, I think this opposition is flawed. As I read it, post-dramatic theatre is not so much a move away from drama as such (the famous Greek *drân*) as a move away from the dominance of the text in theatre practice. This might be a first way of disentangling the notion of theatre from that of performance: while theatre is often heavily dependent on a text (a drama, a play, a script, etc.) – performance and performance art are fundamentally set against any form of linearity or of a script which would pre-scribe what there is to be experienced or understood. Unlike a Shakespeare drama, which you might steep yourself in before going to the theatre in order to better grasp the subtleties of plot, character and language, there isn't necessarily any text you might want to read before going to a performance event. Rather than doing away with drama, figures like Tadeusz Kantor, Jan Fabre, The Wooster Group or Romeo Castellucci have reinvented and displaced it, I would say. There has never been any better illustration of Ortega y Gasset's old claim that "man is a drama" (Ortega y Gasset 1961, pp. 113 and 205) and that philosophy should start anew from this *drân*.

But before you answer, let me also comment on another important point you raised. If I understand you correctly, it makes no more sense to speak of a private theatre than it does to speak of a private language. The (in)famous 'theatre of representation' of classical epistemology à la Leibniz or Locke, so often decried by 20th-century philosophy, where the mind is depicted as some empty stage upon which ideas playact imitations of occurrences in the empirical world, could be reread in this light: even within the closed setting of the mind conceived of as a *camera obscura* (or a Leibnizian *monad* without windows), there has to be a form of self-reduplication between the mind as a stage director and the part of the mind that plays the part of the audience. But if we leave aside for now this problem of philosophical epistemology (and of the "theatre of representation", which leads us back to Plato's allegory of the cave), the question of the "theatre of ideas" remains topical. We could identify two different concerns: philosophy, on the one hand, with its desire to embody (concretize, actualize, personify) its abstractions, and theatre, on the other, which feeds on ideas, as you say, but also amounts to much more than the direct translation of an idea.

S. K.: To my understanding, the 'theatre of ideas', together with your beautifully pointed theatre illustrations, as well as Leibniz' *monads* or Locke's *camera obscura*, work as metaphors to describe the human incapacity to capture what Kant defined as the eternal difference between reason and intellect, between the human capacity to create rules that oblige us to truth, and our incapacity to understand why this is possible (cf. Kant 1998). Following this, we could re-draw your theatrical imagery and make reason perform as the director and the mind represent the actor, doubled by spectators who are allowed to choose which part they want to identify with or adopt. But this also shows why we have to be careful when arguing with the metaphoricity of theatre – because it can have a deep philosophical impact. I hope to make it clear here when I try to summarize that in a philosophical context, the term 'theatre of representation' refers to identity and to abstractions of truth, and perhaps also to the 'presence of truth', but in a theatrical context, it refers to 'estrangement of reality'. Listening to your descriptions of the performative turn in philosophical discourse (or philosophy as a discipline) in terms of beginning to personify its abstractions, to embody its thinking and to actualize its concepts – am I right to conclude that the performative turn in philosophy is where it begins to reflect upon its doing and thinking in terms of its psychological, social and spatial conditions? Because this leads me to think of Bourdieu's descriptions of the social determination we are subject to, and the social fields that confine our social and, not least, intellectual freedom (Bourdieu 1984, 1990). But I am not sure of the consequences for the intellectual matter of thinking. Does performance philosophy evoke questions about its own psychosocial conditions, and try to integrate them into thinking, and perhaps also into new forms of performing philosophical lectures? If so, then we might be about to experience the unification of theatre and philosophy, especially since there is a huge difference between post-dramatic theatre and dramatic theatre as such, namely concerning the significance of the body and the significance of the word. There is no need for drama, as founded on Aristotle's unity of action, time and space, and the elements of exposition, climax and catastrophe (cf. Aristotle 1968); no need for a text even to perform theatre anymore, because performative acting has developed. Dramatic acting and speaking points to a meaning outside the theatrical body, while performative acting and speaking identifies the body and the meaning signified by the theatrical body. This marks its contrast with performative acting onstage.

It is not so much a process of opposing aesthetics but of integrating aesthetics that allowed post-dramatic theatre to emerge, at least since Robert Wilson created his famous work *The CIVIL warS*[2] in the early 1980s, a twelve-hour-performance, never performed as a whole.[3] "Post" indicates not only that the validity of the dramatic text is challenged, but that an aesthetic development has taken place which insists that in order to create a theatrical event, there is no need for drama anymore. There is not necessarily a distinction between theatre as a drama-driven performance, creating a linear narration on stage, and performance art as a contradiction of everything that would describe the other. Both are theatre, because both signify the basic theatrical agreement that one party is acting and one party is watching, and theatricality evolves out of the actor-performer being conscious of their playacting body.

Although theatre is still produced in some places as if no aesthetic, performative revolution ever happened, in current theatre aesthetics, contemporary theatre directors know how to handle text in a post-dramatic way, a choreographer using text for their dance piece, in a more or less representational way. But intertwining varying aesthetics leads to new requirements the spectator has to meet. The spectator is now expected not only to know *King Lear*, but to be able to understand why *King Lear* might be performed by a woman giving a speech written by Jelinek rather than Shakespeare. The spectator has to decode a broader variety of texts and aesthetic languages that have come to the stage. But the spectator is also invited to discover the personal instruments they need to interpret what they observe happening on stage. This is the political impact of deviating from the dramatic text on, in and with the theatre: it is an implicit demand to provoke the spectator's personal fantasy and to make sense of their observations. It is no accident that theatre artists like Castellucci, Fabre, Kantor, but also Elfriede Jelinek or Christoph Marthaler have their provenance in the visual arts or music (Castellucci, Fabre and Kantor were first educated in painting, Jelinek and Marthaler in music and composing). Post-dramatic theatre began with questioning the ability of the text to still be a *signifier* of truth, and the ability of theatre to claim something like truth. These are genuinely political and aesthetic aspects of the development of the cultural politics of theatre institutions.

E. A.: It sounds as if, in the European theatre world, some of the heated aesthetic controversies of earlier decades have now subsided, making space for a more liberal range of aesthetic options. And I imagine you would probably also include, beyond the classical staging of drama and post-dramatic performance, other forms of theatre such as documentary theatre, archive-based theatre, participatory practices with nonprofessionals or phenomena like citizen theatre (*Bürgertheater*), etc. However, even if the 'prohibition years' might be over today, where avant-garde theatre-makers would define their art dialectically by opposing it to the other kind of theatre they consider preposterous, the theatre world still yields crucial debates regarding aesthetic form. To quote Saint Paul: even if everything is allowed, not everything is edifying.[4] While this might surprise you, I see a significant difference here between the situations theatre finds itself in and that of institutional philosophy. Theatre (like any other art) cannot do away with a reflection on its own form. I guess few would contest this. Regarding philosophy, on the other hand, I tend to see the opposite tacit consensus: mainstream Anglo-European academic philosophy has found for itself a certain standard form of publishing, writing and debating which might include extremely varied positions in terms of content, but which is excruciatingly homogeneous in terms of its form. There is so rarely any debate on the 'form' of philosophy and this certainly explains in part why something like 'performance philosophy' has become appealing to some. Since you ask what is meant exactly by 'performance philosophy', I would have a hard time giving a precise answer, and other people in this volume will certainly be more qualified to do so. But I don't want to steal myself away from the challenge either, so I will tentatively suggest the following definition: if philosophy was always about questioning, its questioning has usually taken the form of a 'what?' question (what is Being? What is truth? What is happiness? etc.). In contrast to this, performance philosophy stresses the 'how?' 'How', that is to say, 'where' and 'when', 'who', with what words, in what context and with which voice, are such questions asked? (Significantly, Deleuze associated questions like these to what he called the 'method of dramatization'. Cf. Deleuze 2004.) When we ask questions like 'who?', 'where?' and 'when?', there is, of course, a sociological dimension, and no wonder Bourdieu sprung to your mind. And if this interrogation and its implications on power relations were merely sociological, you would be right to wonder to what extent this can be called a philosophical exercise.

When Bourdieu questioned the 'scholastic attitude' of the philosopher, he claimed he wasn't doing this as a philosopher but merely as a social scientist; and when Foucault questioned the philosopher's discourse on madness, he claimed he was doing so from the strict perspective of the historian (in both cases, there was deliberate bad faith at stake, of course). Modernity might be defined by a division of labour necessary in knowledge and science too. Nonetheless, I believe such specializing tendencies can also be detrimental to the overall critical endeavour.

This leads me back to the fundamental issue you raise: *to what extent is philosophy still philosophical when it questions its own conditions?* Maybe, in order to avoid misunderstandings with regard to the notion of (social or historical) condition, we should prefer the more neutral notion of 'form'. How do ideas take shape and what does it mean to give them a certain form rather than another? This reflection has almost completely disappeared from contemporary academic discourse. At best, it has become a matter of neuro-philosophy, which is yet another way of outsourcing the issue to a non-philosophical context. If theatre and all forms of corporeal expression have something to tell us, it is how the 'what' and the 'how' cannot be dissociated: the content (the idea) cannot be disentangled from its sensible, located embodiment, from its voice, tone, prosody, etc., since both are coextensive, and subtracting one from the other would amount to killing both. After all, all prominent philosophers searched for the appropriate form for their thoughts, using or sometimes even inventing new styles and formats, from Parmenides' poems and Plato's dialogues via Aquinas's thought architecture and Montaigne's *Essays*, or Nietzsche's aphorisms all the way to Wittgenstein's protocol sentences in the *Tractatus* and Heidegger's *Fugen* in the *Beiträge*. In the 20th century, we learned that this coextension is dangerous: the very point about the 'power of the better argument' is that it can be put forward by anyone, regardless of their voice, social position and authority. This is maybe the most fundamental stratum in philosophy's antitheatricality: by fighting theatricality, philosophy championed a certain understanding of universality and abstraction and, indirectly, of emancipation. Would you agree or how should we read philosophy's conflictual relationship with its own form?

S. K.: I do agree with your statement that philosophy has its 'prohibition years' yet to come. Nevertheless, I want to insist on the impact that the social attitude has on the value of the spoken word. While it is not always so much about *what* is said as about *who* is saying it, the 'how?' question, on stage and in philosophy, is also of utmost importance. In times like ours, the discrepancy between the speakers' social standpoint and, accordingly, their form of speaking, becomes even more crucial the more heterogenic the group of speakers becomes. Even if the performative turn does not end by reflecting the philosopher's social dimension and rather emphasizes the impact the form has on the idea, there is a question of power at issue in how one can manage the unfolding of one's 'power of the better argument'. Thinking about performativity must include the (self-) reflection of the performing subject. So, it might not surprise you that I refuse to claim that the 'prohibition years' in theatre are over; they continue in a transformed manner. As a result of performative forms merging into theatre, controversies might have stopped in terms of debating over the form, but only to transform into questions regarding the space in which theatre takes place. As a consequence, for a few years now, we have been able to observe new conflicts about what kind of theatre space is deemed appropriate for what aesthetic form of theatre, with the black cube increasingly being abandoned for new venues. The claim is to create new forms by establishing new spaces, and also to demand of theatre that it leave its familiar spaces to be set free for more heterogenic forms of theatre for a 'new' public not traditionally accustomed to visiting theatre spaces. This corresponds to all the diverse forms of theatre you previously described. Implying that the theatre venue as a public space has a crucial impact on what is to be performed in it, we can observe a kind of 'spatial turn' preoccupying theatre art and opening up arguments on artistic and moral authority, on what is to be represented on and by the stage, which has now been discovered to be a 'bourgeois' place, possessed and 'occupied' by an 'elite from former times'. (Speaking pejoratively of elites from an elitist standpoint is very *en vogue*, by the way…)

This development affects the form. As a crisis of authority can be said to characterize our times, we can compare the crisis of political representation to the aesthetic crisis of the representational theatre. While theatre deals with the transformation of space and thereby with a transformation of performance and the character of theatre itself, philosophy reflects on transformations of the form by the idea, accentuating its performative approach to truth as a universal concept. At least we find philosophy and theatre in similar, albeit contrary, difficulties. Now, both deal with questions of – to put the accent on Foucault here – *governmentality* (Foucault 2007), just as at their incestuous beginnings 2,500 years ago. Both deal with truth and power, but with contrasting approaches. No wonder Plato refused to accept the poets – he feared they might be the philosophers' mightier opponents. However, the antitheatricality of philosophy, originating from an age-long argument about the appropriate form philosophical discourse must take in order to unfold its impact, had its very starting point in tragic theatre. If theatre tends to find its answers before its questions (Lukács 1971), philosophy finds the questions to its answers in Greek tragedy. Greek tragedy describes humanity's emancipating from a self-created image of truth, from God as the concept of unity. Theatre as well as philosophy are genuine modes of emancipation. Tragedy is a metaphor for truth, if you will, and philosophy has the means to analyse this metaphor as a poem, as well as in terms of an answer for which it still has to formulate the appropriate question. In other words, in its beginnings, philosophy represents the coming-into-concept of theatre, and was born of tragedy. This is why I would expect the performative turn in philosophy to discover theatre to be its sensible sibling.

E. A.: Much food for thought here. Let's set aside the debate about whether all theatre forms are now freely available in all institutions or not, as you seem to imply. (Personally, I find it worth noting how strong the public resistance has been to performance and event-oriented approaches in theatre in Western Europe, coming from both a very conservative audience, such as the response to the nomination of Matthias Lilienthal at the *Münchner Kammerspiele*, as well as from the progressive cultural scene, such as in Chris Dercon's case at the Volksbühne in Berlin[5]). Certainly, the urgency to rethink the issue of space and of the speakers' identities is palpable all over the place: 'where' can theatre be relevant again, and 'who' should be acting in whose name? Needless to say, this crisis of aesthetic representation – of the spaces and stages of representation as well as of the actors of representation – interlocks with a crisis of political representation. This is also why in a sense, the attempts by performative (or should one perhaps say, project-based, as opposed to text-based) theatre to have the subjects concerned playing their own role on stage – think of *Rimini Protokoll* – are so highly ambivalent. If a person stages their own daily life (say as a migrant in Europe or as a ragpicker in Istanbul), is this per se an emancipatory, reflective move? Or is this just another perverse form of identity politics, where minorities are cast to perform their assigned social identity? Let's name the elephant in the room here: what are we to do with the question of the 'spectacle'? If thinkers from Plato via Rousseau to Guy Debord have demonized the spectacle, that is because, indeed, it subordinates truth to the issue of power, an infinite replication of the same, through an endless parade of simulacra. Masks cannot but mask the real thing – whence philosophy's theatrophobia, starting with Plato allegedly burning his early theatre plays according to Diogenes Laertius, and its looking daggers at its sensible sibling (as you nicely put it), with whom it sanctimoniously denies any kinship. But of course, there's also the other tradition, the one associated with Nietzsche, who knew very well that the love of truth is itself a tragic endeavour. Rather than believing in a space devoid of power, which would only be dedicated to an argumentative progression towards knowledge, he recalled that truth and power have always been indissociably intertwined, and that the pertinent question is rather *which* powers to use and *how*. Powers – tragic or ecstatic – that would allow us to be *more* or otherwise than what we are now. Whatever is profound needs a mask, says Nietzsche, and maybe today, in our society of spectacle, we are still desperately in want of an understanding of what exactly that means.

S. K.: I could not agree more, but I must add to your short report on Matthias Lilienthal's approach to *Münchner Kammerspiele*, for I believe it typifies what you described as the subordination of truth to the issue of power, disregarding better judgment. When forcing one to take sides with either a concept-based or drama-based theatre, that kind of model would aim at demolishing the kind of theatre art which Lilienthal considers "art crap", by which he labels a theatre that represents the 'bourgeois theatre' of a 'former-to-be' public. To me, an emancipatory approach to theatre means that there is no illegitimate audience and no illegitimate form of theatre, but a legitimate legacy for experimenting to find out what forms are appropriate as a means of deviating from common perceptions of reality. However, at this present moment in time, we have to state that a theatre that claims certain art forms to be the good ones is at risk of confusing minorities with elites, quantities with masses (Ortega y Gasset 1930) and the bad with the evil (Nietzsche 2014). As a result, theatre is no longer about an opposition between concept-based and drama-based theatre; it is no longer about truth, but rather about representation and space, and when it comes to representation – as we have stated before – the question of power arises: artistically, politically, and morally. In this respect, there is no more good or bad theatre, but, according to Nietzsche, good or evil theatre, making demands of truth onstage. So, I would like to thank you, Emmanuel, for calling the elephant by its name. Truth, named as truth onstage, is not truth anymore. This is one of the most trivial insights in decoding theatre, because theatre *is* masking, *is* pretending-to-be/-act, *is* figure-ing, *is* estrangement, *is* re-presenting something that we, the audience and public, can possibly, but not necessarily decode as true or real or profound. This is why the discourse on performativity was invented and why questions regarding the authenticity of stage action are necessarily raised, and particularly regarding the discrepancy between truth and authenticity per se. Neither philosophy nor theatre art is about opposing forms at all, but about how theatre or philosophy – no matter what their form – can contribute to provoking new perceptions of reality or meanings of truth.

It is all about reality onstage, we must never forget that, but also about a masked reality and about masking reality. A theatre that seeks to contribute to questions of emancipation and identity has a great need for philosophy to actualize a social understanding of truth, and to perpetuate the difference between power and truth. Let me conclude our conversation with a quote by the greatest philosopher of theatre in claiming its truth: "*Life is a tale told by an idiot, full of sound and fury, signifying nothing*".

Notes

1 The focus here is on developments in contemporary Western/European philosophy and theatre.
2 Robert Wilson, *The CIVIL warS. A tree is best measured when it's down*, 1981–1984.
3 Cf. film documentary by Howard Brookner, *Robert Wilson and the Civil Wars. A Documentary.* Unisphere Pictures, 1987. Cf. also: Shvetsova (2007).

4 Cor 6, 12.
5 Note: Director Matthias Lilienthal was appointed director of a major German theatre institution in Munich, the *Kammerspiele* in 2015. His performance-oriented approach to theatre, and its move away from traditional 'straight' theatre, met strong resistance. At the same time, in Berlin, at the legendary *Volksbühne* theatre, that had long been associated with its director Frank Castorf and his radical, also performative, but still drama-based theatre, the secretary of culture presented a personality coming from the fields of visual arts – the Belgian curator Chris Dercon – as Castorf's successor. The nomination led to a year of turbulences and debates about the gentrification and managerialization of the cultural sector in Berlin, eventually forcing Dercon to resign.

References

Aristotle. 1968. *Poetics*. Oxford: Clarendon Press.
Bourdieu, Pierre. *Distinction*. 1984. *A Social Critique of the Judgement of Taste*. Cambridge: Harvard University Press.
Bourdieu, Pierre. 1990. *The Logic of Practice*. Stanford: Stanford University Press.
Brookner, Howard. 1987. *Robert Wilson and the Civil Wars*. A Documentary. Unisphere Pictures.
Deleuze, Gilles. 2004. "The Method of Dramatization" [1967]. In *Desert Islands and Other Texts. 1953–1974*. ed. David Lapoujade, trans. M. Taormina. New York: Semiotexte, pp. 94–116.
Foucault, Michel. 2007. *Security, Territory, Population: Lectures at the Collège de France 1977–1978*. Basingstoke: Palgrave Macmillan.
Kant, Immanuel. 1998. *The Critique of Pure Reason*. New York: Cambridge University Press.
Lehmann, Hans-Thies. 2006. *Postdramatic Theatre*. London: Taylor & Francis.
Lukács, Georg. 1971. *The Theory of the Novel*. Cambridge: MIT Press.
Nietzsche, Friedrich. 2014. *On the Genealogy of Morality*. Stanford: Stanford University Press.
Ortega y Gasset, José. 1930. *The Revolt of the Masses*. New York: W.W. Norton Company.
Ortega y Gasset, José. 1961. *History as a System* [1941]. New York: Norton.
Shevtsova, Maria. 2007. *Robert Wilson*. London: Routledge.

17
AESTHETICS OF [THE] INVISIBLE
Presence in Indian performance theory

Sreenath Nair

The question of ephemerality in current Performance Studies scholarship needs a different critical framing and vocabulary – not to debate the relationship between the archive and performance, but to understand the nature of the spatiotemporal dimensions of how the *invisible* emerges and operates in the flesh of performance. In this essay, I wish to focus on the philosophical insights of Indian performance theory, arguing that the notion of "presence" in the *Natyasastra*[1] cannot be conceived, in the strict Derridian sense, as the traces of the play of absence[2] (Olson 2011, p. 215), but the dismissal of it: performance as the presence of excess. In order to do this, I intend to outline two sets of critical observations that further contextualise the investigation of the ontology of the body in performance. Firstly, I examine the *Natyasastra*'s concept of visibility and presence, showing how embodiment and imagination inform the foundational discourse of the emotive experience (*rasa*[3]) of performance. Here, I turn my attention to Peter Brook's production of *Battlefield* (2015), to situate the discussion of ephemerality, arguing that the performance exists only in the fictive and imaginary world, and hence, the 'real' in performance cannot be misunderstood as physical existence. I will also recount the articulation of an ontology of absence by Indian logicians such as Gautama (600 BCE–200 CE) to emphasise the way in which [the] invisible gains the same ontological status as the visible in Indian performance theory. Following this, my second set of observations will shift the emphasis from the body in performance to the act of perception to identify a gap in current debates on the ontology of performance. Finally, I argue that Indian performance theory, through the idea of the experience of art as *rasa* or taste, offers new ways of understanding the material base of [the] invisible in performance.[4] In this way, I will argue, performance functions as heterotopia, the "other site" (Foucault 1986, p. 24) where imagination, both in terms of creation and perception, gains a new ontological dimension, in which the fictive becomes 'real' when the performance takes place. This, I will suggest, is the aesthetics of [the] invisible, by which performance creates excess rather than its own disappearance as 'trace'.

Following Peggy Phelan's oft-cited yet still controversial affirmation that "performance's only life is in the present … [and that it] cannot be saved, recorded, documented" (Phelan 1993, p. 147), Performance Studies scholars have actively debated the purported ephemerality of performance from a range of critical view-points. Comprising a range of complex associations between moments of encounter, interaction, perceptual engagement and imagination, that constantly create and recreate past and present, visible and invisible, the enigmatic nature of performance's "presence" as a temporal event continues to trouble critical discourse. And indeed, this enigmatic relationship between the visible and the invisible also informs some of the key philosophical debates in Indian performance theory and practice, from the theory of *rasa* in the Natyasastra, to performance practices such as *Kutiyattam*[5] and *Kathakali*.[6] 'Visibility' and 'seeing' are, to a great extent, gestural and embodied in the above-mentioned classical Indian performances.[7] That is, in this context, 'seeing', visibility and presence are not conceived strictly as material conditions related to objects and things. The *Natyasastra*, in many ways, proposes the idea of the actor's body as 'optical mechanism', which is capable of generating and delivering embodied visibility for the audience in performance. The visual field of performance, in this sense, greatly depends on the presence of the actor's body and functions as the performative means to structure the way the audience 'see' things and events, as well as what is being 'seen' in a performance. What does that mean when we say the body becomes the 'optical mechanism' in the course of a performance? It initially means that the performer's body displaces the objects and things from the performance space. The disappearance of the objects and things in a performance, on the one hand, generates 'absence', the absence of the material world associated with the performance. But, on the other hand, this voluntary displacement of the objects and things in the performance causes the emergence of the body that is perpetually kinetic and visually symbolic. As a result, the mimetic mediation of the body, in the course of the performance, causes the reappearance of objects and things in the flesh strictly at the symbolic and imaginary levels that make the dichotomy of 'presence' and 'absence' problematic. In this process, performance creates a new world of 'reality' that is concomitantly fictive and affective.

Im-mediate and mediate

The notion of ephemerality remains a recurring theme in Performance Studies. Could a performance (whether live or recorded) escape from mediation, or is the live always a re-enactment and a recreation and therefore a mediated reproduction of its own; as Philip Auslander argues (Auslander 1999). Rebecca Schneider offers a critical overview of the debate between Phelan and Auslander. Both Phelan and Auslander share the notion that the temporality of liveness is the "im-mediate" (Auslander) or "manically charged present" (Phelan). If, for Phelan, performance "marks the body as loss", for Auslander, liveness marks the body as always already referential, a kind of accumulation machine in relation to the mediatisation it cites and incites (Schneider 2011, p. 92).

Auslander disagrees with Phelan's assertion that performance "will not be repeated", suggesting that although not recorded, the live is always a re-enactment, and "a recreation of itself at one remove, filtered through its own mediatized reproduction" (Auslander 1999, p. 31). Reflecting on the apparent disagreement as outlined earlier, Schneider makes a clear observation that "the two are in closely aligned agreement: the live does not record" (Schneider 2011, p. 92). After a careful examination of the genealogy and appearance of the term 'ephemerality' in Performance Studies (through the works of Schechner (1965), Siegel (1968), Blau (1982), Phelan (1993), Roach (1996) and Muñoz (1996)), Schneider raises concerns about the epistemological reductionism underlying the history of the debate, suggesting that 'we limit our understanding of performance [...] to [a] patrilineal, West-identified (arguably white-cultural) logic of the archive' (Schneider 2011, p. 97). She continues that the conceptualisation of 'time' in the current archival debate of performance is linear: namely, 'that it cannot reside in its material traces and hence "disappears"' (Schneider 2011, p. 98).

The notion of performance as disappearance, which is predominantly situated within the curatorial practice and "pressure" to understand performance as "savable", is more of a concern for museums, galleries and the art market than it is for theatre (Schneider 2011, p. 98). Taking her critical position further, Schneider argues that the equation of performance with disappearance is deeply political in the sense that it caters to the "ocular hegemony" of "the 'I' of the Western Cogito" (Kobena Mercer in Schneider 2011, p. 98): a tradition that assumes that truth is only what is visible, and gaze is the only appropriate way to access 'reality' through knowledge. For Schneider, the entire discourse of performance as disappearance is rooted in the fear of the destruction of "the original". In order to argue that performance does not disappear, Schneider draws examples from rituals, and from Tavia Nyong'o, to suggest that there are "affective transmissions of showing and telling" (Schneider 2011, p. 104) and that performance is a ritual act that generates access rather than disappearance through other modes (Schneider 2011, p. 104). It is important to note that Richard Schechner's contact with Indian performance – ritual, classic and modern – since the 1970s helped him circulate many of the central concepts of Indian performance knowledge in his early writings[8] (Nair 2017). Indeed, several of his major ideas – such as "restored behaviour" and "transportation/transformation" – were introduced in the late 1970s and early 1980s in the context of the traditional Indian performance, *Ramlila*. It is also this context in which Schechner's well-known aphorism: "Olivier is not Hamlet ..., but also he is not *not* Hamlet ..." (Schechner 1983, p. 95) emphasises the denial of the 'real', suggesting that performance always occurs in a liminal space.

I am in complete agreement with Schneider's critical position in three main respects: (1) the theory of disappearance is a largely Western approach that finds its origin within the philosophical tradition of 'ocular hegemony', and that substantiates the superiority of gaze over other modes of knowing; (2) the logic of the archive is logocentric in a manner that devalues oral histories, the traditional knowledge base and cultural circulation practices within indigenous societies; (3) the body in performance naturally inherits multiple modes of "affective transmissions" – sensory and embodied – beyond writing and memory: an idea which is overlooked in much of the current debate on the ephemerality of performance.

However, despite the fact that Schneider's critical positions are consistent and thoroughly informed by the major philosophical traditions in the West, there is a strong sense of material reductionism in her understanding of performance as a spatiotemporal event. On the one hand, she argues that performance "plays the sediment acts and spectral meanings that haunts material in constant collective interaction, in constellation, in transmutation" (Schneider 2011, p. 102), meaning that the performance only occurs through the constant 'play' of appearance and disappearance through repetition that makes it citational. On the other hand, Schneider affirms that the disappearance of performance "negotiates" and "perhaps becomes materiality" (Schneider 2011, p. 105), meaning that each occurrence of disappearance passes through and recreates materiality: the argument, which, essentially, reinitiates nothing but the ontological claim. Although I agree that performance constantly transfigures and repositions the material base – bodies and objects – in time and place, "the live body bearing the spectre" (Schneider 2011, p. 110) or the ephemerality of the performance cannot be considered as the material base of the performance. While examining Phelan's phrasing that performance "*becomes itself through*" disappearance, Schneider asserts that it is different from an "ontological claim of being", and "even different from an ontology of being under erasure" (Schneider 2011, p. 105). As she further argues, in this sense, performance, as a medium, negotiates a material entity through the process of disappearance. Schneider's position neither clarifies its distinction from the Derridian notion of 'trace', nor explains how disappearance passes through as materiality. Moreover, the spectral metaphor in Schneider only reconfirms the deconstructionist epistemological position that meaning is something that disappears constantly in the signifying process through the repetition of signifiers as traces (Schneider 2011).

The spectre is to be seen by the spectator and what is being transfigured in the act of seeing is the live body that carries the spectre, meaning that performance can only be understood in terms of the process in which it is being seen. This also means that performance is a transformational object and once the transformation is triggered through the act of seeing, the people, places and objects within the framework of performance will obtain a new spatiotemporal dimension, which is 'distorted' or 'made impure' by the act of seeing.[9] As a result, what is being created as performance through the act of seeing does not exist beforehand and hence, performance as presence delivers new 'realities' and new knowledge, both emotive and experiential, in each of its occurrences as excess. The questions of ephemerality, in this way, can only be processed in the context of perception. It is this insight which is largely missing from the current debate on the ontology of performance as outlined earlier: performance does not exist without perception, in the first place, to be lost.

My point of departure here is that if we consider the act of perception as something that triggers the performative act, it is equally important to ask *where* the performance takes (its) place. Acts of perception are complex phenomena that engage multiple spatialities and temporalities. As such, if it is commonly accepted that performance requires a perceptual and hence imaginary place in order to be unfolded, then the notion of materiality and the fear of disappearance attached to it become meaningless. Again, if it is the act of perception that makes the spectre alive and visible, then what is being forgotten and displaced is the body that carries the spectre, and not the other way around. Finally, since it is impossible for the body that carries the spectre to enter into the visual field of the spectre, the basic assumption of performance as disappearance seems nonsensical, because there is no materiality to be lost in a 'performance': the fictive is the 'real' and hence it is excess rather than loss.

Aesthetics of (the) invisible: Peter Brook's *Battlefield*, a case study

The shift of focus from the "ocular hegemony" of spectacle to the sensory experience of taste (rasa) as presence remains central to the discourse of Indian performance theory. I have already discussed the concept of rasa as the embodiment of experience elsewhere (Nair 2015). The literal translation of the word is taste and the definition closest to the meaning of it is the "very essence of" something. According to Bharata, the mythical author of the Natyasastra, rasa refers to the very essence of the experience shared between the performer and the spectator when they come in contact with each other in a performative context (Nair 2015, p. 139).

Across its 36 extensive chapters, the Natyasastra provides a meticulous analysis of the various textual and psychophysical elements that create the experience of rasa in performance. The primary elements that constitute rasa are known as determinants (*vibhava*),[10] which consists of two performative elements: (1) the physical world, including persons, places and objects in which all the emotional responses are based (*alambana*); and (2) specific environmental factors that trigger emotional responses (*uddipana*). Performance, according to the Natyasastra, consists of visual and kinetic clues for the audience to extract the "essence" (not the spectacle) of what is being seen, through a series of perceptual mimetic interactions (*anubhava*). Rather than relying on the objective physical dimension of performance, the discourse of the Natyasastra focuses on perceptual interaction as a means of accessing "the very essence of" things as new knowledge (*bhava*). The act of seeing in performance, in this way, creates a whole 'new' world of meaning and sensuous knowledge that does not exist elsewhere, and cannot be accessed without the ocular function being in contact with the physical world of performance. I now bring the following case study to further illuminate how the lack of spectacle in a performance reinforces other modalities of perception and stimulates reflective spectatorial experience. The questions that remain in *Battlefield* are: why are we hearing these rather unconnected, irrational and non-linear stories and what experience can the audience gather from their performance? The stories raise questions about deeper meanings of the human condition; they offer no answers, leaving the audience not only to create the visual field of the stories, but also to rewrite them to make new connections.

Thirty years after the production of *Mahabharatha,* Peter Brook revisits the Sanskrit Epic to tell us the aftermath of the war between Pandava brothers and their cousins in *Battlefield*. Yudhishtira, the warrior prince, recognises that "victory is defeat": millions of dead bodies litter the ground; widows are roving the battlefield in search of the mutilated bodies of their hacked men to piece together. The prince who won the war falls into a deep agony. How should he rule this conquered land, full of miseries? How can he bring peace to his country? In *Battlefield*, Brook does not recreate objects, things, places, atmospheres and people the way they usually represent the 'true' nature of the story. Instead, what we see in the performance is the role play of actors narrating multiple stories: of a disputatious snack, a fatalistic worm and a materialistic mongoose. All take place on a bare stage where there were a few poles and brightly coloured fabrics left with the actors to play their characters in between story telling. One actor can be several things at once, at the same level, on the same bare stage: a King, a man, a snack and a worm. Nothing prevents the audience either from following the story or emotionally engaging the moral agony of Kunti, the Mother Queen who lost her son; or Yudhishtira, the warrior Prince, who unknowingly killed his brother. Using four actors and a musician, Brook and Estienne, his collaborator, evoke strong visual images on the stage: a misty and dark landscape of the battlefield; rain clouds; blood; mutilated bodies in the dusk; shadows; widows; the river Ganges; a mother sets her son afloat and sees him come back years later to join in the battle and die; a king weighs himself against a pigeon by progressively shedding his own flesh to stop the eagle killing its prey; a worm trying to cross a crowded road and is crushed by the chariot wheel and so on. Brook uses the simplest means to stage his text: four bamboo sticks and three pieces of cloth – a bold move, particularly at a time when theatre is heavily dominated by technology and large-scale stage craft.

The negation of objects and things in the creation of the *mise-en-scène* becomes an aesthetic approach in Brook's *Battlefield*. Brook's strategy – to nullify the scenographic elements in the play – makes two things apparent:

1. The actor becomes more prominent and the body becomes the site of the imagined visual field of the performance.
2. The audience becomes more receptive in co-creating the visual field of the performance, which is otherwise visually absent.

When the stage becomes empty and when the body becomes the single object of audience perception in a performance, the actor is destined to use the body as a mechanical device to generate imageries, objects, landscapes, characters and events that are physically invisible, but experientially visible and emotionally tangible. The *Natyasastra* addresses this spectatorial ambivalence between the body, the distinction between objects and things and their inevitable non-presence in space, in multiple ways. One might list a number of categories here, but I want to focus on two for further discussion:

1   Audience-led aesthetic discourse: The *Natyasastra* places the audience at the centre of the discourse, to foreground perception as a means of meaning-making. In this process, theatre only takes place within the audience's participatory engagement with the performance.
2   Actor-led performance practice: The *Natyasastra* offers a micro-corporeal training approach to train the body with all its possibilities: the eyes, the face, the hands, the foot, the breathing, all trained in a minute and detailed fashion to make the body capable of creating illusions on its own without depending on scenography and technology. Objects, things, places and people are reimagined and re-presented in and through the "optical mechanism"[11] of the body.

The major conceptual and theoretical issues presented in the discourse of Indian performance theory revolve around the idea of an intersubjective mimetic interaction between the performer and the spectator. The apparent minimalism and lack of material presence in performance problematise the conventional ontological claim that performance is the physical outcome of its material conditions; and that these are the factors which create aesthetic experience, rather than the imaginational transaction with the audience through the act of seeing. I would call the perceptual process of the latter 'the ontology of imagination'.

In *Battlefield*, the actor occupies the space between real and imaginary, gesture and thought, visible and invisible. This space is visually and performatively kinetic, "something that not only exists in time, but which exists in a significant, special, performative and ephemeral time" (Reason 2006, p. 9). Placing itself in the ambivalence between presence and absence, the entire performative function of the actor's body in *Battlefield* makes the invisible visible. The act of seeing becomes experiential rather than ocular, insofar as the body in performance becomes more evocative than representational. When the actor's body becomes evocative, the performance becomes unmediated and the act of perception and audience experience do not seem to be restrained by the object-world of spectacles. Hand gestures (*Mudra*) in Classical Indian Performance, for instance, are essential movements, and the deliverance of their meaning is embedded in the kinetic energies of the hands. Although the shape and composition of the hands are important in mudra practice, it conveys meaning through non-representational movements. A mudra is a 'thing' composed of a number of spatiotemporal properties such as tempo, duration, rhythm, geometrical patterns of the hands and eye movements. In *Kutiyattam,* for example, the *oornanabha* mudra is used to show a number of things such as 'flames', 'taking a bath' and 'radiance', of a person or a thing. The same mudra is used to create three different meanings and mimetic actions.

Similarly, in *Battlefield*, the gaze is directed towards the onlooker as in the mirror: "I see myself there where I am not, in an unreal, virtual space that opens up behind the surface" (Foucault 1986, p. 24). As Foucault observes, the mirror is "a placeless place … a sort of shadow that gives me my own visibility to myself" (Foucault 1986, p. 24). No visual signifiers help the audience to locate a real physical place in the performance. The battlefield, as a thematic location, becomes more of a metaphor than an ocular entity, which places the performance outside of all representational places, although "it may be possible to indicate their location in reality" (Foucault 1986, p. 24). Performance, in this sense, remains a heterotopia, borrowing Foucault's term, where I, as the spectator, "counteract" and "reconstitute" "other sites" and temporalities, to create 'reality' without a material base attached to it: "that enables me to see myself there where I am absent" (Foucault 1986, p. 24). Theatrical encounter, in this sense, continues to be a sensory "joint experience" of [the] invisible spectacles. In the following section, I will further develop the metaphor of the mirror in Indian philosophies of perception, to argue that the invisible gains the same ontological status as the visible in Indian performance.

The ontology of (the) invisible

Indian logicians thought carefully about the ontology of absence. According to the Nyaya philosophy of Gautama (600 BCE–200 CE), the world exists in two domains: presence (*bhava*) and absence (*abhava*). Everything present has a name and a form and can be understood in terms of substance (*dravya*), quality (*guna*) and action (*karma*). Absence (*abhava*) has four categories: relational absence (*samsargabhava*), mutual absence (*anyonyabhava*), pre-absence (*prag-abhava*) and absolute absence (*atyanta-abhava*). The Universe has been categorised in two sets: one set of positive entities (*bhava padartha*) and another set of negative entities (*abhavapathartha*). This implies that there are positive referents and negative referents in the visible world. Thus, there is a particular rose in the garden, for instance, and there is the absence of that rose too in the world. The absence of the rose is as 'real' as the 'presence' of the rose because the rose, which carries a name and a form, is essentially constituent of elements, and the absence of it does not mean nothing, but only the reconfiguration of the particular 'form' into elements or displacement of it from the present dimension of time and space. The rose, when it is absent, does not lose its name or substance and as a result, Gautama argues, presence and absence are equally real and hence, existent entities. Absence is not fictitious. As a matter of fact, the rose is real because it is present. The absence of the rose is also real, because there cannot be an absence of a fictitious entity: only the real can be absent.

Rasa clarifies the performative implications of Gautama's analogy. According to the Natyasastra, rasa derives from *bhava* – or latent emotional memory – when the audience come in contact with performance. *Bhava* is non-present and cannot be accessed without the mediation of performance. Indeed, in this sense, the ultimate aim of a performance is to bring forward (*abhinaya*) the relevant *bhava* to the audience through performance. Humour, for instance, is the *bhava* of laughter, the rasa, which is a visible present entity embodied in performance. Humour is an emotional referent, which cannot be accessed without the interactive engagement of a performance context. From the standpoint of Abhinavagupta, the 10th-century commentator on the Natyasastra, humour is rediscovered as a form of knowledge through the performative utterance of laughter, "through introspection [...] at the time of perception of an object [laughter, in this context] of the world" (Pandey 2006, p. 276). It is clear in this discussion that the performative process of rasa remains a kinetic and symbolic act of perception that makes the invisible visible through the means of mimetic engagement of the body. What is crucial to understand in this discussion is the epistemological foregrounding of the invisible as the material base of performance. This means that, what is being made visible as the performance is the "very essence" of its physical existence as a form of knowledge, not the physical presence (performance) itself simply because the performance only takes (its) place in the imaginary site of the onlooker. Indian performance studies, in this way, undertake some serious philosophical discussions on *taste* as the metaphor of the invisible sensory experience: an experience which is tactile and that presupposes objective reality and visibility as a necessary condition of its existence.

Performance as excess

As I have already observed, absence maintains a powerful critical trajectory in Indian performance theories, and emptiness (*Sunyata*)[12] has never been considered as void or nothingness. Absence is "not static but dynamic" and "pulsate[s] with [an] upsurge of creative energy" as the place of "first motion" and "self-reflection" (Pandey 2006, p. 650). In the Kashmiri Sivite philosophy of the Kula system, *sunyata* is considered as a place from which all creation proceeds, and where we might gain the intuition of the nature of the 'real'. It is also understood as a place of freedom (*moksha*) from the material world and limited actions, meaning that emptiness is the place of non-logical cognition and a necessary condition that connects external and internal sensory perceptions (Pandey 2006, p. 687). Let me make explicit the connection between the concept of *sunyata*, as the place of creation, and the theory of rasa, as the performative process of making the invisible visible. Both share the common epistemological ground that presence of any kind as a form of knowledge is a creation taking place in the "virtual place" of self-reflection as the image in the mirror, which is 'real' in appearance and experience. Unlike the concept of 'trace' in which presence is 'always already' marked by its absence, the performative utterance of rasa produces excess, in which meaning is not attached to the display of objective signifiers. On the contrary, the presence of the body in performance always creates something new.

In his theory of recognition (*pratyabhijna*), Abhinavagupta brilliantly exposes the philosophical process underlying the act of meaning-making, arguing that the moment of recognition involves both "removal of the veil" and "identification of mental images" in relation to the object of perception. As he further explains, remembrance and recognition are two different activities altogether: remembrance is recollection of a former object of mental perception, whereas recognition requires simultaneous existence of the recollection of the object of perception and its presence in the present time (Pandey 2006, p. 300). It is useful to bring Abhinavagupta's own analogies to bear on this discussion. At one time, someone has seen the King riding an elephant and been impressed by the sight of it. Sometime later, the same person seeing the elephant alone will also remember the King, who is already absent in the present sight of the elephant due to the law of association. The presence of the elephant is marked by the absence of the King and, according to Abhinavagupta, remembrance, in this way, involves recollection and associations between the presence of objects and their mental image in the past.

Recognition, on the contrary, entails a complex perceptual mechanism in Indian philosophy for which another analogy might aid our understanding. Devadatta is known to a person as a friend in the past and on seeing him again, after a long time, the person could not recollect his friend at once, but recognises him after a while. The person could not recollect Devadatta at first sight because he possesses a different mental image of him, but after a short while of perceptual processing and self-realisation, the knowledge came to the person that it was Devadatta who was standing in front of him. According to Abhinavagupta, in this example, there is a perceptual gap between the actual moment of perception of the object (Devadatta) in the present and its recollection in the past (previous mental image). A great deal of information, imagination and intuition went into the process of recognition for the person to recognise his old friend as Devadatta and hence, close the gap in perception. For Abhinavagupta, the moment of recognition is the creation of 'new knowledge' in present time, which fills the perceptual gap that has no correlation with the existence of the object in the past or in the present in the recollected mental image. The "new knowledge" occupies a "new dimension" of space and time outside the past/present continuum (Pandey 2006, pp. 422–427).

It is commonly understood that a tree is absent in a seed, but seeing a tree when seeing a seed presupposes a great deal of imagination in creating the physical existence of the imagined (new knowledge), which can be made visible and tactile through corporeal responses (*anubhava*) using the physical (*angika*), verbal (*vachika*), scenographic (*aharya*) and emotional (*satwika*) components to attribute objective reality to an idea (NS 6:19). Two metaphorical terms, "the removal of the veil" and "light" (*prakasha*), constantly appear in Abhinavagupta's discourse on presence, suggesting that any reappearance of objects in present time occupies a new dimension of space where a further layer of information is added as excess to the moment of recognition. Interestingly, the metaphors of 'light' and 'removal of the veil' seem to be more embodied and performative as distinct from the linguistic notions of 'sign' and 'trace': the former suggest the performative utterance of excess, whereas the latter reverse the process into a non-embodied linguistic disappearance. In this sense, Derrida presupposes a philosophical error in the discourse of 'trace' as disappearance, whereas the act of perception, in Indian performance theory, implies uncovering and re-inventing, which needs 'light' (self-reflection) to reveal the true existence of the object that makes the invisible visible. Derrida confirms this philosophical position later in his writings, saying that "mediate objective perception is reserved for sight and hearing which requires the mediation of light or air" (Derrida 1981, p. 19). When discussing the theory of recognition, Abhinavagupta uses the same metaphor of the mirror as we see in Foucault, to elucidate the point that 'reality' appears in art as reflection in the mirror through self-recognition (Pandey 2006, pp. 323–324). Abhinavagupta adds further that the mirror does not reflect in the darkness, so it needs 'light' (*Prakāsa*) to 'unveil' the 'true' appearance of the object of reflection. The vision of the 'tree' which is absent in the seed, in Abinavagupta's analogy, not only remains as the excess mediated by the act of seeing but also reverses the entire poststructuralist discourse on "trace" [tree] as absence.

To close the discussion, I would like to stress the point that the invisible gaining the same ontological status as the visible and perceptual reflection/experience prevailing over sight are two core philosophical concepts underlying the entire aesthetic debate in Indian performance theory. In the debate surrounding rasa as the metaphor of taste, the question one could ask is: what do we see in theatre where there is nothing much to see on stage? Rasa problematises the optical relationship between the object and perceptual experience, suggesting that the body in performance has no control over the knowledge that it creates (Pandey 2006, p. 409) and that 'reality' is constructed in the mirror space, the interactive perceptual space of the audience, through the act of seeing. It implies that reality is imagined and reimagined by the audience, in theatre, each time differently through corporeal terms, since "it is not possible to be certain that our knowledge is correct" (Pandey 2006, p. 410). Derrida notes that "the sense of taste … [is] more subjective than objective … [and] is activated when the organ of the tongue, the gullet, and the palate come in touch with the external object" (Derrida 1981, p. 23). Derrida's insight shows that the experience of art as taste proposes a 'new ontology' that separates objects from *mise-en-scene,* and spectacle from the act of seeing. Performance is not an object of the gaze, but an "other site" of participatory engagement in which the audience becomes creator and the imagination gains a 'new ontological' dimension: fictive replaces tangible physical reality. It is this reflective process that makes the invisible visible. In *Battlefield* or the gestural practice of the hands (*Mudra*) in Classical Indian performance, what is being seen is not what is being experienced by the audience. In Derrida's analogy, the tongue needs to touch the external object to experience the taste, and yet the experience of taste is not strictly bound to any ontological basis in reality in a conventional sense. With the concept of rasa as the experience of taste, the fundamental insight that Indian performance theory contributes is that performance possesses a tremendous temporal force that brings performer and spectator into active engagement, both in terms of creation and perception, and where the fictive becomes 'real' in performance. In this way, the *invisible* emerges and operates in the body of performance as excess, rather than declaring its own disappearance as 'trace'.

Notes

1. The composition of the *Natyasastra* is attributed to Sage Bharata, the legendary mythical author who dates back to between 200 BC and AD 200. Written in Sanskrit, the text contains 6,000 verses, in 36 chapters, discussing a wide range of philosophical and practical aspects of theatre.
2. In Derrida, the notion of presence is the outcome of the play of traces that operates in *difference*. For him, trace is not presence, but is a presence that "dislocates, displaces and refers beyond itself" (Derrida 1998, p. 167). The trace can neither exist nor become present, "because it is always overtaken by effacement, which makes the trace disappear" (Olson 2011, p. 251). See more details in Derrida (1998).
3. The concept of Rasa is central to the Natyasastra. Literally meaning taste, the idea proposes that aesthetic experience is perceptual and sensory, offering lots of emphasis on the audience as the creator of the meaning of performance. See more details in Nair (2015).
4. 'The Aesthetics of [the] Invisible', as a term, first appeared in a conference paper, which I presented at the International Federation for Theatre Research (IFTR) in Stockholm in 2016. Regarding the square bracket in the title, grammatically speaking, 'the' is the definite article and 'invisible' is a non-definite phrase, so it is my choice to keep the definite article [the] in square brackets.
5. *Kutiyattam* is the only remaining Sanskrit theatre of India, preserved and practised in the temple theatres of Kerala known as *Kuthambalam*. Scholars claim that the history of its practice goes back to between AD 1 and AD 3.
6. A major form of Indian classical dance developed in Kerala during AD 15.
7. Elsewhere, I discuss the ways in which the hand gestures are used in classical Indian performances to tell stories and enact situations (Nair, "Mudra: Choreography in Hands" in *Body, Space & Technology*, 2/2013). In *Kutiyattam*, 'The stories of Krishna', a series of solo female performances depicting the stories of the God Krishna, the actress enacts the moonlight at the bank of River Yamuna in a subtle and romantic way through mudras. After a deep and intense lovemaking, the heroine mistakenly tries to grab a long white patch of moonlight, thinking that her garment is the moonlight, by far the most wonderful moment in this episode. The gestural enactment of the performer shows the river, the banks, moonlight, her garments and finally the act of grabbing the moonlight mistakenly. In fact, by means of mimetic gestures, the performer initially displaces the objects and things from the performance space to bring them back into the imagination of the audience.
8. In my interview with Schechner for the *Indian Theatre Journal*, 1:1, he spoke about his contact and familiarity with Indian philosophy and performance practice, which informed the development of performance theory in his writings in the 1970s and 1980s. See more details in "Conversation with Richard Schechner" in *Indian Theatre Journal*, 1:1, 2017, pp. 5–18.
9. Repetition as 'second time' is a concept which frequently appeared in the works of Derrida, Deleuze and Foucault suggesting that the 'second-time' is 'impure' due to lack of originality. See Derrida for details: (1978), "The Theatre of Cruelty and the Closure of Representation" in *Writing and Difference*. Chicago: The University of Chicago Press. In this essay, Derrida argues that Artaud's theatre is impossible because it rejects representation to propose a spectacle of origin without repetition, the second-time. See also Deleuze (1994) *Difference and Repetition*. London: Continuum for further details on the concept of repetition.
10. According to the *Natyasastra* (200 BC–AD 200), the aesthetic experience of rasa is a combination of Determinents (*vibhava*) that are characters and situations; Consequence (*anubhava*), that are embodied emotional responses of the characters against the situations, largely considered as histrionics and the Transitory mental states (*vyabhicari bhava*), that are subdominant emotions that intensify the dominant emotion such as crying when you are extremely happy, but however, the tears don't mean that you are sad. These elements when combined (*samyoga*) cause rasa relish. See for more details: Nair (2017) *The Natyasastra and The Body in Performance: Essays on Indian Theories of Dance and Drama*. Jefferson, NC: McFarland.

11 Gilles Deieuze (2006, p. 339) when discussing film viewing uses the term "optical mechanism" and I further develop this term in the aforementioned essay to discuss the hand gestures in Indian dance, the ways in which the gestural practice of the hands creates meaning. I discuss the concept of the body as "optical mechanism" elsewhere and see for more details in Nair, "Mudra: The Choreography in Hands" in *Body, Space & Technology*, 11:2, 2013.
12 Literally meaning emptiness in Sanskrit, the word refers to the doctrine of fundamental nature of all things widely discussed in Hinduism and Buddhism. The exact philosophical meaning for the term is much wider and deeper and systematically developed in various philosophical traditions.

References

Auslander, P. 1999. *Liveness: Performance in a Mediatized Culture*. New York: Routledge.
Blau, H. 1982. *Take Up the Bodies: Theatre at the Vanishing Point*. New York & Urbana: University of Illinois Press.
Deleuze, G. 1994. *Difference and Repetition*. London: Continuum.
Deleuze, G. 2006. *Two Regimes of Madness*, ed. David Lapoujade, trans. Ames Hodges & Mike Taormina. New York: Columbia University Press.
Derrida, J. 1981. "Economimesis" in *Diacritics*, Vol. 11, No. 2 (Summer), pp. 2–25.
Derrida, J. 1998. *Of Grammatology*. Baltimore: Johns Hopkins University Press.
Foucault, M. 1986. "Of Other Spaces" in *Diacritics*, Vol. 16, No.1 (Spring), pp. 22–27.
Muñoz, J.E. 1996. "Ephemera as Evidence: Introductory Note to Queer Acts" in *Women and Performance: A Journal of Feminist Theory*, Vol. 8, No. 2, pp. 5–16.
Nair, S. 2013. "Mudra: Choreography in Hands" in *Body, Space & Technology*, Vol. 2, ISSN: 1756–4921.
Nair, S. 2015. *The Natyasastra and The Body in Performance: Essays on Indian Theories of Dance and Drama*. Jefferson, NC: McFarland.
Nair, S. 2017. "In Conversation with Richard Schechner" in *Indian Theatre Journal*, Vol. 1, No. 1, pp. 5–18.
Olson, C. 2011 (April). "The "Difference" That Makes All the Difference: A Comparison of Derrida and Sankara" in *Philosophy East and West*, Vol. 61, No. 2, pp. 247–259.
Pandey, K. C. 2006. *Abhinavagupta: An Historical and Critical Study*. Varanasi: Chaukhamba Amarabharati Prakashan.
Phelan, P. 1993. *Unmarked: The Politics of Performance*. New York: Routledge.
Pisharoti, N. 1987. *Bharata Muniyude Natyasastram (The Natyasastra of Bharatamuni)*. Thrissur: Kerala Sahitya Academy.
Reason, M. 2006. *Documentation, Disappearance and the Representation of Live Performance*. London: Palgrave.
Roach, J. 1996. *Cities of the Dead: Circum-Atlantic Performance*. New York: Columbia University Press.
Schechner, R. 1965. "Theatre Criticism" in *The Tulane Drama Review*, Vol. 9, No. 3, pp. 13–24.
Schechner, R. 1983. *Performative Circumstances from the Avant Garde to Ramlila*. Calcutta: Seagull Books.
Schneider, R. 2011. *Performing Remains: Art and War in Times of Theatrical Reenactment*. London: Routledge.
Seigel, M. B. 1968. *At the Vanishing Point: A Critic Looks at Dance*. New York: Saturday Review Press.

PART III

Methods, techniques, genres and forms

18
PERFORMING PHENOMENOLOGICAL METHODOLOGY

Maxine Sheets-Johnstone

To follow a phenomenological methodology is to carry out an analysis of experience by way of an exacting procedure. The procedure is an ongoing and wholly interconnected flow of investigations, and of discoveries, revelations, wonderings, questionings, rethinkings, elaborations, and so on, in the course of the investigations. The word "act" is indeed misleading to apply to phenomenology and phenomenological methodology. It is misleading from a number of points of view, most obviously because it tends to name rather than to describe. In so doing, it basically specifies X as an instance of such and such, the such and such being the act of eating, for example, of writing, sawing, pushing, hesitating, reveling, and so on. The specification, in fact, conceals the very dynamics of the phenomenon in question—the very dynamics of eating, writing, sawing, hesitating, and so on, even if those named acts are, in turn, reduced to other acts: to chewing, for example, and swallowing in the act of eating. Acts are indeed one-dimensional identifications of a known or knowable *doing* of some kind, a fact that incidentally makes it easy to respond to the not uncommon question 'What are you doing?' 'I'm picking up this suitcase,' someone might answer, or 'I'm pulling this tooth.'

One might readily respond that performance is precisely a doing of some kind: it is *signing* a document, it is *hugging* a friend, it is *painting* the kitchen, it is *playing* the violin in an orchestral concert, and so on, but as noted earlier, and to be elaborated further later, the performative doing in each instance is specified as no more than a one-dimensional identification, a one-dimensional identification that fails to describe what is actually being experienced. Real-life, real-time experiences have a distinctive dynamic. *Signing*, for example, is not only dynamically different from *hugging*, but any particular instance of *signing* has itself a distinctive dynamic, certainly in terms of the person who is signing, but certainly too in terms of the document being signed, the situation in which the signing is happening, the people who are present at the signing, and so on. Whatever the dynamics, they are qualitatively inflected, and it is precisely that qualitative structure that makes the performative doing the distinctive performative doing that it is. The nature of that qualitative structure will be set forth in a later section. A further introductory aspect concerning "acts" is of concern here and warrants attention.

A specifically philosophic question may be asked in response to allusions to phenomenological 'acts.' The specific question puts philosophy in general on the spot, asking "what is the nature of a philosophic act?" An answer to that question is given in an article titled

'Does Philosophy Begin (and End) in Wonder? Or What Is the Nature of a Philosophic Act?' (Sheets-Johnstone 1999a/exp. 2nd ed. 2011). Quotations and references are made to a range of well-known persons who have written in one way and another about wonder—Sir Charles Sherrington, Paul Valéry, and Martin Heidegger. Sherrington points out that childhood wonder 'soon lapses' and 'The wonderful ... is soon taken for granted' (Sherrington 1953, p. 100). Valéry asks, *'why not one turn more?'* in writing of the spiraling shells of molluscs (Valéry 1964, p. 11; italics in original). Heidegger asks, 'Why are there essents [i.e., existent things] rather than nothing?' (Heidegger 1961, p. 1). Moreover with its focus on the connection between wonder and 'philosophic act,' the article specifically references classic philosophers. Both Plato and Aristotle remark on the fundamental connection of philosophy and wonder. Plato straightforwardly states, '[The] sense of wonder is the mark of the philosopher' (*Theaetetus* 155). Aristotle takes a more nuanced, motivational perspective. He observes, '[I]t is owing to their wonder that men both now begin and at first began to philosophize' (*Metaphysics* 982b12), though he too later states that philosophy is for those who are at leisure and that philosophy has no purpose other than itself (*Metaphysics* 982b23–28). In light of these classical comments, one may surely ask whether one must be a philosopher in order to wonder, but one may surely also ask whether wonder does not involve the body and indeed even animate it, thus engaging the philosopher—or whoever—in a 'philosophic act' of some kind. As the article shows, one may readily in this context recall and cite the words of two different but equally remarkable persons whose descriptions of wonder are strikingly complementary. Leonardo da Vinci writes of his experience before a great canyon: 'Standing there, I was suddenly struck by two things, fear and longing: fear of the dark ominous cavern; longing to see if inside there was something wonderful' (da Vinci 1959, p. 19). Eugen Fink, Edmund Husserl's assistant for many years, wrote:

> Wonder dislodges man from the prejudice of everyday, publicly pregiven, traditional and worn out familiarity ... drives him from the already authorized and expressly explicated interpretation of the sense of the world and into the creative poverty of not yet knowing.
>
> *(Fink 1981, p. 24)*

Wonder does indeed displace one from the familiar everyday world and into what may be described as a 'longing to know' and thus to an erasure of 'the creative poverty of not yet knowing.' Precisely along the lines of longing and of not yet knowing, the following sections of this paper elucidate the actual practice of a phenomenological methodology and show in the process how the actual practice is a particular kind of performance.

Performing static and genetic analyses and the initial procedure of bracketing

It may certainly sound odd to speak of performing a methodology, but producing a phenomenological analysis of experience is in fact a veritable performance: it is definitely not an act or even a series of acts. Like any performance, it requires vigilance, exactitude, perseverance, alertness, dedication, and myriad other qualities, all of which cohere *in an ongoing and wholly interconnected investigative flow* that in this instance is, as indicated, punctuated by discoveries, revelations, wonderings, questionings, rethinkings, elaborations, and so on. To see this process in detail, we will begin by consulting Husserl's original and continuing expositions of phenomenological methodology. In doing so, we will see that a phenomenological methodology constitutes a performance in-process-of-being-created. The performance is thus not something that has been rehearsed and then performed as per rehearsed, neither it is an improvisation that runs along in a wholly spontaneous, impromptu manner. As we shall see, it follows a certain methodological protocol. Nevertheless, akin to typically rehearsed or improvisatory performances, a phenomenological methodology is performed for an audience, an audience of colleagues who validate the investigative findings or question aspects of the findings, raise basic concerns about the findings, and so on. Colleagues validate or question not simply on the basis of reading the results of the methodological investigation, but on the basis of themselves methodologically performing the particular investigation and of finding supportive or conflicting evidence with respect to their own investigation.

In the broadest sense, phenomenological methodology addresses the question of how the world, in all its complexities and intricacies, comes to be constituted. The performance of the methodology may be in the service either of elucidating epistemological origins or of elucidating the essential nature of a worldly phenomenon. Husserl terms the former phenomenological inquiry 'genetic,' the latter 'static,' the latter inquiry being focused not necessarily on something unmoving, but on something being readily available for investigation, a phenomenon in its own right.[1] As its name suggests, what a static phenomenology elucidates are invariant structures of a phenomenon. Such structures are discovered through an eidetic analysis, which not only may but rightly includes imaginative variations of the phenomenon in question (Husserl 1980, pp. 26, 28, 48–49; 1983, p. 11, 157–159). Husserl originally viewed a static mode of inquiry a "leading clue" (Steinbock 2001, pp. xxxv–xxxvi) to a genetic mode of inquiry, but later came to the realization that a constitutional history was present in both, or in other words that knowledge is built up in each instance. He thus describes the intimate and intricate relationship of a static phenomenology to a genetic phenomenology, a relationship that Anthony Steinbock sets forth in fine and substantive detail (Steinbock 2001).

It should perhaps be explicitly mentioned that the practice of a genetic phenomenology has nothing to do with genes. Being focused precisely on epistemological origins, it constitutes a 'regressive inquiry' (Husserl 1970, p. 354). Husserl's dynamic conception and description of this mode of inquiry, including its epistemological benefits, are notable. Husserl writes:

> In our phenomenological-kinetic method we have ascertained the fundamental distinction among merely material thing, animate organism, and psyche, or psychic Ego, which dominates all apprehension of the world, and we have studied it at the same time with respect to its phenomenological primal sources.
>
> *(Husserl 1980, p. 1)*

Moreover, he later specifically contrasts 'our phenomenological-kinetic method' with ontological methodologies, which, he points out, take objects as "fixed," and are in this sense "katastematic" rather than kinetic (ibid., p. 117): katastematic methods take what is present as wholly present, solid, firmly established entities. In pinpointing the contrast, he vividly describes the kinetic nature of phenomenological methodology. He states:

> The phenomenological-constitutive consideration takes the unity in the flow, namely as unity of a constitutive flow; it follows up the movements, the flows, in which such unity and every component, side, real property of such unity is the correlate of identity. This consideration is in certain measure kinetic or 'genetic.'
>
> *(Ibid.)*

In short, in bypassing ontologically anchored katastematic methodologies, Husserl recognizes the constitutional history of all human knowledge: 'Every unity of cognition, in particular every real one, has its "history" or also, correlatively speaking, the consciousness of this real thing has its "history"' (ibid.). Husserl in fact outlines the specific nature of a phenomenological-kinetic inquiry when he raises the question of the origin of geometry and thus limns the nature of the inquiry's performance. He writes:

> [O]ur interest shall be the inquiry back into the most original sense in which geometry once arose, was present as the tradition of millennia, is still present for us, and is still being worked on in a lively forward development; we inquire into that sense in which it appeared in history for the first time—in which it has to appear, even though we know nothing of the first creators and are not even asking after them. Starting from what we know, from our geometry, or rather from the older handed-down forms (such as Euclidean geometry), there is an inquiry back into the submerged original beginnings of geometry as they necessarily must have been in their 'primally establishing' function.
> *(Husserl 1970, p. 354)*

As is apparent, Husserl's concern is with a new and developing form of knowledge, hence 'the acquisition of spiritual accomplishments which grows through the continued work of new spiritual acts into new acquisitions' (ibid., p. 355). Such acquisitions, he emphasizes, move forward through tradition: 'Our human existence moves within innumerable traditions. The whole cultural world, in all its forms, exists through tradition' (ibid., p. 354). New and developing forms of knowledge may, however, be basically not spiritual accomplishments, but practical accomplishments. Where the investigative concern is in fact with new and developing *human practices*, 'spiritual accomplishments' enter in and are recognized not for their own sake, as in purely epistemological inquiries, but as accomplishments integral to the new and developing practices as, for example, in investigations of the origin of tool-making (Sheets-Johnstone 1990). A genetic phenomenology can thus concern itself with an elucidation of evolutionary as well as cultural knowledge.

What all phenomenological investigations and analyses require, however, is the procedure of bracketing. For example, in an investigation of the origin of verbal language or the origin of counting, one brackets any and all theories and asks what is basic in the very birth of the phenomenon. One thus ceases to take for granted anything about the phenomenon, asking instead how the very idea of the phenomenon arose and what meanings were integral to that idea. One discovers, for example, that an awareness of oneself as a sound-maker was integral to the origin of a verbal language and that bipedalism or "twoness"—as also in two ears, two eyes, two arms, and so on, not to mention bodily sides—right and left, front and back—was integral to the origin of counting (ibid.). As noted earlier, the regressive inquiry in these instances is not uniquely concerned with "the acquisition of spiritual accomplishments" in the new and developing knowledge, but in the acquisition of practical accomplishments in the new and developing knowledge, thus in the acquisition of corporeal-kinetic capabilities, capabilities that are themselves anchored in new and developing awarenesses. As played out in real-life, real-time, the capabilities constitute distinctive performances: the making of a tool; the articulation of a particular sound and sequences of interrelated sounds, which both singly and together are meaningful; the designation of precisely "how many," whatever the entities involved; and so on. In present-day terms, the capabilities play out in a surgeon's tool-using skill in performing surgery, in a student's speaking skill in giving an oral summary to a class of his or her field work, in an accountant's counting skill in putting together a financial report. Such skills are obviously informed by spiritual accomplishments of one kind and another, accomplishments that are tethered in a foundational sense on bodily learnings of one kind and another and are in this sense anchored in corporeal-kinetic capabilities.

What bracketing opens is a field of inquiry uncluttered by the classic five-finger version of the origin of counting, for example, asking instead to begin with: where did numbers come from? Equally, in bracketing, one is no longer held captive by the notion that the origin of language lies in increased brain size or in hunting practices that enhanced survival, or that 'arbitrary elements' were at the foundation of human speech. What is discovered through bracketing, for example, is that no language can be spoken for which the body is unprepared, which means a sensory-kinetic lifeworld was basic to the origin of language, precisely as in the recognition not only of oneself as a sound-maker but of different bodily articulatory dynamics in the making of different sounds and the relationships of those dynamics to the dynamics of worldly life (Foster 1978, 1990, 1996; Wallace 1881, 1895; Sheets-Johnstone 1990, 1999b/2009).

Bracketing is challenging: received wisdom and dictionary definitions can be seductive. One need only think of movement as a 'change of position.' Bracketing can in fact enter in again at any point in the investigatory process. Because the practicing phenomenologist understands the need for and significance of bracketing in a phenomenological methodology, he or she heeds any intrusion and puts aside once again all presupposed knowledge. Thus, from the beginning and throughout, bracketing poses a singular challenge in the actual practice of phenomenology, namely, the challenge of languaging experience in the process of performing phenomenological methodology. The challenge arises precisely in having made the familiar strange and thereby confronting the absolute newness of the phenomenon. Everyday or common professional words used to name or to describe no longer qualify. Such words typically name and tag a verb to the name, as in flowers are growing, and tree limbs are bending. The concern is mainly with objects and what they are doing, not with *dynamics*, or in other words, not with a *phenomenological-kinetic method* that 'follows up the movements, the flows,' both in terms of the object itself and the consciousness of the object. In the context of describing the nature of the relationship between body and world, subject and object, Husserl in fact states, 'consciousness of the world ... is in constant motion' (Husserl 1970, p. 109).

Clearly, a singular challenge also arises in the fact that one does not know what will eventuate in the course of the investigation. There is indeed in the course of the performance a "creative poverty of not yet knowing" (Fink 1981, p. 24). Furthermore, precisely because one does not know what one will find, one does not know where the finished investigation will lead, what new doors it will open. There is, in short, a continual spiral of inquiry. In effect, there is no end to phenomenological inquiries and to the performance of phenomenological methodology.

Phenomenological reduction

Phenomenological methodology is performed by a "disinterested spectator" who has willfully, by his or her own choice, removed him/herself from the everyday world in a "free act" (Husserl 1983, pp. 55, 291; 1989, pp. 267, 282; see also Sheets-Johnstone 2011).[2] It is in and through this free act of suspension that the phenomenologist is able *to inquire* into the nature of the everyday world, inquiring as to how we come to our knowledge of it, how we come to the meanings and values we ascribe to it. Whatever the object of inquiry, the investigator, having spontaneously suspended everyday practicalities and exigencies, is spontaneously living in the experience itself, taking it in its full sensuous form and following both the dynamics of that form and the experiential import of that form from beginning to end. The further step in phenomenological methodology, the phenomenological reduction, consists precisely in that investigative labor.

A critical point warrants attention in this context, namely, a concern with what Merleau-Ponty reprovingly claims is "incomplete," namely, phenomenological reduction. When he states, "The most important lesson which the reduction teaches us is the impossibility of a complete reduction," he rests his methodological claim on his ontological claim that body and world are already there (Merleau-Ponty 1962, pp. xiv, 198). His claims, however, are wide of the mark. As pointed out elsewhere (Sheets-Johnstone 2017, p. 7):

> The phenomenological reduction is in the service of constitution, that is, in the service of bringing to light how meaning and value come to be, how, through active and passive syntheses, through horizons of meaning and sedimentations, and so on, we come to make sense of the world. The *existence* of the world and the *existence* of body are not in question in the practice of phenomenology; both are present in their full reality. *What phenomenological methodology provides is a pathway to understanding how that reality is constituted.*

As we have earlier seen, Husserl in fact terms this genetic phenomenology of constitution, this historical mapping, a "phenomenological-kinetic method" (Husserl 1980, pp. 1, 117–118): it moves through the layers of meaning that constitute sense-making. Those who take the path thus undertake a methodological performance. In doing so, they move through layers of meaning that phenomenological reduction makes possible and that constitute constitution.

Husserl's writings indeed meticulously counter Merleau-Ponty's "important lesson." In his elucidations of the phenomenological reduction that opens a transcendental field, Husserl painstakingly points out in an exacting fashion:

> Within my field of transcendental phenomena [i.e., within the 'transcendental-phenomenological reduction … by means of which the natural attitude, the attitude of inner psychology, is transformed and becomes a transcendental attitude'] I no longer have theoretical validity as a human Ego; I am no longer a real Object within the world which I accept as existing, but instead I am posited exclusively as subject *for* this world. And this world is itself posited precisely *as* I am conscious of it in some fashion or other, *as* appearing to me in a certain way or as believed, predicatively judged, valued, etc.[3]
>
> *(Husserl 1989, p. 413)*

By specifying in exacting terms the nature of the relationship of subject-world in the reduction, Husserl in fact shows how reciprocal understandings may be formed between phenomenological psychology and transcendental phenomenology, that is, between the "natural" and the "transcendental," and what he views more broadly as between empirical science and transcendental science.

What the reduction illuminates are in fact basic aspects of everyday worldly experience that commonly pass unnoticed in the course of everyday experience and unremarked in empirical science. 'If-then' relationships (Husserl 1989, p. 63) are prime examples of such oversight. Husserl describes many instances of the relationship—e.g., '[I]*f* the eye turns in a certain way, *then* so does the "image"; if it turns differently in some definite fashion, then so does the image alter differently, in correspondence' (ibid.). He furthermore describes this sensory-kinetic relationship as a '*two-fold articulation*: kinesthetic sensations on the one side, the motivating; and the sensations of features on the other, the motivated' (ibid.; italics added). Multiple references, elaborations, and emphasis are given to 'two-fold articulations.' For example:

> '[E]xhibitings of' are related back to correlative multiplicities of kinesthetic processes having the peculiar character of the 'I do', 'I move' (to which even the 'I hold still' must be added) …. [A] hidden intentional 'if-then' relation is at work here …. [I]t is in this way that [the exhibitings] are indicated in advance, in expectation, in the course of a harmonious perception. The actual kinestheses here lie within the system of kinesthetic capacity, which is correlated with the system of possible following events harmoniously belonging to it.
>
> *(Husserl 1970, pp. 161–162)*

What the performance of phenomenological methodology affords is clearly an insight into just such body–world relationships that ground knowledge of the world. Indeed, while the body may be 'all there' as Merleau-Ponty claims (Merleau-Ponty 1962, p. 198), we humans have to learn our bodies and learn to move ourselves (Sheets-Johnstone 1999a/exp. 2nd ed. 2011). While we come bodily and moving into the world, neither our bodily form nor our movement and the world are fully fleshed out. In short, neither we nor the world is a ready-made, much less a ready-made duo.

Specific insights of Husserl are again of moment in this context, particularly his consistent description of living beings as 'animate organisms' and his epistemological specification of the developmental structure of animate capabilities. With respect to the former, through his 'phenomenological-kinetic method,' Husserl describes 'the fundamental distinction among merely material thing, animate organism, and psyche, or psychic Ego, which dominates all apprehension of the world, and we have studied it at the same time with respect to its phenomenological primal sources' (Husserl 1980, p. 1). The term '*animate organism*' is indeed found throughout Husserl's writings. Living beings, both human and nonhuman, are recognized as *animate* forms of life. Thus, Husserl's further insight into the developmental structure of animate capabilities is not surprising. Through 'regressive inquiry,' Husserl discovers precisely that 'I move' precedes 'I do' and 'I can.' Movement and indeed thinking in movement (Sheets-Johnstone 1981, 1999a/exp. 2nd ed. 2009, 2011) inform our developmental capacities in infancy and early childhood. They are plainly evident in an infant's turning its head away from a spoon filled with food that an adult wants to put into its mouth, for example. From a developmental standpoint, spontaneous head-turning—'I move'—precedes specific awareness of movement in turning one's head—'I do'—just as specific awareness of movement in turning one's head precedes an infant's voluntarily turning its head to avoid being fed whatever is on the spoon an adult is trying to put into its mouth—'I can.' Kinesthetically felt and kinesthetically cognized experiences clearly ground the faculty that Husserl identifies as the "*I-can* of the subject" (Husserl 1989, p. 13), a faculty that engenders a repertoire of movement abilities and possibilities.

Especially in light of Husserl's insights by way of a phenomenological-kinetic methodology, it becomes all the more evident how the foundational animate phenomenon of movement is readily lost in talk of action and behavior, not to mention of embodiment and enaction. Such talk commonly bypasses recognition of the living dynamics of life itself, the myriad dynamic patternings of movement and their situational variations that inform everyday life. A direct attention to movement anchors us in just such dynamics and directs us to the pan-animate animation that is at the core of life. Moreover, that same direct attention awakens us to the fact that a concentration on motor skills and motor control—in essence, on a motorology—and that a concentration on the brain—in essence on a single organ of the whole body that demotes real-life realities to sensori-*motor* phenomena—predispose us to ignore both the defining feature of animate life itself, namely, animation, and the defining fact of animation, namely, that animate organisms move in synergies of meaningful movement. What phenomenological reduction affords are precisely insights into just such animate facts of life. Brief but pointed consideration of further aspects of the reduction will elucidate just how these insights are possible.

Whatever the phenomenon, it is a sensuous presence of some kind. As such, the complexities and intricacies of its sheer presence can be described, described, of course, as bracketed. It is on the basis of its sheer presence that meaning or meanings arise, meanings that go beyond the sheer presence. Something as simple as a cup or a key can be so described. What becomes apparent in reducing either phenomenon to its sheer presence is what Husserl describes as sedimentations and horizons, that is, earlier and circumstantial experiences of a cup or a key that resonate meaningfully in present experience. One thus discovers a certain history of the present cup and the present key. In addition, one comes to recognize what Husserl describes as internal time consciousness, namely, retentions and protentions inherent in experience, retentions, and protentions that are part and parcel of the internal history of consciousness and that experientially ground memories and expectations. Through phenomenological reduction, one thus arrives at what Husserl describes as the *noema* and the *noesis*: on the one hand, the object as meant; on the other hand, consciousness in the fullness of its perceptions and cognitions that ground the intentional structures of constitution and meaning.

Summary thoughts on performing phenomenological methodology

In his exposition of phenomenology, Husserl states, 'Phenomenology in our sense is the science of "origins," of the "mothers" of all cognition; and it is the maternal-ground of all philosophical method: to this ground and to the work in it, everything leads back' (Husserl 1980, p. 69). In effect, by way of bracketing and phenomenological reduction, phenomenology discloses the nature of consciousness in perception and cognition and the accrual of meaning in the process of constitution. The individual labor involved in the performance of phenomenological methodology is personal, but the knowledge emanating from it exceeds the personal, and this is because, when carried out assiduously, the performance eventuates in foundational knowledge, knowledge that elucidates the complex and intricate dimensions of subject-world experience both in static and genetic phenomenologies, hence the history of subject-world knowledge and the essential nature of human experience for all.

Notes

1 For an example of a static phenomenology and its elucidation of the essential nature of a phenomenon, see *The Phenomenology of Dance* (Sheets-Johnstone 1966/2015).
2 For an elucidation of the ways in which the "disinterested spectator" plays a central role in both phenomenological methodology and aesthetic experience, see Sheets-Johnstone (2019).
3 The transcendental has to do precisely with constitution, with meaning-giving, hence with exacting analyses that go beyond whatever is sensuously present—be it a house, a chair, a tree, or whatever. The analyses answer the question of how the sensuously present comes to be known, judged, valued, and so on. Hence, the first step in the practice of phenomenology requires bracketing what is transcendent such that the familiar becomes strange.

References

da Vinci, Leonardo. 1959. *Philosophical Diary*, trans. Wade Baskin. New York: Wisdom Library.
Fink, Eugen. 1981. "The Problem of the Phenomenology of Edmund Husserl," trans. Robert M. Harlan. In: William McKenna, Robert M. Harlan, and Laurence E. Winters (eds), *Apriori and World: European Contributions to Husserlian Phenomenology*. The Hague: Martinus Nijhoff, pp. 21–55.
Foster, Mary LeCron. 1978. "The Symbolic Structure of Primordial Language." In: Sherwood L. Washburn and Elizabeth R. McCown (eds), *Human Evolution: Biosocial Perspectives*. Menlo Park, CA: Benjamin/Cummings, pp. 77–121.
Foster, Mary LeCron. 1990. "Symbolic Origins and Transitions in the Palaeolithic." In Paul Mellars (ed), *The Emergence of Modern Humans: An Archaeological Perspective*. Edinburgh: Edinburgh University Press, pp. 517–539.
Foster, Mary LeCron. 1996. "Reconstruction of the Evolution of Human Spoken Language." In: Andrew Lock and Charles Peters (eds), *Handbook of Symbolic Evolution*. Oxford: Oxford University Press, pp. 747–772.
Heidegger, Martin. 1961. *An Introduction to Metaphysics*, trans. Ralph Manheim. Garden City, NY: Doubleday/Anchor.
Husserl, Edmund. 1970. *The Crisis of European Sciences and Transcendental Phenomenology*, trans. David Carr. Evanston, IL: Northwestern University Press.
Husserl, Edmund. 1980. *Ideas Pertaining to a Pure Phenomenology and to a Phenomenological Philosophy, Third Book*, trans. Ted. E. Klein and William E. Pohl. The Hague: Martinus Nijhoff.
Husserl, Edmund. 1983. *Ideas Pertaining to a Pure Phenomenology and to a Phenomenological Philosophy, First Book*, trans. F. Kersten. The Hague: Martinus Nijhoff.
Husserl, Edmund. 1989. *Ideas Pertaining to a Pure Phenomenology and to a Phenomenological Philosophy, Second Book*, trans. Richard Rojcewicz and André Schuwer. Dordrecht: Kluwer Academic.
Merleau-Ponty, Maurice. 1962. *Phenomenology of Perception*, trans. Colin Smith. New York: Routledge & Kegan Paul.
Sheets-Johnstone, Maxine. 1966/ 50th anniversary ed. 2015. *The Phenomenology of Dance*. Philadelphia, PA: Temple University Press.
Sheets-Johnstone, Maxine. 1981/1999a/exp. 2nd ed. 2011/2009. "Thinking in Movement." *Journal of Aesthetics and Art Criticism* 39/4, pp. 399–407. Expanded version of article in *The Primacy of Movement* (Chapter 12) and in *The Corporeal Turn: An Interdisciplinary Reader* (Chapter II).
Sheets-Johnstone, Maxine. 1990. *The Roots of Thinking*. Philadelphia, PA: Temple University Press.
Sheets-Johnstone, Maxine. 1999a/exp. 2nd ed. 2011. *The Primacy of Movement*. Amsterdam/Philadelphia, PA: John Benjamins.
Sheets-Johnstone, Maxine. 1999b. "Sensory-Kinetic Understandings of Language: An Inquiry into Origins." *Evolution and Communication* 3/2, pp. 149–183. Included as Chapter IX in *The Corporeal Turn: An Interdisciplinary Reader*.
Sheets-Johnstone, Maxine. 2009. *The Corporeal Turn: An Interdisciplinary Reader*. Exeter: Imprint Academic.
Sheets-Johnstone, Maxine. 2011. "On the Elusive Nature of the Human Self: Divining the Ontological Dynamics of Animate Being." In: Wentzel van Huysteen and Erik P. Wiebe (eds), *Interdisciplinary Perspectives on Personhood*. Grand Rapids, MI: William B. Eerdmans Publishing, pp. 198–219.
Sheets-Johnstone, Maxine. 2017. "In Praise of Phenomenology." *Phenomenology & Practice* 11/1, pp. 5–17.
Sheets-Johnstone, Maxine. 2019. "Phenomenological Methodology and Aesthetic Experience: Essential Clarifications and Their Implications." In Stuart Grant, Jodie McNeilly-Renaudie, Matthew Wagner (eds), *Performance Phenomenology*. Cham: Palgrave Macmillan, pp. 39–62.
Sherrington, Sir Charles. 1953. *Man on His Nature*. New York: Doubleday/Anchor.
Steinbock, Anthony. 2001. "Translator's Introduction." In *Analyses Concerning Passive and Active Synthesis*, trans. Anthony Steinbock. Dordrecht: Kluwer Academic, pp. xv–lxvii.
Valéry, Paul. 1964. "Man and the Sea Shell." In *Aesthetics*, trans. Ralph Manheim. New York: Pantheon Books (Bollingen Series XLV.13), pp. 3–30.
Wallace, Alfred R. 1881. "Anthropology." *Nature* 204, pp. 242–244.
Wallace, Alfred R. 1895. "The Expressiveness of Speech, or, Mouth-Gesture as a Factor in the Origin of Language." *Fortnightly Review* (1 October 1895), pp. 528–543. http://people.wku.edu/charles.smith/wallace/S518.htm

19

DARING TO TRANSFORM ACADEMIC ROUTINES

Cultures of knowledge and their performances

Jörg Holkenbrink and Anna Seitz

Since the 1990s, the Center for Performance Studies (ZPS) at the University of Bremen has carried out projects that facilitate an artistic orientation in academic contexts. Closely affiliated with the ZPS in Bremen is the *Theater der Versammlung* (Theater of Assemblage) (TdV), one of the first research theaters in Germany. TdV brings together students, scholars from all faculties, and professional performance practitioners to work together on a range of theoretical themes and questions that arise within various academic contexts, using the methods and means of performance. This allows for an intensive collaboration with people whose expertise is in a wide range of different discourses. The performances that emerge from this interdisciplinary process have been presented and discussed throughout the German-speaking world and beyond.

The following dialogue is the result of an encounter between philosopher and theater scholar Anna Seitz, and Jörg Holkenbrink, director of the ZPS and artistic director of the TdV. In this conversation, they discuss various ways in which a dramaturgical lens can help to enhance performative methods of research, teaching, and learning at the university where standardized processes of linearization that threaten the very principles of higher education are increasingly becoming habitualized to negative effect. Key to their fresh approach is an understanding of the mutual responsibility that both actors and audience (in the case of a performance) or teachers and students (at the university) carry, and the inherent risks of failure and vulnerability at play in both contexts. Touching on various formats of knowledge production (as opposed to mere transfer), as well as on the role of certain dramaturgical principles (including attentiveness to atmosphere and setting the stage for surprise), their dialogue explores the importance of being conscious of differences when transgressing the boundaries between practical-aesthetic and theoretical dimensions of presentation and assembly.

Holkenbrink: In *Puer Robustus*, his philosophy of the troublemaker (*Philosophie des Störenfrieds*), Dieter Thomä lets us know: "Anyone who employs the imagination to approach experience with concepts becomes active as a threshold entity" (Thomä 2016, p. 146). In the summer of 2014, at the Center for Performance Studies of the University of Bremen, you, Anna, led a dramaturgy project on the topic of the networked generation. The project involved a number of events, including the usual formats of academic knowledge production, but it also dared to break out of the academic routine in several respects. This breaking-out began with the twenty participating students being selected such that as many different areas of study as possible were represented. Students from the fields of biology, comparative and European law, digital media, English-speaking cultures, educational sciences, German studies, history, computer science, arts education, cultural studies, comparative literature, philosophy, political science, and psychology were brought together to examine the question of what it could mean for them to be called "the networked generation," each from the perspective of their own field. In that context, you set them the unusual task of choosing real or fictional prominent "network figures" from literature, film, games, or theoretical treatises to be their imaginary friends and to attend seminars with them that would enable them to find the trail of the concept or metaphor of the network. After attending the seminars, the students then joined into a continual dialogue with their imaginary friends about the content of the seminars, which they then worked out in written form. These explorations subsequently led to an unexpected shift in the direction of research. Participants in the project worked with a combination of socio-politics (which speaks of the network in the context of a potential "social death"), mythology (which speaks of the Parcae, the three Fates, the one who spins our life thread, the one who measures it, and the one who cuts it), and current technological utopias (transhumanists in particular, an influential movement in the United States, are trying to overcome the inevitability of aging with the aid of, among other things, artificial intelligence and its further networking). Within the large frame of the theme "Networked Generation," drawing on these various sources gradually led to the crystallization of a transdisciplinary question: "What does networked life have to do with death?" The insights gained and the materials worked out over the further course of the project ultimately formed the basis for the presentation of *Am seidenen Faden* (On the silk thread), a performance that the *Theater der Versammlung* (Theater of Assemblage) continues to present as a work-in-progress at *trauerraum bremen*, an alternative funeral parlor, and which is seen as a continuation of the project by other means.[1]

When I think about the course of the project again, it strikes me how much imagination and judgment, reason and intuition, practical-aesthetic as well as theoretical approaches and forms of representation are all interwoven. It reminds me of Homi Bhabha's concept of hybridity as a figure of thought for a hybrid form of systems that have until now been separate, of which Doris Ingrisch writes:

> The difference between such hybrid approaches and additive or pluralistic ones lies in the willingness to allow touching and changing or, more precisely: to intend them. Reciprocal learning is a prerequisite and hence an attitude in which the so-called Other is regarded with appreciation.
>
> *(Ingrisch 2013, p. 35)*

Now, Anna, as initiators of such projects, we can be seen from the academic order as trouble-makers, as malcontents, or as marginal figures. According to Dieter Thomä, this raises "the question of the direction of fit: Who adapts to whom? Does order make short work of the disturber of the peace, or does the latter cause it to change, does the trouble-makers cause an upheaval?" (Thomä 2016, p. 18). Let us assume for a moment that we are in fact disturbers of the peace in the best sense: Are there manifestations of crisis in academic education that can be understood better from the margins? And to what extent does the disturber of the peace, or trouble-maker, in his or her precarious marginal position seem "vulnerable, wounded, and wounding"? (Thomä 2016, p. 151).

Seitz: What does it mean, in light of the current university landscape, to be a disturber of the peace in this field? I believe there is, for the moment, no "peace" that one could disturb.

What there is, is uniformity, an evening or leveling out. But leveling out is something different from peace. It does not amount to a *granting of equal rights* but rather to an *equalizing* of diversities. Giving something equal rights is an act of empowerment, but making something equal means smoothing it out, sanding down its corners and edges, and hence can be seen as a violent act of cutting, and, yes, that is something that I would certainly like to disturb. Performative strategies are ideal to this end, because they are in a position to show what is missing. Moreover, we should not forget that a culture of knowledge cannot be thought of except as performative. Knowledge that is not "performed" is mere information. To paraphrase Paul Watzlawick: one cannot *not* act performatively. After all, everything has a performance; everything is performative. What we want to call a "performative act," however, is a *consciously designed* act, a "showing doing" (Schechner 2002, p. 28). An exhibited action that *shows* itself *showing*, or *reveals* itself *revealing* (Prange 2002). Showing or revealing also means addressing someone and hence also showing interest in sharing something with the other person. Whether the context is artistic, pedagogical, academic, or other, "revealing oneself revealing" always involves a dimension of the naked, the unprotected, the vulnerable. Revealing oneself revealing is daring to interact, and as such an act of courage. It means putting trust in the judgment of others. A performative act is always an act of trust, trust in oneself and in the other. A performative act plays with the possibility of failure and with the risk of being rejected, in the hope of it working, of one being understood and connecting.

I often speak of the necessity of increasing performative methods of research, teaching, and learning at the university, because I observe with concern how processes of standardization are manifested in processes of linearization that scarcely allow deviation. Meanwhile, these processes of linearization have become manifest, in turn, in other social institutions as well, where university graduates as decisionmakers apply what they have learned: to even out through linearization. Such dynamics can sometimes have terrible consequences, for example in the area of health and social services, as shown in Ken Loach's film *I, Daniel Blake* (UK, 2016). The noble goal of standardization processes at universities is, of course, to *guarantee* the *success* of methods of research, teaching, and learning. Under that maxim, it might seem a little strange to argue for risk and failure. Why should people subject themselves to the risk of rejection and the possibility of failure in performative acts? My first answer is this: in order to be able to surprise themselves and others with an object, an event. It ought to be obvious why this makes sense. In contrast to the research, teaching, and learning methods at universities, in life, things don't necessarily evolve in a linear fashion, and it can't hurt to practice being surprised. Moreover, isn't it also the case that realization (in the sense of coming to know or understand something) involves encountering the surprising insight of a truth? And are we not then preventing the possibility of this kind of understanding when we eliminate risk and failure and hence surprise?

For example, in the project you mentioned at the beginning, it was important to me that the students talked about things that really interested them and not just about things they believe they *ought to* find interesting. Finding out what really interests you can be a difficult research task in itself and is closely linked to a certain sense of nakedness and the risk of failure. When I research what really interests me, I am also revealing myself revealing and accepting the risk of failure and especially of rejection. The students of this seminar were particularly brave, because from the beginning, I worked with the slogan "death as a method." After all, I needed a kind of code in order to convey to the students what the project was really about and that I was interested in their interests and that wasn't just the usual empty talk but that I honestly meant it. This is why before the first workshop (i.e. before we actually met in person for the first time), I gave them the task of bringing along "last words": that is, of researching (not writing) a text that they felt expressed some aspect of themselves so powerfully that they might choose it if they had the opportunity before dying to communicate something publicly to humanity or to one human being. So it was no surprise that finitude and death came up repeatedly as tropes over the course of the project. Not because we had started with last words but because—seen from the perspective of life—death has the positive quality of provoking a readjustment of standards. The limited goals we spend most of our days chasing, such as, for students, earning "credits," all these lose their meaning when faced with finitude; they recede into the background. You could say they make space, open up a perspective for the things we find truly important. The question is: Why is this disturbing?

Can you, Jörg, follow my chain of associations from "nakedness," exposure, to surprise in relation to performative acts? What, in your eyes, is the added value or necessity of the performative?

Holkenbrink: It goes without saying that performing artists expose themselves in the theater and thus make themselves vulnerable, because it is a fundamental aspect of their profession. It is perhaps more necessary to explain that an audience at a performance can also expose itself and thus make itself vulnerable. Research and teaching at universities and academies are always a form of performance and hence there is a risk of harm, which all of those involved feel daily, without, as a rule, grappling with the associated effects and consequences. In your chain of associations of nakedness, exposure, and surprise, you emphasize the *productivity* of exposing yourself in performative acts. But if universities and theaters are primarily established as battlegrounds, isn't it high time finally to reflect on the conditions and possibilities of disarmament negotiations that could expand the latitude for the productivity of nakedness, as you call it, or reorganize the relationship between being protected and being exposed, as I like to call for? The educational sciences use the concept of the secret curriculum. The idea is that in addition to the official curriculum, the official education, there is also a secret learning, a secret education. While the official learning has an identifiable education with a certain intention, secret learning is structurally anchored, often happening unconsciously with individuals adapting to institutional structures. I once tried to take this concept from educational research and apply it to the theater, speaking of the secret curriculum of the admission ticket. Isn't it true that by constantly buying tickets the audience secretly learns to ignore its responsibility for the quality of a performance because it has "bought" the right to unilaterally judge the acting of the performers, the direction, the stage, and the dramaturgy? If we want to regain the theater as a site of *common* understanding of questions important for life, then there is no getting around thinking about how the possibility of a multilateral "disarmament" can be presented as an invitation rather than an obligation. And this challenge can also be applied to our initial theme: being conscious of differences when transgressing the boundaries between practical-aesthetic and theoretical approaches and forms of presentation.

Seitz: Could you describe the presentation of such an invitation using the concrete example of the aforementioned performance *Am seidenen Faden* (On the silk thread)? Who is disarming in these performances and how?

Holkenbrink: The Theater of Assemblage/*Theater der Versammlung* performs at the points where science and art intersect. One aspect of the process of rehearsing and performing as a process of research involves studying atmospheres and finding differentiated approaches to them. In this particular production, when the phase of staging began, we identified two risks we definitely wanted to avoid: first, that the theme "What does (networked) life have to do with death?" be treated in a fashionable, superficial, or purely objective way and, second, that the audience not be overwhelmed emotionally or, worse still, depressed. So we set ourselves the task of creating an atmosphere that enabled all involved to question life by grappling with their own finitude and to come out of the performance feeling strengthened. The choice of a performance space played an important role in this regard. The *trauerraum bremen* funeral parlor, as a living site of calm reflection in the center of a lively neighborhood, itself radiates a warm, pleasant, and open atmosphere, in which family members and friends of a deceased person can find the space and time that make it easier to accept the reality of their death. During the phase of research and exploration, the actors worked as, among other things, assistants at funeral ceremonies at the *trauerraum*, which enabled them to experience its approach to design and atmospheres. These experiences were then used in the rehearsal process. For example, they influenced how the audience was greeted, the arrangement of the space, the structuring of time, the acting, and how the discussion after the performance was opened up in the form of a "memory stage" on which the audience members could, if they wished, allow spontaneous images from the performance to enter their mind's eye and then be conveyed to the other people present. Here, the performance does not really involve a continuous storyline or narrative. Instead, it lines up fields of association in which the audience can connect the external images of the staging with their own imagined images. Because these associations and their combinations can be arranged and perceived in very different ways, what we have found is that most viewers experience the exchange afterward as extremely enlightening. Within this basic atmosphere of openness, however, the atmospheres can also change. Serious, sad, and cheerful phases and moments alternate; though to what extent this happens, or when and how often cannot be predicted. The three Fates, who already appeared in the dramaturgy phase, control and weave together the diverse elements of the evening. As "the drunken sisters" (Thornton Wilder), they spin the thread of our lives in a contemporary way: sitting at a computer, like modern DJs. They "program chance" by interweaving or reprogramming in real time the digital codes of their Web or weaving machine—a machine that can, by means of recordings and other forms of playback, sonic interruptions, and interventions, among other things, crucially influence the flow of the performance and the study of the life patterns addressed in it. Against the backdrop of information technology and digital media in our project, the composer Joachim Heintz invented this sound machine, which during the performance enters into an interactive exchange with the performers and the audience and whose programs repeatedly lead to unpredictable changes. The staging is also a fragile collage of performatively presented poems, whose fleeting presence is put in play. The audience also controls the performance, for example, by introducing moments of silence and inaction. There is an opportunity to try out lying in a coffin. The performances are designed as a joint research process in which the oppositions of active and passive, doing and enduring are made fluid. In the field of philosophy, Gernot Böhme contrasts the idea of autonomy with that of sovereignty:

> If the autonomous human being understands himself from the perspective of its self-determination and regards everything that threatens this self-determination and calls it into question as not part of him, then the sovereign human being is one who can allow something to befall him.
>
> (Böhme 2012, p. 7)

Studying atmospheres and finding differentiated approaches to them, playing with the active and the passive, with doing and enduring, are examples of why it makes sense to link theoretical approaches and forms of depiction with practical-aesthetic ones. The artistic interventions do not illustrate a preexisting theoretical insight. Rather, they represent a kind of interruption in the usual scholarly formats, one which opens up a creative space and makes it clear how much the emotional influences research. Lived experience and knowledge are combined in the research process. Cooperative scholarly seminars participate in the performance. And if we see to it that academic and non-academic audiences mix, and that different generations meet at the performances, then this can be understood as an invitation to "disarm" that helps bring together different cultures of knowledge into a dialogue (see also Holkenbrink & Lagaay 2016).

Seitz: If I have understood you correctly, Jörg, you are arguing for strategies of presentation and forms of assembly that make us conscious of a mutual influence that is always present in performances and shared responsibility for the entire process *while at the same time making it unavailable*. If we now transfer this idea back to the performances of knowledge in the academic realm, it suggests that, just like in the theater, there could be a secret curriculum here too that causes us to forget the mutual influence, the simultaneity of doing and enduring, of responsibility and unavailability and so still tempts us to speak of producers and recipients and now perhaps even of providers and customers. Just as there can be no theatrical performance without an audience, there can be no seminar, no lecture, without students, and no conference paper without listeners, who in a process of mutual influence produce something together that at the same time eludes the control of the individual. If one considers courses or conferences from this perspective, it is surely surprising that most participants by no means act as if they shared responsibility for the success of an academic event. In fact, it seems rather as if there was a knowledge provider who delivers goods whose reception can be accepted or refused by the customer. Mutual influence, in the sense of an "autopoietic feedback loop" (Fischer-Lichte, 2004), seems to have fallen out of fashion; that is, contemporary academia has lost interest in the emergent exchange of knowledge or thoughts, of discourse, including its ability to surprise and thus produce new ideas. We recognize a good theatrical performance by whether it stimulates thinking, and whether it is pugnacious; in the current academic landscape, by contrast, a good theory almost presents itself as being indisputable, not abiding contradiction, which would contrast with the dialectic ambition of the production of knowledge in some paradigms. For that reason, criticism is being welcomed less and less, and is—on the contrary—often perceived as degradation (something to which you alluded, Jörg, in your association with the battlefield and your proposal to disarm). But shouldn't performances of knowledge also be trying to stimulate thinking? Shouldn't they have the ambition to open up spaces for thinking rather than presenting definitive results of thinking? The way the academic landscape is currently presenting itself is, of course, nevertheless produced together by all participants. As I said before, one cannot *not* act performatively. The question is simply whether or to what extent this is a conscious or unconscious process. What I call the linearization of research, teaching, and learning methods often leads to "performative contradictions": that is, forms or formats that contradict their own content. Holding a multiple-choice exam on the importance of applied learning in educational processes would be one such example. Content-wise students are expected to learn that applied learning is important, but simultaneously, in a more or less subliminal curriculum, the *form* in which they are evaluated teaches them that learning by rote is still more important, because that's what earns them credits. Psychologically, they end up in a sort of double-bind situation that entails a paradoxical instruction for action (Watzlawick et al. 1967). The task of performative methods of research, teaching, and learning would then, in my view, be to sensitize people to contradictions of this kind. It would mean to encourage a "school of perception," and strive for formats with *performative evidence* that make it possible for people to experience that performances of knowledge are also incumbent on the knowledge of autopoietic feedback loops.

We would all benefit from experiencing situations in which it makes a difference *who* has assembled for a performance of knowledge, and in which it is noticeable how those assembled are influenced by the situation as well as, conversely, have an influence on it themselves. It is a question of acknowledging the balance between what is planned and how things actually emerge. According to this view, performative methods of research, teaching, and learning would not exclude surprises but rather welcome them, which I regard as a necessary condition for cognitive processes. It would be about *making* oneself vulnerable in order to *cause* something to happen, in other words, about being sensitive and receptive to the unknown. Therein also lies the opportunity to confront different forms of knowledge, such as scientific and artistic knowledge, or cognitive and sensory knowledge. When different forms of knowledge are brought into dialogue with one another, one all but provokes the moment of emergence and contingency; a space of possibility results in which something can happen because gaps form, because the gears do not mesh seamlessly; interferences result, incalculable superpositions of wave movements that reinforce each other or cancel each other out. Therein lies opportunity and risk. It then becomes an act of responding to and approaching one another, in which different forms of knowledge reveal mutually the marginal zones of their logics; that is to say, they offer a performance of knowledge in the sense of vulnerability.

Holkenbrink: What consequences can be drawn from our reflections thus far on the theme of "knowledge cultures and vulnerability" for the evolution of university education, for imaginative and productive play with the "rules" for studying? With an eye to self-exposure, the education scholars Thomas Ziehe and Herbert Stubenrauch offered the following observation of everyday life at the university back in the 1980s:

> The risk of being evaluated, criticized, upset, and injured by the new cultural ambitions has to be addressed, both outwardly and inwardly. It seems to us that this sort of protective mechanism lies in the widespread tendency to *withdraw* one's own actions. Those who do not expose themselves cannot be pinned down either. Those who cannot be pinned down avoid possible aggressive depreciation. [...] As withdrawn and unclear as the behavior called for is, often the mortality with which the behavior of others is judged can be just that clear and aggressive. Precisely those who behave in very withdrawn and very unclear ways can thereby reveal a way of thinking and judging that constantly moves in dichotomous opposites and patterns of categorization! Those who expose themselves, those who stand out, are quickly said to be "dominant," "placing themselves in the foreground," "boasting." The group watches over itself, indeed does not allow anyone to step out of line.
>
> *(Ziehe and Stubenrauch 1982, pp. 102ff.)*

The linearization of research, teaching, and learning methods that you have observed, Anna, may have increased today this hidden, aggressive protective stance which, conversely, may even be partly to blame for the linearization. By contrast, anyone who wants to encourage a "willingness to allow touching and changing" (Ingrisch) in the fields of knowledge production must, on the one hand, be prepared to look out for rifts within the institutions and, on the other hand, have the courage, inventiveness, and energy to organize the flow of streams of knowledge through these cracks. For example, in Bremen, Performances Studies can, programmatically, only be studied in combination with studies in another department. There was a conscious decision not to set up a Master's program. The structure of studies is set up in a way that students from different departments come together to work on interdisciplinary projects and bring the subject matter from their specialties into the performative work of the center. Conversely, the students are taught performative methods that they can learn to apply to their specialist backgrounds. They begin to productively relate practical-aesthetic and theoretical approaches to reality to one another—an ability that they can also use later in their professional practice. This professional practice can, on the one hand, lie in the artistic field, in which the integration of different forms of knowledge is becoming increasingly significant. On the other hand, it is reasonable to assume that competencies that until now have been specific to the arts will play an increasingly important role in non-artistic professional fields as well (see Goehler 2006). Another possibility is being a performer while also working in a second or third profession. The American co-founder of Performance Studies as an academic discipline, Richard Schechner, imagines a wealth of such theatrical connections in his writings on the anthropology of the theater, in which performing artists have a second or third profession:

> but this does not mean that his skills as a performer are amateurish; far from it, a connection to a community may deepen all aspects of his art. The flexible treatment of time and space—the ability of one space to be transformed into many places through the skills of the performer more than through the illusionistic devices of the scenographer—goes hand in hand with a transformational view of character (role doubling, role switching) and a close contact with the audience [...].
>
> *(Schechner 2003, p. 185)*

Seitz: In conclusion, we can say, following Julian Nida-Rümelin, that our education system should find its way back to equal recognition of different forms of knowledge (but without equalizing or leveling out their differences):

> Our education system as a whole is a bit shaky cognitively, because it does not focus on the formation of personality. The individual way of life represents not just cognitive abilities—that would be an intellectualist error—but also emotive sensitivity, aesthetic approaches to the world, emphatic assumptions of ethical practices, abilities to judge, decide, and adopt emotional stances in equal measure. Accordingly, our education system needs fundamental reform.
>
> *(Nida-Rümelin 2014, p. 64)*

His reference also applies to the connection between education and the image of human beings, so that we should ask what image of the human being, what normativity, forms the basis for our education system? And do we agree with it? It is an interesting idea in this context that anthropology traditionally viewed human beings as fundamentally distinct from animals. When viewed as distinct from animals, our rational abilities are overemphasized, leading to the shakiness that Nida-Rümelin criticizes. I believe, therefore, that it is time to develop an anthropology that views human beings as distinct from *machines*, which focuses again on our capabilities for situationally justified assumptions, for deviation, for sensitivity and hence also calls for a democratization of forms of knowledge or leads to an "unconditional university" in Derrida's sense (Derrida 2005). We could ask what is the difference between artificial intelligence and artistic intelligence? That would also mean making it clear that machines follow rules and people make exceptions, raising the question: How can we teach this ability to make distinctions (instead of teaching how to act like a machine)? How can we teach and learn something like *translinearity*, that is, situationally based subversion which represents itself in the recognition of moments, in inclusion and exclusion, in the capability of emergence and is reflected in respect and equal recognition of different forms and cultures of knowledge?

Translated from the German by Steven Lindberg and Alice Lagaay

Note

1 See https://www.tdv.uni-bremen.de/performances.php, 30.09.2019.

References

Böhme, Gernot. 2012. *Ich-Selbst: Über die Formation des Subjekts*. Munich: Wilhelm Fink.
Derrida, Jacques. 2005. "The Future of the Profession or the Unconditional University." Trans. Peggy Kamuf. In *Deconstructing Derrida: Tasks for the New Humanities*. Ed. Peter Pericles Trifonas and Michael A. Peters, pp. 11–24. New York: Palgrave Macmillan.
Fischer-Lichte, Erika. 2004. *Ästhetik des Performativen*. Frankfurt am Main: Suhrkamp.
Goehler, Adrienne. 2006. *Verflüssigungen: Wege und Umwege vom Sozialstaat zur Kulturgesellschaft*. Frankfurt am Main: Campus.
Holkenbrink, Jörg and Alice Lagaay. 2016. "Performance in Philosophy / Philosophy in Performance. How Performative Practices Can Enhance and Challenge the Teaching Of Theory." In *Performance Matters* 2.1, pp. 78–85. https://performancematters-thejournal.com/index.php/pm/article/view/38/54
Holkenbrink, Jörg and Anna Seitz, 2017. "Die subversive Kraft der Verletzlichkeit – Ein Dialog über Wissenskulturen und ihre Aufführungen". In *Wissenskulturen im Dialog – Experimentalräume zwischen Wissenschaft und Kunst*. Ed. Doris Ingrisch, Marion Mangelsdorf, and Gert Dressel, pp. 97–110. Bielefeld: transcript Bielefeld.
Ingrisch, Doris. 2013. "Intuition, Ratio und Gender? Bipolares und andere Formen des Denkens." In *Ratio und Intuition: Wissen/s/Kulturen in Musik Theater Film*. Ed. Andrea Ellmeier, Doris Ingrisch, and Claudia Walkensteiner-Preschl, pp. 19–43. Vienna: Böhlau.
Nida-Rümelin, Julian. 2014. *Der Akademisierungswahn: Zur Krise beruflicher und akademischer Bildung*. Hamburg: Edition Körber-Stiftung.
Prange, Klaus. 2002. "Zeigend sich zeigen: Zum Verhältnis von Professionalität und Engagement im Lehrerberuf." In *Lehrerbildungsreform: Leitbilder einer alltagstauglichen Lehrerbildung*, ed. Toni Hansel, pp. 111–122. Herbolzheim: Centaurus.
Schechner, Richard. 2002. *Performance Studies – An Introduction*. New York: Routledge.
Schechner, Richard. 2003. "Toward a Poetics of Performance." In: idem, *Performance Theory*, pp. 170–210. New York: Routledge.
Thomä, Dieter. 2016. *Puer Robustus: Eine Philosophie des Störenfrieds*. Berlin: Suhrkamp.
Watzlawick, Paul, Janet Beavin Bavelas, and Don D. Jackson. 1967. *Pragmatics of Human Communication: A Study of Interactional Patterns, Pathologies, and Paradoxes*. New York: Norton.
Ziehe, Thomas and Herbert Stubenrauch. 1982. *Plädoyer für ungewöhnliches Lernen: Ideen zur Jugendsituation*. Reinbek bei Hamburg: Rowohlt.

20
RESONANCE OF TWO

Karen Christopher

A particular configuration in which to think

This is a duet. A duet between you and these words. This is a duet between me from ages ago and you right now. If it is being read aloud to a group of people, this is a duet multiplied. A duet embedded within that duet is between the speaker and these words. And another between those eyes and that mouth.

When I declare it is a duet, I am creating a position, a specific geometry, that includes and excludes, that puts a spotlight on a particular, and that establishes a zone of importance or influence. I find the duet form appealing, frightening, engrossing, vexing, irresistible, and influential and I wonder about the origin of the power and intimacy of two.

By making a series of performance duets, I endeavoured to see what the form affords.

Collaborative performance-making takes many forms: sometimes, there is no director, with all decisions and plans and guidelines arrived at through consensus; sometimes, there is a director who facilitates the working process; sometimes, that director also performs in the work, sometimes not; sometimes, the work begins with a standard theme or focus; sometimes, it begins with a search for a focus. What collaborative performance-making does not do is start with a completed script which is used as a map or template or is put over people like a glove. It is an area of tremendous variability. As part of this, formal constraints, whether practical or aesthetic, exert influence over the process. And, just as all media configures what it mediates, the conditions and methods of a working process become embedded in the work itself. (For the work discussed here, practical constraints included the duet form itself and the rule that all ideas brought into the studio were to be developed by both partners such that all material in play came under joint "authorship"; aesthetically, the material conformed to what is possible in real time and space with the actual performers present and no one pretending to be someone or somewhere else; both parties had to consent to material presented in the finished performance work with the understanding that tolerance for material important to only one of the partners was preferable to keeping only a narrow angle of acceptance in which both parties unreservedly loved all of it. Our overarching principle was to try everything proposed by either of the partners and while each had veto power over any element of the work, that veto was only used when all other avenues of negotiation failed. We tried to maintain an interest in what felt native to the work as material developed and to learn an internal logic that could be used to justify inclusion or exclusion of new material or configurations of it. Ideally, something left out was done by a mutual agreement even if only one member desired its exclusion. The same should be true of its inclusion.) A working process creates a specific and distinct language. The language that is brought forth in the course of a making process becomes the language with which the work speaks and is the language of transmission to the audience during the performance event.

I have recently been engaged in making collaborative duets on which I have worked with a few different partner artists. On each of these projects, the people involved worked through consensus to create a level playing field between us where listening and contributing material culminated in a completed performance work. What I mean by consensus is interchangeable with what I mean when I talk about agreement. Using either of these words in reference to making performance work, I refer to the practicalities of the work: which foot to use and how many times, where to look, and how to look. It is less useful to attempt agreement on where the meaning lies and the right and wrong of things—but we can agree on which story to tell and how long to let the water dry before speaking again. We do have to agree which direction to look but we don't have to see the same things or to think about what we see from the same point of view—agreement is always about the practicalities: when we should meet and where and when to start working and how. And we have to agree when to stop making and start showing the work. Furthermore, agreement on decisions made doesn't necessarily happen without discord in the process and it doesn't mean that there aren't methods of persuasion, influence, bargaining, or outlasting the other partner. Agreement is made because the parties feel that continuing together is better than not continuing together. Sometimes, the human with the strongest resolve wins the day. The solid agreement comes without resort to bullying or blackmailing each other and for each party to operate with generosity and tolerance for difference of opinion. This essay describes some distinct qualities I found specific to working in pairs on collaborative duet performance compositions.

I am using the word "duet" rather than "duo." "Duo" refers to the two individuals involved and the "duet" is the form of what happens between them—the composition that is the product of their combined effort.

Any form affords a particular quality of attention, a certain comfort level, and a distinct geometry of option. A size gives on to this affordance and also a vibration. Just as a shape or a colour can be influential, the framework, the grid, and the airspace of a form have an influence on the nature or quality of interaction undertaken within it. Volume or number of individuals involved in a plan dictates the vibration or resonance of the project working conditions. In the end, unless it folds or unravels altogether, every well-made plan conforms to conditions that win out as a result of negotiations, or fail to budge after the urge to resist wears out.

Different numbers of people require different metres

What I say and how I say it is a finely calibrated event which depends quite a lot on how many people are present. Even without overt communication, our behaviour is affected by the number of people we are with. Consider the lift: a small room which carries us vertically through tall buildings, causing us to be confined with others with whom we have no business or history—nothing in common except that we are travelling through floors of a building. How is it if we are alone with someone in that tiny room and how does it change if just one more enters when the doors open? If I give a public lecture or talk, I am acutely aware that my tone and manner are different for a gathering of six people than for a gathering of 20 or 30. A talk planned for an audience of nine requires recalibration when, on the day, 60 people show up. But if I have only one person in the audience, even if I don't know the person, this is no longer a public talk. It is too intimate for that.

No majority rule, no mitigation between points of view

I have used the duet form as a way of flattening hierarchy in the collaborative making of performance works. Hierarchies arise from interpersonal power dynamics, past history, differing experience levels, social conventions (popular behaviours), and individuals' willingness to expose weaknesses or vulnerability or suffer a loss of dignity. Some people think faster or are more assertive or willing to take creative risks than others. If a hierarchical relation diminishes an individual's sense of agency, ideas become fugitive. Loss of agency stifles impulse and the ability to make connections and give voice to thought. A duet presents the clearest, simplest way of practising equality with other people—working on it one person at a time. The presentation of the duet itself becomes a model of that levelling for the viewers of the duet composition.

If there is no one to settle disputes, if there is no mitigating voice between opposing positions, then agreement or accommodation might be reached through persuasion or tortuous obstinacy. Or maybe the two people put off the decision for a later time. It is also possible that one of those people has more confidence than the other and it is also possible that one of them feels that the greater experience or, conversely, the freshness of youth of the other means that one or the other should take a step back. But if there is to be an actual flattening of hierarchy, then it doesn't come because the "winner" of disagreements is the one who is better at arguing or the less tolerant or less afraid of mistakes or more patient. Agreement has to come freely and fairly as a result of one or the other seeing fit to step back. The only way this can happen freely and without resentment is if the climate between the two is already fostering equality. Maintaining a level field calls for constant practice, a high level of attention, and the humility to say let's do it your way and see what happens. Small practices of faith make this possible.

When one of my duet partners, Sophie Grodin, and I started working together, we had to reckon with a 27-year age difference between us. She was still at university. I was teaching on an MA course at the same institution where she was on a BA course. The age difference between Sophie and me affords a clear view on management of difference which is usually more subtle between people of a similar age. One way to flatten the hierarchy is to honour—even privilege—difference and to value the presence of discord or disagreement. Rather than agree to the same point of view, the agreement becomes about how to keep both.

There are small mechanisms that reinforce this practice. We were working in English which is my first language but not Sophie's. As part of our work on the project *Control Signal* (2013), we planned to include a portion of the performance text in her first language, Danish. This was to be spoken by me. She had to teach me how to say it. Sophie fancied this incapacity of mine be played out in front of the audience, so we performed a version of me not knowing the text in Danish each time we performed that section. I had to disregard the possibility of memorising the Danish translation and let Sophie supply those words to me in front of the audience. This demonstration of humility allowed the audience to read me as less experienced in spite of my grey hair. As part of our warm-up, we practised a clapping pattern. Sophie was much better at it than I was. This became significant. We worked to refrain from making assumptions about what each other was capable of. We listened to each other especially closely during disagreements with an eye towards finding a way to make both of

Figure 20.1 Sophie Grodin (left) and Karen Christopher (right) in *Control Signal* (2013). Jemima Yong

Figure 20.2 Sophie Grodin (left) and Karen Christopher (right) in *Control Signal* (2013). Jemima Yong

us satisfied with whatever outcome we settled on. This meant that each of us was open to persuasion and said yes to things we might not have otherwise. This meant that we both practised patience and worked with an open mind. It meant being clear about whether I want to win or make work: if I crush my colleague, I will have a broken person to work with.

We sit opposite each other at the table. I want her to have a good idea as much as I want myself to have one. I want to work with someone who is going to make me better, and if my idea is found wanting, we need at least half a chance that she will have one that moves us. If we can spark it, the dynamic between us provides a fuel. Initially, it is heavy going.

Let's say we are soggy brained—it is after lunch, we are slow and looking away into the middle distance. It is taking hours. We are trying to write a text that will deliver some information about a particular historical figure. We want to use the events surrounding her life and what happened to her but it is possible that our audience will not know her or will not have enough context to feel the impact of our material unless we deliver enough information for them to locate the world we are operating within. But we don't want to slow down. We don't want to go to school desks in the middle of a performance. There is a velocity we have to keep up, pressure on the audience, their attention, and if we don't keep up this velocity, their heart rates will fall to a place where we can't get them back. We also need this velocity ourselves in the studio. We have a text we are working with which is meaningful to us but which has no place in the world of the material we are working with and yet it delivers an idea that we like *(the idea that there are unspoken rules a society operates within and if we don't pay attention to them, we can sometimes behave—automatically, without thinking—in ways we don't intend)*. So, I say, let's use this text as a template to say what we want to say about our historical figure. We will simply replace key words and write it "in the style of" the pre-existing text. This idea made no sense to Sophie. Because I am suddenly incensed that she doesn't understand me *(how is it possible after so many days working together? It feels like a tiny exposure, a disloyalty, an abandonment that is seismically shifting how I feel about working with another person)* and as I'm looking to contain some kind of fusion happening within me, I take the page on which the text is written and I prove that it will work by doing it for her. I write it by speaking it. And she sees it. She sees it because she is full of attention now and I rise to the occasion because I am also full of attention and full of energy fuelled by the conviction that I can prove it to her—prove that my idea will work. And in this moment, preceded by more than two hours agonising over writing tired expository approaches, we feel a sense of triumph. Each of us has made this possible; it is spark and fuel in an oxygen-rich atmosphere.

Working with someone twisting to the right as I twist to the left actually holds the two of us together in the way that twisting fibres make a rope giving us enough contradiction to keep us on our toes. I don't experience derailment on my own as much as I do in the presence of another person. This derailment or some form of uncertainty puts our minds on alert. We wake up and experience accelerated thinking, not actually thinking in words but intuiting through sensation, producing through the nervous system a response that we understand only after we have made it. The moment of being misunderstood, of gasping at a dead end after following a misconceived assumption, of feeling alone in the company of another, produces a jump start that wakes up the active mind. Problem solving is instinctive. Being at a loss provokes the instinct to regain solid ground. Working on a duet involves swinging between cultivating careful communication on the one hand and persuading ourselves to be comfortable with uncertainty on the other.

Working with two is bicameral, a legislative body with two chambers. It's akin to managing to see through a pair of binoculars. Our views are slightly askew by just about the difference between the point of view from my left eye and the one from my right. And it applies to the audience as well: if they are reading us, they are using each of us as a ballast or reference point for the other. Everything we project pings off the other as if checking the connection between us like a computer. The audience is drawing comparisons; the audience is taking exception to one, and is feeling a growing allegiance to one or the other. We give each other a context within which the audience compares us. We are seen in relief; we are each other's backdrop. If the group includes more than two, the tendency is for an individual to be spotlighted against a crowd of others.

In interviews with David Sylvester, the British painter Francis Bacon talked about painting portraits; he said that he preferred not to have a live model present while he was painting. He felt that he did an injury to them. He painted best from memory or from photographs. He said that the presence of the person in the room made him feel like they were being made to suffer. He worried that the subject felt his painting did them an injury. It was distracting to commit this perceived injury with their own flesh and breath and blood vibrating in front of him. He became preoccupied with the discomfort of live models. This projection of discomfort interfered with the free ranging of the painter's plans. He talked in terms of sensation. He was painting sensation, painting what could not be seen, invisible forces (Sylvester 2016, pp. 45–49). His portraits contain impossible states of conflation between people and things, with rupture or stretched or twisted heads or bodies and, in the case of his portraits of Pope Innocent X (after a painting by Velasquez), excruciating facial expressions of torment. He needed to be alone for this transaction to take place. I think he was creating a bond with the image itself—a duet with the painting coming into being. He didn't want any influence to interrupt his connection with the painting.

I looked at the interviews between Sylvester and Bacon because they are referenced in *The Logic of Sensation* (2003): Gilles Deleuze's analysis of Bacon's work, in which he focuses a chapter on the coupled figures which feature in many of Bacon's paintings. These figures appear to consist of two entities in collision with each other. Sometimes, it is two people, sometimes a person and an object. There is a sense of two entities acting upon each other with shape-changing force. They are mingled by it. They become entangled or enmeshed. In Bacon's paintings, there is violence in the mixing of two.

Deleuze adopts Paul Klee's description of painting: defining its main task as the attempt to render invisible forces visible, closely relating *forces* with *sensation* (Deleuze 2003, p. 56). Deleuze observes a coupling of two figures in many of Bacon's paintings and describes the communication between their two levels of sensation. Equating sensation with vibration, he suggests that the relationship between these two levels of sensation creates a resonance (p. 45). In some cases, these are two distinct objects whose vibrations create a resonance between them; in others, this resonance is happening between "crushed bodies included in a single figure" (p. 65). Deleuze observes that this resonance creates a rhythmic coupling that does not admit a third. The presence of a third figure (often as part of a triptych) becomes an attendant whose rhythm remains apart. Deleuze goes on to cite a similar dynamic in written word and music (pp. 66–73). This resonance of sensations is also generated in live performance. I relate it to the work that two people do with each other, both in the composition of a duet in the studio, and with the participation of the audience in the performance.

The resonance of two may be felt as a sensation and an operative part of an artistic notion or theory, but it is also *a physical fact*. The architecture of the human ear produces the perception of a third tone as a result of being exposed to two tones produced outside the ear canal. Upon hearing two tones of different frequencies, a third or a fifth apart for example, the resonance of these two tones within the chamber of the ear kicks off an extra vibration which we experience as sound without there being an external source for its production (Wolfe 2011). The third tone is the difference in frequencies of the two original tones, a 'difference tone,' or a 'Tartini tone' — named after violinist and composer Giuseppe Tartini, who discovered in 1714 that if two related notes were played simultaneously on a violin, a third sound could be heard. Tartini used this phenomenon as a tool for tuning (Encyclopaedia Britannica 2018). Vibration is the key to the difference between a partnership of two and any other number. It is akin to the confrontation of variant sounds, the sounds that make our ears tingle and invent a third.

Resonance of two

A body becoming something else

The quiver is a movement performed in the duet, *Control Signal*. When the audience enters the performance space, this movement is already in motion. Performed by me, standing facing front towards the seating bank, just to the left of centre in the performance area, the quiver is a small but insistent action. The performance of it requires a consistent side-to-side motion of the hips which is allowed to spread to the whole torso by dint of it all being connected. That is, nothing else is moved intentionally, but the shoulders and therefore the arms, the knees and therefore the heels are also moving. The performer attempts to keep the head still and the eyes looking straight forward, without appearing to stare at something in particular. The effect is of a physical hum, a purring engine, a constant rattle. It is a small action with a constant rhythm.

Figure 20.3 Sophie Grodin (left) and Karen Christopher (right) in *Control Signal* (2013). Jemima Yong

Figure 20.4 Sophie Grodin (left) and Karen Christopher (right) in *Control Signal* (2013). Jemima Yong

Originally, it was composed as a response to the question: What never stops? The composition of the entire piece began with an investigation into lines of electricity, in our bodies, and through the air around us. This led to material connected to the ways electricity has been used to control unruly people and animals, and material focused on vibration or pulse. The quiver takes on various meanings as the piece goes on and is performed a number of times by both performers standing side-by-side or at different positions within the space, but at the beginning of the performance, it stands as a signal that there will be some mysterious, or at least invisible, forces at work. In "Consider this," an essay by Mary Paterson written in response to *Control Signal,* she refers to the quiver in a number of ways including as "a body becoming something else" (Paterson 2013). Eirini Kartsaki describes it in the introduction to her book *Repetition in Performance*: "both performers start to shake, to vibrate, to move with control from side-to-side. Grodin and Christopher shake their arms . . . moving as if they do not know they are moving. They both look ahead" (Kartsaki 2017, p. 3). The way Sophie's hand closest to me moves at a speed and rhythm that matches mine while her outer arm works at a slower speed and different rhythm sets up a counterpoint to my steady, almost mechanical rattle. We undoubtedly affect each other but the manifestation of the effect is various and not always predictable nor matching. In some ways, a counterpoint is more productive than a correspondence as it provokes definition of territory or justification of difference or contradiction. The resonance between two vibrations is most engaging when it produces a new element itself. Kartsaki points out that it seems a force is acting upon the two performers. And she highlights that, as she watches, this invisible force begins to act upon her as well (p. 5).

A pressure of attention

I perform behaviour specific to a duo. I will not behave in the same way when it comes to the performance of tasks if I am alone. Though I may let myself down over and over again without much push, when working in concert with someone else, I will struggle as much as it takes not to let that person down. It is not always possible to succeed but I will put in as much effort as I can to live up to my part in a combined effort. This is partly to do with pride—an effort to show what I can do; with competition—I can do as well as or better than the other; compassion—I don't want to fail to satisfy a need; responsibility—I don't want to break a contract whether tacit or spoken. But it is also to do with the kind of influence people have on one another. The contagion of attitude and diligence and a spirit of work build a membrane only as strong as the demonstration of commitment to the work by the individuals involved. This is particularly true for a partnership of two. Three or more might pull along a sluggish partner but if there are only two on the job, a lack of commitment to the work from one member becomes a drag on the energy of the partnership. If they accept the challenge, it means a pressure of attention is working on both parties.

With a group of three or more, there is a dispersal of attention; it is less intimate. Duos are confined in points of focus, whereas with more than two, the points of focus multiply more rapidly. Duets lack access to a high volume of chaos which requires more simultaneity than two can provide. In larger groups, there is greater affordance for thinking in terms of generalities and mass demonstration. There is a cacophony of vibration once you step from two to three. Two are still distinct from one another, greater numbers blur distinctions, and clarity requires careful engineering.

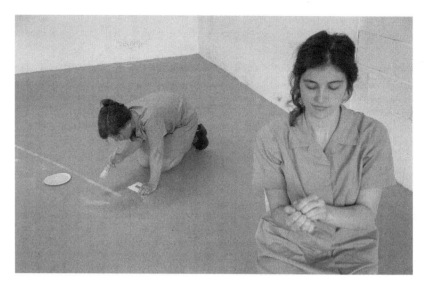

Figure 20.5 Karen Christopher (left) and Sophie Grodin (right) in *Control Signal* (2013). Jemima Yong

In the pursuit of flattened hierarchies, there is not only interpersonal hierarchy to consider, but there is also a hierarchy among the material elements of the performance. Mastery of meaning among and across movement, choreography, spoken word, sound, image, and dynamism necessitate a greater control over the people, objects, and materials in a larger group. More cooperation is summoned, more confinement of individual licence to make decisions in a moment, more to consider in terms of planning and action. This applies similarly in studio sessions (both for composition and rehearsal) as well as in performance before an audience. Imagine two of us looking to the right at the same time with our gaze at the same level, moving with the same speed and tension. Multiply that by five and imagine how many different thoughts reside in those ten heads and how many ways there are to be distracted or less than willing or not quite at full attention. The reality of getting ten heads to turn in exactly the same way, at the same time, is that those ten heads have been pounded into submission (willingly, most likely) by numerous repetitions and some strenuous insistence on the part of an outside eye. It is not a better or a worse situation, but it has a different history and a different subliminal effect.

Everyone has two bodies

The duet composition sets up a vibration, has its own rhythm, requires keen attention from both parties—it ceases to be a group if either member of the duo looks away, drops out, loses connection—a quality not shared by other denominations. Taking the other eye in the bicameral view, between two parties, there is no witness, no tie-breaking opinion—the account of their meeting is between them alone and each has only their own word for how they came together and what transpired. It is a configuration which demands faith and responsibility, trust and confidence, and a willingness to accept the generative force of difference. The intimacy of two affords the possibility of experiencing how entangled the well-being of the other is to the well-being of oneself.

In her book *The Second Body* (2018), Daisy Hildyard suggests that these days everyone has two bodies—the actual flesh body and the body that is in and of the whole world. In the context of a worldwide network of ecosystems, the second body is "your own literal physical and biological existence," a global presence that is larger and more fluid than your flesh body—a version of you that is part of everything.

When I began working on duets and searched for a way to think about the form, I worked with the idea of self and other as the guiding principle that governed both my relationship with my collaborator and the two of us with the audience. It seems that each single part of duo can be multiple. Single units are not stable but like cells, we divide and multiply. If I am here and also everywhere, says Hildyard, then I am responsible for the well-being of the whole:

> Your first body could be sitting alone in a church in the centre of Marseille, but your second body is floating above a pharmaceutical plant on the outskirts of the city, it is inside a freight container on the docks, and it is also thousands of miles away, on a flood plain in Bangladesh, in another man's lungs.
>
> *(Hildyard 2018, p. 25)*

Notions of ecology and the distribution of bodies relate to performance, and these examples help me see that when we are talking about observing bodies in a room, we are reading more than what is readily legible in a conventional sense. In a mass-produced photo book, I often gazed into as a child I particularly remember a series of photos featuring two people standing together. Underneath each of them, the caption read: "these two form a multitude." This moved me greatly but I didn't really understand why. I liked the idea that two people meant all people. I was thinking about synecdoche, these two people standing in for others the way the hand stands in for the whole body in the phrase "all hands on deck." As an adult, when I found the book again, I realised that these couples are all male/female couples from different races and ethnicities, and the implication is that they could procreate and thus produce a whole race. It was one of those blind spots that protected a notion somehow dear to me but which was beside rather than part of what its source intended. We all can and do create scaffolds for knowing and believing what we wish to know and believe, and we can be fluid with the application of this capacity.

I am thinking with words, I am thinking with my body; if I am in a context, then that context is also part of how I am thinking. I am thinking as a member of a duo. I am thinking through a form involving two people. That is a particular way of thinking.

References

Deleuze, G. 2003. *Francis Bacon: The Logic of Sensation.* Translated by Daniel W. Smith. London/New York: Continuum.
Encyclopaedia Britannica. 2018. 'Giuseppe Tartini' [Online] https://www.britannica.com/biography/Giuseppe-Tartini#ref11458 Accessed 23 August 2018.
Hildyard, D. 2018. *The Second Body,* 2nd edition. London: Fitzcaraldo Editions.
Kartsaki, E. 2017. *Repetition in Performance: Returns and Invisible Forces.* London: Palgrave Macmillan.
Paterson, M. 2013. 'Consider This' [Online] https://marypaterson.wordpress.com/2013/12/08/consider-this-control-signal/ Accessed 9 October 2019.
Sylvester, D. 2016. *Interviews with Francis Bacon.* London: Thames & Hudson.
Wolfe, J. 2011. 'Tartini Tones and Temperament: An Introduction for Musicians' [Online] https://newt.phys.unsw.edu.au/jw/tartini-temperament.html Accessed 23 August 2018.

21
LYING FALLOW
Anonymity and collectivity

Rajni Shah

This is an invitation from Mary Paterson, Rajni Shah, Susan Sheddan, and Tiffany Charrington to join a group of 30 people for a series of conversations called *Lying Fallow*.

Lying Fallow will take place over seven months, and will involve a series of three gatherings in different London locations, which will each respond to the following questions:

- How might alert quietude, not knowing, and listening be seen as spaces of change, rigour, and possibility?

- Where and how might the idea of 'lying fallow' be actualised and given value within contemporary society?

- What becomes possible in those times when it may seem to the outside world as if we are doing or producing nothing?

At each gathering, we will return to the same questions within a different frame. This means that while the location, the season, and the light in the room will change, our conversations will become acts of returning. As hosts, Mary, Rajni, Susan, and Tiffany will ensure that the events are carefully and generously held, but the conversations that emerge will be shaped by the people who attend and the ways in which each person wishes to participate.[1]

---

1 Excerpt from 'Lying Fallow: An Invitation', Rajni Shah Projects <http://www.rajnishah.com/lying-fallow> [accessed 21 September 2019].

Lying fallow

Each time we met, we were a little less bound to narrative.

Lying fallow

Lying Fallow is a project that was difficult to describe when we were creating it, and remains difficult to describe as it grows through time.

It was a spacious project.

Its defining feature was its alliance with stillness

and with silence

as a series of attempts to do less in the company of others.

These pages take the form of a kind of poetry, which might feel frustrating in the context of a companion/guide.

But then, frustration was a big part of what we experienced.

Frustration was, I think, a big part of the thinking.

You know how sometimes people try to use a poetic form to describe something indescribable, and it ends up being more frustrating because there is no common ground between you?

I know.

But I think it could be worth a try.

Lying fallow

1. A straw bale room, on a city farm. November.

Lying fallow

After the first session on my train journey home my mind was trying as we are taught to label the experience and put it in a box.

I have a young family and a hectic schedule so understanding fallowness or even practising fallowness became something to think about.

I thought about fallowness during the dishes,

        while playing with my children

    and it all kind of started to mean being present.

Not thinking more than within the moment.[2]

---

2   Wajid Hussain, reflections on *Lying Fallow*.

2. An empty library, inside a university. February.

Lying fallow

Three months passed and we met again.

Although most people still hardly knew each
 other we greeted each other as old friends.

And for some reason it no longer mattered to
me that my public profile was not recognised.

I had been recognised in a different way.[3]

---

3   Anna Minton, reflections on *Lying Fallow*.

Lying fallow

3. A large studio, with windows looking over East London. May.

Linear time has done its trick of leaping forwards
towards a point called an end.

But in cyclical time, we are just beginning.⁴

4   Genevieve Maxwell, reflections on *Lying Fallow*.

Lying fallow

[Whenever I write about it, I find myself mired in doubt. The idea that one might prioritise and dedicate energy to a practice of not-doing dulls against the fact that the world sorely needs activism and change right now. I cannot resolve this in my head. But at the same time, I know that something profound happened during those gatherings. We were beside each other, often disagreeing or presenting very different emotional experiences, quietly, with a listening that remained
in the room
in our bodies
in the world   without over-extending itself.

Fallowness most commonly refers to land that is cultivated but not tasked with growing. It exists within a world that is measured and ordered by agricultural laws and colonial frameworks. There is a sense of the un(re)productive, or the unyielding, in its meaning. But in the context of fallowness this lack of production is always held within parameters that are based on a carefully constructed cycle of productivity: in agricultural terms, fields lie fallow for a certain period of time in order to regain fertility, and to be put to work again. In fact, in its original meaning, 'fallow' means 'ploughed land' and only later, 'land ploughed but not planted'; in this original meaning, then, 'fallow' is not even defined by a lack of productivity but by a lack of visible productivity specifically within a cycle of cultivation. What does it mean to cultivate fallowness within this moment? Was it refusal
       resistance
alternative
       or none of these?

Not thinking more than within the moment feels like a lot of other narratives that are around these days: narratives of mindfulness that turn out to be consumerist. But what does it mean to practise this alongside others? Something about the structure of the project meant that its 'work' continued between the times when we met, and continues to continue even now.]

I am always in movement between these two places.

(who I am matters, because it informs how I think. whatever they tell you, remember that it matters who you are, how you have lived, what your ancestors did or did not experience, where you tread, what body you bring, what voice, what clothes, what smell. and while none of those things, while no things belong to us, we carry and hold them through a lifetime, they move us)

I am always in movement between these two places. One of them is a place of great clarity. Also, efficiency, articulacy, groundedness, and vision. The other is a place of flight, of imagination, of dreaming, and of things that would never make themselves seen in this collection.

And this text, seemingly a chapter in a Companion to Performance Philosophy, seemingly about a project I co-devised and co-led, called *Lying Fallow*, is also the movement between – between your reading, your time, your privilege and suffering, and these words – between my own states of being – between my desire for clarity, and my desire for flight. Then also I think: what if these words could allow someone to put the book down, do nothing, and wait?

Put the book down, do nothing, and wait.

Who is alongside you?

22
PLAY IN PERFORMANCE PHILOSOPHY

Alice Koubová

It is difficult to grasp the relationship between performance philosophy and play in one short chapter. The main reason for that difficulty lies in the character of the concepts involved. When studied individually, performance, philosophy, and play are described variously as ambiguous (Sutton-Smith 1997, p. vii), amphibolous (Spariosu 1989), as essentially contested concepts (Strine, Long, and Hopkins 1990, as referenced in Carlson 2018, p. 1), as concepts with unclear meaning and definition (Turner 1974), and as having incredible structural complexity (Sutton-Smith 1997, p. 195) or a wide range of significance (Schechner 1973). In other words, we do not know exactly how to define or delineate "play", "philosophy", and "performance", although we use these terms, perform them, link them together, and explain one in terms of another. Apart from our central focus here on the composition of "performance philosophy", there are also many other conceptual constellations in existing sources, such as the philosophy of play described by Ryall, Russell, and MacLean (2013), McConachie's performance play (2011), play and performance as explained by Lobman and O'Neill (2011), Gerstmyer's play performance or play as performance (1991), Schechner's term performance as play (2006, p. 89), and the ludic performance theory mentioned by Sutton-Smith (2001, p. 192), to name but a few. The goal of this chapter, however, is not to give a general account of the relationship between play, performance, and philosophical thinking, but to investigate the function of play within the performance philosophy field. Performance philosophy already offers a particular perspective not only on how to interpret, but also how to invent and perform the relationship of performance and philosophy.

In accordance with this perspective, I understand performance, philosophy, and play as conceptual agents whose meaning is generated in their relational constellation, through their use, and in their impact. I am not interested so much in explicating the essence of play, but in reflecting on how performance philosophy acts if regarded through the lens of play. We may also ask: how does philosophy change through the ludic experience in performance? These issues must be investigated within the act of play, rather than from an isolated, distanced position. However, they also require a certain positioning within the problem, a sort of clear attitude, in order to avoid arbitrariness, a play with words, or a philosophical spectacle. But this makes the whole task even more intriguing – it becomes ethical. What sort of attitude should we adopt in this situation of multiple degrees of freedom if we want to avoid cynicism and indifference while at the same time eschewing a return to a rationalistic illusion of transcendence and the totalitarianism of a singular truth? How can playfulness navigate between escapism and a deadly serious attitude, and help move performance philosophy towards a better self-understanding?

My aim is to shed light on this complex topic in three steps. First, I will summarize the crucial characteristics of play that can be used in the further understanding of the relationship between play and performance, and describe existing approaches to this relationship. Second, I will present performance philosophy as a field that emphasizes the need to reinterpret philosophy through performance and I will propose some additional aspects of that ethos generated by the phenomenon of play within performance. Finally, as a particular attempt to practise ludic performance philosophy, I will outline some of the important organizational approaches undertaken at the conference "How Does Performance Philosophy Act? Ethos, Ethics, Ethnography", which was held in 2017 in Prague.

Play and performance: research approaches

The investigation into play and performance is often connected with a third phenomenon, ritual. The interplay of these three phenomena can be analysed either synchronically or diachronically. Play became a subject of systematic study at the end of the 19th century in the works of Herbert Spencer (1855), Karl Groos (1898), and M. Lazarus (1883) (not to mention the relatively isolated account on the play drive in Friedrich Schiller's [(1794) 1954] work, or Immanuel Kant's [(1790) 1914] account of free play). The interest in play and playing as a social, anthropological, and philosophical phenomenon grew into the "ludic turn" in the 1930s (Sutton-Smith 1997, p. ix). Play was regarded as a key element of human culture, the basis of human emotional and moral development, the principle of creativity, and even as the primary characteristic of human beings, as such.

Performance, in contrast, emerged as an important notion only during the second half of the 20th century, and it is often mentioned in the context of the analysis of play (especially in the works of V. Turner [1969] and E. Goffman [1959]). In order to understand performance, descriptions of play structure are often used (e.g. embodiment, time and space framing, challenging borders between the real and the imaginary, art and reality, subject roles, ambivalence between conservative and creative function, etc.). For this reason, many theoreticians propose performance as a "particular form of the play activity" (Lobman and O'Neill 2011, p. viii), as an "important subcategory of play" (Sutton-Smith 1997, p. 192), or it is claimed that performance developed from play. Performance is understood to be a repetition of play on a restricted scale. In order to use these ideas for our goal of investigating play within performance philosophy, let us now focus uniquely on those aspects of play that are repeated (or recycled and adapted) by performance and developed in performance philosophy.

Selected aspects of play

In his book *Homo Ludens* (1938), Johan Huizinga, a key thinker in play studies, focuses on play in "its social manifestations, … as social play" (1949, p. 7). In this, Huizinga approaches what will later be called performance. He formulates the basic characteristics of play in the following way:

> Play is a voluntary activity or occupation executed within certain fixed limits of time and place, according to rules freely accepted but absolutely binding, having its aim in

itself and accompanied by a feeling of tension, joy and the consciousness that it is 'different' from 'ordinary life.'[1]

(p. 28)

Play is, according to Huizinga, "the absolutely primary category of life" (p. 3) and should be studied "as a special form of activity, as a 'significant form', as a social function... and social construction" (p. 4).

The important feature of play is its localization outside the architecture of purposes, both rationally intellectual ones and irrationally instinctive ones. Play, as Huizinga puts it, "is valid beyond the norms of reason, duty and truth" (1949, p. 139), "it stands outside the immediate satisfaction of wants and appetites, indeed it interrupts the appetitive process. It interpolates itself..." (p. 9). In other words, play, as a social function and as the primary category of life, is neither reasonable nor immediate. On the contrary, it interrupts these attitudes through its own interpolation. How is this interpolation and interruption achieved? Huizinga answers clearly:

> This intensity of, and absorption in, play finds no explanation in biological analysis. Yet in this intensity, this absorption, this power of maddening, lies the very essence, the primordial quality of play... the fun-element characterizes the essence of play.
>
> (p. 3)

Through maddening, play interrupts the system of immediate satisfactions, which is not the same as rational or moral interruption. Play provides distance that is produced through absorption and that interrupts our tendency to satisfy immediate wants. It is exactly this ability to become absorbed, to succumb to the intensity of play, and to leave the projects of immediate normative behaviours, which characterizes, according to Huizinga, the human who plays: *homo ludens*. Play interrupts the system of reference to extrinsic motives. It interpolates and is beyond good and evil itself, and in this sense, it is affirmative. If we accept that playfulness is a given characteristic of human beings and of their ability to function socially, without it being defined in terms of reason or morality, would there be any difference between a mad human being absorbed in play and an animal?

Huizinga surprisingly claims that this question is irrelevant. His perspective is that there is no need to make any strict delimitation between human and animal, as in terms of play, none exists. To quote:

> Animals have not waited for man to teach them their playing. We can safely assert, even, that human civilisation had added no essential feature to the general idea of play. Animals play just like men.
>
> (1949, p. i)

Play is a meaningful activity because it is fun, not because it confirms the primacy of a human being or of any philosophical subject. The fun of play is not deduced from other categories of life. It has no purpose outside of itself. In this sense, it is purposeless. It is useless for our projects and goals; we do not achieve anything through playing. Only as such, as purposeless, it is superabundant. The immediate satisfaction and orientation of purposes is interrupted in play in favour of complexity, differentiation, and superabundance. Play offers more than what we immediately need. Therefore, Huizinga proclaims, "we must be more than merely rational beings, for play is irrational" (p. 4).

How can we use this analysis of play to enrich our understanding of philosophy in general, and of performance philosophy in particular? Although Huizinga clearly says that play is inferior to reason and seriousness because it is irrational and "only play", he refuses to subordinate play to reason and seriousness. Instead, he puts play in some respect above them: "Play may rise to heights ... that leave seriousness far beneath" (1949, p. 8). Play in its autotelic and superabundant character stays paradoxically below and above rational seriousness, duplicating it twice instead of reproducing it, and interrupting it through a non-trivial gesture in two directions. Play always arises secondarily, and it is relational, dependent on what precedes it or surrounds it. Play needs the mundane in order to re-enact or imitate the mundane, to protest against the mundane, to step temporarily outside the mundane, or to satirize the mundane. However, only as this secondary parasite-like lampoons, does it become the above-mentioned absolutely primary category of life, the source and nourishment of both human and animal life, an activity with its own wit and fun.

How to approach this phenomenon philosophically? In the moment when philosophy discovers play, play doesn't allow it to exist unequivocally. For when we start to think philosophically about play, play will only interrupt us, lampoon us, provoke us, and make problems from above and below. In this way, it opens a field for philosophy that is not reasonable and autonomous, but complex, dependent (on play that itself depends on thinking), and fun. However, if we succumb to play in the philosophical accounting of it and so proclaim play and philosophy to be one thing, then the game is over for both play and philosophy. This ambivalence in thought caused by play is not a theme or problem waiting to be solved; it is an invitation to a transformation in thinking.

Play performance

Having analysed and developed some characteristics of play, let us now inquire into how play can link to performance. As mentioned earlier, several approaches consider performance a particular part of play. Bruce McConachie proposes, for instance, an evolutionary-diachronic approach and claims that play is a condition of performance: "Our impulse to craft performances and to engage with the performances of others comes from our evolutionary heritage of play" (McConachie 2011, p. 35). He agrees with classical accounts of play provided by Huizinga (1949) and Caillois (1961), and adds that performance is a type of play in which mental self-projection is emphasized, or, in other words, where the capacity "to embody and perform a subjunctive reality as a part of... play" (e.g. as if I were a music star, as if I were a frog, as if I were you) is paramount. "The ability to simulate alternative, imaginary, and future worlds", in which the "self" appears consciously twice and integrates this possibility of conscious doubleness of self, provides, according to McConachie, "the cognitive foundation of all performances" (McConachie 2011, p. 38). Marvin Carlson (2018, p. 5), in his famous book on performance, defers to Bauman (1989), assuming that regardless of many conceptual disagreements on what performance can mean, performance always implies "consciousness of doubleness".

Consciousness of doubleness does not consist in external observation, but in double consciousness of self. For this reason, performance does not provide mimesis of reality, but play about the play, or "action about actions" (Sutton-Smith 2001, p. 194), because "it communicates by its own stylized character that it is a play reality, not an everyday reality" (ibid, p. 195). McConachie concludes: "Performance is a type of play that entails conceptual integration" (2011, p. 43). To complete his argument, he presents ritual as the last element in the development of the structure of play, i.e. as an extension of performance, "the sprout" growing "from the branch of performance" following the line of subjunctive activity (ibid, p. 46).

In contrast to the diachronic approach, the synchronic description, proposed, for instance, by Richard Schechner (2006, p. 89), claims that performance is not merely a part of play. Rather, Schechner places performance on the continuous line between the polarities of play and ritual. Ritual thus represents a social activity that is more serious than a mundane one and that influences reality "from above", as it were. Play, however, is less serious than the mundane, it is below it, and fulfils the function of asocial amusement with this temporary lack of seriousness. Performance, says Schechner, combines these two activities: "Playing, like ritual, is at the heart of performance", and "In fact performance may be defined as ritualized behaviour conditioned/permeated by play". Finally, he identifies the presence of a "double gap" in consciousness within performance that yields to a strengthening of self-reflexivity (2003, p. 260). Surprisingly, Schechner's claims about performance do not differ greatly from what Huizinga says about play. Both refer to an activity that interrupts reality in two directions at the same time whilst influencing it, in turn. The stress on subjectivity, self-reflexivity, and double consciousness makes Schechner's assertions close to the diachronic claims, as well.

Ludic performance philosophy

What can we learn from these descriptions with regard to a philosophy that seeks to respect the function and agency of play and performance? Let us repeat that play is a purposeless, secondary activity dependent upon serious reality, and yet, as such, it becomes a primary category of life. Performance is then that play which brings to awareness the embodied complexity of self-relationship and consciousness of doubleness. Performance, as play on play, repeats play, and at the same time alters this chain of repetitions. It not only performs at a distance from the mundane, but also plays with this distancing. It intentionally tests, plays with the borders of play, restored behaviour, and shows how much this playing on play reinterprets subjectivity. This reinterpretation concerns not only the concept of subjectivity in thinking, but the philosophical subject enrolled in the process as such. Ludic performance philosophy leads to a transformation of the thinking subject. It investigates performatively how one thinks if one is thinking from a secondary position, from the side. This secondary state of being is based in a saturation of the question of subject, not in a form of masochism. The subject in ludic performance philosophy is neither the point of departure, nor the leading idea. It is not the central point of reference or an authority of thought, but it does not surrender itself to any asubjective flow either. It has fun. Through the maddening power of play, the performance philosopher can, firstly, live a meaningful experience (i.e. have fun); secondly, interrupt the system of immediate satisfaction of philosophical wants and appetites; and finally, enter the transitional space of play (see Winnicott 2005) and develop an ethics of ambivalence that through "exercising into the transformation" (see Elberfeld 2007, p. 28) maintains the character of superabundance and excitement.

I claim that this exercise of the subject's secondary position, which is superabundant and not masochistic, brings to the fore a special form of democratic thought process. Equality of genres of knowledge, of subjects involved, and of methods is not based in this case on the rationalistic idea of the autonomy of individuals (genres, subjects, and methods), their mutual independency, or respect and consequent responsibility for their individual deeds and results. Equality here is rather a consequence of an awareness of the always dependent, opaque, framed, rule-bound, and unequal relationships in (academic, artistic, and general) society.[2]

This idea of equality and its consequent ludic ethics is not a form of triumphalism. Its focus on subjectivity situated in the secondary position is both a hope and a danger. The fun of play touches on power relations that are not always funny at all. Hence the need for exercising, negotiating, transforming, and attempting to avoid showing any good will-to-power.[3]

Case study: how does performance philosophy act?
Ethos, ethics, ethnography

In accordance with the basic methodology of performance philosophy, these reflections are derived not only from abstract thinking, but also from practice – through a chain of activities. My own research into the ludic character of performance philosophy has been undertaken through the organization and participatory observation of nearly twenty non-standard academic events occupying the borders between conferences, artistic performances, lectures, and workshops. Most of these events are summarized online[4] or in the form of chapters and articles (for instance, Koubová 2015, 2017, 2018, 2019).

In this section, I wish to present observations accomplished during the preparation, organization, and evaluation of the 3rd Biennial Performance Philosophy Conference, entitled "How Does Performance Philosophy Act? Ethos, Ethics, Ethnography", which took place in Prague in 2017. The programme organizing group (Carolin Bebek, Alice Koubová, Alice Lagaay, Simon Makhali, and Anna Seitz) applied a specific multilayered approach to the event summarized in the conference manifesto (Lagaay and Seitz 2018, pp. 103–105), proposing:

1 To consider the conference itself as a performance and to investigate the ethos of its performativity as a first instance or case study;
2 to de-hierarchize various cultures of knowledge and their respective formats;
3 to call upon participants to act as ethnographers and to engage with various parts of the conference as participant observers, in order to become aware of professional blindness;
4 to democratize the output/input and to encourage real dialogical exchange by facilitating maximum space for thinking and talking together; and
5 to avoid consuming knowledge, but to interactively generate it.

I propose to see these dramaturgical items as an interpolation of the social play referred to as a "conference". The dramaturgy suggests going beyond the strict pre-given programme and giving a generous free time-space, called "fields" or "artistic dinners" to the participants in order to enable flow emergence, interaction, and in-situ happening. At the same time, it proposes to the participants to become ethnologists, or to observe what happens within that setting to distance themselves from simple flow, which includes both normativity and "here and now" experience. This dramaturgy interrupts the classical conference setting both from above and below and privileges a self-reflective approach that is "fun". In the context of preparing the conference, reflection on where the organizers should situate themselves was a further playful task: how to initiate the conference without dominating it? How do organizers remain in a secondary position and create a safe playground that participants will be able to take over, inhabit, explore, and develop? These questions were basically exercised, tested, and experimented with an approach that yielded many transformative insights. The extensive anonymous feedback collected at the end of the conference confirmed how the topics of ethos, performative self-reflexivity, and transformation in free space were regarded as more important than the exchange of knowledge-commodity. Surprisingly enough, the word "play", even "ludic", echoed in the feedback, without it having been emphasized in the conference manifesto or other parts of the programme. Here is the anonymous feedback that corresponded with the topic of this chapter:[5]

- Playfulness in action: the form of playing developed the creativity that we experienced. We were not forced into it. We were not compelled to be comics.
- An atmosphere that made people forget about competitiveness. Instead of showing off, they were curious and wanted to learn from the presenters.
- The reassurance that it is okay to fail enabled participants to experiment. It is not necessary to be constantly in control: we can be vulnerable.
- We experienced how PP can be an ethical act.
- The ethics of encounter was present. Sociology of relationships, of what happens in the room…
- The experimental and ludic setting and the careful people.
- The openness of the expansive time sessions and the very fact that the word experiment was enacted through the conference. It gave me a feeling that anything could happen and I appreciated the spirit of the community in this setting.
- Ethics, ethos, ethnography becoming alive in the doing of the conference.
- All the experiments that broke the standard conference session organization format were very welcome. The best thing was to have so much time for discussion without hurry.
- Allowing play.
- That it was an experiment – making testing self and failure valuable if not required.

I propose that this last comment be considered as the concluding statement of my chapter, as it could hardly be restated better.

Acknowledgement

This article was written with the support of the Czech Science Foundation grant No. 16-00994Y "Performativity in Philosophy: Contexts, Methods, Implications" carried out at the Institute of Philosophy, Czech Academy of Sciences.

Notes

1. Huizinga's definition is not the only one, and it has faced criticism by other scholars. The aspect that we want to focus on here, however, has not been widely criticized.
2. Here, I refer to a vast field of "care ethics" developed since the 1970s. See Gilligan (1982), Held (2006), and Noddings (1984) for some examples.
3. I have discussed other aspects of this fragility of power distribution, in terms of the quest for the neutral, secrecy, the phenomenon of the 'uncanny', and distance through expression, in my discussion with Alice Lagaay; see Koubová and Lagaay (2014).
4. https://alicekoubova.academia.edu
5. Here, the language of the feedback has been edited lightly. The original and complete feedback is available on the webpage http://web.flu.cas.cz/ppprague2017/feedback.html. All comments herein appear as they were originally written, with no additions or corrections.

References

Bauman, Richard. 1989. "Performance." Vol. 3 of *International Encyclopedia of Communications*, edited by Erik Barnouw et al., 262–266. New York: Oxford University Press.

Caillois, Roger. 1961. *Man, Play and Games*. Translated and edited by Meyer Barash. New York: Free Press.

Carlson, Marvin. 2018. *Performance: A Critical Introduction*. London: Routledge.
Elberfeld, Rolf. 2007. "Transformative Phänomenologie", *Information Philosophie*, Vol. 5, 26–29.
Gerstmyer, John S. 1991. "Toward a Theory of Play as Performance: An Analysis of Videotaped Episodes of a Toddler's Play Performance." PhD diss., University of Pennsylvania.
Gilligan, Carol. 1982. *In a Different Voice: Psychological Theory and Women's Development*. Cambridge, MA: Harvard University Press.
Goffman, Erving. 1959. *The Presentation of Self in Everyday Life*. New York: Doubleday.
Held, Virginia. 2006. *The Ethics of Care: Personal, Political, and Global*. 2nd ed. New York: Oxford University Press.
Huizinga, Johan. 1949. *Homo Ludens: A Study of the Play-Element in Culture*. London: Routledge.
Kant, Immanuel. (1790) 1914. *The Critique of Judgment*. Translated with Introduction and Notes by J. H. Bernard. 2nd ed. London: Macmillan.
Koubová, Alice and Alice Lagaay. 2014. "Performing the Impossible in Philosophy." *Encounters in Performance Philosophy: Theatre, Performativity and the Practice of Theory*, edited by Laura Cull Ó Lagaay Maoilearca and Alice Lagaay, 39–62. London: Palgrave Macmillan.
Koubová, Alice. 2015. "Performance (in) Philosophy: Gnothi seauton." *Formen der Wissensgenerierung, Practices in Performance Art*, edited by Manfred Blohm and Elke Mark, 129–140. Oberhausen: Athena.
Koubová Alice. 2017. "The Sacrifice and the Ludic Stance Reflected Through the Theatre Practice of the 20th Century," *Filozofia* 72, No. 6, 451–462.
Koubová Alice. 2018. "Ludic Philosophy in Brecht's Drama and Prose", *The Brecht Yearbook*, Vol. 42, edited by Tom Kuhn, David Barnett, and Theodore F. Rippey, 51–64. Camden House.
Koubová Alice. 2019. "Le jeu: entre art, humain, inhumain," *La notion d'humanité dans la pensée contemporaine*, edited by Anne Alombert and Camille Chamois, 259–274. Paris: Presses universitaires de Paris Nanterre.
Lagaay, Alice and Anna Seitz, eds. 2018. "Wissen Formen, Performative Akte zwischen Bildung, Wissenschaft und Kunst." *Erkundungen mit dem Theater der Versammlung*. Bielefeld: transcript Verlag. http://web.flu.cas.cz/ppprague2017/manifest.html (1.9.2018).
Lobman, Carrie and Barbara E. O'Neill, eds. 2011. *Play and Performance*. Vol. 11 of *Play and Culture Studies*. Lanham, MD: University Press of America, 1998–2018.
McConachie, Bruce. 2011. "An Evolutionary Perspective on Play, Performance, and Ritual", *The Drama Review: TDR* 55, No. 4, 33–50.
Noddings, Nel. 1984. *Caring: A Feminine Approach to Ethics & Moral Education*. Berkeley: University of California Press.
Ryall, Emily, Wendy Russell, and Malcom MacLean, eds. 2013. *The Philosophy of Play*. London: Routledge.
Schechner, R. 1973. "Performance & the Social Sciences: Introduction", *The Drama Review: TDR* 17, No. 3, 3–4.
Schechner, Richard. 2003. "Ethology of Theatre." Chap. 7 in *Performance Theory*. London: Routledge.
Schechner, Richard. 2006. *Performance Studies: An Introduction*. 2nd ed. Abingdon: Routledge.
Schiller, Friedrich. (1794) 1954. *On the Aesthetic Education of Man*. Translated and edited by Reginald Snell. New Haven, CT: Yale University Press.
Spariosu, Mihai. 1989. *Dionysus Reborn: Play and the Aesthetic Dimension in Modern Philosophical and Scientific Discourse*. Ithaca, NY: Cornell University Press.
Spencer, Herbert. 1855. *The Principles of Psychology*. London: Longman, Brown, Green and Longmans. http://oll.libertyfund.org/titles/1394.
Strine, M. S., B. W. Long, and M. F. Hopkins. 1990. "Research in Interpretation and Performance Studies: Trends, Issues, Priorities." *Speech Communication: Essays to Commemorate the Seventy-Fifth Anniversary of the Speech Communication Association*, edited by G. Phillips and J. Wood, 181–204. Carbondale: Southern Illinois University Press.
Sutton-Smith, B. 1997. *The Ambiguity of Play*. Cambridge, MA: Harvard University Press.
Turner, Victor. 1969. *The Ritual Process: Structure an Anti-Structure*. Chicago, IL: Aldine.
Turner, Victor. 1974. "Liminal to Liminoid, in Play, Flow, and Ritual: An Essay in Comparative Symbology", *Rice Institute Pamphlet - Rice University Studies* 60, No. 3, 53–92.
Winnicott, Donald. 2005. *Playing and Reality*. London: Routledge, 2005.

23
LANDSCAPE PERFORMANCE

Tess Denman-Cleaver

Landscape performance practices attend to more-than-geographical aspects of landscape via an expanded understanding of it as subjective, experiential and temporal. As such, landscape performance may be non-sited: taking place in an auditorium or studio, and may include touring work. Thus, landscape performance includes performances that operate beyond the limitations of site-specific practice's concern for where a performance takes place. Mike Pearson defines site-specific performance as performance in which "the site becomes the dominant signifier rather than simply that which contains the performance" (Pearson 2010, p. 19). While 'site-specific' generally refers to performance that takes place at a specific site, 'landscape performance' provides a broader definition that includes performance primarily concerned with landscape, though not necessarily presented in specific locations.

Landscape performance, as understood within my own artistic practice and within this collection of writings on performance philosophy, is also a philosophical practice, that is, a performance practice concerned with what landscape is, how we experience, understand or know it, and with the development of different modes of being with(in) landscape. If, as Andrew Bowie asserts, "the practice of philosophy [is] making sense of making sense" (Bowie 2015, p. 52), then landscape performance is the practice of making sense of landscape. In its philosophical endeavour, landscape performance may take the form of relatively traditional studio theatre work in which the focus is on the sensory and experiential aspects of space, language or sound rather than a narrative structure, or it may adopt the format of a walk or participatory event occurring outside of an auditorium context, for example. In defining landscape performance, my aim is not to restrict the forms in which this practice might manifest, but rather to provide a language with which to articulate performance philosophy practices motivated by an aim to question understanding and experience of landscape in its widest sense.

Landscape performance looks to the performative turn in cultural geography for expanded definitions of what landscape is. For instance, John Wylie's 2007 review of landscape scholarship describes how, within the performative turn, phenomenological influences have particularly supported landscape to be understood as a "milieu of engagement and involvement [which] takes shape within the realms of human perception and imagination" (Wylie 2007, p. 147). This understanding is in opposition to traditional conceptions of landscape as being at a distance to a spectator (as in landscape painting), or as measurable and map-able space (as in cartography). In *The Temporality of Landscape*, Tim Ingold indicates his allegiance to this phenomenological perspective by rejecting "the division between inner and outer worlds – respectively of mind and matter, meaning and substance – upon which [Cartesian models of landscape] rest" (Ingold 1993, p. 154). Jo Vergunst suggests that phenomenology, in its rejection of dualistic conceptions of mind and matter, offers a "holistic approach to person-and-environment" that emphasises process and experience (Vergunst and Árnason 2012, p. 4). In my own artistic practice – through projects such as *Project R-hythm* (2014)[1] and *Alice in Bed* (2013)[2] – landscape performance emerged from a series of attempts to stage or perform landscapes that were phenomenological in their emphasis on subjective experience (of both artist and audience), rather than spatial or geometric dimensions.

This chapter shares extracts of three texts that I developed through three different landscape performance projects, each of which entailed working and writing with different landscapes. As a collection, they represent a performance writing practice that operates through performative engagements with place. The artistic processes were configured to elucidate or draw out the nature of our experience of landscape and question what landscape is beyond geographical phenomena. Each extract attempts an enactment of particular landscape philosophies as read in selected philosophical texts or texts which the projects read "as philosophy", whether or not they are conventionally categorised as such.[3]

The first extract is from a project developed in collaboration with Laura Cull Ó Maoilearca entitled *The Sea, Lies Open* (2015). This project – which culminated in a sound installation and series of performative walks – considered the role of landscape in the writings of Nietzsche, and developed its own landscape philosophy and writing through performative engagements with bodies of water. The second extract is from *Time Passes* (2017): a performance writing and installation project that took its cue from philosophical readings of the novels and diaries of Virginia Woolf. As a performance gesture, *Time Passes* is an act of striving beyond the human-centric phenomenologies of landscape referenced in the aforementioned definition of landscape performance. The final project, *Town Hall Meeting of the Air* (2018), draws on Gertrude Stein's notion of landscape plays and her earlier 'cultivated motor automatism' writing experiments (Stein 1898) to respond to the dynamics of a town hall. *Town Hall Meeting of the Air* brings an example of a performative engagement with place that recalls ideas of landscape which emerged in postdramatic theatre, from Stein through to Richard Foreman, Robert Wilson and The Wooster Group.

The Sea, Lies Open (2015)

The Sea, Lies Open was a collaboration between myself and Laura Cull Ó Maoilearca for the festival *PHILOSOPHY ON STAGE #4* (Vienna 2015).[4] It took the form of a publication of performance texts, a performance installation and a series of group walks around Vienna at dawn, midday and dusk. Together, these works considered the relationships between walking and thinking, landscape and health, horizons and aphorisms in Nietzsche's life, work and influence. The performance texts were developed through a process of correspondence in which rules for writing were applied to both collaborators; letters were to be written at dawn, midday and dusk. Writing was generated during a point of encounter with a particular landscape at that time of day: walking near one's home, lying in a bath, standing on a church tower or swimming in the sea. *The Sea, Lies Open* is an example of a collaborative landscape performance practice that values non-sedentary writing gestures as a mode of performative and philosophical engagement with place. Development of *The Sea, Lies Open* included investigations into the relationship between body, landscape and writing: walking-writing and writing conducted in relation to specific physical contexts or movements. The activities were aimed at drawing out the effect of particular contexts, including the artists' bodies, on thinking and writing processes. The extracts shared here address the motivations of the project, and in doing so illustrate some of the central and defining questions of landscape performance.

★ ★ ★

Dear T.

As a consequence of my condition, I am only able to walk for short distances and slowly, taking regular breaks and avoiding sharp inclines. Whilst I might hitherto have been inclined to see this as a limit, I now remind myself that such physical states in fact signal new styles of thought. As a philosopher who has traversed many kinds of health, and keeps traversing them, I have passed through an equal number of philosophies; when I walk, I simply cannot keep from transposing my states every time into the most spiritual form and distance: this art of transfiguration *is* philosophy. We philosophers are not free to divide body from soul, inside from outside…

And yet what an error it would be to refuse limits altogether, to lose ourselves in the pretensions of ceaseless overcoming! This is where the real challenge lies: overcoming the temptation to respond to limitation as a challenge to be overcome! I know of no other way for now, but to describe it as a kind of *openness* that does not enclose.

Once, all I wanted was to swim to the horizon. Fooling myself, like so many ancient philosophers, that I could hurl my javelin off the edge of the world and come to know the space beyond – one way or another. In my middle age, I no longer imagine such capture as the purpose of thought, nor of my writing for that matter. There too, where once I cursed the flagging body of language that could not keep up with the pace of my experience, the weakness of words to grasp the wondrous horror of the unlimited, my present self delights in finding new words to help me pay attention to the world once more, and takes pleasure in the failure of my descriptions to exhaust the landscapes before me, within me. *The sea is in my blood*, I told them – these poor land-locked creatures. But perhaps I said as much with my endless slide show – a never-ending catalogue of the sea, which can always be looked at from another angle, a new perspective.

Forgive me! I have already diverted from the task at hand, to share with you my latest urgent thought, namely:

> we must find ways to stop them from focussing on seeing all the time

Already it is too much the way of things to settle for philosophy as the practice of good housekeeping: tidying spaces, mending fences, defining boundaries. When one speaks of limits, all they see is a line in the sand. I know that I have been a victim of this mapping too – but now, my friend, it is up to us to locate the boundaries of time as well as space, to walk such that we might at least *sense* – without seeking to overcome – the thresholds of our hearing, our touch, the peripheries of all our senses, not as walls between spaces but as other kinds of horizon altogether.

There is a kingdom of wisdom from which the logician is banished!

As I know you understand, I am not saying that we should think of ourselves as entering it by other means. It is rather that to swim to the edge now must mean something other than trying to capture foreign lands to make them our own.

I must stop now…

Yours, L

★ ★ ★

Dear L,

From soft deep blue towards slight violet. For fear of scalding myself there is too much cold water. As we know, all deep knowledge flows cold, but this feels decidedly surface upon entering. I suspect I have failed to achieve your dissolving-of-self due to a lack of extremity. Or maybe this is an imaginative failure on my part.

Each time, upon immersion, I anticipate the blurring of inside and out, expect my skin into only a figure of my imagination, and each time, instead, I picture your calves as my calves dip into the milk-soft pool, and I sink up to my neck.

I'm writing this letter, I realise, not to you, but from and within your words, attending all the time, also, to the movement of my world... *Enveloped now in the rose glow of Northumbrian sands...* Swimming, drifting through body and bathwater, between his water cycles and the changing of light against the window, wandering amongst your thoughts I sense that we have learned this movement from him. And I, at least, have begun...

pigeons next, the beating of wings imitated by the ratching of shutters in the gentle green or aquamarine. Dunnock friend calls patiently as the wash of city hum floods in. I know his company well, though he is likely unaware of my listening from the water.

... to live with you, in this way, upon entering the water and attending to the fluidity of writing.

Man may be a disagreeable creature at this early hour, but certainly woman-immersed-in-water is a softer being all together, if this letter is anything to go by. Maybe it's her surface nature, her changeable stormy film that is inclined to this gentle time of day, when one can hang between surfaces and drift, with just a glimmer of the depth, in a domestic simulacrum. From here the sky is in formation on the bricks of the buildings and in the glass of the windows and I push myself to imagine the deeper change this suggests, push out beyond the reflection and the visual phenomena, reaching deep into the body itself, to feel the soft-deep-blue-slight-violet-rose-glow-sea-glass-green with the movement.

Tomorrow dawn will be a very different matter all-together as I will travel to a land famed for its lack of light; I don't imagine I will feel at home there, but look forward to reporting back on its effect.

Yours, T.

★ ★ ★

The correspondence, as well as the walks that took place during PHILOSOPHY ON STAGE #4, constituted a thinking with Nietzsche's landscapes, the landscapes he writes and the role of walking in his own philosophical practice.

In English, the words 'aphorism' and 'horizon' are etymologically linked, with aphorism coming from the Greek, *aphorizein* "to mark off, divide", from apo- "from" and *horizein* "to bound". In content and form, Nietzsche's writing keeps coming back to the matter of horizons, testing the cultural and physiological limits of philosophy, and of the human, through his own varied thinking practice. *The Sea, Lies Open* was initially informed by a shared interest in the role of the sea as a bounding yet unbounded presence, as a horizon with which to write, walk and perform. The project asks *how does landscape think? And how can we think alongside landscape in practices of walking, writing, and performance making?*

Time Passes (2018) continued this line of thought in relation to the fictional landscapes of Woolf.

Time Passes (2017)

This project took as its starting point the central section of Woolf's novel *To the Lighthouse*. In response to Woolf's text and its implications for phenomenological thought, *Time Passes* was an attempt to create a performance landscape that is absent of humans.

To the Lighthouse (1927), *The Waves* (1931), *Mrs. Dalloway* (1925) and *Jacob's Room* (1922) are at the centre of the handful of revisionist readings that position Woolf as a European and anti-Cartesian thinker. A. O. Frank distances Woolf from G. E. Moore and the Pateresque school of thinking that her Bloomsbury peers occupied (Frank 2001, p. 21), arguing that Woolf's relationship to European Continental philosophy has been neglected due to the historic dominance of narrative realism and biography within literary criticism (ibid., p. 12).[5] Despite *To the Lighthouse* sitting at the heart of these anti-Cartesian readings of Woolf, very little attention has been given to the novel's central section 'Time Passes', or the implications of that text for phenomenology and landscape. My project focused on this section as a key source and I conducted a reading of Woolf through an act of performance making which positioned her philosophy in opposition to the residual anthropocentrism of phenomenologies of landscape used by cultural geographers and anthropologists such as Ingold.

In 'Time Passes', Woolf tells the story of the Ramsey family's island house as it stands unoccupied for a number of years, during which WW1 begins and ends and keeps the family from returning. With the family gone, Woolf "imagine[s] the world in the absence of the human eye" (Briggs 2006, p. 146). We hear of distant marriages and the deaths of certain family members lost to war, age-related illness, and childbirth. News of the novel's absent human characters is relayed to the reader in the form of parentheses, reminiscent of the character-limited text of telegrams. The presence of people is contained within these brackets, while the movement of the story continues to occupy the empty house; the narrator remains with the landscape.

Woolf commented on the particular challenge of writing 'Time Passes' in her diary on Sunday 18th April 1926:

> I cannot make it out—here is the most difficult abstract piece of writing—I have to give an empty house, no people's characters, the passage of time, all eyeless & feature-less with nothing to cling to.
>
> *(Woolf 1980, p. 75)*

Woolf tells the story of the empty house through an account of the processes of dust and decay, and the movement of light and shadow.

The texts shared here take the form of a diary. They include borrowed phrases and moments from Woolf's own diary as well as 'Time Passes'. They were developed through a process I would consider as a correspondence with Woolf, rather than a study of her, and build upon the approach to writing with landscape understood as intersubjective begun in *The Sea, Lies Open*. The texts then formed the basis of a series of performances and performative installations that took the landscape philosophy of Woolf's writings as a guide for a performance making practice that challenges and develops the conception of landscape offered by cultural geography's performative turn.[6]

★ ★ ★

Monday, 16th January 2017

We are a train of three vast cars plunging northwards. In my suitcase I have all of Virginia Woolf's diaries, novels and essays, a disappointing biography & some complete holes.

Moving backwards, I wonder which other of us is you. I wonder if your luggage will be as substantial as mine. I ponder the patterns of work inhabited by our fellow passengers, maybe returning home to fill a space, half a bed, a hot bath, arms, which, stretched out the night before, have remained empty.

As we enter the Cairngorms, it becomes grey and the wind on the water's surface turns to ice. We keep looking at the sky as it begins to fade: soft-fleecy.

On the first night we walked, close, in the dark. The tension of our new relationship stringing us together; anxiety concerning what the other wants, questions of whether one's own wishes will be inhibited by how the other imagines this situation will reveal itself. Your sleeve warm inches away from my arm.

Treading together, away from the streetlights, we fell silent. Maybe concentrating, maybe unsure, maybe taking in the gloaming snow or the blinding light of the house up ahead; into whose garden we could be about to trespass.

A front window & a light burning.

It's almost too dark to see.

Are you nervous? Am I nervous? Your nervousness encourages me.

Every step on the frozen earth is a dare, daring one another to move away from the lights, moving away from the orientation of a starting point, giving our weight to the potential of ice underfoot. Every step a question which, when asked, commits us to innumerable risks. It is an odd road to be walking. One can hardly tell which is the water and which is the land, when I am her and when I am me: who is leading. Not for the first time the possibility of turning back is aired.

Out and out we go, further and further, until at last we seem to be on a narrow plank, perfectly alone, over the sea.

Wednesday, 25th January 1915

Your birthday.

I don't know when I have enjoyed a birthday so much – sitting at tea we decided three things: the first place to take Hogarth, if we can get it; in the second, to buy a printing press; in the third to buy a Bulldog – probably called John.

We acknowledged the local significance of the day with a Haggis and some whiskey, but decided to celebrate with you. We talked about the dark; the substance of your darkness, the presence of your absence, and the fullness of your nothing moving through the house.

Your nothing thinks.

Nothing stirs in the drawing room and certain airs undertake a years-long process of questioning – wondering – asking – nosing round doors – contemplating permanence and durability with the movement of light and the prying of the wind and the noise of the sea.

We asked one another, "does darkness move through your work and what is it made of?"

"What are you doing with time and how do 'inside' and 'out' relate in the things, in the events, in the structures that you create?"

Taking our cue from Woolf, we asked "where is, [and] what are the bounds of consciousness in your practice?"

Friday, 22nd December 2017

Standing in the house with the wind and the rain with the sea and the earth and setting up an echo which chimed in the air and made it full of vibration, it is clear to me that your things are not symbols: they are things – things that think, think with us, things without us or with their own centre from which they know and shape the world.

How once the looking glass had held a face; had held a world hollowed out in which a figure turned, a hand flashed, the door opened, and went out again – this is not "the emptiness of death [...] the transition from consciousness to unconsciousness, from life to death, from peace to war".[7] Our things do not perform a hierarchy, in which the human being sets the measure for the liveliness of all beings.[8]

Certain airs have detached from the body; one fold of the shawl loosened, swings to and fro. I must still grope and experiment, but this afternoon with the crystals, encouraging your dog away from a game of catch with a pendulum, I had a gleam of light.

Your nothing is weighted differently.

Looking back, nothing, it seemed, could survive the flood, the profusion of darkness which, creeping in at keyholes and confidence, washed away preoccupations, stole days and returned nights, swallowed up here a jug and basin, there a bowl of red and yellow dahlias, there the sharp edges and firm bulk of a chest of drawers, a plan. These days have been water, ruffled by the wind into atoms of ice against the cheek.

Then your empty house, forming round us like a still pool.

* * *

Town Hall Meeting of the Air (2018)

Elinor Fuchs credits Gertrude Stein with the introduction of a landscape language to theatrical practices that differed from the existing dramatic tradition (Fuchs, cited in Lehmann 2006, p. 81). Lehmann suggests that postdramatic theatre directors "Richard Foreman and Robert Wilson carried a use of language inspired by Stein into the theatre" (Lehmann 2006, p. 63).

In her 1935 essay "Plays", collected in *Lectures in America*, Stein describes her discomfort during a trip to the theatre as a result of the sense of 'syncopation' caused by the time of the performance being different to that experienced by the audience. Stein explains in "Plays" that her own texts for performance are written in such a way as to counter the temporal dynamics of traditional theatrical form, and thus avoid the syncopated experience she describes having as a child at the theatre. As Davy describes:

> As playwright [...] Stein abandoned the conventional narrative attributes of drama and conceived the static or "landscape play." In a landscape composition each element has equal weight and is as significant as the whole.
>
> *(Davy 1978, p. 116)*

In response to a perceived disconnect between spectator and dramatic action in the theatre, Stein conceived of performances that the audience would experience as landscapes. In Stein's plays, theatrical "structures are arranged not in lines of conflict and resolution but on the multivalent spatial relationships" (Fuchs cited in Lehmann 2006, p. 81). Landscape performances, like Stein's landscape plays, attend to the temporal quality of audience experience and give parity to different media and perspectives.

Town Hall Meeting of the Air drew directly on Stein's landscape plays as a form and on automatic writing practices described in an early essay written by Stein when she was a medical student at Harvard. The project used this borrowed methodology to develop the approach to writing with landscape that emerged through *The Sea, Lies Open* and *Time Passes* and create a performance composition in which divergent elements had parity, and language was intended to support an experience of landscape rather than narrative.

What follows is an extract of a text I performed at Middlesbrough Town Hall (UK) as part of Middlesbrough Art Weekender 2018. The piece takes the printed form of a play script, echoing Stein's landscape plays, but where distinctions between voice, stage direction and characters are disrupted. It incorporates fragments of archive material from the Teesside Archives, which include historic council minutes and development plans for the new town hall built in 1989.

★ ★ ★

Act III.
  Scene II.
  A moon is ruined – covered over with footsteps used up and hanging. The moon has seen us whole and had enough has gone off with a flight of cows – face scrubbed and quivering innards half raw and waning the moon is aching in our smoked cold glasses the moon is crescent and will not be renewed – is past caring. Fading cobalt. Practicing coping strategies to endure. The moon is darker, is the beginning of a violent storm. The moon is a shadow down low and powerful, is afloat in a crystal bowl is held in the hands of everybody all over. The moon is cool skin unclothed of sun and waiting – tried and counting – howling toward the end.
  Act IV.
  Scene I.
  Fourth character (a woman who sounds like a meeting). Open quote.
  A figure of justice, complete with sword and balance, which had a pedestal on a window-sill near the police court entrance has disappeared. It was feared that justice might have an undignified fall.
  First character (a woman who looks like a country). Open quote.
  Ornamentation has been sacrificed in the interests of safety.
  Twelfth character (everybody anywhere all over). Open quote.
  Justice is a full-sized sculpture of a woman. Real justice is full sized, real justice is a woman, real justice is a sculpture of compassion, is an arm pushing into the dark and the clay. Justice is an endless knot of wants and looping back to look forward and trying. Justice is trying, is a phone call away – justice is footsteps moving through the empty house next door, justice is bus money, is good weather, justice is no such thing as bad weather, is a ceiling not less than 8 feet 6 inches high, is pockets, is sliced ham and pease pudding, justice is a lunchbox, is a syrup, is up shit creek, justice is a real pea souper, justice is so thick all we can see is our own lights pushing into the dark and the clay, justice is falling into the dark, is falling hard onto the marble floor, justice is shoulder hard onto the marble floor, cheek bone onto the steps to the police court, justice is an undignified fall, real justice is undignified, real justice is fear, real justice is feared, real justice is sacrificed in the interests of safety.
  Act V.
  Scene I.
  Fourth character (a woman who sounds like a meeting). Open quote.
  Any other business?
  Close quote.

★ ★ ★

Thinking with landscape through performance

Each of these projects, of which text extracts are shared here, presents modes of thinking *with* and making sense of landscape in the context of a performance philosophy practice. They use writing – the gestures and performative activity of writing – to engage with, articulate and shape landscapes. In the processes shared, the focus is on the 'thinking with landscape' that occurs through performance making, rather than in the performance event itself. All three projects did include events and public performances, within which other modes of thinking and shaping landscapes were employed. Most prominently, each of the projects engaged with the effect that writing and communication technologies have on how we experience and understand landscape. As with Stein's landscape, these events gave parity to different elements and media, at the same time as frameworks were developed to support the audience's own thinking with the landscape of the performance event. Thus, at the heart of this practice, throughout making and presentation, is an emphasis on thinking *with* rather than *about* landscape. It is this epistemological positioning of equivalence that defines landscape performance, and positions the practice within performance philosophy.

Notes

1. See https://tessdenmancleaver.com/portfolio/project-r-hythm/
2. See https://tessdenmancleaver.com/portfolio/my-project/
3. The practice of reading a text "philosophically" is illustrated below with the project *Time Passes* (2018), in which the writing of Virginia Woolf was read through a performance-led enquiry into the implications for how reality, experience and landscape are conceived in Woolf's thinking. Another philosophical reading of a text beyond the traditional philosophical canon was conducted in *Alice in Bed* (2013), which staged Susan Sontag's play according to the implied phenomenological conception of reality that text presents.
4. See https://homepage.univie.ac.at/arno.boehler/php/?p=9130
5. In A. O. Frank's *The Philosophy of Virginia Woolf: A philosophical reading of the mature novels*, Frank argues that Woolf's later novels, such as *To the Lighthouse*, demonstrate an attitude that is in opposition to the influence of Pater and readily used to position Woolf in relation to philosophical thinking of her day. Frank denies the notion that Woolf was an aesthete along with contemporaries such as Roger Fry, asserting that her writing is concerned with "various types of rationality, the competence of different modes of understanding and some vital existential questions" (Frank 2001, p. 21).
6. *Time Passes* has been presented in the form of performances at Scottish Sculpture Workshop (Aberdeenshire), Paul Melon Centre (London), M_HKA Gallery (Antwerp) and Tate St Ives.
7. Briggs 2006, p. 149.
8. Kirkkopelto 2016, p. 52.

References

Bowie, A. 2015. 'The "Philosophy of Performance" and the Performance of Philosophy'. *Performance Philosophy* 1, pp. 51–58.
Briggs, J. 2006. *Reading Virginia Woolf*. Edinburgh: Edinburgh University Press.
Frank, A. O. 2001. *The Philosophy of Virginia Woolf: A Philosophical Reading of the Mature Novels*. Budapest: Akadémiai Kiadò.
Ingold, T. 1993. 'The Temporality of Landscape'. *World Archaeology: Conceptions of Time and Ancient Society* 25 (2), pp. 152–174.
Pearson, M. 2010. *Site-Specific Performance*. Hampshire and New York: Palgrave Macmillan.
Vergunst, J. and Árnason, A. 2012. 'Routing Landscape: Ethnographic Studies of Movement and Journeying'. *Landscape Research* 37 (2), pp. 147–154.
Woolf, V. 1980. *The Diary of Virginia Woolf: Volume 3 1925–30*. Bell, Q. eds. London: Hogarth Press.
Wylie, J. 2007. *Landscape*. London and New York: Routledge.

24
RE-TELLING THE SELF
The lived experience of modern yoga practice

Theodora Wildcroft

Defining the terms: yoga, performance, and practice

Millions of practitioners around the world currently engage in a multitude of practices that they all call 'yoga', a term that covers a vast diversity and rich history of practice, philosophy, and belief. The Sanskrit word itself has a sense of 'discipline' or 'deliberate connection' (De Michelis 2008: 17–18). As the product of complex encounters between India and the rest of the world, yoga can be this and more: a physical and mental practice for health and well-being; a metaphysical system describing the ongoing creation of the universe; a devotional, ritual practice (Newcombe 2013: 72); or a system of ethics and other social practices for righteous living.

While there are many diverse movement practices that maintain pop cultural appeal, and many wellbeing practices that have mainstream interest, few of them have reached the high level of penetration into popular culture of yoga. Contemporary yoga thus describes a lived practice that is highly diverse and often inward-focused, whilst its reflection in popular culture is highly uniform and performative. Elite physical practitioners effortlessly demonstrate acrobatic poses and slim serenity under the gaze of Instagram and YouTube followers, and are, in turn, mimicked by models in adverts for everything from yoghurt to life insurance. More dedicated yoga practitioners are often focused on more than the physical performance of the pose. Yoga teachers are encouraged to make overt reference to yoga philosophical tenets in their practices, their classes, and their representation of the practice to potential students. They meditate on the nature of identity and consciousness, whilst also seeking ways to externalise that quest into social media self-representation. The result is a doubling of vision and visualisation: the ideal selves of contemporary interpretations of yogic philosophy and contemporary aspirational lifestyles blur into a single goal. Within practice, and on social media, the practitioner seeks to perform imperturbable wellness, serene calm, and effortless abundance as an ideal that they then aspire to in the mundane, off-scene spaces of daily life.

Thus through the aspirational vision of slender, female flexibility and privileged calm, images of yoga dominate the marketing of a number of extremely profitable international industries (Hauser 2013: 6; Lavrence and Lozanski 2014: 77). Yet, the differences in form and intention between yoga as a marketing meme, yoga as a personal practice, and yoga in transmission to others can be glaring (Goldberg 2015; Klein 2015). In response, this chapter considers those same fault lines between the experience and the presentation of yoga through the lens of social media. My aim is to consider the in/visibility of lived experiences of the body, and the eternal conversation between the private and public nature of yoga as a practice.

To do so, I will be taking the idea of performance into the realm of social interaction, and into personal practice, with the following questions. How does the nature of performance change when the performer's stage is their lived environment? Who is the implied and actual audience for practitioners sharing images of their practice? This chapter will also involve consideration of the idea of 'practice', defined here as deliberate actions subject to disciplined repetition. Doing so implicates a (multi)cultural history of obedience, mimesis, and self-transformation that is witnessed by the evolution of textual, visual, and social media, but ultimately always carried by bodies.

Yoga, perfection, and the gaze

The pre-modern roots of what is often called modern postural yoga are complex and diverse (Mallinson and Singleton 2017: ix; Singleton 2013: 39). Many pre-modern texts on yoga emphasise an ideal of absolute isolation for practice (Powell 2017). In contrast, since the redevelopment of the practice for modern, mass consumption, the transmission of practice has been largely achieved via group teaching. Despite this, both individual practice and a personal relationship with a teacher are still held by many dedicated practitioners to be the gold standard for the authentic transmission of yoga. The orientalised, idealised images of an Indian ascetic alone with their practice, and a devotee at the feet of their guru, still haunt each Instagram image of a usually white, female practitioner on a beach in Bali, and every large urban studio hosting the contemporary, transnationalised 'guru' for audiences of hundreds (Black 2016: 25). Whilst the recommendations by pre-modern yoga philosophers that practice should be isolated and overseen by a perfect yet absent teacher were characterised as preliminaries to practice, what cannot now be known is whether such recommendations became aspirational or foundational to the actual performance of practice.

Enhancing this idealisation of an isolated practitioner, who is yet in intimate relationship with a perfect teacher, is a persistent evocation in yogic philosophy of supernatural powers gained through the practice, often associated with sight. Pre-modern guides to practice attribute a range of divine rewards to practices of physical austerity, including an omniscient or destructive gaze (Mallinson 2018; Mallinson and Singleton 2017: 259). Such a gaze could, by implication, be capable of effortlessly empowering and regulating the practice of devotees at a distance.

The blessings of esteemed spiritual teachers are still broadcast to devotees via the gaze, or *darśan*, of the guru (Langford 2004: 29; Strauss 2008: 55). Western students, who may spend mere weeks with an Indian guru, invoke the power of their gaze to sanctify career-long practice (MacGregor 2012: 31, 41, 70). Whilst few transnationally famous yoga teachers inherit the status or mythical powers of such holy figures, the porousness between the physical, emotional, and spiritual benefits of the practice cast a discernible aura of divine serenity, otherworldly beauty, or supernatural virility over the superstars of contemporary yoga culture. Only the form of such idealised bodies has changed, to be largely white, Western, young, and female, although even ancient texts on yoga promote such benefits to the practice as restoring vitality and virility to the dedicated male, Indian body (Mallinson and Singleton 2017: 222).

Yoga's most devoted practitioners have always held an ambivalent relationship to the visibility of their practice. Whilst the *practising* of yoga idealises spaces of intimacy or isolation, the *performance* of yoga has long been part of publicising its benefits. To this day, ascetics can be found performing physical feats across India, attracting donations and adherents, and demonstrating the more supernatural outcomes of practice (Bevilacqua 2016). For Indian ascetics and transnational influencers alike, the practice of yoga is also the proof of its benefits: both the discipline that trains the body, and the supernatural results that follow. Such proof in performance is rendered possible by the power of the guru's gaze, but also regulated and sanctified by the same. In this sense, performativity is the harmony of aspiration and result, within a practice that maintains a considerable belief in the miraculous possibilities of disciplining movement and posture. The audience for such performances is the public, but is also divinity itself, through the guru's omniscient gaze. Both the gods and the groundlings are watching.

In the modern era, a succession of technological developments in media enabled widespread changes in the reach of such yoga-related performances. Swami Sivananda was the first major guru to offer spiritual initiation to his international followers via postal order, in the 1980s (Strauss 2008: 53). Innumerable small printing presses based in ashrams and yoga shalas continue to widen the reach of a guru's teachings beyond their physical presence. These technologies are largely broadcast-based, with content and instruction being disseminated outwards in one direction only. To achieve this, teachings must be standardised and simplified to fit the medium. As Singleton (2010: 163) explains, many of the now dominant schools of modern postural yoga benefited from the rise in commercial photography. Anyone with a photographic guide to such practices could follow along at home, and newly trained yoga teachers had a manual of form to refer to.

BKS Iyengar's 'Light on Yoga' (1965) remains one the most influential and includes extensive instructions written by the modern guru for how junior teachers and students themselves can bring non-standard bodies into 'correct' physical alignment. This modern renaissance of yoga practice was heavily influenced by colonial and corporeal discipline, and the standardisation and anatomical alignment facilitated by photographic comparison (Gilman 2014: 69; Sarbacker 2014: 106). The visual culture of yoga in the modern era thus contributed to the dominance of physical cultural ideals based upon a largely static, aesthetic ideal of posture, linked to moral rectitude and productivity (Jesson 2017). The photographic process itself acquired the corrective power of omniscience, through comparison and the systematised reproduction of the ideal human form.

Pre-modern students and adepts were largely expected to find their balance alone. Instruction was commonly transmitted via verbal authority: the adept is to do as the guru says, rather than as the guru demonstrates. By the turn of the millennium however, mass transnational yoga brands had developed systems of ever more intricate postural alignment in which the authority for student bodily experience, as well as any associated meaning-making, was subject to the comparative gaze of expert instructors. Typical examples include online advice for both students (Peacock 2017) and teachers (Loupe 2018), and teacher training manuals (Friend 2008). Platonic ideals of form proliferated these diverse and conflicting processes of universal alignment that sought to govern practice. This enabled each school to assert both the uniqueness of the system on offer and the universality of its application.

An aesthetics of correction and the performance of near-supernatural physicality, fuelled by disciplined repetition of the practice, combine spiritual and biomechanical justifications that have been a source of productive tension in yoga discourse for over a hundred years (Alter 2005: 119). Contemporary alignment schools of yoga are thus able to connect the aesthetics of good posture to reinventions of sacred Tantric geometry, in which the idea of universal alignment becomes contiguous with a universal blueprint for the human form that once realised, like the beneficent gaze of the guru empowered through practice, confers not just good health, but material abundance and spiritual realisation.

A perfect exemplar of these dynamics at play exists in a promotional clip for David Regelin (2014). During the film, a reassuringly fit, masculine body uses Platonic-inspired, overlaid graphics of perfected geometry to correct an already slim, normative, and above all pliant female form, to achieve nebulous ends associated with general health and wellbeing. All that is required from the student is complete surrender over the most subtle details of their physical form to the critical examination of a teacher. As each teacher carefully adjusts each student's body for maximum physical and spiritual alignment, in each performed practice, the modern guru bestows a kind of remote artistry of perfection through each teacher thus trained, much as a celebrated artist might use assistants to recreate arresting installations from mundane objects in galleries across the world.

Post-lineage yoga

If alignment and standardisation in yoga were encouraged by the development of visual media, more recent developments in the democratisation of practice have been enabled by the rise of social media. In my research, I have proposed the term 'post-lineage yoga' to describe a growing development of contemporary yoga that moves to different degrees beyond lineage, and looks beyond historical practice and precedent for the authority to determine practice (Wildcroft 2019). Post-lineage environments are spaces to share yoga practice and culture that look further afield than lineage or brand for their inspirations and sense of practice community. For many who have become uncomfortable with self-definitions grounded in an institutional identity, post-lineage yoga is an opportunity to discover themselves as part of a subculture beyond their immediate community of practice, to join a diverse and often chaotic network of local scenes and online groups, grounded in the creativity of real-world crossings and dwellings (Tweed 2006: 75). And although post-lineage networks are often supported by face-to-face meetings, in the post-lineage era, conversations on social media have been most effective in dethroning the omniscient, centralised gaze of authority that governs modern yoga brands and lineages.

John Friend's Anusara Yoga system combined intricate, universalised alignment with ideas of sacred geometry and neo-tantric philosophy (Williamson 2013: 219). The 2012 fall of Anusara Yoga, once one of the largest yoga schools in the world, is now remembered as a fall from grace precipitated by personal scandal (Williamson 2013: 210). But once Anusara teachers started to question Friend's personal integrity, they also started to share very different results to the practice. Facebook threads began to fill with stories of injuries both acute and chronic, significantly contributing to a loss of confidence in this, and eventually many other universal systems of alignment (Poole 2012). Just as the modern era supplemented the single gaze of each omniscient guru with multiple systems of universal, reproducible alignment, so social media replaces both, with peer networks of algorithmic surveillance (Kitnick 2015: 220). Nonetheless, the power of performing yoga, and the gaze of the audience, persists.

The natural body

New media technologies continue to enable many of the interpersonal conversations at the heart of yoga peer networking, but also more fraught, even aggressive interactions between yoga subcultures with very different values and priorities (Horton 2015, 2016). The tensions between orthopraxy, commodification, and real-world practice are not resolved in a post-lineage environment, nor via democratised media. On Facebook, yoga teachers share the practical details of upcoming events and courses, and discuss the thornier issues of norms and ethics governing practice. On Instagram and YouTube, however, the performance of yoga as practice dominates, and every yoga teacher can be a self-publishing self-promotor.

Video content platforms have also enabled the aesthetic re-animation of practices once promoted as a series of static shapes. The notion of corrective postural alignment has regenerated into growing subcultural approval for 'natural' movement that mimics developmental and evolutionary actions. Through such sympathetic magic, practitioners move like a baby learning to crawl, or like a wolf travelling soundlessly through the forest, to achieve youthful and primal regeneration (Potolsky 2006: 139). Such practitioners commonly film themselves and share the results in online spaces. Although the clips are meant to be instructional, they are also performative proof, once again, of the benefits of disciplined practice, for an audience whose gaze confers influence over the mundane world. In a typical film by Cameron Shayne (2016), this muscular teacher flows effortlessly between yoga poses, martial arts movements, and simian tumbling, but no actual instruction for the practice is offered. The potential student can only witness and admire.

Although modern postural yoga is a global phenomenon drawing on Indian roots, much of its axiological framing originates in the Anglophone world. The idea of an untamed, pre-civilised body, uncorrupted by contemporary life, thus holds faith with orientalised fantasies of ancient practitioners living rugged lives in mountain caves. In reality, the very idea of a 'natural' body would have been anathema to many pre-modern Indian adepts, practising to produce a living self that is uncorrupted by material existence (Mallinson and Singleton 2017: 326).

From upright bodies, to Platonic alignment, and from images of wellness to imitations of other-than-human movement, for contemporary practitioners in urban centres worldwide, the ideal bodies of modern postural yoga are indelibly marked by the shadow of indolent decadence that results from our engagement with a modernised, Westernised culture. Mainstream media messages agree, claiming that smart phones are ruining our posture, and sitting will make us obese. The shift to 'natural' movement is, therefore, also a response to an over-stimulated and over-surveilled, globalised and yet Anglophone culture, seen to be rapidly evolving out of our control (Black 2016: 28).

Biography and hagiography

Platforms such as Instagram and YouTube have enabled the rise of the elite yoga practitioner, whose popularity is based not in their esoteric or alignment knowledge, but instead in living a life that can be witnessed and mediatised. The resulting aesthetic packages ideas of the natural and authentic far beyond the performance of physical practice, as part of an inspirational lifestyle of organic food and unspoilt environmental beauty (Lawrence and Lozanski 2014: 80). Yoga social media 'influencers' repeatedly and repetitively perform such aspirational identities online. An Instagram search for '#yogaeverydamnday' produces an endless stream of such images in which every post is evidence of their wellness and abundance, via raw vegan breakfasts, sunset-lit perfect hand balances, and smiling families. This regular practice for the smart phone as witness is endlessly performed with just the right balance of genetic privilege and authentic grittiness for each practitioner's followers to believe in.

Beyond Instagram, and as part of what Joseph Alter calls "transnational refractions of globalized gurudom" (2013: 63), most contemporary yoga teachers are expected to share edited biographies when publicising their work, rendering the performing self into both marketable product and testimonial. As Jeffrey Kripal writes, the life of a revered religious figure is a hermeneutical process. Hagiography, as the "writing of the holy", is about "experiencing the holy in memory and text" (Kripal 2001: 36). Guru hagiographies select biographical facts to promote their teachings, via a linear narrative that often includes early spiritual inclinations, dedication to a lineage, miracles and magical powers, and the guru's death as deliberate liberation (Venkatesan 2014: 568). The life of the teacher becomes a guiding star that followers can continue to steer by, even post-mortem. In the process, any instances of behaviour that contradict the narrative are excised from history. The self-authored promotional biographies of transnationally famous teachers mimic this practice (for example, see Bruni 2018; MacGregor 2018b), and the religious power of both the guru and the teachers that disseminate their teachings persists as long as the collective, hagiographic narrative of the lineage is maintained.

What thus separates such yoga teachers from other wellness entrepreneurs is their perceived position within a chain of memory that links the gaze and performance of teacher to student, guru to adept (Hervieu-Léger 2000: 123). Within the confusing diversity of contemporary practice in which anyone can perform for the gaze of social media, stories of in-person transmission are an anchor for perceptions of authenticity, a sanctification of the powers performed via not just gaze, but touch. The direct presence of the teacher mimics the traditional dissemination of spiritual power via a single touch or glance from a powerful guru, known as shaktipat (*śaktipāta*) (Caldwell 2001: 47; Jain 2012: 10). The results of transmission in the form of wellbeing and abundance can be performed for the digital masses, but transmission itself, like practice, necessitates more than the omniscient gaze. If we watch David Regelin's performance of teaching again, we see that transmission also requires the performance, and thus the recollection, of moments of physical intimacy between student and teacher. As a result, while contemporary yoga wrestles with democratising teaching hierarchies, those teachers, who can demonstrate the charisma associated with a near-supernatural practice and physical presence, continue to hold significant power over the student experience, promising miraculous transformations if the student can move beyond the virtual to surrender to the touch of the right teacher (Featherstone 2010: 196).

Aspirations of abundance

As one such teacher, with over a million followers on Instagram, Kino MacGregor's short autobiography is filled with references to gaze, to touch, and to transform (MacGregor 2012: 27, 33, 35). Her own teacher's gaze and touch are life-changing, and far more so than any verbal instruction she received (MacGregor 2012: 54). The healing thus provoked transforms how she sees her own body, her place in the world, and the stories she is able to tell about herself as a result (MacGregor 2012: 15, 68, 109).

In recent years, controversy has regularly erupted in response to MacGregor's social media presence. When she suffered a hip injury, there were debates in yoga-related media spaces in which the 'authenticity' of her self-presentation was called into question, because her Instagram account had not paused in its daily uploading of elite postures performed in idyllic environments (Hudelson 2015; Remski 2015). In 2018, the man she continues to invoke as her (late) teacher, Pattabhi Jois, was publicly accused of multiple sexual assaults. Her response was criticised for minimising the harm he had caused in order to maintain her own hagiographic version of her origin story (MacGregor 2012: 9), as shown in the comment threads at MacGregor (2018a) and Brown (2018). Her biography contains glowing descriptions not just of healing, but of surrendering her physical agency to the guru (MacGregor 2012: 35), and ends with an exhortation to her readers to mimic her journey:

> Buy your airline ticket before you doubt yourself. Just jump, heart first, into the moment, into the light of spiritual fire. The rest will, honestly, work itself out.
> *(MacGregor 2012: 115)*

In 2016, MacGregor joined the online feed at Periscope (https://www.periscope.tv/KinoYoga/1YqGoWzdzYQGv), to bear witness to her life, in real time, for hours each day, blurring the line further between performing and living, between identity and hagiography. In her biography, she states that her deepest connection to the practice is in isolated, personal practice (MacGregor 2012: 65). Yet, her million Instagram followers, her active YouTube account, and her adventures with Periscope reveal an obsession with self-performance, and with being witnessed. The self-produced image that is Kino MacGregor leaves no space between brand and personal life. The million-eyed gaze of social media feeds not just her identity, but the blessings that result from practice in the form of financial reward and approval, but only as long as she keeps practising, keeps performing.

Yoga brands continue to trade on the aesthetic performance of unworldly practitioners, enlightened gurus, and saints in seclusion. This despite the fact that some lineages are now multinational corporations wrestling with historical accusations of abuse and intergenerational power struggles, trading on the orientalised past of a country that is a rising power in the technology industry, with a large and cosmopolitan middle class. Thus, the path to success as a yoga teacher that Macgregor's biography sets out is not based in her evident brand or business knowledge (Javid 2018; MacGregor 2018c), nor is it paved with luck or privilege, insight or accomplishment in the practice. In her narrative, it is a result of the continued performance of 'humility' and 'discipline'. Deference is inseparable from her connection to Ashtanga Yoga (MacGregor 2012: 107) and inseparable from her online identity. Despite the numerous rifts in continuity between pre-modern and contemporary yoga practice (Mallinson and Singleton 2017: ix), the privileged and white, mostly female bodies of Instagram yoga stars choose to believe that they mimic a practice performed for thousands of years by unbroken lineages of male, Indian ascetics. Post-industrial loft spaces now stand in for the jungle or roadside shrine, and the teacher performs their prostrations online, to the image of their guru on an altar, for the witness of social media.

The transformation of biography into hagiographic self-performance is the active, ongoing price each yoga teacher may have to pay to enter the gig economy (Lagaay and Koubova 2014: 51). In the narrative framing of such practice, anecdotes of revelation and transformation rise like bubbles in a world that is not composed of surfaces and depths, but agency-denying illusions and the active creation of the self and world as a unified whole: that which yogic philosophy calls *māyā* and *mokṣa* ("Maya" 2018; Mallinson and Singleton 2017: xiii). Neoliberalism has transposed these ancient ideas into a religion of abundance in which potency and privilege are a state of mind, supernatural rewards are the result of positive thinking and a Protestant work ethic, and social media 'influencers' are transformed into near-divine figures, living lives of unquestionable beauty, power, and benevolence (Leckey 2015: 211; Kilroy 2017: 169). Thus, the superstar, supernatural stars of yoga social media must keep repeating their performance of immanent becoming in order to reinforce a personal brand increasingly inseparable from their lived identity. They are suffused with the aura of divinity because they perform the miraculous. And they must be seen to bow in submission to their own absent teacher, in order to maintain the flow of blessings through them. Above all, they must reframe any touch, any connection, any conversation initiated in either the studio or the digital space as a blessing, no matter how intimate, self-violating, or confusing. The uncertainties and indignities of a non-supernatural life cannot be seen to contaminate their performance.

May Google and Facebook, Instagram and YouTube deliver us into post-human abundance via the daily divine touch of likes and mentions in the comment thread (Kulwin 2018; Steyerlpp 2015: 443)? And yet when the power-delivering gaze of public attention moves on, what does it take with it? The performance space of social media is a function of a pact between influencer and follower similar to that between actor and audience (Potolsky 2006: 75). Such performative identities can only survive through the willing and repeated performance of suspended disbelief by thousands of followers.

The end is always ob-scene

Our life histories can often be reframed as quest narratives, in which any "serious disruption in life's prospects and expectations can offer some people an opportunity to remake themselves" (Sparkes and Smith 2011: 363). As Megan Devine (2015) writes, "what cannot be fixed must be carried". Within the quest narrative, as in hagiography, the central character becomes an avatar whose past life is told in the service of its continuing present. When the narrator is the person who lives the narrative, such stories make meaning, and through that meaning, can make it easier for life to continue. Similarly, post-mortem life narratives can provide a handle of meaning for those left behind to grasp. Meaning-making in either case is both contagious (Kramer 2014: 228) and laminar: the grit of one's suffering and the incomprehensible life experiences of others are laminated in layers of narrative and practice, of witnessing, imitation, and performance. Each one is intimately formed from both the body and its ecology. Identity and meaning are formed through accretion, hardened through the fierce power of the gaze of others. What is left behind is a curated landscape of self-portrait and self-narrative that is somehow both inseparable from, and yet non-contiguous with the lived experience of the performer. In yoga, the performance of the teacher lives on instead in the mimesis of the student, in the disciplined performance of ongoing practice, in the memory of divine perfection, and the hope of the ideal self to come.

Movement is semiotics and experience. Method and practice are a repository for memory, a record of discipline. Movement can be identity freighted with personal history, a palimpsest of repertoire that spreads through entrainment and mimesis into a culture of contagion veined in its transmission with vectors of power, history, and empathy. The gaze of the charismatic teacher, and the multiple gaze of social media, watches as we move with, move for, and bow before others. The practitioner repeats their performance of the practice, again and again, in a chain of memory made from body to body, teacher to student (Hervieu-Léger 2000). With each practice, the practitioner demonstrates their allegiance to an inherited philosophy of perfection. With each witness, they take another step towards it.

References

Alter, Joseph S. 2005. 'Modern Medical Yoga: Struggling with a History of Magic, Alchemy and Sex', *Asian Medicine*, 1: 119–46.

———. 2013. 'Shri Yogendra: Magic, Modernity, and the Burden of the Middle-Class Yog.' In Mark Singleton and Ellen Goldberg (eds.), *Gurus of Modern Yoga* (Oxford University Press: Oxford), 60–82.

Bevilacqua, Daniela. 2016. "Let The Sadhus Talk. Ascetic Practitioners of Yoga in Northern India." In *Yoga Sadhana, Yoga Darsana* (Jagellonian University: Krakow), academia.edu.

Black, Shameem. 2016. 'Flexible Indian Labor: Yoga, Information Technology Migration, and U.S. Technoculture', *Race and Yoga*, 1: 22–39.

Brown, Jason. 2018. "Kino MacGregor – "Conflicts and Confluences" – International Yoga Teacher, Founder of Miami Life Center and OMstars." In *J. Brown Yoga Talks*. Accessed 16/01/2018. https://www.jbrownyoga.com/yoga-talks-podcast/2018/4/kino-macgregorAccessed 16/09/2018

Bruni, Diane. 2018. 'About Diane Bruni', Accessed 16/01/2018. https://dianebruni.com/about-diane-bruni/.

Caldwell, Sarah. 2001. 'The Heart of the Secret: A Personal and Scholarly Encounter with Shakta Tantrism in Siddha Yoga', *Nova Religio: The Journal of Alternative and Emergent Religions*, 5: 9–51.

De Michelis, Elizabeth. 2008. 'Modern Yoga: History and Forms.' In Mark Singleton and Jean Byrne (eds.), *Yoga in the Modern World Contemporary Perspectives* (Routledge: London), 17–36.

Devine, Megan. 2015. 'Everything Is Not Okay'. http://www.refugeingrief.com/support/audiobook/.

Featherstone, Mike. 2010. 'Body, Image and Affect in Consumer Culture', *Body and Society*, 16: 193–221.

Friend, John. 2008. *Anusara Teacher Training Manual* (Anusara Press: The Woodlands).

Gilman, Sander L. 2014. '"Stand Up Straight": Notes toward a History of Posture', *The Journal of Medical Humanities*, 35: 57.

Goldberg, Michelle. 2015. 'The Brutal Economics of Being a Yoga Teacher', Accessed 07/12/2017. http://nymag.com/thecut/2015/10/brutal-economics-of-being-a-yoga-teacher.html.

Hauser, Beatrix. 2013. 'Introduction: Transcultural Yoga(s). Analyzing a Traveling Subject.' In Beatrix Hauser (ed.), *Yoga Traveling: Bodily Practice in Transcultural Perspective* (Springer International Publishing: New York), 1–36.

Hervieu-Léger, Danièle. 2000. *Religion as a Chain of Memory* (Rutgers University Press: New Brunswick).

Horton, Carol. 2015. 'Yoga Selfies on Instagram: Reflections of a Curious Onlooker', Accessed 13/04/2015. http://carolhortonphd.com/yoga-selfies-on-instagram/.

———. 2016. 'Yoga 2016: Fragmented, Contested, Reimagined', Accessed 04/02/16. http://yogadork.com/2016/01/19/yoga-2016-fragmented-contested-reimagined/.

Hudelson, Emma. 2015. 'Leave Kino's Hip Alone', Accessed 16/07/2015. http://www.thebuddhiblog.com/leave-kinos-hip-alone/.

Iyengar, B.K.S. 2004 (1965). *The Illustrated Light on Yoga: Yoga Dipika* (Rupa HP: Pune).

Jain, Andrea R. 2012. 'Branding Yoga', *Approaching Religion*, 2: 3–15.

Javid, David. 2018. 'The Truth behind Kino's Letter', Accessed 24/03/2018. https://www.elephantjournal.com/2018/03/the-truth-behind-kinos-letter-paul-javid/.

Jesson, Thomas. 2017. 'Upright and Uptight: The Invention of Posture', Accessed 10/04/2017. https://medium.com/@thomas_jesson/upright-and-uptight-the-invention-of-posture-fe48282a4487.

Kilroy, Robert Thomas. 2017. 'Lacan through Lacoue-Labarthe and Nancy: From "Modernist Myths" to Modernism as Myth', *L'Esprit Créateur*, 57: 160–173.

Kitnick, Alex. 2015. 'Everybody's Autobiography.' In Lauren Cornell, Ed Halter and Lisa Phillips (eds.), *Mass Effect: Art and the Internet in the Twenty-First Century* (Mit Press: Cambridge, MA).

Klein, Melanie. 2015. 'Yoga and Body Image Coalition', Accessed 12/08/2015. http://ybicoalition.com/.

Krämer, Sybille. 2014. 'Connecting Performance and Performativity: Does It Work?' In Laura Cull and Alice Lagaay (eds.), *Encounters in Performance Philosophy* (Palgrave Macmillan UK: Basingstoke), 223–237.

Kripal, Jeffrey J. 2001. 'One Lifetime, Many Lives: The Experience of Modern Hindu Hagiography', *History of Religions*, 40: 396–398.

Kulwin, Noah. 2018. 'One Has This Feeling of Having Contributed to Something That's Gone Very Wrong', Accessed 03/07/2018. http://nymag.com/selectall/2018/04/jaron-lanier-interview-on-what-went-wrong-with-the-internet.html?utm_source=fb&utm_medium=s3&utm_campaign=sharebutton-t.

Lagaay, Alice, and Alice Koubova. 2014. 'Performing the Impossible in Philosophy.' In Laura Cull and Alice Lagaay (eds.), *Encounters in Performance Philosophy* (Palgrave Macmillan UK: Basingstoke), 39–62.

Langford, Jean. 2004. *Fluent Bodies: Ayurvedic Remedies for Postcolonial Imbalance* (Oxford University Press: New Delhi; New York).

Lavrence, Christine, and Kristin Lozanski. 2014. "'This Is Not Your Practice Life': Lululemon and the Neoliberal Governance of Self', *Canadian Review of Sociology/Revue canadienne de sociologie*, 51: 76–94.

Leckey, Mark. 2015. 'In The Long Tail.' In Lauren Cornell, Ed Halter and Lisa Phillips (eds.), *Mass Effect: Art and the Internet in the Twenty-First Century* (Mit Press: Cambridge MA).

Loupe, Emily. 2018. '10 Tips for New Yoga Teachers', Accessed 16/01/2018. https://www.doyouyoga.com/10-tips-for-new-yoga-teachers/.

MacGregor, Kino. 2012. *Sacred Fire: My Journey into Ashtanga Yoga* (Harmony: Edinburgh).

———. 2018a. 'Ashtanga Yoga—Accountability, Acceptance and Action in the Arena of Sexual Appropriateness and Hands-On Assists by Kino MacGregor', Accessed 16/09/2018. https://www.kinoyoga.com/ashtanga-yoga-accountability-acceptance-action-arena-sexual-appropriateness-hands-assists-kino-macgregor/.

———. 2018b. 'Kino MacGregor', Accessed 16/01/2018. https://www.kinoyoga.com/about/kino-macgregor/.

———. 2018c. 'When One Big Company Picks on One Yoga Teacher', Accessed 24/03/2018. https://www.elephantjournal.com/2018/03/a-battle-for-the-heart-of-yoga-when-big-companies-try-to-buy-yoga-teachers-and-sometimes-succeed-kino-macgregor/.

Mallinson, James. 2018. "SOAS Centre for Yoga Studies Launch." In (School of Oriental and African Studies: London).

Mallinson, James, and Mark Singleton. 2017. *Roots of Yoga* (Penguin Books: London).

"Maya." 2018. In *Encyclopædia Britannica* (Britannica Academic: Chicago, Illinois).

Newcombe, Suzanne. 2013. 'Magic and Yoga: The Role of Subcultures in Transcultural Exchange.' In Beatrix Hauser (ed.), *Yoga Traveling: Bodily Practice in Transcultural Perspective* (Springer International Publishing: New York).

Peacock, Ryan. 2017. 'The A-to-Z Guide to Yoga Cues', Accessed 16/01/2018. https://www.yogajournal.com/teach/a-to-z-guide-to-yoga-cues.

Poole, Katy. 2012. 'The Vicious Vocal Minority vs. John Friend', Accessed 12/08/2015. http://www.elephantjournal.com/2012/05/the-vicious-vocal-minority-vs-john-friend/.

Potolsky, Matthew. 2006. *Mimesis* (Routledge: New York; London).

Powell, Seth. 2017. 'Advice on Āsana in the Śivayogapradīpikā', Accessed 13/07/2017. http://theluminescent.blogspot.co.uk/2017/06/advice-on-asana-in-sivayogapradipika.html.

Regelin, David. 2014. "Geometry of Yoga." Accessed, 30/3/2019. https://www.youtube.com/watch?v=nm8CnPFLXD4.

Remski, Matthew. 2015. 'Kino's Hip: Reflections on Extreme Practice and Injury in Asana', Accessed 13/07/2015. http://matthewremski.com/wordpress/kinos-hip/.

Sarbacker, Stuart R. 2014. 'Reclaiming the Spirit through the Body: The Nascent Spirituality of Modern Postural Yoga', *Entangled Religions*, 1: 95–114.

Shayne, Cameron. 2016. "BDK Calisthenics Animal Slow Motion Study." In YouTube.com. Accessed 17/03/2016. https://www.youtube.com/watch?v=nm8CnPFLXD4

Singleton, Mark. 2010. *Yoga Body the Origins of Modern Posture Practice* (Oxford University Press: Oxford).

———. 2013. 'Transnational Exchange and the Genesis of Modern Postural Yoga.' In Beatrix Hauser (ed.), *Yoga Traveling: Bodily Practice in Transcultural Perspective* (Springer International Publishing: New York).

Sparkes, Andrew C., and Brett Smith. 2011. 'Inhabiting Different Bodies over Time: Narrative and Pedagogical Challenges', *Sport, Education and Society*, 16: 357–370.

Steyerlpp, Hito. 2015. 'Too Much World.' In Lauren Cornell, Ed Halter and Lisa Phillips (eds.), *Mass Effect: Art and the Internet in the Twenty-First Century* (Mit Press: Cambridge, MA).

Strauss, Sarah. 2008. '"Adapt, Adjust, Accommodate" The Production of Yoga in a Transnational World.' In Mark Singleton and Jean Byrne (eds.), *Yoga in the Modern World: Contemporary Perspectives* (Routledge: London), 49–72.

Tweed, Thomas A. 2006. *Crossing and Dwelling: A Theory of Religion* (Harvard University Press: Cambridge).

Venkatesan, Archana. 2014. 'Making Saints, Making Communities: Nayaki Svamikal and the Saurashtras of Madurai', *South Asia-Journal of South Asian Studies*, 37: 568–585.

Wildcroft, Theo. 2019. 'Patterns of Authority and Practice Relationships in 'Post-lineage Yoga'', Open University. PhD Thesis. Awarded 2019. Available at http://oro.open.ac.uk/59125/.

Williamson, Lola. 2013. 'Stretching toward the Sacred: John Friend and Anusara Yoga.' In Mark Singleton and Ellen Goldberg (eds.), *Gurus of Modern Yoga* (Oxford University Press: Oxford), 210–231.

25

THE THINK TANK

Institution as performance

Sonya Dyer

Think tanks affect our political and social realities in ways both tangible and intangible. They shape our lives by setting the trajectory of acceptable political thought, and other aspects of public life, including determining priorities for scientific and medical research and informing public policy and human behaviour, through advocacy and the dissemination of ideas. They are arguably the main way those of us living in advanced economies are exposed to 'new' ideas (which may in fact be recycled old ideas). Here, I do not mean to suggest that we have all consciously consulted a think tank. Rather, I want to invite consideration of the ways in which the work of think tanks often determines priorities for public funding, which includes the support of arts and culture. Also consider the increasing number of research-based entities within the university system funded by wealthy individuals or groups, which, either explicitly or otherwise, operate in the manner of, think tanks, generating and disseminating ideas with the intention of influencing public life.[1] In this chapter, I will not attempt to provide a comprehensive account of the contentious history of the think tank. Instead, I will draw out the performativity of the think tank as a form and critically examine some of the ways in which the form is being used by contemporary artists working within the expanded field of performance, including my own practice.

However, before I embark on this analysis, it is useful to begin with some understanding of what a think tank is, or – more importantly – what a think tank *does*: how it performs its function. So, what is a think tank? Notable examples include the Fabian Society, Demos, the Adam Smith Institute and Chatham House. The etymology of the phrase derives from a colloquial term for the brain first used in the early 1900s (Online Etymology Dictionary 2019). According to standard dictionary definitions, a think tank is variously defined as: "an institute, corporation, or group organized to study a particular subject (such as a policy issue or a scientific problem) and provide information, ideas, and advice" (Merriam Webster Dictionary 2019); or, alternatively, as "a research institute or organization employed to solve complex problems or predict or plan future developments, as in military, political, or social areas" (Dictionary.com 2019). This distinction between studying and solving, prediction and providing information is, I would suggest, often a generative and constructive one within contemporary arts practice using the think tank model.

In his book, *What Should Think Tanks Do? A Strategy Guide to Policy Impact,* Andrew Selee describes the work of think tanks as "getting new ideas into the public sphere or shaping the way that policymakers and the public understand issues": a process which necessitates planning, research and "a respected institutional or personal reputation" (Selee 2013, p. 5). Selee's four critical resources for success are "human resources, financial resources, partnerships and reputation (brand)" (Selee 2013, p. 15). In other words, he believes that the success of a think tank's performance depends on being able to hire the right people, having people to give you money, making friends with the most useful people and being a voice that is listened to. Selee goes on to state that "successful think tanks develop systematic approaches to planning for impact… so that they make the greatest possible difference on public ideas and policy decisions" (Selee 2013, p. 4).

This description conjures up images of the bright young things dashing about *The West Wing*, or the shiny, smiling faces of New Labour (whose rise was charted in partnership with the Institute for Public Policy Research, or IPPR, a centrist think tank). It may also bring to mind the USA-influenced free market advocate think tanks that aided Margaret Thatcher's rise to power in 1979, a time when the model's ascendency was becoming apparent. I am thinking here of the Centre for Policy Studies (CPS), the Institute for Economic Affairs (IEA) or, perhaps most famously of all, the Adam Smith Institute – all founded in the United Kingdom in the period from 1974 to 1977. As Andrew Rich notes, the number of think tanks "quadrupled from fewer than 70 to more than 300 between 1970 and the turn of the century" (Rich 2004, p. 4) in the USA, and the Thatcher revolution was an influential part of this conservative wave. Equally, it is arguable that these conservative think tanks worked, if not in concert, then at least in sympathy, with each other across the Atlantic – national borders being no barrier to ideas. Whilst the UK cannot claim the same number of think tanks as the United States, I'm not convinced that we cannot claim a similar degree of impact. That is to say, from academia to policy research, cultural advocacy and political agitation, a plethora of think tanks, from the Thatcher era onwards, influence our everyday lives now as never before.

The think tank in contemporary art practice – local, national and international

The think tank model reoccurs in different forms of performative, collaborative and the so-called 'socially-engaged' arts practices. In this section, I will briefly address some examples of think tanks created in the context of contemporary art – foregrounding a series of projects, which have been particularly influential on my own thinking. They represent distinct variations of the model, and highlight ways artists have used institutions of research as tools for the performance of institutional legitimacy. Each project represents a different relation to capitalism, subject-object, neo-colonial/gentrification agendas, community building and notions of the local, national and international. Each lends itself to a different form of performativity, and constructs different publics for their works. Of course, many intersect between various categories.

I am interested in the performativity of the institution. What does a think tank allow these projects to do, that other forms of organisation cannot? How do artists utilise this institutional form to create works that at least attempt to be both inside and outside overarching superstructures (larger institutions, colonial legacies)? And what happens to the think tank, itself, when it claims the role of art? In other words, can art transform the potentiality of the think tank?

The Institute for Human Activities (IHA)

The Institute for Human Activities (IHA), a research project set up by Dutch artist, Renzo Martens, in 2014, initially sought to, in his own words, "gentrify"[2] Lusanga, a town in the Democratic Republic of the Congo (near a former Unilever palm oil plantation), via art capital.

The word gentrification has troubling implications, particularly in a formerly colonised region of the world with an extreme inequality of wealth distribution. Indeed, one of the major critiques of gentrification, particularly the Floridian[3] model so prevalent within UK arts policy in the early part of the 21st century, was that the surplus value created by the 'creative class' was not in fact shared with the locals, but used to push them out. This raised the question of what possible motives could there be for a white, European artist to initiate a project espousing gentrification in Africa?

The copy on the website has significantly altered in tone since I first accessed it in 2015, and gentrification is no longer mentioned as its aim. Instead, it now describes itself as a:

> research project, initiated by a Dutch artist Renzo Martens and developed at the KASK – School of Arts in Ghent. IHA's goal is to prove that artistic critique on economic inequality can redress it – not symbolically, but in material terms.... (IHA) facilitates the global dissemination of the artworks created with the CATPC, the profits of which return directly to the Congo to support the makers and their families, as well as community projects in Lusanga.
>
> *(IHA 2017)*

This framing now positions the IHA's role as providing 'artistic critique', and also indicates the local community as the main beneficiaries of the economic outcomes of the project. The model is thus: locally based artists produce works, most commonly using materials derived from cacao farming. These works are then exhibited and sold in significant Western art institutions, with the profit derived from these sales going back to the artists. It is unclear precisely what percentage of sales returns to the artists. Of course, there is also cultural capital, which I would argue largely, or even entirely, resides with Martens, himself – his name is recognised, and 'allows' the Congolese artists access to these spaces.[4]

The IHA website uses terms such as "global economic segregation" and "local free zone", describing the Congolese plantation workers' "artistic engagement with plantation labour". This new language marks a significant shift in the self-description of IHA's aims and partnerships from its inception, which is to be cautiously welcomed, as it suggests a less 'colonial' relationship between the Dutch artists' symbolic, cultural and economic value and those of the Congolese people involved.

There has been a strong critique from anti-colonial scholars and artists regarding the IHA, Martens' relationship to it and the Congolese community in which it is based. Certainly, the 'white saviour' cliché was at least initially (and perhaps still is) fully utilised within the operations and performance of IHA as an institution, with Martens as its figurehead. Most commonly used in relation to cinema (and indeed certain charitable and philanthropic activities), the white saviour complex describes the self-serving actions of a white person who supposedly seeks to help non-white people or persons, particularly – but not exclusively – those in Africa. It is a colonial relationship, with the non-white person/people in a subservient role, benefitting from the white persons largesse and inherent goodness. The white saviour is a well-used trope in cinema, where a heroic white character rescues abject people of colour from their miserable plights, often whilst learning valuable insights about themselves. Even when the film is supposedly about, for example, trans-Atlantic enslavement (Amistad 1997), inner city children (Dangerous Minds 1996) or African-American domestic workers (The Help 2011), the subjectivity and sheer goodness of the white character is the dominant note.

Equally, some of the language initially used by Martens was questionable. I once attended a talk at the ICA in London, where Martens repeatedly referred to the Congolese workers as 'those people' or 'these people' and claimed 'these people' thought of him as 'a God'. To me, it appeared that Martens (as the dominant public face of the organisation, and the embodiment of white, male privilege) had embraced with glee the role of the colonial overseer – or if one is to be generous, colonial benefactor. Is this the model of social relations needed for the 21st century?

It appears that, in the intervening years, Martens has modified his position and learned to critically examine his privilege in respect to working in/with one of the most impoverished communities in the world. By placing himself in the position as that community's conduit to the wealthy Euro-American art world (and potential access to life-changing capital) in which he has made his own not inconsiderable wealth, the power relations, colonial historical memory and contemporary North/South power differentials are sometimes painfully re-encoded and re-enacted. But might they yet be reimagined altogether?

The Silent University and *Our Neighbours: with Tania Bruguera*: towards community

The Silent University (2012–present) and *Our Neighbours* (2018–2019) are both examples of artists utilising their creative capital in support of engendering cross-cultural collaboration, explicitly speaking to the current question of Europe's response to issues of migration. Turkish artist Ahmet Ogut developed *The Silent University* with the support of the Delfina Foundation and Tate Modern in 2012, as a "solidarity based knowledge exchange platform by refugees, asylum seekers and migrants... led by a group of lecturers, consultants and research fellows" (The Silent University 2017). *The Silent University* operates by partnering with arts organisations (mainly galleries) for the production of workshops, courses, performances and other discursive, public-facing work. It provides opportunities for highly skilled refugees, asylum seekers and migrants to utilise their skills in their 'host' countries where – because of their status – they are currently unable to do so. Its politics is timely, as Europe faces the ongoing political reality of migration in its various forms.

Our Neighbours: with Tania Bruguera forms part of the Cuban artists' 2018 Hyundai Commission for the Turbine Hall at Tate Modern. It was programmed as part of Tate Exchange, a social practice-focused platform at Tate, for which Bruguera is the corresponding lead artist for the 2018–2019 activity year. A working group, *Tate Neighbours*, consisting of a roughly demographically accurate group of 21 people from the local area, met on a bi-weekly basis for the six months prior to the commission's unveiling. *Tate Neighbours* became an in-house think tank, working with relative independence from the main Turbine Hall commissioning process, but responsive to it. Participants were paid an equal amount for their time, and directly engaged not only with each other, but the artist herself and members of Tate staff, including the Director, Francis Morris.

During this intensive, and undoubtedly challenging period of focused collaboration and communication, *Our Neighbours* utilised the think tank's potential to influence and affect transformation in ways that are materially apparent to the visiting public, at least in the short term. For example, focusing on the idea of neighbourliness, and the physical and emotional experience of migration, this project instituted a rewriting of the Tate's Terms and Conditions (accessed when signing up to use their Wi-Fi) inviting the public to identify their interests and commit to action in the service of civic responsibility.

Most radically, they also lobbied for, and won, a name change in the building, traditionally offered in exchange for large donations from benefactors. Instead, during the project year, the entire Boiler House extension was renamed after Natalie Bell, a local community activist, selected by the *Neighbours* as a mark of respect and recognition. This renaming was made permanent in October 2019 (The Art Newspaper, 4th October 2019). Thus, the think tank's knowledge generation capacity reimagines the possibility of the civic superseding the monetary in terms of social value.

ABIFR

My own project, the *…And Beyond Institute for Future Research* (ABIFR) is a think tank, creating possible futures. The Institute draws upon a range of experiences and talents to centre marginalised subjectivities (particularly those of Black women) within narratives of space travel and futurity. Its premise owes much to Hakim Bey's notion of the 'temporary autonomous zone' (Bey 1991, p. 2) and other forms of Utopian thinking, both fictional and non-fictional. I set up the ABIFR in 2014 (although nascent iterations began in 2012) as an evolving work intended in large part to allow space for my practice to interrogate the dearth of Black women depicted in the science fiction movies I consumed.

This project continued my long-standing interest in public research as a form of practice (first developed during *The Paul Robeson Research Station* at the Site Gallery in 2011). The think tank became an attractive proposition – a place where I could test and distribute ideas in the public realm. I was interested in the way think tanks operate as organisational structures concerned with the production, propagation and advocacy of forms of knowledge, potentially influencing public policy. I wondered how a think tank might be employed in the service of the imagination.

I had previously worked with, and been approached by, various think tanks as a writer and cultural commentator, and I felt I had a strong understanding of the role they played in civil society. My ambition therefore was to consider whether the propagandising potential of the think tank could be utilised as an artwork to rethink whom and what space travel and the future was for. How could I insert Black women as the face of the future? The work produced by ABIFR should therefore be seen as building a body of public knowledge, often within ephemeral or performative frameworks, arising from visual arts practice. It utilises my curatorial and organisational skills, in addition to the performative pedagogy that forms much of my practice.

A significant point of difference between ABIFR and the traditional think tank is that it is primarily composed of one person – myself – with the potential for working with collaborators on a project-by-project basis. I choose to work with the think tank as a form, as a way of embracing the research-based nature of my practice by making the research itself the form. Developing ABIFR provided space for me to incorporate the elements of my curatorial work (at this point, my main source of income) that felt most generative to my practice, including the reproduction and distribution of ideas, the politics of exchange and the uses of propaganda. The think tank's role in conferring institutional legitimacy on ideas and its capitalist, colonialist origins also provide a subversive potentiality for ABIFR.

As a think tank, ABIFR is able to consider and subvert the nature of the institutional invitation. For example, with *The Claudia Jones Space Station* ("CJSS") (2017), ABIFR invited locally based groups and individuals to take up space within the institutions during the projects, offering workshops, talks and other discursive spaces to the wider community. The think tank became a host within a host. It was named after Claudia Jones, the pioneering

Trinidad-born activist, writer and newspaper editor who, amongst other things, set up both the Notting Hill Carnival in 1966 and the first significant Black newspaper in the UK, the West Indian Gazette and Afro-Asian Caribbean News in 1958, as well as advocating for decent housing more generally. This act of naming continued my ongoing interest in the potentiality of monumentalising – of how naming things after neglected figures might reinvigorate their memory.

Equally, Space Stations are places where people from different disciplines and different parts of the world can live and work together for a set period of time, working on individual research, as well as generating collective knowledge. The CJSS was inspired by the possibilities of creating such a space, inspired by the key aspects of Jones' public life.

Originally, my research considered the possibilities of what an intersectional space programme might be, and creating an organisation for that purpose seemed an obvious choice. In subsequent years, the work has moved more towards reimagining the history of space travel, beginning with the HeLa[5] cells that were sent into space on the Korabl-Sputnik 2 satellite by the Soviet Union in 1960. Taken from the body of Henrietta Lacks – a young African-American mother and farmer – HeLa cells are deemed 'immortal' due to their constant reproducibility – they can reproduce under pretty much any circumstances and have become the gold standard for medical research. In 1951, Lacks had a particularly aggressive form of ovarian cancer and was treated at John Hopkins Hospital, at that time the only hospital that would take Black patients in the area. There is some contention as to whether Lacks consented to her cells being taken. However, they were subsequently shared amongst the scientific community and became monetised – although Lacks and her family were themselves not compensated, and the origins of these miraculous cells were obscured. These cells became the first human materials in space, arguably marking the beginning of human space travel.

The story of HeLa cells in Space forms part of a trilogy of influences fuelling ABIFR's ongoing body of work, *Hailing Frequencies Open*. Alongside HeLa is the under-reported history of actress Nichelle Nicols (the original Nyota Uhura in *Star Trek*), utilising her status as a science fiction icon to initiate an astronaut diversification programme for NASA during the Space Shuttle era of the 1970s. Nicols' work developed the first American woman in Space, Sally Ride, as well as the first man of African descent in Space, Guion Bluford, in 1983.

The third part of the trilogy is the Greek myth of Andromeda. There are various versions of the story, but effectively, Andromeda was the daughter of the Ethiopian King Cepheus and Queen Cassiopeia. When her mother declares her daughter to be the most beautiful girl in the known world (or more beautiful than the Nereids), Poseidon sends a sea monster to ravage Ethiopia and Andromeda is chained naked to a rock to avenge the angry Gods. In the story, Perseus eventually rescues Andromeda. In European art history, Andromeda is always depicted as white, despite the story taking place within Ethiopia, and authors such as Ovid and Sappho explicitly referencing Andromeda's dark skin tone. Additionally, Andromeda is the name of a star constellation. This work is building a world where the HeLa cells are still in Space.... and heading towards Andromeda. ABIFR's work of reimagining the origins of space travel is also a means of reinvigorating its future.

The ABIFR has many of the visual characteristics of a traditional think tank, such as a logo and a slogan: "We Make the Future". The 'we' constitutes recognition of its key purpose to centre the marginalised and displace homogeneity, but one can also read 'we' ambiguously, attending to its exclusions. Who are *we*? Unlike political think tanks, and similar to many arts-based organisations, ABIFR seeks to affect the commons, rather than government, politics and policy. ABIFR occupies a space between fact and fiction, fantasy and reality.

Space think tanks

As I discovered in my research for ABIFR, the field of space travel is heavily populated with think tanks, particularly as federal funding to NASA decreased from the 1970s onwards (The Guardian 2011). Over the past decade, there has been an exponential growth in private spaceflight companies such as Virgin Galactic, Space X, SpaceDev and Blue Origin, and even NASA has sought to leverage its own capacities in partnership with private companies (NASA.org 2019a). Dr Mae Jemison is the principal officer of the *100 Year Star Ship* project (100yss.org 2017), which aims to make human interstellar travel possible within 100 years. When I first started to develop the ABIFR in 2012, the *100 Year Star Ship* was a significant inspiration. In the early days, the project team consisted of six people, four of whom were women, three of whom were Black. The team has since expanded, but the affective charge of seeing so many women – most of them Black – involved in this initiative proved monumental. I realised I had not seen this before, and the reality of it was overwhelming. I returned to the 'About Us' page on their website often, just to confirm and remind myself that this was reality.

Companies such as Elon Musk's Space X and Richard Branson's Virgin Galactic have already advertised for, and booked, clients for imminent private spaceflights. By making space tourism possible, space travel will no longer be an activity for highly trained fighter pilots, scientists or engineers, and will instead become a feasible holiday choice for the super-wealthy. Much like flight in the early 20th century, one can now conceive of space travel as one of many holiday options in the not too distant future. Surely, colonisation is not too far away thereafter.

The problematic language of 'conquer' and 'colonisation' betrays the imperial genesis of much of Western-dominated space exploration. NASA's online library has a whole section devoted to 'space colonisation', for example, and a quick Google search of the term results in over 299,000,000 references at the time of writing (NASA.org 2019b). It is the language of the kinds of forces that enslaved, annexed, tortured and underdeveloped the Majority World during the period of colonisation, and in economic and political terms continues to do so. Therefore, challenging this language – and thinking about more cooperative models of community building – is essential to ABIFR. ABIFR occupies a space between these commercial ventures, the political think tank, and in conversation with other artist-led projects, it looks to the commons and to the real stories of women whose contributions to futurity are neglected, in conversation with their fictional counterparts.

Recognising the systems of privilege the artist with any modicum of visibility and success does have access to – the art gallery and art funding, the ability to travel internationally, acuity with language, access to like-minded people – ABIFR develops opportunities to develop propaganda, distribute images and create public spaces for performative pedagogy within the expanded field of performance.

I suggest that it is this performative pedagogy that provides space for the relationship between performance and philosophy to be realised and enacted through the think tank. The educational properties of the think tank, the research institute are subverted, reimagined, reconstituted and potentially radicalised by creating a performative dynamic between 'audience' and 'institute'. Performance philosophy – that is, thought generated and disseminated through performance and performativity – can transform a traditionally static and passive relationship between publics and think tanks into a form of call and response where the 'expert' and the 'receiver of information' swap places, or indeed sometimes are, or can become, the same person. The institution is performance.

Notes

1. As an example, the University of Oxford careers service website emphasises how 'exciting, influential and fulfilling' working at a think tank can be. It posits think tanks as 'research institutes that seek to play a key role in making and influencing global, regional and national policy' and goes on to claim 'think tank researchers influence public opinion and public policy'. Think tanks based at Oxford include the Future of Humanity Institute (supported by funders as diverse as Elon Musk and the Leverhulme Trust).
2. Whilst the term 'gentrify' no longer appears on the IHA website, it is still referenced elsewhere, including Martens' Wikipedia page https://en.wikipedia.org/wiki/Renzo_Martens, accessed 11th March 2019.
3. I am referring to the work of American urban studies theorist Richard Florida, whose book *The Rise of the Creative Class* (2002) had a significant effect on New Labour cultural and economic policy in relation to the 'creative industries'. In brief, Florida asserts that high concentrations of artists, tech workers and LGBT people, amongst other 'high Bohemian's', raised an area's economic profile. Florida's work is generally regarded as being integral to legitimising gentrification policies, which have been critiqued as social cleansing and ethnic cleansing. One of the ironies of such policies is that most artists cannot then afford to live in these areas, post-gentrification. Most impactfully, nor can much of the original working-class communities with deep ties to the area.
4. It should also be noted that IHA is now also in partnership with the Cercle d'Art des Travailleurs de Plantation Congolaise (CATPC) as referenced earlier, which was founded in the South of the DRC in 2014. Described as a grassroots platform, this organisation is led by a named group of Congolese plantation workers, an ecologist and a smaller group of Kinshasa-based artists.
5. What is now commonly known about HeLa largely derives from Rebecca Skloot's book *The Immortal Life of Henrietta Lacks* (2011), although it is worth noting that some relatives contest many of the books assertions about the family and the circumstances under which the cells were taken.

References

100yss.org. 2017. The 100SS team, 2017 [Online]. Available at: https://100yss.org/mission/team, Accessed 11th April 2017.

Bey, H. 1991. *T.A.Z: The Temporary Autonomous Zone*, Autonomedia: New York.

Future of Humanity Institute, University of Oxford. 2019. 'Support FHI' [Online], Available at: https://www.fhi.ox.ac.uk/support-fhi/, Accessed 5th October 2019.

IHA. 2017. Institute for Human Activities [Online], Available at: http://www.humanactivities.org/en/, Accessed 10th April 2017.

NASA.org. 2019a. 'NASA Establishes New Public Private Partnerships to Advance U.S. Commercial Space Capabilities' [Online], Available at: https://www.nasa.gov/press-release/nasa-establishes-new-public-private-partnerships-to-advance-us-commercial-space, Accessed 12th March 2019.

NASA.org. 2019b. NASA HQ Library [Online], Available at: https://www.nasa.gov/centers/hq/library, Accessed 12th March 2019.

Rich, A. 2004. *Think Tanks, Public Policy, and the Politics of Expertise*. Cambridge University Press: Cambridge. doi:10.1017/CBO9780511509889.

Selee, A. 2013. *What Should Think Tanks Do? A Strategic Guide to Policy Impact*, Stanford University Press: Stanford.

Silent University.org. 2016. *The Silent University* [Online], Available at: http://thesilentuniversity.org, Accessed 10th April 2017.

Site Gallery. 2011. *The Paul Robeson Research Station* [Online], Available at: http://www.sitegallery.org/site-platform-sonya-dyer/, Accessed 7th April 2017.

The Art Newspaper. 2019. 'Tania Bruguera's 2018 Turbine Hall commission becomes permanent at Tate Modern' [Online], Available at: https://www.theartnewspaper.com/news/tania-bruguera-s-turbine-hall-commission-becomes-permanent, Accessed 5th October 2019.

The Guardian. 2011. Datablog- NASA Budgets: US Spending on Space Travel since 1958 UPDATED [Online], Available at: https://www.theguardian.com/news/datablog/2010/feb/01/nasa-budgets-us-spending-space-travel, Accessed 11th April 2017.

University of Oxford. 2019. 'Think Tanks: About This Sector' [Online], Available at https://www.careers.ox.ac.uk/think-tanks/, Accessed 5th October 2019.

26
TOUCH

Naomi Woo

In this text, I suggest that the practice of philosophy and the act of performance are both instances of touching and being touched, just as touch is a technique that informs them. The text focuses on my own encounters with the technique of touching in performance, which come primarily from the piano keyboard: where touch is both a physical process and an elusive sonic quality. It is telling that the word touch is also used metaphorically to speak about thoughts and emotions. Here, I engage with all three of these capacities—embodied, audible, and emotive—to consider the tactility of Performance Philosophy.

Technique: the repeated touch[1]

When the pianist strikes the same key more than once in a row, in English, we refer to the phenomenon—and the technique—as 'repeated notes'. In French, though, the word for a key is 'une touche'—a touch. And so both sounding phenomenon and technical skill bear the name 'repeated touches'—*les touches répétées*. This technical skill is notoriously difficult for pianists to master. Its execution changes from instrument to instrument, so every new piano requires learning a new dynamic of action. Equally, both the pianist and the piano have physical limits as to how fast they can move. Of course, Deleuze reminds us that even the possibility of repetition is not as straightforward as it might seem. 'To repeat is to behave in a certain manner, but in relation to something unique or singular which has no equal or equivalent' (Deleuze 1994, p. 1). In order for the note to repeat, it must be, in some respect, 'the same', but it also cannot be the same: it must be singular.

> And perhaps this repetition at the level of external conduct echoes, for its own part, a more secret vibration which animates it, a more profound, internal repetition within the singular [...]. They do not add a second and a third time to the first, but carry the first time to the nth power.
>
> *(Ibid.)*

This is curiously true of musical repetition, and in particular the musical repetition of a single pitch. The pitch is defined and sustained by a particular vibrating sound wave. This wave carries within it the possibility of persistence. However, persistence is not in itself repetition, for repetition requires a break in the sound and a new start. And so, it is the singular vibration that allows for the pitch to be repeated, not through addition but instead through subtraction—through the absence of sound followed by its re-appearance.

In this quality of singularity, it is crucial that repeated notes cannot be exchanged: the first note and the second or third or fourth note are not commensurable. Rather than exchange, Deleuze suggests that 'theft and gift' are the 'criteria of repetition' (ibid.). In this context, I recall Derrida, for whom giving is also the condition of a very different phenomenon: touch. He reminds us that the French verb *'tendre'*—in English, to tender, or hold out, offer—means 'to give what is given without giving up' (Derrida 2000, p. 94). Etymologically, it is related to extend, pretend, attend—in all cases a touching that retains its own identity and specificity. To extend is to give and keep. To pretend is to take on alongside, not instead of, the self. To attend is to bring oneself—gift oneself—in time. In the same way, repetition for Deleuze involves both a giving across time and a preservation of that which is given. Touching and repetition, then, are both kinds of giving, and it is for this reason that I have chosen to investigate 'touch' in the context of repeated notes, to see what the suggestive contact between touching and repeating has to offer.

Given that the hand stays fairly static, the technique and phenomenon of repeated notes can appear quite simple from the outside. The hand remains in place, and so the execution poses none of the challenges of awkwardly stretched hand positions or mastering wide leaps. The primary oppositional force in this kind of difficulty comes not from the body itself, but rather from the instrument. When a finger strikes a key at the piano, the action is transmitted through levers, bolts, and joints. Eventually, the motion arrives in the hammer, a felt-tipped block of wood that is raised toward the string, just at the moment that the damper (which keeps the string from resonating) is lifted off: a note sounds. The hammer bounces right back after striking the string (otherwise, it would act as a damper and soften the note) but as long as the key is depressed, the damper remains at a distance. When the finger leaves the key, the damper returns to its role and the note ends.

The intricacy of this mechanism—as it is called in technical terms, the 'action' of the piano—means that so many invisible things must happen in the split second between the first note and its repetition, and that the action is easily jammed or stuck. In order to combat this effect, the piano-maker Sébastien Érard invented in 1821 a mechanism known as 'the double escapement' (Ehrlich 1990, p. 111). With this mechanism, after the note is struck, the hammer does not return all the way to its resting position, but instead is reset, and at-the-ready; there are fewer actions that need to happen inside before the note can be struck again. Even still, pianists often struggle with repeated touches, as there is tremendous potential for the touch to fail. When the touches are going smoothly, a seamless succession of repetitions, I am aware that my hand both retains its connection to my body, while also becoming part of the instrument's action. Like Érard's double escapement mechanism, an effective succession of repeated notes in the hand behaves as an *extension*—an addition to the action of the piano that makes a new phenomenon (repeated notes) possible. In order to make the notes sound evenly and clearly, the body appends itself to the instrument, working alongside it.

Different technical approaches are possible to smooth out this process. In the famously challenging opening of Ravel's 'Scarbo', the low repeated note is often performed with first three fingers (thumb, pointer, and middle finger) all constantly in contact with the key, and the hand is as if stuck to the key itself, bouncing up and down as the key itself bounces (c.f. Bricard 1990, p. 5). In the most common repeated note technique, though, different fingers relinquish contact with the keys in order to take each other's place—commonly, for example, the middle finger, followed by the pointer finger, followed by the thumb. Although in this case, the hand is not completely stuck to the keys, the reason the technique of replacing the fingers works so well is that the time it takes to transfer from one finger to the next corresponds with the natural bounce speed of the keyboard. The fingers thus feel as if they are part of the action of the keyboard. It is at once disconcerting—a feeling of being outside of myself—and deeply satisfying.

Elaine Scarry reminds us that the disembodying phenomenon of touch is closely connected with pleasure:

> If [the woman] experiences across the skin of her fingers...the feel of the fine weave of another woman's work, or if she traces the lettering of an engraved message and becomes mindful not of events in her hands but of the form and motivating force of the signs, or if that night she experiences the intense feelings across the skin of her body not as her own body but as the intensely feelable presence of her beloved, she in each of these moments experiences the sensation of 'touch' not as bodily sensations but as self-displacing, self-transforming objectification; and so far are these moments from physical pain, that if they are named as bodily occurrences at all, they will be called 'pleasure', a word usually reserved either for moments of overt disembodiment, or, as here, moments when acute bodily sensations are experienced as something other than one's own body.
>
> *(Scarry 1987, p. 166)*

The fingers in contact with the keys, when the repetition goes smoothly, are experienced in this way—as not the body but the keyboard—tended and extended. The body itself is only felt when something goes wrong. A glitch or a falter, in which a repeated note fails to sound or a finger slips, suddenly makes the pianist aware again of their body as a sensing organ, rather than an instrumental extension. When an error occurs, I feel a jolt and make a conscious adjustment to my body, until I can regain the sense of being part of the machine. For Scarry, a sensation of touch that is felt within the body, rather than beyond it, is the experience of pain. 'If a thorn cuts through the skin of the woman's finger, she feels not the thorn but her body hurting her' (ibid.).

Repeated notes can also be disembodying in another way. Some pianists claim that the trick to mastering these repeated touches is to assimilate multiple sounding notes into a single gesture. Rather than treating every touch as intentional—as the product of a conscious, linear relationship from synapse to the tip of the digit—multiple notes are grouped into one intention. This technique—in its use of multiple fingers and grouping of multiple notes—creates what might be thought of as an extra finger. The repeating fingers together form a new digit that touches repeatedly, even as in their singularity their touch is not successive. Peter Szendy (2016) describes the possibility of such created digits using the term 'effiction', which refers to bodily forms, organs, and digits created by the instrument. Szendy is particularly interested in the keyboard in this respect, for unlike a wind instrument, or even a stringed instrument, keyboard fingering is completely arbitrary: any finger (or any appendage—see David Rakowski's piece *Schnozzage*, for example) can play any note on the keyboard. Because of this, the use of the digits at the instrument fabricates 'phantom limbs' (*membres fantômes*), which—as 'effictions'—are both 'effective' and 'fictional' (Szendy 2016, p. 15). There is no real sixth finger, created by the two, or three, or four that repeat, but nonetheless, such a finger acts.

Indeed, studies of Braille readers—who use three fingers to touch their alphabet—have shown that from a neurological perspective, such fictional fingers are not so far-fetched. According to one study, 'the cortical somatosensory representation of the fingers is topographically disordered' (Sterr 1998, p. 4417), although we might equally replace disordered with extended or enhanced.

When researchers touched one of the fingers, the Braille readers would often misperceive which of their fingers was being touched. Through such touches, we see that body is not only disembodied and extended beyond itself, but also re-embodied in new ways.

This suggests to me that such touches—and touch at the keyboard in general—cannot be thought of as linear. There is much more to touching the piano, and touching the piano in succession, than the contact of a single finger with a single key. The digits multiply themselves such that their interaction with the instrument becomes not only digital, but also analog: not only buttons that are down or up, but also a continuity in which digits are blurred and blended (see also Moseley 2015). Moreover, the quality of the pianist's touch relies on their capacity to listen, on the sound that the piano emits. This sonic feedback further complicates the analogousness of touch, as sound has its own surrounding tactility. Frances Dyson reminds us that

> to hear is also to be touched, both physically and emotionally [...]. In listening, one is engaged in a synergy with the world and the senses, a hearing/touch that is the essence of what we mean by gut reaction—a response that is simultaneously physiological and psychological, body and mind.
>
> *(Dyson 2009, p. 4)*

Equally, Pauline Oliveros' sonic meditations suggest that to touch can also be to hear, when, for example, she calls us to 'walk so softly that the bottom of [our] feet become ears' (Oliveros 1974).

As an extension of the instrument, the pianist strikes the key with a digit, is touched by the resulting sounding phenomenon of the hammer against the string, responds to the physical feedback of both the finger and the ear, and—in the brief time during which the action resets between two successive repeated notes—adjusts and resets her own body before touching once again. Through repetition, touch multiplies in time. And through repetition, touch also multiplies in space, existing across multiple points of contact with the body. So repeated touch brings up a series of questions about touch that might guide an investigation in other domains: is touch singular or is it multiple? Is it analog or is it digital? Is it possible to speak of *the* sense of touch?

Form: the pianist's touch

The question of the singularity of the sense of touch has been a part of philosophical conversation about the subject since Aristotle's memorable investigation in *De Anima,* in which he inquires not only as to whether touch is a single sense or a group of senses, but equally exposes touch's lack of a singularly definable sense organ (see also Paterson 2007). Indeed, at the very least, it seems necessary to consider instead the senses (plural) of touch. Equally, as Mika Elo points out, we must be careful with the senses of 'sense', which is also a multiplicity, encompassing both the body and the mind (cf. Elo and Miika 2018). At the piano, this intersection of touch and knowledge can be sensed linguistically, in the use of the term 'touch' to also refer to the pianist's faculty and ability. A pianist with 'a good touch' does not only make a good sound but is also skilled in a more general sense. Even the recognition of touch as a technique emphasizes the link it draws between the mind and the body.

Touch at the piano also refers to an elusive sonic quality that is deeply personal and affective. A pianist might have a 'sensitive touch' or even a 'magic touch', and a pianist's performance can 'touch' the audience emotionally. The relationship between touch and affect, of course, extends beyond the piano, and is a theme of much writing and philosophical literature about touch (as it is in writing about affect). In *Touching Feeling*, Eve Kosofsky Sedgwick reminds us that

> the same double meaning, tactile plus emotional, is already there in the single word "touching"; it is equally internal to the word "feeling". I am also encouraged in this association by the dubious epithet "touchy-feely" with its implication that even to talk about affect virtually amounts to cutaneous contact.
>
> *(Sedgwick 2002, p. 17)*

This affective quality brings to mind the way in which touch tenders a relationship between a body and the world. Let us re-examine the pianist's repeated notes in context. Whether in the opening of Ravel's exuberant and haunting *Scarbo,* or in the clean, exactitude of a Scarlatti Sonata, or as an improvised gesture—on stage, the pianist's touch extends not only to the instrument but also outward, to the listeners. The sound reverberates in the space and among the bodies of the audience as it returns to the listening pianist, whose keyboard touch is affected by the touch of its sonic feedback. The presence and placement of listeners—in any size or kind of space—change and affect the sonic vibrations, as these vibrations touch and are absorbed by their bodies. When Benjamin Piekut states, memorably, that 'every musical performance is the performance of a relationship' (Piekut 1998, p. 2), it is worth considering the extent to which that relationship is literally a relationship of sonic touching, even as it is also a relationship in which listeners are emotionally touched by a performer's presence. If nothing else, performance is related to touch because—as Elizabeth Harvey writes—it also 'relies upon contiguity or proximity for its operations' (Harvey 2016, p. 2).

And yet, touch is not only confined to proximity, as Sarah Jackson emphasizes in her exquisite reflection on poetic touch, in which she draws out 'the non-contact at the heart of touching' (Jackson 2011, p. 171) through Anne Carson's *The Beauty of the Husband: a fictional essay in 29 tangos.* Jackson aptly points out that the very genre of the tango invoked in Carson's title already combines distance with touch—a dance that originated as 'the dramatic expression of resistance to political and racial hegemony' (ibid., p. 174) and keeps bodies separate while still intimate. Indeed, distance is maintained too in the act of translation—in the gap between music and dance in any such genre, as well as in the gap of poetic composition to a musical and choreographic form. Carson touches music and dance with her poetry, but in such a way that the distinctions between the genres are held apart: we are not confused as to whether Carson's tangos are poetry, music, or dance.

In this way, we recognize how touch is also an act of setting apart and marking borders. According to Derrida, touching 'must touch on the untouchable' (Derrida 2000, p. 6) and in so doing also defines its untouchable separate parts. Take, again, the pianistic body, touching the repeated notes. In contact with the piano, the pianist's body is configured as an extension of the keyboard, and her limbs rearranged to suit and respond to the specific technical touch at play. But what of the pianist's body prior to the keyboard? Outside of the relationship to the keyboard, there is no pianist-body. Instead, it is the touch at the keyboard that creates the very body that touches it. As Szendy writes:

> what does *having* a body, and a body that is *mine,* really mean when I lift my hands from the keyboard, and, in this suspended time, little by little, the vibrations, tacts, and contacts dissipate, and the innervations slowly come undone….
>
> *(Szendy 2016, p. 1)*

Equally, it is in the act of touch that it marks *itself* out as a distinct entity, while creating the very bodies that are both demarcated and joined by touching. In this respect, we might call touch 'performative'. Just like, in Austin's performative theory, much is revealed about the action when it goes wrong—the body is most obvious, not in successful touches but rather in the misfires of touch, when it fails to speak the note or strike the key. Touch becomes itself as it acts, and acts beyond its mere content—to share a touch with another person is much more than the contact between palm and shoulder, just as the touch of the finger at the instrument acts beyond the mechanism of the instrument, which transforms from pure mechanism into action. Therefore, touch is performative, negotiating—as per Elin Diamond—'between a doing and a thing done' (Diamond 2015, p. 1).

Method: touching Performance Philosophy

Performance, too, is touch, tending—Derrida's 'giving that is given without giving up'—which brings me to the subject of this chapter: touch as a 'method, technique, genre, or form' of performance philosophy. In this investigation, the pianist's encounter with touch at the instrument (inevitably, my own encounter) has demonstrated a multiplicity within touch, in its porous capacities as sense, sound, knowledge, and affect, and shown how touch itself appears at the limits between these senses. Furthermore, it has explored touch as enacting a kind of relationship, showing that insofar as music and performance are relational experiences, it is through literal and metaphorical touch—imaginative relationships between two bodies—that such relationality is enacted. Finally, it suggests a close relationship between touch and performativity, suggesting that performance is a productive mode with which to understand touch.

Beyond the fact that philosophical investigations of touch have formed part of this analysis, by what means might touch inform this elusive, emergent discipline, whose name already suggests an equal contact between the two nominal forms of 'performance' and 'philosophy'? In his non-manifesto for the field, Esa Kirkkopelto writes that

> performance philosophy opens up a field in which performance, performance makers and performers can make contact with philosophical thinking without the advocacy of intermediary disciplines and in equal dialogue with them, learn to think in their own terms, and become understood by others.
>
> *(Kirkkopelto 2015, p. 2)*

I have already given away part of my answer in the question, for I think that one important gesture is simply to think performance philosophy as a means by which two bodies of thought and thinking can touch each other. I am inspired here by the 'pathic touch' of Laura Gröndahl and Sami Santanen, who—like Derrida—suggest that touch is always a recognition of the incompleteness of touching contact (c.f. Elo and Miika 2018). Touch also cannot exist without being touched by the other—it is reciprocal, and thus also requires recognition of an unknowable otherness, just as it allows for intimate extension. At the intersection of performance and philosophy, we see touch emerge at the limit; as Anne Daly writes of dance criticism, 'it is a surpassing gesture, like Pollock's excursive stroke, the one that touches without making contact' (Daly 2002, p. xvi).

Kirkkopelto also calls for performance philosophy to be enacted 'in a way that indicates both the possibility of change and a way to bring it about in critical relation to the given institutional order of things' (Kirkkopelto 2015, p. 3). Privileging touch in our forms of thinking and performing allows us to engage with a form of critical performance philosophy that is eternally present and political. I am reminded of Fred Moten and Stefano Harney, for whom politics encompasses 'hapticality, the capacity to feel through others, for others to feel through you, for you to feel them feeling you' (Harney, Stefano, and Fred Moten 2013, p. 98). Audre Lorde, as a Black lesbian feminist, saw 'the erotic'—the capacity 'to share the power of each other's feelings' (Lorde 1978, p. 58) —as a powerful tool against oppression. Via the erotic, she claims, 'not only do we touch our most profoundly creative source, but we do that which is female and self-affirming in the face of a racist, patriarchal, and anti-erotic society' (ibid., p. 59). By centering touch as a crucial method of the discipline, we remember and are called upon to use performance philosophy as a form of challenge.

It is ironic that touch might hold such critical potential for performance, philosophy, and thought in a context in which touch is also seen as the 'next frontier' for technology. In the technological realm, the haptic promises more efficient and effective means of messaging, knowing, and (no doubt) buying, and—as Mika Elo writes—privileges a direct relationship between touch and visuality, sense-perception and certainty (Elo and Miika 2018, p. 56). In this context, can we redeem and recall the opposing capacity of touch to critique, unlearn, and break apart? To harness touch purely for its productive capabilities ignores that its strength lies in the dialectic between these poles—indeed, between Scarry's pain and pleasure. If we keep touch in mind as a point of critical contact within and between performance and philosophy, perhaps we will also keep our minds in touch, feeling through and with each other our capacity for performative critique and critical performance philosophy.

Note

1 The material in this chapter was first presented at 'Thinking Through Touch', a lecture-performance in collaboration with Sasha Amaya and Cam Scott, that was produced by tick tock and performed at Performance Philosophy Prague in 2017.

References

Bricard, Nancy. 1990. 'The Piano Music of Ravel', in: Nancy Bricard (ed.). *Ravel, Gaspard de la Nuit: Three Poems for Piano by Aloysius Bertrand*, New York: Alfred Music.
Daly, Ann. 2002. *Critical Gestures: Writings on Dance and Culture*. Middletown: Wesleyan University Press.
Deleuze, Gilles. 1994. *Difference and Repetition*, trans. by Paul Patton. New York: Columbia University Press.
Derrida, Jacques. 2000. *On Touching — Jean-Luc Nancy,* trans. by Christine Irizarry. Stanford, CA: Stanford University Press.
Diamond, Elin. 2015. *Performance and Cultural Politics*. New York: Routledge.
Dyson, Frances. 2009. *Sounding New Media: Immersion and Embodiment in the Arts and Culture*. Berkeley: University of California Press.
Ehrlich, Cyril. 1990. *The Piano: A History*. Clarendon Paperbacks, Oxford: Oxford University Press.
Elo, Mika, and Miika Luoto, eds. 2018. *Figures of Touch: Sense, Technics, Body*. Helsinki: The Academy of Fine Arts at the University of Helsinki.
Harney, Stefano, and Fred Moten. 2013. *The Undercommons: Fugitive Planning & Black Study*. Brooklyn, NY: Autonomedia.
Harvey, Elizabeth. 2016. *Sensible Flesh: On Touch in Early Modern Culture*. Philadelphia: University of Pennsylvania Press.
Jackson, Sarah. 2011. 'Dis-Tanz: 29 Tangos', *Oxford Literary Review*, Vol. 33, pp. 167–187.
Kirkkopelto, Esa. 2015. 'For What Do We Need Performance Philosophy?'. *Performance Philosophy*, Vol. 1, pp. 1–3 <http://www.performancephilosophy.org>

Lorde, Audre. 1978. 'Uses of the Erotic: The Erotic as Power', in Audre Lorde: *Sister Outsider. Essays and Speeches*. Berkeley: Crossing Press, pp. 53–59.

Moseley, Roger. 2015. 'Digital Analogies: The Keyboard as Field of Musical Play', *Journal of the American Musicological Society*, Vol. 68, pp. 151–227.

Oliveros, Pauline. 1974. *Sonic Meditations*, American Music. Sharon, VT: Smith Publications.

Paterson, Mark. 2007. *The Senses of Touch: Haptics, Affects and Technologies*. Oxford: Berg Publishers.

Piekut, Benjamin. 1998. *Experimentalism Otherwise: The New York Avant-Garde and Its Limits*, California Studies in 20th-Century Music. Middletown, CT: Wesleyan University Press.

Scarry, Elaine. 1987. *The Body in Pain: The Making and Unmaking of the World*. Oxford: Oxford University Press.

Sedgwick, Eve Kosofsky. 2002. *Touching Feeling: Affect, Pedagogy, Performativity*. Durham, NC: Duke University Press.

Sterr, A., et al. 1998. 'Perceptual Correlates of Changes in Cortical Representation of Fingers in Blind Multifinger Braille Readers', *The Journal of Neuroscience: The Official Journal of the Society for Neuroscience*, Vol. 18, pp. 4417–4423.

Szendy, Peter 2016. *Phantom Limbs: On Musical Bodies*, trans. by Will Bishop. Oxford: Oxford University Press.

27

IN-BETWEEN: A METHODOLOGY OF PERFORMATIVE PHILOSOPHY

Thoughts on embodiment and the public (with Helmuth Plessner) reflecting the philosophy-performance-festival [soundcheck philosophie][1]

Eva Maria Gauss and Katrin Felgenhauer

Introduction

There are two observations that guide our interest: the first is that Western academic philosophy does not sufficiently take into account that we always philosophize as persons, i.e. as physical and social beings. The second is that while philosophy exists as a discipline in academic practice, it also has a special proximity to everyday life and life in general, which is not adequately realized in academic practice. In other words, academic philosophy lacks the reflection of its own habitus. We intend to recognize these aspects as an essential part of philosophizing: reflection of the embodiment of thinking, on the one hand, and its social integration, on the other. It is in this sense that we understand our research as an instance in Performative Philosophy. It is decisive that the following theoretical reflections are based on practical concerns and experiences. Consequently, we will elaborate first on the *context* of our thoughts.

In the German-speaking world, the term *Performative Philosophie* (Performative Philosophy) was probably first introduced in 2012 in the context of the second edition of the festival series [soundcheck philosophie].[2] With the initial project dedicated to "communicative formats of thinking" (*Vermittlungsformate des Denkens*), which provided funding for the first two festivals, the goal was to bring together scholars and artists who were doing philosophy in certain explicitly performative ways, for instance, on stage, in artistic forms, addressing the public (as opposed to a purely academic audience) or with a particular connection to life experiences. Following the first edition of the festival, we came across the term Performative Philosophy and found it fitting for what we were trying to do. On the one hand, we wanted to expand the conventional ways of doing philosophy, which are too limited to a few forms of expression and communication (university lectures and conversations in seminars, essays and academic publications). On the other hand, we wanted to open up a critical approach to philosophizing by understanding thinking as an aesthetic phenomenon.

The initial project [soundcheck philosophie] started with the following questions: "Does a social discourse on complex theoretical questions require new forms of communicative representation?" and "To what extent can the stage be a laboratory for thinking?" For the first two editions of the festival, there was a focus on displaying the communicative prerequisites and possibilities of forms of expression and formats of conversation, beside the concern for a general exploration of the relationship between philosophy and art. Since then, we, the authors of this text, have come to clearly understand Performative Philosophy as a methodological approach to philosophy which necessarily involves an addressing of the question 'what is philosophy?' Moreover, if Performative Philosophy claims to contribute to the discipline of philosophy, our experiments on stage, in conversation and in other forms must critically address the criteria set by this academic field of knowledge. For a rough orientation, we can specify the relation of Performative Philosophy to the concrete project [soundcheck philosophie], and we can also specify the relation between Performative Philosophy and Performance Philosophy to the project [soundcheck philosophie]. The project [soundcheck philosophie] can be seen as one activity among others within the more general field of Performance Philosophy. We consider the field of Performance Philosophy as primarily concerned with the relationship between performance and philosophy. It refers to, and might address more strongly, other fields of knowledge and tradition, like other humanities or artistic practices, than explicitly academic philosophy, which we consider as a central point of reference and address for Performative Philosophy. Accordingly, we understand Performative Philosophy as a form of theoretical reflection, as a methodological approach with a self-grasping movement in thinking that can also be applied to work in the academic and social practice of philosophy outside of universities. And coming back to the developing project: at this point in time, we wish the festival [soundcheck philosophie] to be dedicated to the cultivation and development of this methodological approach. In this respect, the festival can be seen as part of the explorative field developing and conceptualizing Performative Philosophy, and Performative Philosophy as an articulation of a methodological perspective in the field of Performance Philosophy.

Since the first two editions of the festival [soundcheck philosophie], the debate on the conceptualization of Performative Philosophy has continued. As organizers, curators and contributors, the questions about criteria in the diversity of approaches and formats have both theoretical and practical significance. For example: What demands have to be met for something to become an act of philosophical thinking? What is a dramaturgy of thinking? How much prior knowledge may or may not a philosophical performance presuppose? Which formats are better, which are less appropriate for philosophically thinking together? What situations at all enable us to think (together)? With regard to the practical impact of these questions, curating itself is a form of collective artistic research: how to approach a topic, whether approaches to understanding and joint exchange can be found at all, and ultimately the whole dynamic of the festival, depends strongly on which contributions are invited, how they are arranged and how they are reflected upon with the audience. Each edition of [soundcheck philosophie] is therefore preceded by intensive working meetings and workshops, which serve to present and discuss possible contributions and to try out new formats. Even though there is no agreement among the protagonists of Performative Philosophy regarding the prerequisites to be fulfilled in order for what is shown and communicated to constitute philosophical thinking, we can find these two key aspects in all contributions shown at the festival: thinking is considered bodily and social – or stated more broadly: as involving the public.

Let us now move on to a theoretical reflection on (but also *from* the practice of) Performative Philosophy. The two concepts that we would like to let resonate together – embodiment and the public – are central concepts for Performative Philosophy in general and so they are too in the philosophy of Helmuth Plessner (1892–1985). Following on from Husserl and Dilthey, Plessner develops a cultural philosophy in the interweaving of phenomenological and hermeneutic methods that takes its approach from the human being as a *living* being and is thus, alongside philosophers such as Maurice Merleau-Ponty, Emmanuel Levinas or Bernhard Waldenfels, representative of a philosophy of the body. Plessner seeks to establish a "new philosophy" that is able to "comprehend the human as the subject object of culture and as the subject object of nature" (Plessner 1928, p. 70).[3] All human creativity or work of the mind "crosses with the level of [their] bodily existence" (ibid., p. 71). From this double aspect of human existence ("excentric positionality"), Plessner derives the programme of his philosophical method. His central question about the relationship between mind and nature is answered, apparently in cultural philosophy: culture is embodied mind. Plessner's philosophy is characterized by the fact that he neither thinks dualistically (soul and body as separate entities), nor does he conjure a unit monistically, but he recognizes the common experience of the separation of inside (soul) and outside (body) in order to understand their entanglement and inherent rupture.

If philosophizing can be understood as a bodily activity and if (philosophical) thinking can (also) be public, how can this be adequately thought about in the context of an academic article such as this? In the following, our usual writing and reading habits are slightly interrupted by graphically contrasting the two sides of the theoretical core as parallel columns – an intermediate space is created; bridges might appear. It is up to the reader to decide which aspect to start with or continue reading, or whether to switch between the two. Please enjoy the reading experience in which the two interdependent concepts, side by side, touch in confusion and conjunction.

Thinking in Public

During the first edition of the festival [soundcheck philosophie], a matinée entitled "Thinking in Public" invited people to discuss the question of whether thinking must necessarily be considered public. To approach this question within this framework it is important to clarify (a) what we mean in saying thinking is public, (b) how we understand the concept of the public and (c) in what modality thinking acts in public.

(a) With the concept of public thinking we want to grasp a thinking that does not operate in a closed system. It is recognized that no object can be fully understood within any theoretical system, i.e. the object is autonomous from the theoretical reference. In this respect, there is a gap between reference and object.

Embodying Thinking

At the public conference "Saying or showing: Embodying thinking? Showing Thought?" during the second festival, contributors presented their work exploring various forms of expression of philosophy. Processes of embodying thinking are central in this research, as the body is the first medium of any expression. But what exactly is embodying thinking? To address this and the general question of embodiment, following Plessner, we can discuss three different aspects: (a) body, (b) expression and (c) expressivity.

(a) The relationship of the human to their own body is the cardinal question of Philosophical Anthropology. Plessner begins in his hermeneutic-phenomenological method with the distinction between inorganic and organic bodies in order to comprehend human life.

This gap is essential for a thinking that we want to understand as public thinking. That is to say, if the gap, the in-between, is closed in the precondition of a principle or mediated in a third position, public thought can no longer be spoken of. Helmuth Plessner can be drawn upon to understand the meaning of the in-between more precisely. For a start, he speaks about philosophy as a public science in order to say that **there is no such thing as philosophy as such but different philosophies with regard to object and method** (Plessner 1947, pp. 170ff.). Compared to the natural sciences, which are entitled to enquire into the condition of possibility of their objects, philosophy must abstain from this question (cf. Plessner 1931, p. 171). Only then can a researcher be open minded to the things themselves, because how they appear and are experienced cannot be decided a priori: the objects of philosophy must be approached as unfathomable and not bound to a transcendental point that obscures their manifestation. But only a thinking that accepts itself as unfathomable too, that is, that does not presuppose an ego-transparent subjectivity, can remain open in such a way that even the unexpected can appear. Such an attitude requires the commitment of one's own bodiliness (*Leiblichkeit*) which serves as the resonant surface of affection (cf. 'bodily resonance' – *leibliche Resonanz* – Breyer 2015, pp. 48ff.). Unlike the scientific subject-irrelative form of intuition which lowers the phenomenon, an intuition which is open to phenomenal richness must necessarily be subjective. In other words, **epistemologically, a thing only appears in itself in a public space that is constituted by different fleshly subjects**. Insofar as objects are on public display, they are exposed. The idea that objectivity means "exposed to everyone" is introduced in Husserl's phenomenology (Husserl 2012, p. 124). However, Husserl acts on the assumption of a transcendental intersubjectivity. Here, we argue for a real intersubjectivity of various concrete subjects. We believe that such an approach to public thinking needs to be tested practically, again and again.

Inorganic bodies are space-filling, their boundary is the transition from one materiality to another; **organic bodies, on the other hand, are space-maintaining, their boundary belongs to the body and is an exchange organ for contact with the environment. Man now knows about his boundary as an area of expression.**

Consequently, all expressive behaviour is culturally shaped, which is obvious in phenomena such as clothing and acting, but is also the case in the individual shaping of "natural expression" in the form of habitus. This basic structure is doubly reflexive: **On the one hand I am as a body (in space), on the other hand, I am in and with body.** Both aspects (body-being and body-having) are real and incompatible, as the experiences are each in their own right – there is no reconciling and unifying mode. The human *knows* about this double aspect. In a double detachment from his/her own body s/he is set in relation to him/herself. S/he is captured in the dilemma (hiatus), not suspended in a third position. An individual who is "positionally triply characterized" (*as* body, as *in* or *with* a body, and "as the point of view from which it is both") "is called a person" (Plessner 1928, p. 365). Note: To be *in* or *with* a body is the same but often indicated as the difference between having a body and being a body. Furthermore this is a slightly different description of the distinction between *body* and *lived body* (*Körper vs. Leib*) than is commonly known. The lived body here is always an experience of the self-dividedness of body and lived body. Volker Schürmann (2019, pp. 241–242) points out that Plessner focusses on the *relationship* between body, lived body and third aspect person. Each of these three dimensions is to be understood as bodily, which means to focus on the process, *the doing* in physical self-objectification. This differs from other phenomenologies of the body. The question is, **how do we deal with this situation, how do we express it?** So, the work involved in exploring the bodily side of doing philosophy must involve research into (1) the articulation of philosophy as always corporally bound communication, that means a certain kind of interaction,

Insofar as a concrete public is actively constituted and transformed in philosophy performances, philosophy performances are capable of working on the concept of public thinking. This requires, however, a theoretical concept of the public that is open to such transformative processes.

(b) An approach to understanding the public primarily as an exhibition space can be found in Plessner's concept of *excentric positionality* (Plessner 1928). According to Plessner, the intentional structure of our experience is excentric. That is to say that we not only experience, but we experience our experience – we perceive ourselves as being perceptive in the world. I am the *subject* of my experiences and, at the same time, the *object* of my experiences in the knowledge of them. In the interlinking of the inner perspective and the outer perspective, I know about my own interactions with the environment and perceive myself as a living being exposed in the world. However, the knowledge of our environmental relation does not mean that the relation is in any way rationally *available* to us: the interlink does not form a sphere of its own, like the Kantian pure rationality or the Hegelian ghost, but is as *in-between* just the hiatus, i.e. "the empty transition of mediation" ("das leere Hindurch der Vermittlung") of body and soul (ibid, p. 365). Elsewhere Plessner refers to the in-between as the sphere of behaviour (Plessner 1925, p. 88). Now, **if we understand this in-between as the public sphere, we hereby first and foremost do not refer to a normative sphere but to the simple fact that something is revealed** (cf. Plessner 1960, p. 213). So this approach to publicity does not argue for a specific society with certain conventions. And that is why we can use this consideration to distinguish two basic elements of the public: we can distinguish between the familiar and the unfamiliar; between the ordinary and the extraordinary (cf. Waldenfels 1997, pp. 77ff.). **Contrary to many theories of the public that postulate a third instance (discourse, norm, convention, habitus) which acts as the mediating measure for the social participants, a concept that understands the public primarily**

(2) the physical processes of following a thought and (3) the shapedness of thinking by our bodies. One initial challenge is to think all aspects of this self-objectivation. The greater challenge is to understand and practice this body-bound, reflexive, basic structure itself as a mental (*geistige*) activity of philosophy.

(b) Following the notion of "expression" (*Ausdruck*), we will now try to understand what this embodied philosophy could be. How do I communicate to others in expression? How the medial relationship is constituted is paramount in this regard. The gap between one person and another is unbridgeable. However, it is not the assumption by analogy that I see others as persons that enables me to understand others, but it is the human structure that allows one to get in touch with others. To describe this, Plessner introduces the terms "spirit", "we-sphere" and "shared world", used almost synonymously. **It is the sphere of the "we" which strictly understood has to be named "spirit"** (Plessner 1928, p. 377) **and in which "all human matters meet"** ("*alle menschlichen Dinge sich begegnen*"). It is the sphere of the shared world (*Mitwelt*), in which the mediation of an inner world (soul) and an outer world (body) becomes visible. The co-world has no specific substance (like inner world and outer world), but rests on its specific structure of revealing the opposing relationship between inner world and outer world in the sphere of the spirit. **Expression is therefore not to be understood as the "bulge" of an "inside", but as a border relationship, as a producing-interaction-relationship with the world around us**, in which the acting subject themselves is situated in the world and against the world (ex-centric, in and outside their centre). In this sense, communication – including that of philosophy performances – does not function as a transport of information, but as an encounter in-between. Language is often indicated as a characteristic of the human being, but this is only a concise form of expressivity among others. Plessner notes for philosophy a "tense relationship to language" as an exhibition space includes the revealed thing in itself: **It is not sacrificed to a systemic thought.** I can therefore take into account that there is something about it that eludes me (my control). This elusiveness (*Unverfügbarkeit*) is particularly evident in the phenomena of failure. Likewise it becomes clear in the phenomenon of surprise. However, we must then understand these phenomena in their own right and not as, say, deviations from the so called "normal". Therefore we have to train our attention – something that Bernhard Waldenfels, as well as Plessner, points out. Both refer to the capacity of the arts to cultivate an attention that can be alienated, i.e. that can be addressed by the extraordinary (cf. Plessner 1953, pp. 99ff.; c.f. Waldenfels 2006, pp. 105ff.). **Philosophy performances are capable of training and challenging our attention.** This training can be seen as a basic condition for a public space that is kept open as a place of appearance. By renouncing the transcendental question of the possibility of the phenomenon, we release the view of its concrete reality, that expresses itself by itself. Now what is left to ask is what this means for **the way in which thinking becomes public** in

(Plessner 1947, p. 189), for the human being "a specific tense relationship to their own body" (ibid. 1946, p. 64) – both result from the necessity of expression and the knowledge that the expression is inadequate.

It is good to remind oneself that linguistic expression – including that of philosophy – is basically a special form of animal contact behaviour (Plessner 1967, p. 475). Having this basis of language in mind, the challenge is to think what it might mean to get in touch with others in doing philosophy. Linguistic expression is the human-specific ability to communicate *about* something. Consequently, a philosophy that understands itself as a behaviour of expression and a thinking movement would have to play with the specific dilemma of the *about*, that "the presence of what is meant is felt in the wrapping of what is said" ("*in der Umhüllung des Gesagten gespürt*") (ibid. 1967, p. 476). It is possible for human, in perceiving their limitation, to grasp their limitation (cf. ibid., p. 463).

Sometimes in philosophical performances artistic expression is used to show how limited language is. But in Performative Philosophy artistic expression seeks to have what is said truly coincide with what is meant – something that is never quite possible in language itself (cf. ibid., p. 476), but can be brought to its limits **performative play.**

(c) Let us now return to Plessner's concept of excentric positionality. From the postulate of an excentrically structured intentionality, it follows that the relation of a human being to their environment seems to be more complex than, for example, and without ascribing value, that of an animal. In contrast to humans, animals perform their environmental relation in *natural naturalness*. Humans, on the other hand, as they know about their relation with the world, perform it in *natural artificiality* (Plessner 1928, pp. 383ff. Natural artificiality, *natürliche Künstlichkeit*, is one of three fundamental anthropological laws that Plessner states.) To emphasize the artificial character of the human-world interrelation we may say that **each and every human activity can be seen as a performance** (cf. Schechner 2002, pp. 22ff.).

(c) Expressivity is the term in which human contact behaviour in spirit becomes a concept in Plessner's philosophy and in which the term embodiment stresses the social and bodily dimension. The terms expression, expressivity and embodiment are closely related and emerge one after the other in the genesis of Plessner's work where they are successively concretized. Their different accentuations can be summarized as follows: while expression refers to the concrete behaviour of (all) living beings (whereas in human expressions spirit and body are interwoven), expressivity stands for the basic situation that is specific to humans. In his later works, Plessner uses embodiment to describe not only concrete bodily expressive behaviour but also its social dimension.

In other words, human vitality is expressive: I cannot *not* behave or communicate, as Watzlawick says. For Plessner, expressivity is an essential human feature, which is wider than the classical characteristic of language. However, language has a special position in the field of expression for Plessner. Through language, the expressive relation in which the human lives within the world is grasped in expressions (Plessner 1928, p. 340). Thus, language provides the "true existential proof" ("*wahre Existentialbeweis*") for the excentric position (ibid). But expressivity means more than the ability to speak – a capacity which representatives of a language-analytical approach too quickly equate with rationality, which is understood, in turn, as non-expressive disembodied thinking. However, what interests Plessner is the relation of the human to his/her/their body (especially themed in Plessner 1941). **The essential feature of expressivity is based on the double detachment of one's own body: I experience myself as a body within a body** – as a private ego to which I attribute thoughts and psychic constitutions, and as an embodied public ego. **Knowing that both I's are I does not help to cover the gap between me and me.** Here one can find a reason why I may seem foreign to myself – a human peculiarity that is interesting for psychopathological research (cf. the works of Thomas Fuchs) and with which it is possible to play on stage (cf. Valerie 2016; Plessner 1948). It follows, first, that thinking is not an ability of a self-identical subject. To that extent, instead of unifying thinking in a transcendental origin or telos, it seems more interesting to **focus on the gap between me and me, me and you. The in-between vanishes when I postulate a transcendental principle**. In order to focus on the in-between, the following is important. Namely that **thinking must be considered as bodily**. Whenever thoughts are expressed, however conventionally that may be – in books, within a presentation, in a lecture – they are realized within a form and the form cannot be separated from the content, because it only results in the realization (Plessner 1928, p. 415).

The expression of the "**embodiment-function of the senses**" (ibid. 1970, pp. 370–384) **acquires meaning quite basally, which is to say that the human gives meaning to their world through concrete physical performance and effort.** To understand human nature, we must therefore start from the broad and abundant varieties of expression and understand the intertwining of mental and physical expression components (cf. ibid. 1941, p. 215). Doing philosophy is a specific cultural activity and one should be attentive to the embodying work in doing philosophy, as it is only in work that the (mental-bodily) organization of the senses appears; **we need to understand "spirit as work embodied in performance"**(*Geist als in Leistung verkörperte Arbeit* (ibid. 2003, p. 318, cf. ibid. 1970, p. 384). The concept of expressivity, which Plessner describes from cultural behaviour of expressions, language, up to historicity, is formulated in the anthropological basic law of "mediated immediacy: immanence and expressivity". Expressivity goes hand in hand with the experience of immanence, the experience of contents of consciousness. The basis for both (the innerworld aspect of immanence and the outerworld aspect of expressivity) is the borderline experience of mediated immediacy, which is already present in the relationship of a human being to their own body. **The mediation goes through them, because they must carry out the mediation from their particular position**: "The knowledge of the object is the mediation between himself and him" (ibid. 1925, p. 404). **Thus, expressivity is described as the necessary behaviour of a living being for whom the world is objective.** The work of acting is called embodiment, as it shows us the entanglement of having and being a body and the activity that is needed to handle this double relationship. Therefore acting gains an important explanatory status in Plessner's work. Imitation is part of this craft and, like objectivation, so too is the ability to achieve distance in relation to oneself.

So thoughts are performed,
or,
in other words,
**there is a performative process
by which
thinking
becomes public.**

If one pays

attention

to thinking
as a performative process,
as is the case in philosophy performances,

the in-between itself
can become thematic for
Performative
Philosophy.

If one's relationship to one's own body is normally instrumental in expressively mediated contact with others, it becomes self-reflexive in imitation – we are thrown back on our body (cf. ibid. 1961, p. 452). Imitation does not, therefore, amount to a poor copy, but can serve as a powerful means in shaping social reality. It is not just re-iteration in time, but constitutes the embodied process of being human – throwing them back to the basic situation of being doubly detached from their own body. What's more, it is fun! Performative Philosophy may be understood by analogy as the attempt to throw us back on ourselves in expressively mediated linguistic contact. **What would it mean to understand acts of Performative Philosophy as imitations of philosophical thinking – connected to a certain pleasure in attention?**

Conclusion and outlook

What might be the characteristics of philosophy performances and what experiments are we as philosophers (always already) called upon to carry out? By outlining Plessner's concepts of "embodiment" and "the public", we wanted to reflect on a methodological approach of Performative Philosophy – not least in order to gain an orientation for our own work and to critically develop it. As curators, observers, participants or contributors in the festival [soundcheck philosophie], we are always asked to consider what makes a performance into an act of philosophy or under what circumstances do we experience philosophical thinking in public. One could claim that every good piece of art touches and brings us into common thinking. But what might be the specific modality in which *philosophical* thinking touches and brings us together? Instead of delineating what philosophy is, what another form of theorizing might be or what good art, play, thinking at all, etc., are, we would like to make explicit what we are challenged to do. It is not enough to realize that philosophy is (always already) performative; we have to develop a practice of this insight, for instance by critically questioning the performative conditions of philosophy – systematically in academia (from the perspective of institutions and traditions), as a certain way of grasping the phenomenon of performativity (from the perspective of epistemology) and as a practice of understanding the performativity of our shared world (from the perspective of the social world). For now, we understand Performative Philosophy as a methodological approach, which is significantly characterized by the movement of self-distancing (double detachment from one's own body). The self is in the world and at the same time against the world. Consequently, when speaking about the body, the world or history, the philosopher always brings along her body, her world and her history. This is how a cultural-scientific practice of self-reflection is systematically incorporated into philosophy: not only as a self-reflective movement, we propose, but also with a view to exploring and developing a whole range of human expression phenomena as modes of academic philosophical thinking. This thought is understandable for a philosophy that is open to rhetoric. Of course, in terms of the acquisition of knowledge and communication, rhetorical modes of presentation and stylistic devices then have to be understood and used as fundamental parts of understanding. And the view that rhetorical form is a part of thinking could find its way more into academic practice. A conscious use of styles of presentation of philosophical thought in text and speech could be more strongly implemented in academic education. However, there is room for a more radical consideration of the exploration and practice of a body- and life-bound reason in philosophizing – understanding human expressivity in a broad sense without forgetting to acknowledge language as a specific kind of expression. The consequence of this is that it cannot be a matter of a singular method, but of *methods plural* that need to be further developed within philosophy. Performative Philosophy is an approach to doing philosophy, always already performative itself – by grasping its own performative conditions in order to develop thoughts.

In other words: How would it be, if we understood Performative Philosophy as a *theoretical approach* and at the same time as a *practical attitude* to grasp the peculiarities of philosophizing by making this activity the subject of critical confrontation in the phenomena of its embodiment? Ultimately, the resulting play with embodiments could be considered as an invitation and opportunity to pursue a philosophy that is *fun*. And it could also be an invitation to follow a philosophy that seeks touch and contact. After all, the in-between is not to be understood as some third thing that comes between us and separates us dualistically. Rather, it is a border that separates *and* connects – a place of encounter where one makes contact with others and two directions diverge: one that throws one back upon oneself and one that opens one up to something else. In this sense, communication *about things* takes *place between us*. Maybe it would be helpful for the understanding and practice of philosophy that in considerations of truth and knowledge, one includes the concept of "understanding between us". In this sense, the gap between the columns might remind us of the work and wonder that need to happen in order to reach comprehension.

Notes

1 This text is based on a previous version first published in Czech; see Gauß and Felgenhauer (2013).
2 See www.soundcheckphilosophie.de. First held in Halle/Saale (Germany), *[soundcheck philosophie]* (the square brackets should remind of the spelling according to phonetic convention) is an ongoing festival organized by the association Expedition Philosophie e.V. It now takes place every three years in Leipzig, Germany. The initiators of this project were Matthias Kaufmann, Rainer Totzke and Eva Maria Gauß; the first two festivals (2011 and 2012) were funded by VolkswagenStiftung in a programme for the public communication of science and the humanities. Around forty contributors were invited to the first event. For further reflection on the intention, format and content of the festival, see Gauß and Totzke (2015). According to our understanding of Performative Philosophy, the development of theoretical positions is necessarily tied to testing and development in practice and must be expressed in the form of philosophical articulation. See also Tiedemann and Totzke (2019), where the term *"Performatives Philosophieren"* is introduced in the field of didactics in philosophy.
3 Translations from German by Felgenhauer & Gauß – the language has been gently adapted to meet current conventions for a gender-sensitive language. Plessner's main work, "Levels of Organic Life and the Human" (1928) has just recently been translated by Millay Hyatt (Plessner 2019).

References

Breyer, Thiemo. 2015. *Verkörperte Intersubjektivität und Empathie: philosophisch-anthropologische Untersuchungen*, Philosophische Abhandlungen Vol. 110. Frankfurt: Klostermann.

Gauß, Eva Maria & Felgenhauer, Katrin. 2013. Meziprostory: K čemu jsou filosofické performance? Úvahy o ztělesnění a veřejnosti filosofického myšlení (Interspaces: Philosophical Performances. What for? Embodiment and the publicity of philosophical thinking). *Filozofia*, vol. 68, No 5, Bratislava: IRIS, pp. 402–411.

Gauß, Eva Maria & Totzke, Rainer. 2015. "On Performative Philosophy – 10 impulses for discussion from [soundcheck philosophie]," in: *Performance Philosophy*, Vol. 1, pp. 74–94.

Husserl, Edmund. 1931/2012. *Cartesianische Meditationen. Eine Einleitung in die Phänomenologie*, Philosophische Bibliothek Vol. 644. Hamburg: Meiner.

Plessner, Helmuth. 1923/2003. "Die Einheit der Sinne. Grundlinien einer Ästhesiologie des Geistes," in id. *Anthropologie der Sinne*, Gesammelte Schriften Vol. III. Frankfurt am Main: Suhrkamp, pp. 7–315.

Plessner, Helmuth. 1925/2003. "Die Deutung des mimischen Ausdrucks. Ein Beitrag zur Lehre vom Bewusstsein des anderen Ichs," in id. *Ausdruck und menschliche Natur*, Gesammelte Schriften Vol. VII. Frankfurt am Main: Suhrkamp, pp. 67–129.

Plessner, Helmuth. 1928/2003. *Die Stufen des Organischen und der Mensch. Einleitung in die philosophische Anthropologie*, Gesammelte Schriften Vol. IV. Frankfurt am Main: Suhrkamp.

Plessner, Helmuth. 1931/2003. "Macht und menschliche Natur. Ein Versuch zur Anthropologie der geschichtlichen Weltansicht," in id. *Macht und menschliche Natur*, Gesammelte Schriften Vol. V. Frankfurt am Main: Suhrkamp, pp. 135–234.

Plessner, Helmuth. 1941/2003. "Lachen und Weinen. Eine Untersuchung der Grenzen menschlichen Verhaltens," in id. *Ausdruck und menschliche Natur*, Gesammelte Schriften Vol. VII. Frankfurt am Main: Suhrkamp, pp. 201–387.

Plessner, Helmuth. 1946/2003. "Mensch und Tier," in id. *Schriften zur Philosophie*, Gesammelte Schriften Vol. IX. Frankfurt am Main: Suhrkamp, pp. 52–65.

Plessner, Helmuth. 1947/2003. "Gibt es einen Fortschritt in der Philosophie?" in id. *Schriften zur Philosophie*, Gesammelte Schriften Vol. IX. Frankfurt am Main: Suhrkamp, pp. 169–191.

Plessner, Helmuth. 1948/2003. "Zur Anthropologie des Schauspielers," in id. *Ausdruck und menschliche Natur*, Gesammelte Schriften Vol. VII. Frankfurt am Main: Suhrkamp, pp. 399–418.

Plessner, Helmuth. 1953/2003. "Mit anderen Augen," in id. *Conditio Humana*, Gesammelte Schriften Vol. VIII. Frankfurt am Main: Suhrkamp, pp. 88–104.

Plessner, Helmuth. 1960/2003. "Das Problem der Öffentlichkeit und die Idee der Entfremdung," in id. *Schriften zur Soziologie und Sozialphilosophie*, Gesammelte Schriften Vol. X. Frankfurt am Main: Suhrkamp, pp. 212–226.

Plessner, Helmuth. 1961/2003. "Der imitatorische Akt," in id. *Ausdruck und menschliche Natur*, Gesammelte Schriften Vol. VII. Frankfurt am Main: Suhrkamp, pp. 447–457.

Plessner, Helmuth. 1967/2003. "Zur Hermeneutik nichtsprachlichen Ausdrucks," in id. *Ausdruck und menschliche Natur*, Gesammelte Schriften Vol. VII. Frankfurt am Main: Suhrkamp, pp. 459–477.

Plessner, Helmuth. 1970/2003. "Anthropologie der Sinne," in id. *Anthropologie der Sinne*, Gesammelte Schriften Vol. III. Frankfurt am Main: Suhrkamp, pp. 459–477.

Plessner, Helmuth. 2003. "Selbstdarstellung," in id. *Schriften zur Soziologie und Sozialphilosophie*, Gesammelte Schriften Vol. X. Frankfurt am Main: Suhrkamp, pp. 302–341.

Plessner, Helmuth. 2019. *Levels of Organic Life and the Human: An Introduction to Philosophical Anthropology*. Translated by Millay Hyatt. New York: Fordham University Press.

Schechner, Richard. 2002. *Performance Studies: An Introduction*. London: Routledge.

Schürmann, Volker. 2019. "Max Scheler und Helmuth Plessner – Leiblichkeit in der Philosophischen Anthropologie," in *Leiblichkeit. Geschichte und Aktualität eines Konzepts*, ed. Emmanuel Alloa, Thomas Bedorf, Christian Grüny and Tobias Nikolaus Klass, 2nd revis. and exp. ed. Tübingen: Mohr Siebeck, pp. 241–258.

Tiedemann, Markus & Totzke, Rainer. 2019. (eds.): *Performatives Philosophieren. Themenheft, Zeitschrift für Didaktik der Philosophie und Ethik*, Volume 41, No. 2. Bamberg: C.C. Buchner.

Valerie, Susanne. 2016. *Actors and the Art of Performance: Under Exposure*, trans. Laura Radosh with Alice Lagaay. London: Palgrave Macmillan.

Waldenfels, Bernhard. 1997. *Topographie des Fremden: Studien zur Phänomenologie des Fremden 1*. Frankfurt am Main: Suhrkamp.

Waldenfels, Bernhard. 2006. *Grundmotive einer Phänomenologie des Fremden*. Frankfurt am Main: Suhrkamp.

28
AFRICANIST CHOREOGRAPHY AS CULTURAL CITIZENSHIP
Thomas 'Talawa' Prestø's philosophy of Africana dance

'Funmi Adewole

In the introductory chapter of *Black Performance Theory* (BPT), Thomas F. DeFrantz and Anita Gonzalez explore how the thinking about 'black identity and representation' alters from one historical period to another within and between performance tropes (DeFrantz and Gonzalez 2014, p. 1). The authors consider the theorisation of 'Africanist aesthetics' by art historian, Robert Farris Thompson (1974), as one of the milestones in the formulation of this scholarly field. Thompson identified a number of traits which encapsulated the 'philosophies of beauty and ethics' in West African dance, which could also be found in African American culture. With this concept of Africanist aesthetics, the authors suggest, emerged 'the possibility to theorise black performance in terms of its own ontologies' (DeFrantz and Gonzalez 2014, p. 4). This category has expanded since Thompson theorised it and as other researchers continue to identify similarities between African and diaspora dances[1]. Additionally, several have used this aesthetic category as the starting point for theoretical, ethnographic, historical and philosophical analyses[2]. My interest is in the philosophical basis of choreography with Africanist aesthetics – particularly here, Thomas 'Talawa' Prestø's philosophy of Africana dance.

In this chapter, my focus is on choreography produced for the stage in the northern hemisphere. My proposition is that we view choreography as a practice of cultural citizenship[3]. I argue that this approach offers a way of engaging with the philosophical context of Africanist choreography. Secondly, I discuss the work of Thomas 'Talawa' Prestø from this vantage point. Prestø – who is of Trinidadian, Norwegian and African American heritage – started Tabanka dance ensemble in Norway in 1997. He registered it in 2007 when he decided to make it a full-time professional outfit. I write about Prestø due to his strategic involvement in shaping the cultural sphere for choreography that is based on African and diaspora forms in Norway and internationally. Additionally of interest is his choreographic approach which is informed by Africana philosophy. My main focus in this essay is his piece *I:Object* (2018).

Cultural citizenship and performance philosophy

To think of choreography as a practice of cultural citizenship is to focus on its power as a representational or 'symbolic form': with 'dialogic' propensities which generate language, as people invested in the practice engage in deciphering its meanings in a 'shared cultural space' (Hall 1997, p. 10). As Judith Hamera reminds us:

> Aesthetics are inherently social. The formal properties and presumptions intrinsic to the production and consumption of art are communicative currency developed by and circulating between artists, audiences and critics, binding them together in interpretive communities serving as bases for exchange in public and private conversations that constitute art's relational, political and affective lives.
>
> *(Hamera 2007, p. 3)*

However, the 'communicative currency' of a choreographic practice can be limited and constrained within institutional settings, which is why dance practitioners exercise their cultural rights as including the 'power to name, construct meaning' and 'to throw into question established codes and to rework frameworks of common understanding' (Stevenson 2003, p. 4). Citizenship is performative (Hildebrandt and Peters 2019 p. 5). An artist has to act as a citizen of the artistic community in order to have any impact on its artistic discourse. Cultural rights are extended when dance practitioners create performances (as their works are discursive), and also when they make statements about their artistic visions, and carry out activities which generate public and institutional interest in their work.

With globalisation, culture is increasingly organised in 'diverse networks' which supersede national boundaries (Stevenson 2003, p. 17). Theatrical dance is one such network. It is linked and partly sustained by educational establishments, archives, venues and the media, and national and global circuits of dissemination where people of all cultural and racial backgrounds seek representation. If no meaningful exchange is instigated, then a representational practice is not effective in that institutional space (Hall 1997, p. 10). The exercise and extension of cultural rights are pertinent within institutional settings, since an artist's success or failure at representing him or herself on their own terms has cultural, political and economic consequences.

This idea of choreography as a practice of cultural citizenship foregrounds the role of theatrical dance in the public sphere. It is a view that tests the possibilities of performance philosophy because it suggests a way of generating dance histories that focus on how dance practices come into being in the public sphere. According to Laura Cull, performance philosophy offers the opportunity to interrogate 'what it is *to philosophize* and *to perform* beyond disciplinary boundaries and beyond the dominant narrative of their histories' (Cull 2014, p. 33). Choreography as cultural citizenship makes the interaction between dance practitioners, institutions and audiences in the creation of meaning, and in struggles over meaning in choreography, a significant part of our theatrical dance narratives. It decentres Euro-American dance histories as a measure of artistic evaluation and opens up the possibility of exploring philosophies of performance through the politics of representation.

My professional experience, working within organisations which support the professional practice of black dancers, has shown me that histories of theatrical dance which document the ideas, theories or praxis of practitioners of Africanist choreography can hardly be generated where no institutional support or recognition is given to the importance of that knowledge (Adewole 2005, p. 14). The struggle over meaning is real. Even cultural policies, which are formulated to construct a professional context for dance, can erase the meanings that practitioners propose for their work – whether intentionally or not (Adewole 2017, pp. 135–136). Africanist choreography, as indicated by the aforementioned definitions, is a very broad category. Some choreographers and dance practitioners prefer terminology that is more specific to their artistic vision. However, the vantage point proposed here posits this site of struggle as a route to dialogue and meaningful exchange with the choreographer or dance practitioner's vision and how they articulate their practices both verbally and physically.

Africanist choreography and philosophies of continuity

Choreographers who describe their work as drawing from African and diaspora forms of dance position their aesthetics as central to the systems of representation that constitute their choreography. This differs from an approach to dance-making where Africanist aesthetics are drawn upon choreographically, but their cultural origins are made invisible (Gottschild 1998, p. 48). Certain choreographers – such as Zab Maboungou and Alphonse Tierou, who consider the articulation of their philosophy of practice to be part of their choreographic labour – are aware that the aesthetics of their choreography (which are associated with social, ceremonial or ritual practices) might be considered as 'other' in performance contexts that have been shaped by dominant Euro-American discourses. They do not make choreography in order to fit into Western discourses of art, but to address existential questions which, no doubt, mean that they will also engage with Euro-American aesthetics. Paulo Freire's concept of 'praxis' appropriately describes their rebuttal of colonial discourses and their production of knowledge through dance-making, guided by the requirements of the cultural or artistic problem at hand (Freire 2005, pp. 73–79).

I would argue that attending to the artistic vision of the choreographer of Africanist choreography, as opposed to focusing on its hybridity or liminality, provides a richer understanding of the work. 'Double consciousness' – a term used to describe the incorporation of codes which place the artistic practice both 'within and outside of the dominant culture' (Barson 2010, p. 10) – is considered a defining feature of black artistic practices. It can be misleading, however, to posit obvious juxtapositions of Africanist and European techniques in Africanist choreography as the key to understanding the choreographic work. As a representational practice, choreography can draw on a range of sources, but its meaning is not located in the separation of its parts so much as in what they come together to indicate. In many choreographic works, 'double consciousness' is contextualised within what I describe as discourses or 'philosophies of continuity'. Continuity of cultural legacy is an important trope in African and diaspora cultural production (Nettleford 1994, p. xv). Pan-Africanism, Afrofuturism, the worldviews proposed by specific cultural practices, as well as postulations and questions arising from personal or lived experience have the power to forge artistic visions through which the choreography should be viewed. Artistic vision assembles multiple sources in pursuit of cultural continuity, across historical time and geographical borders, between performance contexts and indeed discursive formations.

The African American choreographer, Alvin Ailey, for example, wanted to insert his work into American modernism whilst honouring his 'ancestral legacy' (DeFrantz 2004, p. 21). The gamut of dance techniques that he drew on for *Revelations* (1960) – 'Jazz dancing, balletic positions, Graham, Horton, Humphrey, Brazilian stance, West African musicality and complex rhythmic meter and a fundamental African American musicality' – achieved coherence through an artistic vision forged through a commitment to 'cultural memory', which situated him amongst the black modernists of the 1950s (DeFrantz 2004, p. 25). Likewise, Diane McIntyre – a choreographer whose work spans the concert stage and musical theatre – is described as working a 'blues aesthetic', which 'speaks of affirmation in the face of adversity' (Goler 2002, p. 207). The blues aesthetic manifests in her explorations of the relationship between music and dance in jazz. Her vocabulary is eclectic, merging 'modern dance movement, African American social dance forms, African dance steps and everyday gestures', with music styles ranging from 'classic and avant-garde jazz' to 'hymns and rhythm and blues' (Goler 2002, p. 209). The features of 'double consciousness' that appear in the work of the aforementioned choreographers create overlaps with theatrical genres from the Euro-American tradition of theatrical dance, but do not make their work derivative (as is sometimes claimed).

The critical analysis of artistic work, which is a significant aspect of cultural production, would benefit from an engagement with a choreographer's wider professional practice and the 'interpretive communities' it fosters. A critic is not required to *like* a choreographer's work. However, the critic should aim to be situated in the same conversation as the choreographer; otherwise, the risk is that reviews are merely an uninformed expression of (often Eurocentric) tastes – as we shall see in an example I touch on later.

The rest of this chapter focuses on Thomas 'Talawa' Prestø, the founder and lead choreographer of the Tabanka African and Caribbean Peoples' Dance Ensemble, Norway. However, rather than doing a conventional piece of performance analysis, I want to focus mainly on how his philosophy of dance is enacted in and by the activities he organised around the production of *I:Object* in 2018[4].

The cultural citizenship of Thomas 'Talawa' Prestø

Prestø entered the consciousness of the Norwegian general public in 2010, when he made the strategic decision to enter his company – Tabanka dance ensemble – into *Norway's Got Talent*. The company were runners-up; however, Prestø is now known internationally as the creator of the Talawa dance technique. The Talawa technique is one of the few codified techniques that coordinates the movement qualities and sensibilities of Africa and the Caribbean into technical configurations. It is a meta-technique, in that it maps multiple dance forms. Training enables the dancer to find entry points into dancing in traditional performance practices; in commercial dance and as an artistic representational form, Prestø describes technique as 'a validating institution' which 'releases privilege' (Prestø 2019, p. 16). He points out that a dancer who has twenty years of training in African dance diaspora forms is considered less of an expert than a dancer who has a three-year certificate from a dance academy, which acts as proof of training in a dance technique. The development of the Talawa technique has enabled Prestø to train and work with a community of dedicated dancers who are able to perform to standards set by both commercial and artistic programmes.

Prestø's choreographic practice tests out ideas of citizenship. Artistic citizenship is generally defined in terms of projects in which professional artists create opportunities for non-artists or disenfranchised groups to participate in art-making as a means of gaining a sense of empowerment (Hildebrandt and Peters 2017, p. 8). However, whilst not negating the importance of such projects, this is not Prestø's focus. His project is to fight for an inclusive artistic discourse of dance and to open up this system of representation to accept the thinking of people of diverse cultural backgrounds. To be absent from artistic discourse is to be excluded from a public sphere where debates about beauty, ethics, invention, histories and belonging are taking place. Prestø acts as an advocate for ethnic minority groups in Norway, in terms of how they are represented online and in the media. He initiates discussions about art, identity, visibility and agency, by posting clips of dance, articles and images. He has 72,000 followers on social media – some of which could be described as being part of his 'communities of practice' (Wenger 1999, p. 72). These include academics, other dance practitioners and artists who are equally interested

Africanist choreography

Figure 28.1 Thomas Prestø, *I:Object* (2018). Tale Hendnes/Tabanka dance ensemble and Dansens Hus, Norway

in Africanist aesthetics and artistic practices. In 2019, Prestø undertook a Master's degree in Choreography in 2019 at the Oslo National Academy of the Arts: one of the few black people in Norway to gain this qualification in the history of the establishment. In studying for this qualification after having already established an international career, Prestø was aiming to deepen his understanding of the cultural politics of contemporary dance and gain further access to this field. The transnational audience interested in Prestø's work was almost invisible to the contemporary dance scene in Norway when he embarked on this postgraduate work.

Generating discourse for *I:Object* (2018)

I:Object was a production by Tabanka Dance Ensemble which had a run at the Dansens Hus, an important contemporary dance venue in Oslo, from the 1st to the 4th of November, 2018.[5] The title of the piece is a double statement referring to the objectification and agency of the black subject. In terms of themes, it spanned topics ranging from the transatlantic slave trade to Black Lives Matter and the #me-too movement against sexual harassment. Performed to recorded music and recorded spoken word, the messages and themes of the production are direct and assessable. Due to the movement vocabulary of the production however, Prestø decided to invest a considerable amount of time and personal finance in generating an appropriate discourse for the reception of his work. At the time of the production, according to Prestø, there was very little discourse about choreography based on African and diasporic forms in dance in Norway. Performances featuring Africanist aesthetics tended to be categorised as 'urban dance' or were targeted at children. There was no mainstream training centre or higher education course on choreography with Africanist aesthetics, although it could be researched under the category of 'folk dance'. This meant that Tabanka dance ensemble, and other companies who performed African and Caribbean dance, did not feature in the discourses which analysed performances in terms of choreography, aesthetics, meaning or creativity.

The activities Prestø organised to generate a discourse around *I:Object* were geared to disrupt complacent viewing of the production. The audience were offered a different set of concepts than those of the 'urban' or 'folk' through which to encounter African diaspora dance. For example, Prestø actively sought to produce this new discourse by organising pre- and post-show talks with Professor Brenda Dixon Gottschild – a notable African American dance scholar. These events created a forum for different publics interested in his work to meet, including those who were interested in his technique classes or in online conversations (who would not normally visit the Dansens Hus or belong to the conventional contemporary dance audience). He also published an edition of *HÅRSÅR*, his company's occasional magazine, containing articles about the experiences of black Norwegians, interviews with eminent choreographers such as Zab Maboungou and texts on Tabanka dance ensemble's artistic mission and approach. He also engaged members of his communities of practice in discussions about his work, which resulted in online conversations and review writing.

The invisibility of black bodies in artistic dance discourses in Norway was one of the key issues addressed in the public talks. How dance forms are represented in scholarship has a significant impact on the dance profession for those who practise them. As Monica J. Casper and Lisa Jean Moore attest, there are 'social and economic consequences of visibility and invisibility (of bodies) as they relate to the privileges and benefits of citizenship' (2009, p. 10). For her part, Brenda Dixon Gottschild's pre-show talk addressed how the treatment of 'the dancing black body' constitutes a 'measure of culture' that reveals what is valued and repressed in a given society. Elsewhere, Dixon Gottschild has analysed how some Euro-American dance criticism has described African-derived forms as 'primitive', and made but scant acknowledgement of the fact that jazz and postmodern dance in America are influenced by African diaspora forms (1998, pp. 48–51). Prestø then invited two Norwegian choreographers, Belinda Braza and Knut Aril Flatner, to respond to Dixon Gottschild's lecture[6]. On the whole, jazz in Norway is not recognised as having African diaspora roots or Africanist aesthetics. Both these choreographers produce work that is influenced by dance forms and aesthetics from the African diaspora; however, it is not contextualised as such in the academic curriculum. The pre-show talk and the panel sought to initiate a conversation about the need to re-vision the art dance histories in Norway to include bodies of colour, histories of cultural exchange, appropriation and misappropriation.

The choreography of *I:Object* (2018): heritage, polycentricism and 'revitalizing the exhausted body'

Prestø describes his choreography as 'Africana dance', because his investigation of African and diaspora forms follows the aims of Africana philosophy. According to Lewis R. Gordon, Africana philosophy is a trans-discipline, which encompasses African, African American and Afro-Caribbean philosophy, and gathers together reflections of thinkers across disciplinary boundaries about the position of the black human being in the world. On the whole, these reflections are gathered to address questions of 'how Africana people should be studied' and to challenge 'Eurocentric approaches to human studies' (Gordon 2016, p. 86). For Prestø, contemporary theatrical dance is about creating choreographic conventions which enable the transmission of critical ideas and values which he has identified within African and diaspora forms, and which remain relevant to black communities transnationally. His productions draw on aspects of Western dance theatre, but he does not consider Western aesthetics or dance technique as symbolic of modernity. Prestø's contemporary dance expression is created from a dialogue with tradition, rather than a rupture from it. This temporal dialogue is one of the philosophical ideas he investigates choreographically. As he writes in *HÅRSÅR*:

> Heritage is a result of the dynamic interaction between past experiences, the future and the present. This understanding of the term implies the collective nature of heritage as something common shared by a group of people. This forms a basis for connection and a common space of urgency and imagination.
>
> *(Prestø 2018, p. 7)*

In the spirit of exercising cultural citizenship, Prestø actively promoted the emergence of 'interpretive communities': inviting members of his communities of practice to discuss choreographic ideas he was exploring during the rehearsal process.

I was credited as 'advisor' for the production, but my role would be better described as 'feed-backer'. I watched clips of rehearsals and discussed with Prestø what I was seeing and sensing. This provided Prestø with a space to reflect on his work. In discussions with Prestø, we agreed that his approach to staging *I:Object* could be described as 'polycentric'. There was a bobbinet upstage that dancers would perform both behind and in front of, and in many sections of the work, there was usually more than one scenario taking place at any point in time – one behind the bobbinet, another up stage and another centre or down stage. Polycentricism can refer to many different phenomena, but the compositional structure it references here is an African cosmology where the unborn, the living and the dead are considered as co-existing and interacting (Akinyela 2005, p. 241). In *I:Object*, the structure proved to be an innovative and effective means of commentary on the psychic and the social. It enabled Prestø to juxtapose scenes to depict different dimensions at once: the physical alongside the spiritual world, different historical eras side by side and different events taking place in the same historical moment but in different places. The structure of the piece was also designed to prompt audiences to critically reflect on their own practice of spectatorship. For example, Prestø told me that he hoped audience members – whenever they were forced to choose which scene to watch – would consider why they had decided to pay attention to one thing and ignore another. A particularly powerful instance of this occurs in the choreography when the audience is laughing along with a group of female dancers who are dancing in a circle, possibly in a market place, bantering and gesticulating as if joking with one another. Suddenly, upstage, behind the bobbinet, appears a man with a rope around his neck in a spotlight – a victim of a lynching. The women continue to banter and dance.

The performance style of *I:Object* is also informed by an Africana principle. 'Revitalizing the exhausted body' is a term coined by Prestø to describe his approach to directing the performance of the dancers to achieve an expression of 'soul': the unashamed display of emotion, be it pain, anger, happiness or joy. The performer engages in energetic dancing, in combination with Caribbean grounding techniques, the performance of codes that exist in certain rituals and a specific use of the body's weight, until he or she passes through exhaustion and is re-energised. It produces an intense, visceral performance style. The sensory is political in Prestø's view of art. In discussing the sensory, he also cites Jacques Rancière's description of art's 'ethical-political potential'. Rancière describes the arts as enabling a 're-distribution of the sensible' and having the ability to contest 'the existing distribution of what can be seen and heard, and by whom' (Prestø 2018, p. 8). Prestø's recourse to Rancière could be read as a means of providing an intercultural context for his work, and also as a way of framing the emotional expressivity of the production in political terms, in order to challenge ideas that overt expression takes place in the absence of thought.

Figure 28.2 Thomas Prestø, *I:Object* (2018). Tale Hendnes/Tabanka dance ensemble and Dansens Hus, Norway

After the run ended, the Dansens Hus issued a statement on its website about the online attention and debate provoked by *I:Object*. Most shows at the venue only get one review, they noted, but by the end of November 2018, *I:Object* had already received four, which presented some radically different responses[7]. These included Diese Nunes' reply to Andrea Csaszni Rygh who, while comparing the production to the Marvel film *Black Panther* (2018), described it as traditional, boring and lacking in innovation (Rygh 2018). Nunes argued that Rygh had deliberately ignored the discourse around the production and her review was an uninformed expression of her tastes (Nunes 2018). Margrete Kvalien, writing for the online music magazine *Ballade.no*, also wondered why a production like *I:Object* was only appearing on Norway's main stage fifty years after Alvin Ailey's *Revelations* (1960). She described *I:Object* as her first experience of watching a production with Africanist dance aesthetics, outside of popular entertainment, which addressed political issues, including 'institutional racism' in Norway. She considered the choreography well composed, the dancing as an expression of rhythmic and physical force and the performance as continually switching between the articulations of deep pain and great entertainment. For her, the production was a dialogue between 'the stage and the (dance) hall' (Kvalien 2018). And finally, Tia Monique Uzor, a dance scholar of British-Caribbean heritage, who visited Norway to see the piece, situated it within the African diaspora tradition of using creative expression as a form of resistance and commemoration. For her, *I:Object* stood out for its technical excellence, the unapologetic expression of emotion, the investigation of women's grief and the framing of art as a conduit of healing (Uzor 2018).

In conclusion, then, I propose that Thomas Prestø's philosophy of dance is performed not only in his choreography, but also in how he engages with his professional context. It is informed by a reflection on the intersections of transnational histories of the African diaspora and Norwegian cultural politics. His Africana choreography performs his investigations into black expressive cultures, and corporeality articulates performance concepts embedded in African and Caribbean forms. The philosophy of performance in the public sphere is tangible through the politics of representation which renders visible invisible histories of artistic ideas.

Notes

1. African and diaspora dances and dance practices include social, ceremonial and ritual dances from Africa and countries wherever people of African descent live. Internationally known social forms from Africa and the African and diaspora dances and dance practices include social, ceremonial and ritual dances from Africa and countries wherever people of African descent live. Internationally known social forms from Africa and the diaspora are Sabar, dance hall and hip-hop – as feature in commercial and theatrical dance projects around the world. There are dance techniques created by drawing from these forms of dance such as the Acongy technique created by the Senegalese modern dance pioneer Germaine Acogny and L'Antech created by the Jamaican choreographer and scholar L'Anoinette Stines. The aesthetic features shared by these various dances and techniques are called Africanist aesthetics.
2. A number of dance scholars (Welsh-Asante 1994; Gottschild 1998; DeFrantz 2002; Osumare 2007) have used Africanist aesthetics as the starting point for theoretical, ethnographic, historical and philosophical analyses. Features commonly quoted by the aforementioned scholars are the presence of flexed feet, bent knee, flexible spine, polyrhythmic and polycentric movement, high-low effect, the aesthetic of the cool, call and response. Choreographers draw on these forms and aesthetics in different ways guided by their philosophical and artistic interests.
3. Citizenship has been used as a method of analysis for performance in Africa and the Caribbean also. Yair Hashachar (2018) has written about cultural citizenship as a drive behind the organisation of African Pan-African festivals in the late 1960s in Africa as part of post-independence celebrations. Additionally, Yvonne Daniel (2011) writes on citizenship and popular dance in the Caribbean and wider diaspora.
4. This article focuses on only aspects of Prestø's philosophy of dance and only aspects of the choreography of *I:Object*. I was a feedbacker on *I:Object* and Presto gave me permission to draw on our conversations to write this chapter.
5. Hus, Danses. https://www.dansenshus.com/artikler/mage-lovord-til-tabanka. Accessed December 8th 2018.
6. Belinda Braza trained as a jazz dancer and transitioned to hip-hop. She is a house choreographer for a major venue called Det Norske Teater, whilst Knut Aril Flatner is one of the two members of the company Subjazz, and one of the four main jazz teachers at the Oslo National Academy of the Arts.
7. My review of the show appeared after the aforementioned date. See the reviews online here, https://www.dansenshus.com/artikler/mage-lovord-til-tabanka.

References

Adewole, F. 2005. Dance Theatre and African Identities: Crossing Physicality and Academia. In *Dance Heritage: Crossing Academia and Physicality*. Proceedings of 7th NOFOD Conference. Reykjavik April 15–18 2004, pp. 12–26.

Adewole, F. 2017. 'The Construction of the Black Dance/African Peoples' Dance Sector in Britain: Issue Arising for the Conceptualisation of Related Choreographic Practice'. In Christy Adair and Ramsay Burt (eds.) *British Dance: Black Routes*. London and New York: Routledge, pp. 125–148.

Akinyela, M. 2005. 'African Cosmologies'. In: Molefi Kete Asante and Ama Mazama (eds.) *Encyclopedia of Black Studies*. Thousand Oaks: Sage Publications, p. 241.

Barson. T. 2010. 'Introduction: Modernism and the Black Atlantic'. In: T. Barson and P. Gorschlutter (eds.) *Afromodern: Journey through the Black Atlantic*. Liverpool: Tate Liverpool, pp. 8–25.

Casper, M.J. and Moore, L.J. 2009. *Missing Bodies: The Politics of Visibility*. New York and London: New York University Press.

Cull, L. 2014. 'Performance Philosophy – Staging a New Field'. In Laura Cull (ed.) *Encounters in Performance Philosophy*. London: Palgrave Macmillan.

Daniel, Y. 2011. *Caribbean and Atlantic Diaspora Dance: Igniting Citizenship*. Urbana, Chicago and Springfield: University of Illinois Press.

DeFrantz, T. 2002. 'African American Dance: A Complex History'. In: Thomas F. DeFrantz (ed.) *Dancing Many Drums: Excavations in African American Dance*. Madison: University of Wisconsin Press, pp. 3–33.

DeFrantz, T. 2004. *Dancing Revelations: Alvin Ailey's Embodiment of African American Culture*. Oxford: Oxford University Press.

DeFrantz, T. and Gonzalez. A. 2014. From "Negro Expression" to "Black Performance". In: Thomas DeFrantz and Anita Gonzalez (eds.) *Black Performance Theory*. Durham, NC: Duke University Press, pp. 1–5.

Freire, P. 2005. *Pedagogy of the Oppressed*: 30th Anniversary edition. New York and London: Continuum.

Goler, V. 2002. '"Moves on Top of Blues": Diane McIntyre's Blues Aesthetic'. In: Thomas F. DeFrantz (ed.) *Dancing Many Drums: Excavations in African American Dance*. Madison: University of Wisconsin Press, pp. 205–233.

Gordon, L.R. 2016. *Disciplinary Decadence: Living thought in rying Times*. New York and London: Routledge.

Gottschild, B.D. 1998. *Digging the Africanist Presence in American Performance: Dance and Other Contexts*. Westport, CT: Greenwood press.

Hall, S. 1997. *Representation: Cultural Representations and Signifying Practices*. London: Sage.

Hamera, J. 2007. *Dancing Communities: Performance, Difference and Connection in the Global City*. New York: Palgrave Macmillan.

Hashachar, Y. 2018. 'Guinea Unbound: Performing Pan-African Cultural Citizenship between Algiers 1969 and the Guinean National Festival'. *Interventions* Vol. 20, No. 7, pp. 1003–1021, https://doi.org/10.1080/1369801X.2018.1508932

Hildebrandt, P. and Peters, S. 2019. 'Introduction: Performing Citizenship: Testing New Forms of Togetherness'. In: Paula Hildebrandt, Kerstin Evert, Sibylle Peters, Mirjam Schaub, Kathrin Wildner and Gesa Ziemer (eds.) *Performing Citizenship: Bodies, Agencies, Limitations*. Germany: Palgrave Macmillan, 1–13.

Kvalien. M. 2018. 'Den "svarte" kroppens rause raseri', *Ballade* [Online]. Published 12.11.2018, Available at http://www.ballade.no/sak/den-svarte-kroppens-rause-raseri/ Accessed 16 October 2019.

Nettleford, R. 1994. 'Foreword'. In: Kariamu Welsh-Asante (ed.) *African Dance: An Artistic, Historical and Philosophical Inquiry*, Trenton, NJ/ Asmara, Eritrea. African World Press Inc., pp. xiii–xviii.

Nunes, D. 2018. 'Tabanka tar plass: La oss snakke om scenekunstkritikk', *Golden Mirrors Arts* [Online]. Published 12.11.2018, Available at https://www.goldenmirrors.org/single-post/2018/11/12/Tabanka-tar-plass-La-oss-snakke-om-scenekunstkritikk Accessed 16 October 2019.

Osumare, H. 2007. *The Africanist Aesthetic in Global Hip-Hop: Power Moves*. New York: Palgrave Macmillan.

Prestø, T. 2018. *HÅRSÅR*. Oslo: Tabanka Dance Ensemble.

Prestø, T. 2019. *Talawa Technique: Ancient Power – Modern Use*. Tabanka Dance Ensemble. Unpublished company document.

Rygh, A. 2018. 'Tabanka tar plass', *Scenekunst* [Online]. Published 6 Nov 2018. Available at: http://www.scenekunst.no/sak/tabanka-tar-plass/ Accessed 16 October 2019.

Stevenson, N. 2003. *Cultural Citizenship: Cosmopolitan Questions*. Kents Hill: Open University.

Uzor, T. 2018. 'A Liberation of the Soul: *I:Object* – Tabanka Dance Ensemble' [Online] Available at https://tiamoniqueuzor.wordpress.com/2018/11/21/a-liberation-of-the-soul-iobject-tabanka-dance-ensemble/ Accessed 16 October 2019.

Welsh Asante. 1994. *African Dance. An Artistic, Historical and Philosophical Inquiry.* Trenton, NJ/ Asmara, Eritrea. African World Press Inc.

Wenger, E. 1999. *Communities of Practice: Learning, Meaning and Identity.* Cambridge: Cambridge University Press.

PART IV

Figures

29
RŪMĪ

Will Daddario

To embrace Jalāl al-Dīn Rūmī as a performance philosopher is to offer a direct challenge to many Western philosophical beliefs and practices, and I want to impress upon all of us who identify as performance philosophers the necessary and salutary effects of this challenge. Though he lived eight centuries ago, Rūmī's presence is exquisitely palpable today through his poetry, even through the fog of translation and across the vertiginous terrain of cultural difference. Situated in his time and place, however, Rūmī's spiritual message and ecstatic, irrational, anti-philosophical approach to truth override the New Age, feel-good image of him that led to his status as "best-selling poet in the U.S." (Ciabattari 2014). It is the historical, actual Rūmī whose figure I would like to trace here.

The first challenge to Western philosophy comes from Rūmī's identity as a devout Islamic mystic whose method of investigation bypasses rational inquiry in favor of *tasting* the world so as to gain "direct perception and experience of a thing as opposed to conceptual knowledge about it" (Dagli 2016, 43). Rūmī's "philosophy" here is thus closer to what we might call theosophy and confronts us with the specific type of knowing cultivated through a deeply spiritual attunement to the mysteries of the world. The Sufi practices of fasting and, especially, the ritual "audition" and dance known as *samā* guided Rumi into his immediate perception where, once directly apprehending the quiddities of things, he would dictate his discoveries in the form of poetry (Lewis 2000, 309).

The phrase "directly apprehending the quiddities of things" is actually misleading since, and this is the second part of Rūmī's challenge, the poet openly rejected the received tradition of the *fālsifah*, Arab and Persian thinkers who utilized the technical vocabulary of Ancient Greek philosophers. To follow Rūmī requires partaking, instead, in the way of the *taṣawwuf*, which Islamic mystics understood as the "institutionalization of the spiritual life in both its practical and theoretical aspects as rooted in the Quran and Sunnah" (Dagli 2016, 12; see also Zarrabi-Zadeh 2016, 7). The word "mystic" even sets us out on the wrong path since it evokes the Medieval Christian tradition of figures like Meister Eckhart, Ignatius Loyola, and Hildegard von Bingen and leads back ultimately to the Ancient Greek word μυω (to conceal or to close, as in to close one's eyes for a ritual ceremony), thereby fastening a (Westernized) Greek origin to Rūmī's mode of thought. Here, in fact, lies the third challenge to Western philosophy since to eschew the Ancient Greek origin to Islamic philosophy is to re-open the Eastern lines of thought that hail from Zoroastrianism and grow through the Illuminationist practices of exciting figures like Shihāb al-Dīn Abū al-Futūḥ Yaḥyā ibn Ḥabash ibn Amīrak al-Suhrawardī (1154–1191), thereby commanding philosophers to cultivate experience journeying to the imaginal realm of inner vision or else succumb to the vanity of exoteric knowledge.

True, Rūmī would have been familiar with the largely Aristotelian and Neoplatonist doctrines passed into his hands through the translations of Ancient Greek texts (which had first been translated into Syriac and then into Arabic by the scholars in, first, Alexandria and, then, the "House of wisdom" (*Bayt al-hikmat*) in Baghdad). To emphasize this line of transmission, however, is to overlook the inheritance of *gnostic* experience bequeathed to Rūmī by his father Bahā al-Dīn Valad, his first spiritual teacher Sayyed Borhān al-Din Mohaqqeq, and then his great love Shams al-Dīn Tabrīzī for whom Suhrawardī seems to have been influential (Corbin 1977, 16; Jackson 2014, 19; Lewis 2000, 85–89, 101–102, 135–200). Likewise, while Rūmī's knowledge of jurisprudence (*fiqh*) and Islamic law (*Sharī'ah*) enabled him to begin his career as one of the respected "men of knowledge" (*ulama*) within the Hanafi branch of the Islamic sciences, Rūmī's proclivities for the way of the *taṣawwuf* helped him to transcend the scholarly understanding of his religion and find a deeper connection with The One. As such, we need to resist the temptation to see in Rūmī either a "philosopher" in the strict sense or (as is common today) a pantheist and shockingly contemporary New Age poet espousing free love. Instead, I recommend that we approach him as a gnostic theosophist whose praxis of poetry enabled him to hollow himself out like a reed flute to be played by God.

The challenge of Rūmī is a kind of tempering fire for the field of performance philosophy, which espouses a radically "democratic" approach to thinking such that "all thoughts are equal," a phrase that evokes John Ó Maoilearca's and Laura Cull Ó Maoilearca's work with François Laruelle's non-standard philosophy. Opposed to the top-down, authoritative pronouncements of Philosophy, non-standard philosophy "sees philosophical thinking as both a performance *and* a physical tendency or spatial *activity*" that seeks neither to transcend ignorance nor to reach ontological certainties but, instead, to witness thought as it unfolds from the immanent real (Ó Maoilearca 2015, 6; emphasis in original). As such, without the goal of reaching knowledge, the doing of thinking takes center stage and the materiality of thinking practices compels our focus. That is, performance philosophy generally, and in particular its non-standard philosophical comportment, challenges us to feel thought from within, to transpose that tactile experience into words, images, sounds, and other media, and then to re-organize our understanding of *philosophy* and *performance* based on our findings. What better way to test this operation than to turn to a 13th-Century Sufi poet whose vision of the world clashes so profoundly with Western, secular, rationalist philosophical views and the typical representational aesthetic counterparts to those views? We have no direct connection between Rūmī and visual art, no Islamic theater tradition held up as a model for understanding his work. The art we encounter is an outpouring of poetry that, despite its beauty and provocative imagery, continually returns to the primacy of silence over speech and directs the listener to turn away from words toward the essence of Being. If Rūmī is a performance philosopher, then the field is truly wide open for performance philosophy insofar as it would entail a performance philosophical practice devoid of the most common artistic touchstones and philosophical vocabulary.

In this short writing, I would like to present Rūmī specifically as a performance philosopher of grief, a guide to the nexus of love *and* loss where, upon arrival, we vanish and affirm our weak agency within the vast nothingness of Being, which Rūmī understands as a kind of workshop from which multiplicity spins out from pure unity. The journey to this place, named *Alast* in the Quranic tradition, is Rūmī's sole occupation and, therefore, demands that we, as students of Rūmī, shift our attention to the work of journeying. Henry Corbin frames the journey through the term *ta'wil*, an Arabic word that connotes the leading-back to one's origin through the science of spiritual direction and divine inspiration. "He who practises *ta'wil*, therefore, is someone who diverts what is proclaimed from its external appearance (its exoteric aspect or *zahir*), and makes it revert to its truth, its *haqiqah*'" (1977, 12). The opening lines of Rūmī's *Masnavi* help frame this practice within the poet's unique vocabulary:

> Listen to the reed how it tells a tale, complaining of separations—
> Saying, "Ever since I was parted from the reed-bed, my
> lament hath caused man and woman to moan.
> I want a bosom torn by severance, that I may unfold (to such
> a one) the pain of love-desire.
> Every one who is left far from his source wishes back the
> Time when he was united with it.
> *(Trans. R.A. Nicholson 1926, M1 5)*

The matter of return (Arabic: *rujū'*, Persian: *bāzgasht*) is primarily a matter of orientation. Through the science of *ta'wil*, the individual first turns toward the pain of the initial separation, embarks on the spiritual practice outlined within the *batin*, or esoteric aspect, of the Quran, seeks a guide to maintain sight of the path, and proceeds to the source through ascetic practices and meditation.

Rūmī's guide was Shams al-Dīn Tabrīzī. A curious figure occluded by the narratives of Rūmī's hagiographers and Western historiographers, Tabrīzī's passion, intellectual acumen, and violent end has led to comparisons with Socrates. Coming as he did from the tradition of Qalandars, he was likewise viewed by some as a Cynic whose charismatic truth-talking helped him gain access to people of such renown like Rūmī. These comparisons, however, lead again to the Ancient Greek tradition and, as such, we would be wise to find an alternative framework through which to view this persona and his relationship with Rūmī.

The Quran, again, provides a helpful word: *qutb*. Corbin's translation of the word as "mystical pole" reveals Tabrīzī as the axis around which all esoteric truths oscillate, a spiritually perfect node whose light serves to guide fellow travelers back home (1977, 191). Roy Jackson summons the title *al-insān al-kāmil*, Perfect Man, when writing about Tabrīzī, a term that comes from the highly influential "Akbarian School" of Ibn al-'Arabī (1165–1240) for whom the Perfect Man was nothing less than "the physical manifestation of God" who "embodies all the perfections of the universe" (Jackson 2014, 80–81). Prepared with both *qutb* and *al-insān al-kāmil*, we can ascertain the Rūmī-Tabrīzī couplet as a spiritual unity through which perfection can be understood and the Love of the Divine directly encountered. Hence, another challenge for performance philosophers today: what would it mean to abandon academic institutions, immerse ourselves in the pursuit of esoteric knowledge, and seek out psychagogical relationships such as that between Rūmī and Tabrīzī?

Lewis tells us that prior to the arrival and embrace of Tabrīzī, Rūmī had never practiced the ritual of *samā* (2000, 172). This means that what appears as Rūmī's most obvious "performance," i.e. his whirling dance, chanting, and creation of the poetry for which he is the most well-known, was a direct result of his prolonged exposure to the *qutb*. We can think of Rūmī's dancing as a kind of hollowing out. The center point around which he rotates when engaged in *samā* becomes the empty core of the reed flute through which the Divine will breathe and create music. The images that appear in the poetry, therefore, are not merely metaphors or parables or illustrative devices (though they are *also* those things). They are primarily, it seems to me, events witnessed within the imaginal realm to which Rūmī had access by merit of his existence as one of the "*zuhhād* (ascetics), *'ubbād* (pious devotees), *muhaqqiqūn* (men of realization), *'urafā'* (knowers or gnostics)" (Dagli 2016, 12). This imaginal realm, the *'alam al-mithal,* made visible to the West through Corbin's scholarship, "is intermediary between the intelligible world of the beings of pure Light and the sensible world; and the perceiving organ proper to it is the active Imagination" (1969, 1977, 213). The imaginal realm is a separate ontological layer of reality that Western philosophy has intentionally forgotten (Chittick 1989, ix). It is not a pejorative realm of "imagination" akin to the Platonic simulacrum but, rather, a world of autonomous "Forms and Images" that disclose themselves to the few who are prepared (Corbin 1977, 213). The *samā* opened the portal to the imaginal realm and Rūmī's partnership with Tabrīzī sharpened the poet's vision within that stratum of reality.

Thus, we come face to face with Rūmī's theosophy for which we in the West might lend the phrase a "performance philosophy of everyday life," with the caveat that, in this case, this phrase must retain an Islamic inflection. To submit ourselves to the teachings of Rūmī, we would need to treat his poetry as an extension of his Sufi ritual *samā* and, furthermore, understand that the goal of following Rūmī would be to undertake the *fanā',* or annihilation, that exists as the endgame of spiritual perfection. This is, to be sure, an "irrationalist" performance philosophy, one given over to the "mystic" and gnostic tradition (Zarrabi-Zadeh 2016, 174). For those who truly hear Rūmī's words, however, none of these predicates and adjectives really matter, since the promise of following such a path is true knowledge of love and oneness. What ir-, non-, or suprarational methodologies are we willing to employ in order to learn from Rumi's insights? What would university education look like if it was modeled on the ascetic practices of this Persian, Islamic poet? These are questions that, if pursued rigorously, would create neither a fundamentalist nor a conservative performance philosophy but the one that reaches beyond the dichotomy of immanence and transcendence to the heart of oneness.

References

Chittick William C. 1989. *The Sufi Path of Knowledge: Ibn al-'Arabi's Metaphysics of Imagination.* Albany: State University of New York Press.
Ciabattari, Jane. 2014. "Why is Rumi the best-selling poet in the US?" *BBC Culture Online.* 21 October 2014. Accessed 10 July 2018. http://www.bbc.com/culture/story/20140414-americas-best-selling-poet.
Corbin, Henry. 1977. *History of Islamic Philosophy.* Translated by Liadain Sherrard and Philip Sherrard. London; New York: Kegan Paul International.
———. 1969. *Alone with the Alone: Creative Imagination in the Sūfism of Ibn al-'Arabī.* Princeton, NJ: Princeton University Press.
Dagli, Caner K. 2016. *Ibn al-'Arabī and Islamic Intellectual Culture: From Mysticism to Philosophy.* Routledge Sufi Series. New York: Routledge.
Jackson, Roy. 2014. *What Is Islamic Philosophy?* New York: Routledge.
Lewis, Franklin D. 2000. *Rumi—Past and Present, East and West: The Life, Teaching and Poetry of Jalâl al-Din Rumi.* Oxford, England: Oneworld.
Ó Maoilearca, John. 2015. *All Thoughts Are Equal: Laruelle and Nonhuman Philosophy.* Minneapolis; London: University of Minnesota Press.
Rūmī, Jalal al-Dīn. 1926. *The Masnawí of Jalálu'ddín Rúmí.* Edited and Translated by Reynold A. Nicholson. Volume 2. Cambridge, England: Cambridge University Press.
Zarrabi-Zadeh, Saeed. 2016. *Practical Mysticism in Islam and Christianity: A Comparative Study of Jalal al-Din Rumi and Meister Eckhart.* Routledge Sufi Series. Edited by Ian Richard Netton. London; New York: Routledge.

30
ADRIAN PIPER

Lauren Fournier

In 1971, the American artist Adrian Piper performed a work entitled *Food for the Spirit* in her New York City studio apartment. In it, she read Kant's *Critique of Pure Reason* as part of a private performance for one—herself. A young woman of colour, Piper made this work at a time when, even as marked social and political changes were taking place with the civil rights and feminist movements of the late 1960s, the conceptual art world remained largely, in her words, "a white macho enclave, a fun-house refraction of the Euroethnic equation of intellect with masculinity" (Piper 1996b, p. xxxv). Working as an artist at a time when Kantian aesthetics still held sway in the American art world—via the modernist art critic Clement Greenberg and his formalist take on Kant's philosophical system—Piper used performance as a way of metabolizing dominant art discourses and philosophical frameworks through the body.

Piper has a multi-decade history of experimenting across media and forms to realize her deeply considered, conceptual work. As she works in performance—including live performance, performance for the camera, text and image work, and other modes—Piper metabolizes dominant art and philosophical discourses, generating artwork that is both philosophically rigorous and resonant with an anti-racist feminist politics and aesthetics of self-imaging.

Staged in the artist's studio, Piper's *Food* sees her ritualistically move between the following actions: monastically reading Kant's *Critique of Pure Reason,* scribbling notes in the margins of the book, and taking selfies of herself using a Kodak Brownie camera and a mirror. Questions at the heart of Kant's philosophy—namely, the relation between the self as an appearance or "mere representation" and the self as a "thing in itself"—find new resonance in Piper's performance (Kant 1781, pp. 426–427). Through physically performing the actions of reading, study, and self-imaging, Piper conceptually processes the critical discourses of her time.

Piper first came to Kantian philosophy after she finished art school at the School of Visual Arts in Manhattan, and was told by her peers that she should read Kant since he was, in their view, taking up the kinds of ideas that Piper was taking up in her performance (O'Neill-Butler, 2018). And, it turned out that her peers were right—Piper would go on to study philosophy, completing a Bachelor's in philosophy at the City College of New York, and then a Master's (1977) and Doctorate (1981) in philosophy at Harvard, with periods of study abroad in Germany during the late 1970s.[1] Particularly taken by Kant's philosophical vision, Piper's engagement with Kantian philosophy continued through to the present. In 2013, she published the monumental tome *Rationality and the Structure of the Self, Part 1: Kant* as part of a two-book series with *Rationality and the Structure of the Self, Part II* on Hume—with whom she was in philosophical disagreement, generally aligning herself with the Kantian view on things. But it is in *Food* where we find the trace of her first engagement with Kantian philosophy, with the artist reading Kant's first *Critique* as an artwork in itself.

In her artist statement for *Food*, which frames the work in terms of its larger conceptual thrust, Piper configures Kantian philosophy as that which "was shaking the foundations of my self-identity" (Piper, 1971). In doing so, she introduces a fundamental problem of the divide between the demands of philosophy on the one hand, and the physical, spiritual, and emotional needs of the artist's embodied self, or "I," on the other. This statement by Piper is preserved in the Adrian Piper Research Archive Foundation in Berlin along with the rest of the performance documentation,[2] including the marked up *Critique of Pure Reason* and Piper's photographs, and it reads as follows:

> Private loft performance continuing through summer, while reading and writing a paper on Kant's *Critique of Pure Reason,* fasting, doing yoga, and isolating myself socially. Whenever I felt that I was losing my sense of self due to the profundity of Kant's thought, I went to the mirror to peer at myself to make sure I was still there, and repeat aloud the passage in the *Critique* (underlined on following pages) that was shaking the foundations of my self-identity, until it was just (psychologically manageable) words. I recorded these attempts to anchor myself, by photographing myself and tape-recording the reiterated passages (the tape has since been destroyed). These attempts did not succeed, so I eventually abandoned them, and just studied the *Critique*. Upon finishing the paper, I found I could not look at or think about the *Critique of Pure Reason* for two years afterwards.
>
> *(Piper, 1971)*

It is this fear of losing her self that comes with the practice of reading Kantian philosophy in isolation that sparks Piper's movement towards the mirror with her camera, prompting her to take self-portraits to ensure that she still physically "exists" as a body with a reflection. "Whenever I felt that I was losing my sense of self due to the profundity of Kant's thought" is rich in what it offers to an unpacking of autotheory as a contemporary feminist practice with roots in body art and performance. In Piper's conceptual and performance-based work, the act of self-portraiture is turned to as a remedy for the effects of (analytic and continental) philosophy (and theory): photographing the self becomes a means of grounding oneself empirically in space and time lest one be (literally) taken away by the (metaphorical) effects of Kant's philosophy of transcendental aesthetics.

Piper describes the self-portraits and voice recordings[3] as attempts to anchor herself in space and time. The artist activates conceptual art as a flexible, practice-based framework within which she can stage the reading of Kantian philosophy as a mode of consumption and metabolization, where Kant's philosophy of the transcendental aesthetic is configured as nourishing matter "for the Spirit." She ritualistically enacts a conceptual transubstantiation whereby Kantian philosophy is rendered sustenance or "food" that the artist will figuratively (and, in light of her fasting, somewhat literally) subsist on over the course of the performance. The embodied metaphor of philosophical sustenance is in sustained tension with the notion of "spirit" as abstracted from the body—like the tensions sustained within Kant's own philosophy, itself unresolved and continually debated within and beyond an international community of Kant scholars.

Food is as much a practice of the artist seeking to know or understand herself, as it is a practice of the artist seeking to know or understand philosophy—and the resulting work, a pioneering artwork in the history of American conceptualism, embodies the ideas Kant was introducing with his philosophical system. Take, for example, Kant's theory of the transcendental aesthetic, where he distinguishes objects into phenomena and noumena, where "phenomena" is what we perceive (representations, 'mere appearances') through the senses and noumena is the 'thing in itself' or the unknowable. Kant famously conceives of objects in space and time as representations or "merely appearances," and as space and time themselves as "appearances." Just as Kant's philosophy of aesthetics "attempts to suture the impossible chasm" that exists between sensation as subjective and cognition as objective (Jones 2012, p. 27) between sensibility and understanding, so too does Piper's practice as a pioneering conceptualist and a feminist body artist work to suture the chasm that exists between self-imaging and philosophizing, a chasm ripe with tension and paradox in the larger histories of Western art, philosophy, and theory.

In her discussion of self-imaging in contemporary art, Amelia Jones observes that "Kant notes clearly our desire for 'empirical representation' that led Descartes, among others, to describe the body as a secondary representation of the self, the locus of the 'I think'" (Jones 2006, p. xiii). Kant desired "empirical representation" as part of his philosophical project that ultimately sought to square philosophy with empirical science. Through her performance and self-portraiture, Piper provides evidence in the form of a photograph as a kind of "empirical representation" of her existence in the world. Could it be that self-imaging is a paradoxical attempt at empiricism situated in the liminal and potentially irresolvable space between "subject" and "object"—one that extends beyond the feminist politics of objectification to broader philosophical questions of ontology? As a human body in space and time, Piper is an "object[s] of an experience" and therefore "nothing but appearance[s], i.e., mere representation[s]" (Kant 1781, pp. 426–427). But she is also an object of representation, foregrounded as such through the act of photographing herself. The resultant selfies—documentation of this performance—are material traces of an act of Kantian evidencing. They show Piper working through these philosophical questions through the specificities of her own body—racialized and gendered in ways that are read differently than, say, the supposedly "neutral" art historical body of an able-bodied, cisgender, white man.

Works like *Food* show Piper as a performance artist embodying her own self as a site for philosophical critique; other works, like her ongoing *The Mythic Being* performance (1972–1975), entail the use of performative personas and alter-egos as a mode of social and political critiques. Made a few years after *Food for the Spirit,* Piper's *The Mythic Being* sees the artist performatively engage in "what (Audre) Lorde called 'acting like a man'" (Bowles 2007, p. 621), taking on a drag alter-ego male of colour who behaves in hyperbolically masculine ways, acting out scenes based on Piper's own life. From 1973 to 1975, Piper would take out advertisements in *The Village Voice* and publish her image-text works as *The Mythic Being*—an example of artists staging conceptual art interventions in venues like newspapers and TV. Pairing image and text in a way that extends the latently discursive aspects of a referentially philosophical work like *Food* to a more literally discursive degree, Piper would stage these performance photographs of herself in drag with handwritten thought-bubbles, marked out in charcoal and oil crayon. Located in the newspaper, without the more obvious framings of an art gallery or museum space, readers would stumble upon these conceptual art interventions—opening Piper's performances to yet another aspect of New York City public life.

The text that Piper uses in this series—which she juxtaposed with these drawn-on, performative drag photographs—includes statements that the artist wrote as a teenager in her journal a few years prior. Like the meditative aspect of *Food,* with Piper's monastic study of the philosophical text, these *Village Voice* works were tied to a personal, embodied, and performance-based practice of mantra. Piper would take the phrase that she published in *The Mythic Being* thought-bubble for that week, and would repeat it to herself over the course of that week—with that utterance serving to guide her actions as she moved through the world, making art and philosophizing. There was a cathartic aspect to *The Mythic Being* performances as well; referencing Jean-Paul Sartre's *Being and Nothingness* ("A person frees himself from himself in the very act by which he makes himself an object for himself"), Piper explained that, "The experience of the *Mythic Being* thus becomes part of the public history and is no longer a part of my own" (Piper 1975c).

Adrian Piper embodies a present-day practice of performing philosophy, moving through the world with the fervent curiosity of an artist and a philosopher, and working adeptly across media and forms. From the late 1960s through the present, Piper's performance practice serves as a necessary site through which the artist can process philosophical problems that are long-debated or difficult to resolve in the twinned worlds of contemporary art and academia—from the Kantian notion of the transcendental aesthetic, to the ways that certain bodies are read in public space. Her performance practice also becomes a site for taking up the politics of philosophy and theory in the twentieth through the twenty-first century, with Piper's subjectivity and embodiment—as an artist of colour, and as a woman—serving to stage confrontations that are often sympathetic and ambivalent to her so-called objects of critique. Through performing philosophy, Piper creates complex works of art that engender new insights into modern and contemporary political and aesthetic issues and historical philosophical debates.

Notes

1 Piper studied philosophy at the University of Heidelberg from 1977 to 1978.
2 As a private performance, *Food* is particularly dependent upon documentation for people to view the work long after the performance took place. As documentation, it functions as an archive of the effects that philosophy has on Piper as a black female artist working in early 1970s America. The didactic panel contextualizing *Food* in Tate Modern's sprawling group exhibition *Performing for the Camera* states: "The original presentation included 44 pages of a paperback edition of Kant's text torn out and annotated by Piper" (Tate Modern 2016). I have accessed these pages through the Adrian Piper Archive in Berlin, where they have digitized scans of the original text that Piper marked up over the course of the private performance as archival material and performance detritus.
3 The self-portraits exist to this day as documentation, being preserved in the Adrian Piper Research Archive Foundation in Berlin and also being shown in exhibitions, such as the large-scale group exhibition "Performing for the Camera" in 2016 at the Tate Modern. The tape recordings, however, have "since been destroyed" (Piper, *Food*).

References

Bowles, John. 2006. "Adrian Piper as African American Artist." *American Art* 20, no. 3: 108–117.
———. 2007. "'Acting Like a Man': Adrian Piper's Mythic Being and Black Feminism in the 1970s." *Signs* 32, no. 3: 621–647.
———. 2011. *Adrian Piper: Race, Gender, and Embodiment.* Durham, NC: Duke University Press.
Jones, Amelia. 1998. *Body Art/Performing the Subject.* Minneapolis: University of Minnesota Press.

———. 1999. "Art History/Art Criticism: Performing Meaning." In *Performing the Body, Performing the Text,* edited by Amelia Jones and Andrew Stephenson, 39–55. New York: Routledge.

———. 2006. *Self/Image: Technology, Representation, and the Contemporary Subject.* New York: Routledge.

———. 2012. *Seeing Differently: A History and Theory of Identification and the Visual Arts.* New York: Routledge.

Jones, Amelia and Adrian Heathfield, eds. 2012. *Perform, Repeat, Record: Live Art in History.* Bristol, England: Intellect.

Kant, Immanuel. 2007 [1790]. *Critique of Judgment.* Edited by Nicholas Walker, translated by James Creed Meredith. Oxford: Oxford University Press.

O'Neill-Butler, Lauren. "Adrian Piper Speaks! (for Herself)." *The New York Times.* 5 July 2018. Web. https://www.nytimes.com/2018/07/05/opinion/adrian-piper-speaks-for-herself.html

Piper, Adrian. 1971. "Food for the Spirit" [artist statement]. Berlin: Adrian Piper Research Archive Foundation. A scan of the physical artist statement was provided to the author via e-mail courtesy of the archivist of the Adrian Piper Research Archive Foundation on 12 August 2016.

———. 1974a. *Talking to Myself: The Ongoing Autobiography of an Art Object.* Hamburg: Hossman.

———. 1974b. Untitled Statement. In "Make a Political Statement." *Art-Rite* 6 (Summer): 24.

———. 1975a. *The Mythic Being: Doing Yoga* [artist statement]. Adrian Piper Research Archive Foundation. http://www.adrianpiper.com/art/the_mythic_being-doing_yoga_2.shtml

———. 1975b. *Some Reflective Surfaces* [artist statement]. Adrian Piper Research Archive Foundation. www.adrianpiper.com/vs/sound_surfaces.shtml

———. 1975c. *The Mythic Being: Getting Back* [artist statement]. Generali Foundation. http://foundation.generali.at/en/collection/artist/piper-adrian/artwork/the-mythic-being-getting-back.html?nomobile=#.XXkY8FB7lE4

———. 1981. "Food for the Spirit, July 1971." *High Performance* 4, no. 1: 34–35.

———. 1985. "Two Conceptions of the Self." *Philosophical Studies: An International Journal for Philosophy in the Analytic Tradition* 48, no. 2: 173–197.

———. 1987a. "Moral Theory and Moral Alienation." *The Journal of Philosophy* 84, no. 2: 102–118.

———. 1987b. "Flying." In *Adrian Piper: Reflections 1967–1987,* edited by Jane Farver. New York: Alternative Museu, 19–24.

———. 1991. *What It's Like, What It Is #3.* Adrian Piper Research Archive Foundation. www.adrianpiper.com/art/What_Its_Like-What_It_Is.shtml

———. 1993. "The Logic of Modernism." *Callaloo: A Journal of African Diaspora Arts and Letters* 16, no. 3: 574–578.

———. 1994. *The Hypothesis Series, 1968–1970* [press release]. Paula Cooper Gallery, New York. www.paulacoopergallery.com/exhibitions/adrian-piper-the-hypothesis-series-1968-70/installation-views

———. 1996a. *Out of Order, Out of Sight: Selected Writings in Meta-Art 1968–1992, Volume I.* Cambridge, MA: MIT Press.

———. 1996b. *Out of Order, Out of Sight: Selected Writings in Art Criticism 1967–1992, Volume II.* Cambridge, MA: MIT Press.

———. 2006. "Intuition and Concrete Particularity in Kant's Transcendental Aesthetic." In *Rediscovering Aesthetics: Transdisciplinary Voices from Art History, Philosophy, and Art Practice,* edited by Francis Halsall et al., 1–20. Redwood City, CA: Stanford University Press.

———. 2012a. "NEWS (September 2012)." adrianpiper.com/news_sep_2012.shtml

———. 2012b. *Thwarted Projects, Dashed Hopes, a Moment of Embarrassment.* Adrian Piper Research Archive Foundation, September. www.adrianpiper.com/news_sep_2012.shtml

———. 2013. *Rationality and the Structure of the Self Volume II: A Kantian Conception.* Adrian Piper Research Archive Foundation. http://www.adrianpiper.com/rss/index.shtml

31
DIOGENES

Yunus Tuncel

The best examples for performative philosophy in the Western tradition come down to us from the Cynics, especially Diogenes who is the main subject of this essay. Our main source for his life and performative actions is Diogenes Laertius's *Lives of Eminent Philosophers*. The emergence of the Cynics is shrouded in mystery, because not much is known about their founder, Antisthenes. What comes down to us about the Cynics is mostly about Diogenes of Sinope who, according to legend, was banished from his home city, for debasing the currency, and moved to Athens. The Cynics shared similar concerns with other post-Socratic schools, such as the search for the good life, for the good state, and for truth-telling, but they departed from them in the way they stood against social conventions, in the way they associated with animals and the animal world, and in the way they did philosophy. Instead of relying only on the power of words, 'logoi,' they also used acts, often shameless acts, not to mention humor and witticism.[1] These acts had certain performative value and created bridges between thinking and being, between mind and body, and between the performer and the observer. Cynics have often been criticized for not having philosophical rigor; however, academic philosophy has become sterile and stagnant, detached from life and culture, for the sake of "rigorous" thinking. We can ask how, in our age, we can do performative philosophy with the depth and rigor that thinking demands. In what follows, I will present some of the Cynic acts, those of Diogenes of Sinope, the first known performance philosopher in ancient Greece, as reported by Diogenes Laertius, while keeping in mind the question raised earlier, and discuss how they engage the body at the level of primordial registers, which are ecstatic, aggressive/violent, transgressive, erotic, and metaphoric. In this way, we can also understand how Diogenes the Cynic could contribute to performance philosophy.

Ecstatic. Ecstatic is to be understood in the Dionysian sense, which Nietzsche designated to be crucial to Greek dramatic performance, as symbolized by the dancing and singing chorus. He recognized this ecstatic/animal function in the satyr and the satyr chorus of Greek theater, which formed a bridge between the animal and the human worlds (Nietzsche, 1968).[2] There is also the satyr chorus through which a link to animality is established. Acting like animals, raising animals to a higher status, is an important sign of the Cynics, contra the condemnation of the animal to a lesser status in and through the civilizing process. The Cynics' association with animals, primarily with dogs, is indicative of their mode of living according to nature and also their capacity and actuality to lose themselves in other beings and become unified again, which is the core function of the Dionysian. We can read Cynic acts as ecstatic acts in which an attempt is made toward the other to become one with that other. Being like an animal or acting like an animal constitutes such a bridge. One example from Diogenes' life is reported by Laertius: "At a feast certain people kept throwing all the bones to him as they would have done to a dog. Thereupon he played a dog's trick and drenched them" (Laertius 1925, p. 49). Shameful acts are performed to jolt others, so as to move them out of the ordinary into the extra-ordinary. However, ecstatic acts establish a bond between the performer and the audience, creating the original unity of spectacle.

Aggressive/violent. Spitting in someone's face, beating with a staff, and urinating on someone are some of the aggressive Cynic acts. In the first episode, Diogenes, while visiting a magnificent house, was asked by his companion not to expectorate, upon which he cleared his throat and discharged his phlegm on the man's face (Laertius 1925, p. 35). In the second episode, he called out for men; when people showed up, he started beating them with his staff saying "It was men I called for, not scoundrels" (Laertius 1925, p. 35). In another episode, a man, knowing that Cynics are associated with dogs – this was a source of common joke with Cynics – threw a bone at Diogenes; in turn, Diogenes pissed on the man (Laertius 1925, p. 35). Violence, as Artaud[3] understands it, exists in spectacle to shake and enervate the whole spectacular field. In archaic societies, sacrificial rituals were performed to bring the community together around the sacred object: an object that was feared and revered at the same time. Although there is no evidence as to what types of sacrificial rituals the Cynics practiced, other than what was accepted at the time, there is an indication for their violent acts, perhaps as sublimated sacrifice or as agonistic practices that were common in ancient Greece at the time. One such story from Laertius recounts, "And when a man, who was very superstitious, said to him, 'With one blow I will break your head;' 'And I,' he replied, 'with one sneeze will make you tremble'" (Laertius 1925, p. 51). Breaking heads and making tremble were common occurrences in the combat games of ancient Greece. The Cynics were no strangers to such games and used their symbolism.

Transgressive. Transgression is a significant aspect of the Cynic performance, as it was for Greek tragedy. Transgression is to go beyond the established norms, the everyday and the ordinary. The Cynics were known as debasers of the coin, an act with which Diogenes was charged in his home city, Sinope (Laertius 1925, p. 23), and which came to symbolize the dominant Cynic gesture. Transgression is the second half of the human story, complementing the world of taboos, as Bataille claims in many of his works, but most significantly in his *Erotism*. One significant aspect of Cynic culture that separates Cynics from the rest was their shameless acts. Shamelessness meant to break down the ordinary taboos in the public sphere by urinating, masturbating, exposing private body parts (this must have been very easy for ancient Greeks with their light clothing), and acting like animals. They claimed that these taboos did not conform with our nature, that is, our animal nature, and were bound to be transgressed. These gestures are visceral and can often be shocking to the everyday audience, as Cutler observes (Cutler 2005, pp. 142–145).

Erotic. Eroticism in the domain of sexuality can be likened to the total artwork in the domain of arts. It activates and brings together all human functions in the sexual life of a human being; in the erotic act, one becomes fractured yet whole again. Therefore, erotic spectacles are needed to cultivate an erotic culture. However, such spectacles must be bound within a mythic context and, as a result, have a cult value. For instance, in Greek tragic performances, the satyr play had such a function. To what extent the Cynics like Diogenes intended their acts to be erotic is hard to assess. However, their sexual acts, such as masturbation in public and invocations of adultery, can be read as erotic signs. Many areas of ancient Greek culture were eroticized: specific cults and gods, the athletic culture, the war culture, the symposia, and some of the schools of philosophy (like that of Socrates). We can assume that the Cynic sexual acts, such as public masturbation, used certain erotic signs and symbols in order to be 'provocative' and thereby to break down the existing thought/action patterns and to create "embodied thoughts." Our prejudices, or doxa as the Greeks called them, are often coagulated not only in words but also in our psychosomatic functions and emotional make-up. To jolt and shift them, an extra-ordinary act is needed, an act that, while being unique, will resonate with the spectator and will elicit a response. In this way, a new embodied thought may arise, with a new constellation of mental and psychosomatic forces.

Metaphoric. Another important contribution of Cynic gestures to performative philosophy is their attack on ordinary beliefs and concepts. The effect was probably similar to the skeptic suspension of judgment, but even more radical than that, if one is forced back to an *original* metaphorical act of word formation. In other words, Cynic attacks can help break down our inherited thought patterns and concept formations, by calling into question the process of transference in and through which images and sounds come together. It is necessary to understand *transference* in its broader context than the meaning evoked by language and psychoanalysis. Many Cynic acts can be construed as interceptions into perception to break down the existing image-sound patterns. Since these interceptions consist not only of words but, more often than not, of gestures, they can have a variety of effects on the other side. And these effects can dissolve ordinary perception. One legend that strikes me as a good example of Cynic interception is as follows:

> When one day he was gravely discoursing and nobody attended to him, he began whistling, and as people clustered about him, he reproached them with coming in all seriousness to hear nonsense, but slowly and contemptuously when the theme was serious.
> (Laertius 1925, p. 29)

Here, whistling draws attention with which he attracts and at the same time repels the crowds.

Performance in any form, mimetic or non-mimetic, cannot be only a mental activity, just as human beings are not merely walking minds. All human functions, mental or physical (and more often than not, they are hard to separate), belong together, and must be sustained holistically in spectacle and performative philosophy. Since philosophy is the domain of thinking, it can easily tend to fly into the abstract domain and establish itself as separated from the body, as superior to the body, which is rooted in what Nietzsche, a recent Cynic, calls the "Despisers of the Body," and in ascetic idealism as a mode of interpretation and will to power. Such a temptation must be resisted and bodily regimes in performative philosophy must be cultivated to anchor thinking unto the body, since the body and bodily functions are primary and the animal human is silent, and has no say over its "human" destiny. Nietzsche's Cynic performance philosopher, Zarathustra, says: "But the greater thing — in which you do not want to believe — is your body and its great reason: it does not say I, but does I" (Nietzsche 2005, p. 30).

In conclusion, it is extremely difficult to practice Cynic shameless acts in academic philosophy in our age.[4] First, Cynics have been derided by society because of their "immoralism," and by philosophers because of their lack of rigor for doing "real philosophy." Second, their reliance on bodily performance led them to be marginalized under the regimes of ascetic idealism; they would be considered outcasts by medievals. Third, the academic environment, with its formal rules in confined spaces, is not conducive to the performance of Cynic acts. And yet, despite all of these factors, Cynicism remains highly significant both for performance and performance philosophy. Most Cynic acts, or what may resemble them, especially in the way presented earlier, occur, to list only a few from our times, in the works of performance artists such as Jaime del Val (the use of nudity), Marina Abramović (transgressing limits), Oleg Kulik (offending the spectator and jolting his/her sensibility), Hermann Nitsch (the use of animal sacrifice and blood), and Artaud (the use of violence in theatrical setting). In their works, performance and philosophical wisdom come together. I am not suggesting that we imitate Cynic acts today. However, we can learn from ancient Cynics like Diogenes, and bring performance, action, and life to philosophical practices, without necessarily weakening the rigor of thought, as the critics of Cynics have argued. In other words, we need to look at Cynics from a different perspective – from the standpoint of the needs of philosophy of performance today – and include bodily actions and witticism in the way we philosophize. In this way, by bringing philosophy and performance together, we will be able to invigorate philosophical practice and bring thoughtful depth to performance.

Notes

1. There are many examples of Cynic humor; here is one of them from Diogenes: "On being asked by a tyrant what bronze is best for a statue, he replied, "That of which Harmodius and Aristogiton were moulded" (Laertius 1925, p. 51).
2. Dionysian Greeks, as Nietzsche presents, gives us one of the best examples of "live performance" in the form of "embodied interaction" as opposed to mediatized performance (Krasner & Saltz 2006, p. 10).
3. Half a century before Artaud, Nietzsche called for externalization of cruelty in their appropriate outlets within the economy of a culture, although Nietzsche's framework is broader than theater. For Nietzsche, this would be "refined cruelty" (Nietzsche 1982, pp. 17–18).
4. Most Cynic acts would be subject to prosecution by courts and/or university regulations. One would not last very long as a professor if one urinated on a student, even if there was a Cynic or a philosophical context to doing so. In my work, instead of using shameless Cynic acts, which would be difficult, I simulate their teachings by using gestures, saying out of the ordinary things to take my audience out of their comfort zone, introducing unusual practices (unusual for that setting), and establishing personal bonds with my audience.

References

Bataille. G. 1986. *Eroticism*, translated by Mary Dalwood, San Francisco, CA: City Lights Publishers.
Cutler, I. 2005. *Cynicism from Diogenes to Dilbert*, Jefferson, NC: McFarland & Company.
Krasner, D. & Saltz, D. eds. 2006. *Staging Philosophy, Intersections of Theater, Performance, and Philosophy*, Michigan: University of Michigan Press.
Laertius, D. 1925. *Lives of Eminent Philosophers, Volume II, Book VI: Diogenes*, Cambridge, MA: Harvard University Press.
Nietzsche, F. 1968. *The Birth of Tragedy*, translated by Walter Kaufmann, New York: Vintage Press.
Nietzsche, F. 1982. *Daybreak*, translated by R. J. Hollingdale, Cambridge: Cambridge University Press.
Nietzsche, F. 2005. *Thus Spoke Zarathustra*, translated by Graham Parkes, Oxford: Oxford University Press.

32
A DICE THROWER

Mischa Twitchin

As may be noticed, this article is composed of twelve paragraphs, so that one could participate in its composition by throwing dice to decide in which order to read them. Using the dice, one could choose to eliminate each number from future possibilities, until all twelve paragraphs had been read, or adopt the alternative constraint of re-reading paragraphs until finally each has been read at least once. Although adding the two numbers of the dice to make one is more usual, one could also read the two numbers together, thereby expanding the field of possibilities from 11 to 66, rather than 2 to 12. After all, the reader need not be confined here to the role of what John Cage called a 'contractor', interpreting text according to an academic 'morphology of continuity' (1987 [1958], p. 36). As these paragraphs are read successively with the dice (rather than remaining simultaneous), the reader might then discover unforeseen continuities by chance. For interest changes when simultaneity is overtaken by succession – when the sense that any order could both be and not be at the same time gives way to the sense that there is one order or another; or when a combinatorial reading is overtaken by an expositional one. Following the example of Michel Foucault, one might say then: 'The thought-event is as singular as a throw of the dice; the thought-phantasm does not search for truth, but repeats thought' (Foucault 1986, p. 179).

Does the figure of a dice thrower simply repeat discussion of 'the difference between a world with chances in it and a determinate world' (James 1884, n.p.), participating in a debate about (ir)responsibility – whether on earth or in heaven? God does not play dice, according to Einstein, but, according to Nietzsche, god is dead (cf. Nietzsche 1978). Beyond belief, the question is often posed, in both moral and epistemological terms: Is anything possible then? Even 'performance philosophy'?! The least we can say of the latter is that it is not reducible to an opposition between its terms – such as one used to hear regularly repeated at conferences, dividing participants into 'theorists' and 'practitioners'; the former supposedly speaking an arcane language, a new Latin in which academic privilege asserted itself, and the latter supposedly plain speaking. These clichés have since been displaced by the institutionalisation of 'practice as research' (PaR), where performance philosophy surely offers a more interesting conceptual example than academic attempts to define PaR, instead of actually practising research; that is, engaging with 'outcomes' that are not already known and merely reported on for an ever-expanding industry of academic 'assessment'. In this case, philosophy functions as 'doxography' (Deleuze and Guattari 1994 [1991], p. 80) and performance as simply its 'qualification'.

'Indeterminacy' is the title of a lecture by John Cage (printed in 'excessively small type… to expose [its] intentionally pontifical character' (1987 [1958], p. 35). The lecture explores the variables in terms of which indeterminacy can be conceived, both in composition and performance, without being arbitrary in a 'subjective' rather than a structural (or impersonal) sense; that is, without abandoning the contingent to the simply accidental, or the combinatorial to the merely random. Here, the dice removes the temptation of improvisation, as a falling back into 'subjectivity' distinct from chance – into an arbitrariness that is not formal but, all too often, conventional; just as so much academic writing simply reiterates what is expected of its discipline.

Conceptual personae already include the Idiot and the Madman (in Deleuze and Guattari's account [1994 (1991), p. 70]), so why not add the dice thrower – as a figure of and for performance philosophy? What relation might this persona have, then, to the Nietzschean itinerants who will gather at a future Asses Festival to celebrate, with laughter and drink, in remembrance of the eternal return (rather than in communion with divine eternity)? What relation might a dice thrower have to the fate of that ancient practitioner of performance philosophy, the lover? 'Lucky' in one domain but not both, would he or she be more or less melancholy than the gambler? And what relation might she or he have to the ascetic or the aesthete?

'Every thought emits a throw of the dice' ('*toute pensée émet un Coup de Dés*') is the last line of a poem by Stéphane Mallarmé, whose very title tells us that 'a throw of the dice does not abolish chance'. Between chance and thought comes composition – as the possibility of aleatory combinations, with indeterminate 'outcomes', rather than those disciplined by linear, sequential, or deductive consequences. An image of and for thought, Mallarmé's 'dice throw' offers a displacement of those alternatives, expressive of their performance, that have become basic concepts of philosophy: the Cartesian *cogito* and the Socratic *gnothi seauton* ['know thyself']. The subject of the dice throw (as, here, that of performance philosophy) is not, however, bound in a closed circle of individuality – for the 'I' is not what it imagines. The claim of consciousness to define itself is a wish to deny itself, exposed in a dynamic relation with what is unconscious. As Deleuze and Guattari note: 'Conceptual personae are also true agents of enunciation. "Who is 'I'?" It is always a third person' (1994 [1991], p. 65).

Tyche is a god of many names, according to Dio Chrysostom: 'Her impartiality has been named Nemesis; her invisibility, Elpis; her inevitability, Moira; her righteousness, Themis – truly a deity of many names and many ways' (*Discourses*, 64, 8). As Giorgio Agamben comments on this citation of Chrysostom: 'Tyche is not only chance; no matter how contradictory this may seem to us, she is also destiny and necessity' (2018 [2015], pp. 16–17). We are born under these signs, Tyche and Ananke, who were represented for the ancient Egyptians by the moon, as it affects our bodies, and by the knot (ibid., p. 4). In the absence of the divine, the secular still entrust themselves to the necessity of chance, even though the invention of humanity seems paradoxically limited to an infinity that changes nothing in reality.

How to distinguish between a dice thrower and the dice throw itself; the poet from the poem; the performer (or even the philosopher) from the performance? Following his suggestion that '[t]he only way to escape contingency would have been to have become just as eternal and infinite as the latter', Quentin Meillassoux, in his reading of Mallarmé's *A Dice Throw* poem, comes to questions such as these: 'But how? How to be, oneself, all the options of a throw? How to incorporate the dialectical structure of Chance, which, like the speculative Infinite, contains in itself the contradictory totality of alternative possibilities?' (2012 [2011], p. 128) Fundamentally, in Meillassoux's view, 'reading this apotheosis, we understand that the poem is quite simply in the process of doing what it describes' (2012 [2011], p. 44). *A Dice Throw* has what he calls – in quotation marks – a 'performative' dimension, in the becoming act of the text (ibid., p. 116). With its curious Heideggerian overtones, the thrower becomes the thrown; that is, perhaps, a possible instance of 'performance philosophy'.

Rolling the dice, there are two numbers that never come up: zero and one. This is gratifying, as it means that a throw of the dice is not reducible to the digital binarism with which contemporary culture is so infatuated (in which the consumer becomes the 'human face' of computational capitalism). The persona of the dice thrower belongs to a world before super-computers changed the meaning of calculation in games such as chess and Go. (Imagine, for example, *The Seventh Seal* remade as a version of the Turing Test, as if the dream of Providence were but a delusion of AI.) A dice thrower offers a persona of and for the *savoir-vivre* of a world before predictive texting and automated decision making; he or she has no digital profile to 'like'. And yet, there is always a zero in play with the dice roll – in the time before the dice settle and the resulting numbers transform possibility, momentarily, into actuality. Zero, nothingness, the presentiment or echo of being, remains the potential of distinguishing each number, not simply from the others but from itself. (One might prefer, indeed, to read the silences between these paragraphs and meditate simply on one's own thoughts.) Perhaps the pleasure of rolling the dice is in this very suspension of being, as a way of experiencing time? The time not of performance or philosophy; but that of performance philosophy, of 'an interpenetration of these opposites… which is more characteristic than either' (Cage 1987 [1958], p. 36).

One paragraph here only 'follows' another within a certain concept of time, which gives weight to the sense of wager or hazard in the roll of the dice – whether wanting to avoid it or, perhaps, wishing to cheat it. The point is not that the throw is resolved or sublated by the resulting number – but that the throw is an event in which the number, the outcome, remains indeterminate. The question or the wager, then, takes on a new vibrancy of thought, as a reading (or performance) that does not simply 'follow' from it, as its 'preconceived object' (Cage 1987 [1958], p. 31). This sense of a chance that is never abolished is what distinguishes the so-called 'analytical' philosophy, grounded in logic, from the so-called 'Continental' traditions of thought. The former eschew complexity in favour of 'clarity', associations in favour of deductions, the 'literary' (or 'artistic') in favour of the literal, and constellations in favour of conclusions. (It is perhaps no accident that performance philosophy seems to find so little resonance in analytic traditions.)

What might be the genealogy of this 'thought-event' of the dice throw that refracts chance and determinacy, necessity and repetition – as instances of performance philosophy? But if we are without souls would any genealogy of such wagers be simply meaningless? If we are composed only of that 'humorous sadness' evoked by Jacques (in *As you like it*) – being merely a handful of the atomists' dust, lacking that quintessence invoked by Hamlet – does the gamble of a dice throw mean anything to anyone? And as for the relation between a dice thrower (as a performing philosopher) and the Chinese Book of Changes, or the casting of palm nuts in Ifa Divination, that would have to wait for the thirteenth paragraph of this essay.

Entering into Pierre Klossowski's simulacrum of the myth of Diana and Actaeon as a modern novel (in 'the presumptuous and impious will to appropriate myth through the mediation of language' [1998 (1980), p. 70]), we find that the hunted hunter is said to have 'dreaded chance: he wanted to anticipate destiny, to become its accomplice, to coincide with destiny with all his willpower… a mad overestimation of free will at the expense of grace…' (ibid., p. 69). In the 'ruse' of a 'literalistic application of the analogy of being', Klossowski exposes the mistrust of a 'facile elevation of a tangible reality to the level of a spiritual truth' (ibid., p. 70). Where a roll of the dice is made to invoke such a truth, whether of destiny or 'simply' chance, the very casting of the dice means to forego the possibility it promises. This is the scene of Nietzsche's 'eternal recurrence'; no one escapes their destiny, precisely because they do not have one, unless and until they 'own' it. (Oedipus, for example, calls himself a 'son of Tyche' [cited in Agamben 2018 [2015], p. 16].) In an age where calculation rules, there are those who believe that 'neuro-science' is the new phantomachia – with all the fervour of those who still want to kill that which they proclaim to be dead: the soul. For them, the subject and the world, being and difference, are separate phenomena, rather than constellations of twins.

Research, resistance, return, reality, relativism, roll, recursive, representation, reductive, refusal, relation, reading.

References

Agamben, Giorgio. 2018 [2015]. *The Adventure*. Trans. Lorenzo Chiesa, Cambridge, MA: MIT Press.
Cage, John. 1987 [1958]. 'Composition as Process (Indeterminacy)', in: John Cage: *Silence*, London: Marion Boyars.
Deleuze, Gilles and Guattari, Félix. 1994 [1991]. *What Is Philosophy?* Trans. Graham Burchell and Hugh Tomlinson, London: Verso.
Foucault, Michel. 1986. 'Theatrum Philosophicum.' Trans. Donald Bouchard and Sherry Simon, in: *Language, Counter-Memory, Practice*, ed. Donald Bouchard, New York: Cornell U.P., pp. 165–196.
James, William. 1884. *The Dilemma of Determinism* (available as a pdf from https://www.uky.edu/~eushe2/Pajares/JamesDilemmaOfDeterminism.html [last accessed, 23.09.18]).
Klossowski, Pierre. 1998 [1980]. *Diana at Her Bath*. Trans. Steven Sartarelli, New York: Marsilio Publishers.
Meillassoux, Quentin. 2012 [2011]. *The Number and the Siren*. Trans. Robin Mackay, Falmouth: Sequence Press.
Nietzsche, Friedrich. 1978. *Thus Spoke Zarathustra* (Pt. IV). Trans. Walter Kaufmann, Harmondsworth: Penguin Books.

33
OPEN TEXT – OPEN PERFORMANCE
Hélène Cixous and Ariane Mnouchkine

Elisabeth Schäfer, Esther Hutfless and Gertrude Postl

There is a significant shared moment between the philosophical and prosaic–poetic writings of Hélène Cixous and the theatrical praxis of Ariane Mnouchkine at Théâtre du Soleil: a fundamental and radical openness towards the 'other' and the future. This makes both their individual and collaborative works a promising starting point for a discussion of the ethical-aesthetical as well as the transformative potential of performance philosophy.

The French director Ariane Mnouchkine was one of the founders of *Théâtre du Soleil* – a cooperative theatre company established in 1964. From its beginning, the Soleil has pursued a politically transformative theatrical approach: to criticize and transform classical theatre production, including its commercialization and its hierarchies, to question societal developments and to intervene politically (cf. Miller 2018, pp. 7–8), as indicated in the company's programme of 1975: 'We want to reinvent the rules of the game that unveil daily reality by showing it not as familiar and immutable, but as surprising and transformable' (Stevens 2016, p. xiii).

The collaboration with the author, philosopher and dramatic advisor Hélène Cixous – famous for her poetic fiction, her writings on deconstruction and literary criticism, and, most influentially, for establishing *écriture féminine* as a style of writing – began in 1985 and still exists today. Her texts, similar to the work of the Soleil, resist fixed meanings and monolithic significations; they break with the common rules of grammar and punctuation and intervene in the symbolic order. Manifold intertextual references and citations, as well as the use of different languages, open her texts for new, unexpected and hidden meanings.

This article will centre on the notion of 'openness' as common ground between Cixous' writings and Mnouchkine's theatrical praxis at the Théâtre du Soleil. Cixous' texts, including those she wrote for the stage, are characterized by a radical openness, challenging the idea of a singular authorship – they have no clear beginning or end, they cannot be attributed to any particular literary or theoretical genre and they encourage the reader to actively interact with the texts. Similarly, the stage productions of the Soleil engage in a comparable openness by escaping the textual closure and completion typical for traditional plays. By approaching a play's textual features as continuously changing citations, by relying on the input of the ensemble and by blending life and art (the company work closely together but they do not live together constantly as has been the rumour since the 1970s[1]), the words spoken on the stage – together with the aspects of production – are an ongoing process, each performance differing from the previous one. Cixous and Mnouchkine – each in her own way but especially when working together – create a milieu of unenclosed textual and performative processes which affect the concepts of text and writing and also of performance and theatre practice. These processes are porous, open and dynamic, engaging the reader and spectator in never-ending surprising and unexpected ways.

Investigating how the mentioned openness manifests itself in Cixous' writings, as well as in Mnouchkine's understanding of theatre, will necessarily also be an investigation of the relationship between text and performance. What does it mean to talk about a performative text? What is the role of the text/language for performance? In short, we will have to expand the meanings of the notion of 'text' as well as 'performance' in order to grasp the openness involved in both instances. For Mnouchkine, the bodies of the performers become signs; they can therefore be read as text, while for Cixous, every text is imbued with a performative quality as she understands texts as deeply connected to the body: 'Write your self. Your body must be heard' (Cixous 1976, p. 880).

Mnouchkine's theatre work can be described as 'open' in all its facets. She is famous for choosing politically charged material; for her employment of different performance styles and theatre traditions (in particular Asian theatre, such as *Nō* or *Kabuki*, but also the *Commedia dell'Arte* and inspirations from various modernist European theatre and performance theories); for a refusal to present a coherent linear narrative with a clear beginning and end; for a focus on the actors rather than the text; for using an archive of texts and narratives rather than one singular text; for the place given to improvization on the part of the actors; for a focus on the production process rather than the final product; for a multi-ethnic and multi-cultural outreach (with respect to troop members as well as languages spoken) and for attempts to reach out to the audience (physically, emotionally, intellectually) by transforming a given textual material via its performative embodiment through the actors (a kind of 'translation' process for which the actors serve as translators or mediators). The collaborative and strictly egalitarian structure of the company is central for this production concept in that it can be viewed as enabling this 'translation' work rather than being a mere outside condition for what eventually will take place on stage. Overall, the Soleil productions blend form and content, aesthetics, ethics and politics.

Mnouchkine uses the term 'metaphor' to describe the transformative processes she aims to engage in order to reach the audience.

> (T)hat the theatre is metaphor, metaphor of gesture, of the word, and that what's beautiful in theatre is when an actor transforms a feeling, a memory, a state or a passion. No one sees pure passion unless the actor transforms it into performance, that is to say into a sign, into a gesture.
>
> *(Mnouchkine & Simon 2005, p. 101)*

According to Mnouchkine's production concept, an inner state has to be made visible (accessible to the audience) through the body of the performer so as to establish 'a sign'. Thus, the body itself becomes a kind of 'text', something that has to be read or deciphered by the spectators in order to undergo the transformative process that Mnouchkine intends. However, the performing body as sign/text does not reveal the individual inner state of a respective actor but rather becomes a representative for a larger historical event.

It is for those reasons that Mnouchkine rejects psychological realism or psychological theatre, productions which confirm for the audience what they already know. Instead, Mnouchkine wants to take the audience out of their everyday reality, and wants to de-familiarize them via aesthetic means through what she calls 'theatrical theatre'. In the words of Judith G. Miller, '(T)heater should take us to the life obscured by everyday reality […] theater moves us to a transcendent realm, to an undefined but felt metaphysical space' (Miller 2018, p. 40). Mnouchkine's preferred means to accomplish 'theatrical theatre' and to generate an 'aesthetic shock' (idem, p. 43) are the stylized movements and gestures of Asian performance techniques and the use of masks and make-up. Masks, together with strong make-up, hide the facial expressions that are associated with psychological realism; they are themselves signs and help to turn the performing body of the actor into a sign as a whole. According to Mnouchkine, 'working correctly with masks allows bodies to become forms, figures, and signs – or easily readable visual images' (idem). Hiding the face of the individual actor through stylization and already coded visual cues creates the effect of an alienation necessary for the transformative process on the side of the audience.

As stated already, the production process is crucial for the openness inherent in Théâtre du Soleil productions. From the choice of material and questions regarding the presentation of a given material, to text, costumes and *mise-en-scène*, all the way to decisions as to who plays which part – all is the result of a collaborative interaction between the individual members of the group. Furthermore, the audience is given the opportunity to observe the actors in their preparation for the stage which undercuts the illusory aspect of the performance and its status as a finished product (comparable to Cixous appearing and disappearing as the author of her texts within those very texts). Due to the importance placed on collaboration, improvisation, ongoing revisions and audience involvement, no Soleil production is like the other.

However, the unfinished quality of each production – also seen within the writings of Cixous – does not entail that meaning is arbitrary or signification of a random occurrence. Given the importance placed on the sign, Théâtre du Soleil productions lend themselves to a semiological approach with signs to be encountered on different levels: the level of the literal text (in itself a collaborative, unfinished creation, or, in the case of an authored text, for example, by Hélène Cixous, the result of many revisions in response to input from the group), the level of the body of the performer (including movements, gestures, facial expressions or masks and make-up) and the level of visual images provided by production elements. One could claim that every Théâtre du Soleil production is a multi-layered 'text' which, due to its openness, has to be deciphered on different levels at the same time, with the different qualities of signifying structures influencing and determining each other.

The 'openness' characteristic in Hélène Cixous' texts makes her the perfect collaborator for the Théâtre du Soleil. Comparable to the production process for Mnouchkine, for Cixous the very act of writing itself is collaborative. She states, 'The books for which I am the scribe belong to everyone' (Cixous 2005, p. 188). Indeed, her open-ended process is neither determined nor controlled by the position of the author. Rather, the writer gives herself over to the contingencies of the activity of writing without a clear sense of what the final product will be. 'My book writes itself' (idem, p. 191), '(w)hen I write I do nothing on purpose, except stop. My only voluntary intervention is interruption. Breaking. Cutting. Letting go' (idem). In a similar way to Mnouchkine's productions, the body plays a central role for the signifying project: 'A desire to write rises in my body […] The entire body readies itself' (idem, p. 192). While in Mnouchkine's productions it is the body of the performers which signifies, in Cixous' case the body is always already involved in the creation of a text in that, for her, writing is not a mental but a partially physical, unconscious activity. The source for what is written is the secret, that which is not consciously known, that which is not visible – analogous to Mnouchkine's use of masks, her use of archives of multi-cultural forms of theatrical expression, of historical, political and mythological narratives and figures and various motives of a shared social imaginary which all have in common that they hide and reveal at the same time.

Cixous' explicit reference to the unconscious as a prime source for any work with language, thus for writing and accordingly also for the theatrical (Cixous views the theatrical as simultaneously the unconscious, the spiritual and the political) (cf. Miller 2018, p. 42), does not find an exact correspondence in Mnouchkine's reflections on her own work. However, the role of the unconscious can be located within different aspects of the production process: the actors can only achieve what Mnouchkine wants them to achieve if they are willing to open themselves to an unconscious reservoir of voices, gestures and movements; the theatrical effects also target the repressed desires and fears of the audience to initiate a possible transformative change; and last not least, the way the Soleil approaches historical material can, to a certain extent, also be described in terms of an unearthing of the respective political and cultural repressed.

Furthermore, Cixous just like Mnouchkine – in all her texts, not just those written for the stage – refuses a coherent, linear narrative. Instead, her texts could be described in terms of a compilation of narratives, different strings of stories woven together. These stories are intersected by philosophical reflections, political assessments, memories, biographical facts and references to historical or everyday events. Continuously throughout, references and allusions are made to other authors – indicated or not, described as 'intertextual allusions' (Stevens 2016, p. xviii). It is attributable to those particular features that Cixous' text cannot be categorized by any genre or specific type of text. Rather, the telling of different stories, or parts of stories in one text, in combination with the rich plethora of sources, connections and links, establish what might be called a 'plurality of voices' (equivalent to the use of different languages in the later productions of the Soleil).

Another vital commonality between Mnouchkine and Cixous is their urge to give voice to 'the other' (another variation of openness) – be this women, non-Western populations, the foreigner or stranger, those excluded from the great historical narratives; all that feature in the unknown, unsaid, unconscious underpinnings of established cultural norms. While this concern for 'the other', in Cixous' case, centres around (but is by no means limited to) women, the unconscious, and that which conventionally cannot be said, for Mnouchkine, it is the non-Western, in particular Asian 'other' that influences her work. This renders every one of Mnouchkine's productions to be a representation of 'the other' in a myriad of different ways: such as the device of incorporating masks, elements of Asian theatre traditions and geo-political problems that highlight the othering of non-Western continents.

Openness is what Cixous' and Mnouchkine's projects share. They each work to open up a space in which a multiple corpus of texts, bodies, signs, languages and so on can unfold. Viewing this corpus in terms of its performativity allows a focus on its effects on readers, the audience, others; in short, on the world. *Performance Philosophy* explicitly seeks to think, embody and perform an immanent entanglement of the arts *and* philosophy: '[…] contrary to a deeply rooted belief, the book is not an image of the world. It forms a rhizome with the world […]' (Deleuze and Guattari 2004, p. 12). In this way, Cixous' and Mnouchkine's projects can be seen to form open rhizomes with the world. They work productively with multiple meanings and ambiguities; they approximate things without eliminating or violating them; they work with multiple layers of narrations, imaginations, languages, conscious and unconscious archives involving all the senses. Their work exceeds monolithic significations and is emanating in all directions; it addresses multiple histories of exclusions. An alternative mode of intellectualism is established which does not exhaust itself in ongoing criticism but calls for productive, positive and vital forces to intervene. Such interventions shift and transform the political, social and also symbolic orders. These positive and vital forces are particularly relevant for the encounter with 'the other', which is never threatened with destruction, degradation, annihilation or appropriate classification. Starting from the philosophical assumption that meanings, aesthetic forms, signifying practices, signs gestures are generated immanently out of the open rhizomatic relations shared and repeated with others in the world, the understanding of Performance Philosophy, as realized in the projects of Cixous and Mnouchkine, is based on the power of citations and the radical openness of the event.

Note

1 Here, we refer to an email correspondence with Franck Pendino who is currently in charge of the theatre's archive.

References

Cixous, Hélène. 1976. 'The Laugh of the Medusa.' *Signs*, 1 (4): 875–893. https://doi.org/10.1086/493306
Cixous, Hélène. 2005. 'Writing Blind: Conversation with the Donkey.' Translated by Eric Prenowitz. In: Hélène Cixous: *Stigmata. Escaping Texts*. New York: Routledge, pp. 115–125.
Deleuze, Gilles, and Félix Guattari. 2004. *A Thousand Plateaus*. New York: Continuum.
Miller, Judith G. 2018. *Ariane Mnouchkine*. New York: Routledge.
Mnouchkine, Ariane and Simon, Alfred. 2005. 'Of Loss and Liberation. From an interview with Ariane Mnouchkine by Alfred Simon.' In: David Williams (ed.) *Collaborative Theatre. The Théâtre du Soleil*. New York: Routledge, pp. 97–104.
Stevens, Lara. 2016. 'Editor & Translator's Introduction.' In: Lara Stevens (ed.) *Politics, Ethics and Performance. Hélène Cixous and the Théâtre du Soleil*. Melbourne: re.press, pp. xi–xxiv.

34
ROGER FEDERER

Einav Katan-Schmid

The men's singles final of the Australian Open 2017 was an eagerly awaited performance. After an interval of almost six years, Roger Federer and Rafael Nadal, two of the dominant male tennis players of the current era, were back to compete against each other for victory in the championship. Both players had suffered injuries and missed a large part of the previous season. Crowds again gathered to witness with great anticipation the iconic rivalry between the two champions at the final of this famous grand slam tournament. The match lasted over three-and-a-half hours. Federer won the first set (6:4), Nadal won the second (6:3), then the third set went to Federer (6:1), and the fourth to Nadal (6:3). The match proceeded into a deciding fifth set.

I take up the commentary at this point.

Nadal wins a first break point and takes the lead (3:1). His movements are explosive and decisive. It seems that he knows instinctively where to aim; he puts all his guts into it. Federer's serve is just as explosive and precise, but he appears to be quiet and calm. He breaks back (3:3), in turn, to take the lead. His movements seem effortless. During the ensuing rally, his body is agile and his feet are sprightly; he seems to anticipate the ball as he swiftly moves towards the net. His backhand is especially beautiful; he delivers a powerful volley, streaming force into the shot and then releasing it into a flow from both arms. At the peak of tension, the audience at Rod Laver Arena is ecstatic; people shout and whistle. Nadal seems to be nervous and makes a rare double fault (4:3, 40:0). Then, he channels his emotion into his serve, winning the next point with a strong forehand. "He's just a pure competitor", says Lleyton Hewitt, the commentator, showing his appreciation for Nadal. Nadal takes the lead on the momentum; his mighty serves overpower Federer's game, pushing him towards a series of forced errors (4:3, 40:40). Nevertheless, Federer still seems calm. His movements are free and he enters into the flow of Nadal's serve, as if this is not so much a duel but more a duet. He mixes his shots, trying to send a forehand down the line, but Nadal anticipates it and returns the ball. Federer changes tactics and starts to pass the ball in a sequence of cross-court shots with Nadal. As soon as the structure is established, Federer disrupts it, and with a surprising forehand, he sends a winner down the line. Nadal is too late to reply. It seems as if Nadal has been caught out by the pattern he mistakenly thought he was leading and has been surprised by its sudden discontinuity. Federer reclaims the lead and eventually wins the game (5:3), the set (6:3), the match (6:4, 3:6, 6:1, 3:6, 6:3), and his 18th grand slam championship.

Roger Federer is one of the most acclaimed athletes of our times. In line with iconic sportspersons like Nadia Comaneci and Mohammed Ali, his innovative performance advances the sport he plays, inspires many, and is lauded for both its kinaesthetic beauty and its excellence. David Foster Wallace famously compares Federer's somatic grace to a ballet, analyses his intelligence as "both flesh and not", and defines witnessing his playing as a "religious experience" (Wallace 2006). Christopher Jackson highlights the importance of Federer to the history of tennis, sport in general, and contemporary culture, by situating his beautiful appearance in the history of art and defining Federer himself as an artist (Jackson 2017). As a figure for performance philosophy, Roger Federer's tennis embodies contemplative action and the symbiosis between thought and practice. Federer presents a vivid example through which to consider the relationship between artistry, contemplative knowing, physical wittiness, genuineness, and transformative creativity.

Creativity, artistry, and contemplation never occur in a void. They need the context of both a knowledge-system and a lived experience. Tennis is a sport of protocols, rules, and traditions. The forms of behaviour, the formalizations of the game, and the analysis of the successful tactics of former champions are there for the individual player to follow, to recognize, and to strive for. It is in the protocol that players must shake hands with their opponent and with the chair umpire at the end of each game. It is within the rules of the game that the serve must hit the diagonal service court, and, in terms of tactics, it is well-known that Pete Sampras' technique of serving generates enormous power and spin from a relaxed bodily presence, so opponents cannot easily predict the movement of the ball. When a player learns how to play the game, they learn physically how to behave. The practice of sport is a physical knowledge-system which guides the individual player in how to feel, how to appreciate impressions, and how to coordinate objectives, sensations, and moods within the experience of the game. Nonetheless, a knowledge of tennis is not a mere custom for the player to wear and to execute as-is. Tennis is a matrix of information, which raises tensions and challenges for a player, who must comprehend and solve these challenges with their own body, mind, and spirit. While the protocols require sportsmanship, the competition is based upon rivalry. There are two opponents but only one winner. The aim of the game is to win, rather than to be beautiful, strong, or nice to one's opponent. Aristotle refers to the Olympic Games thus:

> it is not the most beautiful and the strongest that are crowned but those who compete (for it is some of these that are victorious), so those who act win, and rightly win, the noble and good things in life.
>
> *(1994–2009; [c. 350 BC], Book 1, §8)*

The attempt to win is important because it sets new challenges for the player to face experientially. In tennis, without competition, there would be less room for overcoming obstacles, and expressing creativity and artistry. Since both parts aim to win over the other, the opponents bring two contradicting goals to the court. Facing their opposition, they must lead their objective wisely while deconstructing the other's plan. While striving to win, the player must decipher their rival's game, deconstruct it, and redirect the ball's movement. They do it consciously and experientially. If a ball does not go the way a player planned, they must readjust its spin. Sometimes, they cannot do that, so they must review their tactics. When they fail to fulfil their aim, they need to renounce all tendencies towards frustration, anger, or self-doubt in order to concentrate on the next chance. Players should live through experience; they need to be at the same time free and composed in order to perform their best understanding within any given moment. For the purpose of winning, they must be attuned and attentive to their aims, their emotions and their opponents, while remaining sufficiently detached to be in control of the game. The challenge of tennis is even more puzzling given the speed of the game. Players perform decision-making "in the blink of an eye" (Papineau 2017, pp. 25–40) – as fast as they perceive, see, and feel the ball.

Knowledge regulation is performed immediately while playing. However, it takes years of training and reflection, incorporating an understanding of connections between behaviour and results, before a player is a genuine and receptive thinker in action. It is apparent that Federer's contemplative thinking has led him to reach high levels, to improve as a player, and to enjoy success for more than a decade. His post-match press conferences analyses are often very precise – how the ball moved, why a forehand at a certain moment would have been a better choice than a drop shot, which weakness he recognized in himself or in his opponent during the game and how he tried to overcome it or to use it in his favour, and so forth. These reflections demonstrate the active thinker he is on and off court. In the film *Strokes of Genius*, Federer defines playing as problem-solving. He states that a perfect game is impossible to achieve. He describes how when he was young, he strived for perfection too soon, trying to imitate the shots of great players before he had the physicality and the knowledge to achieve the results he wanted. His early ambitions resulted in frustration (Douglas 2018, 00:43). In his first years on tour, Federer was known for his temper, while nowadays he is acknowledged for his calm mood. Compared to other players, it is very rare to see him responding emotionally on court. As described earlier, when Nadal's game forced Federer's errors at the Australian Open 2017 (4:3, 40:40), it seemed that his calmness and patience at this critical moment enabled him to win the next point.

Federer's attitude is interlocked with his versatility as a player. While his sportsmanship and respect for opponents and for the game are widely recognized, his gamesmanship is just as developed. Stephen Potter defines gamesmanship as "the art of winning the game without actually cheating" (2015 [1947], p. 8). The most important feature of gamesmanship is to use playfulness in order to break the flow of the opponent. Federer's attempt in the eighth game of the fifth set was to win Nadal's service game. He needed to disrupt the movement that Nadal had initiated. His forced errors reveal that the power and the spin of the ball were too commanding for him to readjust them immediately into his original plan. At this point, he calmly modified his tactics so that he could further play within Nadal's service game and interrupt it. According to Potter, one principle of gamesmanship is to make the opponent believe that they control the game. By entering into a long rally with Nadal (4:3 40:40), Federer gives Nadal a reason to perceive that Federer is merely reacting to Nadal's shots. It seems that once Nadal believes he controls the momentum, Federer breaks the flow. Federer transforms the game of tricking the opponent into playful artistry, with volleys like a 'tweener' (a shot in between the legs), hitting the ball behind his back, or making a sneak attack from the net, surprising his opponent's second serve with a fast return towards the base line (a move which is known as Sneak Attack By Roger, or in short, 'SABR'). His contemplative and developed attitude of playfulness is entertaining because of the physical wittiness it generates. However, it has also become a key element in his winning and in his ability to sustain his performance at high levels over time. He foresees the game and reacts to the ball before the rival and the audience realize the disruption of the opponent's flow. Furthermore, the flow of his experiential insights and the spiritual beauty of his game could not be as vibrant as they are without him having trained his body and mind to the extent of developing the deep-felt as well as reflective understanding of what playing tennis means to him. A tennis game is a challenge with the risk of losing in front of an audience and playing it demands the bravery of facing failures. As Federer admits in an interview with Andy Roddick, although people might think of him as a naturally effortless player who is not competitive, he is nevertheless gritty and motivated by the joy of winning – "I think I'm more in the part where I love winning" [more than he hates losing] (Fox Sport, August 28, 2013). His playfulness is advanced because it is at once a tactic, a mental attitude, and a personal value.

In the *Nicomachean Ethics*, Aristotle fosters personal values like courage and temperance as complete knowledge and as practical wisdom since the virtuous person deliberately puts their general understanding of well-being into action and contemplates it within practice. As the philosopher writes:

> The attribute in question, then, will belong to the happy man, and he will be happy through his life; for always, or by preference to everything else, he will be engaged in virtuous action and contemplation, and he will bear the chances of life most nobly and equally decorously, if he is 'truly good' and 'foursquare beyond reproach'.
> *(Aristotle 1994–2009 [c. 350 BC], Book 1, §10)*

Federer's performance is philosophically beautiful and wise for the same reasons it is aesthetically pleasing; his movements express his comprehensive understanding. In *Strokes of Genius*, Nadal says that he admires Federer's style: "even if you are someone else's fan you have to be able to recognize excellence and Federer is excellent in every sense". For Nadal to understand Federer is to know what tennis is about (Douglas 2018, 1:22), I add to his statement – to watch Federer play is to realize what knowledge is about. The quality of the engagement he brings into the court is a performative act of undertaking personally the meanings of values and actions. His thoroughgoing movements are skilful, reflective, sensitive, immediate, articulated, and innovative. Both flesh and not, he deciphers and enacts the variable conditions of a game and of himself as an agent of activity and thought. More than a physical capacity, his kinaesthetic beauty is a comprehensive understanding. In playing, he performs clarity concerning the involvedness of all knowledge components – he knows the "why" and the "that" of the game and of himself not less than he knows "how" to play it and how to conduct his actions – and it is strikingly affective. The performance philosopher Roger Federer might not use written words as his medium of reflective thought; however within tennis, he performs wisdom and knowledge-invention.

References

Aristotle. 1994–2009 (c. 350 BC). *Nicomachean ethics*. Translated by W. D. Ross. Cambridge, MA: *The Internet classics archive*. Available at: http://classics.mit.edu/Aristotle/nicomachaen.html (Accessed: September 1, 2017).
Douglas, Andrew. 2018. *Strokes of genius: long live rivalry* [documentary film], The Tennis Channel, USA.
Fox Sports. August 28, 2013. *Roger Federer 1 on 1* [Online Video]. Available at: https://www.youtube.com/watch?v=mzP8-4D0o9w (Accessed: September 1, 2018).
Jackson, Christopher. 2017. *Roger Federer: portrait of an artist*, London: Eyewear Publishing.
Papineau, David. 2017. *Knowing the score: how sport teaches us about philosophy (and philosophy about sport)*, London: Constable.
Potter, Stephen. 2014 (1947). *The theory and practice of gamesmanship. Or, the art of winning games without actually cheating*, London: Bloomsbury Reader.
Wallace, David Foster. 2012 (2006). 'Federer: both flesh and not', in: David Foster Wallace: *Both flesh and not*, New York: Back Bay Books, 5–36.

35

26 MESOSTICS RE AND NOT RE JOHN CAGE

Anthony Gritten

These mesostics work through some recurrent themes from Cage's work. They are what Cage called '100% Mesostics': between two consecutive capitalised letters, neither of the two letters may be used. That there are twenty-six mesostics is a homage to Marcel Duchamp and James Pritchett: the former was the subject of two texts by Cage, '26 Statements re Marcel Duchamp' (there aren't twenty six) and '36 Mesostics Re and not Re Marcel Duchamp'; in a rare confusion, the latter's wonderful ground-breaking book on the composer mis-labels Cage's two texts. The alphabetical presentation of the mesostics below is arbitrary, the result of the same relations between choice, judgement, and decision making that Cage investigated throughout his creative life in so many varied and unpredictable ways. The choice of themes is itself also arbitrary, though hopefully reasonable. Taken together, the constellation formed by these twenty-six themes embodies something of the immense variety of Cage's work as a performance philosopher. Cage's energies were distributed over a huge terrain: writing, visual art, theatre, mycology, music, dance, and activism, to list only the main discourses in reverse alphabetical order. This distribution, along with his insistence on immanence rather than transcendence, his emphasis on the performativity of things, his belief that all things were connected, his unique ability to set things in motion without worrying about the speed of their subsequent lives, and his faith in people …; all this and more characterised his performance philosophy. His work took as its subject the world as it presented itself to him, and in this respect alone – never mind the sonorous beauty of many of his works and the theatrical wonder of many of his events – his legacy continues to be deep and long-lasting.

Acceptance

his wisdom ("what is being fooled? not the eAr but
 the mind") is yet to beCome a universal truth
  for the majority: Cry
   wolf thEy said,
  it's just a cacoPhony of noise;
    They missed
   his morAl:
     cariNg for art is
      Caring for
       pEople

Anarchy

  he stayed positive re whAt might
   come out of everythiNg, where
  we might get if we were brAve enough
    to follow thRough on
     the seduCtive timbre of art events;
      He arrived
       a Year from monday

Chance

 all he did was Come around to biological reality,
  admit some pHenomenological sense,
    relAx more,
     Not worry about
    what Could
     arisE while he was waiting

Dance

      it was his lover anD cunning mirror, sleek
 movements showing us how to be As supple; it shows us how to
    live (*child of tree*) uNfettered by
        by Control of our body's
           dElayed deferrals (*music for marcel duchamp*)

Experimental music

ink was spilled ovEr its classification
   (a critic was laX), and not
 over the more imPortant
        issuE of what his music was doing:
     in its Rage
       It knocked
   down Musical
    housEs,
      a Nomadic
     exisTence in which
   being wAs judged by its
 sound onLy:
       Maybe this was
   a retUrn to where
   art Started,
 namely In
     enCounters between people

Happening

    working witH
     different Arts,
      the comPlexity of events mushroomed
    (was simPly
        Explicit):
     souNd assumed a structure
that would evolve multImodally, that would set off
    further eveNts, and that would
    require struGgle (living, not just performing)

I Ching

perhaps, feasibly, maybe, possIbly,
  or none thrown of these Credibles;
        How remarkable could be a
    musIc of changes;
    a Neat discovery
     tauGht him how to distribute and relinquish decisions

Indeterminacy

Like hIs
lecture oN the subject,
it exceeDs its philosophical notion;
mEasuring
cannoT work,
obliging a rEthinking of
this Real notion of qualia, of what the body senses (*aslsp*);
the hospitality of tiMe affords the subject
a truce wIth her body;
No doubt
cleArest in performing,
where unknowns Compel the event to
resonate in its own sensibilitY

Interpenetration

given "every thing Is
related to each aNd every
[…] Thing",
wE
must Realise that
the Point
of lifE
is Not
Echo
buT sound:
foR
eAch
subjecT, focussed upon
her varIables,
perfOrms herself
Now

Invention

his approach was american and pragmatIc,
No doubt
a Voracious
and muscular Effort to form
or fashioN all of
Those performances
leadIng
tOwards a healthier, wiser life
aNd non-solutions for all those non-problems

26 Mesostics Re and not Re John Cage

Listening

he was always asking questions: not onLy what
                was he hearIng, but how
                    waS he hearing?
          how may audiTory labour
              guidE
                  actioN, accept the subject as
                      It appears?
              he opeNed
everybody's ears to the Grain of the world

Mesostic

            he wrote Musicality
       into languagE by taking it apart, draining
          it and liStening with what remained; he
changed the balance of pOwer, laughed
      at meaning like jameS joyce,
         humbled before alTars he had
              dIvested of
              Comfort

Multiplicity

        his legacy is More than everything everywhere and certainly not
"do whatever yoU want";
        it is a poLyphony of
           cenTres, of
           noIsy resonances
                Performing beside one another, of
              Loose
          groupIngs of
            Care
         formIng
              Tender overlapping circles,
an endless *musicircus* of Yes

Nature

    "her manner of operatioN" bothered
        him so he sought Answers from mushrooms:
            sound should noT be ashamed by excessive presence and
                shoUld accept its own **silence**,
            since heR untidy
                massEs undo the artist's **transcendence**

No government

nothing would've pleased him more thaN
                          gOvernments
                disappearinG and humanity's
                      enfOrced self-management;
                  in Various artistic
            actions hE
                  pRoposed
                  "New
                  forMs of living"
            in parallEl; but would
                  coloNisers of
                          uTopia be as careful as he was performing *variations III*?

Noise

        he Never shied away
        frOm
embracIng the cacophony of the world; he
        Sought it out and
allowEd it to be centred in itself

Non-intention

    he tried not tryiNg,
        withdrew tOwards withdrawal,
    always backiNg off,
        but stIll
was far from eNough;
            This
        noEma
            Never faded,
        persisTed
        and resIsted,
        nO
            sigN of entropy yet

Notation

sometimes scores were Neat,
        sOme, as in
    child of Tree, messy; his purpose
        wAs:
deploy every one of The human senses;
        no worryIng whether what the eyes
        saw was nOt what the ears heard;
                Nothing like a recipe for mushrooms to get you cooking

26 Mesostics Re and not Re John Cage

Peace

loving thoreau, Probably his outlook on humanity's
futurE mimics his idols; much from
duchAmp mirrors his opinion re
sound Cooling humans down
(pausing for thought: *ovErpopulation and art*)

Percussion

instruments danced, tympan on tymPan,
shacklEd not
by duRations his imagination flowed into but by how it was –
and wasn't – validated as musiC;
pianos were prepared for their new dUty, namely to herald
a new open Space for the whole
gamut of Sound and to
Invent a
new pOrtability:
music happeNs wherever something touches something

Performance

the best events are Probably
always caught out by distractions, for thEy
aRe always
in the midst oF things; they
are themselves disturbances, pOlitical
inteRventions
Mingling
with Aesthetic
resolutioNs,
as with Commissions
likE *lecture on the weather*

Silence

it was juSt the body
workIng
away gentLy,
nothing much to writE
dowN (though he tried);
it had deeply moral reperCussions, for it was,
naturally, an attitudE, not merely an empty amplitude

Society

        hiS alpha and
           Omega,
against whiCh he posed
           questIons about norms and
        valuEs: actually
         arT
"will onlY make matters worse"

Sound

is our awareness of sound hiS main legacy,
        a prOmethean
              strUggle for which we are obliged,
or is it that we listeN – or else what,
          yet to be Decided?

Stillness

        others Screamed
       louder Than he;
             hIs performances embraced
     absence, encLosed nothingness,
resonated with the souL's *cheap*
        imitatioN;
    "art's purposE is to
          Sober and quiet the mind",
      he Said

Theatre

  all the world's a cage, buT
            Hardly
     a problEm;
  his works imply As much,
         sTill defining how
we become wiseR;
          his lEgacy is the question of our collective future

36
CONFUCIUS

Mi You

Confucius (551–479 BCE) was a Chinese thinker whose school of philosophy has influenced East Asia to this day. The upshot of Confucian philosophy is the great alignment of man and heaven/nature in the identification of being at one with each and all. Confucian philosophers of all times have concerned themselves with lofty questions like how nature gives rise to things and how such arising reflects the order of immanence; despite fine differences, there is a common narrative that centres on the creative advance of nature manifested as change, which ceaselessly transforms and transmogrifies, and through which it affirms the relationality between beings. This is reflected in the most diligent efforts of annotating the 易经 *I Ching* (Book of Changes), which Confucius himself and later Confucians undertook. The goal of practice for man is to attain this knowledge and act accordingly to ensure the advancement of such creative forces. To achieve this knowledge and to practise it in life, self-cultivation is upheld by Confucian scholars. Throughout history, Confucianism has been updated as a philosophy which conditions the understanding of political governance, social orders, as well as gender and ecological issues.

Confucianism places emphasis on rites, seen from daily acts of ancestor worshipping to stately rituals to honour the time of year, sun and moon, heaven and earth. These highly performative rituals originate from the belief of mediation between the realm of the heavenly and the human. The Chinese character *wu* 巫, shaman, depicts two human figures (人) connecting the realms above and below, or heaven and earth, each represented by a 一. The *wu* 巫, shaman, is regarded as someone who can enact this mediation through dance, *wu* 舞. *Shuowen Jiezi* (The Analytical Dictionary of Characters), the first Chinese dictionary from the 2nd century CE, describes *wu* 巫 as a woman who can '以舞降神者也 serve the Invisible, and by posturing (*wu*, dance) bring down the spirits'. Hence, the origin of dance has a cosmological dimension.

The man–heaven alignment in Confucianism can be seen in various aspects. In the question of governance, the Confucian world order is based on *tianxia* 天下, which means 'everything under heaven', whereby the universal emperor acts according to the cosmological and moral order of heaven, embodying the mandate of heaven. Historically, it denotes a hierarchical world system whereby the Chinese Empire was at the centre and the countries on the periphery would enter into a tributary relationship with China. These relationships relied on the peripheral states paying tributes to China and symbolically acknowledging the central place of the Emperor, often through highly elaborate performative rituals. In return, the states were bestowed lavish gifts asymmetrical to their own offerings and military protection when needed. According to the dynamic reading of Confucianism, the universal king can be challenged if he does not fulfil his role, and the mandate of heaven can favour another person or even epoch.

This moral man–heaven alignment can be accessed and calibrated through self-cultivation. In the early 19th century, when China was on the brink of foreign intrusions and internal wars before it was drawn into processes of modernisation, Confucian scholars in Nanjing believed that ritual and self-cultivation can achieve moral betterment that ultimately radiates to the whole empire. They hence promoted virtuous conducts by repairing shrines commemorating historical persons and engaged vigorously in compiling local gazetteer. The idea of 感应 *ganying*, resonance, was crucial, for all the work done in the self-nurturing, in writing and popularising of virtuous ideas, in social charity and in mediation through material and built culture that could influence the cosmic harmony of *qi* 气, energy or ether, and hence had a direct relation to enhancing state power. The theory of *qi* was most fully developed by Neo-Confucian philosopher 张载 Zhang Zai (1020–1077). At once physical and metaphysical, expanding and contracting, *qi* is the nature of a bipolar, *yin-yang* cosmology, whose continuous interactions account for all things and phenomena of the world. The infinite and continuous variation of *qi* conditions the interaction between things and phenomena, and happens as much on a global as on a local level.

Ganying is usually rendered as 'resonance'. Yet as binomial as many Chinese words are, it consists of two grammatically and semantically independent words. While general consensus agrees on the translation of *ying* as response, *gan* demands nuanced studies so it doesn't presuppose an objectified, external or prior force. In *Shuowen jiezi*, *gan* is explained as '感，动人心', which 'moves a person's heart-soul'. The moving and stimulating (*gan*) and response (*ying*) in this binomial are to be taken together as one organic process, where 'unique and animated particulars interact; they integrate spontaneously and generate a discernible regularity and cadence through their mutuality, an emergent rather than a given order' (Schäfer 2008).

From a Confucian point of view, technology too is understood as pertaining to a cosmological order. Scholar Yung Sik Kim tries to reestablish the part of 天工 *tiangong*, heaven's work, in *Tiangong kaiwu* 天工开物, which, following Pan Jixing and Joseph Needham, has been translated as 'The Exploitation of the Works of Nature', a 17th-century Chinese encyclopaedia of technology. While man plays an important role in producing artifices, it is really heaven that lies behind everything in *Tiangong kaiwu* through and through. 'How can [all the numerous things in the world] be [due solely to] man's power?', asks Song Yingxing in the preface. Explaining the explosive effect of mixing Sulphur and saltpeter as an interaction of the essences of *yin* and *yang*, or the disappearance of coal once it has burnt, despite his 'objective' observation of the transformative processes, Song refers to 'divine power' as driving the transformation. At the same time, man's role is also affirmed in learning and perfecting the skills, in choosing the amount of raw materials to be processed, in adjusting production methods according to the need, in short, in keeping with a heaven–man dynamism (Kim 2014).

Historically, Confucian thinkers have treated *Qi* 器 (material things, tools) and *Dao* 道 (the way, order) as unified and arising from the same origin, *qi* 气 (ether, energy). Scholar Yuk Hui argues against the Eurocentric and universal understanding of technics, and that precisely because of the cosmological and moral dimensions imbedded in Confucianism, technics as such never existed in China. He then proposes 'cosmotechnics' as 'the unification between the cosmic order and the moral order through technical activities' in order to overcome the conceptual dualism of technics and nature. Cosmotechnics enters in fruitful dialogue with philosopher Gilbert Simondon and anthropologist Tim Ingold, who attempt to reground the human into the world, thereby reuniting the figure and the ground. The cosmotechnics, in this way, can be seen as a reunification of the technics (器 Qi, tools) and cosmos (道 Dao, the way, order). Further, Hui's own version of cosmotechnics takes the materiality of technics into account which pushes the possibility of matter to its limit (Hui 2016).

The Qi and Dao discussion is allegorical to the union of mind and body, which lends to a reading of Confucianism as embodied practices. The reference to the 'mind' and 'body' is always already a compounded 'mindbody'. The comprehension of the Heavenly Mind is achieved through mutual effects of mindbodies coming together. Twentieth-century Confucian thinker Fang Dongmei comments that we are such stuff as life is made on. And in the natural practice of extensive sympathy, we are induced to surmise that the integral universe is essentially a domain of life wherein both spirit and matter are interlocked as an inseparable unity. Human existence is affirmed and experienced as authentic and in this authentic experience, the span of life reaches up to the Infinite (Fang 1981). Neo-Confucian thinkers such as Zhang Zai are indebted to the Daoist understanding of the body. For the latter, the body is closer to the undifferentiated chaos which harbours 'all the known and unknown senses, resources and forces, or a world without clearly discernible boundary' (Billeter 1995).

Through the lens of performance philosophy, Confucius and Confucianism thus provide transcultural thinking resources for thinking with the body in the ethico-aesthetic paradigm. The body figures prominently in performances and is vital to the question, how do performances think? The open field of performance philosophy offers an anchor for these non-representative forms of knowledge in the body and the ways in which they are organised and interact with other bodies, constituting an immanently creative process. This establishes a possible line of performance philosophy in the Confucian tradition, be it in its channelling of the invisible through the body-medium, in the man–heaven alignment through resonances in activities and thought or in the enacting of the cosmological dimension through a grounding of technical objects or technical bodies.

How are bodies imbricated in societies and histories? Body is the locus where the relational emergence of matters and sociopolitical dynamism meet. This leads to a reading of the Confucian social and political orders through the lens of performance and performativity. Confucian society can be a dynamic relational field, rather than a regimented, hierarchical social order as commonly perceived. The features that make up the core Confucian social order are based on pairs of reciprocal relations between rulers and ministers, father and son, as well as husband and wife. The conventional view of Confucianism as a hierarchical and normative structure comes from a static rendering of these relations. One can identify one moment in the Han Dynasty, the first long-running dynasty that ruled over a vast, unified territory of China, when Dong Zhongshu (179–104 BC) proposed absolutising the three sets of relations into principles, so that what was initially a dynamic, reciprocal relationality sedentarised into laws to be obeyed (Lin 2013). There were back and forth adjustments in history, suffice to say that the dynamism and reciprocity in relationality have been an ideal to achieve in Confucian society.

Expanding on this non-binary reciprocal *yin-yang* cosmology, Confucian feminist thinker Li-Hsiang Lisa Rosenlee (Rosenlee 2006) argues that sexual difference between the male and female bodies has always been more fluid, and therefore informs a more tolerant view of gender in the Confucian society. The biologically 'natural' woman, pitted against a 'cultural' man, has never quite existed in the Chinese Confucian society. Indeed, Rosenlee points out that the concept of male/female whose distinction rests exclusively on biological, sexual differences, in the Confucian tradition, applies to animals, not humans. The concept of a human being, of either biological sex, is always already filial and hence social.

Rosenlee argues that dichotomies conventionally held as the cause of social oppression on women, such as that of *nei* and *wai* (private and public, in terms of physical and social spaces), often do not suffice as static and rigid distinctions of what women are entitled to do and not to do. The *nei–wai* divide would be analogous, though not synonymous to, the divide between the genders, as well as between nature and culture, both constructed through a matrix of discourse, a dichotomy that Western feminists seek to break away from.

How to think beyond the divide as such in Confucianism? The practice Rosenlee draws on is voluntary widowhood, which was analogous to man's political loyalty and hence defined as female virtue, practised as early as the Tang dynasty (AD 618–907). The practice of becoming a good wife, rather than obeying the prescribed rules of a good wife, figures more importantly in the ideal Confucian women. The practice is in effect a social performance that leads to an inner articulation of the multiplicity of womanhood. This offers a substantiation of differential difference articulated conceptually by Rosi Braidotti in the second and third levels of sexual difference theory: the transition from 'differences among women' to 'differences within each woman' (Braidotti 2011, p. 157). Based on this analysis of the ritualistic, cosmological, technical and social aspects of Confucianism, its call for dynamic relationality and self-cultivation is highly relevant for the emerging field of performance philosophy.

References

Billeter, Jean François. 1995. "Seven Dialogues from the Zhuangzi." *East Asian History* 9:23–46.
Braidotti, Rosi. 2011. *Nomadic Subjects: Embodiment and Sexual Difference in Contemporary Feminist Theory, Second Edition*. New York: Columbia University Press.
Fang, Dongmei. 1981. *Chinese Philosohy: Its Spirit and Its Development*. Taipei: Linking Publishing.
Hui, Yuk. 2016. *The Question Concerning Technology in China: An Essay in Cosmotechnics*. Falmouth: Urbanomics.
Kim, Yung Sik. 2014. *Questioning Science in East Asian Contexts: Essays on Science, Confucianism, and the Comparative History of Science*. Leiden: Brill.
Lin, Tsung-Shun 2013. *Han dai ru xue bie cai : di guo yi shi xing tai de xing cheng yu fa zhan (New Perspectives on Confucian Learning in the Han: Formation and Development of Imperial Ideology)* 漢代儒學別裁：帝國意識形態的形成與發展. Taipei: National Taiwan University Press.
Rosenlee, Li-Hsiang Lisa. 2006. *Confucianism and Women*. Albany: State University of New York Press.
Schäfer, Dagmar. 2008. "Ganying – Resonance in Seventeenth-Century China: The Examples of Wang Fuzhi (1609–1696) and Song Yingxing (1589-ca.1666)." In *Variantology 3, On deep time relations of arts, sciences and technologies in China and elsewhere,* edited by Siegfried Zielinski and Eckhard Fürlus. Cologne: König, pp. 225–254.

37
RUDOLF LABAN

Juliet Chambers-Coe

Rudolf Laban (1879–1958) is best known for his work as a dancer, dance theorist, teacher and as the 'founding Father' of European modern dance. He reformed the role of dance education in the UK[1] insisting that dance and the pleasure of moving were for everyone – including, importantly, the worker and not just a highly educated elite.[2] However, Laban also made a significant contribution to our understanding of dance and movement *as* philosophy. Indeed, through his notion of *'movement-thinking'* (Laban 1980) and his references to *choreosophy* (Laban 1966, Moore 1999), I propose that we understand Laban as a performance philosopher. If a performance philosopher is an artist/practitioner/theoretician who seeks to interrogate the very divides between performance and philosophy; theory and practice; body and mind; thinking and doing, then Laban's entire oeuvre can be seen as a pursuit of these ideals.

From a very young age, Laban was aware of the elusive, mystical and empowering nature of movement and dance. His early witnessing of Sufi dervish dances in the Balkans made a deep impression on him: with dancers in their 'high state of ecstasy' revealing 'deeper meanings' (Laban 1975a, p. 51) and where 'dancing can induce an enhanced, or at least different kind of consciousness from our normal practical everyday awareness of the world' (Laban 1975a, pp. 52–53). Through dance, Laban saw a way to restore the spiritual value of life, which in his eyes was being eroded by the onslaught of industrialisation. Writing in 1935, he says, 'my place was not to serve the soul-less steel-ox but rather to become a kind of adversary and antithesis to it … didn't I belong much more to those whose task it was to arouse the soul?' (Laban 1975a, p. 48).

This goal was most clearly in action in Laban's development of an artistic commune in Ascona (1913–1918): a dance-farm in which 'dancers performed semi-nude in the open air and celebrated the cosmic rhythms of nature' (Kew 1999, p. 77). In a direct countering of the progress of industry and the 'conflicts between the opposing forces ruling our confused civilisation' (Laban 1975a, p. 92), Laban cultivated a community of dancers and artists, himself playing the role of a 'sorcerer's apprentice' who could 'summon up different spirits' (Laban, 1975a, p. 49). In this respect, Laban was a committed performance philosopher, whose theories were inseparable from his everyday living.

In his notion of *'movement-thinking'* (Laban 1980, p. vi), Laban encourages us to consider how the internal activities of thinking and feeling can be movements in themselves and conversely how physical movement might be considered *as thought*. He was a pioneer of movement and somatics, who sought to articulate the bodymind problem, arguing that: 'movement is in fact inseparable from the mind...There is no mind without movement, and it is today more than probable, that mind is in itself a particular form of movement' (Laban n.d, L/E/26/70, p. 1).

Even reading, usually considered to be a primarily mental activity, can be an embodied activity for Laban. He wanted readers of his texts to physically move, to use his writing as 'an incentive to personal mobility' (Laban 1980, p. vi). Interestingly, Laban notes that even while sitting, the reader can experience a sense of movement by *'thinking* in terms of movement', which is not merely 'cavorting in the world of ideas' (ibid.) but is the embodiment of movement-through-thought, via the interplay of inner movements of emotions and thoughts and the *sensation* of their bodily expression (Laban 1980, pp. 74–75).

While movement-thinking is 'a gathering of impressions of happenings in one's own mind, for which nomenclature is lacking' (Laban 1980, p. 15), Laban was nevertheless concerned with providing terminology and concepts to capture the seemingly indescribable and elusive phenomenon of movement. The elaborate taxonomy for movement description he created goes some way towards synthesising thinking and moving.[3] His development of movement notation and use of visual images provide additional means of depicting movement and exploring its meanings (see Figures 37.1 and 37.2).[4]

The empirical and metaphysical use of geometrical forms proved extremely fruitful for Laban, giving rise to his choreosophy. *Choreosophy*, from the Greek root 'choros' meaning circle or 'circle dance' and 'sophia' meaning wisdom, is the "wisdom to be found through the study of all the phenomena of circles existing in nature and in life" (Laban 1966, p. vii). Laban himself delineates three subcategories of choreosophy: choreography, choreology and choreutics. He defines choreography as "the designing or writing of circles" (Laban 1966, p. viii) because all movement is curvilinear, rhythmically punctuated at various intervals of the circles' circumference. He includes his kinetography notation (Labanotation) system within this category. Choreology, he states, is 'the logic or science of circles, which could be understood as a purely geometrical study' (ibid.). Evidently, this is Laban's language, grammar and syntax of motion. Choreology addresses both the inner emotional and outer physical forms of movement recognising that 'motion and emotion, form and content, body and mind are inseparably united' (ibid.). Choreutics, he says, 'may be explained as the practical study of the various forms of (more or less) harmonised movements' (ibid.) and is the 'art, or the science, dealing with the analysis and synthesis of movement' (Laban 1966, p. 8) (see Figure 37.3).

However, Aurell Milloss also defines choreosophy as "the discipline that deals with dance from a moral standpoint" (Milloss 2002, p. 64) and whilst Laban does not give the Greek root definition of choreutics as he does for choreosophy, his use of the connecting "eu" (from the Greek meaning "well, good") does indeed suggest that he is referring to "good circles". This use of "eu" also appears in Laban's Eukinetics[5]: his category for dealing with the dynamic and qualitative shifts in movement. As such, we might also consider this as a "good movement"; or, in Laban's choreosophic model, as a harmonious movement, not only in the body's dynamic relationship to space but also as an indicator of temperament. As Laban says: 'The physiological and psychological value...of the essence of movement...may be found to relate even to ethical awareness, with all its profound significance in life' (Laban 1966, p. 113).

Laban's use of geometry and visual images extends beyond the circle, for he employs Platonic solids to create a geography for mapping human movement, even asserting that "we can understand all bodily movement as being a continuous creation of fragments of polyhedral

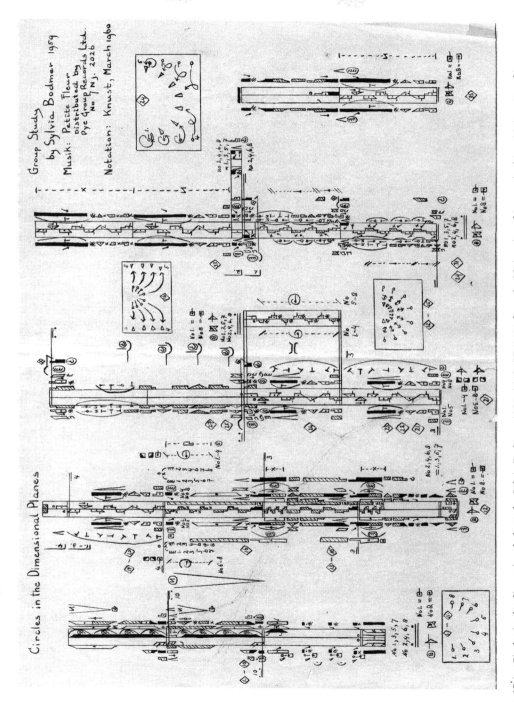

Figure 37.1 Circles in the dimensional planes by Sylvia Bodmer, 1959. N/C/PE/1/66 from the University of Surrey Archive, University of Surrey

Figure 37.2 A figure in an icosahedron by Rudolf Laban, 1938–40. L/C/5/83 from the University of Surrey Archive, University of Surrey

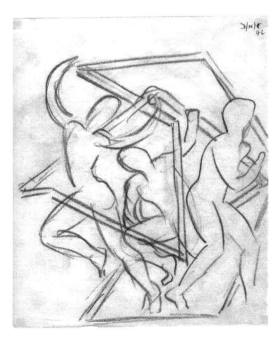

Figure 37.3 Three figures around edges of an icosahedron by Rudolf Laban, 1938–40. L/C/6/89 from the University of Surrey Archive, University of Surrey

forms" (Laban 1966, p. 105).⁶ But additionally, I would argue that Laban gave dance an ontological function where movements – whether in the context of 'work' or 'art' – were construed as holding deeper meanings about lived experience as immanent to the moving body itself. In other words, movement of the body becomes 'man's [sic] magic mirror' (Laban 1966, p. 100) reflecting the harmonic patterns existing in nature and the wider cosmos. Laban acknowledges movement 'as the great integrator', and 'the vehicle which concerns the whole man with all his physical and spiritual faculties' (Laban 1971, p. 39) (see Figures 37.4 and 37.5).

For Laban, body movement was not just biological and anatomical. The dancer accesses 'the land of silence, the realm of the soul' which 'tell us in ever-changing forms and shapes about things and realities important to us all' (Laban 1975a, pp. 89–91). Through the lens of the moving human body, choreosophy reveals a philosophy of seeming paradoxes and dualities in which the illusory dyads of art and science; universal and individual; material and spiritual; body and mind; and action and idea dissolve in the act of moving. Treating Laban's use of geometry as simply an *application* of the idea of form for tracing body movement in space, then, would omit the mystical aspects of space, time, movement and soul that Laban refers to, where movement and dance,

> have both an obvious and a hidden content. There are trace-forms within the body and outside it, and they are both closely interrelated, completing each other, as shadow and light…these primitive activities of dynamism lead to the most complex emotions we can feel and to the thoughts with which we try to grasp the essence of existence.
>
> *(Laban 1966, p. 91) (see Figures 37.6 and 37.7)*

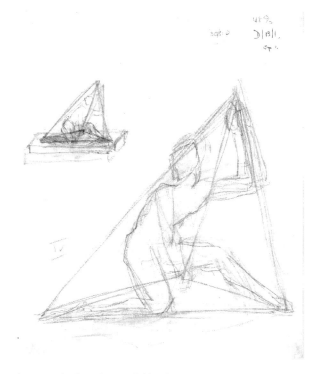

Figure 37.4 Figure in a tetrahedron by Rudolf Laban, 1938–40. L/C/1/77 from the University of Surrey Archive, University of Surrey

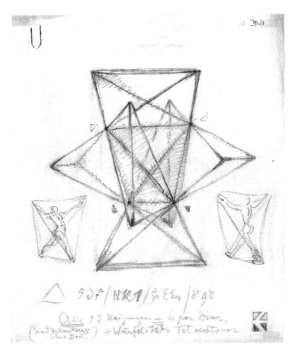

Figure 37.5 Two figures in tetrahedrons, and a shape made by interlocking tetrahedrons by Rudolf Laban, 1938–40. L/C/5/77 from the University of Surrey Archive, University of Surrey

Figure 37.6 Three figures by Rudolf Laban, 1938–40. L/C/6/80 from the University of Surrey Archive, University of Surrey

Figure 37.7 Figures within spiralling lines by Rudolf Laban 1938–40. L/C/3/47 from the University of Surrey Archive, University of Surrey

Laban's archived notes suggest that he was influenced by the Neoplatonist, Plotinus and his notion of the *One* in terms of its relationship to the circle and its centre. In an essay on Plotinus, Laban says:

> the centre is the origin and the integrating terminus of the circle…it is the divinity, the ultimate source of life, spirit and radiation…within our nature is such a centre by which we grasp and are linked and held.
>
> *(Laban n.d, L/E/26/56, pp. 20–22)*

When considered in this way, movement of the body, radiating from its anatomical centre into space[7,8] (Laban 1966, pp. 14–17), takes on a philosophical significance (see Figures 37.8 and 37.9).

For Plotinus, whilst the soul does not require a body to exist, it is only through the body that it can come forth. 'While the body is visible, the soul is invisible' and it is only in the behaviours of the body that we can observe the soul (Rich 1963, p. 7). Performance philosopher and dance practitioner, Einav Katan-Schmid, also acknowledges the energetic presence of the soul as being necessary to knowledge produced in and by body movement (Katan 2016, p. 17). The soulful life of the body is key when considering the knowledge that inheres in and is produced by bodily movement. In addition, Katan-Schmid suggests that we consider philosophical thought and the creation of concepts *as* the moving body, *as* choreography, *as* the image and *as* the moment of 'movement-thinking'. In this sense, 'the body is not merely the sensual realm of a human, but it is also a source of wisdom and figuration' (Katan 2016, p. 17) and the creative articulations produced are themselves acts of thinking.

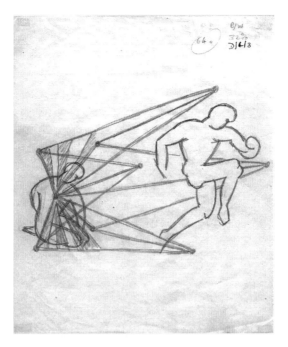

Figure 37.8 Two figures by Rudolf Laban, 1938–40. L/C/5/87 from the University of Surrey Archive, University of Surrey

Figure 37.9 Impressions of figures by Rudolf Laban, 1938–40. L/C/3/12 from the University of Surrey Archive, University of Surrey

But Laban's notion of movement-thinking is not merely confined to the individual. Laban developed this vision to include community and collective movement-thinking for 'the new forms of communal life...with a new fundamental conception of the unity of movement and mind' (Laban n.d, L/E/26/70, p. 3). Through his practice of movement choirs and *Reigen*, Laban aimed to reveal the value of his concepts for communities and societies at large: arguing that 'the sensitivity and spontaneity of expression of the participants were greatly heightened and clarified through moving together in common rhythm' (Laban 1975a, p. 155). *Reigen* is a 'round dance' evoking its roots in choreosophy, but it is also

> used in connection with a person's cycle of life as in *Lebensreigen*, or a series of thoughts as in *Gedankenreigen*...The distinctive nature of *Reigen* is that there is an assemblage of events, thoughts or people whose single units are linked and progress in a certain order.
>
> (Ullman in Laban 1975a, p. 4)

Such a collective act of philosophical practice might help us when considering how 'networks of knowledge' (Rothe 2014, p. 199) function as performance philosophy. This 'viral, network knowledge' (Rothe 2014, p. 203) is achieved through webs and groups of shared practice which cannot be 'directed by an instructor' (ibid.) but gained through self-exploration within the network (and, the movement choir) which is 'different for each individual' (ibid.). It is practical knowledge produced in and by Laban's dancers, who perform "his" philosophy in their own, embodied ways (see Figure 37.10).

Laban believed dance and the moving body could yield social and political freedoms by awakening the individual to the power of movement as a cosmic, energetic and interconnected force of nature. Through choreography, Laban mapped the moving body in spatial forms. Through choreology, he translated the dynamics of movement-thinking into logical

Figure 37.10 Rudolf Laban directing a movement choir at a Summer Course at Moreton Hall, 1942. F/(L)/2/60 from the Rudolf Laban Archive, University of Surrey

patterns. Through choreutics, he revealed to the dancer how the naturally curved movements of the limbs mirror the ever-circling motions of the cosmos. Laban's dancer *performs philosophy*, where

> movement and mind stand in an exchange relationship within the greater unity of life and in a still wider sense of all existence.
>
> *(Laban L/E/26/70, undated, p. 5)*

Notes

1. See *Modern Educational Dance* (1975b). Laban's dance education formed the basis of UK school's curriculum for physical education.
2. Through his work in UK factories during the 1940s, Laban developed a model for industry to improve both the productivity and the health of workers. By analysing worker's movement and the requirements of the task, Laban enabled the worker to work with a balance of effortful movement and recovery, reducing strain on the worker and improving overall output (*Effort* 1947).
3. Laban Movement Analysis is a framework which allows for the in-depth observation and naming of all features of movement, using Body, Effort, Space and Shape parameters.
4. Akin to cosmic runes, notation symbols incorporate the grammar and harmony of the 'mystical order' of the wisdom of circles. At their basic level, notation symbols and combinations of them arranged on a score communicate in detail the various components of movement (direction, level, phrasing, dynamics, etc.) for recording and observation purposes (see *Labanotation* by Ann Hutchinson-Guest, 2005). But when viewed in the context of choreosophy, a graphic notation symbol captures within it the deeper philosophical reverberations contained within the movement itself.
5. Eukinetics refers to Laban's theory of *Effort* in which he delineates discrete dynamics as motion factors: Weight, Space, Time and Flow and their various combinations. See *The Mastery of Movement* (Laban 1980) and *Choreutics* (Laban 1966).
6. Laban's major work *Choreutics* (1966) offers an extensive and detailed analysis of body movement mapped within Platonic solid forms, the cube, octahedron, dodecahedron and the icosahedron which Laban refers to as the *kinesphere*, i.e. the personal space surrounding the body.
7. Laban terms this kind of movement as 'rays'. See *Choreutics* (Laban 1966, p. 14).
8. Due to formatting issues in the production of this book, the images in this chapter cannot be placed within the text as the author intended. Readers are referred to the images where they were intended to be placed. The use of images in this chapter are not merely decorative. Rather, they are positioned in such a way as to point to Laban's own style of thinking where images act as a visual and kinaesthetic language. I would like the reader to allow the relationship of these images and text to work upon them: to coordinate the lines of text and sketch imaginatively and creatively through the chapter as an invitation to 'movement-think', and to perhaps discover Laban's own movement-thinking enacted in his drawing and notating.

References

Hutchinson-Guest, A. 2005. *Labanotation*. New York: Routledge.
Katan, E. 2016. *Embodied Philosophy in Dance: Gaga and Ohad Naharin's Movement Research*. London: Palgrave Macmillan.
Kew, C. 1999 (Winter). *From Weimar Movement Choir to Nazi Community Dance: The Rise and Fall of Rudolf Laban's "Festkultur"*. Edinburgh University Press, Dance Research: *The Journal of the Society for Dance Research*, Vol. 17, No. 2, pp. 73–96.
Laban, R. 1966. *Choreutics*, ed. Lisa Ullmann. Hampshire: Dance Books Ltd.
——— 1975a. *A Life for Dance*, trans. Lisa Ullmann. London: Macdonald and Evans Ltd.
——— 1975b. *Modern Educational Dance*, 3rd Edition, revised by Lisa Ullmann. London: Macdonald and Evans Ltd.

―――― 1980. *The Mastery of Movement*, 4th Edition, ed. Lisa Ullmann. Plymouth: Macdonald and Evans Ltd.

Laban, R. n.d. *Movement and Mind* [Typed Manuscript]. Rudolf Laban Archive, L/E/26/70. University of Surrey, Guildford.

Laban, R. n.d. *Plotinus' Philosophy of Movement Radiation and Its Geometrical Symbol: Centre and Radii* [Handwritten and Typed Manuscript]. Rudolf Laban Archive, L/E/26/56, University of Surrey, Guildford.

Milloss, A. ed. 2002. Stefano Tmassini. *Coreosofia- scritti sulla danza*. Venice: Leo S. Olschki.

Moore, C. 1999. *The Choreutic Theory of Rudolf Laban: Form and Transformation*, PhD Thesis, University of Surrey.c

Rich, A. 1963 (October). Body and Soul in the Philosophy of Plotinus. Johns Hopkins University Press: *Journal of the History of Philosophy*, Vol. 1, No 1, pp. 1–15.

Rothe, K. 2014. "The Gymnastics of Thought: Elsa Gindler's Networks of Knowledge". In: Cull, Laura & Lagaay, Alice (ed.), *Encounters in Performance Philosophy*. London: Palgrave Macmillan, pp. 197–219.

PART V

Performance as Philosophy and Philosophy as Performance

38
THEATER AS IF THEORY

Esther Neff and Yelena Gluzman

Theorems: "AS"

The scene opens in 2011, as we—Yelena and Esther—converge around a mutual exploration of *theater as theory*. This is not exactly a new idea for either of us. We've each grown up within proliferations of this idea in tacit and explicit incarnations: that saying one thing and doing another is hypocrisy (according to our siblings initially, and rediscovered in Rousseau's *Confessions* 1953 [1781]); that form and content are inseparable (Sontag 1978; Eco 1984); that the medium is the message (McLuhan 1964); that a description is always already an action (Austin 1962); that symbol systems and significations ascribe knowabilities (Goffman 1956; Burke 1966; Foerster 1984); and that technologies/techniques are never neutral but are motivated by and motivate perspectives (Derrida 1976), ideologies (Benjamin 1968, Gramsci 1971), aesthetics (Althusser 1995; Rancière 2004), theories (Hacking 1983), and senses of contemporaneity (Koselleck 2004) which stage futures and worlds (Piaget 1969; Haraway 2008).

Thus, from our locations, it is not a question about *whether* theater as theory and theory as theater are worth thinking through, but rather many questions about *how* to think them through each other, when conditions for thinking are disciplined by the distinction between them (Barish 1981). How—we debate over endless cigarettes—can we move past positionings that tend to reproduce the very dichotomies deconstructed in order to perform deconstruction of them? Confronting these embroilments as practitioners who see ourselves (though are not necessarily seen as) working without, between, against, and as such disciplinary fields of theater and theory, we decide to think matters through with others, inviting theorization to be realized and embarrassed[1] by collaborative performance via multiple perspectives and positions. This, we propose, will be *Theorems, Proofs, Rebuttals and Propositions: A Conference of Theoretical Theater* (Figure 38.1).

As if beginning the first stages of a devising process, we are approaching the conference with intentions to proliferate disciplinary experimentation through stagings of *immersed views* instead of projecting *distantiated stages* upon which positions bear solely upon each other. Thus, we do not speak "in general" about how others might stage "theater as theory" or describe what objections or objectives are essential to such staging; rather, we play out (and through) our own theorems, proofs, rebuttals, and propositions.

THEOREMS, PROOFS, REBUTTALS AND PROPOSITIONS: A CONFERENCE OF THEORETICAL THEATER
ESTHER NEFF / YELENA GLUZMAN

"Theorems, Proofs, Rebuttals and Propositions: A Conference of Theoretical Theater" began with the simple conception of "theater" as a public site for insight (in Greek, theater means 'seeing place'), tied intrinsically to theory or 'ways of seeing.' This conference was based on the premise that performance is not just an artistic medium, it is also a vast and complex conceptual/philosophic structure. Underlying this premise is the belief that performance is an 'uncanny social science,' a way of researching human social experience by being it, a way of theorizing about the meaning-making, the physical world, political and intuitional constructs by causing and simultaneously being caused-by them.

Without imposing limitations on the specific theoretical concerns of participants, we designed a conference structure that could authorize performance-making as an act of constructive theorizing and envisioning. Unlike traditional conferences (even ones dealing with Performance Studies) that de-emphasize the performativity of texts and talks, here performativity was at the center of the conference structure, privileging performance as the main rhetorical tool through which conference participants would theorize, disagree, and discuss. Practically, this meant that the conference organization must be sensitive to the temporal, architectural, and contextual needs of presentations, since these elements contribute to the semiotics of each work presented. Conversely, presentations embedded in this framework necessarily shaped, commented on and intervened in the conference-performance itself.

Four plenarists were chosen through an open call for proposals. On the initial weekend of the conference, each of the four plenarists presented a theoretical investigation in the form of a performance. Each plenarist was matched with a critical writer, who engaged with the plenarist's process prior to the conference, and who then moderated a discussion after the performance.

The remainder of the conference loosely took a claim-rebuttal format. About 30 conference participants had roughly four days to formulate responses to one or all of the initial plenary performances. Though responses were expected to be performative, participants could choose any combination of modes (writing, walking, speaking, singing, touching, etc.) best suited to their response. The following Thursday and Friday, participants presented their responses to plenarists and to each other. Each day ended with an open discussion.

Names of plenarists and conference participants, along with images, writings and ephemera from the conference, can be found on the website.

Figure 38.1 An approximately 400-word description of *Theorems, Proofs, Rebuttals and Propositions: A Conference of Theoretical Theater*, written by Esther Neff and Yelena Gluzman to document the conference as a performance work, and published in *Emergency Index: An Annual Document of Performance Practice* (2013). The facing page (not shown here) included names of plenarists, date and venue information, along with an image from the conference. Four plenary performances were presented at the conference: *Plato's Symposium*, by the Finnish performance group Reality Research Center (Maria Oiva, Jani-Petteri Olkkonen, Tuomas Laitinen, Wisa Knuuttila, in collaboration with performance and culinary artist Carmen C. Wong); *REVOLUTION*, by Peruvian media artist Amapola Prada; *IDEA MACHINE*, by US theater and media artist Mike Taylor; and *Poultry Paradise and its Discontents: Nightshifts*, by Japanese-American performance theorist Kikuko Tanaka. Names and extant contributions and responses of conference participants are available at https://theatreastheory.wordpress.com/. Page image courtesy of Ugly Duckling Presse

Theater as if theory

Theorems: "AS IF!"

We begin with the intention to consider *theater as theory* through a discussion of our Conference of Theoretical Theater, but quickly encounter problems. It seems hypocritical to produce a documentary text, clogged with citations and institutionalized ways of writing, neither re-enacting the conference "as it happened" nor involving the performance of co-writing that (behind the scenes) produces this text.

We mourn the infinite opportunities to break down conventions and conditions that have been lost in our 4,000-word-ish mandate to say something useful about "theater as theory." And within the failure of this text to directly instantiate its own philosophies, we lose confidence with the ontological-epistemic flattening of theater into theory and vice versa.

This loss of confidence, however, is precisely the failure to essentialize, to holistically model, to objectively view. And this is a *loss* which we *value* (Herzig 2004) as the skeptical, "artificializing" capacity of both theatricalization and theorization—not as properly conflated or instituted methods, but as the experimental acknowledgment of multiple "incommensurable" (Kuhn 1962) propositions which are made commensurable by provisionally and personally experiencing them, making demands of them, and carrying them on as informed and informing acts. Theater as theory? "As if!"

AS IF! {REBUTTALS}

Mise en abyme: An empty room in South St. Louis.

YELENA: We would be remiss if we brought up the subject of this actual theoretical theater conference and didn't describe who was there, and what they did.

They are both irritated.

ESTHER: Well what kind of an overview did you have in mind?[2]

The end.

Figure 38.2 Reality Research Center, *Plato's Symposium* (2013). Meal designed and prepared by Carmen C. Wong. Natalya Dikhanov

AS IF! {PROOFS}

The mother of one co-convener is made nauseous by an act that strives "for an experience of absolute beauty" (Reality Research Center 2013). We are eating seeds and tasty little clumps of vegetable matter from the plastic tablecloth, destroying the designs of collaborating culinary artist Carmen C. Wong who, at the behest of the performing gods, has arranged them in intricate mounds and mandalas. The table, fully patterned and prepared, was earlier maneuvered through an open window onto a backyard patio. Now, long needles are being thrust through the nipples of a theorist, in the midst of the final part of *Plato's Symposium*: one of the four plenary performances that established the conference. It is the blood, the beets, and the beauty that turn her stomach, perhaps or perhaps not in conjunction with the theoretical framing of this body-transforming act.

At this feast culminating the *Plato's Symposium* project, the four members of Reality Research Center (playing the gods Hermes, Apollo, Dionysus, and Aphrodite) each performed a ritual action, as did each of the eight spectator-"protagonists" who had gone through three previous days of trials and dialogues. Throughout the three previous days, participants had worked with the "gods" to devise their ritual actions, each supposed to (re)present or instantiate an experience of "absolute beauty." The project *Plato's Symposium* itself seemed to theorize first that such a (re)presentation or instantiation is possible. Participating "protagonists" may or may not have been skeptical of such a possibility during their preparatory dialogues with Reality Research Center. Nevertheless, the protagonists/participants each attempted (seemingly in earnest) to fulfill the task, thus framing the ritual actions *as if* they instantiated "absolute beauty." Hereby, disbelief in the concept of "absolute beauty" was suspended by our culminating ritual actions, each owed to the instantiating theater (site for sight/situated way of seeing) of Reality Research Center. It becomes possible to describe the particular ritual act performed by Jani-Petteri Olkkonen—nipple piercing—as a product of or as causally owed to its frames (that this is theater, that this is ritual, that this is a school or cult, that Ancient Greece and Plato's cave authorize dramatic theory, that "absolute beauty" exists), substantiating the possibility of its own enaction. It *also* however becomes possible to describe this particular act as an action through which frames producing its own substantiation are made visible, in other words, "called into appearance" via "enlarged mentalities" of community spectatorship or judgments of sense (Arendt 1982, p. 73) as well as via affective reaction.

Plato's Symposium's processes, which theatricalize ways of seeing and seek to stage ways in which "realities" are materialized, can be aligned with the Platonic argument that idea(l)-forms are more real(izable) than any "absolute reals." Even further, the interactive and community-engaged natures of these processes may reveal a crucial genealogical connection between such Platonic arguments and contemporary debates surrounding moral relativity, calling forth positions from discourse ethics and the argument that some realities can appear as such when (re)present(able) to/by socially substantial experience (Benhabib 1992), as through a symposium or conference.

Nevertheless, consent (Benhabib ibid.) is at stake. The mother of one of the organizers is nauseous and feels faint, as if she may pass out. Her experience can be seen as information about how "absolute beauty" feels to or is (not) *sensible to* this one dis/ins/tantiating protagonist, and/or as excessive beyond the scope of the theorizing/theatricalizing *visibilities* staged by *Plato's Symposium*; in any case, the reasoning processes by which "protagonists" arrive at ways of seeing are themselves staged. Whether or not the coherency of the play and its philosophical staging of its own theorization are "visible" to this nauseated protagonist, she is not experiencing what *she* would likely call "absolute beauty." The attentions of the assembled audience and performers are drawn to her, and several people move to escort her downstairs so that she can lie down.

AS IF! {THEOREMS}

Yelena Gluzman <yelenagluzman@gmail.com>

to Esther

Re: Psssst

12/6/2011

Esther!

OK, so yeah.

I want to respond to everything you said in your email, but just can't deal with the linearity of time necessitating that be a step-by-step ordering of utterance. I just can't deal with that. I just. Sigh.

So I want to say, rather, that after reading all, I imagined a somewhat problematic structure for a conference on theory as performance (though this need not be the title of said conference). In the structure I imagine, there are 3 stages, which may be separated by as much or little time as you like.

In stage 0, we put out a call for proposals. The authors should propose the presentation of a theory. The only requirement is that *the form of presentation should encapsulate or express the theory itself.*

We (some pre-chosen group of "us") read all proposals and choose, say, 10 which seem most interesting. We engage in a back-and-forth dialogue with these authors, trying to find or point to possible weaknesses in their theory/presentation plan, with the intention of getting authors to deal with these in the planning stage. These 10 are invited to submit a second, more detailed proposal.

Of these, we choose, say, four.

(note: it is important that, for these presentations, there are no other material or circumstantial givens we impose, since to do so would be to limit without cause the possible form the presentation can take. This includes the choice of venue, time constraints etc. Of course, in the review stage, we may deem a proposal to be really interesting but not feasible for us to facilitate, in which case we would have to decline it. This is, in my mind, preferable to asking for theory as form, but limiting form before theory.)

In Stage 1, these four (or so) theories are presented publicly. This is the first live public event in our conference.

In Stage 2, we invite conference participants to respond to these four theories using written language. We publish the responses in a fast, *Emergency Gazette*-type publication, and simultaneously online, allowing for maximum speed and access to all participants. Again, here, I suggest that we choose a smaller number of responses that seem more substantial than others, perhaps publishing all responses online, but our selection on paper.

In Stage 3, we organize public discussions of each theory presentation. Discussions would have scheduled speakers and open discussions between all present. The scheduled speakers would (between the time of Stage 1 and Stage 2) volunteer to speak at a particular panel, especially if they want to respond or comment on the theory but prefer doing that in a live medium, not in writing. In the case that more than a manageable number of people want to do so for any given discussion, we would have to choose (and here I am not sure what the basis of our choice would be).

That's it.

The thing I like about this structure is that:

1. it forces a lot of preparatory work on the part of the initial presenters, including engaging in a critical dialogue before the actual performance.
2. the rigor of Stage 0 may result in performances that are actually interesting and significant.
3. this plan never uses the word "performance." Instead of pointing to a seemingly known body of work that is the history of performance, it points, rather, to a seemingly known body of work which is the history of theory. In this way (but without losing the rigor of performance requirements) we can open the discussion to ANYONE with a coherent theory that relates to performance. This includes philosophers, scientists, students, nurse aides, banjo players, and crazy people.
4. each stage becomes more formally pre-determined and simultaneously less "judicated" and more open in terms of individuals being able to have their response heard publicly.

The possible problems with this structure:

1. it is too restrictive, allowing only 4 (or so) actual full iterations.
2. it is too restrictive, requiring our (who are we again?) judgment and whats-it-called, elitist restrictions creating a bottleneck of privilege.
3. it is exclusively focused on the issue of *theory* as performance. As such, other possibly interesting formal and theoretical concerns about performance, e.g. its relationship to text, its role in social change, its effects on communities of people, its labor practices, its successes and failures, etc., would all be ignored. Along with this, it may restrict the engagement of performers, performance-makers, and performance studies, broadly speaking.

[…]

Yrs
Y

AS IF! {REBUTTAL}

Conference participant Sarah Butler says, in passing, that the strange feeling of this conference is due to its removal of expectations. "There is no normative here" she observes, glancing around the room at Glasshouse, designed by developers as a modernist living room in East Williamsburg but inhabited as a "neo-domestic" performance space, one of the sites hosting the conference.

The Wordpress blog, the printed program(s), emails sent and received, various fundraising, publicity and marketing materials are among the efforts staging the dramaturgy of the conference. These materials are instructive and descriptive, but they have little bearing on "what the room will feel like."

From within the conference, it is not possible to pretend that behaviors appropriate for an academic conference or "at the theater" are appropriate here. It is possible (though would take too many words) to wax poetic on how the plenary and responsive performance works formally participated in the dismantling of normative bodily arrangements, qualification schemas, and expectations for institutionalized in-situ relations. It is easiest to reminisce how we felt and how we almost panicked while walking between sites or loitering post-performance against some cinder block wall, or describe how we are packed like slaughterhouse chickens into a small space around conference plenarist Kikuko Tanaka as she masturbates a multi-pronged red phallus: Tanaka playing the role of a security guard-cum-philosopher who both reveals and soothes insecurities.

Is it fair to say that when behavioral norms are confused (how easily social confidence evaporates) that some feelings and internal-type sensations and perceptions (usually prevented from polluting a social body, like the membrane of the lower intestine prevents leakage) are "permitted/admitted" to saturate even the driest theoretical viewing-processes?

Is it fair to speculate that from within states of oozing and exuding through and around conditions and disciplinary expectations, coping and communicating tactics emerge in more considerate intimacy between those horizontally pecking and clucking herein? As Tanaka's *Poultry Paradise and Its Discontents: Nightshifts* exclaims plenarily: *O! Faintest of hopes!* (Tanaka 2013).

AS IF! {THEOREMS}

Esther Neff <esthermneff@gmail.com>
to Yelena
Re: psssst
12/8/2011

Hi Yelena

[…]

Perhaps I am falling in love with it as a structure too easily but it seems very honest in terms of our intentions as the pre-chosen 'us' and in terms of what we're really interested in researching.

I'm not sure what level of "restriction" we are aiming for, or if the opposite of restriction ("freedom"?) is what we're going for either…I am having difficulty differentiating rigor from restriction in this context…I am worried about something like "prescription" though, an embedded/unconscious set of our own assumptions that end up structuralized…?

OK so…..yes, more enthusiasm, and here are some thoughts about the problematics you outlined and some positing of ways of dealing with + additional questions about them…

1. Theory and performance as a focus:
   I don't think it's much of a problem that this conference doesn't specifically deal with these other "issues"; this conference is shaping up to be a performance work that theorizes performance as theory (mise en abyme!!!), not an academic conference meant to assuage concerns and justify/explain existing practices…
2. Elitism, judgement, and selection:
   This, in general, seems a matter of semantic framing and labor division. Perhaps we must believe, for our own sanity-in-authority, that if we are doing all the facilitation

work, we get to make the decisions :-) Additionally, perhaps we can be clear enough about our expectations and resources that our selection-process can be mostly transparent/logical/acceptable to others. (maybe this lattermost is naïve on my part... this is one of the problems with organization/directing/composing/writing at all times, so no matter what we do we may continue to wonder who the hell we think we are...)

The "*back and forth dialogue*" part of stage 0 after selection of the first 10 seems the stickiest part. I think it would be most interesting perhaps to do the critical honing of the first 10 proposals in person, as a private group, as the 10 artists + us? The final decision of which 4/5 would be ours (artists still must formalize their final presentation in writing after the in-person dialogue) but the discussion would be collective, that way everyone hears all the concerns and can benefit from observation of/participation in the constructive processes of others, even if their work is not selected for full presentation. This, I think, would further strengthen the "judication arc" you mention, esp its "private to public" transition....?

[…]

Ok that's all for now...

[…]

e

AS IF! {PROPOSITIONS}

Mike Taylor's plenary presentation, *IDEA MACHINE*, addresses the temporal conditions of transformative theater by experimentally traversing lived and restored experience. To do this, Taylor, in a day-long workshop, develops and deploys a series of "compression techniques." Taylor proposes that these compression techniques operate as methodological principles for quickly composing events on stage, transforming concepts into actions, and communicating with an audience in manners designed to "achieve sufficient G-force to break through the merely personal to the shared space" (Taylor 2013). In her words, she is interested in "audience transformation technology."

These compression technologies are themselves compressed by Taylor's years of experience making theater, positing that "a performance must make its case in far less time than it takes for an idea to permeate a culture" (Taylor ibid.). This chapter is such a compression: it takes significantly less time (to read) and less space (in words) than did "the conference," *while* proliferating potentials for the conference's commitments to permeate more broadly. Indeed, elements of Mike's technique-testing processes can be seen as an embedded criticism of how the conference fails to compress its own contexts into codes of commitment, ones that might achieve sufficient force to fuel this text through the ephemeral/particular/personal into "a" or "the" shared disciplinary space.

What are these "ways" and "senses" through which "theatrical disciplinarity" (un)does itself within the instantiated/instantiating context of the Conference of Theoretical Theater? Taylor's proposal takes up the paradigm of algorithmic computers, setting performers before microphones, seemingly staging bodies as if they are processors of "ideas." Yet against assumptions of automaticity, *IDEA MACHINE* emphasizes ways in which the internet is dependent on dynamic users and their own culturally located interpretative processes. For example, one "compression technique" involves what Taylor calls "affective disruption" (or, she says, "oblique extra-lingual category dilemma") suggesting that disciplinarities, networkings, and static/stable networks must perpetually be theatrically (re)determined as meaningful, always

Figure 38.3 Mike Taylor, *IDEA MACHINE* (2013), workshop at the Collapsable Hole, with project cast and conference participants. Hilary Sand

in *some relation to* programmatic (culturally embedded?) codes and commitments held and performed by users, or persons. Usership determines the pathways of the network, even as userships are compressed and articulated by the network they shape. Through *IDEA MACHINE*, this mutual dependence made it difficult to differentiate users (the "merely personal") from network ("the shared space"), calling their distinction into question.

The question of transformation haunted *IDEA MACHINE's* post-show discussion and the remainder of the conference, challenging us to question it as a goal, as a social or artistic good, as a potentially identifiable phenomenon. In its perpetual return as conceptual terminology (technology?), "transformation" demanded acknowledgment even as motion, particularity, time, and subjectivities ever-unmade its compression into a simple change-state machine.

AS IF! {PROP(OSITION)S}

Tuomas Laitinen <emailaddress@gmail.com>

to Esther, me, Yelena

Some Things

9/6/2013

Hi!

We still miss a couple of things. Do you think you might have these / we could get these or some of these tomorrow from Panoply?

- one armchair

- one mirror

- two extension chords (one over 10 meters + one 5 meters)

- massage table from Panoply

- one spotlight + the tripod (which came from Materials for arts)

- something to cut metal wire with

- some wood to make a bridge for the food from the window to the back yard

See you soon,

T

from: Yelena Gluzman <yelenagluzman@gmail.com>

to: Culture Push, Clarinda, Esther

Re: Theater Theory Conference – help with payment

9/19/2013

Christina (and Clarinda & Esther),

I am following up about refunds to conference participants. Though I was going to mark up the spreadsheet you sent, it is read-only, so I am attaching one exported from jotforms. The column that says "CULTURE PUSH" is the one for you guys to process the refunds; there are 13 paypal refunds and 2 checks that you should tear up. This should leave $100 (minus whatever fees you are charged by paypal) and if you could write that amount as a check to me, that would be great. Make the check out to Yelena Gluzman, and my address is [...].

If you don't mind emailing me a snapshot of the torn-up check, I will forward it to the people so they know we will not cash their checks :).

For the people who paid through BPT, I will refund them by writing and sending checks.

Thank you so much for fielding the financials for us; we couldn't have pulled it off without your help. Conference participants were really positive about this revolving fee system, and I think it systemically encouraged commitment all the way through. Thank you!

All my best,

Yelena

Kikuko Tanaka <emailaddress@kikoworld.net>

to me, Yelena

3/4/2013

Hi Esther-

Of course, I can help both preparation and staffing at the benefit. Are you considering documenting the lecture? That's something that I can help too. Maybe we can use a mic and recorder to have clearer sound along with video documentation. I'm also willing to help more physical staffs like bar-tending etc, depending on your needs.

Excited!

Best,

Kiko

AS IF! {PROOFS}

Amapola Prada's plenary presentation, an installation/performative video triptych, posits that revolutions can be private, mundane, alterior, interpersonal, aesthetic. Prada is not asking *if* they can be, or "exploring" this (im)possibility; Prada is proving that they can be. Prada's proof is, precisely, that if even one person experiences something as revolution (even something that seems epic, often recognized only when it's happening on a grand political scale such as Revolution), it is really happening. Furthermore, Prada herself is the proof that revolution has and is and can be a party of one. One small person standing in the middle of the street as the day passes from dawn to dusk. One daughter living in an embodied matriarchy, an adult suckling her mother's breast. Individual sexual beings who give and take genders, nothingness scooped away from their crotches with oversized wooden spoons/paddles. Each video documents and testifies to its own (literal and conceptual) positions *as if* each is testimony of the real (Prada 2013).

Figure 38.4 Installation view of Amapola Prada's *REVOLUTION* (2013) at Glasshouse Projects. Hilary Sand

It is one thing for an authorized US American white cis male critic (for example) to "lead" (Fried 1980) readers through interpretations of Prada's work in a major art publication and/or for us to describe it here. It is another for the artist to describe their intentions, beliefs, and theories as part of their work. It is yet another thing for audience members—those subjected by and subject to the work as carriers of its mimetic forces through and beyond embodiments—to recognize and articulate some meanings and resonances they feel and experience through and as the work, even to compare and contrast these with the theories articulated by the artist (for instance, through and as part of discursive sessions involved in/ by and respecting authorship/authority of the artist and the work).

In other words, if modes of production and dissemination of works are not aspects of the theorizations/theatricalizations present in and performed as/by the work, ways of seeing are not seen and heard in their own ways, and perhaps they can't be seen or heard at all (Spivak 1988). Further complexity lies in the communication of and through *forms, modes,* and *structures* themselves, and the potential staging of embodied processes that situate (p)articulations.

By identifying this complexity, one need not be arguing that dominant institutions should tell audiences what an artist says their work means. Rather, the argument is that performances of institution and discipline (as theatricalized verbs) can structurally enable (a) work's positions and perspectives to be recognized, heard, and seen as such, in and upon their own terms and forms and modes of communication. If an artist is making work that sees itself as "wholly open to interpretation," a multiplicity of interpretations can be contextually and conditionally enabled. If an artist is theorizing via their work, theorizations may be *theatricalized and performed through and as* the work's modes of production, framing, and generation of expectations for attending, listening to, and interpreting performativities as theorizations.

(Re)propositon: "AS IF" (Hypocrits)

Re-read the above text and underline the parts that seem to you like "theory."
End scene.

We struggle with *acts of defining*, and their slippage into epistemic and ontological singularity (Moten and Harney's "onto-epistemic encyclopedia," 2011 or Foucault's "all encompassing and global theories," 1998). We fear that a simple union of "theater" with "theory" could beget definitive descriptions of each as institutionalized and total disciplines, reproducing bifurcated conditions for methods of research, staging, and analysis, and at the same time conflating theater theory into a sexy singular *Theatrum Mundi* inside which all stagings wholly condition one another toward emergence into marketability as intellectual product. This, precisely, is what our orientation around theatricality and theorization sought to unsee and undo, and the reason we now seek to reformalize "as" into something that stages its own provisionality while insisting on the (f)act of its realization.

By shifting our orientation to "as if," we look away from *mise-en-scène*, with its presumption of a single proscenium (bringing up debates of whether by "nature" or "design") that gives coherence to a singular real, and instead toward *mise-en-abyme*, inviting procreation of (f)acts. "As ifs" are ways of seeing which are made meaningful to and via the idea(l)s of assembled, embodied practitioners and participants, worlds which are (idealistically) framed to enable and invite ways of seeing rather than contain or conclude them.

In lieu of a conclusion, then, we end by reviewing the logics of theater/theory through the lens of "as if."

In our attempt here, "as ifs" operate not as claims of knowledge but as "invitations for *acknowledgement*" (Hejinian 2000, p. 2) beyond dichotomies of artificial vs. real, suspending disbelief in that which is pre-conceived as insensible, illegible, or illegitimate (Scott 1998). Theater *as if* theory, we suggest, communicates on temporary, consensual bases (as within improv's "Yes, and…"), thereby instantiating and substantiating ways in which implications of "uncanny" forms and ideations may be experimentally (Ihde 1977) or agonistically (Mouffe 2013) researched through implementation. Implementation is important here, since it is not only the proliferation of ways of seeing that are at issue, but also their embarrassed consequentiality.

Thus, the suspension of disbelief that conditions "as ifs" need not imply that acknowledgments and suspensions are enacted by sidelined audience members who can always return to "more believable" pre-or-post-conditions, or that theatrical roles can be discarded as easily as they are taken up, as Butler suggests in order to specify performativity by counter-distinction with theater (Butler 1988, 1993). It is the performativity of theater and the necessary embodied theatrics of the performative (Gluzman 2017) that shift the "as if" from a relativist language game to a matter of, and for, survival.

In this essay, and in our work more broadly, we pursue how theater "as if" theory can perform what Donna Haraway described as "a critical practice for recognizing our own 'semiotic technologies' for making meanings, *and* a no-nonsense commitment to faithful accounts of a 'real' world" (Haraway 1988, p. 579). We feel that provisional acts of theater as if theory cannot be wholly undone/unseen once (re)marked from within the ways a situation seems to those within it. We are wondering if it follows, then, that (un)certain irrevocability *demands* (or at least frames subsequent enactments as) responses and responsibilities.

Notes

1 See "opera of operations" *Embarrassed of the Whole: EotW* (2020) by Panoply Performance Laboratory (PPL) through which embarrassment is theatrically theorized as exposition, excavation, disenchantment, disenfranchisement, dislocation, illegibility, illegitimacy, signification of dissidence, the "guilty conscience of imperialist traditions of rationalism" and as a "hole," wound, or orifice in "zeitgeists" and meta-narratives.
2 cf. Figure 38.1.

References

Althusser, L. 1995. *Sur la reproduction*, Presses Universitaires de France, Paris.
Arendt, H. 1982. *Lectures on Kant's Political Philosophy*. Edited and with an interpretive essay by Ronald Beiner, University of Chicago Press, Chicago.
Austin J. L. 1962. *How to Do Things with Words,* Harvard University Press, Cambridge.
Barish, J. A. 1981. *The Anti-theatrical Prejudice*, University of California Press, Berkeley, Los Angeles, London.
Benhabib, S. 1992. *Situating the Self: Gender, Community, and Postmodernism in Contemporary Ethics*, Routledge, New York.
Benjamin, W. 1968. "The Work of Art in the Age of Mechanical Reproduction" from *Illuminations*. Schocken Books, New York, pp. 217–251.
Burke, K. 1966. *Language as Symbolic Action: Essays on Life, Literature and Method,* University of California Press, Berkeley.
Butler, J. 1988. "Performative acts and gender constitution: An essay in phenomenology and feminist theory." *Theatre Journal* 40: 519–531.
———. 1993. "Critically queer." *GLQ: A Journal of Lesbian and Gay Studies* 1(1):17–32.
Derrida, J. 1976. *Of Grammatology* (trans. Gayatri Chakravorty Spivak), Johns Hopkins University Press, Baltimore & London.

Eco, U. 1984. *The Role of the Reader: Explorations in the Semiotics of Texts,* University of Indiana Press, Bloomington.

Foerster, H. 1984. *Observing Systems,* Intersystems Publications, Cambridge.

Foucault, M. 1998. *The History of Sexuality: The Will to Knowledge,* Penguin Books, London.

Fried, M. 1980. *Absorption and Theatricality: Painting and Beholder in the Age of Diderot,* University of California Press, Berkeley.

Gluzman, Y. 2017. "Research-as-theatre: Positioning theatre at the centre of PAR, and PAR at the centre of the academy." In Annette Arlander, Bruce Barton, Melanie Dreyer-Lude, Ben Spatz (Eds.), *Performance as Research: Knowledge, Methods, Impact.* Routledge, Abington, UK and New York, 123–150.

Goffman, E. 1956. *The Presentation of Self in Everyday Life,* Penguin Random House LLC, New York.

Gramsci, A. 1971. *Selections from the Prison Notebooks of Antonio Gramsci* In Q. Hoare and G. Nowell-Smith (Eds.), International Publishers, New York.

Hacking, I. 1983. *Representing and Intervening: Introductory Topics in the Philosophy of Natural Science.* Cambridge University Press, Cambridge.

Haraway, D. 1988. 'Situated knowledges: The science question in feminism and the privilege of partial perspective'. *Feminist Studies* 14(3), 575–599.

———. 2008. *When Species Meet,* University of Minnesota Press, Minneapolis.

Harney, S., and Moten, F. 2013. *The Undercommons: Fugitive Planning & Black Study,* Autonomedia, New York.

Hejinian, L. 2000. *The Language of Inquiry,* University of California Press, Berkeley, Los Angeles, London.

Herzig, R. 2004. 'On performance, productivity, and vocabularies of motive in recent studies of science'. *Feminist Theory, 5*(2), 127–147.

Ihde, D. 1977. *Experimental Phenomenology: An Introduction,* Putnam Press, University of Michigan, Ann Arbor.

Koselleck, R. 2004. *Futures Past: On the Semantics of Historical Time,* Columbia University Press, New York.

Kuhn, T. 1990 [1962]. *The Structure of Scientific Revolutions,* University of Chicago Press, Chicago.

McLuhan, M. 1964. *Understanding Media: The Extensions of Man,* Routledge, London.

Mouffe, C. 2013. *Agonistics: Thinking the World Politically,* Verso, London, Brooklyn, NY.

Neff, E. and Gluzman, Y. 2013. "Theorems, proofs rebuttals and propositions: A conference of theoretical theater." In Yelena Gluzman and Sophia Cleary (Eds.), *Emergency Index: An Annual Document of Performance Practice Vol. 3.* Brooklyn: Ugly Duckling Presse, pp. 420–421.

Panoply Performance Laboratory. 2020. "Embarrassed of the Whole (EotW)", Ugly Duckling Presse, Emergency Playscripts Series, Brooklyn.

Piaget, J. 1969. *The Mechanisms of Perception,* Basic Books, New York.

Prada, A. 2013. *REVOLUTION,* Theorems, Proofs, Rebuttals, and Propositions: A Conference of Theoretical Theater, New York City.

Rancière, J. 2004. *The Politics of Aesthetics: The Distribution of the Sensible,* Continuum, London.

Reality Research Center. 2013. *Plato's Symposium: Mysteries of Love,* Theorems, Proofs, Rebuttals, and Propositions: A Conference of Theoretical Theater, New York City.

Rousseau, J-J. 1953. *The Confessions of Jean-Jacques Rousseau* (trans. J.M. Cohen), Penguin Books, London.

Scott, J. C. 1998. *Seeing Like a State: How Certain Schemes to Improve the Human Condition Have Failed,* Yale University Press, New Haven.

Spivak, G. C. 1988. 'Can the Subaltern Speak?', *Die Philosophin,* 14 (27), 42–58.

Sontag, S. 1978. *On Photography,* Farrar, Straus and Giroux, New York.

Tanaka, K. 2013. *Poultry Paradise and Its Discontents: Nightshifts,* Theorems, Proofs, Rebuttals, and Propositions: A Conference of Theoretical Theater, New York City.

Taylor, M. 2013. *IDEA MACHINE: Experiments in Theatre Techniques for Audience,* Theorems, Proofs, Rebuttals, and Propositions: A Conference of Theoretical Theater, New York City.

39
DANCE AS EMBODIED ETHICS

Aili Bresnahan, Einav Katan-Schmid and Sara Houston

Introduction

In this chapter, we propose that one of the many possible ways that dance might embody philosophic thought and discourse is via embodying ethical practice. Each author contributes a different perspective on the relationship between dance and ethical activity. We invite the reader to go through this account in two ways: as separate ideas and as interrelated thoughts.

Katan-Schmid views 'dance' as a metaphor for 'embodied ethics'. She analyses dance as an embodied activity of decision-making which regulates the tension between co-existing physical dynamics. Following from the idea of 'dancing', she asks us to think of 'embodied ethics' in performative terms – as a contemplative activity.

In her section, Bresnahan shows how dance practice provides examples of applied ethics within traditional Western philosophical categories of both virtue ethics and consequentialist ethics.

Houston argues that dance can encompass an ethics of care. She demonstrates how dance with an ethic of care involves attentiveness, putting the person before the form, and for the dance artists to give up a degree of control and autonomy over the work made.

As a mutual account, it is our view that dance contains practices – including but not limited to dancing – that constitute ethical activity along all of the lines discussed earlier, be they metaphoric of ethical action, applied directly towards a goal of human flourishing or societal good, or an ethics of care for and with one another. Dance, on all of our accounts, contains careful, thoughtful work on balance, self-development and attentiveness to the needs of the whole while contemplating, comprehending and considering the essentials of any individual part within. As such, we together have views that themselves exist in relations with one another and are not in contradiction, although we are aware that we have by no means exhausted the possibilities for dance as embodied ethics here. We invite you to think through dancing with us as you try on the views expressed below.

Dancing as a metaphor for embodied ethics
Einav Katan-Schmid

I ask the reader to view 'Dance as Embodied Ethics' as a metaphor. I invite an understanding of one thing: 'dance', in terms of another: 'embodied ethics'. As I sense it, this metaphor *feels* quite actual. Moreover, I am aware that the shared instinctive feeling here – that dance interweaves aesthetic knowing with ethics – is timely (see Bannon 2018) and does not stand alone. George Lakoff and Mark Johnson, for example, state that the metaphor of dancing is an alternative to the current war-like culture of argumentation. They ask their reader to imagine 'a culture where an argument is viewed as a dance, the participants are seen as performers, and the goal is to perform in a balanced and aesthetically pleasing way' (Lakoff and Johnson 2008 [1980], 5). I would like to further develop this image and to suggest that 'dance' enables thinking of decision-making in terms of embodied comprehension of dynamic interrelationships. Thus, tacit and contemplative decisions are made beyond rigid definitions.

My notion of 'dancing' here is schematic. I draw from my knowledge – as fragmentary and contextual as it is – a broad sense of 'what dancing *means*'. I am aware that there are mock combat dances, that not all training-cultures are ethical and that some stylistic expressions do not aim to please their viewers. However, I look here at 'dancing' as a general idea. In its broadest far-reaching sense, 'dancing' is the human activity of moving aesthetically. Like all other physical techniques, dance movements are both social and personal (Mauss 1935). In addition, while dancing, bodily movements are tailored to their aesthetic purposes and their performance is neither practical nor existential (Valéry 1957 [1938], pp. 1390–1391; Katan-Schmid 2016, pp. 57–59). So, bodily movements in dance are self-referential and are conducted due to an exchange between knowledge, sensitivity and imagination. Thus, as I view it, 'dancing' holds three characteristics, which are significant for human understanding: it is personal, cultural and reflective at the same time.

Take, for instance, a pirouette as a metaphorical component of 'dancing'. In order to regulate balance within a spin, a dancer needs to swiftly move the leg into a passé, to rise into a relevé, to find the position of the arms, stretch up and contract the core of the body and, critically, fix the gaze onto one focal point while constantly moving and whirling. There is a technical know-how – acquired through practice during the experiential history of training – but every time anew there must be an activation of knowledge through feeling, interpreting and fine-tuning to the present momentum. A dancer jumps into the experience of a pirouette without having full control over all the instants of movement in advance. Attentiveness is required to both the environmental conditions and personal capacities in that moment so as to transform and direct the body into effective movement. This process involves many small moments of decision-making which are both embodied and consciously felt. The activity is contemplative; to dance is a process of feeling, tacitly analysing and attuning dynamics.

American Pragmatist philosopher, John Dewey, defines the intelligence of an artist as maintaining a perceptual balance between doing and undergoing (Dewey 1980 [1934], p. 47). In line with Dewey's definition of aesthetic perception, within dancing a dancer activates a genuinely felt understanding of what the movement needs and accordingly regulates the aesthetic balance between leading and responding to bodily forces. Achieving the pirouette demands a correlation of the understanding of what is happening physically with the imagining of the future development of this movement and so leads *towards* this development. Leading the progression of movements, feeling their momentum and undergoing the complexity of current dynamics are relevant to a successful performance in any imaginable kind of dancing.

Maintaining aesthetic balance implies embodied agency (Bresnahan 2014a; Merritt 2015) of a dancer who contemplates doing because it involves tacit-attuned decision-making within the feeling for the dance. In line with Lakoff and Johnson's metaphor (2008 [1980], p. 5), the actual work of dancing is an aesthetic labour of sustaining immediate understanding regarding what a movement needs in order to lead into the fulfilment of that movement. 'Aesthetically pleasing', as Lakoff and Johnson phrase in their metaphor as the goal of a dance, is a regulative idea, which leads the aesthetic balance between directing dynamics to undergoing their current momentum. This work demands a constant attunement of self-dynamics, knowledge, sensitivity and an understanding of the mutual related effect of all current undergoing aspects of the dance. Not all movements aim for the spinning of the pirouette, but in all dancing activities I can think of, there is a common process of adjustment between knowing and feeling in order to coordinate a rhythmic flow (or a break of it) from a variety of dynamics. Beyond stylistic taste, graceful dancing expresses the sensitivity of the embodied agency of the dancer who is responsible for a continuum of swiftly made decisions and knowledge regulation.

'Dance' – or more precisely: 'dancing' as 'embodied ethics' – is an image worthy of inquiry according to what we think of ethics in an ever-developing world of knowledge and of diverse and disunited experiences (Bannon 2018, p. 28; Tong and Williams 2018). The image of dance offers a view on the interrelation of dynamics in regard to traditions (like the technique of performing a pirouette), the effective knowledge they embody (finding operative bodily tensions for leading a spin) and the sensitivity for existing – always exceptional – conditions for fulfilment (like regulating momentary feelings of collapse into a spin). In any act of dancing, such knowledge must be re-enacted, re-comprehended and re-adjusted in relation to present momentums and their progressions. What if we understand, for instance, social engagements as a dance, with balanced communication as their regulative goal and ethics as the contemplative activity of leading towards fulfilment? In this case, ethical decision-making could be understood in terms of sensitivity for diversity of dynamics, leading them towards a mutual exchange. The metaphor of thinking on 'embodied ethics' in terms of 'dancing' leads me to think of the embodied agency of a person who conducts decision-making within an enduring attentiveness for the interrelations of co-existing, often disunited, social forces rather than a mere following after pre-formed norms. In case we consider communication as a regulative goal, 'embodied ethics' could be seen as an activity of recognising one's own knowledge, reconsidering and re-adjusting it in relation to new information that manifests within an exchange.

Dance as applied ethics

Aili Bresnahan

In Western philosophy, theories of ethics often fall under one of three traditional categories:

1. Virtue ethics theories of what is good for human beings, construed in terms of character development or virtue (Aristotle's idea of *eudaimonia* or human flourishing).
2. Consequentialist theories of what is good for others or of human society overall (as in, for example, John Stuart Mill's theory in *Utilitarianism* and, in contemporary form, John Dewey's philosophy).
3. Kantian deontological theories based on what is right in accordance with universal principles that are true for human beings (see *Grounding for the Metaphysics of Morals*).

It is not difficult to imagine how dance practices might be construed as an ethical action on the first two of these theories, so it is only these two that I will address here. Regarding virtue ethics theory, dance can contribute to human flourishing by helping human beings to develop their physical, artistic and civic capabilities. Dance can also help us to flourish by helping us to experience a *katharsis* of the emotions. According to Aristotle, *katharsis* occurs when we experience strong emotions such as pity or fear when watching tragedy, which helps to purge us of negative and excess feelings (Aristotle 1984 [c. 335 BCE], p. 230, 6.1449b22–27).

An example of dance as Aristotelian tragedy is exhibited in the photo below. Boston Globe staff writer, Evan Allen, describes it this way:

> At first, the dancers were joyful, leaping in circles and wrapping in a bear hug the young man portraying slain 12-year-old Tamir Rice, who was shot to death by Cleveland police at a playground in November 2014.
>
> But then the drumbeat turned staccato, his body jerked, and the other dancers rushed him in attack. He fell dead, his white shirt now smeared with black paint to symbolize bullets.
>
> *(Allen 2016)*

Dance is also a practice with consequentialist benefits. First, the kind of dance regarded as fine art can create 'higher pleasures'. In Mill's view, higher pleasures are those that require faculties of intellect, education or feelings that are worth more due to their qualitative value than are the lower pleasures of animals in their contribution to overall societal good (see Mill 2017 [1863], pp. 5–6). However, it can be argued that even 'lower' forms of dance, such as some forms of pole dancing, can contribute to the overall balance of societal pleasure.

In the late 19th century and early 20th century, John Dewey held a consequentialist theory of ethics which held that the results of an action for human life determine whether it is a moral action or not (Dewey 1985 [1932], p. 295). His ethical theory also requires that these actions spring from a human self that is motivated by the desire to help rather than

Figure 39.1 Demetrius Burns laid on the ground while playing the part of Tamir Rice during an interpretive dance at the Black Lives Matter rally at the TD Garden [Boston]. CRAIG F. WALKER/GLOBE STAFF

harm others (Dewey 1985 [1932], p. 295). Dewey treats art, including the performing arts, as primarily aimed towards the creation of heightened and unified aesthetic experiences. If we find that these experiences can constitute what is good for human life, then it is a short step from this to the claim that dance is an ethical action (see Bresnahan 2014b). Indeed, Dewey acknowledges that dance can affect people in ways that have deep ethical import for the creation of social good. Dewey points out, for example, that:

> Cooperation and sympathy are fostered by the activities of *art*. Some of these activities are spontaneous, but most of them serve some definite social end and are frequently organized for the definite purpose of increasing the unity and sympathy of the group. The hunting dance or the war dance represents, in dramatic form, all the processes of the hunt or fight, but it would be a mistake to suppose that this takes place purely for dramatic purposes.
>
> *(Dewey 1985 [1932], p. 45)*

Indeed, the Black Lives Matter movement in the United States – a grass-roots civil rights action group 'whose mission is to build local power and to intervene in violence inflicted on Black communities by the state and vigilantes' – has inspired dance, poetry and song as part of its efforts to build community and morale among its members, as well as to express its social and political message (Black Lives Matter website; see also Lavington 2016; Schaefer 2016). Dance troupes in connection with Black Lives Matter and other ethically engaged groups have used dance as a form of protest action in public spaces, such as in front of police stations and other government organisations whose behaviours they wish to change (see Saldivar and Easter 2017). These examples show that dance can count as an ethical action in the service of the good.

Dance as ethical engagement and connection with others

Sara Houston

1   Nora's eyes light up and she extends her hand upwards to a young man, who has his arm outstretched towards her. He takes hers, swinging gently to the music of Frank Sinatra. Nora has dementia. She always attends her care home's weekly dance class. Her carers claim this is the highlight of her week.
2   Bienvenue has fled his homeland and now lives in a guarded refugee camp in Chad. He thanks God that the dance company NDam Se Na comes every few months to dance with them. Today, the dance group freestyles, sharing a circle like a hip-hop cypher. Bienvenue's torso moves back and forward in rapid motion, his arms held out to the side as he steps into the ring, taking over from another dancer who finishes with a helicopter spin. His fellow dancers clap and sing out the rhythm.
3   Eva dances several times a week. She has Parkinson's. She works with choreographers attending her city's arts programme. She shows me a film she's made with choreographer Fabio Novembrini. Her fine-boned body, its delicacy enhanced by the tremors she experiences, is buried in a pile of red-gold autumn leaves that crackle as she moves.

These vignettes are illustrations of socially engaged dance in action.[1] They are examples where dance artists or companies work with community groups through dance. I say 'with' and 'through' to emphasise that this is not dance being 'taught' *to* people as transmissions of knowledge from teacher to pupil; rather, they are illustrations of the use of movement to communicate, to share movement ideas, to integrate, to create, to form relationships, to invent together. These cases are instances of participatory art that are relational, where the sense and intention of relating is one of the most important factors in the process of making dance.

The individuals featured earlier have all felt the disintegration of something that has been integral to their sense of humanity, their sense of self as a capable actor: Nora's mind, the loss of home for Bienvenue, the deterioration of Eva's control of her movement. To work as a dance artist with people who experience vulnerability requires sensitivity to their needs. I suggest that ethics of care (Noddings 1984) are required to address this in the making of art. Performance scholar James Thompson describes art as having ethics of care, or a form of aesthetics of care, as 'a set of values realised in a relational process that emphasise engagements between individuals or groups over time' (Thompson 2015, p. 437). This requires dance artists to be 'attentive' (Tronto 1993, p. 127) whilst creating work with dance participants. By 'creating', I am referring not only to the process of making a performance work, but also the physical process of dancing, of deliberately moving through and carving out space. The practice of attentiveness in socially engaged dance contexts requires knowing or sensing how each participant is doing that day. Particularly for people caught up in a situation that potentially makes them vulnerable, each day may bring its own set of challenges and emotions. In order for their circumstances not to overwhelm and for the dance session to be successful – in terms of being 'safe', welcoming, open, respectful, inclusive and enjoyable – the practice of dancing needs to mould itself *around* people, rather than being an inflexible structure into which people fit. This is a different conception to much conventional dance teaching that often uses structures to mould bodies to the technical demands of the form. Essentially, in socially engaged dance practice, the person comes before the form.

Person before form means, in practice, a number of different things.

For example, firstly, even before participants enter the dance space, the session needs to be accessible to them: Are they physically able to get to the session and once there, can they get in, or feel that they are catered for and welcome? How does Eva recognise that the opportunity of working with a professional choreographer is for her? Where there are barriers to participation, dance remains exclusive.

Secondly, the dance artist needs to be flexible in approach, to be open to jettisoning the session plan or differentiating movement for individuals. If Nora's symptoms are worse on any particular day, she may not be able to do what was planned. Instead of assuming she cannot join in, a different movement can be imagined that retains the essence of the original idea. So, for instance, instead of foxtrotting around the room, Nora might stay seated and wave a scarf to the lilt of the music. The dynamic swing is still there in the trace of the scarf. The dance artist needs to come to the space with the question 'how might everyone in this room feel included in the dance?', rather than 'how am I going to teach everyone to dance?'. Enacting notions of inclusivity and openness marks out the session as socially engaged.

In facilitating people to feel included in the dance, it is also about the dance artist giving up autocratic pretensions. Although there are varying degrees of control relinquished by the dance artist within socially engaged dance, it is characterised by a sharing of creativity. Specifically, a sharing of creativity here means participants making decisions, such as what movement they do, how they move and themes used. The effect of this is that the participant may feel they have a voice and presence.

The contemporary dance company NDam Se Na works in refugee camps. They specifically embrace types of movements and dances familiar to the refugees and encourage participants to create using their own ways of moving. With this principle, the company acknowledges the cultural worth of these dances, thus signalling to participants the value of their own heritages and knowledge. In taking a step back, the dance artist may instead offer a voice to a different 'other', in this case, a group of people who have few legal rights or representation.

Performance projects also may be conducted with socially engaged values. Eva is performing in Novembrini's film; they have been in dialogue for some time. Novembrini attended Eva's dance sessions, participating alongside those with and without Parkinson's. They have been sharing ideas and Eva recognises her bodily need to keep moving, as well as her interest in artistic practices. The decision for Eva to dance for Novembrini offered her an identity that was separated from her disease but acknowledged her specific movement qualities influenced by Parkinson's.

Routinely working with attentiveness and encouraging embodied connectivity is an ethical approach to dancing with others. This approach cultivates practices of listening and responding, as well as a readiness to accommodate the 'other'. It allows the dance artist to connect through recognising the value of what participants bring to the process. Moreover, attending to access and inclusion may more broadly address some of the barriers that traditional pedagogies in many dance forms have erected that actively exclude or marginalise groups and individuals.

Conclusion

As shown earlier, it is our view that dance has an inherent capacity to promote embodied ethics in a variety of ways: as a metaphor for a balanced and attentive process of ethical decision-making, as applied ethics in the service of what is good for human beings and as an ethic of caring for others. Further, it is our view that this application is necessary. We hold that without extending ethics from an abstract notion into applied understanding, without addressing in concrete ways the inclusion of others who are often excluded from society, then 'ethics' is an ineffectual concept – a disembodied framework – without application and true value for human life. The dance practices we have discussed not only embody dancing then, but ethics; they help to give ethics moving, breathing life. In this way, there is a sense in which we have made ethics *dance*.

Note

1 Socially engaged dance and community dance are interchangeable terms. Here, I use the term socially engaged dance in order to stress the notion of social engagement on the part of the dance artist.

References

Allen, Evan. 2016. January 2nd. "Our Children Can't Play in Peace," the *Boston Globe*, https://www.bostonglobe.com/metro/2016/01/02/black-lives-matter-protests-dance-death-cleveland-year-old/9UWjRNlOX5kcHuSWGoR8OI/story.html, accessed July 25, 2018.
Aristotle. 1984 [c. 335 BCE]). "Poetics," in *The Rhetoric and the Poetics of Aristotle*. I. Bywater (trans.), with an introduction by Edward P. J. Corbett, New York: The Modern Library, McGraw Hill Inc., 221–266. [Note: The citations from Immanuel Bekker's 1837 edition of this text has been retained in the body of the text for ease of reference.]
Bannon, Fiona. 2018. *Considering Ethics in Dance, Theatre, and Performance*, London: Palgrave Macmillan.
Black Lives Matter website, https://blacklivesmatter.com/about/, accessed July 23, 2018.

Bresnahan, Aili. 2014a. "Improvisational Artistry in Live Dance Performance as Embodied and Extended Agency", *Dance Research Journal* 46 (1): 84–94.

Bresnahan, Aili. 2014b. "Toward A Deweyan Theory of Ethical and Aesthetic Performing Arts Practice", *The Journal of Aesthetics and Phenomenology* 1 (2): 133–148.

Dewey, John 1980 [1934]. *Art as Experience*, New York: A Perigee Book.

Dewey, John 1985 [1932]. "Ethics", in *John Dewey: The Later Works, 1925–1953, Vol. 7*. J. Boydston (ed.), with an introduction by A. Edel and E. Flower, Carbondale: Southern Illinois Press, pp. 1–18.

Kant, Immanuel. 1994 [1785]. "Grounding for the Metaphysics of Morals", in *Ethical Philosophy, Second Edition*. J.W. Ellington (trans.), Indianapolis/Cambridge: Hackett Publishing Company, Book I, 1–65.

Katan-Schmid, Einav. 2016. "Purposiveness without Purpose", in Einav Katan-Schmid: *Embodied Philosophy in Dance: Gaga and Ohad Naharin's Movement Research*, London: Palgrave Macmillan, pp. 57–64.

Lakoff, George and Mark Johnson. (2008 [1980]) *Metaphors We Live By*, Chicago: University of Chicago Press.

Lavington, Theresa. 2016. "Dance for Black Lives Matter", YouTube, https://www.youtube.com/watch?v=nkKMA3MSANk, accessed July 23, 2018.

Mauss, Marcel. 1994 [1935]. "Techniques of the Body", in *Incorporations*, J. Crary and S. Kwinter (eds.) New York: Zone Books, pp. 455–477.

Merritt, Michele. 2015. "Thinking-Is-Moving: Dance, Agency, and a Radically Enactive Mind", *Phenomenology and the Cognitive Sciences* 14 (1): 95–110.

Mill, John Stuart. 2017 [1863]. *Utilitarianism*. J. Bennett (ed.), Early Modern Texts, http://www.earlymoderntexts.com/assets/pdfs/mill1863.pdf, accessed July 23, 2018.

Noddings, Nel. 1984. *Caring: A Relational Approach to Ethics and Moral Education*, Berkeley: University of California Press.

Saldivar, Steve and Makeda Easter. 2017. April 28th. "These L.A. Dancers Are Changing the Way People Protest", *The Los Angeles Times*, http://www.latimes.com/la-et-cm-street-dance-activism-20170420-story.html, accessed July 23, 2018. [See link for story and for video footage of the dancing discussed.]

Schaefer, Brian. 2016. Nov. 30. "Dance in the Age of Black Lives Matter", *Dance Magazine*, https://www.dancemagazine.com/dance-age-black-lives-matter-2307047358.html, accessed July 23, 2018.

Thompson, James. 2015. "Towards an Aesthetics of Care", *Research in Drama Education: The Journal of Applied Theatre and Performance* 20 (4): 430–441.

Tong, Rosemary and Nancy Williams. 2018. "Feminist Ethics", in *The Stanford Encyclopedia of Philosophy*. Edward N. Zalta (ed.), https://plato.stanford.edu/archives/sum2018/entries/feminism-ethics/.

Tronto, Joan C. 1993. *Moral Boundaries: A Political Argument for an Ethic of care*, New York: Routledge.

Valéry, Paul. 1957 [1938]. "Philosophie de la danse", in: *Paul Valéry: Oeuvres. Tome 1. Théorie poétique et esthétique*, Paris: Gallimard, pp. 1390–1403.

40
PHILOSOPHY ON STAGE

Arno Böhler and Susanne Valerie [Granzer]

Perspective I
Doing aesthetics
Arno Böhler

What is arts-based philosophy?

Arts-based philosophy is a concept of philosophy in which *poiesis*, the process of letting something come into being (becoming), is considered the core performance of philosophy. When practising arts-based philosophy, one *"takes care of an event"* (Böhler and Manning 2014, p. 14), and one curates future becomings.

In this context, philosophy is no longer a solely theoretical, contemplative practice of thinking, as it was in ancient Greek times, but an approach to bodily *staging* things (res): staging ideas, the promise of a future to come or a new grouping of bodies. In this sense, it amounts to *doing aesthetics*. It is not so much a case of analysing somebody's relation to already existing empirical objects at hand (as in Baumgarten's and Kant's understanding of aesthetics), or of philosophizing about one's relation to objects that have already emerged in the past. It is a question, rather, of productively researching the genesis of things to come that have *not yet* been staged in the ontogenesis of time but that are, *perhaps*, capable of being generated, induced, invented, created, constructed and produced in the course of future becomings (natura naturans).

An arts-based philosophy *performs* aesthetics. As such, it is a mode of philosophy that goes beyond the mere mental representation of an idea, in that it seeks to stage the 'thing itself' – empirically, physically, bodily – in nature,[1] and not just in a mind. Arts-based philosophers mime (*anukāra*, cf. Böhler 2016, p. 11) the productive force at work in nature (natura naturans), in the same sense in which nature itself does no imagining, but actually produces trees, human beings and black holes in the course of her ongoing evolutionary becoming in time and space.

It follows then that if arts-based philosophers are concerned with the genesis of new social entities, they must be interested, like artists, in the material becoming of such new social forms in time and space. They strive to stage the genesis of such entities (their becoming), by calling forth their future appearance, in a generative sense, both artistically and inventively. If Paul Klee considers art to be a form of *making* things *visible* (Deleuze 2003, p. 56), arts-based philosophy considers art to be a generative field *of making things appear* in time and space. It can therefore be characterized as a form of *Speculative Materialism*, a philosophical approach of which both philosopher-artists and artist-philosophers can be considered *virtual precursors* (cf. Böhler and Granzer 2017, pp. 198–199), researching as they both do, the performativity of future becomings.

With Deleuze, one can call the *tension* at work in such an in-*tention*-ality, which actually addresses a future *tense* to come, the *virtual* dimension of our corporeal being-in-the-world. It is a dimension of time, unfolded in every living body capable of transcending the present and past tense in the direction of a future tense. This virtual dimension of time comprises everything which is *not yet actual*, yet is nevertheless a *real* dimension of any body, insofar as that body is able to address a future *to come* in order to be presented. The staging of future becomings never takes place in the future, but in the here and now, in the midst of our empirical relations to other human and non-human bodies with whom we share our bodily being-in-the-world. Therefore, the *doing of aesthetics*, operative in arts-based philosophy, can also be regarded as a radical form of empiricism (cf. for example, Deleuze 1994, p. 47; James 2012, pp. 30–31). It is no positivistic empiricism, however, for it is not limited to analysing already given empirical facts ready at hand (natura naturata), but oriented towards the artistic empiricism of virtual becomings as they are on their way to happening, perhaps. Indeed, one never knows beforehand whether the *full* empirical constitution of a virtual genesis will take place in the future or not. But even though future becomings are contingent, they can be felt beforehand in *pre-sentiments*, in which their future *presentation* is emotionally and conceptually anticipated (*mathemata*) before the thing itself emerges empirically in time and space. (Inventors of the mobile phone, for example, already *lived* the future tense of its becoming, before the reality of the device made its appearance ready at hand in the present.)

The time zone of the dangerous perhaps

When Nietzsche claimed in *Beyond Good and Evil*—a text with the telling subtitle *Prelude to a Philosophy of the Future*—that the "new category of philosophers to arrive, those, whose taste and inclination are the reverse of their predecessors" will be "in every sense philosophers of the dangerous Perhaps" (Nietzsche 1998, p. 6), he clearly indicated that a philosophy *of* the future is structurally confronted with the dangerous time zone of the *perhaps*. It is dangerous because in this virtual dimension of time, *the taking place* of a future is *actually* at stake. Perhaps it will be presented, perhaps not. This uncertainty is constitutive if one addresses the genesis of virtual becomings. Any virtual "object" oscillates, ontologically, in a time zone between being and non-being in a state of contingent becoming.

Arts-based philosophers curate precisely this in-between, this insecure and precarious time zone of the dangerous perhaps. One could call this the maieutic, in the sense that the generative character of arts-based philosophy is the one in which one follows one's artistic appetite (*conatus*) to invent the material genesis of something or somebody so that it appears in time and space. In this respect, arts-based philosophers perform an aesthetic inversion of the Socratic method. While Socrates was a midwife helping to determine the truth value of propositions in respect to different claims made in dialogues, arts-based philosophy tests and experiments virtually the genesis of future becomings. *One day,* it will probably be possible to *see* it happen, the future one is longing for – *eventually*, it will be possible to inhabit it, perhaps. Live in it, perhaps, intuit[2] it, perhaps.[3] It is obviously a precarious, insecure stage which emerges from *doing* aesthetics.

The promise of artist-philosophers: Nietzsche's post-Socratic inversion of Platonism

In order to induce the arrival of arts-based philosophy as an untimely form of performing philosophy, Nietzsche was forced to conceptualize the conceptual persona of the artist-philosopher. It would have to be somebody willing and able to actually perform arts-based philosophy and thus take care of the genesis of a new performative way of doing philosophy in alliance with the arts.

In this struggle, Plato, "the greatest enemy of art Europe has yet produced" (Nietzsche 1989, p. 154), plays a crucial role. It is historically his philosophy that produced the *antagonistic* relation between art and philosophy, a model which, according to Nietzsche, still prominently determined the relation between the regimes of art and philosophy in his own era. If there is some truth in Whitehead's claim that the entire European history of philosophy can, at its best, be considered a footnote to Plato (cf. Whitehead 1979, p. 91), then Europeans are not just working on history of philosophy while deconstructing Platonism; we are deconstructing a prominent figure in the context of the genealogy of the *contemporary regime* concerning the relation of art and philosophy that still dominates European thinking today (cf. Heidegger 1991, pp. 200–201; Whiel 2012; Böhler 2017).

Plato versus Platonism

Plato's life can be taken as a telling example of what is at stake in this reversal of Platonism. We know that Plato, in his early days, was an artist, a playwright. It was only after he had met Socrates that he decided to put an end to his artistic persona and burn all his works in order to become a follower and disciple of Socrates. To become a Socratic philosopher, Plato obviously thought that he had to give up on his former existence as a playwright. Both conceptual personae were apparently no longer able to live together in peace in his person; he felt compelled to choose. Either he was to become an artist *or* a Socratic philosopher. The relation between art and philosophy thus became antagonistic. Henceforth, Socratic philosophers were to assume, in a Platonist manner, that they had to exclude, probably even displace, any artistic impulse to generate artefacts materially, if they intended to become serious, decent, "proper" Socratic philosophers. To be an artist-philosopher was clearly not an option either for Plato or, later, Platonists. It would appear to be impossible, in the context of Plato's image of thought, that one might be and become both an artist *and* a philosopher: artist-philosopher, philosopher-artist, artistic researcher. However, it is more than obvious that within Plato himself the distinction was never clear-cut. Even after having given up his first career as an artist, the skills he had thereby acquired clearly survived in his second career as a Socratic philosopher; they are obviously detectable in the midst of his philosophical oeuvre: in the dramatic form of the dialogues, in the fictional characters he created and in the eloquent description he offers of the material settings within which the discussions take place – the market square, outside the city walls of Athens, under a tree, etc. (cf. Puchner 2010, p. 47).

Certainly, one rarely finds this dramatic style in the writing of Socratic philosophers today, probably because these days most of them do not look back on a first career in the arts. They have become pure scientists, as it were, people who, unlike Plato, no longer perform a crossover of philosophy and art but concentrate on pure logic, refined and purged of any artistic or mythological aspect... What a mess!

While Plato might have assumed that he had to abandon his existence as an artist in order to become a Socratic philosopher, Nietzsche assumed precisely the opposite: that he had to overcome the conceptual persona of a merely Socratic philosopher in order to become an artist-philosopher. This is in fact one crucial aspect of Nietzsche's famous reversal/inversion of Platonism. He had to, metonymically, replace the ascetic figure of the Socratic philosopher by his newly invented aesthetic concept of the artist-philosopher (cf. Böhler 2017).

Philosophy on Stage: a research forum for cross-disciplinary strategies between art and philosophy

The research festival series *Philosophy on Stage* – which we, Granzer and Böhler, have created over the past twenty years in the course of several research projects sponsored by the Austrian Science Fund (FWF)[4] – attempts to experiment with new forms of cross-disciplinary strategies by way of which new alliances between art and philosophy are conceptually and artistically staged in performances, lecture-performances, interventions, etc., to keep alive Nietzsche's promise of a *productive* friendship between art and philosophy.[5]

In contrast to a Platonist, that is, antagonistic view of the relation between art and philosophy, *Philosophy on Stage* promotes a *cross-disciplinary perspective* on the regimes of philosophy and art, assuming that they have never been clearly distinct, or that one regime would never have existed entirely separately from the other.

As in Plato's own philosophical opus, so the festival *Philosophy on Stage* thus encourages art to re-enter the realm of philosophy again. We also see this with reference to Indian culture, where the arts and philosophy have never been considered entirely independent of each other in themselves but have generated in relation to one another in the course of a historical process of differentiation [the legend of Patañjali is a nice example of this (cf. Jayaraman 2012) or the tantric philosophy of Abhinavagupta (cf. Ramakrishna Kavi 1984)].

At our post-Socratic and post-Platonist research festival *Philosophy on Stage*, philosophers thus do not have to burn and destroy their artistic persona while doing philosophy. On the contrary, they are invited, even called upon, to incorporate artistic practices and methods into their philosophical research. For the conceptual persona of the Socratic philosopher does not have to be rejected entirely if one becomes an artist-philosopher. It can still live and survive within an artist-philosopher, but in the context of arts-based philosophy, it will simply be considered as one layer or manner of performing philosophy, one dimension among others. Artist-philosophers certainly still reflect, contemplate, analyse and argue about the truth value of propositions. They do not reject and thereby *reverse*, but *inverse*, the reflective awareness of Socratic philosophers in their bodily being-in-the-world in relation to others (Da-sein). For them, the Socratic way of doing philosophy is just one way of doing philosophy. There are others, even more primordial and elementary ways of accessing becoming, such as the generative approach of *doing* aesthetics considered in the first part of this text.

Cross-disciplinary strategies: becoming bi...

Claiming that the field of philosophy is entirely different from the field of the arts amounts to a clouded, overly simplified and confused conceptualization of the factual proportion between A (art) and P (philosophy). Such a view overlooks the fact that the respective fields always already inhabit bridging connections in which art and artistic practices *show up in the midst* of philosophy and philosophy *shows up in the midst* of the arts. Many philosophers have used performative practices to make a thought emerge on their mental stage: thinking in the dramatic form of dialogues (Plato), writing in aphorisms that make a philosopher dance (Nietzsche), developing a technology of text-montages which leads one to express one's thoughts (Wittgenstein), probably even not writing at all, but drawing people into discussions on the market square (Socrates), developing an *écriture féminine* (Cixous), or, from the perspective of an artist, questioning the relation of being and non-being, which has been a problem considered in the history of philosophy for thousands of years (Shakespeare). Without such cross-disciplinary strategies, many philosophers and artists would not have been in a condition to give shape to their thoughts at all. Would Shakespeare ever have become the cosmopolitan artist he was if he had not philosophized in his plays?

Our research festival *Philosophy on Stage* attempts to deliver a research platform for artist-philosophers/philosopher-artists ready and willing to literally exist *in-between* the regimes of philosophy and the arts. They are called to generate lines of flight, bridging both disciplines in a chiastic crossover of regimes. Artist-philosophers and philosopher-artists are therefore *ontologically bi:* an in-between of art *and* philosophy. They travel between both regimes, like Hermes, bringing the news of a hybrid form of doing art and philosophy by virtue of actually performing untimely relations, alliances, concepts and artefacts between them, disrupting the inherited antagonistic model of the Platonist conception of the relation between art and philosophy.

Philosophy on Stage consequently stages the promise of a contemporarily still young and untimely post-Socratic and post-Platonist crossover between art and philosophy. It actually performs thereby the genesis of the concrete, speculative becoming of a new generative image of thought in the making.

Perspective II

Being in love with art & philosophy
A fucking sublime dilemma[6]

Susanne Valerie [Granzer]

Biographic note one: starting point

Our relation to the world and the disconcertment of being that differentiates us from ourselves and, paradoxically, at the same time makes us one with ourselves was already electrifying from an early stage. It hit. Perhaps the process can be described as an endless movement that grasps you. Or as lightning striking out of a clear sky. Not unlike sudden love befalling someone. Nobody asks for your permission. It just happens, hits. An event which is psychically and physically seizing, it gets under the skin, hits you right at the heart, becomes sensorily virulent – and life is turned upside down. "Oh, to be able to see the top of one's head!" Georg Büchner's Leonce muses (Büchner 1971, p. 209). This results in a break, a rupture of what has been so far. Life gapes open, the world gapes open, time gapes open. Everything becomes doubtful, and a window opens, a view. Something drags and feels like it's being dragged, something is seen, perceived under the pathos of the moment. A kind of pre-reflective occurrence which is understood intuitively, illustratively by looking at it. Listening to this pathos, pursuing it, giving in to it and ad personam giving testimony to it, whatever this will have meant once is without doubt. It is an occurrence which is spontaneously affirmed. Its yes is a promise given while being obtained at the same time. A promise the future happily shouts into the present, thus changing the past. As yet without emergency. Just a happy end with no end. Is this not like the soul being injected with love?

Biographic note two: trigger theatre

Life unfolds in this maelstrom, this labyrinth where both Minotaur and Ariadne are rulers. There is no way back to suit and tie, to skirt and blouse. Along with this, a passage is opened to theatre and philosophy. Everything else is excluded. In the beginning, for a long time, it is the stage that provides a rich reservoir of world. But soon it becomes clear that despite one's joy of spectacle and performance, *a truth that slips only into refined ears* (Nietzsche 2005, p. 180) is seldom heard among actors. Eventually, it gets boring.

However, the creative process of acting is fascinating. It makes you an addict. Its darkness troubles and makes you wonder in equal measure. For the bewildering experience on the stage has encountered an event beyond one's disposal (German: *unverfügbar*) – and here a sublime dilemma is born: yesterday's leap of joy at successful acting, which flowed so easily, simultaneously gives way to a feeling that yesterday's success never happened, and that it is simply impossible to repeat. Success evades feasibility, and evades the will. Questions and ever more questions start to burn. One is as light as a bird one moment, as heavy as the earth the next. Fuck!

The German word *unverfügbar* means unavailable, but there is also the phrase *sich fügen*, which means to yield. A *Fuge* in German is a gap and at the same time a joint. There is also the polyphonic and complex principle of musical composition called *Fuge* – the fugue in English. The meaning of the verb *fügen* ranges from obedience to occurrence, and a *glückliche Fügung* is a happy coincidence we are *unverfügbar* (inevitably) exposed to: serendipity. *Unfug* (nonsense, mischief) and *Befugnis* (authority) also chime in. Thus, contradicting meanings swing towards and bounce off each other in the paradox of simultaneity.

The question about the performative art of theatre now starts to rumble. Apart from the many professional skills one needs in acting, ultimately it is the lived-body in its beingness-in-the-world that is at stake on stage. Could we not come to the conclusion therefore that *how* one performs one's existence is the specific challenge for art at the theatre, and that this is what determines its quality? After all, is it not our *capacity to be* that is on screen in the art of acting, and that awakes our daily mode of being from its dream, from sleep, from everyday life? Did this result in a connection to our first start, back in the past, which had left such impressive traces? If so, then it must have been then that the same attraction *of the possibility of being* made an appearance, like the promise of love?

However, being firmly rooted in the earth, how or thanks to what is this flight possible when acting on stage? Is it a coincidence? Do we have to *eat of the fruit of the tree of knowledge again to fall back into a state of innocence*? *Do we have to traverse the infinite*, as Kleist would have it (Kleist 2010, p. 313)? But how is this supposed to be possible? Is there a clear path to it? A satnav? A method? Some form of know-how? A *techné*? No, there is not. This is what we are told by self-observation and by observing others. No, there is no such path or method, although there is much necessary knowledge, so many techniques and important know-how.

Wanting to grasp and understand that which will not fit. Learning how to understand and accept that which, by means of creative acting, joyously happens, *is* able to be – and is also what will vanish over time. Thus cursed, desired *posse esse*.

Biographic note three: trigger philosophy

Philosophy now moves into focus. It promises a deeper understanding of the phenomena of life, of the play of forces and how they relate to each other, of the forces that started moving without beginning or end, in which everyday language loses its way because it lacks the words. Philosophy. The word alone is inspiring. Is it not, like the act of thinking as such, erotically charged?[7] *Philein* means to love, *sophia* means wisdom. Could philosophy not be read as a kind of *amour fou*, as the craving for the knowledge of *how one becomes what one is*, while shamelessly, without recourse to a fig leaf, exploring the bareness of life?

Driven by this passion, philosophy is studied alongside theatre. However, soon a new dilemma occurs. With all due respect to the High Schools, it is there that this stage actor once asks spontaneously: *Those behind the desk, aren't they the wrong cast? Why is it Faust's famulus, Wagner, who enters and not Faust himself?* This is confusing. Sobering. Is the intellect fleshless? Without passion? Neutral, grey, in other words: objective? But then, what is thinking without a body, without sensuality? Surely, mind and body are not apart. Yet of course, there are even examples of this. Then, there are the texts, books, talks and discussions. Later the philosopher friends...

Philosophy maintains its attractiveness. Its siren call does not lose its allure. Just follow the white rabbit into the uncertain, and hoppity-hop, one finds oneself behind mirrors. A line has been crossed to something while at the same time catching up with it. This can only be tried out and practised, again and again. It requires life and art as a laboratory, it requires thought as a dare, it requires experimenting on stage, the play of chaos and order, the change from pathos to epoché. The driving force of the first elementary experience does not stop unfolding its suction, and no longer does it allow for any non-commitment. Not with art, nor with thought, nor with life. A promise is made to the becoming, to the different, to the unavailable.

Questions about subjectivity and fate now make their entrance and exit, their conflict is not just a private issue, not even one's own personal happiness, not even the allotment garden, has been dismissed. A view from the perspective of time takes turns with a view to eternity. The power of discourses flickers and buzzes in mind, belly and sex. They make us wonder. They want to be filtered and classified. To be thoroughly understood and tested. Both in mind and heart.

Oh yes, the heart! That obnoxious, dismissed entity. Sentimentally burdened. Conservatively burdened. Morally burdened. Indeed, a *corpus delicti*. It is on the black list. An image appears from memory. It shows two frowning intellectuals, and harsh words reverberating about a gingerbread heart with *amor fati* written on it – *how dare you!* (cf. Böhler and Granzer 2011). The prejudice works. Not even Nietzsche's laughter is helpful here, and neither is Ariadne of the small ears.

Biographic note four: Philosophy on Stage

Art and *philosophy* are the love couple of this life's journey as a lucky incident. They do not become tired of each other; no habituation paralyses their mutual interest. On the contrary, again and again, they inspire each other anew, they are joyous and curious about each other, also quarrelling, but based on and led by one and the same libido, a *friendliness of the heart* (cf. Hölderlin 1996, p. 103). It represents the active power of affirmation. A yes that is uttered not once, but again and again, as a promise keeping itself and being renewed by this keeping. Ladies and Gentlemen, this has nothing to do with sentiment and kitsch.

Consequently, the first beginning has never stopped being a driving force for the field of art, for philosophy and for the search for a way of life. How to bring them together? Expression is sought in the writing of texts following an *écriture féminine*, and also inspired by elements of the old home, the theatre – and gradually, resolutely, the traditional stages are replaced by the format of *Philosophy on Stage*.

Following Nietzsche, *Philosophy on Stage* may be considered an attempt at a *prelude of a philosophy of the future* dedicated to a kind of post-Platonic thought. It is about a *gay science*, philosophy and art jointly looking for new ways and being brought together in a laboratory of the future. By way of a variety of experiments and test runs, not the ascetic ideal of the sciences, the bodily dimension of untimely thought is exposed and indeed risks itself so as to better unmask the (superstitious) belief of the metaphysicians regarding the contradiction of values and to learn how to refute it in new ways (cf. Böhler and Valerie 2017).

As the *conceptual persona*, at the heart of *Philosophy on Stage,* there is Nietzsche's character of the *artist-philosopher*, and vice versa, the character of the *philosopher-artist*. Both have disengaged from philosophy's traditional resentment towards art *and* from art's resentment towards philosophy. By way of free interplay, there is the attempt to return its sensitivity and vulnerability to philosophy and to give back to art the dimension of thought and discursive sharpness. This involves preliminary work in laboratories, where fields are created that, both intellectually and emotionally, discursively and sensually, work out their own views, and their own insights into the history of thought and each topic.

The process does not spare one's own self as if one's thoughts were unconcerned with one's own 'I' when living one's life. Thus, together with all participants, the artists, the philosophers and the audience, there is the attempt to create a common field rooted in affirmation, in hospitality, in welcoming, in cordiality. No individual I is predominant, but *Philosophy on Stage* is dedicated to following through with the fact that one's existence is always a co-existence with others, existence being rooted in being *singular plural* (cf. Nancy 2000), without levelling any differences or levering out any dissent, but carefully risking the border regions of being-with.

In the course of this process, *Philosophy on Stage* insists in the *heart* as a fellow actor and understands this claim as a subversive act. In the Nāṭya Śāstra, the oldest known text of the Indian culture on theatre, the focus is on "one having a heart" (*sahṛdaya*, cf. Bäumer 2016, p. 92). And please, who is to say that it has been decided once and for all that Saturn is more powerful than Venus? The tyrant needs the slave's gloom to maintain his power, as we read in Spinoza (cf. Spinoza 2007, p. 6). Once more it makes sense to quote Heiner Müller (cf. Valerie 2016, p. 99) who considers fear the final, defining horizon in the alliance with the audience. Under the spell of the fear of death, whose victim all of us one day will be, the spectator does not see living people on the stage but the future dead. An eerie idea. Given the event of the creativity of ecstatic acting on stage, given the potency of life happily exploding in its immanent self-affirmation, Heiner Müller's interpretation is only one side of the truth. Who will be finally triumphant in the pathos of this experience, life denying itself or affirming itself? That is the question of a life's story. It is elementarily impressive, sublime – and also fucking bewildering.

Notes

1 Nature in the sense that Spinoza uses in his *Ethics*. In this context, culture is just a specific region of Nature. It is the region of the Anthropocene, where humanity acts (natura naturans) upon Nature (natura naturata) within Nature (as the one substance of being which Spinoza equals with God, God sive Nature).

2 Spinoza's third kind of knowledge, *intuition*, is the kind of knowledge by way of which one *intuits* the staging of a single entity sub-species aeternitatis. That is to say, the appearance of something in its relation to the *eternal* ontogenesis of Nature herself, which Spinoza equals with God.
3 This is precisely the reason why the Greek term *ousia* (essence) privileges the presentation of something in the present tense.
4 https://homepage.univie.ac.at/arno.boehler/php/?page_id=1244, date accessed 1 September 2018.
5 View the video recordings of the research festivals *Philosophy On Stage* #1–#4 online: https://homepage.univie.ac.at/arno.boehler/php/?page_id=841, date accessed 1 September 2019.
6 Translated from the German by Mirko Wittwar.
7 Cf. Nietzsche 1998, p. 3: "ASSUMING that truth is a woman—what then?"

References

Bäumer, Bettina 2016. 'Die flüssige Natur der ästhetischen Erfahrung.' In: *Polylog. Zeitschrift für interkulturelles Philosophieren*, 35: Berührungen. Zum Verhältnis von Philosophie und Kunst, pp. 89–95.

Böhler, Arno. 2017. 'Immanence: A Life…Friedrich Nietzsche.' In: *Performance Philosophy Journal*, Volume 3, Issue 3: Philosophy On Stage. The Concept of Immanence in Contemporary Art and Philosophy, pp. 576–603.

Böhler, Arno. 2016. *Polylog. Zeitschrift für interkulturelles Philosophieren*, 35: Berührungen. Zum Verhältnis von Philosophie und Kunst, pp. 7–33.

Böhler, Arno and Valerie, Susanne. 2017. 'Corpus Delicti#2. Untimely Precursors'. In: P. de Assis and P. Giudici (eds.) *The Dark Precursor. Deleuze and Artistic Research. Vol. I: Sound and Writing*. Leuven: Leuven University Press, pp. 193–213.

Böhler, Arno and Manning, Erin. 2014. 'Do We Know What a Body Can Do? #1'. In: A. Böhler and K. Kruschkova and S. Valerie (eds.) *Wissen wir, was ein Körper vermag? Rhizomatische Körper in Religion, Kunst, Philosophie*. Bielefeld: transcript, pp. 11–22.

Böhler, Arno and Granzer, Susanne Valerie. 2011. *Corpus delicti. Denken, ein Ort des Verbrechens*, Lecture Performance in the Context of the Research Festival Philosophy on Stage#3, Haus Wittgenstein Vienna, November 24th –27th, https://homepage.univie.ac.at/arno.boehler/php/?p=4417, date accessed 1 September 2018.

Büchner, Georg. 1971. 'Leonce and Lena'. In: Georg Büchner: *Danton's death. Leonce and Lena. Woyzek*. Trans. Victor Price. New York: Oxford University Press, pp. 73–104.

Deleuze, Gilles. 2003. *Francis Bacon. The Logic of Sensation*. London/New York: Continuum.

Deleuze, Gilles and Guattari, Felix. 1994. *What Is Philosophy?* New York: Columbia University Press.

Heidegger, Martin. 1991. *Nietzsche. Volume I: The Will to Power as Art*. San Francisco, CA: Harper & Row.

Hölderlin, Friedrich. 1996. 'In a Lovely Blue.' In: *Friedrich Hölderlin: Selected Poems*, 2nd expanded edition. Newcastle upon Tyne: Bloodaxe Books, pp. 103–104.

James, William. 2012. *Essays in Radical Empiricism*. Auckland: The Floating Press.

Jayaraman, M. (transl.). 2012. *Patañjali-caritam. The Legend of the Sage Patañjali*. Chennai: Krishnamacharya Yoga Mandiram.

Kleist, Heinrich von. 2010. 'On the Theater of Marionettes.' In: P. Wortsman (ed.) *Selected Prose of Heinrich von Kleist*. New York: Archipelago, pp. 264–274.

Nancy, Jean-Luc. 2000. *Being Singular Plural*. Stanford, CA: Stanford University Press.

Nietzsche, Friedrich. 2005. *Thus spoke Zarathustra: A Book for Everyone and Nobody*. New York: Oxford University Press.

Nietzsche, Friedrich. 1998. *Beyond Good and Evil. Prelude to a Philosophy of the Future*. New York: Oxford University Press.

Nietzsche, Friedrich. 1989. 'On the Genealogy of Morals.' In: W. Kaufmann (ed.) *On the Genealogy of Morals and Ecce Homo*. New York: Vintage, pp. 15–200.

Puchner, Martin. 2010. *Platonic Provocations in Theater and Philosophy*. Oxford/New York: Oxford University Press.

Ramakrishna Kavi, M. (ed.). 1984. *Natyashastra. With the Commentary of Abhinavagupta*. Baroda: Oriental Institute.

Spinoza, Baruch de. 2007. *Theological–Political Treatise*. Cambridge: Cambridge University Press.

Valerie, Susanne [Granzer]. 2016. *Actors and the Art of Performance. Under Exposure*. Trans. Laura Radosh with Alice Lagaay. London: Palgrave Macmillan.

Whiel, R. 2012. 'Nietzsches Anti-Platonismus und Spinoza.' In V. Waibel (ed.). *Affektenlehre und amor Dei intellectualis. Die Rezeption Spinozas im Deutschen Idealismus, in der Frühromantik und in der Gegenwart*. Hamburg: Meiner, pp. 333–350.

Whitehead, Alfred North. 1979. *Process and Reality*. New York: Free Press.

41
PAS DE DEUX
Écriture Féminine Performative

Tina Chanter and Tawny Andersen

TC: My favourite statue in London is called *Jeté*. It is balanced on a white pillar so that the dancer soars through the air, as if he is ready to leap across the Thames. Any visitor to the Tate Britain who has arrived by tube, exiting Pimlico station, must have passed this ethereal figure, who floats above the street, the angles of his limbs rearranging the light several feet above your head. Whoever curated this outdoor statue by Enzo Plazotta in such an inspired location understood that David Wall, the ballet dancer who informs Plazotta's statue, is throwing himself into thin air, abandoning himself to the movement of his body, flinging his future into a void. The silhouette of his leap is cast against the sky, so that as you circle the statue, the clouds are cut into singular shapes, which take your breath away. There is such joy, such grace, such lightness in the taut muscles, the pointed fingers through which the light of day filters, the tilted face searching the sky. It is a leap of faith. A leap of innocence into nothingness, into an empty time, an empty space, into the unknown. It is a leap from the past into a future. It breaks with perceptible horizons.

"Your horizon has limits", says Irigaray, addressing Nietzsche, whose concept of the overman she interrogates for its attachment to the earth, its commitment to high peaks, its obsession with the beyond, and its appropriation of the figure of women to perform a mirroring function (Irigaray 1991, p. 4). Irigaray's observation occurs within the context of her engagement of philosophy as a site of forgetting of the elements. In *The Forgetting of Air*, for example, Irigaray puts into question Heidegger's discourse of Being and his attachment to the earth by recuperating air as its condition, as exceeding and grounding all 'saying', as prior to 'clearing' (Irigaray 1999, pp. 3, 5, 19). In doing so she approaches the 'open' as that which 'does not stretch out like a perceptible horizon' (Irigaray 1999, p. 56). Just as Irigaray calls on Heidegger to exceed his own thinking of the Open and of the clearing (*Lichtung*), so she calls on Nietzsche not to allow his philosophy of becoming or going beyond to become stultified. As she puts it in *Marine Lover of Friedrich Nietzsche*, "And (you) find yourself a captive in a prison universe. Horizon, house, body or soul closed upon themselves. Surviving, no doubt. But stopped dead in your becoming" (Irigaray 1991, p. 67).

Plazotta's leap doesn't succumb to Irigaray's complaint against the arid world Nietzsche conjures for his Zarathustra: a world of bridges, attached to the 'meaning of the earth' (Irigaray 1991, p. 13). It is a leap that has read neither Nietzsche nor Heidegger nor Kierkegaard. It is a breaking through. A breaking away. A breaking into something new, outside the confines, restraints, shackles, boundaries that hem in possibilities and put up barriers. A rendering visible the invisible lines that define the limits of what can be heard, seen and done. A breaking of perception. It makes me think of transitivity, of doing, acting, performativity. It is a remoulding, remaking, reshaping. Citing the past in a way that doesn't mimic it, but makes it into something new. It is, as they say, a leaping for joy.

I wanted to show you this statue. I thought, as a dancer, a ballet dancer, and a thinker, you'd appreciate it. I wanted you to look up at this dancer who flies from his pedestal right across the sky, beckoning those who will to look to the clouds he points toward, a canopy over the river we've begun to see through Turner's water and sky scapes.

Critical of Nietzsche's dance because it remains 'within the same' (Irigaray 1991, p. 44), Irigaray addresses Nietzsche as follows: 'If I didn't have to carry your burdens, I should walk more lightly toward my time. And if I didn't have to bear your ills, how I should dance!' (Irigaray 1991, p. 24). Perhaps Plazotta's *Jeté* is emblematic of such a dance. A joyous leap. A leap of pure pleasure, maybe even *jouissance*. Lighter than air, suspended in the clouds. Communing with the sky, making envelopes for the sky's drama in the midst of the drama of its leap. In throwing himself off his pedestal the dancer unlocks previously unknown, unheard of horizons, beckoning us to follow him on his wholly unpredictable leap through time and space. Only the flimsiest swathe of material attaches him to the earth, to his stone plinth, as he disregards the solidity of the ground from which he leaps and abandons himself to a moment in time in which everything might be renewed.

TA: "The sky's doing its thing again", you said, simultaneously suspending and grounding our dialogue about Nietzsche, Turner, and false idealization in what some might call the 'Real'. Like many of our exchanges, that day's discussion transpired over the course of a promenade through central London. It began in Bloomsbury, continued through Holborn and into Soho, and culminated on the South Bank of the Thames, where we went our separate ways for the evening. There on the bridge, halfway between the Victoria and Albert Embankments, though, we experienced what I since have come to understand as the failure of language in the face of the trauma of nature. The term 'trauma' is somewhat misleading here, in that the sky was by all means beautiful: a post-human poetics playing out above our heads; Turner's canvasses embodied; a live landscape painting. It was performativity without representation, as if this were not a paradox (and therein lies a possible source of our silence as we stood staring at the horizon).

I don't know how many times you have walked beneath *Jeté*—on how many occasions your gaze has circumnavigated its form, or how many different skies you have seen cut or rearranged by and through its negative spaces—but I imagine that it must be many. As an embodied, cognitive action, perception is a highly particularized and performative *process*. It is what enables meaning to emerge, what invites us to respond to solicitation and to be affected by this representation of a dancer executing a *grand jeté*.

A symbol of virtuosity and vigour, this step (*un pas*, en français) is one of ballet's fundamental semiotic building blocks. It appears countless times in every work in the classical repertoire, from *Swan Lake* to *Giselle* to *Don Quixote* to *Romeo and Juliette* to *La Bayadère*. Like all signs, the *jeté* functions by virtue of what Derrida named its 'iterability'—i.e. its combination of sameness and difference, repetition and alterity. The etymological root of this neologism, Derrida explained in his 1971 "Signature Event Context", is the Sanskrit word *itara*, meaning 'other' (Derrida 1988, p. 7). There is an otherness that permeates every enunciation: you speak/act through me, and I, through you, making iterability (and, consequently, relationality) a defining feature of performativity.

It is its iterability that enables the grand jeté to traverse multiple classical ballets and migrate into contemporary styles, just as it is its iterability that allows it to be performed by different dancers across generations, cultures, and continents. It is this quality, too, that allows it to cite 'the past', as you so aptly write (and here I am citing you), "in a way that doesn't mimic it, but makes it into something new". This inherent structural duality ensures the gesture's ability to be disengaged from its initial context of enunciation and to signify within new contexts. Performativity, then, is about giving form, but it is also about *trans*forming; it is, as the prefix trans- suggests, about extending across and beyond, as exemplified by the dancer in your favourite sculpture.

In the case of *Jeté*, the citationality at play involves a kind of intra-semiotic translation, in that the gesture is moved into another medium, another system of signs; what was of the vocabulary of dance now inhabits the realm of sculpture. De-contextualized and re-contextualized (context, as we know, is always indeterminate), it is set in stone and placed into the scenography of London's urban landscape, where it offers itself up to be interpreted by passersby.

By some sort of serendipity, I saw this sculpture before you spoke to me about it. I first stumbled upon, or rather under, it while on my way to the Tate Britain. When I did, I lingered beneath it with my neck craning backwards in space (in modern dance lexicon, this position is called a 'high lift') trying to apprehend it. Thinking back, the transformation of *Jeté's* spectators' bodies produces a micro-choreography that could be said to constitute a by-product of the sculpture. In J.L. Austin's terms, this invisible theatre is a 'perlocutionary effect' of the sculpture's 'illocutionary force' (Austin 1975, pp. 91–101). This subtle shift in my physique served as a gentle reminder that looking and perceiving are embodied activities and that, as such, they are highly individual and contingent. No universals, no truths, in the encounter between the flesh of the body and the flesh of the world.

TC: Did you ever perform a grand jeté in any of those ballets, *Swan Lake*, *Giselle*, *Don Quixote*, *Romeo and Juliette* or *La Bayadère*? What did it feel like? Did you feel like you were on top of the world? That you could leap over rivers? Is such a leap gendered, do you think? What would it mean for it to be gendered? You haven't really told me much about what your body did when it danced. You've told me you like to walk, that you walk a lot, now that you no longer dance every day, you've told me that you became frustrated performing the choreography of others, but not what it was like to dance, to feel yourself dancing. Did your discomfort with choreography (usually the choreography of men, perhaps) resemble Irigaray's, with the mirroring function she ascribes to Nietzsche's women when she asks him, "Why don't you give her leave to speak?" (Irigaray 1991, p. 32). Whether dancing can be adequately glossed by speaking is in question, of course. Perhaps to dance is rather a way of writing the body, a mode of *écriture féminine*? If the body is written into the corpus of literature and philosophy by Irigaray and Cixous, does dance write the body into space such that it rearranges how we see it, how we feel it, how we know it?

We are all thrown into a world over which, initially, we have no control whatsoever. We are dependent, vulnerable, at the mercy of others. Some of us are cared for in such a way that allows us to flourish, to develop horizons, cultural futures full of promise and possibility, while others lack such horizons. Plazotta's dancer takes up this being thrown into the world and makes it his own. He is able to take the risk of remaking the form of a jeté, into a free flowing leap that breaks with formal training and constraints even while adhering to them. It is as if he has thrown away his safety net, metaphysical and otherwise, in the supremacy of a leap that springs from the confidence of knowing what it is to jump and to be caught and held, and which therefore has been able to go beyond any expectations, a going beyond—but a going beyond *of what* exactly? Could it be the kind of going beyond that Nietzsche intimates in his discussion of Zarathustra? Not quite. "Life is what matters to me, not the beyond", says Irigaray (Irigaray 1991, p. 18).

In her bid to recall him to the immemorial waters of the sea, which she associates with women, understanding it as "Too restless to be a true mirror" (Irigaray 1991, p. 52), Irigaray contests Nietzsche's association of woman with eternity (Irigaray 1991, pp. 42–43).

> You had fashioned me into a mirror but I have dipped that mirror in the waters of oblivion…I have washed off your masks…scrubbed away your multicolored projections and designs, stripped away your veils and wraps…I have even had to scrape my woman's flesh clean of the insignia and marks you had etched upon it. That was the most painful hour. For you had so deeply implanted these things into me that almost nothing was left Almost nothing to let me rediscover my own becoming beyond your sufferings All that was left [was an] I want to live.
>
> *(Irigaray 1991, p. 4)*

Irigaray has done more than most to bring into question those myths that seem to have such a hold over us, challenging them, rejuvenating them, reiterating them. You pick up on the necessary alterity that is built into the etymology of iterability, noting the Sanskrit derivation from *itara*. I like that. Perhaps we should write *ita*rability from now on (following Derrida's example in his spelling of 'differance' to signal delay, deferral), to underline its inevitable alterity. The itarability of performativity. Perhaps we should write it with an 'a', but still pronounce it as usual, so it sounds the same. We can write itaration, but say iteration.

TA: Is a leap gendered? This is a difficult question. I'm not sure if it is the leap, the word, the gesture, the sign in itself that is gendered. Perhaps it is the way in which that movement is lived, performed, and contextualized that makes it so. In her 1988 "Performative Acts and Gender Constitution: An Essay in Feminist Theory and Phenomenology", Judith Butler described gender as "an identity tenuously constituted in time—an identity instituted through a *stylized repetition of acts*" (Butler 1988, p. 519). It is the act, then, that stylizes, produces, genders the body, but the act itself could be performed, reiterated, in myriad ways—it could be subverted, reappropriated, displaced.

Interestingly, in her preface to the 1999 republication of *Gender Trouble*, Butler reports that she took her initial inspiration for her theory of gender performativity not from Derrida's reading of Austin, but instead from his reading of Kafka's *Before the Law*. The Derridean-Austinian lineage would only come into play explicitly in *Gender Trouble's* sequel, the 1993 *Bodies That Matter*, when Butler drew upon Derrida's theory of the iterability (*ita*rability) of the semiotic signifier to propound a theory of the iterability of the embodied gesture. In the 1999 preface, however, Butler states that when reading Derrida on Kafka, she wondered if we do not labour under similar expectations before gender as we do before the law. In her eloquent words, the anticipation of "an authoritative disclosure of meaning" actually "conjures its object" (Butler 1999, p. xv).

Ballet always involved labouring before ideals and forms (or ideals of forms). It was a doing, a re-doing, an undoing. Like gender, it always involved a certain degree of failure. I grew up in front of a mirror. Whatever that does to one's psyche is perhaps best exemplified by the particular tension between ego and insecurity that seems to characterize so many dancers. A product of the European Renaissance, traditional classical ballet was, historically, a very elitist, misogynist and white art form. One need only recall the heteronormative narratives about frail princesses saved by their princes that dominate the classical repertoire, or the glorification and institutionalization of an extreme thinness attainable only through anorexia and/or drug use ("I need to see bones", Balanchine proclaimed, as he knocked on the sternums of his *corps de ballet*), or the near complete absence of racial diversity, or the pitifully small number of female artistic directors and choreographers in what is primarily a women's field, to substantiate this claim.[1] I did ballet for years when I was young, but I moved into contemporary dance as soon as I could. It would be naive to say that that field is immune to the power dynamics that characterize classical ballet. There too, dancers are often overworked and underpaid, offered solos in exchange for sex, and subjected to all kinds of precarity.[2]

And yet, despite all this, yes; there was an immense freedom and an incomparable pleasure that I have not experienced elsewhere or since. It was so empowering to inhabit my body so fully, to become a vessel for characters, states, and energies, to ride adrenalin, to transgress limits, to be looked at within the safety net of the stage, and to learn how to orient a spectator's gaze. I think what I miss most about dancing is the feeling of being completely and totally absorbed by something—of being 'in the moment' in a way that fundamentally altered my phenomenal temporality.

TC: I really like what you said about context and Cixous and Butler in relation to my probably somewhat idiotic question, is a leap gendered? I knew there was something facile about my formulation even as I wrote it, but I let it stay there on the page. It is good that I took a chance, inviting you to say something more scholarly than I could muster at the time. And you did, you brought my question into the realm of plausibility, so thank you for that. It feels a bit risky, doing this, jumping, leaping into the unknown with you, not knowing quite where this exchange is going to land. Ceding control. And being okay about doing that. For once in my life. For once in my writing. Letting writing become ours. A bit scary, but also a lot of fun. It loosens things up. Of course, you are completely right about the contextualization of gendering in a leap, or anything else for that matter.

TA: When reflecting on Irigaray's practice of critical mimesis in a 1998 interview, Butler proposed that the feminine, for Irigaray, could be understood as a method of reading (Cheah et al. 1998, p. 19). In the same breath, however, she pointed out that Irigaray rarely reads women writers, and that there is a mode of identification at play in her relationship to the male writers that she reads. I would add that this relationship is not only identificatory, but also sexualized (I am thinking of the very title *Marine Lover*). For Butler, the implied heterosexuality in Irigaray's reading practice limits its critical potential.

I have recently been revisiting this question of the gendering of reading and writing practices and considering how we might construct a dialogue between the historical iterations of *écriture féminine* and contemporary permutations of performative writing. I have always felt that something is lost in translation when we qualify Cixous' early work as "essentialist". In her canonical 1975 "The Laugh of the Medusa", she states that the only inscriptions of feminine writing that she has encountered in French literature are those authored by Colette, Marguerite Duras, and Jean Genet (Cixous 1976, p. 879). Given her inclusion of Genet in this short list, we might conclude that *écriture féminine* was always already open to queer enactments; in other words, it was always already performative.

I am curious as to whether there is an alternative interpretation of Irigaray's mode of feminine reading that is not foreclosed by a normative heterosexuality—one that does not limit reading to a reading of the (sexual) Other, one that makes space for different modes of difference. Could we speak of a *lecture féminine*, just as we speak of an *écriture féminine*? Could such critical mimetic praxes serve to reduce the temporal, geographical, cultural distances between performative accounts of gender identity and philosophical configurations of the feminine?

TC: You and Butler are of course completely right about the heteronormativity of Irigaray's texts such as *Marine Lover*. As for *écriture féminine*, to claim sexual difference as a foundational, transcendental horizon in some way would be to produce, in the same gesture, the constitutive others of a white, middle class, heteronormative feminism. Yet, I wonder whether to say that *écriture féminine* was *always already* open to queer enactments might be to risk an erasure of the justified critiques by feminists of colour such as Barbara Christian (1988). Christian felt excluded not so much by the vaguely psychoanalytic framing of French feminism as a riposte to Lacan, as by the academic authority that accrued to French feminist theory through an erasure of feminist spaces that had been opened up by black feminist (or womanist to use Alice Walker's term) voices. Insofar as castration theory is bound up with the entry into language, speech is "governed by the phallus" (Cixous 1976, p. 881), considered "phallic" (Kristeva 1985, p. 165), symbolic meaning is marked as masculine in advance, and bound to sexual difference as foundational. Even if French feminism interrogated this view of language, there is a sense in which its very interrogation relegated all other differences, including racial difference, to a secondary, sometimes invisible, status.

So how far should we read *écriture féminine* as anticipating its own re-itarations and how far should we hold it accountable to traditional authorial standards? Should we allow it to depart whatever authority might have been invested in the signatories of its original texts, however white, heteronormative or cisgendered they might have been? Perhaps we need to resist a linear narrative (how many waves of feminism do we have now, is it three, four, or more?) that suggests first there was French feminism, then there were its critics, now we all live in some big, happy intersectional family. Mobilizing the vocabulary of disidentification allows us to take up a version of French feminism that would not be sanitized, whose imperialism and colonialism would be interrogated, while its anti-sexist discourse is engaged as a still valuable yet mediated identification (Muñoz 1999, p. 9). What, to borrow Muñoz's formulation, might it mean to work on and against the ideology of French feminism, which is itself a counter-ideology, to excavate it in a way that "tries to transform" its "logic from within"? (Muñoz 1999, p. 11).

Perhaps I love *Jeté* so because, with one step, it slices through all the phases of history, scholarship and critique, transcends the boundaries of gender somehow, just by doing what it does, being what it is. Somehow unclassifiable ontologically, sexually, and gender-wise, it flies away from categories. Maybe this was what was behind my idiotic question. *Jeté* seems to somehow mix up the categories and come up with something entirely new. It does not bound from mountain peak to mountain peak, it leaps into the air, in a leap that, as you pivot around it, bounces from cloud to cloud, as if the sky were a trampoline, as each new perspective opens up. As you point out, it is as much a framing of one's own bodily perception, one's own body, as it is a creation of envelopes of sky.

By thinking about *Jeté* in the light of the questions raised by *écriture féminine*, not by sanitizing its exclusionary aspects but by transforming its logic from within, we are not seeking to drive a wedge between what Plazotta's dancer does and whatever it was Cixous or Irigaray might have meant. We are allowing Plazotta's dancer, who soars above us in an ever-moving silhouette against the sky, to open up new envelopes for thought that do not comply with racism, do not acknowledge the lines it draws, but tap into the energy of a disidentificatory mimesis.

TA: I am grateful for your rigorous response to my last passage and I appreciate how you push me to rethink my use of the expression 'always already'. Words, of course, matter. This is perhaps especially true in the context of a discussion of a mode of language that produces that which it describes—one whose essence (if it is not a contradiction to speak about the essence of that which resists the very notion of essence) is its ability to wield extra-linguistic effects. Words can be tools, but they can also be weapons. Pain and humiliation are some of the possible perlocutionary effects of the illocutionary speech acts of racial slurs, misgendering, hate speech, and other forms of verbal abuse.

To be clear, I am by no means insinuating that sexual difference is a more foundational or primary mode of difference than racial difference is. In suggesting that "The Laugh" opens *écriture féminine* to queer enactments, I wish to propose that Cixous' conception of "the feminine" anticipates performative accounts of gender identity.

What is so experimental and exciting about "The Laugh" is that Cixous employs a mode of writing that performatively enacts the ideas that her text describes. What is difficult about it is that, in adopting a literary/poetic/theatrical/performative style, she resists making clear theoretical arguments. That *écriture féminine* should, from its inception, subvert logical argumentation and truth conditions and preclude direct signification also aligns it with a mode of writing that has since been labelled 'performative'.

For performance theorist Della Pollock, performative writing is bound up in the question of how meaning is produced: "Writing as doing displaces writing as meaning; meaning becomes in the material, dis/continuous act of writing" (Pollock 1998, p. 75). For Pollock, such writing is 'evocative' (it "uses language like paint"), 'metonymic' (it displaces meaning by highlighting the differences between the signifier and the signified), 'subjective' (it "defines itself in/as the effect of a contingent, corporeal, shifting, situated relation—and so itself as shifting, contingent, contextual"), 'nervous' (because of its intertextuality, its nonlinearity, its use of pastiche), 'citational' ("it figures writing as rewriting" and "quotes a world that is always already performative"), and 'consequential' (it posits language as an action that has effects) (Pollock 1998, pp. 75 and 80–85). For queer and performance theorist Peggy Phelan, performative writing must "risk poetry" (Phelan 1997, p. 11).

What is the risk that poetry presents philosophy? It is my hypothesis that enacting performative writing allows women philosophers, queer philosophers, trans philosophers, Indigenous philosophers, philosophers of colour—i.e. all of those navigating the margins of what remains one of the most patriarchal, white, and heteronormative fields in the humanities, with a means of enacting both discursive resistance and embodied transgression. In other words, it allows for the inscription of subjectivity in text and celebrates the particularization of the subject, while also blurring the ontological boundaries between art and philosophy.

You are, of course, right to draw attention to French theory's blind spot with respect to postcolonial theory. I have been thinking about this subject in relation to Cixous' conflation of woman and blackness. "Because you are Africa, you are black", the author writes in "The Laugh", addressing 'women' in general. For Cixous, blackness, which becomes a metaphor for the 'dark', 'dangerous' spaces of women's writing, is 'beautiful' (Cixous 1976, pp. 877–878). However, the evocative, poetic, and indeterminate quality of the writing and the lack of explicit acknowledgement of imperialism—all the stranger due to Cixous' complex relationship to both France and Algeria—makes these formulae problematic. Are race and ethnicity performative? I would venture that the answer is yes—to some extent. But not in the same way that gender is. What intersectionality has taught us is that these markers of identity cannot be compartmentalized when thematizing a subject's experience; we must acknowledge that each mode of oppression is specific, and its context unique.

I have often wondered what makes certain forms of mimesis critical, or what it is that invests certain performative praxes with disruptive potential. It seems to me that you are onto something with your notion of 'disidentificatory mimesis' in which Muñoz and Irigaray 'meet'. This notion strikes me as a wonderfully productive one with which to tease out the structural ties between performativity and mimesis—two concepts that, Elizabeth Grosz suggests in the interview I referenced above, constitute "attempts to generate an anomaly that produces a new future..." (Cheah et al. 1998, p. 40).

A text or choreography written in such a mimetic/performative manner would not remain 'within the same' (as per Irigaray's critique of Nietzsche), but would break out of repetition/mirroring and shift 'perceptible horizons', as you write of the dancer in *Jeté*.

TC: Whether this text accomplishes such performativity perhaps will have been decided by its readers.

Notes

1 In her 1992, *Women and Dance: Sylphs and Sirens*, Christy Adair highlights the power imbalances between men and women in the field of dance, demonstrating that it is predominantly men who occupy the positions of choreographers and directors. A 2016 *New York Times* article reported some very depressing statistics on this subject: of the 58 works performed by the New York City Ballet that season, not one was choreographed by a woman. Similarly, none of the works performed by London's Royal Ballet were authored by a woman. Of the two dozen ballets performed by Russia's Bolshoi Ballet, only one was choreographed by a woman (and even this piece was co-authored with a male choreographer). The American Ballet only featured one work by a woman that year (https://www.nytimes.com/2016/06/26/arts/dance/breaking-the-glass-slipper-where-are-the-female-choreographers.html). Statistics on racial diversity in ballet are equally disheartening: in 2012, Russia's Bolshoi ballet had no black dancers amongst its cast of 218; England's Royal Ballet had four amongst its cast of 96, and the English National Ballet had two out of 64 (https://www.theguardian.com/stage/2012/sep/04/black-ballet-dancers). It was only in 2015 that the American Ballet Theatre promoted its first black woman, Misty Copeland, to the position of female dancer.

2 In the past year, the effects of the #metoo movement have begun to be felt within both classical ballet and contemporary dance, where a culture of bullying, humiliation and sexual exploitation is being challenged. See the following articles for further reading: https://www.theguardian.com/stage/2018/jul/16/dance-ballet-metoo-culture-bullying?fbclid=IwAR15fZAhbpysi4zh-Fh337pL-h1NvgPAgGyxImUzcghH488UAyX8bhM47YhA, https://www.bbc.com/news/world-us-canada-45437643, https://www.nytimes.com/2018/09/23/arts/dance/20-jan-fabre-dance-metoo.html?fbclid=IwAR-E2IivEkULz90hh7WuCoIVYU6Wt2A7I.

References

Austin, J.L. 1975. *How to Do Things with Words*. Second edition. Cambridge: Harvard University Press.
Butler, J. 1988. 'Performative Acts and Gender Constitution: An Essay in Phenomenology and Feminist Theory'. *Theatre Journal*, 40 (4), pp. 519–531.
Butler, J. 1999. *Gender Trouble: Feminism and the Subversion of Identity*. 2nd ed. New York: Routledge.
Cheah, P., Grosz, E., Butler, J. and Cornell, D. 1988. 'The Future of Sexual Difference: An Interview with Judith Butler and Drucilla Cornell'. *Diacritics*, 28 (1), Irigaray and the Political Future of Sexual Difference, pp. 19–42.
Christian, B. 1988. 'The Race for Theory'. *Feminist Studies*, 14 (1), pp. 67–79.
Cixous, H. 1976. 'The Laugh of the Medusa'. Cohen, K. and Cohen, P. (trans.). *Signs*, 1 (4), pp. 875–893.
Derrida, J. 1988. 'Signature Event Context'. In: *Limited Inc*. Evanston: Northwestern University Press.
Irigaray, L. 1991. *Marine Lover of Friedrich Nietzsche*. Gill, G. (trans.). New York: Columbia University Press.
Irigaray, L. 1999. *The Forgetting of Air*. Mader, M.B. (trans.). New York: Columbia University Press.
Kristeva, J. 1985. 'Oscillation between Power and Denial. An interview by X. Gauthier'. August, M.A. (trans). In: Marks, E. and de Courtrivon, I. (eds.). *New French Feminisms*. Brighton: The Harvester Press, pp. 165–167.
Muñoz, J. 1999. *Disidentifications*. Minneapolis: University of Minnesota.
Phelan, P. 1997. *Mourning Sex: Performing Public Memories*. New York: Routledge.
Pollock, D. 1998. 'Performative Writing'. In: Phelan, P. and Lane, J. (eds). *The Ends of Performance*. New York: New York University Press, pp. 73–103.

42
ONANISM, HANDJOBS, SMUT
Performances of self-valorization

Fumi Okiji

I will interrogate the onanistic spirit that innervates the socio-economic configuration we live through. My interest is in how performances of self-valorization excite capitalist exchange society at its every register. Capitalism is a system of self-valorization. The capitalist is a "self-made man." And the worker, a self-sustaining partner in exchange. These acts of *apparent* self-valorization, in fact, depend on the reproductive labor of the homeworker, invisible and unaccounted for, and on the mnemonic impositions placed on hyper-visible and symbolically overdetermined surplus populations, such as the black poor. This may be why the permutation of this self-valorizing performance captured by the term "black excellence" sounds like a cruel joke.

On a freestyle tribute to the late Nipsey Hussle, fellow rapper and entrepreneur Jay-Z tells the crowd "Gentrify your own hood before these people do it / Claim eminent domain and have your people move in" (Jay-Z 2019). This succinct exhortation speaks for a generation of hip-hop entrepreneurism, and, more particularly, allows a "glimpse" into the Hussle's extra-musical vision, at least as Jay-Z understands it. An uneasy marriage of investment and philanthropy—material accumulation, local community activism and an update on symbolic racial uplift. Hussle, an artist whose music was entwined with the social sinew of the Crenshaw area of South Los Angeles, acquired a range of property, including a barber's, a burger restaurant and a fish market—key venues of sociality (Jennings and Kelley 2019). What does it mean to "gentrify [one's] own hood"? What are the ethical implications of the now-wealthy buying up private and commercial properties in an area that they have long called home? Should this be understood as gentrification? The modest twitter storm triggered by Jay-Z's words, that I must reiterate, were strung together on the fly, tended to focus on the inaccuracy of the comment, particularly the choice of the word "gentrify" to describe acts of black capitalism and self-empowerment, and/or community building, depending on how you read Hussle's legacy (and, ultimately, on your faith in the American Dream). The now almost obligatory (always inane) debates that these virtual encounters generate over the definition of a particular word, in this case obscured a more interesting, long-standing one, concerning the contradiction to be found in a black elite's embrace of a system that relies on the material elevation of a few at the expense of communal forms of social and socio-economic organization.[1] Gentrification might not have been the appropriate term—black-determination, seemingly, the underlying personal objective of Hussle's community enterprises. Jay-Z's "gentrify" may be best understood as a slip, something that was not meant (but *really* meant). The buying up the neighborhood in order to "improve" (it)—as evidence of a certain will to excel or valorize—is well-partnered with an artistic genre that appropriates the lived experience of poor black folk, selling it onto the general social field, the agents of this primitive accumulation at times, rewarded by admission to exchange society.[2]

There is no reason to give Jay-Z the benefit of the doubt, if there is doubt that the call was anything but a morsel of capitalist moralism. (The migration of black respectability—meaning here the sanctioned modes of black public appearance, from the cultural and social into the economic—is entirely in keeping with the more general decline of Protestant-tinted secular morality, that, historically, worked to obfuscate the avarice that the Dream expects of all those in its pursuit.) Back in 2011, on the track "Murder to Excellence," Jay-Z could not deliver the message in starker terms. He, "dress[ed] in Dries and other boutique stores in Paris," is the spokesman for "the new black elite" and applauds their "excellence" (Jay-Z and West 2011). More recently, on "The Story of O.J.," Jay-Z is unapologetically acquisitive, and invites us to aspire to be, too. The tune weaves an ode to accumulation—wealth propagates as if by magic. Consider: "I bought some artwork for one million/… Few years later, that shit worth eight million." And: "I turned that two to a four, four to an eight" (Jay-Z 2017). This is not the repressed underbelly of a Booker T. Washington-style utilitarian thrifty respectability. Not the "exercise of extravagant expenditure" undertaken by the work-sky "N****," narrated by David Marriott in his essay "On Decadence: Bling Bling" (Marriott 2017). This is a sermon on valorization. M-M'. Money makes money. Jay-Z is, apparently, self-made, too. The mysticism of this seeming self-accretion aided by his "pull yourself up by your bootstraps" chides. Reading our minds after sharing his advice on art investment, he responds, "Y'all think it's bougie, I'm like, it's fine" (Jay-Z 2017). He is bougie to our black. And in case we did not catch this vital fact, Jay-Z dissects the speech act for us—our appearance in the work (no "n★★★a" is left unsummoned), our gentrified blackness, *could* be sold back to us, at a paltry "nine ninety-nine," his oeuvre, the blueprint for success, but only if we agree to embrace exchange society ("a million dollars' worth of game") (Jay-Z 2017).

Self-valorization

The spirit that innervates liberal capitalism is self-valorization. This is, of course, a word used by Karl Marx to describe the system in its entirety: "the occult ability to add value to itself […] [B]y virtue of being value" (Marx 1990, p. 255).[3] What is described as "capital mystification" involves concealment of the actual source of this valorization—most readily identified as the free labor the worker performs on behalf of the capitalist, but also to be found in the invisible and unremunerated reproductive labor of the homeworker, and in the symbolic and imaginary work of other surplus populations such as the slave/black.[4] Exploitation (the surreptitious extraction of surplus-value) and valorization (supposed self-valorizing value) are two sides of the same coin. And while these are often mapped onto the worker and capitalist, respectively, it is important to understand that as the spirit that energizes the mode of production, all players admitted to exchange are bound by the imperative to valorize, and, more accurately, to *appear* (able) to self-valorize, to self-(re)produce. In fact, this may be the terms of one's very admittance, worker and capitalist alike. The player in the capitalist market must appear to self-valorize in accordance with the character (material and spiritual) of the system as a whole. They do not, of course, as capital does not. The important thing is that they *appear* to. Valorization is not only descriptive of the material mechanics of capitalism in its entirety, but it also names the spirit of the political economy. It is something one must believe in. One can only play in the capitalist market if one appears (able) to self-valorize.

"make parade of riches"/"conceal poverty"

Hannah Arendt on the requisites for participation in the public realm of ancient Greece: "no activity that served only the purpose of making a living, of sustaining only the life process, was permitted to enter the political realm" (Arendt 2019, p. 37). Arendt's insistence on the strict separation of the political (the province of freedom) from the economic has been well-rehearsed.[5] What is perhaps of more interest with regards the argument unfolding here is how entry into the public sphere is conditioned upon a person's ability to transcend material constraints—showing political freedom to be very much dependent on an individual being "carefree of all worries that are connected with life's necessity" (Arendt 2006, p. 38). The poor, chained to "bodily needs," fall short of the economic liberty required to prepare for and participate in the public realm. They were "not free[,] because they were driven by daily needs (ibid.). Moreover, for Arendt, the tragedy of being poor was the anonymity that poverty brings: "darkness rather than want is the curse of poverty" (Arendt 2006, p. 59). It is not only a practical necessity that prevents the poor from becoming public actors, but also that they are ashamed of their poverty and wish to remain hidden. It is interesting that when the poor multitude do expose themselves, when they "burst into the streets" (as during the French Revolution, for instance), Arendt is ambivalent concerning the value of their political participation, believing the violence of the multitude threatening to the very integrity of the notion of freedom (Arendt 2006, p. 39).

Despite Arendt's desire to protect the autonomy of the political, there is little mistaking the entanglement of socio-economic and political here. (The same imbrication of self-preservation and public exhibition is found in *The Theory of Moral Sentiments* [1759], where Adam Smith, the political economist and moral philosopher, suggests that people were more inclined to show sympathy for actors who "make parade of [their] riches" and, importantly, who "conceal [their] poverty" (Smith [1759] 1822, p. 54)). Notwithstanding the inability of a nascent working class to access genuine political freedom, capitalism requires that all its participants be free. The freedom the worker lacks politically must be staged within the economic sphere in order that they appear a partner in exchange. The system depends on this pretense. As Marx tells it: "All the notions of justice held by both worker and the capitalist, all the mystifications of the capitalist mode of production, all capitalism's illusions about freedom, all the apologetic tricks of vulgar economics, have as their basis the form of appearance discussed above, which makes the actual relation invisible, and indeed presents to the eye the precise opposite of that relation" (Marx 1990, p. 680). While the system rests on an acute lack of autonomy and spontaneity, worker and capitalist, both, are called upon to appear free as part of their demonstration of worthiness. And, I suggest that it is not only freedom performed, but the spirit of the system, self-valorization.

"the economic Relation does not exist"

A key intervention of classical political economists of the eighteenth century was the upending of the mercantilist assumption that "the world's wealth was a finite amount [and that] if someone got more of the cake, someone else would get less" (Bayly 2004, p. 136). In early modern times, a state was enriched through conflict and conquest—war chests funded by trade taxes met the costs in a period of almost continual commercial war. The growth of a country was dependent on the successful contest for the world's limited natural resources. Growth was relational; the prosperity or ruin of a nation state was contingent on, and, in turn, affected that of, its competitors. At this turn into free market capitalism, Adam Smith, David Ricardo and other economists suggested that rather than the zero-sum game of ferocious competition for scarce resource, an economy could, in fact, increase by itself. Through innovations in technology, labor organization and mutually beneficial trade, a national economy was thought to be able to increase independently and to be capable of infinite growth. This, effectively, neutered the economic antagonism between the dominant and the subordinate.[6] As part of her exploration of the socio-economic implications of the lack of (sex) relation at the source of subject formation, Alenka Zupančič insists that this superseding economic model rests on an earth-shattering notion: "the economic Relation does not exist" (Zupančič 2017, p. 31).[7] Mercantilism provides

> the image of a 'closed' totality in which the relation ensures the visibility of the difference (in wealth); if you want more, you have to take it from somewhere, so someone else has to lose. The relation is that of subordination (of the weak to the powerful), but it is still a relation. The new economic idea undermines this (totality-based) relation, while at the same time prizing the productivity of the newly discovered non-relation.
> (Zupančič 2017, p. 31)

All can benefit from this ruptured totality; everyone is capable of increasing their wealth independently.[8]

"invisible handjob of the market"

The "invisible hand" and avaricious prudence are partnered and co-constitutive. The invisible hand of the market looks after the interests of society at large. It ensures that the onanistic pursuit of individuals is checked. The invisible hand of the market is mysterious, and seemingly transcendent, but it can, in a more rationalistic light, be considered the sum (plus, perhaps, the little more that always eludes accounts) of the miscalculations, over-extended ambitions, environmental and social opportunity and disaster, that temper the self-interestedness that Adam Smith considers the making of the ideal society. And for their part, "the butcher, the brewer, [and] the baker" (Smith 2019, p. 14) can wholeheartedly embrace avarice in the knowledge (or rather, belief) that they are "led by an invisible hand to promote an end which was no part of [their] intention" (Smith 2019, p. 423). In "intend[ing] their own gain," butcher, brewer and baker show a fidelity to the market far exceeding that which any conscious governance or policy could achieve. Indeed, the efficiency of the market rests on this myopic prudence. Through this rapacity, with the guidance of the invisible hand, the individual "frequently promotes that of the society more effectually than when he intends to promote it" (Smith 2019, p. 423). Following Smith, we might consider that partners in exchange, in adherence to the spirit of capitalism, "address [them]selves, not to their humanity but to their self-love" (Smith, p. 14). Capital is (seemingly) masturbatory, and calls on its players to be, too.

Invisible handjob of the market. Following Zupančič's lead, I would like to borrow this term from Aaron Schuster to bridge my discussion concerning this model society—one in which all would be infused with this spirit of onanism; one where we would address each other not by way of our common humanity but rather our "own self-love"—and the thought that has driven my deliberations: namely, capitalism's imploration that its participants appear (able) to self-valorize (Zupančič 2017, p. 32). I am taken by the invisibility of the act. Why invisible? Does this not contradict my insistence that capitalism requires that its partners appear able to self-valorize; that they perform their excellence? Indeed, capital and its participants are exhibitionists. They want you to watch. On further reflection, we might say that they do not intend for you to spectate the entire operation, in fact, but only for you to see them come. Zupančič's play with the phrase seems to be in reference to the stimulation of one's own erotogenic zones (a "solitary enjoyment"). A handjob is, perhaps, more often understood as involving (an) other(s). The distinction is key, and the slippage not surprising: the system aims to appear masturbatory but, in fact, depends on the stimulus provided by an unseen facilitator. With this in mind, we might say that the capitalist system as such needs to *appear* to bring itself to orgasm, but, in fact, is very much dependent on a silent (or invisible) "partner" to produce the excess. The invisible labor symbolized by this handjob is, of course, the activities that contribute to the upkeep of the market player. The labor expended on turning the raw goods of sustenance into products and activities of social reproduction—toward the material upkeep of current workers, the rearing of future participants and the emotional support provided in the home—is concealed, hidden at the core in capitalism. Whilst this reproductive labor involves a transferal of goods, labor and sustenance between the worker and homemaker, and perhaps most essentially (re)produces labor power—capitalism's most essential commodity— it does not appear within the political economy. This is taken up by Marx without adequate redress. As Silvia Federici writes, "Marx's analysis of capitalism has been hampered by its almost exclusive focus on commodity production and its blindness to the significance of women's unpaid reproductive work and the sexual division of labour in capitalist accumulation" (Federici 2009, p. 209). The homeworker is a key source of generation of the surplus required for valorization; her work occurs in obscurity. This invisible labor of the homeworker allows the worker to appear worthy of the market. His apparent ability to self-sustain, his apparent self-sufficiency, maintains the illusion that excites the entire (accounted for) system.

The slave is not a worker

This ~~handjob~~wank scam might be thought sufficient to maintain the illusion, and yet the unavoidable qualitative difference between owning the means and material of production and owning, merely, one's own labor power is stark, despite the dictum that the market is blind to one's birth.[9] Alongside an invisible homeworker, the capitalist theology employs a hyper-visible icon of derogation. As a commodity, the slave is barred, categorically, from being an agent able to exchange. A slave is a means of production, someone's property. They do not own their own body. They do not have labor power (to sell). They are not, strictly speaking, a worker—they are not an unpaid worker. A slave represents a non-participatory, passive component of the system, symbolizing what a participant must not be. Despite its suspiciously human countenance, there is no reason to regard its status (commodity and/or means of production) as categorically distinct from cattle or machinery. It is of absolute necessity to the capitalist system that the worker distinguishes himself from such; to distinguish his labor power from his body and being. Labor power and the slave are two commodities. The worker owns his labor power; the slave owns nothing. Regardless of the actual paucity of alternatives, the worker ("free" also from property) must be at liberty to sell, not his body but (and this is important) his labor power. Under capitalist relations, the appearance of freedom and equality between partners of exchange is key. The worker must put distance however symbolic, however imaginary, between himself and the commodity he trades. As with so much in the system, it is this symbolic distance that is the "truth" which allows the worker to be (or seem) worthy of his partnership.

Smut to get off on

Consider:

> Compared, indeed, with the more extravagant luxury of the great, his [the common labourer's] accommodation must no doubt appear extremely simple and easy; and yet it may be true, perhaps, that the accommodation of a European prince does not always so much exceed that of an industrious and frugal peasant, as the accommodation of the latter exceeds that of many an African king, the absolute master of the lives and liberties of ten thousand naked savages.
>
> *(Smith 2019, p. 12)*

In this quotation from *The Wealth of Nations,* Adam Smith summons the figure of the African which goes to work in a number of directions. Most readily, we find a jarring claim that sees a peasant living in greater prosperity than the highest position that one can hold in an African tribe; that of king. While the entire passage is addressing the working poor, the "common labourer" of capitalist society, Smith evokes the peasant here as a subject close enough to an African (king) to bear comparison. He suggests that the inequality between European peasant and African king, in which the former holds the advantage, is not as great as that between the peasant and the European prince. Furthermore, although this may go beyond a straightforward reading, the polemic force of Smith's words allows me to suggest that a qualitative distinction is being drawn between the poor European and African (rich or wretched). The African king is conjured in order to show the upper limit of any estimation an African can obtain. And the designation of the worker (or the peasant standing in for him here) as "absolute master of… [African] savages," in the context of contemporaneous Atlantic trade reinforces the signifying chain, African/savage/slave. As Ian Duncan writes, in a revelatory reading of Smith's passage:

> it requires little reflection to see that African savagery is… part of the political economy of the nation… As Smith knew perfectly well, mid-eighteenth-century Glasgow's commercial wealth was founded on the Chesapeake tobacco and (increasingly) West India sugar trades, and thus on slavery. The elected recognition of that fact occurs here across a syntactical suppression: the European subject *is*, in effect, 'the absolute master of the lives and liberties of ten thousand naked savages,' whether he owns plantations, has shares in the trade, or consumes sugar or tobacco.
>
> *(Duncan 2016, p. 106)*

In quotidian parlance, Smith is assuring the worker, "you may be poor but you are not an African (savage, slave, black)." This is a declaration that echoes uncomfortably into the present day, placed on loudspeaker in this Trumpian era. "Shithole countries," denigration of black protest, clandestine repeal and continued suppression of civil rights all work to maintain this categorical distinction. The message also operates as an exhortation, providing a clearing in the symbolic and imaginary spheres from where the ambiguity that intramural material inequality creates (between, say, capitalist and worker; or the affluent and white poor) can be countered. Lewis Gordon's pithy formulation of white supremacy perhaps says it best: "(1) be white, but above all (2) don't be black" (Gordon 1997, p. 63).

The ever-extending metonymic chain African/savage/slave/black/welfare queen/subprime debtor—which the move from one formally prohibited from market relations to one not worthy of them does not break—is the smut with which the welcomed exchange participant gets off. Black unworthiness of the market is pronounced with elaborate fanfare. The subprime debtor, for instance, is well set up for the fall. She is encouraged to partake of the promises of homeownership and is seemingly received into this market. And yet, through loaded dice of sociohistorical impediment, finance services malevolence and housing discrimination, the black as a subprime debtor will most likely roll low. This complex of disadvantage shows up in the general social field as the "natural" shortcomings of a subject unable to take personal responsibility, and rejuvenates what Fred Moten understands as the "pathologizing discourse within which blackness' insurgent materiality has long been framed" (Moten 2013, p. 243). The debtor is painted as

> a victim of her own impulses, which could be coded as her own desire to climb socially, into a neighborhood where she doesn't belong and is not wanted—the general neighborhood of home ownership, wherein the normative conception, embodiment and enactment of wealth, personhood, and citizenship reside.
> *(Moten 2013, p. 243)*

The blame (criminality, even) attributed to these former "owners" provides contemptible relief against which those worthy of participation can distinguish themselves. This is the obscenity to which the market participant gets off.[10]

Black excellence

Consider these lyrics drawn from Jay-Z's 2011 "Murder to Excellence":

> Black excellence, opulence, decadence [...]
> I stink of success, the new black elite.
> *(Jay-Z and West 2011)*

Black excellence is a peculiar term. The coupling of these two words provides a punchline to a joke retold in each performance the term is used to describe. To avoid any confusion: I am not disputing the achievements—financial, academic or political—of black individuals, or that we might want to celebrate these, particularly in light of the odds stacked against them. Nor am I arguing that the condition of blackness is one of absolute abjection—that black lives as imaged and imagined by the general social field are all these lives can be (or what these lives actually are). Yet, it does seem that the declaration of what should be self-evident—that black individuals can also make money, say smart things and provide leadership—betrays the unease in which these two words sit. We might argue that the term "black excellence" is a performative intervention that seeks to, at once, dispel the unease brought on by its own coupling. We might suggest that it is a reparation of discursive space, a mode of representational warfare. This is a valid remedial response. However, I am most interested in the term's palpable unease and the critical work that this unease does. It is not impossible, but it takes considerable effort to divorce black excellence from the neoliberal spirit of the day. Its most recognizable proponents (for instance, Jay-Z, Beyoncé, the Obamas) show distinction through their ability to accumulate economic and social wealth (their seeming self-valorization) at a time when an assault on the social safety net, on employment and voter rights, under-investment in public services (coupled with exponentially increasing military defense) and the bolstering and further privatization of the carceral industry, helps keep the poor, disproportionately represented by black and brown people, in poverty. As part of the ideological baggage of neoliberalism, excellence tends to refer to the aptitude black individuals show in transcending these trappings of race toward (or by way of) aspirations of full immersion in society. Black excellence performs how one might move toward socio-economic "health," supposedly by way of "hustle" and "grind," by enforcing conventional familial configuration, by celebrating resilience.[11] It attempts to contribute to a fiction that black folk have no reason to believe. It requires that they now feign ignorance concerning the contrivance of a myth that was never meant to take them in, an illusion crafted without them in mind. While the general populace is met with a variety of elaborate ploys to obscure the fact of their powerlessness (consider my ~~handjob~~wank formulation or how patriarchal protection of the sanctity of white femininity serves to control women), black people (historically, and in this contemporary moment) have their subordination pronounced to them in no uncertain terms. Chattel, three-fifths, "No Dogs or Negroes," the war on drugs, Flint, Sandra Bland. The force of these continually refreshing declarations of subordination frustrates any last-minute mystification "black excellence" might hope to achieve on behalf of neoliberalism. The two words continue to stand in opposition, rendering the notion of back excellence forever uneasy. Against the ideological current, and despite itself, the term restates the social antagonism underpinning the system.

Could the term black excellence be gesturing toward something else? Perhaps the specifier indicates a distinct category of excellence—a *black* excellence that calls into question these illusory self-made lives that feed the American Dream. How might this black variety of excellence manifest? Might we observe it in a family who, without shame (and perhaps even need), claims social security funds in defiance of exhortations to perform self-sufficiency (a fallacy for the affluent as much the poor), in awareness that the die is crooked, that the invisible hand requires willful ignorance of the persistence of unequal relations and the antagonisms that compose the society we live in? Or perhaps "black" can be wrested from the overloaded signifying chain, and made to denote opacity or fugitivity: matter(s) that cannot be accounted for—black life beyond the symbolic uses made of it; that which escapes (or is ignored/rejected by) mainstream imaginings. This might be an excellence that evades the hyper-visible antithesis to the self-valorizing market participant, and avoids the self-cannibalizing tendencies of the black neoliberal. But, of course, black excellence, as it is widely understood, does nothing to draw attention to the villainy at the heart of capitalism. It, in fact, helps to conceal its inherent injustice, and this cannot but enact a psychic burden on those who live black lives. Black excellence is an absurd state to perform—its "excellent," supposedly self-valorizing subject providing the titillation for their own wanking off.

Notes

1 Social media hermeneutics call, not for clarity, but for enough confusion to appear, superficially, and to oneself, at least, to have "owned" another. For a sample of the debate, see https://twitter.com/i/events/1122205041522139136?lang=en

2 This is not an Adornoian denigration of popular form. I consider it to be a key site of critical intervention. My focus is narrow and on the neoliberal strain within the music that we hear in some of Jay-Z and Kanye West's work. It is important to understand this as distinct from the tropes

concerning reckless conspicuous consumption—this irresponsible depletion of personal wealth, in fact, runs counter to the prudent avarice discussed in this essay. On "improvement," see Harney, Stefano, and Fred Moten. "Improvement and Preservation: Or, Usufruct and Use." In *Futures of Black Radicalism*, Johnson, Gaye Theresa, and Alex Lubin, eds. Verso, 2017, pp. 83–91.

3 Autonomists such as Tony Negri use the term to refer to the self-determination of the working class.
4 I, of course, have in mind the invaluable feminist interventions of Leopoldina Fortunati, Silvia Federici and Mariarosa Dalla Costa, and others, beginning in the 1970 and continuing on to the present.
5 For instance, see Moruzzi, Norma Claire. *Speaking Through the Mask: Hannah Arendt and the Politics of Social Identity*. Cornell University Press, 2000; Villa, Dana. *Arendt and Heidegger: The Fate of the Political*. Princeton University Press, 1995; Fine, Robert. *Political Investigations: Hegel, Marx and Arendt*. Routledge, 2005.
6 See Pincus, Steve. "Rethinking Mercantilism: Political Economy, the British Empire, and the Atlantic World in the Seventeenth and Eighteenth Centuries." *The William and Mary Quarterly* 69, 1 (2012): 3–34. This essay provides a very useful review of the conventional wisdom on the break between mercantilism and the economic system that followed.
7 It is important to understand the non-relation, not only in reference to sexual matters and activity. Capitalism might be understood as an appropriation and privatization of this fundamental non-relation. The "missing of the binary signifier," the "minus one," is the impossibility, the constitutive negativity that molds the spaces in which all relationships occur. This non-relation is not counter to social ties but is, in fact, "the inherent (il)logic (a fundamental 'antagonism') of the relationships that are possible and existing" (Zupančič, p. 24). Zupančič tells us that the discursive field is characterized as antagonistic. The various contests for power and recognition challenge the authority of Man brought by those who embody difference that occurs here. Yet, its primary antagonism is not due to these confrontations accommodated by the field but to the formal qualities of the space itself.
8 We might add that the thesis of self-expanding economies—the notion that the innovations in production and "new organizations of labour" revolutionized economic growth—is incomplete without acknowledgment that this supposedly intramural surplus was to a significant extent mined from the bodies and futures of workers, homemakers and slaves (this, of course, is putting to one side primitive accumulation). This is the reality that the political theology of capitalism worked at its every register to dispel.
9 "The blessing that the market does not ask about birth is paid for in the exchange society by the fact that the possibilities conferred by birth are molded to fit the production of goods that can be bought on the market. Each human being has been endowed with a self of his or her own, different from all others, so that it could all the more surely be made the same." Adorno, Theodor and Max Horkheimer, *Dialectic of Enlightenment*. Stanford University Press, 2007, p. 9.
10 In a similar turn of argument, Adam Kotsko writes of the "welfare queen" as a latter-day witch, "that racialized figure of sexual license who depletes the public purse with her lavish lifestyle." He continues:

> One might be tempted to dismiss my evocation of her 'demonic' character as a mere metaphor, but a number of the tropes that accumulated around her bear a striking similarity to what we find in an early modern witch-hunting manual.

Amongst her occult capabilities, "the 'welfare queen' has the mysterious ability to cause mass inflation and economic stagnation." The "near-demonic power" she exercises raises a moral panic, and contributes to the effigy of the untouchable that all upright market performers must shun.
11 During his 2013 commencement speech to Morehouse College graduates, Barack Obama urges, "If you stay hungry, if you keep hustling, if you keep on your grind and get other folks to do the same—nobody can stop you." Full speech at https://www.youtube.com/watch?v=e50Tt9qJRQk.

References

Adorno, Theodor and Max Horkheimer. 2007. *Dialectic of Enlightenment*. Stanford: Stanford University Press.
Arendt, Hannah. 2019. *The Human Condition*. Chicago: University of Chicago Press.
Arendt, Hannah. 2006. *On Revolution*. New York: Penguin Books.

Bayly, C. A. 2004. *The Birth of the Modern World 1780–1914*. Oxford: Blackwell, 2004.

Dawson, Michael C. and Megan Ming Francis. 2016. "Black Politics and the Neoliberal Racial Order." *Public Culture* 28, 1 (78): 23–62.

Duncan, Ian. 2016. *Scott's Shadow: The Novel in Romantic Edinburgh*. Princeton: Princeton University Press.

Federici, Silvia. 2009. "The Reproduction of Labour-Power in the Global Economy, Marxist theory and the Unfinished Feminist Revolution." In *Center for Cultural Studies, University of California, Santa Cruz. Seminar Reading for Jan*, vol. 27.

Fine, Robert. 2005. *Political Investigations: Hegel, Marx and Arendt*. New York: Routledge.

Gordon, Lewis Ricardo. 1997. *Her Majesty's Other Children: Sketches of Racism from a Neocolonial Age*. London: Rowman & Littlefield.

Harney, Stefano, and Fred Moten. "Improvement and Preservation: Or, Usufruct and Use." In *Futures of Black Radicalism*, Johnson, Gaye Theresa, and Alex Lubin, eds. New York: Verso Books, 2017, pp. 83–91.

Jay-Z. 2019. "Jay-Z Freestyle Tribute for Nipsey Hussle". B-sides Concert, Webster Hall, New York, 26 April 2019. https://www.youtube.com/watch?v=N4qO9CmzCOg

Jay-Z. 2017. "The Story of O.J." 4:44. Roc Nation/ Universal. 20 April 2019. https://www.youtube.com/watch?v=RM7lw0Ovzq0&list=RDRM7lw0Ovzq0&start_radio=1

Jay-Z and Kanye West. 2011. "Murder to Excellence." Watch the Throne. Roc-A-Fella Records. 20 April 2019. https://www.youtube.com/watch?v=8ZNqRMj4pjk

Jennings, Angel and Sonaiya Kelley. 2019. "Before His Death in South L.A., Nipsey Hussle was Trying to Buy Back His 'hood," in *The Los Angeles Times*. 2 April 2019. https://www.latimes.com/local/lanow/la-me-nipsey-hussle-south-la-20190402-story.html

Marriott, David. 2017. "On Decadence: Bling Bling." *e-flux* 79. http://www.e-flux.com/journal/79/94430/on-decadence-bling-bling/.

Marx, Karl. 1990. *Capital: Volume One*. London: Penguin Classics.

Moruzzi, Norma Claire. 2000. *Speaking through the Mask: Hannah Arendt and the Politics of Social Identity*. Ithaca: Cornell University Press.

Moten, Fred. 2013. "The Subprime and the Beautiful." *African Identities* 11, 2: 243.

Pincus, Steve. 2012. "Rethinking Mercantilism: Political Economy, the British Empire, and the Atlantic World in the Seventeenth and Eighteenth Centuries." *The William and Mary Quarterly* 69, 1: 3–34.

Smith, Adam. 2019. *The Wealth of Nations*. New York: Courier Dover Publications.

Smith, Adam. [1759] 1822. *The Theory of Moral Sentiments*. London: J. Richardson.

Villa, Dana. 1995. *Arendt and Heidegger: The Fate of the Political*. Princeton: Princeton University Press.

Zupančič, Alenka. 2017. *What Is Sex?* Cambridge: MIT Press.

43

EXPLOSIONS OF 'CREATIVE INDIFFERENCE'. SALOMO FRIEDLAENDER, SUN RA, SERENDIPITY AND THE IDEA OF A 'HELIOCENTRE'

Alice Lagaay in conversation with Hartmut Geerken

In 2013, while researching for an article I was writing on the potency of the concept of the 'neutral' (that which is in principle neither 'this' nor 'that'), I stumbled upon a footnote in a book by William Watkin on Agamben (Watkin 2014). It was a reference to a writer I had not heard of before, and the title of the book – *Schöpferische Indifferenz* (creative indifference) – compelled me to look it up. This is how I first came across the philosophical writings of Salomo Friedlaender (1871–1946) also known as Mynona (reverse spelling of the German word for anonymous – *anonym*). What felt like a chance discovery turned out not only to strike a chord with my academic interest in philosophical figurations of the neutral, but it also seemed to resonate with my engagement in performance philosophy on a number of levels. First of all, there were several aspects about the person and biography of Friedlaender/Mynona (F/M) that suggested that he was himself a kind of performance philosopher *avant la lettre* (Lagaay & Thiel 2020): (a) he was an artist-philosopher who wrote scholarly philosophical discourse *and* witty satirical literary tales (so-called grotesques) to embody the central theory he sought to convey; (b) his writings were not just to be read, but to be read aloud, as their sound was often integral to their meaning and he would perform them in the Berlin expressionist salons of the early 20th century; (c) he was an eccentric bohemian who did not abide by the conventions that would have made his acceptance in the academic realm more likely; (d) described in his day as the German Voltaire (Steegemann 1921; Frambach 2003, p. 114), or as the "Charley Chaplin of German philosophy" (Hatvani 1922, p. 508) his theorizing was never for theory's sake alone, but always politically engaged and fervently concerned with the relevance of enlightenment and sound philosophy for people's lives; (e) he tirelessly sought to show the importance of rational thinking and did not shy away from taking significant risks (given the politics of his time and as a Jew) in voicing objection to multiple forms of political idiocy, social injustice and discrimination.

Then, there is the philosophy of creative indifference itself and how the different terms that F/M uses for this idea throughout his extensive writings – *zero point*, *heliocentre*, *magical I*, etc. – can be fruitful in offering a conceptual toolbox with which to explore and elucidate both the differences between performance and philosophy and the theoretical origin of the impulse to conceptualize – and to enact – a synthesis between them. According to Friedlaender, it is from a theoretically indifferent/indifferentiable (no-) point of origin, that creative processes – polar differentiations – are initiated. What strikes me as compelling, thought-provoking and relevant to multiple contemporary discourses and the experience of life in a late capitalist world is the manner in which the concept of creative indifference, describing, as it does, a theoretical zone/non-place of indifferentiation between all differences, both centres the active source of meaning-creation squarely in the self (the "I") *and* simultaneously understands and provides a model to explain that the subject (the "I", the person, the artist, whoever...) is never entirely reducible to their expression, nor indeed even to their identity.

"what have i got to do with herr friedlaender? i am mynona!"
"Some call me mystery, some call me mr. ra"

These two quotes, the first by F/M, the second by jazz musician Sun Ra, are taken from the programme pamphlet of a live radio performance by Hartmut Geerken and The Art Ensemble of Chicago, "Null Sonne, No Point", that was aired on Bayern2Radio on 25th & 26th October 1996. The pamphlet further states:

"*Null Sonne no point* is the combined title of the two radio plays and performances. *null sonne* is a constantly recurring [idea] in Friedlaender's philosophy, depicting the centre, the origin of coordinates, the heart of human existence. This centre is as inviolable as the sun. Were it not, our existence between the poles might be worn away by the trivialities of day-to-day life. Friedlaender's philosophical journey takes us to the centre of human existence and to the sun he wishes to see at its centre, in keeping with the Copernican worldview. Sun Ra's 'no point', on the other hand has utopian characteristics. (…) His philosophical itinerary describes the 'nowhere-home' of outer space by leaving the earth far behind ('this is not my planet'). (…) Although Friedlaender and Sun Ra followed opposite directions in their thinking, they arrive at the same destination. This is apparent even in the titles of their works: the 'I-heliocentre' of Friedlaender and Sun Ra's 'Heliocentric Worlds', and Friedlaender's polaristic opus 'Creative Indifference', or 'The Magic I' (Sun Ra) and 'Das magische Ich' (Friedlaender). Although the text material in *null sonne* was largely written by Friedlaender, and that of *no point* by Sun Ra, there are many analogies between the two plays. This, however, is not intended as a proof of congruence between the two philosophical systems. Yet, it is a fact that both of them stem from a deep dissatisfaction with the state of the world: Friedlaender the Jew, in the era of the Holocaust, Sun Ra, an Afro-American in a society distinguished by a repressive tolerance. Friedlaender and Sun Ra have drawn their conclusions by declaring the earth a meaningless battleground which they rise, self-assuredly, above, assessing the world by their own standards from an individual state of suspension (Friedlaender: 'Only by floating can one trust the abyss'), and refusing to acknowledge death (Sun Ra: 'Give up your death'; Friedlaender: 'I am the death of death'). Thus, in every creative moment, *null sonne no point* becomes a funeral rite for a shoddy death and a celebration of the life lived. The score encourages each musician to begin from point zero and discover something new" (Geerken 1996, pp. 5–7).

I am often asked what performance philosophy is. And I do not have a singular, consistent answer. I am sure it can be lots of things; it can encompass a wide variety of modes of thinking and bring into connection many different academic interests and disciplines, whilst also involving various artistic and performative practices. For me, engagement with philosophical thought, be it within or outside of the academic realm, has to do with finding a way to grapple with life – and death. Grappling with life is, to my mind, essentially philosophical. And it is also essentially performative in that *how* one grapples – which includes the question of when, to what extent and with recourse to which kind of tools one does so, but also, and *just as importantly*: when, why or how one *ceases* to grapple or interrupts one's grappling to allow oneself "to just *be*" – immediately affects one's manner of living. By 'manner of living', I mean both how one experiences life in general, one's attitude and basic ability to take pleasure in and enjoy being in the world, and how one goes about finding out or deciding what one's role in society might be, or, stated in more basic terms, how one chooses (or not) to spend one's time, provided that one has a certain measure of freedom, some scope at least within which one can choose and thus be enabled to lead a life. So, for me, and for the purpose of this article at least, performance philosophy is the name for a philosopher's, or any grappling person's, particular way of living (whatever its characteristics may be). It is the manner in which they may (or may not) choose or be able to integrate or align their grappling, intellectual interest with their mode and style of living, habitual stance, attitude, perhaps also beliefs, that is to say, their way of acting/bearing themselves in the world, in a word: their *ethos*. It is by no means easy to speak of these things without becoming specific or too personal, and the specific or personal might be misleading in this context as the point is not to uphold one particular ethos above another. Performance philosophy, in the sense I am giving it here, is not ideological or dogmatic. Insofar as it seeks to consider a line of connection between *whatever* content and form, or theory and practice, or manner of grappling and ethos of life, one could say that its eye is ethico-aesthetical – or creatively indifferent. Or simply dramaturgical – with life being the play to be performed.

    The anecdote, as a form, offers a means to navigate between the personal and the general. Yet incidentally, it is precisely the relationship between the personal and the general that is at stake here. Indeed, this is where the notion of creative indifference unfolds its most secret potency: by offering a theoretical apparatus by means of which one might begin to understand that that which is most personal (therefore most inwardly specific and unique, most differentiable) is also – paradoxically – that which is most general, universal and *in*differentiable, that is, at its core impossible to label, therefore unmarketable, and *apersonal*. The French language is intriguing and telling in this regard as the word for person – *personne* – is the same as for nobody – *personne*. This might all sound a bit boggling, or even worrying. So let me continue with an anecdote.

    I had published a short article on F/M's concept of Creative Indifference and its possible relevance to performance philosophy in the first issue of the Performance Philosophy journal. The journal was launched in the spring of 2015 during the Chicago conference '*What can Performance Philosophy do?*' (Lagaay 2015). Hartmut Geerken was alerted to the article and contacted me by email soon after its publication. This is how our correspondence began.

    Hartmut Geerken, born in 1939, is a free-jazz musician, composer, writer, publisher, author of radio plays, filmmaker, owner, it is said, of one of the world's largest collection of gongs and a joyful practitioner (so to speak) of 'creative indifference'. He spent twenty years living and working in Greece, Egypt and Afghanistan before settling with his family on the shores of Ammersee in Southern Germany. Geerken has spent the last fifty years collecting, transcribing and publishing (in his own Waitawhile publishing house) the writings of Salomo Friedlaender/Mynona (cf. Friedlaender 2005–2019). This is a phenomenal undertaking given the extent of the task: the Collected Works (*Gesammelte Schriften*), co-edited with Friedlaender scholar Detlef Thiel, will eventually encompass up to forty large volumes. When I heard that Hartmut and his wife Sigi lived close to Munich, I arranged to visit them in the summer of 2015. Their garden was well kept and overflowing with fruit, flowers and vegetables. It reminded me of Mr McGregor's garden in Beatrix Potter's Peter Rabbit. But when Hartmut came around the corner in a sunhat with a beaming smile, I knew instantly that there was nothing to be afraid of. As he came to open the garden gate, for a moment we paused at the threshold. He looked straight at me with a twinkle in his eyes. It seemed to say "Alice! Welcome to Wonderland! So, you've come to talk about Mynona? One step in and there's no turning back…" Anyone who meets Hartmut cannot fail to notice the singular quality of his energy, playfulness, generosity, his light-hearted, infectious *joie de vivre*. I am convinced that there is much to be learned from the spirit and enthusiasm with which he goes about his life and work, much to be learned not just for each of us individually, but for performance philosophy too and *how it might act.*

Alice Lagaay: Hartmut, can I ask you to take us back to your first encounter with the name Salomo Friedlaender? How did you come across his writings and what was it about them or about his character that urged you to dedicate so much of your life to them? Was it circumstantial, to do with chance encounters and relationships that emerged as a consequence? Or did it also have to do with the content of the work? Can you remember at what point you realized this was going to be life-long endeavour? Was it a sudden realization or a gradual affair?

Hartmut Geerken: It was a gradual process. And a chance encounter of sorts. It was 1966 and I was researching the German writer Victor Hadwiger (1878–1911). I had found the name of the trustee of Hadwiger's estate; it was that of an anarchist philosopher called Anselm Ruest (1878–1943), a follower of Max Stirner. Anselm Ruest had been living in exile in France at the time of his death. After a long search we discovered the whereabouts of his widow, but she died only shortly after we had managed to get in touch with her. A neighbour in the last place where she had lived remembered that Ruest had a daughter who worked as a cleaner in a hospital in Avignon. So my wife, Sigrid Hauff (1941–2018), and I drove to Avignon, where we managed to find the daughter of the trustee of Victor Hadwiger's estate. She did not recognize the name Hadwiger, but she did tell us that she needed to sell her mother's house urgently and that she did not know what to do with all of her father's papers that were still in it. She was delighted and relieved when we offered to take them on the spot – she was going to throw them all away anyway. We had arrived in the nick of time! So, we drove back to Germany with our little VW-beetle full to the brim with all the letters and papers of a refugee who had fled Hitler's regime. Once we got home, we perused all the papers, but found no mention or trace of Hadwiger as we had originally hoped. Instead, there were lots of letters from a whole host of cultural contemporaries like André Gide, Raoul Hausmann, Alfred Kerr, André Malraux, Heinrich Mann, Arthur Segal, Paul Zech… And amongst these, there were also pages and pages of correspondence from a certain Salomo Friedlaender, who happened to have been a cousin and brother-in-law of Anselm Ruest. We were particularly fascinated by all the material relating to Friedlaender – it wasn't just letters, there were stories and all sorts of documents. And from that time on, I began to devote myself with increasing intensity to this Friedlaender, more than to any of the other writers collected in Ruest's archive of correspondence. I began to write to all his relations and acquaintances throughout the world, all those who had survived the Third Reich, asking them to send me any letters or other materials they might have pertaining to Friedlaender. I bought everything I could find on the autograph market or in antique shops, and located any mention of him that could be found in archives and libraries. One thing perhaps worth mentioning here: at first the focus of my interest was in his *literary* works. I published lots of his literary grotesques and novels. It was only after encountering Detlef Thiel, with whom I later began co-editing Friedlaender's "Collected Works", that a path opened up for me to his philosophical writings. This contact came about as a result of my interest in the Afro-American musician and philosopher Sun Ra, whom Detlef Thiel also admired, as did I. At first, I was drawn to the literary grotesques, a form of storytelling that Friedlaender himself had helped to shape, and that he wrote and published under the pseudonym *Mynona*. These texts challenged my understanding of what literature could be. *This* literature was provocative, sarcastic, devoid of taboos, unabashed, and full of impudent humour. In fact, for Friedlaender, the grotesques weren't purely literary works at all, as I later found out; he considered them rather as practical applications of his philosophy, "*eine Nutzanwendung seiner Philosophie*" (Thiel 2011, p. 49).

Alice Lagaay: I'm interested in this observation that Friedlaender considered his literary texts to be an application or a form of embodiment of his philosophy. I wonder if this relatedness could be pushed even further so that the notion of creative indifference could actually be presented as a kind of motto or ethos by which (perhaps by force of circumstance) he lived. It seems to me that there is also a kind of creative indifference in the manner in which you describe your own discovery of the box of correspondence which ignited your interest in beginning to collect his writings in the first place. Whilst deliberately looking for something else, this other material falls into your hands, as it were, and then all you have to do, in a way, is recognize the opportunity, pay attention to your curiosity and intuition, follow the signs. This, it seems to me, is a description of what it can often mean to be an artist-researcher or performance philosopher. Friedlaender was a philosopher, but he clearly held quite some disdain for the "academy", which, in turn, failed to take his work seriously enough to offer him a university post. He liked to call it "akadämlich" – translatable as "acadumbic" (e.g. Friedlaender 2010, p. 207). Is it possible that his incompatibility with the gatekeepers of the university had to do with the fact that his theory, although extremely theoretical and speculative, was far from merely 'theoretical'? Again and again he describes the practice of creative indifference – the deliberate turning inwards towards a central point of indifference within one – as a conscious action, an exercise to be repeatedly tried. Indeed the style of his writing itself, its dogged insistence, the manner in which it returns tirelessly although at times not without a sense of frustration and anguish, to gnor again at the same theme, but from a slightly different perspective, presents itself less as a particular *saying that* than as a certain life-practice. So although profoundly theoretical, and although he tussled and argued with multiple figureheads of scholarly philosophy (Nietzsche, Bergson, Einstein, Sartre to name but a few), his philosophy is not reducible to an abstract concept but calls to be lived, embodied, and experienced by the 'I' who tussles with the idea of the middle, the central point, the heliocentre. "My philosophy isn't a mere philosophy anymore, it is life itself", he writes in a 1937 letter to Lothar Homeyer (Friedlaender, vol. 29, p. 142, my translation). Did this make him all too eccentric for the university, I wonder? Or as an artist-philosopher, is one perhaps *bound* to be eccentric, marginal, queer in relation to conventional academia?

Hartmut Geerken: It stands to reason that there was no place for Friedlaender in traditional academia. He was dismissive of all outdated institutions and it wasn't just there that his position was "between the chairs", so to speak. It was the same with regard to his position on political, societal and religious questions (cf. Thiel 2012; Moran 2011). His philosophy did not sit well with the conditions of polarization which characterizes such institutions. Friedlaender was certainly one of the only thinkers, perhaps even *the only* philosopher of the modern age, to call for a positively revolutionary change in one's manner of thinking, one that would render obsolete any recourse to national pride, religion, the allegiance to any political party or the relevance of skin colour, one that would guarantee global freedom by means of a development of Kant's "for Eternal Peace". What fascinated me then, and still does now, is that Friedlaender's philosophy *begins* at the very point where his philosophizing colleagues seemed to see the culmination of thought.

Alice Lagaay: Friedlaender's prolific writings are driven by a tireless need to repeat his central idea of creative indifference (which he has lots of different names for: "the nought of the world", "the absolute", "∞", "I", "ego", "heliocentre"...), approaching it from multiple angles, again and again. Would you say that there is something about the idea or principle of Creative Indifference that resonated with an attitude to life that you already had, or was Friedlaender something of a teacher to you?

Hartmut Geerken: Without going into great detail I would like to call Friedlaender's philosophy of creative indifference a scientifically grounded *philosophy of life* which, based on his reading of Kant's "opus postumum", culminates during his exile in Paris in his most important work, "*Das Magische Ich*" (Magical I). Of course Friedlaender has rubbed off on me in all sorts of ways (though not entirely). When you dedicate half a century to somebody's writings, collecting, transcribing and digitalizing tens of thousands of pages of handwritten pages and typescripts, it is unavoidable that one surrenders oneself to the other in a certain sense. Whenever I sat at my mechanical typewriter back then (or when I sit down to work at the computer now) I had the feeling of communicating with a good old friend that knew much more than I did. I learnt so much from him. From antiquity to the modern age, he was well versed in everything: the natural sciences, literature, philosophy, para-phenomena etc., and he could draw lines of connection between all these realms. This became evident after his whole library was lost in the war. Even when he had no access to any books, his writings were permeated with quotations in classical Greek, Latin, English, French, Italian. He knew so much off by heart! He was no doubt one of the last great polymaths, not just at home in *one* subject. I always had the utmost respect for the breadth of his knowledge.

But perhaps already as a schoolboy I had something of an inkling of or a predisposition towards creative indifference: I would often say goodbye to my school friends and do my homework on my own sitting up on a branch of an old beech tree in the woods near where we lived. On my way home, I would pick wild mushrooms (I have always been a passionate mushroom gatherer). I was always a happy child, even when after the war we were hungry for years. I often had the feeling that my state was one in which everything was tied up into one point, as if there was something there that was a kind of explosion. It's possible that this predisposition goes back to a strange story from my childhood. During the Second World War after every bomb attack in my home city of Stuttgart, I would go to the park close by and collect all the bomb splinters and fragments that could be found in sinkholes on the ground. One day I found the blind shell of a phosphorous bomb that had failed to detonate. With three or four friends, we must have all been about five or six years old, I carried the bomb to a wall, pressed the red button of the grey hexagonal object and threw it against the wall. On the third attempt, the bomb finally exploded, spewing a metre-long streak of burning phosphorous away from us, thankfully not towards us. I had wanted to know what would happen! Perhaps there is a certain riskiness involved in living indifferently (in Friedlaender's sense of the term).

Alice Lagaay: I'm interested in this consideration that there is a form of courage or daring[1] involved in living "indifferently". When people hear the word "indifference" they might tend to think instead of a kind of detachment/non-caring attitude. It does not seem intuitively plausible that there could be an "ethics" of indifference. And yet to read Friedlaender is to encounter a writer profoundly and courageously engaged with the politics of his time. What conclusions or indeed lessons can be drawn from this? Can there be an ethics of indifference?

Explosions of 'creative indifference'

Hartmut Geerken: I'm sure that, throughout the history of humanity, there are innumerable cases of individuals who have reached a kind of indifference that they might refer to with the tag of an "ethos" depending on the influence of whatever religion. Really I would prefer to avoid the word "religion" here, but I can't think of a better word right now. I'm thinking of shamanistic and energetic rituals, "grey magic", voodoo, Sufism, mysticism etc. Perhaps "ethics" is not the right word here either, perhaps it should be replaced by "ethopoeia", the process of a person's mental/spiritual constitution, in the course of which transmitted expressions, beyond the realm of academia, can be impersonated. A resonant "approximation", a kind of "thereabouts" would seem to play a role here; a thereabouts that could perhaps be equated to Friedlaender's zero point/heliocentre, as something that – as a non-place – can never be fully inhabited or precisely located but that one can only ever oscillate around. Thelonious Monk, for instance, was a pianist who was actually quite a bad piano player, but his sounds always hit the mark. Or Hanns Eisler. He was a terrible pianist and singer, but an excellent composer... It seems that a certain state of creative indifference can be reached through all sorts of different circumstances. It would be worthwhile to investigate the role of the pineal gland in achieving creative indifference, in other words to look at the part played by the unconscious in bringing about strange serendipitous coincidences, whereby a kind of explosion occurs in the merging of Kairos and Chronos.

Alice Lagaay: Hartmut, you are something of a hybrid artist/scholar yourself. Is there a parallel here to the person of Friedlaender/Mynona? It seems to me that this is something that both F/M and you share with perhaps all those who identify (one way or another) with performance philosophy (cf. the description of hybridity as a quality of performance philosophy in the introduction to this volume). Not fitting in to a particular category, or combining knowledge and experience from different realms and bringing them into a form that has no label as such, this way of being no doubt comes with certain challenges, but can also be liberating too, wouldn't you say?, as it becomes a question of defining one's own rules – as opposed to following already established principles. How relevant in this regard is the notion of creative indifference to your own working practice? Has your intimate involvement with F/M's philosophy become something of an ethos – a way of living for you? Can you describe this relation, perhaps with some examples?

Hartmut Geerken: You call me a hybrid artist? Well you're right! The only publisher that I still work with is the Berlin-based *Hybriden Verlag*! A hybrid artist/author/philosopher cannot draw solely on received methods of creative indifference. I have a habit of always carrying a little notebook and pen in my jacket, shirt, coat – whatever I am wearing. Wherever I am, at the corner of a street, on the loo, in the cinema, in bed, on a train, in an airplane (not yet under water!) I take notes and write down keywords. In the past I would then sit at my typewriter, now I sit at the computer, and write the notes out. This transcription process can take place at any time of the day or night. My wife Sigi would say: you write big books but I never see you writing! Friedlaender left 170 notebooks all filled with philosophical content and multiple journals and diaries in which he kept a note of everyday events. One can really imagine how in Paris, in the cold unheated room, he would lie in bed scribbling down notes that he would later transcribe and expand into legible print. I know that when I write my notes, I am in a kind of state outside of time. It's as if the thought that I am writing down were to disappear into "the outer darkness" if I were not to grab hold of it and note it down. Perhaps this kind of moment points to something like the creative indifference that Friedlaender constantly sought to declare as a utopian normal state. In free improvised music something similar can happen. When several musicians improvise together, the most beautiful moments occur as a kind of swarm intelligence. All the musicians suddenly move in precise simultaneity following unintended routes, like a murmuration of starlings in the red evening sky.

Alice Lagaay: I gather that for many years another passion of yours has been the music of Sun Ra – in fact you can claim, I think, to be the only Caucasian to have had the privilege of performing live on stage with Sun Ra Arkestra. Tell us about your relationship to Sun Ra – both the person and the musical phenomenon. What role has this played in your life? Is there a connection between Sun Ra and Friedlaender (& are *you* perhaps the point of indifference between them?!)

Hartmut Geerken: At the end of the 1950s I was 17 or 18 years old. I had a simple crystal radio and some army headphones left over from the war and I would use these to listen to the jazz programmes by Joachim Ernst Berendt, Germany's most famous jazz "king" at the time. I remember two broadcasts in particular: a concert by Billie Holiday and one by an Afro-American musician called Sun Ra. At the time, in America, Sun Ra had just one LP out and two singles. I can't remember what the music was that was played on the radio that time, but I remember very clearly one sentence the DJ said. Berendt said that Sun Ra was a musician who polarized the critics into two extreme camps. Some considered him a musical genius and as the next big thing in jazz; the others dismissed him as a charlatan. For a while he didn't really play much of a role in my field of interests. But when in 1966 I was sent to Cairo to work for the Goethe Institute, I suddenly remembered him. I bought everything that Sun Ra had published up until then – and I got the idea that it would be great to invite the Master to his spiritual homeland, which was Egypt. I got no response to the letter I addressed to his label. But in December 1971 a musician colleague of mine told me that Sun Ra was "in town" and staying at Mena House Hotel at the foot of the pyramids. So I immediately jumped in the car and drove to Gizeh. On an arterial road I saw a dark-skinned man in non-Egyptian clothing hitching a ride in the direction of the pyramids. I stopped the car, he got in and we started talking. We introduced ourselves. His name was John Gilmore! We were both properly surprised. I was surprised that none other than John Gilmore was in my car – I knew his music off by heart from all the Sun Ra records I had. And he was surprised to get into a stranger's car in Cairo and find someone there who knew his music! When we arrived at the hotel, Sun Ra was in the lobby wearing all his robes and chains. Gilmore introduced me to him and maybe because in this foreign land he saw in me a kind of accomplice, we agreed to meet for breakfast the following day. I had only invited Sun Ra, but he turned up with 25 musicians – his whole 'arkestra'! I couldn't organize a concert that fast so I proposed to them that they play at my house. We cleared everything out of the living room and invited a good 25 or so well-heeled folk (at around 100 Euro per person) – and after the concert I was able to give Sun Ra a good wage! My house was in a suburb of Cairo, in Heliopolis (another strange coincidence of sorts). And I know that for Sun Ra it was a very significant occasion to be able to play in the city of the sun, the pharaonic ra's place of worship.

In terms of how it was to be with him, Sun Ra was really quite a "normal" person – apart perhaps from his tendency to launch into tirades. Above all, he had a really great sense of humour with Dadaist impulses. He had a contagious laugh – he could laugh until he was short of breath. His eccentricity, by the way, which was often ridiculed by critics, had nothing to do with American show: its roots were African. Anyone who has personally witnessed the rituals they derive from, would experience and understand his performances in quite a different light. His weren't really concerts in the conventional sense of the term, they were rituals in which language, song, theatrical elements, dance, acrobatics, frills and furbelows all combined into a musical event. Sun Ra Arkestra, a truly unique phenomenon, must be seen in its historic significance alongside the big bands of Duke Ellington or Count Basie. In 1946/47 Sun Ra played and arranged music in Fletcher Henderson's legendary orchestra, and in the second half of the 20th century, alongside The Art Ensemble of Chicago, he was hugely influential in the whole development of the "New Thing".

Sun Ra wasn't just the director of his arkestra, he was also a lyric poet and a philosopher. I published his poems in a 530-page volume called "The immeasurable equation" (Geerken 2005). This side of Sun Ra too is part of his whole concept with African roots. Indeed, he was certainly no representative of the compartmentalized thinking typical of the West, but rather for a flowing together of currents more analogous to chaos theory. In this mode of being and creating, self-organizing dissipative orders come about and dissolve, the left-overs leading to yet new orders that again emerge and disintegrate. Seen as a whole, Sun Ra's creativity is perhaps better described with recourse to physical or chemical concepts than with musical references. He once told me that words are like chemicals: if you bring two corresponding words together it can lead to an explosion.

Note

1   Cf. Chapter 19, "Daring to Transform Academic Routines", by Jörg Holkenbrink and Anna Seitz in this volume.

References

Friedlaender, Salomo. 2005–2019. *Gesammelte Schriften*. Vols. 1–38. Edited by Hartmut Geerken & Detlef Thiel. Herrsching: Waitawhile.

Frambach, Ludwig. 2003. "The Weighty World of Nothingness: Salomo Friedlaender's 'Creative Indifference'," in: Spagnuolo Lobb, Margherita and Nancy Amendt-Lyon (eds.): *Creative License. The Art of Gestalt Therapy*. Vienna: Springer-Verlag, pp. 113–127.

Geerken Hartmut & The Art Ensemble of Chicago: Progamme pamphlet for *null sonne no point*. interactive media performance aired on 25th and 26th October 1996, live on Bayern2Radio.

Geerken, Hartmut. 2005. *Sun Ra. The Immeasurable Equation. The Collected Poetry and Prose*. compiled by James L. Wolf and Hartmut Geerken. Herrsching: Waitawhile.

Hatvani, Paul. "Für Mynona" in: Friedlaender, Salomo. 2005–2019. *Gesammelte Schriften*. Vols. 1–38. Edited by Hartmut Geerken & Detlef Thiel. Herrsching: Waitawhile, Vol. 8, p. 507–508.

Lagaay, Alice. 2015. "Minding the Gap of Indifference. Approaching Performance Philosophy with Salomo Friedlaender (1872–1946)". *Performance Philosophy* Vol. 1, pp. 65–73.

Lagaay, Alice & Detlef Thiel (eds.). 2020: *The Critical Introduction to Salomo Friedlaender-Mynona. 20th Century Performance Philosopher*. London: Rowman & Littlefield International.

Moran, Brendan. "Politics of Creative Indifference". *Philosophy Today*, Vol. 55, No. 3, pp. 307–322.

Steegemann, Paul. 1921. *Zwei Jahre Verleger. Von Laotse bis Dada*, Hannover: Steegemann.

Thiel, Detlef. 2011. "'Sokrates der Idiot' - Friedlaender/Mynonas Rehabilitation". *Perspektiven der Philosophie* Vol. 37, pp. 41–74.

Thiel, Detlef. 2013. *Maßnahmen des Erscheinens. Friedlaender/Mynona im Gespräch mit Schelling, Husserl, Benjamin und Derrida*. Nordhausen: Traugott Bautz.

Watkin, William. 2014. *Agamben and Indifference. A Critical Overview*. London/New York: Rowman & Littlefield.

44
IN THE MAKING – AN INCOMPLETE CONSIDERATION OF THE FIRST DECADE OF *EVERY HOUSE HAS A DOOR* 2008 TO 2018 AS PERFORMANCE PHILOSOPHY

Will Daddario, Matthew Goulish and Lin Hixson

Table 44.1

Philosophy in columns/ Performances in rows	Methods	Materials	Structures	Parallel
Scarecrow (2018)	1	11. LH A paper leaf falls	21	31
This is not a dream (2017)	2	12	22	32
MERCUA (2017)	3	13	23	33. LH subvocalization
The Three Matadores (2017)	4	14	24. MG dramaturg's introduction	34. WD start form nothing
Exhaust the possible final trunk show (2016)	5	15. Program text	25. Bumper sticker image	35
Caesar's Bridge (2014)	6	16	26	36
Testimonium (2013)	7. MG dramaturg's introduction	17	27	37
9 Beginnings (2012)	8. LH remake	18	28. WD question	38. MG response

Reader's Guide to chart contents
    Rows: Ten *Every house* performances in reverse chronology
    Columns: Four categories of philosophical engagement
        Methods – informing collaborative methods of generating performances
        Materials – informing performance materials, physical or conceptual
        Structures – informing performance time and space structure
        Parallel – informing discourses alongside performances

Methods

7. *Testimonium*
Dramaturg's introduction – MG

Hello and welcome. My name is Matthew Goulish. I am the dramaturg for *Every house has a door*, and I will give a brief introduction to the performance.

We began with *Testimony*, an unfinished work of over 500 pages, by American poet Charles Reznikoff. Reznikoff, who had a background in law, collected, compiled, and revised courtroom transcripts of testimonies from hundreds of criminal cases or cases of workplace negligence, spanning the years 1885 to 1915, from various regions of the United States. We selected a six-page extract as our starting point. Shortly thereafter, the publisher denied us the theatrical rights to present those six pages, or any part of the work, in public. The unexpected gift of this denial commenced our creative process in earnest, forcing us to transform and rewrite the poems, knowing what we now know, or thinking what we now think, about law, justice, and the Objectivist poetry of Charles Reznikoff. What is the function of testimony? What is the reason? What can we say about law and poetry, or *as* law and poetry, and objects, and objectivity?

We decided to attempt a weave of the modes of recitation, movement, and music, a weave that invites three distinct ways of listening, or three kinds of attention. To recitation as words heard. (Bryan enters.) This is Bryan Saner. To movement as words made visible, made material, taken literally. (Stephen enters.) Stephen Fiehn. And to music, I mean songs, as words made melodic. (Tim, Theo, Bobby enter.) The band Joan of Arc. And to weave them at three radically contrasting levels of volume. We have provided a supply of earplugs. [Distribution moment] There is also a lyric book, so you can read along if you want, during the songs.

Baruch Spinoza was a philosopher who lived from 1632 to 1677. He wrote on ethics, in the form of a geometric proof. His book *Ethics demonstrated in the geometric* was an inspiration to Charles Reznikoff. We tried to follow that course, to unfold it out of the original, and to fold it into our performance. Because Reznikoff sought to reveal the extraordinary within ordinary words, with reports of commonplace suffering, using "words in their daylight meanings," and he did so by writing *sub specie aeternitatis*, under the aspect of eternity. Can we distinguish his lucidity from his objectivity from his ethics? We want to trace that geometric equality, and that performativity; what the words say, and what the words do, what they might do, to us when we listen. The title of our performance is the Latin name for the last line of a contract, in which the signers state that they are who they say they are. We thought it sounded like an old-fashioned musical instrument. *Testimonium*. (Stephen starts.) Dignity, objectivity, sincerity, and poetry, even music, rough and precise. And so many people, so many names. The poet signs his name with a simple loop at the R. He suspects the existence of justice, clear and commonplace, and as provable as geometry. He tries to fashion it in words, to bring it near, to deliver it as a demonstration, an invention, a necessary recollection. These are the things between which we fall, and then we pick ourselves up again. Stephen has started.

8. 9 Beginnings
Comments for Remake Symposium, Saturday Sept. 15, 2012, Arnolfini, Bristol UK – LH

We began by looking at beginnings of performances that took place in a space where the audience was seated. What constitutes a beginning in this configuration? The documents we watched, DVDs or online videos often began with the audience entering the space or even before the audience entered the space, when the performers were preparing for the audience to enter the space. All these things were fascinating and offered many possibilities for material in creating a performance. But, in the end, we took what we perceived as the artist's intention of a beginning. The moment after the audience grew quiet in anticipation.

We agreed to use a stopwatch, viewing each work for three minutes. Matthew would call time (three minutes) and we would look closely for an ending to the beginning, a point where there was no turning back, a place where the performance took a different direction or commenced on another path. On adopting this system, we saw variations. There were beginnings that were clearly only one minute and some seconds long and there were beginnings that announced their ending, such as a performer saying "Part 2" after seven minutes.

In the process of selecting which archival performances we would use to make a performance, we gravitated toward three kinds of beginnings. Those that began with an introduction, telling you something about the performance or how to view it before it began, like a pre-show announcement; those that began with a more ritualized, nonverbal activity using time or duration as a means to gather the audience's scattered energy into a more directed focus; and a third, *in medias res*, a beginning that drops the audience into the middle of something, into the disoriented feeling that the performance began before they arrived. We gathered three performances for each type and used this as a form.

When making the performance, I was reminded of the words of the writer Hélène Cixous: *Writing leaves nothing it touches intact...* For once we touched these nine performances, they broke apart. But the intention in the breaking was to allow space for the original to ghost the remake.

I was also reminded of Fanny Howe's beginning line of an essay she wrote called Bewilderment. She writes, *What I have been thinking about, lately, is bewilderment as a way of entering the day.* Her essay goes on to ruminate and circle around this statement eloquently in relation to her poetry and fiction.

I take her line out of context and consider how bewilderment resonates with how I would describe the beginning of making a performance. It is important to me that I do not know how to control what I am initiating or that I do not understand where I am going. I need to feel that the material is more than or larger than what I think I can handle. I am in search of a performance that exceeds, defies, and punctuates what I know. Bewilderment guarantees that I need others to find my way.

10. *Let us think of these things always. Let us speak of them never.*
Conceit – WD

Every house offers a new typology for the human actors on stage for *Let us think of these things always. Let us speak of them never*: non- and semi-performing performers.

If non- and semi-performing performers, then what do we become? Non- and semi-auditing audience members? Non- and semi-spectating spectators?

The conceit requires analysis.

For *Every house*, the non- and semi-performing performers leave their labor as wholly performing performers to acquire new functional roles as facilitators, translators, mediators, stage-hands, stand-ins.

What new roles, then, do the non- and semi-auditing/spectating attendees acquire? They become, precisely, the conceit of the performance.

"Conceit" requires analysis.

From the Latin *conceptus*, "to take in and hold." As conceit of the performance, the non- and semi-auditing/spectating attendees take in and hold a new relation with the material of performance itself (as opposed to developing the "meaning" or proprioceptively perceiving the "affect" of the performance, which, I might argue, is the work of the wholly auditing audience and wholly spectating spectator).

Matthew describes the non- and semi-performer as a guide, of sorts.

> Theirs is a dance with history.
> Their dance, like an essay on the page, traces the journey of discovery that the mind makes through a subject.
> Their non-performer performances in fact seem, as a style, necessary to bring about this relation with the material of the subject.

I am, in fact, a non-auditing audience member of *Let us think of these things always. Let us speak of them never.* I never saw the performance. I continue to unfold, rather, astride the performance in the role of philosopher. So too did I function as a pre-spectator when I attended the lecture at the University of Minnesota where Matthew and Lin discussed the work of this particular performance.

With what then do I dance?

My dance is with the living history of the performance, one that eminates out beyond the present performance itself. My dance, like a prognostication of a reality yet-to-come, foretells what the performance might still become. My non-auditing auditing and non-spectating spectating in fact seems, as a style (of thinking?), necessary to bringing about the hope of a relation with the material afterlives of these things of which we always think but never speak.

Materials

11. *Scarecrow*
A paper leaf falls – LH

A paper leaf falls differently each time it falls. Sometimes, it spins. Sometimes, it takes off. Sometimes, it launches into the air. Then drops. Matthew, performing in *Scarecrow*, sets the paper leaves in motion, pitching and sending them afloat. In turn, the leaves animate Matthew. He swivels, flicks his wrist, bends his knees, and lets go. It is here in the air that the mystery occurs. For one cannot control where the leaf falls. One time it is here. Another there. Between hand, paper, air, and floor, a micro-event occurs like a falling star.

What follows is a list of some of the materials in *Scarecrow* –

Hand-cut paper leaves
Horsehair
A coconut
Dirt
Slime made from Metamucil
Fresh leaves from the florist
Lettuce
Tricycle tire inner tubes
Velvet
Plastic red and yellow circles
Essi Kausalainen
Matthew Goulish
Three children ages 8–11

In *Scarecrow*, attention moves from thing to thing, focusing on combination rather than selection, moving away from metaphor and the transfer of meaning toward the singular and the unfamiliar.

                                    Horsehair
                            horsehair on a shirt
                         horsehair shirt on man

                                         Toes
                                  toes tiptoe
                           toes tiptoe backwards
toes tiptoe backwards while holding arching man in a horsehair shirt

                                     Coconut
                             a massive coconut
toes tiptoe backwards holding arching man in a horsehair shirt
            while a massive coconut teeters on his fingers

                                       Dirt
                     dirt in hand of kneeling girl
toes tiptoe backwards holding arching man in a horsehair shirt
            while a massive coconut teeters on his fingers
      dirt in hand of kneeling girl thrown under man's heels
                creates and a path in advance

This additive process of amalgamation allows degrees of likeness and degrees of difference to entangle. It designates a site to observe presences of difference and presences of likeness on a continuum. It attempts to direct the eye to that point where horsehair meets human chest; where coconut and human fingers link; where dirt and heel cooperate; and more importantly, where the unknown adheres to and pervades the known. In this no-man's land perhaps possibilities exist where one might re-envision the sense of what it means to be human.

15. Exhaust the Possible – the final Trunk Show
Program text

The exhausted person exhausts the whole of the possible. Does he exhaust the possible because he is himself exhausted, or is he exhausted because he has exhausted the possible? He exhausts himself in exhausting the possible, and vice versa. He exhausts that which, in the possible, *is not realized*. He has had done with the possible, beyond all tiredness, "for to end yet again."

– Gilles Deleuze, *The Exhausted*, tr. D. W. Smith & M. A. Greco

Structures

24. *The Three Matadores*
Dramaturg's introduction – MG

April 10, 2015 work-in-progress introduction
  Performance Philosophy Conference, Logan Center, University of Chicago
  Hello and welcome. My name is Matthew Goulish, and I am the dramaturg for *Every house has a door*. I will introduce the performance this evening. This is our first public showing of *The Three Matadores Project*, a performance that we began working on last year, and that we hope to complete and premier in fall, 2016. We will show a sequence of about 40 minutes this evening. I will give that some context for you, but first I want to thank Laura Cull and Will Daddario for inviting us to present here. Thanks to John Muse and everyone at the Logan Center, and everybody who worked so hard to make this conference happen. In particular, we at *Every house* are grateful for the concept of performance philosophy, and for the organization's aspiration – that is less to engage philosophy to enlighten performance, or performance to illustrate philosophy, than to uncover how they entangle; how performance philosophizes and how philosophy performs. We are not alone in this trending aspiration. The philosopher Alva Noë boldly proclaims in his latest book that "Art and philosophy are one" (Noë 2012).
  I want to take the opportunity of this invitation to try to reflect on how we see our work situating in relation to that notion of the oneness of art and philosophy, and in relation to performance philosophy's stated goal.
  If we consider philosophy the practice of bringing the knowledge of a spectrum of disciplines into alignment with the most advanced among them, then taking the side of philosophy might mean a resistance to the fragmentation of knowledge, despite the necessity of fragmentation as a form of disciplinarity. Philosophy levels the demand that all disciplines must contend with the advances of the others, and philosophy leads in that practice. Another way to say it is *philosophy has no knowledge of its own*. It has only modes of thought for reconciling the knowledge advanced by other fields. By knowledge, I mean aggregates of facts and feelings. I will propose now that performance as we desire it aspires to that same mission. I suppose that means that we understand performance as a form of creativity that might provide a forum for such diverse reconciliation; that the conditions under which its creativity comes into existence might be constructed in such a way as to force this reconciliation, as wayfinding amid continual reorientation.
  Our approach to this aspiration, I hope, might be apparent in two specific ways. The first of these is the selection of material that will guide the performance, as a form of curation. For *The Three Matadores*, we began with the writing of the poet Jay Wright, with the

understanding that that writing will in a sense live three lives in the performance. We will attempt to stage the writing in a theatrical sense. We will also respond to the writing, or engage selected words or phrases of it as generative, when devising our original performance gestures and sequences that will also become part of the finished performance. Finally, we hope to frame the writing as significant independent of our treatment of it, as a docent would in a museum standing before and attesting to the value of a painting.

On that note, I will take a moment to introduce the extraordinary work of the poet Jay Wright. Mr. Wright, born in Albuquerque, New Mexico in 1934, lives in Bradford, Vermont. His distinctions include a MacArthur Fellowship, a fellowship from the Academy of American Poets, a Lifetime Achievement Award from the Before Columbus Foundation, a PEN New England Award, and being the first African-American writer to receive the Bollingen Prize in Poetry awarded every two years from Yale University. He writes from the multi-cultural imagination, his poetry a complex weave of Southwestern American imagery and history, West African mythology, quantum physics, and numbers theory. As Mr. Wright tells it, he is not weaving these elements. "They are already woven," he says, "I'm just trying to uncover the weave" (quoted in Rowell 2004, p. 95). Last year, I wrote him a letter. I requested his permission for *Every house has a door* to craft a performance out of and in response to a roughly ten-page selection from his 2008 book *The Presentable Art of Reading Absence*. The selection includes a passage that we have come to refer to as The Three Matadores micro-play. This complete episode, rendered in the conventions of playwriting and bilingually in English and Spanish, partly interrupts the flow of the book-length poem. We were fascinated by the complexity and lyricism of the language as it tracked through the stages of a bullfight. The voice of the poetry continues to interject, to assert itself in the play. I phrased the request this way: *If you grant us permission to work with the three matadores micro-play, we would … of course present all the words exactly as written.* After a telephone call with Mr. Wright, who listened and spoke patiently and with absolute generosity, I received a letter granting permission, typed and signed by his wife Lois.

Back to the performance philosophy aspiration, our second approach to, if I might adopt Mr. Wright's phrasing, uncovering the weave of performance and philosophy, is in conceptualizing how the performance as a whole will occupy the same universe as the material selected, how it will reflect or amplify that material's set of concerns as we understand them, and how we will structure and sequence the parts clearly in the time we have and in the room in which we meet.

And with that I will introduce precisely what you will see tonight. I will start with some personal introductions. Lin Hixson is the director and mastermind. Daviel Shy is the Assistant Director, and the costumes are designed and constructed by Sky Cubacub. Tim Kinsella performs the narrator, or the voice of the poetry. Sebastián Calderón Bentin is Matador One, Taisha Paggett is Matador Two, and Stephen Fiehn is Matador Three.

We discovered an approach to staging the matadores play that Lin and I will discuss in some detail in our lecture tomorrow morning. The density of those ten pages led us to conceive of a structure for the performance that involved considering the matadores play part 3 of a three-part performance, and devising the first two parts as four original solo performances presented by the four performers. These solos will frame, elucidate, or respond to in advance, the matadores passage, and will function like steps up to the high platform of the play. Tonight, we will begin with one of these solos – Tim Kinsella's sonic offering – and will progress immediately into those sections of the play that we have thus far succeeded in staging.

I mean to suggest that that structure, that composition, addresses, or tries to address, the performance philosophy mission, as I understand it in this way of demonstrating a reconciliation, or gesture of reconciliation, of advances in different, perhaps competing, disciplines, and of resisting, however awkwardly, the fragmentation that we have come to consider normal.

Anyway, those of you who know me know how much I love the pre-show announcement that threatens to go on forever, know my admiration for beautifully empty phrases like, "Please silence your cell phones." It's a formality, and a tradition, that persists as a way of focusing the mind, individually and collectively, on what is about to happen. We hope to have some time for conversation after, because your reactions will be very valuable to us at this early stage in the work's development. Thank you all for your presence and attention. We will now present what we have so far of *The Three Matadores Project*.

25. *Exhaust the Possible – the final Trunk Show*
Bumper sticker design by Jordan Williams

Figure 44.1   Bumper sticker design by Jordan Williams.

28. *9 Beginnings*
An email exchange, initiated by me (Will) on January 29, 2014 at 5:07pm (Chicago time). – WD

Beginnings, generally speaking, are opportunities for philosophical tuning. I think of your own phrase in *39 Microlectures*, Matthew, where you write that engaging critical minds requires understanding how to understand something. For me, this initial understanding is the act of tuning through which I turn toward the art object/performance. With *9 Beginnings*, I found myself constantly tuning and retuning into the performance, needing to find a new frequency for each of the 18(+) beginnings offered to me. Eventually, I felt that I was not comporting myself to the historical materials/performances cited through your work specifically but, rather, to the concept and performance of beginning as such.

As you considered the audience during the creation of the piece, did you dedicate time to this notion of comportment or ever ask yourselves what precisely the audience might try to tune in to? For example, a performance that compels thought about beginnings in general or about the concept of beginnings will provide different (perhaps more) openings for audience members than a performance about the beginnings of certain, historical performance pieces. If audience members, such as myself, have little to no familiarity with the archival material, then our/my comportment to the performance changes tremendously, and I end up in a different register than an audience member for whom all the archival material triggers personal memories.

Here, I sense a dramaturgical distinction between what I might call "open tuning" and "regular tuning." With the guitar, an open tuning is a tuning of each guitar string to a specific note such that, when played together and before any frets are touched, the notes of the strings combine to form a chord, such as G or D. Regular tuning, by distinction, requires instrumentalists to position their hands on the frets in a specific way in order to make a chord such as G or D. Left untouched, the strings themselves will sound atonal when strummed. If an audience member is provoked into trying to "play" *9 beginnings* as an open-tuned instrument when its arrangement compels the type of "playing" more suited to regular tuning, then the auditing/spectating experience will "sound" quite different. If, however, the performance somehow notifies the auditor/spectator of its open tuning, then that auditor/spectator can comport herself accordingly.

Does this resonate with you?

30. ***Let us think of these things always. Let us speak of them never.***
First, Second, Third – MG
Public presentation, University of Minnesota
October 12th, 2009 (excerpt)

We began to work intuitively, and before too long, made some discoveries, which we then tried to follow in order to allow them to become real, as if the substance of reality requires the permission that we might give to ourselves.

One of these discoveries involved a recurring role of the onstage performer as, to some degree, a non-performer.

We began to occupy functional roles – as facilitators, translators, mediators, stage-hands, stand-ins.

Selma Banich, Mislav Cavajda, Stephen Fiehn, and myself re-enact some, any, or all of the roles simultaneously in the feast scene from the film *Sweet Movie*, directed by Dušan Makavejev in 1974.

The scene captures, documentary-like, a loose ritual in which the members of the commune overseen by the Viennese Aktionist artist Otto Muehl, somewhat inexplicably, devour and destroy a meal together.

They eat, they induce their own regurgitation, one of them urinates into the air, another pulls a beef tongue from his trousers onto the tabletop and attacks it with a cleaver in an act of mock castration, they throw salad leaves at one another, they pour wine like blood onto the table, they wear plates of food on their heads like hats.

They turn themselves inside out, and prove that they are most definitely alive.

But the audience, our audience, only imagines all of that.

The scene plays on a laptop screen, averted from their gaze.

They can hear it, and they can see us enacting it like an elaborate wordless lip-synch, but they cannot see it.

The feast becomes for us an armature of sorts, an ostinato theme behind the table, onto which we attach other choreographic material that departs from and returns to it.

Before the feast, a sequence from a different film had caught our attention.

In this sequence, the American B-movie director William Castle interrupted the story-line of his 1961 film *Homicidal*.

Castle's voice makes a speech that intervenes on the soundtrack, inviting any cowardly members of the audience to leave the cinema if they are "too frightened to see the end of the picture."

"This is the Fright Break," he intones.

He halts the film's narrative progress long enough for a ticking clock to appear onscreen.

He gives the audience 45 seconds in which to flee, before, as he says, we "go into the house."

In "the house," apparently, the titular homicidal person dwells.

Since we had given our new company the name *Every house has a door*, this hesitation at the threshold seemed somehow appropriate.

Furthermore, something in Castle's estrangement effect for the matinee crowd struck a chord in us, a resonance perhaps with this notion of the non-performing, or semi-performing performer – the trait that positions Castle squarely in the borderlands between the other performances in the film, and the members of the audience he addresses.

He appears as a meta-narrator, with the power to slow, but not entirely forestall, the events of the film.

The performance essays of Raimund Hoghe, recently performed here at the Walker Art Center, provide a more contemporary reference point for this approach.

Hoghe composes a performed dramaturgy, in which the subject's extreme constraint – a single piece of music, like Ravel's *Bolero* – allows for a vast unfolding of historical actualities; variations, to use Hoghe's term, touched by this theme.

Under Hoghe's guidance we either hear or hear of renditions of *Bolero*: instances including a performance by the inmate orchestra of Auschwitz; and the recorded accompaniment to the perfect-score ice dancing performance of the champion skaters Torville and Dean at the 1984 Olympics, complete with sportscaster commentary and audience applause.

But what exactly is performed in his show, and who or what performs it?

We may consider the human presences on stage as tour guides of sorts, like Virgils who navigate our way, step by step, through the territory of the performance, in various strata, by turns infernal, purgatorial, and paradisiacal.

Their performance appears secondary, as it allows for a primary performance by these traces of the past, in the form of objects, documentary sound recordings, and carefully calibrated, enacted gestures.

These guides have composed the performance as a trajectory through pre-existing material.

Theirs is a dance with history.

Their dance, like an essay on the page, traces the journey of discovery that the mind makes through a subject.

Their non-performer performances in fact seem, as a style, necessary to bring about this relation with the material of the subject.

In a sense, they perform a sort of puppetry, in which it is essential that they, the performers, do not overtake the subject.

We discover, in watching *Bolero Variations*, that the subject is not Ravel's *Bolero*, but a fault line, a plateau of instability, of similarity, that Ravel's *Bolero* makes visible.

Hoghe's restraint of onstage presence allows the subtlety and force of this discovery to emerge in the course of the deliberately patient duration of the performance.

Perhaps this pinpoints a conundrum of theater: the way virtuosity of any sort, once recognized, becomes the subject, at the expense of, or by way of replacing, or supplanting, the intended subject.

This, in turn, points to a theatrical narcissism, a tendency of performance, or performing, to be about itself, while pretending to be about something else.

The something else that the performance claims to investigate retreats to a sentimentalized background, lurking behind the foregrounded act and presence of the performers.

Let us consider instead presence as mobility; not a thing made, but a thing in the making (Bergson, 2002, p. 338).

[…]

Parallel

33. *MERCUA*
Subvocalization – LH

As a child, I broke words into sounds to identify them. With the act of recognition, I moved to the next and the next. Some words had one sound. Some had five. Like a slow train, I traveled across a track of sounds forming words forming meanings and meanings forming patterns and patterns forming arrivals where fragments coalesced to construct a panorama of comprehension.

To read, I sounded out words and with time, these soundings were internalized. They became silent speech through a natural process called subvocalization. Subvocalization, a fundamental part of reading, involves the involuntary minute movement of muscles associated with speaking and does not involve the movement of one's lips. Subvocalizing never goes away. Micro-muscle tests suggest that its elimination is impossible.

Now, writing about reading, I think again about this process called subvocalization. The activity conjures up a space of possibility and an unexpected creative structure I feel I can use with quotations I have been collecting about reading. When I visualize the procedure, I see a river of sound and words running under a sentence like a viaduct. I see a subterranean nocturnal world adjoining the daylight world of the quote and I see a musical score with hands moving up and down the scales. I take 'subvocalization' as an invitation and use it as a landscape to write *into and under* the quotes.

34. *The Three Matadores*
Start from Nothing – WD

After a performance of *The Three Matadores*, I posed a question to a student.
 "What did you make of that?"
 A smile, symptomatic of bewilderment, crept over the face.
 "Well, I mean, I came at this with nothing, no knowledge of Jay Wright, no knowledge of poetry, and I've never seen a devised performance."
 I asked no more questions, fully satisfied that the work of criticism had begun.
 I hear in my head one sentence from *39 Microlectures*: "Each time we experience a work of performance, we start over from almost nothing."
 It is easy to read this sentence as a declaration of truth instead of what, I believe, it is, namely, a secular prayer. I offer a modest amendment: "May we hope that each time we experience a work of performance, we start over from nothing." With nothing – almost nothing – to filter the words of Wright's *The Presentable Art of Reading Absence*, the student has no obstruction to the everything of the performance.
 This is why I asked, "What did you make of that?" and not "What did you think?" Whereas the latter question permits judgments framed by familiar tropes, the former gestures toward an act of creation that can only begin upon encountering the performance.

Perhaps I phrased the question incorrectly, after all. If the student is reading this, I'd like to rephrase: "What will you make of that?"

38. *9 Beginnings*
Matthew's response to Will, from March 1, 2014 at 1:22pm (Chicago time). – MG

Your framing of the question as tuning reminds me of Gertrude Stein's essay *Plays*. Stein talks about "confusion" between the audience and the performance. She defines confusion as times moving out of phase with one another, creating non-synchronous interference. Familiarity with what is going on onstage, some knowledge that allows for shared meaning, is one of the factors in the degree to which confusion arises. This problem has always manifested itself acutely in our work, since we announce a relationship between our performance and a source. In *9 beginnings*, the sources are actual named pre-existing performances. Confusion multiplies, and the act of retuning becomes one of the major responsibilities of apprehending the performance. As the violinist Irvine Arditti said about John Cage's composition *Freeman Etudes*, the difficulty subsided when he realized the piece was "always beginning."

If I am in the audience, the advent of the source creates an illusion of familiarity in some audience member who is not me. By that I mean that as an audience member, if I have trouble accessing some part of the performance, I might tend to blame this on my lack of familiarity with the source, or exclusion from the community of people, perhaps sitting beside me, whom I imagine are more familiar with the source. I suspect we cannot dispel this illusion completely. I call it an illusion for two reasons: the first directorial, the second dramaturgical.

As director, Lin has the capability of watching every iteration of the performance, especially in rehearsal, as if seeing it for the first time. She can disregard the source or simply forget it. She does not concern herself with it. She has this refined and uncanny skill, that results in, as she would say, not seeing something that is not there. I think she means that some directors see things in their work others do not see – aspects they wish were there, imagine are there, or remember being there because of an association with a source. So for her, the source and the familiarity it brings, the guide to tuning, is something to be escaped in crafting the performance. The resolution then follows the logic discovered in the equation between apprehending every legible element and the feelings evoked by those apprehensions. Everything that appears has a self-contained reason. That reason, or meaning, or feeling, migrates from one element to another over the time of the performance like a relay.

The dramaturgical reason that familiarity is an illusion becomes apparent to those people more familiar with the source. It concerns the compositional defamiliarization, the warping of the material that we attempt. As a dramaturg, I try to keep our version of each beginning in *9 beginnings* guided by the original, to turn to the original when a question arises, but that guidance dictates our claim to the material, manifested in our warping of it. For instance, Sebastián performed Augusto Corrieri's beginning in Spanish after the audience was allowed time to read the English translation. Sebastián performed a physically astute impersonation of Augusto, but Augusto performed in English, for an English-speaking audience. The translation was our response, our insight into his intentions. As Sebastián has said, it reflected the relationship between him and his material through an analogous realizable relationship between us and our material. Hopefully, this technique allows the beginning to stand in for the whole. The performance as defamiliarization machine generates the illusion that some audience member other than me has more familiarity with the material, is seeing it again, thus attunes to it with less effort. In fact, a person who has seen the original may feel the opposite, because the newcomer does not experience the initial shock of Augusto speaking for no apparent reason in Spanish. Maybe the disorientation factor that takes the form of the question: *How familiar exactly am I with this?* makes its demands through the work, of tuning and retuning, especially in this parade of beginnings.

BUT - I suspect one of the reasons this piece was such a crowd pleaser in comparison to our other works is that it structurally retains a built-in rejoinder to this familiarity question, regarding the magic of an artist, known or unknown, commencing an encounter with an audience. Because of the equalizing nature of beginnings, that in their own mode make acquaintance, the familiarity question would have arisen even in the original, even if everybody in the theater had seen all of Augusto's previous works. The first moment announces the arrival of a work equally new for everybody. This particular aspect of this show continues to fascinate me – the recreation of arrival.

39. *They're Mending the Great Forest Highway*
If philosophy. – WD

If philosophy has no knowledge of its own,
    and if performance creatively reconciles multiple knowledges from various field,
    then performance philosophy is not-knowing what one reconciles
    is the seismometer of what will have been reconciled
    is making friendly the doing of thinking and the thinking of doing
    is the subvocalization of a profoundly fecund and embodied reading practice
    is the tuning of being and becoming
    is the consignment of multiplicity within the self, with the understanding that a self, or one's self,
    is part of this multiplicity that one consigns
    is the recreation of arrival

References

Bergson, Henri. 2002. "An Introduction to Metaphysics". In *Henri Bergson: Key Writings*, edited by John Ó Maoilearca and Keith Ansell-Pearson. London: Bloomsbury, pp. 337–348.
Cixous, Hélène. 2003. "The Devil without Confessing Him", *Paroles gelées*, Volume 20, Issue 2, pp. 8–29, quote on p. 11, available at https://escholarship.org/uc/item/0cs123x8
Deleuze, Gilles. 1997. "The Exhausted". In *Essays Critical and Clinical*, translated by D. W. Smith & M. A. Greco. Minneapolis: University of Minnesota Press, pp. 152–174.
Goulish, Matthew. 2000. *39 Microlectures*: In Proximity of Performance. New York: Routledge.
Howe, Fanny. 2003. "Bewilderment". In Fanny Howe, *The Wedding Dress: Meditations on Word and Life*. Berkeley and Los Angeles: University of California Press, pp. 5–23.
Noë, Alva. 2012. *Varieties of Presence*. Cambridge, MA: Harvard University Press.
Rowell, Charles H. 2004. "'The Unraveling of the Egg': An Interview with Jay Wright". In *Jay Wright*, edited by Harold Bloom. Broomall, PA: Chelsea House, pp 85–99.
Wright, Jay. 2008. *The Presentable Art of Reading Absence*. Champaign and London: Dalkey Archive Press.

45
BLACKOUT
Thinking with darkness

Tru Paraha and Theron Schmidt

It begins in blackout.

The theatre begins like every other evening begins with the fading of the lights, to blackout, or at least to darkness. We gather in a place, a place for showing. And the first thing it shows us is darkness.

In a moment, we expect the lights to come up and for something to be seen. A demonstration of some sort. A presentation of action, or a re-presentation, if you prefer. But we have understood that we have entered representation because of the signal given by the lowering of the lights, the implied instruction to silence, and to 'pay attention', to 'watch closely now'. The instruction to 'watch closely' is conveyed by this darkening. And we will know that we are leaving representation when we see this darkness again—perhaps a darkness, realised more fully, when everything goes black at the end of the staged action. Perhaps, hastily, impatiently, we will not linger there but will rush into applause, returning ourselves to this room not as a representation of a room but as an actual room, where we will rise from our actual chairs, and navigate the clumsy actual bodies also trying to leave the room, and go and get some actual dinner.

So, in this moment, we expect the lights to come up and later for them to go back down again. We might say that this moment when we see nothing is the condition for seeing anything.

Let's stay in this moment.

Let's stay here for a while.

This enquiry began for me with what I initially thought was quite a simple observation. As someone who spends a lot of time in theatres, and a lot of time thinking about what theatre is, I became curious about what seemed to be an epiphenomenon of the theatre: its capacity for blackout. But as I sat in the dark, it occurred to me that we need to think about this darkness as part of the technological apparatus of the theatre—certainly in Western naturalist traditions, in which stage lighting and illusionism rely on this kind of architecture, and in which a certain kind of spectatorship is defined precisely by sitting in the dark watching others in the light. Theatre needs a darkened room in order to show us what it wants to show us. And in fact, often the first thing it shows us is darkness, as the lights go down, in a call to attention. That darkness, along with the furniture and architecture, calls us to occupy our mode of 'spectator', to pay a certain kind of attention to things, and to signal that we are now entering the world of representation—which we often will leave again through a corresponding blackout at the other end of the experience.

In other words, darkness is a lighting effect: 'Blackouts [...] are a hallmark effect of electric light in the theatre, unrealizable before the incandescent bulb's full theatrical implementation' (Hurley 2004, 210). If light is a fabricated representation—'brightness pretending to be other brightness', as Bert O. States (1985, 20) glossed Peter Handke—then darkness in the theatre is a representation of darkness. Or perhaps it's more accurate to say that it is one of the conditions that allows representation.

And yet—of course—it's also *actually* darkness. We are really in the dark together—an experience that becomes obvious any time there's a technical problem, and a blackout lasts longer than a few seconds, and the collective audience-body starts to generate a nervous restlessness. In this agitation, perhaps I become aware of the sounds of other people in the audience, their smell and their heat, the fact that we are all gathered together here: the darkness shows us this, too, the fact of being close together in an enclosed space. It's for this reason that a lot of non-naturalist theatre, from Maeterlinck to Beckett and into all kinds of contemporary experimentation, amplifies this 'real' (though engineered) experience of darkness as the subject of its attention. (For an excellent overview of this lineage of 'theatre in the dark', see the introduction to Alston and Welton 2017.)

So I wanted to start thinking about this darkness: the ways in which it is the grounds of representation, the ways in which it exceeds symbolic representation and becomes palpable as experience, and the ways in which we might avoid confronting darkness in our everyday lives, but choose to encounter it in performance.

I come to the darkness from my fascination with horror, from performance genealogies, and philosophical and cultural spaces that feed into my work. As a choreographer, I consider the negative–positive enigma of darkness proposed by Eugene Thacker (2015), who interestingly notes how 'the concept of darkness invites us to think about this basic philosophical dilemma of a nothing that is something' (18). I approach this conundrum in practice through extensive periods of working in endarkened spaces, and with attention to conceptions of darkness. This may be a nocturnal darkness, or dark aesthetics, such as the 'artificial darknesses' of the studio. Choreographic strategies are developed within and out of nonhuman environments (such as shrouded forests, a cave, night oceans, etc.). When working with the dancing bodies of performers, enfleshed acts of occlusion are traced implicating black space as a potency within choreography that is extracted through doing, being, seeing with dark attention. Here, the body presents its own obscurity and a kind of agency that can be experienced as a mo■ment, or dark movement.

From a tangata whenua perspective, we descend from, and are of, Te Pō (darkness perpetual), and there are numerous cosmo-genealogical names for these durations of darkness leading into Te Ao Mārama (the terrestrial world). The extensive gradients of darkness within Māori cosmo-genealogies are indicative of its importance as a transformative state and space of philosophical contemplation for indigenous people of Aotearoa New Zealand. Te Pō can also be considered a tūpuna, or a nonhuman ancestor.

Experimentation with the black-light of the performance space at a material level is a highly satisfying practice—to work with, in, from the dark, but also to *create* a kind of darkness that is distinctively choreographic, not cinematic (for example). This may be partly attributed to the fact that so little of the night, dark space, and black space is permitted or advanced in conventional, urban life. The places that we might occupy or encounter in the city are hyper-illumined to encourage visibility, identification, activity, and surveillance. But there is a *hidden city*, a secret pavilion that surely thrives in darkness, where we come to understand 'the significance of darkness as a medium for seeing and being differently' (Welton 2013, 6).

For the artist-audience, an engagement with black-light or what André Lepecki (2016) astutely theorises as minor light 're-enchants experience through darkness' (79), not as seduction, but as mystery, potentiality. In its media-specific ways of being with darkness, choreography can enable live encounters that expand speculative imagination towards these enstranged realms. I'm particularly interested in voidal bodies entangled within corrupt spaces and bl ckout production strategies. I'm curious about the hiddenness. Through experimenting within dark space, choreography persists as a unique medium for harnessing what Lepecki describes as a 'depersonalized, collective blackness' (78). So, I posit choreography to be an occultist practice requiring the very conditions of darkness in which to thrive, and in which we might also become anonymous. Here, I conceptualise a blackening choreosphere where participants are permitted their own dark, aesthetic experience within a nomadic space—to 'assemble in heterogeneity' to borrow from Deleuze.

Pø xero

You weren't able to distinguish any forms in the night.

the enduring night
the aching night
the night of annihilation
the caesarean night
the night without end
the deadly night
the yearning night
the night of death-sexing
the intensely held night
the night of utterance
the night where nothing is nor ever will
the blackening night
the night of intimate terror
the deep drowning night
Te Pō-mā
Te Pō-mangu
Te Pō-whakaruru
Te Pō-kumea
Te Pō-hakarite
Te Pō-punga
Te Pō-raro
Te Pō-matau
Te Pō-maui

The night is long. It is long; it is when horror opens its dark eyes and lets you experience its endless void. And what was time anyway? back to the blackness of a beginning.

Dark swan

I think things eaten in the dark taste good. Even now, I eat sweets in bed in the dark. I can't see what they look like but I know they taste twice as good. Light, in general, sometimes seems indecent to me. We came into it like that. We showed up dark, and we stayed dark.

Black bear

The body has interiors within interiors. The body has exteriors beyond exteriors. The body corrupts back to black—and the universe was black. A black band separated the black earth from the black sky. All over was just blackness, a layer of blackness. Black intensities of black on black on black feeding on itself? Immense? Immeasureless?

In 2016, I was choreographing a work for the *Undisciplining Dance Symposium* in Auckland. It was a group piece that explored some of the dark aesthetics and conceptual drives that I've mentioned, and which I have conceptualised as horrørChor. After I made this group work, I began to research other choreographers who might also be exploring speculative darkness with concept horror underpinnings. I didn't expect to find anything that specific or relevant because it's not a blood and gore thing; it's nuanced, and it is dance. Dance and horror, or the horror of dance, are not generally explored in this way. It was enlivening to come across Mårten Spångberg's *Natten*, which, as it turns out, was being choreographed and produced around the same time in Stockholm. I watched hours of murky footage on Vimeo and felt elated knowing such a work existed on the other side of the world. I'm inspired by this choreography (that I've never seen) because I had been fantasising about making a xero dark performance that ran from dusk till dawn. Spångberg's work is a large format, seven-hour dance in the dark. I had this strange feeling that he'd basically made the dance I had been dreaming of.

I am drawn to your idea of 'a hidden city', the thrill, maybe, of the darkness, as a source of energy. There are rich literary and cinematic traditions that draw on this energy: noir, most obviously, and horror, as well as ritual traditions, in many cultures. Your 'dusk till dawn' choreography reminds me of a very formative experience I had as a spectator at a Kathakali performance in a rural temple that ran from dusk till dawn, in which I kept drifting off and waking up into a stream of precisely choreographed action. Not speaking Malayalam, I imagine I was like one of the many infants in the audience, with everything unfolding like a dream of infinitesimal gesture. Dawn felt like it was a continuation of the night, as we staggered through it in a haze of diffused and fragmented attention.

We know that somewhere out there lies the hidden city.

Is it the same as this one, but in reverse? All its bright spots turned into dark ones, all its populated spaces now barren and filled instead with the lifeless?

Only empty thoughts walk through its streets, only strays and castaways and the unwanted—

—No, not unwanted, for to be unwanted would be to be known, but rather: un-wantable, un-thought-of, unhoused and without name.

Somewhere out there this dark city, the same as this one.

Is this to say that this is somehow the true city? The one that shows its real, hidden face? I don't think so. It is instead disinterested in the true. It has nothing to show us, only places for thought to become lost, only places for us to disappear, for bodies to become ghosts and for block after block nothing to stop you from drifting ever further and further from proper sleep (*& from your proper self*)…

Blackout

Western philosophy has always been somewhat apprehensive about this hidden city of the night. Plato's cave, of course, is a parable in which darkness stands in for the world of illusion, one that encourages us to come out into the light; and for Kant ([1786] 1996), not surprisingly, darkness becomes a challenge for orientation ('orientation' being a recurring theme in Kant about which Sara Ahmed [2006] has much more to say). Kant imagines that someone has turned out the lights, and perhaps even mischievously rearranged all the objects in the room, but even so, he would be able to orient himself through his subjective experience; and he extends this to valorise pure reason as a guide to orientation when we move from the world of material objects to the domain of concepts and ideas. Reason lights up the darkness. Thinking is impervious to the dark.

The situation gets less straightforward when it comes to the twentieth-century phenomenologists. I found a reference (Himanka 2006) to a note in which Husserl also imagines that the lights have been turned off: if being is given by our intentionality, he asks, then what happens when there is nothing there to be intended? For Husserl, it's important that the objects in the room are still there, not just as a memory, but in a transformed presence, a 'bodily emptiness'. So something curious has happened: the object in the dark has acquired something new, a presence that supersedes its sensory qualities—such that there can be such a thing as an empty appearance. And for Levinas, this negative presence becomes much more profound. He writes, 'When the forms of things are dissolved in the night, the darkness of the night, which is neither an object nor the quality of an object, invades like a presence' (Levinas [1947] 1995, 58). He describes this presence—which is the presence of nothing—as 'an absolutely unavoidable presence', the ground of our existence, which is completely independent of us and needs nothing of us. It's just the 'there is', the *'il y ya'*, into which our 'I' disappears—or rather which invades our 'I', depersonalises us. Levinas vividly describes being unable to sleep, and feeling confined within the fact of one's existence: *present* without anything to be present *to* (65). For Levinas, this state is oppressive, stifling, horrific.

The thinking stops the breathing. I find my breath held by a thought.

Now, too, there is the sound of scratching a tiny itch forward across a page.

The thinking self scurries across the floor like a furtive mammal looking for crumbs.

Next door a visiting friend is breathing heavily in his sleep. I feel like an intruder just hearing him. I shouldn't be hearing this. There shouldn't be a 'me' here.

I try to quiet my thoughts, to think my way back to thoughtlessness. I drink cool water to try to still the body's restlessness. I write in this notebook, my eyes closed, hoping this is just a momentary pause, a small dream that feels real but is really part of sleep. That when I wake it will be as if it didn't happen, and that I am fully rested, and that this will not have been a wasted night, a night spent lost in the wastes.

Entangling notions of horror within choreography and with regard to recent speculative philosophies of darkness allows spaces of encounter where sentient bodies and things might collude more darkly, bizarrely, *and with feeling*. This is a form of attention that a normative, illumined spectacle of dancing bodies has not enabled, particularly within the proscenium arch. In dark attention, knowing's unknowing has a skin of brain that feels all the more directly for not being self-permitted to know in, and as, only the scopic. This is significant when contemplating how choreographic darkness might be distinguished from other mediums such as visual arts, literature, or film. In this context, movement itself becomes another order within the economies of humans and the unhuman.

In practice, this movement is both choreographically structured and contingently arising, so we are always working with the unfathomable, the hidden. It is also conceived as becoming-apart from the apparent agencies that initiate it. In other words, though choreographic darkness may be framed within the conditions between human bodies, unhuman entities, and elements of performance production, that movement is not human per se. It becomes a force operating amidst and upon the multi-dimensional agencies in which the choreography strategises its inception.

Dark movement as force can be conceptually linked with Foucault's notion of power as forces operating in culture. But the concept of dark movement as force means to resist the hubristic telos of power's force, in Foucault's terms. Moreover, this movement has an autonomous quality that affects as a kind of decay. Reza Negarestani (2008) contends that through decay, a 'peaceful (non-annihilative) assault on the ground of power formations is effectuated as a concrete sabotage against the very definition of power' (188). So, I conceive darkness' force, while not concrete, as an ungrounding of hegemonic power in Western theatrical dance and within the contemporary dance 'industry' in which many choreographers have been trained: part of that undoing is an attention to choreographic darkness as unhuman in its agency. Like Negarestani's ethics of decay, it 'ungrounds the very ground upon which power is conducted, distributed and established' (187) and within dance, it degenerates as a body that also exceeds 'the body', and enacts a becoming-disembodied.

To attend to the dancer as an alien body, a prehistoric body, an unhuman body, is something I am attempting to cultivate in the studio and within the contingencies of performance. During such times, I observe how dark movement performs as a liquidity among the more apparently substantial aspects of darkness and beyond the mere novelty of turning the lights out. It becomes a deterritorialised identity and intensifies the displacement of normative agency among humans, the unhuman, and the spaces in which these bodies perform.

You remind me that the topographies of darkness are cultural and political as well as phenomenological and experiential, coalescing around racialist and imperialist structures of power and affect—and affect slides fluidly between the scales of the individual and the aggregate, from fear of the dark to 'Fear of a Black Planet', as Public Enemy so emphatically put it. Like you, I am drawn to these aspects of performance that enable or work towards the deterritorialising of the body and of our states of knowing and feeling—but that aspiration means something different for me, as a white, cis-male, salaried person whose experience of my body and structures for knowing the world have been consistently affirmed and validated throughout my life so far. This is part of what I take with me into the darkness. Even in sleep, I take my privilege with me (whether understood as specific material benefits, or as the absence of deprivation) as part of what is wrapped around this 'me'—even if I experience the Levinasian existential horror of the ultimate groundlessness of that 'I'. And I am held in other grids of subject-formation, too; one of the thoughts that frequently arises when I am in an insomniac vortex is an anxiety around productivity: *if I don't fall asleep, I won't be able to write clearly or teach clearly tomorrow*, and the more that thought goes around, the further away sleep remains. Sleep is reproductive labour, as new parents know very well, and reproductive labour is unevenly distributed and compensated.

Blackout

So if I want to cultivate a 'dark attention', to borrow your evocative phrase, I need to attend to the wider implications of thinking blackness, and of black thinking. 'All thought is Black thought', writes Christina Sharpe (2016, 5), referring to Jared Sexton, who wrote: '1) all thought, insofar as it is genuine thinking, might best be conceived of as black thought and, consequently, 2) all researches, insofar as they are genuinely critical inquiries, aspire to black studies' (Sexton 2012). The work of projects like these is to generalise blackness as a model of thinking and being—'fugitive movement', Fred Moten (2008) calls it—that locates in Black and otherwise undervalued life a paradigm of refusal and countervalent life. I do not mean to suggest that thinking in the dark somehow makes what I am doing Black thinking—that would be a crass appropriation—but to acknowledge and affirm the reorientation being called for by these activist philosophies.

You point to the role that performance can play in opening lines of flight, away from the scripted body and into other modes of being/together, different modes of knowing. I like this idea of 'choreographic darkness'; in the word 'choreography', we can think about the relation between movement and writing as the one that can be understood both ways, not just the writing of the body, but an embodied writing, a performative writing: 'writing as *doing* displaces writing as meaning' (Pollock 1998, 75). In relation to darkness, my own approach to a fugitive writing arose during a lengthy period of insomnia. Repeatedly finding myself awake in the middle of the night, and unable to return to the 'normal' condition of sleep, I felt displaced, anomalous, not-at-home in my own form-of-life.

I decided to start to use that time to write, in an unfamiliar way, without turning on the lights, just allowing my pen to move over the page. To write from within the darkness about the darkness that surrounded me. To write in the dark. To write of the dark. To write from the dark. To write with the dark. Writing—that most ordinary of activities for the philosopher—was here a furtive action, in symphony with the city dogs wandering restlessly through empty streets, the aimless traffic, the small noises of my apartment shifting in the night, and just one more night creature, *the sound of scratching a tiny itch forward across a page*, my hand wrote. This writing formed the basis for a performance work in which I spoke these fragments alongside other writings on darkness inside a blackout theatre, accompanied by ambient recording and faint music. An engineered blackout, yes, a choreography of darkness and sound, taking place in what we might think of as the rest-state of the theatre, the blackout that enables illumination, the blackness of thought.

I should be asleep.

I am lying in the dark thinking about anomaly. This thinking has woken me up, from what was an ordinary night, now made strange.

I should be asleep but instead I am writing, without turning on the lights, from a place in-between sleeping and waking.

I have woken up here and find myself off the grid. What does it look like from here? It doesn't look like anything. It doesn't feel like anything. I don't know how to think my way through this, to think about it, for it is *it* that is about me, literally, that wraps around me, that has become me. That means I don't know how to know.

It is not the same as being sun-drenched, or flooded with light, these things that overwhelm the senses. Here, darkness is capacious, it swallows and engulfs, its appetite is voracious, it consumes everything. It is not just things that may be seen, and that now cannot, that become part of the condition of darkness, that disappear into it, but thoughts, sounds, even thoughtlessness, silence. All fall away. All fall away into the dark.

Composed in xero dark (generally the hours between midnight and dawn), texts arise out of, or independently of live works. These texts may become a poem, or a choreographic score that is not intended to be danced or even uttered. Working choreographically across black space and within a physical privation of light influences textual practices towards the inscribing of darknotes. How might we reveal the fabric of the text that the black-thought is experiencing? What is it that the ▓▓▓▓ is wanting us to think? And how might we voice the unsayable? Neologisms surface in relation to these questions, where words refract a kind of double=crossing, or bilingual blind spot. The creation of performative language materialises as intentional texts whose glossary finds meaning through acts of translation and embodiment. Writing becomes infected by a choreological syncing with peers (philosophers, artists, imagined authors), along with strategies of tran*slang*uaging. Darkness conduits these flows of black-thought. Hidden writing can be a kind of putrefaction that undoes the hegemony of scholarly texts towards cosmoses of ambiguity within the 'dark ground of clarity' (Mika 2015, 62). Such inscriptions may appear to certain readers as bugs or glitches; to others, they may be exotic features. The leak holes in my writing can be directly related to a choreographic practice cultivated within the dark unknowing. Here, the right to conceal is observed, allowing for pages of inscrutability where further elucidation may be deemed unnecessary. This is directly induced by darkness manifesting as the Māori practice of hakaaro huna (hidden thought), or, as the obfuscated, unidentifiable aspect of things that are visible.

minor light

assuming critter-like forms traveling across floor on hands& feet feeling feet as hands& creasing deeply into bodily abysses pausing when tired& breathing without judgement then continuing stalking forwards around perimeter of studio with clear alignment finding a stalking pace neither slow nor fast pedestrian nor formal walking up& down studio as if part of funeral procession then walking backwards with clear alignment& as if part of funeral procession raising arm while walking around perimeter of studio, with clear alignment& as if part of funeral procession, with other arm rotated out ever so (slightly) changing arms rolling down to floor through spine with ease then rolling up through spine with ease feeling vertebrae as string of blackpearls staying open across clavicle& sternum connecting movement& timing of tail with movement of skull shaking wildly through various parts of meatbody while connected to surface finding authenticity of shaking from core of movement's desire trying not to fake it closing curtains, leaving lights off& absorbing studio darkspace allowing dark to become normal as light rolling over large mat across low - mid levels from one end to other finding economy in 5th body organising across floor through spine hips limbs sitbones knees bones of hands feet keeping eyes empty as deadgirl grounding extended balances on leg then alternating finding polar tension through ether limbs including face orbiting on axis with feet together clockwise& anticlockwise orbiting on axis with feet together& raising arm to sky holding iPhone in other hand at same time with torch function on maintaining clear orbits increasing speed expanding eyebones& releasing while orbiting around axis lying on back& dreaming into darkness not knowing what's next& not caring feeling meatpain& doing nothing but feeling

Blackout

The darkness holds the promise of restoration. That from this empty state fullness will be returned, the world will come back to life.

First the sound of birdsong,
    and then traffic,
        and eventually daylight and speech and social beings.

All will be put back like it was. All will be revealed.

We like to think that when the lights come back on, the world will be waiting there for us.
We will move from the darkness onto the stage of our lives.

Let's stay in this moment.

Let's stay here for a while.

References

'Dark swan', 'Black bear', and 'Pø xero:' include lines from: an interview with Hijikata Tatsumi (Tatsuhiko 2000); an interview with Moira Walley-Beckett (Connolly 2015); *'We, who live in darkness'* by Hone Tuwhare in *Deep River Talk* (1993); 'The bear's vision of blackness' by Kathy Acker in *Blood and Guts in High School* (1984); *From the Antipodes: Prologue to a work in progress* by David Karena-Holmes (2003); *Natten* by Mårten Spångberg (2016); and 'Mātauranga Māori (Māori Epistemology)' by Hone Sadler (2007).

Acker, Kathy. 1984. *Blood and Guts in High School*. New York: Grove Press.
Ahmed, Sara. 2006. *Queer Phenomenology: Orientations, Objects, Others*. Durham: Duke University Press.
Alston, Adam, and Martin Welton, eds. 2017. *Theatre in the Dark*. London: Bloomsbury.
Connolly, Kelly. 2015. "*Flesh and Bone* Finale Postmortem: Moira Walley-Beckett Breaks down Claire's Final Answer." *EW.com*. December 27, 2015. https://ew.com/article/2015/12/27/flesh-and-bone-finale-postmortem-moira-walley-beckett/.
Himanka, Juha. 2006. "How Does a Dark Room Appear: Husserl's Illumination of the Breakthrough of *Logical Investigations*." *Indo-Pacific Journal of Phenomenology* 6 (2), pp. 1–8.
Hurley, Erin. 2004. "BLACKOUT: Utopian Technologies in Adrienne Kennedy's *Funnyhouse of a Negro*." *Modern Drama* 47 (2), pp. 200–218. https://doi.org/10.3138/md.47.2.200.
Kant, Immanuel. (1786) 1996. "What Does It Mean to Orient Oneself in Thinking?" In *Religion and Rational Theology*, edited and translated by Allen W. Wood and George di Giovanni, pp. 3–18. The Cambridge Edition of the Works of Immanuel Kant. Cambridge: Cambridge University Press.
Karena-Holmes, David. 2003. *From the Antipodes: Prologue to a Work in Progress*. Dunedin: Maungatua Press.
Lepecki, André. 2016. *Singularities: Dance in the Age of Performance*. New York and London: Routledge.
Levinas, Emmanuel. (1947) 1995. *Existence and Existents*. Translated by Alphonso Lingis. Dordrecht: Kluwer Academic Publishers.
Mika, Carl Te Hira. 2015. "The Thing's Revelation: Some Thoughts on Māori Philosophical Research." *Waikato Journal of Education* 20 (2), pp. 61–68. https://doi.org/10.15663/wje.v20i2.206.
Moten, Fred. 2008. "The Case of Blackness." *Criticism* 50 (2), pp. 177–218. https://doi.org/10.1353/crt.0.0062.
Negarestani, Reza. 2008. *Cyclonopedia: Complicity with Anonymous Materials*. London: re.press.
Pollock, Della. (1995) 1998. "Performing Writing." In *The Ends of Performance*, edited by Peggy Phelan and Jill Lane, pp. 73–103. New York: New York University Press.
Sadler, Hone. 2007. "Mātauranga Māori (Māori Epistemology)." *International Journal of the Humanities* 4 (10), pp. 33–45.
Sexton, Jared. 2012. "Ante-Anti Blackness: Afterthoughts." *Lateral*, no. 1. http://csalateral.org/issue1/content/sexton.html.
Sharpe, Christina. 2016. *In the Wake: On Blackness and Being*. Durham: Duke University Press.
Spångberg, Mårten. 2016. "Natten." https://mdtsthlm.se/archive/2236/.
States, Bert O. 1985. *Great Reckonings in Little Rooms: On the Phenomenology of Theater*. Berkeley: University of California Press.
Tatsuhiko, Shibusawa. 2000. "Hijikata Tatsumi: Plucking off the Darkness of the Flesh." *TDR/The Drama Review* 44 (1): 49–55. https://doi.org/10.1162/10542040051058852.
Thacker, Eugene. 2015. *Starry Speculative Corpse: Horror of Philosophy*. Winchester: Zero Books.
Tuwhare, Hone. 1993. *Deep River Talk: Collected Poems*. Auckland: Godwit Press.
Welton, Martin. 2013. "The Possibility of Darkness: Blackout and Shadow in Chris Goode's *Who You Are*." *Theatre Research International* 38 (1): 4–19. https://doi.org/10.1017/S0307883312000958.

INDEX

Note: *Italic* page numbers refer to figures and page numbers followed by "n" denote endnotes.

Abhinavagupta: discourse on presence 189–190; theory of recognition 190
Abramović, Marina 109, 112; transgressing limits 325
absence 23, 25, 26, 92, 103, 111, 114, 170, 182, 183, 187, 188, 189, 190, 257, 281, 305, 327, 401, 442
absence *(abhava)*: absolute absence *(atyanta-abhava)* 188; mutual absence *(anyonyabhava)* 188; "not static but dynamic" 189; pre-absence *(prag-abhava)* 188; relational absence *(samsargabhava)* 188
academia 6, 209, 273, 295, 320, 419, 421
accumulation 58, 59n1; settler colonial logics of capitalist 53, 55–58
act: of care 45; of *dhikr* 45; doing of some kind 195; equalizing 3; of fasting 45; of perception 185, 186; 'philosophic act' 196; of prayer 45; of seeing 185; of self-portraiture 318, 320n3; of "self sensing" 113; of whirling 45
acting (theatrical) 319, 392
acting intuition 69–75
actor: *An Actor's Work on a Role* 169; *An Actor's Work on Himself* 169; body as 'optical mechanism' 183; craft from the stage 168–171; demanding professional recognition of 171–172; -led performance practice 187
Adorno, Theodor 66, 97
aesthetics: art and philosophy, cross-disciplinary strategies 390; arts-based philosophy 387–388; cross-disciplinary strategies 390–391; of invisible (*see* invisible); *ontologically bi* 391; perception 380; Plato *versus* Platonism 389–390; promise of artist-philosophers 389; time zone 388–389

affect: media/mediality, philosophy of 109–110; and thinking 113–114; transfer of energy and 159
Africa 42, 144, 145, 274, 302, 307n1, 307n3, 403
African American 155, 274, 277, 299, 301, 302, 304, 430
Africanist choreography: Alvin Ailey, African American choreographer 301; *Black Panther* 306; cultural citizenship and performance philosophy 299–300; Diane McIntrye, choreographer 301; double consciousness 301, 302; generating discourse for *I:Object* (2018) 303–307; and philosophies of continuity 301–302; social dance forms 302; Thomas 'Talawa' Prestø 302–303
Afrofuturism 301
Agathon: *Haptesthai* 26; wisdom 26
agency 215, 249, 268, 302, 303, 314, 380, 381, 441, 442
agôn 23, 27
Agra, Lucio 92
Ailey, Alvin: *Revelations* 306
Alcibiades 23, 24
Alembert: *Encyclopedia* 169
Alexander Technique 74
Ali, Mohammed 336
alignment 61, 264, 265, 266, 347, 348, 349, 429, 444
Al-Jabri 144
Al-Jahiz 16n10
Allen, Evan 382
Alter, Joseph 266
Analayo, B. 35
analytic philosophy 85, 318, 328

447

Index

Ancient Greece: 'ancient quarrel between philosophy and (dramatic) poetry' 21; Socrates' performative philosophizing 21; Socratic/Platonic legacy of philosophical performativity 21; 'transgressions'with Oedipus 21

And Beyond Institute for Future Research (ABIFR): *The Claudia Jones Space Station* ("CJSS") 276; dearth of Black women 276; HeLa cells 277, 279n5; Korabl-Sputnik 2 satellite 277; reimagining the origins of space travel 277; space stations 277

Anderson, Laurie: 'Concert for Dogs' 134

de Andrade, Oswald: *The Anthropophagic Manifest* 92; cannibalism 93

angel of history *(Angelus Novus)* 28

Anglo-American Philosophy: dance studies 80; definition of 'art' 77; linguistic turn 77; musical works and performances 78; performance as philosophical medium 80–82; performance thinking 82–84; performing arts 79–80; theorising performance 77–80; value(s) of philosophy of performance 84–85; Western classical music 78–79

Anglo-European philosophy 150, 177

animals/animality 127–138, 322

anthropocentrism 14, 133, 257

anthropophagy 92; Brazilian identity 93; cannibals and 93; 'epistemology of the South' 94; performance philosophy 93

anti-blackness 56

anti-theatrical 6, 9, 179

aphorism 178, 184, 254, 256, 391

application 6, 10, 11, 13, 14, 16, 50, 79, 85, 129, 131, 135, 160, 222, 264, 329, 365, 385, 419

Aquinas 178

Arcades Project 28

Arendt, Hannah: *The Human Condition* 407; notion of freedom 407; tragedy of being poor 407

Ariel (Rodo) 55

Aristodemus 22

Aristophanes: *Clouds* 22; speech on Eros 23

Aristotle 42, 112, 114, 196; *katharsis* of emotions 382; memorable investigation in *De Anima* 283; *Metaphysics* 22; in *Nicomachean Ethics* 338; Olympic Games 336; *Poetics* 21; Principle of Noncontradiction 22; unity of action, time and space 176

art: autonomy of thought 166; concept of 166; definition of 77–78; interdisciplinary practices 129; performs aesthetics 387–388; reality 166; truth in 166

Artaud, Antonin 63, 65, 66; 'ancient cultures' 91; *The Conquest of Mexico* 90; idea of a *Bodenlos*/groundless experience 91; "No More Masterpieces" 67; *The Peyote Dance* 90; theater, "the physical knowledge of images" 65; theatrical fantasy 90; travel to Mexico 90–91; "The true theatre" 65; violence 323

artist-philosophers 61, 388–391, 394, 415, 419

artist-researchers 11, 81, 135, 419

artistic practice 78, 103, 117, 121, 253, 254, 289, 301, 303, 385, 390, 391

artists 6, 11, 88, 94, 111, 112, 119, 120, 122, 123, 128, 130, 132, 162, 166, 170, 171, 172, 265, 317–320, 376, 380, 384, 389, 390, 405, 416; 'artistic research' 129; "elite-artists" 172; intelligence of 380

arts-based philosophy 387–390

Assedic 172, 173n6

Athens: conventions of space and time 23; discursive practices of philosophy and performance 23; knowledge of ignorance 24

atopia, definition 23

attention/attentive/attentiveness 7, 9, 10, 12, 15, 21, 27, 63, 77, 78, 80, 84, 110, 127, 129, 130, 134, 153, 156, 182, 195, 201, 204, 214, 217, 220, 221, 257, 293, 294, 315, 324, 337, 379, 380, 381, 384, 385, 403, 412, 419, 431, 432, 437–442

Atwood, Margaret 59n2, 59n10

audience 5, 9, 27, 46, 49, 50, 58, 62, 66, 80–84, 117, 123, 147, 157, 158, 167, 215, 217, 259, 263, 284, 289, 300, 304, 305, 323, 331, 332, 333, 335, 337, 372, 426, 427, 431, 432, 433, 435, 438, 439, 440

Auslander, Philip 183; temporality of liveness 183

Austin, J. L.: performative theory 285

autonomy 132, 166, 249, 379, 407

Bacon, Francis 218

Badiou, Alain 167

Bakhtin, Michail 152n8

ballet 336, 397, 398, 399, 400, 401, 404n1, 404n2

ballet dancer 397–401

Barad, Karen 72–73; agential-realist ontology 75n4; concept of intra-action and theory of 'agential realism' 75n4

Barba, Eugene 91

Barrio, Artur 92

Barthes, Roland 172

Bataille, G. 323

Bauman, Zygmunt 154, 248

Beckett, Samuel 62, 63, 64; modern drama 66; *Waiting for Godot* 66–67

behaviour–including restored behaviour 7, 10, 102, 135, 184, 214, 220, 249, 267, 272, 291, 293, 294, 336, 337, 367, 383

Being 162n1, 397

being 156; being-in-the-world 112, 304, 388, 390, 417; being-towards-death 97, 102, 141; with darkness 439; exhaustive 6; existence 113; 'fugitive movement' 442; human 144,

150; ignorant 27; kind 3; lover 27; and non-being 391; 'real' 35, 37; sarcastic 27
Bektashi order 48
Bel, Jerome: *Disabled Theater* 83
Benjamin, Walter 5, 21; and aesthetics of thinking 27–29; choreography (the 'bodily writing') of thought 29; Dialectics at a Standstill 28; "Epistemo-Critical Prologue" 29; *flaneur* 24; German Mourning Play 29; N-convolute of *Arcades Project* 28; "On the Concept of History" 32n10; *The Origin of German Tragic Drama* 29; "very crude (*primitivste*) example" 27–28; "What is Epic Theatre?" 27, 30
Bentley, Eric 62
Bergson, Henri 63, 138; *Creative Evolution* 138n1
Best, David 82
Bey, Hakim: notion of 'temporary autonomous zone' 276
Bharucha, Rustom 17n12; analysis of Schechner's ethnocentrism 13
Biet, Christian 167, 168
biography 266–267
Black (identity) 276, 277, 278, 286, 411–412, 442; excellence 411–412; Black Lives Matter movement *382*, 383
blackness 56, 156, 159, 403, 406, 411, 439, 442, 443
blackout: Black bear 439; 'dark attention' 442; Dark swan 439; 'Fear of a Black Planet' 442; minor light 444; thinking with darkness 437–438; *Undisciplining Dance Symposium* 440
Black Performance Theory (BPT) 299, 374
black studies 442
Bloch, Ernst: *The Principle of Hope* 143
Bloom, Harold: "anxiety of influence" 65
Blue Origin 278
Bluford, Guion: first man of African descent in Space 277
body 25, 37, 38, 48, 69–74, 92, 94, 106–107, 109, 112–114, 160, 161, 167, 170, 172, 176, 182–187, 219–220, 254–256, 265–266, 281–284, 290–294, 318, 319, 332, 349, 357, 399–401, 409, 442
bodymind 34–39, 40n3, 72–74, 352
Bohler, Arno 16n9, 16n10, 390
Bohme, Gernot: idea of autonomy 208
Boiler House extension 276
Bonpland, Aime 117, *118*
Bourdieu, Pierre: descriptions of the social determination 176; 'scholastic attitude' of the philosopher 178
Bowie, Andrew 97, 253
bracketing: challenges 199; five-finger version of origin of counting 199; origin of verbal language or origin of counting 198; skills, spiritual accomplishments 198–199

Braidotti, Rosi 350
Brandes, Georg 63, 64
Branson, Richard: Virgin Galactic 278
Brathwaite, Edward Kamau 55, 59n6
Brazil 89, 90, 91, 92, 93, 143, 159, 160, 161, 164n24; way of thinking 92
breath 37, 38, 39, 46, 47, 218, 397, 401, 422, 441
breathing 37, 38, 47, 50, 187, 385, 441, 444
Brecht, Bertolt 21, 63, 168; and appearance of the thinking man 29–31; art of theater 30–31; "A Dialogue about Acting" 66; exilic home in Svendborg 31; *Lehrstucke*, 'Learning Plays' 29; Marxist ideas 65–66; Marxist-materialist approach 29; materiality of the theater 31; *Messingkauf Dialogues* 30, 66; stories of Herr Keuner 29–30; "theatre of the scientific age" 170–171; "thinking-theatre": *Buying Brass* 170, 171
bring forward (*abhinaya*) 188
Brook, Peter 182, 186; *Battlefield* 182, 185–188, 186, 187, 190
Brown, Jason 267
Bruguera, Tania 94
Brustein, Robert 62, 63
Buchner, Georg 391
Buddhism 34, 35, 37, 38, 39, 40, 43
Burckhardt, Titus 44, 45
Butler, Judith 32n9, 57, 135; feminine 401; *Gender Trouble* 400; performative theory of gender 57
Butler, Sarah 370
Byrd, Jodi 55; 'arrivants' 56, 59n6; *Circumdederunt me* 100; notion of cacophony 55

cacophony, decolonial: logics of accumulation 58; *The Tempest* (Shakespeare's) 55–56
Cage, John 326; indeterminacy 327
Caillois, Roger 248
de Campos, Haroldo: friendship with Derrida 93–94; *The rule of anthropophagy: Europe under the sign of devoration* 93
Camus, Albert 64
Canclini, Nestor: "deficient" political and socioeconomic modernisation 91–92
capitalism 53, 56, 59n5, 273, 407, 408, 409, 413n8, 413n9; "self-made man," capitalist 405, 406, 410
care, act of 45
care ethics 251n2
Carlson, Marvin 248
Carr, D.: model of practical reasoning 81
Carson, Anne: *The Beauty of the Husband: a fictional essay in 29 tangos* 284
Cartesian: *cogito* 327
Casper, Monica J. 304
Castellucci, Romeo 175, 177
catharsis 148

Center for Performance Studies (ZPS) 204
Centre for Policy Studies (CPS) 274
Cerrahi order 48
Cesaire, Aime 55
chance 25, 100, 112, 123, 208, 216, 326–329, 340, 401, 415, 418
character 21, 34, 36, 38, 39, 55, 56, 69–71, 121–124, 144, 191n10, 257, 347, 394, 406, 413n11
Charrington, Tiffany 223
Chaudhuri, Una 130
Chekhov, Michael 36, 38, 63
child/child-like 3, 10, 57, 91, 119, 161, 222, 259, 274, 303, 420, 434
Chittick, William 44
choreography: Africanist (*see* Africanist choreography); Aril Flatner, Knut 304; Braza, Belinda 304; 'communicative currency' 300; cultural rights 300; power as representational or 'symbolic form' 299–300; practice of cultural citizenship 299–300; relation between movement and writing 442; thesis 443
choreosophy 351, 352, 355, 359
Christian, Barbara 402
Christianity/Christian theology 89, 140, 148, 150, 313
Chrysistom, Dio: *Tyche* 327
Chua, Daniel 97
cinema 82, 83, 274, 421, 439, 440
circles 123, 127–138, 147, 352, 353, 383n2, 397
In Circles, prelude: attention as interval between two points of compass 127–128; performance, an expanding circle 127; philosophy an expanding circle 127–128; photograph of author *128*
citizen 22, 155, 170, 177, 300
civil rights movement 12
Cixous, Hélène 330; concepts of text and writing 331; conflation of woman and blackness 403; *ecriture feminine* 391; 'openness' characteristic 332; poetic fiction 330
Clark, Lygia 92
Coates, Marcus 135
Cogito 184, 327
cognition 80, 105, 155, 189, 198, 202, 319
cognitive science 202
collaboration 9, 130, 204, 254, 275, 330
collective 3, 122, 123, 147, 150, 161, 267, 289, 359, 438
colonialism/colonial/colonized/colonizer 49, 53, 54, 56, 57, 58, 88, 89, 142, 145, 154, 156–159, 241, 264, 273, 274, 275, 301, 402; *see also* decolonial
"colonial wound" 163n16
Comaneci, Nadia 336
comedy/comic 22, 23

communication 8, 31, 42, 63, 64, 161, 218, 261, 291, 296, 296n2, 376
community 16n9, 99–101, 146, 151, 265, 274, 275–276, 277, 351, 368, 385n1, 405
comparative philosophy 151n1
composition 21, 51n4, 118, 214, 218, 221, 245, 260, 305, 435
concealment 406; *see also* unconcealment
conferences (academic) 7, 9, 209, 250, 326, 371
Confucius: cosmotechnics 348–349; *Ganying* 348; man–heaven alignment 347–348; 'mind' and 'body,' reference to 349; *nei–wai* divide 350; order of immanence 347; Qi and Dao 348–349; relationality between beings 347; ritual and self-cultivation 348; transcultural thinking 349; *yin-yang* cosmology 349; Yung Sik Kim 348
consciousness 43, 70, 84, 100, 102, 138, 198, 199, 202, 247, 248, 249, 258, 262, 294, 301, 302, 327, 351; *see also* self-consciousness
Corbin, Henry 315
corporeality 71, 81, 156, 307
cosmos/cosmology/cosmological 24, 141, 305, 348, 349, 355, 360
creativity/creative 1, 4, 11, 12, 15, 38, 39, 44, 69–71, 81, 121, 128, 159, 166, 189, 196, 209, 215, 246, 251, 265, 274, 275, 290, 303, 336, 347, 349, 384, 392, 394, 423, 429
criticism/critic (art) 12, 50, 63, 77, 94, 235, 257, 285, 302, 304, 317, 330, 334, 372, 376
Critical Art Ensemble: experimental setting and testimony 123; performativity of knowledge 124; *Target Deception* 122, 122–123
Croce, Benedetto 63
cross-disciplinary 390–391; *see also* disciplines
'Cuba until Fidel' (Retamar) 55
Cull O Maoilearca, Laura 16n10, 53, 254, 300, 314; *The Sea, Lies Open* 254
culural citizenship 307n3
Currie, Gregory 79
Cvejić, Bojana 82
Cyropaedia 142
Cyrus: expeditions *(Anabasis)* 142

Daddario, Will 1, 151
Daly, Anne: dance criticism 285
dance 129; as applied ethics 381–383; as Aristotelian tragedy 382; artist 384; black dancers 300; company NDam Se Na 384–385; 'cultural memory' 301; as embodied ethics 379–380; ethical decision-making 379, 381; as ethical engagement and connection with others 383–385; 'folk dance' 303, 304; Gottschild, Brenda Dixon 304; 'higher pleasures' 382; and horror 440, 441; *katharsis* of emotions 382; *Revelations* 301; socially engaged dance and community dance 385n1;

space 384; theatrical 300; 'urban dance' 303, 304; Uzor, Tia Monique 307
'dancing,' notion of: bodily movements 380; human activity of moving aesthetically 380; metaphorical component of 380
Danto, Arthur 79
dark movement 441
Davidson 77
Davies, David: 'pragmatic constraint' 79
da Vinci, Leonardo 196
Davy 259
Day, Iyko: 'aliens' 56
death 23, 43, 54, 56, 59n7, 95n2, 102, 106, 206, 207, 259, 416
deciphering 153, 154, 155, 300, 331, 332
decolonial: decolonizing performance philosophies 12, 53–59; geopolitics of space and censorship 159–162; Sankofa Danzafro's *Fecha Límite* 155–159; significance of Sylvia Wynter 153–155
deconstruction 93, 94, 185, 330, 365
Defense of Poesy (Sidney) 62
DeFrantz, Thomas F. 13, 16n11, 299
Deleuze, Gilles 16n10, 53, 388, 429; 'difference tone,' or a 'Tartini tone' 218; *The Logic of Sensation* 218; Paul Klee's description of painting 218; possibility of repetition 280; *Rhizome* 92; 'theft and gift' 281
Delfina Foundation 275
Delphic Oracle, prophesy of 22
del Val, Jaime: use of nudity 325
'democracy,' idea of 4, 147, 249, 314
Derrida, Jacques 16n10, 100, 190, 211, 281; deconstruction 93; Derridian sense 182; experience of art as taste 190; friendship with de Campos 93–94; *Of Grammatology* 114; notion of presence 191n2; notion of 'trace' 184–185, 191; theory of the iterability 398, 400
Descartes, Rene 319
desire 4, 25, 49, 100, 120, 155, 167, 319, 332, 429
Despret, Vinciane 136
Devine, Megan 269
Dewey, John 380; consequentialist theory of ethics 382–383
dhikr, act of 45
dialectics 15, 23, 25, 28, 29, 55, 209
dialogue(s): complexity of a musical score 141; East–West dialogue 144; education 144; effects of colonialism 145; fact of 'being human' 144; idea of 'organic/organicity' 147; inter-philosophical dialogue 12, 140–151; mythos – logos – dialogue 140–143; 'philosophers,' communitarian role of 143; philosophy of performance 145–150; political and economic hegemony 143; 'professional philosophers,' role of 146; 'universal core problems' 143, 144; world philosophies 143–145

Diamond, Elin 285
Diderot, Denis 168; *Conversations on the Natural Son* 169; empirical approach to theatre 168; *Encyclopedia* 169; in-situ-based thinking 169; *Letter on the Deaf and Dumb* 169; *Paradox of the Actor* 169
difference: cultural 13, 313; identity and 13; philosophical 90; power and truth 180; reason and intellect 176; repetition of 7; sexual 349–350, 401–402; social 13; tone 218
Dion, Mark 119–120; excavation performance 121; *Raiding Neptune's Vault: A Voyage to the Bottom of the Canals and Lagoon of Venice* 120
disagreement 3, 183, 215, 248, 318
disappearance 182, 183, 184, 185, 190, 191, 348
disciplines 1, 2, 4, 6, 13, 14, 16n10, 99, 101, 128, 131, 153, 170, 174, 211, 264, 269, 277, 285, 286, 288, 289, 327, 376, 391, 416, 429, 431; *see also* interdisciplinary
diversity 13, 79, 89, 118, 267, 289, 404n1
Dixon Gottschild, Brenda 304
Dixon, Martin Parker 99–100; inferentialism 101; Quodlibet 106
Dong Zhongshu 349
drama 21, 24, 25, 61–67, 67n1, 67n2, 175, 180, 181n5, 398
dramatist 23, 26, 63, 64, 66, 67
dramaturgy/dramaturg 6, 25, 30, 63, 204, 207, 208, 250, 289, 370, 425, 429, 435
dualism/duality/dualities 42, 43, 69, 93, 349, 355, 399
Duchamp, Marcel 339
duet: agreement 214; collaborative 214; flattened hierarchies 215, 221; lack of access to high volume of chaos 220; performance 213; between speaker and words 213
duos 214; points of focus 220
Dussel, Enrique 12, 140, 143
Dyson, Frances 283

Eckhart, Meister 313; notion of the God 149
ecology 222, 269
economy 172, 268, 325n3, 408, 409, 410; economics 407; self-expanding economies 413n9
écriture féminine 391, 399, 401–403
education 10, 26, 98, 144, 157, 204, 205, 207, 211, 351
ego 142, 201, 291, 294, 319
Einstein 326
Ekuanul Safa 42
elimination 53, 56, 58
Elo, Mika 283, 286
embodiment 39, 46, 75n3, 81, 82, 100, 185, 290, 293, 295, 352, 419
embodying thinking 290–295
Emlyn-Jones, Chris 27

emotion 191n10, 305, 307, 335, 352
emptiness *(Sunyata)* 189
Ender, Eduard 117
entropy 103, 106
ephemerality 182–185, 187, 276, 372; in Performance Studies 183
epistemology 94, 118, 157, 159, 175, 176, 295
equality/equity/equalizing 3, 13, 127–138, 159, 206, 211, 215, 249, 250, 409, 425, 436
Erard, Kit: double escapement mechanism 281
Eros, praise of 22
erotic 286, 322, 323–324
escapism 246
Esslin, Martin 64
Estragon 66
ethics, theories of: care ethics 251n2; consequentialist theories 381; embodied ethics 81, 379–385; ethical 8, 10, 110, 134, 141, 143, 144, 145, 155, 211, 352, 379, 380, 381, 382, 383–385, 405; ethos 246, 250–251, 417, 419, 421; Kantian deontological theories 381; virtue ethics theories 381–382
Eurocentrism: academic Philosophy 12; perspective 13
everyday: "free act" 199; and language 40; life 101, 119, 168, 201, 228, 288, 316, 378, 392, 438; life and emotional intimacy 168; reality 331–332; type/token distinction 85n1; and university discourse 100; worldly experience 200
Every house has a door 2008 to 2018: Comments for Remake Symposium 426; email exchange (Will) 431–432; Exhaust the Possible 429, 431, *431*; *Let us think of these things always. Let us speak of them never* 426–427, 432–434; Matthew's response to Will 435–436; *MERCUA* 434; *Scarecrow* 427–428; *Testimonium* 425–426; *They're Mending the Great Forest Highway* 436; *Three Matadores* 429–431, 434–435
excess 182, 189–191, 409
exclusion 53, 56, 58
exercise 36, 37, 38, 39, 40n3, 135, 249, 300, 419
exhaustion 305
Existence, Three Characteristics of 35, 36; anattā (non-self), anicca (impermanence), and dukkha (suffering) 35
expertise 2, 7, 80, 204

failure 50, 90, 103, 135, 204, 206, 337, 367, 398, 400
Fang, Dongmei 349
Fanon, Frantz 154
fasting, act of 45
Fecha Límite, Sankofa Danzafro: basic rights 155; being, knowledge, and power 156; colonial wound and healing process 158; conjunction of space and time 159; Palacios with 157–158, *158*; pedagogical-performative-philosophical project 158–159; performance of 158; racism and classism 156; traditional celebratory dances and Afro-contemporary technique 157; transfer of energy and affect 159
Federici, Silvia 409
Feld, Alina 149
feminine 43, 148–149, 330, 391, 394, 399, 401–403
feminism 12, 154, 402
Fevered Sleep 130, 133–137, *133*
fiction 79, 131, 205, 256, 276, 277, 282, 330, 389, 412
film 11, 82–83, 94, 98, 129, 205
finitude 207, 208
Fink, Eugen 196
Fisher, Tony 129
Flusser, Vilém: *Bodenlos* 90; influence of existentialism and phenomenology 89–90; *Phenomenology of the Brazilian* 90; *Post-History* 89
Foucault, Michel 154, 187–188, 326; *governmentality* 179; notion of power 441; philosopher's discourse on madness 178
Frank, A. O. 257
freedom/free will 25, 29, 39, 43, 55, 57, 74, 90, 145, 161, 176, 189, 245, 329, 369, 401, 407, 409, 417, 419
Frege 77
Freire, Paulo: concept of 'praxis' 301
Freud 93, 113
Friedlaender, Salomo 415–423
Friend, John: Anusara Yoga system 265
Fuchs, Elinor 66, 259
fungibility 53, 56–57, 58, 59n1
future/futurity 16n10, 28, 31, 58, 61, 66, 89, 140, 144, 150, 156, 157, 159, 162, 170, 248, 276, 277, 278, 305, 326, 327, 330, 365, 387, 388, 392, 394, 397

Galindo, Regina 94
Gautama 182, 188
gaze 24, 43–44, 83, 184, 187, 190, 262–269
Geerken, Hartmut 416–423
gender 53, 57, 81, 94, 98, 347, 349, 400–401
genre 23, 98, 155, 284, 302, 406
gentrification 273–274, 405–406
geophilosophy 6, 53
George, David 36
Gerstmyer, John S.: play performance or play as performance 245
Gestalt Psychology 114
gesture/gestural/gestic 4, 6, 12, 13, 24, 28, 67, 85, 102, 110, 112, 118, 130, 131, 160, 162, 167, 170, 171, 183, 187, 190, 191n7, 248, 254, 261, 282, 284, 285, 305, 323, 324, 331–334, 399, 400, 402, 430, 431, 434, 440

Index

Gide, Andre 418
Gill, Denise 46
globalization: as fable 160, 162; *Mona Lisa* 162; as perversity 160, 161, 162; as possibility 160, 162
global south 12, 16n10, 144, 159, 160
Globe, Boston 382
gnosis: experience 314, 316
God 43, 45, 48, 140, 142, 148, 151, 179, 191n7, 264, 275, 277, 314, 324, 326, 327, 368
Gonzalez, Anita 299
Goodman, Nelson 78, 79, 119; *Languages of Art* 78; performing arts 79; properties of musical notation 78
Gordon, Lewis R. 304
Gosse, Edmund 64
Gouhier, Henri 167
Gracyk, Theodore 80
Gramsci, A. 140, 146, 147, 150; 'caste of the intellectuals' 151n6; 'democratic historian' and 'democratic philosopher' 147; 'philosophy of praxis' 147; religion and religious movements 147–148
Granzer, Susanne 16n9, 390
Greekphilosophy 142, 143
grief 57–58, 307, 314
Grodin, Sophie 215, *216*, 220, *221*
Grondahl, Laura 285
Groos, Karl 246
Grosz, Elizabeth 403
Grotowski, Jerzy 91
groundlessness 442
Guattari, Felix 53; *Rhizome* 92
Guenon, Rene 43

habit 4, 5, 25, 64, 74, 138, 290, 421
Hadot, Pierre 146
Hadwiger, Victor 418
hagiography 154, 267–269
Hag-seed (Atwood) 59n2
Hamera, Judith 300
handjob: "invisible handjob of the market" 408–409; slave is not a worker 409–410
Han Dynasty 349
hannifya 42
Haptesthai (to touch) 5–6
Haraway, Donna 377
Harney, Stefano 286
Hartman, Saidiya 56, 59n1
Harvey, Elizabeth 284
Hausmann, Raoul 418
Heidegger, Martin 145, 196; discourse of Being 397
Heinich, Nathalie 171; vocational regime 172
heliocentre 415–423
heritage 42, 88, 93, 248, 299, 304–307, 385
hermeneutics 145, 147, 290

heterotopia 182, 187
hidden writing 443
hierarchy 16n10, 43, 55, 65, 114, 120, 141, 148, 215, 221, 259
Hildyard, Daisy: *The Second Body* 222
hip-hop 405
history 28, 37, 46, 55, 56, 57, 64, 65, 69, 70, 72, 89, 90, 91, 92, 94, 140, 142–149, 159, 167, 183, 197, 198, 202, 205, 214, 215, 221, 262, 263, 267, 272, 277, 295, 303, 317, 319, 320, 336, 347, 380, 389, 391, 394, 421, 427
Holkenbrink, Jorg: Homi Bhabha's concept of hybridity 205; "knowledge cultures and vulnerability" 210; lived experience and knowledge 209; modern DJs 208; moments of silence and inaction 208; "the networked generation" 205; productivity of exposing 207; *Puer Robustus* 204; secret education 207; Theater of Assemblage/*Theater der Versammlung* 207–208
Hollinghaus, Wade 1
Houston, Sara: dance as ethical engagement and connection with others 379, 383–385
Huizinga, Johan 248, 251n1; *Homo Ludens* 246–247
human or Homo sapiens (the 'wise man')/humanism/humanity 2, 54, 99, 130, 144, 145, 150, 154, 155, 159, 161, 179, 207, 289, 296n2, 327, 384, 403, 408, 421
humour 84, 135, 188, 419, 422
Husserl, Edmund 196, 200, 201, 290; '*animate organism*' 201; genetic mode of inquiry 197; genetic phenomenology 197; katastematic methods 197; phenomenological-kinetic method 197–198, 201; phenomenological methodology 196–197; sedimentations and horizons 202; 'spiritual accomplishments' 198; static phenomenology 197, 202n1
Hussle, Nipsey: extra-musical vision 405
hybridity/hybrid 4, 5, 13, 92, 93, 94, 102, 138n1, 159, 206, 301, 391, 421

Ibsen, Henrik 62, 63, 64, 65; *Brand* 62
idealism 324
identity 12, 13, 14, 22, 37, 50, 64, 78, 83, 90, 93, 94, 95, 98, 104, 114, 136, 141, 154, 156, 157, 179, 180, 197, 262, 266, 268, 269, 281, 299, 302, 385, 400, 401, 403, 416, 442
illusion 11, 29, 34, 35, 36, 37, 38, 40, 84, 171, 187, 246, 268, 407, 409, 412, 435, 440
image 7, 8, 23, 25, 28, 29, 31, 38, 43, 65, 83, 109, 113, 145, 149, 150, 153, 154, 161, 179, 189, 200, 208, 211, 218, 263, 268, 278, 313, 317, 319, 327, 333, 367, 380, 381, 389, 391, 393, 408
imagination 36, 38, 39, 50, 73, 114, 118, 141, 149, 182, 187, 189, 190, 191n7, 204, 205, 253, 256, 276, 305, 316, 333, 380, 430, 439

immanence: Confucius order of 347; performance of 268; philosophies of 16n9

immediacy 294

impossible 2, 7, 73, 84, 92, 138, 161, 185, 191n7, 218, 319, 337, 389, 392, 411, 417

improvisation/improvise 7, 80, 133, 197, 284, 327, 421

in-between: academic practice 288; editions of the festival 289; embodying thinking 290–295; exploration and practice 296; knowledge and tradition 289; mind and nature, relationship between 290; movement of self-distancing 295; *Performative Philosophie* (German-speaking world) 288; philosophical thinking 295; philosophy and art 289; theoretical approach 296; theoretical reflection on Performative Philosophy 290; thinking in public 290–295; Western academic philosophy 288

indeterminacy 97, 107, 136, 327, 328, 342, 403

Indian performance theory 182; hand gestures *(Mudra)* 187, 190; notion of "presence" in *Natyasastra (see Natyasastra)*; ontological status 182; performer and spectator, interaction between 187

indifference, creative: *avant la lettre* 415; concept of 'neutral' 415; grappling with life 417; "Null Sonne, No Point" 416; personal and general 417; philosophy of creative indifference 415–416; Sun Ra's 'Heliocentric Worlds' 416; 'The Magic I' (Sun Ra) 416

Indigo (Warner) 57–58

Ingold, Tim 10, 349; *The Temporality of Landscape* 253–254

Institute for Economic Affairs (IEA) 274

Institute for Human Activities (IHA): 'artistic critique' 274; Congolese plantation workers' 274; critiques of gentrification 274, 279n2; Renzo Martens 273, 275; 'white saviour' cliche 274

intercultural/interculturality/interculturalism 13, 49, 50, 51n9, 109, 115, 145, 305

interdisciplinary 1, 2, 4–5, 6, 11, 129, 154, 204, 210

interpretation 22, 23, 47, 53, 71, 72, 74, 79, 84, 112, 131, 196, 262, 324, 376, 394, 401

interspecies 130

intuition, acting: 'action' 69–70; Belgrano, Elisabeth L. 72–75; concept of Nothingness 72, 75; definition 69, 70; 'external' actions 70; intuition and action 70; self-negation 72, 74; theories on bodily expression 74; 'thing' and 'I,' relation between 70–71; Uehara, Mayuko 69–72; vocal performance philosophy 73

invisible: act of perception 185, 186; act of seeing 185; archive and performance, relationship between 182; im-mediate and mediate 183–185; negative entities *(abhavapathartha)* 188; notion of performance as disappearance 184; ontology of (the) invisible 188; performance as excess 189–191; Peter Brook's *Battlefield*, a case study 185–188; positive entities *(bhava padartha)* 188; visible and invisible, relationship between 183

I:Object: Black Lives Matter and the #me-too movement 303; choreography of 304–307; heritage, polycentricism and 'revitalizing the exhausted body' 304–307; institutional racism 306; performance style of 305; polycentricism 305; Tabanka Dance Ensemble 303; urban' or 'folk' dance 303–304; Western dance theatre 304–305

Ionesco, Eugene: *Exit the King* 84

Irigaray, L.: *The Forgetting of Air* 397; *Marine Lover* 401; mode of feminine reading 401; practice of critical mimesis 401

Islands (Brathwaite) 55

iterability 98, 398, 400

Jackson, Christopher 336

Jackson, Roy: *al-insān al-kāmil*, Perfect Man 315

Jackson, Sarah 284

Jay-Z 405–406

jazz 80, 301, 302, 304, 307n7, 416, 422

Jelinek, Elfriede 177

Johnson, Mark 380–381

Jones, Amelia: self-imaging in contemporary art 319

Jullien, Francois 115

Kafka: *Before the Law* 400

Kania, Andrew: philosophical model of jazz performance 80

Kant, Immanuel 440; *Critique of Pure Reason* 317, 318; "empirical representation" 319; human incapacity 176; 'immortality of the soul' 143; notion of transcendental aesthetic 320; philosophical system 317; philosophy of aesthetics 319

Katz, Helena 160

Kearney, Richard 140, 145; *Anatheism: Returning to God After God* 148–149; 'applied hermeneutics' 145; *Carnal Hermeneutics* 148; 'conflict zones' 146; *Guestbook Project* 146; *Le Monde* 146; 'possible God' 149; 'problem of God' 148; *Reimagining the Sacred* 148; 'thinking in action' 150

Kennick, William 77

Kerr, Alfred 418

Keuner, Herr: 'thinking man' 30

Khan, H. I. 45

Index

Kierkegaard, Soren 63, 64; *The Crisis and a Crisis in the Life of an Actress* 168; *Repetition* 168
Kittler, Friedrich 110; *Grammophon, Film and Typewriter* 110
Klee, Paul 388
Kleist, Heinrich von 392
Klossowski, Pierre 328
knowledge 156; equality of genres of 249–250; of ignorance 24; ignorance *vs.* 26; and intelligences of the heart 45; of jurisprudence (*fiqh*) 314; lived experience and 209; modes of 11–12; performativity of 124; radical equality of 129–130; rewritten 154; and tradition 289; *see also* wisdom
Knowles, Ric: Theatre & Interculturalism 51n9
Kripal, Jeffrey 267
Kripke 77
Kula system 189
Kulik, Oleg 325; offending spectator and jolting sensibility 325
Kurtz, Steve 123
Kvalien, Margrete 306

Laban, Rudolf: Ascona, development of artistic commune 351; body movement 355, 357; choreutics 360, 360n6; circles in dimensional planes *353*; context of 'work' or 'art' 355; directing a movement choir at Summer Course at Moreton Hall *359*; early witnessing of Sufi dervish dances 351; Eukinetics 352, 360n5; figure in icosahedron *354*; figure in tetrahedron *355*; figures within spiralling lines *357*; 'founding Father' of European modern dance 351; geometrical forms and visual images 352–353; impressions of figures *358*; Movement Analysis 360n3; notion of 'movement-thinking' 351–352, 357, 359; notion of the One 357; performs philosophy 360; references to choreosophy 351, 352; *Reigen,* 'round dance' 359; three figures *356*; two figures *356, 358*
Lacoue-Labarthe, Philippe 16n10, 97
Ladder of Love 24–26, 28, 32n7
Laertius, Diogenes 180; aggressive/violent 323; ascetic idealism 324; Cynic acts 322–325, 325n4; ecstatic 322–323; erotic 323–324; "immoralism" 324; *Lives of Eminent Philosophers.* 322; metaphoric 324; transgressive 323
Lagaay, Alice 124, 172, 212; notion of creative indifference 419, 420
Lakoff, George 380–381
landscape: practice of making sense of landscape 253; review of landscape scholarship, Wylie's 253; *The Sea, Lies Open* 254–256; site-specific practices 253; thinking with landscape through performance 261; *Time Passes* 257–259; *Town Hall Meeting of the Air* 259–260
language 3, 4 ,5, 7, 40, 42, 46, 47, 55, 65, 77, 83, 89, 92, 94, 110, 113, 147, 154, 155, 199, 214, 215, 253, 278, 294, 296, 330, 333, 352, 393
Laruelle, Francois 16n10, 129; art, 'thought circularly' 132; critical one and constructive one 131–132; equality of thought, notion of 129, 130, 131; experimental practice 131; non-standard philosophy (or non-philosophy) 129, 130, 131, 132–133, 314; radical equality of knowledge 129–130; roles of artist and theorist or philosopher 132
Latin America: modernity (and democracy) 91; National Projects 92; performance art 94; performance philosophy 88, 95; *Performing from within* 88; philosophy of liberation 144; structural violence 92; *Thinking from outside* 88; 'Thy name is woman' 91–95; Utopia named America 88–91
Law of Identity 22
Lazarus, M. 246
learning: community 99–101; in contemporary university 99; mode of self-presentation or "(in)determination" 99; priorities of the contemporary university 99; STEM disciplines 99; university discourse 100
Legesse, Asmarom 154
Lehmann, Hans-Thies 174, 259
Leibniz: *monads* 176
Lepecki, Andre 439
Leroi-Gourhan, Andre 114; *Gesture and Speech* 114
Le Roy, Xavier 159
Levinas, Emmanuel 97, 290, 441
Levinson, Jerrold 79
Levi-Strauss, C. 143; *Tristes Tropiques* 91
Lilienthal, Matthias: *Münchner Kammerspiele* 180
Lings, Martin 43
listening 10, 48, 73, 74, 102, 103, 176, 214, 256, 283, 284, 343, 385, 391, 425
literature 16, 78, 85, 92, 205, 284, 399, 401, 419, 420, 441
liveness 183
Livingston, Paisley 82
Loach, Ken: *I, Daniel Blake* 206
Lobman, Carrie 245
Locke: *camera obscura* 176
logos: conceptual categorisation of 143; logocentrism 93; rationality of 142; strong 140, 141–142; violence of 141; as 'Word of God' 142
Lorde, Audre 286
loss 2, 90, 105, 185, 215, 217, 265, 314, 367, 384
love 7, 24, 35, 43, 48, 143, 148, 180, 314, 316, 371, 391, 393; *see also* affect
Loyola, Ignatius 313

ludic: character of superabundance and excitement 249; equality of genres of knowledge 249–250; performance philosophy 245; transformation of the thinking subject 249
Lying Fallow 223–244

McConachie, Bruce 248; evolutionary-diachronic approach 248; performance play 245
MacGregor, Kino 267–268
McKenzie, Jon 8, 16n6, 101; "global performance stratum" 101; modes of evaluation 101–102; modes of performance 101; paradigm-shifting 106; *Perform or Else* 102
McKittrick, Katharine 153; *Beyond Human As Praxis* 153
MacLean, Malcom 245
Mahabharatha 186
makam: banning of *tarikats* 46; feeling of 'burntness' 47; influence of Qu'ranic recitation 47; *Melancholic Modalities* 46; Mevlevi order 46; as 'monophonic' 47; tuning remains closer to nature 46; Turkish makam features, levels 47; Western orchestral tradition 51n8
Malalasekera, G.P. 35
Mallarmé, Stephane 327; 'dice throw' 327; *A Dice Throw* poem 327
Malraux, Andre 418
Mann, Heinrich 418
Marber, Patrick: adaptation of Eugene Ionesco's *Exit the King* 84
Marco Pallis 43
Marriott, David: "On Decadence: Bling Bling" 406
Martens, Renzo 273, 275
Marthaler, Christoph 177
Marxism 12, 171; doctrine, specificities of 171
Marx, Karl 63, 406, 407; *Theses On Feuerbach* 63
masculine 148, 265, 319, 402
mask 3, 179, 180, 332, 333, 400
materialism 110
materiality 31, 100, 110, 112, 184, 185, 186, 291, 314, 349, 411
matter 9, 10, 11, 45, 47, 63, 67, 73, 78, 79, 98, 100, 101, 102, 103, 106, 109, 112, 113, 134, 135, 146, 166, 176, 188, 254, 256, 315, 349, 368, 399, 412, 413n8
McCabe, MM 9
media/mediality, philosophy of: affect 109–110; *archi-writing* 114; body as a medium 109, 112–113; creation 109, 111; development of homo sapiens 114; in-betweenness of media 109; materialities of communication 110; 'media landscape' 115; *meta* (in-between) and *dia* (poiesis or bringing forth) 109; notion of the object 115; in objectified world 109, 113–115; and performativity 110; shadow play 111; in Western tradition 112
medium 7, 8, 9, 70, 80–82, 104, 105, 109, 110, 112–113, 114, 399, 439
Meillassoux, Quentin 327
memory 36, 37, 43, 57, 74, 156, 184, 188, 204, 208, 218, 267, 269, 275, 277, 331, 393, 441
Mendieta, Ana 94; *Silueta Series* 94
mercantilism 408
Merleau-Ponty, Maurice 16n10, 23, 200, 201, 290; Gestalt Psychology 114
Mersch, Dieter 109
mesostics 339–346
metaphor 25, 40, 47, 58, 93, 94, 106, 121, 134, 141, 145, 150, 154, 175, 176, 179, 187, 188, 190, 205, 316, 318, 331, 379–381, 403, 428
metaphysics 141, 150
method 6, 14, 57, 72, 121, 129, 138, 138n1, 169, 170, 177, 197, 199, 202, 204, 206, 209, 210, 211, 269, 285–286, 296, 307n3, 376, 392
methodology 14, 98–99, 195–202, 288–296, 316
Mevlevi Whirling 48, 51n4
Meyerhold, Vsevolod 168, 169, 170
Michon, Jean-Louis 43
Mignolo, Walter 144, 145, 163n15; *The Idea of Latin America* 89
Mill, John Stuart 382
Miller, Judith G. 332
Milloss, Aurell: choreosophy, definition of 352
mimesis 248, 263, 269, 401, 403
mind 12, 24, 28, 34, 37, 39, 40n3, 44, 50, 71, 74, 80, 83, 112, 138n1, 142, 146, 150, 174, 175, 176, 216, 217, 254, 283, 290, 293, 322, 336, 349, 393, 406, 431
mindfulness 34, 35, 36, 37, 38, 241
Mnouchkine, Ariane: concepts of text and writing 331; founders of Theatre du Soleil 330; 'metaphor' 331; production concept 331, 333; rejects psychological realism or psychological theatre 331–332; 'theatrical theatre' and 'aesthetic shock' 332; understanding of theatre 331
modern drama: early modernisms 63, 67n2; emergence of 61; European modernist movement 62; playwright as thinker 67; "pre-history of performance philosophy" 61; relationship to philosophy 64; temporalities of 62; theater, and philosophy 62
modernism 49, 63, 67n2, 91, 301
modernity 88–89, 91–92, 178, 304
Moi, Toril 63
Montaigne 178
Montiglio, Silvia 24
Moore, G. E. 77, 257
Moore, Lisa Jean 304
Moten, Fred 286

Motomori, Kimura 71; "formative-expressive-existence" 71, 73, 74–75; "self in itself" 71, 75; theories on bodily expression 74

movement: pulse of *dhikr* 47; sema gathering 47–48, *48,* 49; Tibetan Five Times Rites 47

Muller, Heiner 394

Mullis, Eric 81, 82

Munoz, Beatriz Santiago 94

Museum of Modern Art of São Paulo (MAM) 160

music: centrality of entropy 97; concept of iterability 98; echoing, fading, and dying 102; empirical decline and deterioration of sound 102–103; end(s) of sound(s) 103–106; entropy 103; learning community 99–101; performance philosophy 129; performativity 97, 98; self-absenting 103; Sonic subjectivity 107; sound or musical sound 99; "sound-related phenomena" 102; special body 106–107; special relationship between 97, 106; verbal utterances 98

Musk, Elon: Space X 278

myth: 'production of myths' *(mytho-poiesis)* 143

mythos: defined 140; to logos 140–142

Nadal, Rafael 335; service game 337; *Strokes of Genius* 338

Nancy, Jean-Luc 16n10, 109, 112; act of "self sensing" 113; 'existence,' 'exposure,' 'extension' 113, 115; thinking of bodies 112–113

Naqshabandi order 48

narrative 13, 23, 24, 25, 55, 82, 83, 84, 89, 92, 93, 143, 145, 208, 253, 257, 259, 260, 267, 268, 269, 276, 300, 315, 331, 333, 347, 400, 402

NASA 278; online library 278

Nasr, Seyed Hossein 43

natural body: Anglophone culture 266; media technologies 265–266; pre-modern Indian adepts 266; video content platforms 266; *see also* yoga

nature 2, 4, 11, 14, 34, 36, 45, 46, 66, 70, 77, 78, 79, 80, 81, 82, 83, 94, 106, 114, 117, 118, 120, 123, 141, 143, 166, 175, 182, 183, 186, 189, 195, 197, 198, 200, 202, 21, 254, 263, 276, 290, 305, 323, 343, 347, 348, 351, 352, 357, 359, 387, 394n1, 398, 436

Natyasastra: actor-led performance practice 187; audience-led aesthetic discourse 187; concept of visibility 182; determinants *(vibhava)* 185; emotional responses 185; *Kutiyattam* and *Kathakali* 183; notion of "presence" 182; theory of *rasa* 182, 183, 185, 189, 191n2

Nauha, Tero 16n9

Negarestani, Reza 441

negation 71, 131, 133, 148, 186

neoliberal 163n9, 411, 412

Neoplatonist 357

Nestroy, Johann: *Der Talisman* 168

Nicols, Nichelle 277

Nida-Rumelin, Julian 211

Nietzsche, Friedrich 61, 63, 64, 93, 97, 100, 167, 178, 180, 322, 394; aphorisms 391; association of woman with eternity 400; *Beyond Good and Evil* 388; dance 398; 'eternal recurrence' 329; externalization of cruelty 325n3; famous reversal/inversion of Platonism 390; god is dead 326; Greek dramatic performance 322; landscapes 254, 256; post-Socratic inversion of Platonism 389

Nightingale, Andrea Wilson 26

Nishida Kitarō: 'acting intuition' (*see* intuition, acting); "Kyoto School" of philosophy 69

Nitsch, Hermann: use of animal sacrifice and blood 325

nonhuman 14, 59n9, 110, 130, 133, 388, 439

non-philosophy 26, 53, 129, 130–133, 178

non-self 34, 35, 36, 37, 38, 39, 40, 75

nothingness 72, 75n3, 189, 314, 328, 375, 397

objectivity 122, 123, 168, 291, 425

O'Callaghan, Casey: claim of "sonic realism" 104; position 104; theory of sounds 102

Oedipus: employment of logical reasoning 23; philosophical performances 23; ruler of Thebes 22; 'transgressions'with 21

Oedipus Tyrannus 24

Oiticica, Helio 92

Oliveros, Pauline 283

Ó Maoilearca, John 15, 16n9, 131, 314

onanism 405

O'Neill, Barbara E. 245

O'Neill, Eugene 62, 63, 65

ontocentrism 162n7

ontology/ontological 11, 43, 53, 54–55, 57, 58, 59n2, 75n4, 114, 129, 143, 150, 155, 182, 184, 185, 187, 188, 190, 197, 198, 200, 299, 314, 316, 365, 376, 381, 388, 391, 402, 403

openness 3, 4, 101, 153, 208, 251, 255, 330, 331, 332, 333, 334, 384

open text – open performance: Cixous 330–331; 'intertextual allusions' 333; Mnouchkine 330–332; notion of 'openness' 330; 'plurality of voices' 333; production process 332; Theatre du Soleil productions 330–332; voice to 'the other' 333–334

opera 72, 168

'original Islam,' definition 42–43

Oswald 93

'the other'/otherness/othering 5, 81, 160, 285, 333–334, 398

Our Neighbours 275

pain 157, 160, 282, 286, 305, 307, 315, 402
painting 78, 112, 117, 118, 128, 177, 195, 218, 398, 430
Palacios, Rafael 156, 157
Pan-Africanism 301
paradox 22, 23, 29, 36, 39, 40, 43, 89, 92, 103, 167, 169, 170, 171, 172, 209, 248, 319, 327, 365, 391, 392, 398, 417
participation 29, 134, 158, 218, 372, 384, 407, 411
passive/passivity 9, 10, 92, 147, 161, 200, 208, 278, 409
Passmore, John 77
Paterson, Mary 220, 223
Pauker, Magnolia 129
Paul, Saint 177
Pausanias 25
Pearson, Mike: site-specific practices, definition of 253
pedagogy 7, 29, 144, 156, 158, 206, 276, 278, 385
perception 35, 42, 44, 45, 46, 92, 103, 104, 105, 106, 133, 134, 136, 180, 182, 186, 187, 188, 189, 190, 191, 201, 202, 218, 253, 267, 313, 324, 371, 380, 398, 402
performance art 80, 92, 94, 175, 176
performance philosophy 1; alternative formats 8–10; beyond 'application' 10; beyond – or besides – linearity 8; collaborative authorship 3; companion 3; critical reflection of form 12–13; critical self-reflection 3–4; against "default" systems 10–11; defining 6, 15n1; degree of recognition 1; dramaturgical sensitivity 2; equalizing act 3; expanding canon – decolonizing 12; field 2; Haptesthai (to touch) 5–6; interdisciplinarity 4–5; literature and music 85n1; the live love of wisdom 7–8; methodological self-reflexivity 2; model of practical reasoning 81; modes of knowledge 11–12; multiple overlapping usages 6–7; non-philosophical outside 53; "partaking in the experience of thought" 53; performance thinking 81–82; performer or performance-maker 82; performing and making 80–81; publishers 8; sensitivity to form in relation to content 2; simultaneously 2–3; terminology and translation 5; (un)translatability 5; your companion 13
Performance Studies 1, 4, 13, 91, 92, 94, 102, 128, 147, 182, 183, 211
performance theory 182, 183, 185, 187, 189, 190, 191, 245
performance thinking: actors' identities 83; 'aesthetic dimensions' of film 83; choreographer's choice of material 83–84; 'cinematic thinking' 83; dwindling Ifans 84; 'film' 81–82; kinds of self-conscious 84

performativity: of exploration or research 117–118; of knowledge 124; media/mediality, philosophy of 110; musical performance philosophy 97; simultaneously 2; Socratic/Platonic legacy 21; sounds 104–106
performer 11, 27, 34, 38, 50, 79, 80, 82, 83, 84, 94, 99, 112, 130, 134, 135, 136, 137, 140, 147, 151, 160, 169, 183, 185, 187, 191, 191n7, 207, 208, 211, 213, 219, 220, 263, 269, 284, 285, 305, 322, 327, 331, 332, 369, 372, 380, 426, 427, 430, 432, 433, 439
Phaedo 24
Phelan, Peggy 182
phenomenological methodology: initial procedure of bracketing 198–199; phenomenological reduction 199–202; static and genetic analyses 196–198
phenomenological reduction: body–world relationships 200, 201; free act of suspension 199; 'If-then' relationships 200; motor skills and motor control 202; phenomenological-kinetic method 200; relationship of subject-world 200; 'two-fold articulations' 201
phenomenology 25, 89, 103, 114, 195, 197, 198, 199, 200, 202, 202n3, 254, 257, 291
philosophers 146; 'organic intellectual' 147; professional 146; real 147
philosophical objectivity, myth of 168; imperialism of philosophical meaning 171
'philosophy of praxis' 140, 146, 147
Philosophy on Stage 9
Piekut, Benjamin 284
piano 280, 281, 283, 284, 421
Piper, Adrian: act of self-portraiture 318, 320n3; civil rights and feminist movements 317; *Food for the Spirit* 317, 318, 319, 320, 320n2; Kantian philosophy 317–318; *The Mythic Being* 319, 320; performances-for-the-camera 319; present-day practice 320; *Rationality and the Structure of the Self, Part II* on Hume 318; *Rationality and the Structure of the Self, Part 1: Kant* 318; subjectivity and embodiment 320; *The Village Voice* 319, 320; voice recordings 318
Pirandello, Luigi 63
Pittman, Alex 1
place of freedom *(moksha)* 189
Plato 23, 42, 167, 178, 179, 196; "absolute reals" 368; *Apology* 24, 141; dramatic form of dialogues 391; notion of ascent 24; notion of 'sudden'*(exaiphnes)* 26; philosophical hero's performative behavior 27; vs. Platonism 389–390; Reality Research Center 367; *Symposium* 22, 26
play: "action about actions" 248; conscious doubleness of self 248, 249; ethos, ethics, ethnography (case study) 250–251;

localization 247; ludic performance philosophy 245, 249–250; play performance 248–249; research approaches 246; selected aspects of play 246–248; subjectivity and self-reflexivity 249; understanding of philosophy 248; voluntary activity or occupation 246–247; *see also* ludic
playwright 23, 27, 61–67, 154, 170, 259, 389
The Playwright as Thinker (Bentley) 62
Plessner, Helmuth 290; embodiment and public, concepts of 290, 295; excentric positionality, concept of 292–293; expression, notion of 292
Plotinus 357
poetry/poetic 21, 23, 42, 64, 149, 284, 313, 314, 315, 316, 330, 403, 425, 426, 434
poiesis 93, 109, 387
Polanyi, Michael 114; *The Tacit Dimension* 114
politics 56, 61, 65, 122, 124, 146, 148, 159, 175, 177, 179, 275, 276, 277, 303, 307, 317, 319, 320, 415, 420
Pollock, Della 403
Popper, Karl R.: model of verification 31n2
popular 36, 148, 149, 151n6, 167, 170, 262, 306
post-dramatic 174, 177, 254, 259
postmodern 92, 93, 142, 304
post-structuralism 190
Potter, Stephen: gamesmanship, definition of 337
power 156
'practice as research' (PaR) 129, 326; *see also* artists, artistic research
Prada, Amapola: major art publication 376; *Revolution* 375, *375*
pragmatism 79, 82, 103, 107
praxis 146, 147, 150, 166, 300, 301, 314, 330
prayer, act of 45
presence: *bhava* 188; Abhinavagupta's discourse 189–190
Prestø, Thomas 'Talawa' 299; artistic discourse of dance 302; 'communities of practice' 302; contemporary theatrical dance 304; cultural citizenship of 302–303; *I:Object 303, 306*; Tabanka dance ensemble 302
'professional philosophers,' role of 146
Project R-hythm 254
psychoanalysis 324
psychology 38, 65, 200, 205
psychophysical 38, 40, 185
public thinking 290–295
Puchner, Martin 9

Qadiri order 48
queer 12, 401, 402, 403, 419
Quijano, Anibal 144, 145, 156
Quine 77

race/racism 55, 56, 142, 154, 155, 156, 157, 222, 306, 403, 412
Rahner, Hugo: idea of '*God as play*' 149
Rahula, Walpola 35, 39
Ramlila 184
Rancière, Jacques: description of art's 'ethical-political potential' 305
rasa, theory of 182, 183, 185, 189
rationalism: Greco-Roman emergence of 42
rationality 81, 142, 145, 292, 294
Read, Alan 16n10
realism 257, 331, 332
reason 15, 27, 43, 46, 91, 92, 93, 102, 105, 110, 121, 135, 136, 140, 141, 142, 150, 159, 167, 172, 174, 176, 205, 209, 247, 248, 281, 294, 296, 324, 337, 376, 406, 425, 435, 438, 440
recognition *(pratyabhijna)* 189
Regelin, David 265, 267
'regional' philosophy 150
rehearsal 80, 170, 208, 221, 305, 435
religion 43, 44, 50n1, 146, 147, 148, 149, 151, 161, 268, 314, 419, 421
repetition 191n9
representation 29, 54, 88, 89, 93, 154, 157, 167, 168, 171, 175, 176, 177, 179, 180, 205, 262, 282, 300, 301, 302, 319, 333, 387, 398, 411, 437, 438
research 1, 3, 4, 6, 9, 11, 72–73, 81, 110, 114, 115, 117–124, 129, 134, 135, 136, 169, 204, 206, 207, 208, 209, 210, 246, 273, 276, 277, 390, 391
Retamar, Roberto Fernandez 55
Reznikoff, Charles 425
rhythm 14, 15, 43, 45, 46, 111, 187, 218, 219, 220, 221, 361, 369, 383
Ricardo, David 408
Rich, Andrew 273
Ricoeur, Paul 143, 145
Ride, Sally: first American woman in Space 277
risk 4, 11, 74, 88, 130, 138, 154, 180, 204, 206, 207, 210, 215, 302, 337, 394, 399, 402, 403
ritual 46, 58, 93, 157, 184, 246, 248, 249, 262, 301, 305, 307n1, 313, 315, 323, 347, 348, 368, 421, 422, 440
Roddick, Andy 337–338
Rodo, Jose Enrique 55
Rohr, Richard: *The Divine Dance* 149
Rokem, Freddie 129
Rosenlee, Li-Hsiang Lisa 349–350
Rousseau, J. -J. 167; *Confessions* 1953 365
Rublev, Andrei: icon of the Trinity 149
Ruest, Anselm 418
Ruhaniat Order 48
Rūmī, Jalāl al-Dīn 313; exposure to the *qutb* 315; *fanā* or annihilation 316; father of Mevlevi Order of Sufis 48; founder of the Mevlevi Order of Sufis. 51n6; inheritance of *gnostic*

experience 314; knowledge of jurisprudence (*fiqh*) 314; *Masnavi* 315; merit of his existence 316; nothingness of Being 314–315; received tradition of *fālsifah* 313; science of *ta'wil* 315; Şeb-iArus is yearly celebration of passing of 51n6; Shams al-Dīn Tabrīzī 315; Islamic law (*Sharīah*) 314; and visual art 314; Western philosophy 313
Russell, Wendy 77, 245
Ryall, Emily 245
Rygh, Andrea Csaszni 306

Sahabi Safa 42
Salazar Bondy, Augusto 90; Western/European thinking 90
Santanen, Sami 285
Santos, Milton 159; geography, an epistemology of existence 159–160; mixture of fear and fantasy 161; proliferation of fake news 161
Sartre, Jean-Paul 64; *Being and Nothingness* 320
Scarry, Elaine 282
Schechner, Richard 91, 94, 211, 249; aphorism 184; term performance as play 245
Schiller, Friedrich: "The Stage as a Moral Institution" 65
Schmidt, Theron 3
Schneider, Rebecca 183, 184; "affective transmissions" 184; logic of the archive 184; 'play' of appearance and disappearance 184; position 184, 185; sense of material reductionism 184; theory of disappearance 184
Schopenhauer, Arthur 63
Schuon, Frithjof 43
Schwartz, Wagner 159; capitalism and "primitivism/wilderness," relationship between 160; *Dominio Publico* 161; excerpt of *Transobjeto* 160; *La Bete* 160–161; *Wagner Ribot Pina Miranda Xavier Le Schwartz Transobjeto (2005)* 159
Schwarz, Roberto 91; project of modernity 91
Scribe, Eugène: *La Mansarde des artistes* 171
Şeb-iArus: yearly celebration of passing of Mevlana Jalaluddin Rūmī 51n6
Sefik Can: sheik of the Mevlevi Order 48
Segal, Arthur 418
Segal, Charles 22
Selee, Andrew: *What Should Think Tanks Do? A Strategy Guide to Policy Impact* 272
self-consciousness 84
self, re-telling: aspirations of abundance 267–269; biography and hagiography 266–267; end is always ob-scene 269; natural body 265–266; post-lineage yoga 265; yoga, performance, and practice (*see* yoga)
self-valorization: capitalism 405, 406; exploitation 406

sema (whirling ceremony) 51n6
Sequeira, Jessica 111, 114; *Other Paradises. Poetic Approaches to Thinking in a Technological Age* 111
sexuality: differences 57–58, 349–350, 401–403; eroticism 323–324; harassment 267, 303; objectification 54; reproduction, motherhood, pleasure, and desire 57
Shah, Rajni 223; radical equality 130
Shakespeare 65, 93, 391; *The Tempest* 53–59
Sharpe, Christina 58
Shaw, George Bernard 61, 63, 64, 65; boundary between theater and philosophy 61; "factory of thought" 62; "*I* am a philosopher" 64, 65
Shayne, Cameron 266
Sheddan, Susan 223
Sherrington, Sir Charles 196
Shestov, Lev 63
Sidney, Sir Philip 62, 65
silence 83, 102, 103, 135, 140, 208, 314, 345, 355
Silent University 275
Simondon, Gilbert 349
simultaneity/simultaneous 2, 3, 9, 15, 21, 22, 29, 71, 93, 102, 103, 175, 189, 209, 218, 220, 283, 326, 333, 369, 370, 392, 398, 416, 422, 432
Singer, Milton: "cultural performance" 94
singing 74, 75, 322
Singleton, Mark 264
Sinnerbrink, Robert 83; notion of 'cinematic thinking' 83
Smith, Adam 131, 408; *The Wealth of Nations* 410
smut 410–411
Sneak Attack By Roger ('SABR') 337
Soares, Elza: 'Mulher do Fim do Mundo' 95
social death 59n7
social media hermeneutics 412n1
Socrates 26–27, 42, 114; Agathon's house 22–24; *Apology* 24; as a form of philosophical interruption 26; gnothiseauton 327; ignorance *vs.* knowledge 26; learning as process of recollection 26; market square 391; notion of wisdom as knowledge of ignorance 22; odd behavior (*atopos,* or *atopia*) 23–24, 26; own 'private theatre' 28; performative philosophizing 21; philosophers 389; philosophical performances of 23, 24; piece of wisdom (*sophia*) 26; response to 'riddle' of Oracle 22; stage of the 'theatre of the world' 28; third demonstrative rejection of Agathon 26; transmission of knowledge and wisdom 26
Soldatenko, Gabriel 144
song 74, 80, 149, 150, 157, 158, 348, 383, 422, 425; *see also* singing
Sophocles 65; *Oedipus Tyrannus* 21–22
sound: disturbances and transmission events 104–105; end(s) of 103–106; "non-mental

particulars" 104; "particular individuals" 104; perception 105–106; performativity 104–106; sonic 49, 85n1, 102, 103, 104, 105, 106, 107, 208, 280, 283, 284, 430; sound events 104
Souriau, Etienne 166, 167
de Sousa Santos, Boaventura 94
sovereignty 11, 208
space (outer space) 416; SpaceDev 278; Space X 278
space/spatial: and censorship, geopolitics of 159–162; federal funding to NASA 278; of the *polis* 24; think tanks 278
space travel 276, 277, 278
spectacle 25, 117, 119, 123, 167, 179, 180, 185, 186, 187, 188, 190, 245, 323, 324, 392, 441
speech 23, 26, 55, 111, 118, 177, 199, 296, 314, 402, 434
speech act 98, 112, 402, 406
Spencer, Herbert 246
Spillers, Hortense 57; "one is neither female, nor male" 57
Spinoza, Baruch 425; *Ethics demonstrated in the geometric* 425
spirituality: movement and whirling 47–49; performance philosophy in makam 46–47; spirit 23, 48, 54, 63, 70, 89, 220, 251, 292, 293, 294, 305, 318, 336, 349, 405–408, 411, 418; Sufi philosophy 43–44; Tasawwuf 44–46; transcultural performance philosophy 49–50
Spitzer, Michael 97
sport 336
stage (theatre): doing aesthetics (*see* aesthetics); philosophy on stage 393–394; starting point 391–392
Stanislavski, Constantin 168, 169, 170; *modus operandi* 170
Stein, Gertrude: *Lectures in America* 259; notion of landscape plays 254, 259; theatrical structures 259; *Town Hall Meeting of the Air* 259–260
Steinbock, Anthony 197
Stiegler, Bernard 114; 'externalization' 115
Street, Anna 7, 129
Strindberg, August 62, 63
structuralism 50, 56, 88, 92, 110, 160, 207, 245, 325, 388, 389, 403
Stubenrauch, Herbert 210
subjectivity 70, 89, 102, 103, 104, 105, 106, 107, 159, 249, 250, 274, 276, 291, 320, 327, 373, 393, 403
'subtle body' 51n3
Sufi philosophy: concept of 'an intellect of the heart' 44; critiques of Western philosophy 43; Eurogenetic philosophy 43–44; feminine (mystical) principle 43; knowledges and intelligences of the heart 45; 'original Islam' 43; perennialist thought 50n1; sacred 43; Sufi *murid* 45–46; Sufism 42
sunyata, concept of 189
Sutton-Smith, B.: ludic performance theory 245
Sylvester, David 218
symbolic 57, 109, 110, 114, 119, 121, 143, 183, 188, 274, 304, 330, 334, 402, 405, 406, 409, 410, 412

tactility 280, 283; *see also* touch
Tanaka, Kikuko: *Poultry Paradise and Its Discontents: Nightshifts* exclaims plenarily: O! Faintest of hopes! 371
Tang dynasty 350
Taplin, Oliver 32n4
Tasawwuf or purity 44–46; emotional and mental bodies 44–45; Islamic expression of Sufism 51n2; *murid's* life 50
Tassi, Aldo 34
Tate Neighbours 275
Taylor, Mike: "affective disruption" 372–373; "compression techniques" 372; *IDEA MACHINE* 372–373, *373*; technique-testing processes 372
technology 91, 105, 106, 119, 161, 186, 187, 208, 261, 264, 268, 286, 348, 365, 372, 391, 408
tempo 78, 187
temporality 54, 62, 101, 105, 106, 183, 185, 187, 401
Theatre and Performance Studies 91, 128, 129
theatre: archive-based 177; citizen 177; 'classical paradigm' to 78–79, 80; crisis of political representation 179; definition of 167; documentary 177; dramatic forms 174; in European tradition 65; Konigstadter Theatre in Berlin 168; metaphorical implementations 175; National Theatre in London in 2018 84; peculiarity, singularity, and complexity 168; "post-dramatic" theatre 174, 175, 177; 'prohibition years' 178; 'spatial turn' 179; *Theater der Versammlung* (Theater of Assemblage) (TdV) 204; "theatre of ideas" 174; "theatrical turn" 174
theatricality 23, 27, 176, 178, 179, 376
theology 111, 140, 141, 409, 413n9
theory 6, 7, 8, 10, 11, 15, 57, 59n1, 70–72, 75n4, 98, 102, 103, 104, 105, 106, 110, 114, 129, 131, 132, 153, 162, 169, 170, 174, 182–185, 189, 190, 218, 245, 319, 320, 348, 350, 351, 365–377, 400, 402, 417, 419
The Theatre of Revolt (Brustein) 62
The Theatre of the Absurd (Beckett) 64
theatre-thinking: demanding professional recognition of the actor's role 171–172; essentialisation or instrumentalisation 167; as opposed to "thinking-theatre" 167–168; thinking the actor's craft from the stage 168–171

theatrophobia 179
Theatrum Mundi 376
therapy 148
Theravādin Buddhism: *ānāpānasati,* or Mindfulness of Breathing 37; *'Atthikāyo'* ('This is body!') 37–38; awareness or mindfulness *(sati)* 35–37; 'body memory' 37; 'bodymind' 40n3; *citekaggatā,* 'one-pointedness of mind' 39; continual cycle of conditioned existence *(samsāra)* 34; discourse and practice of *samatha* 39; emptiness of 'self' 39–40; forgetting of 'self,' and realisation of non-self 39; form of practice-based research 35; idea of *anattā* 34; idea of non-self or emptiness 34, 36, 37, 38; idea of 'self' 34; Imaginary Body and Psychological Gesture 39; *Kāyānupassanā,* or Mindfulness of Body 37; liberation *(nibbāna)* 34; *paramattha-sacca,* as 'ultimate' or 'absolute' truth 40; parts of the *Mahāsatipattāna Sutta* 34, 36, 38; place of emptiness *(sunyatā)* 36; practice of *satipatthāna* 38; processes of imagination and visualisation 38–39; process of 'unconcealment' 40; *sammuti-sacca,* as 'relative' or 'conventional' truth 40; Sole or Only Way *(ekayānomaggo)* 36; sutta (or sutra) 40n2; teaching *(dhamma)* 34; Three Characteristics of Existence 35
'thinking in action,' concept of 145
think tank: *And Beyond Institute for Future Research* (ABIFR) 276–277; in contemporary art practice – local, national and international 273; definition of 273; Institute for Human Activities (IHA) 273–275; intention of influencing public life 272; *Silent University* and *Our Neighbours* with *Tania Bruguera:* towards community 275–276; socially engaged practices 273; space think tanks 278; success of 274
Third Reich 418
Thoma, Dieter 204, 205
Thom, Paul: *For an Audience* 79
Thompson, James 299, 384
Thompson, Robert Farris 299
time: and space 23, 176; zone 388–389
Time and Narrative 145
Time Passes 261n3, 261n6; challenge of writing 257–259; fictional landscapes of Woolf 256, 257
touch: 'action' of piano 281; affective quality 284; connected with pleasure 282; elusive sonic quality 283–284; multiple fingers and notes 282; musical repetition 280–281; performance philosophy 285–286; pianist's touch 283–284; piano keyboard 280; poetic touch 284; repeated notes 281–282; repeated touch 280–283

Town Hall Meeting of the Air 259–260
trace 1, 6, 53, 56, 58, 59n2, 62, 63, 65, 92, 94, 107, 119, 121, 182, 183, 184, 189, 190, 191n2, 282, 313, 318, 319, 384, 418, 425, 433, 439
tragedy 22, 23, 141, 151, 179, 323, 382, 407
transcendence 24, 42, 45, 85, 115, 246, 316, 339, 343
transcultural performance philosophy: 'contemporary music' 49; forms of modernism and 'tradition' 49; 'free play of the imagination' 50; 'inter-' or 'transcultural' experiments 49; in 21st-century music and makam today 49–50; transcultural, definition 51n9
transdisciplinary 1, 4, 5, 88, 129, 205, 304
transformation 12, 14, 21, 26, 28, 44, 67, 74, 97, 107, 110, 113, 120, 131, 132, 174, 179, 184, 185, 248, 249, 250, 267, 268, 275, 348, 372, 373, 399
transgression/transgressive 21, 322, 323, 403
translation 5–6, 15, 40, 61, 92, 110, 113, 145, 176, 185, 215, 284, 313, 314, 331, 348, 399, 401, 435, 443
Trebitsch, Siegfried 61
Triau, Christophe 167, 168
Trinity: dance *(perichoresis)* 149–150; 'theory and praxis,' or 'thinking in action' 150
truth 24, 26, 28, 29, 31, 34, 36, 40, 42, 45, 47, 50, 66, 100, 107, 118, 119, 132, 166, 176, 177, 179, 180, 184, 296, 313, 315, 326, 329, 388, 389, 390, 394, 403, 410, 434
Tuck, Eve 58
Tupi tribes 89, 93
Turner, Victor 91

Ulysses 30
'uncanny,' phenomenon of 251n3
unconcealment 34, 40
under-world 24
universal 5, 22, 30, 42, 43, 45, 83, 93, 130, 143, 144, 145, 154, 179, 264, 265, 347, 348, 355, 381, 417
university 44, 61, 99–101, 204, 205, 206, 207, 210, 211, 215, 272, 289, 316, 419
unlearning 4, 128, 136

Valery, Paul 196
value(s) of philosophy of performance: dance and theatre 84–85; transcendent approach or "application" model 85
Vergunst, Jo 254
Vilar, Jean 169
Villiers, Andre: in *Vocabulaire d'esthetique* 167–168
Virgin Galactic 278
virtual 9, 98, 101, 102, 117, 161, 187, 189, 267, 284, 388, 405

visible 9, 15, 26, 29, 45, 119–120, 160; in Indian performance theory 182–190; and invisible, relationship between 183
Vladimir 66
voice 3, 6, 8, 12, 21, 27, 31, 39, 74, 85, 95n2, 100, 110, 111, 136, 138, 144, 156–159, 167, 177, 178, 215, 260, 273, 318, 333, 384, 385, 402, 430, 443
von Bingen, Hildegard 313
von Humboldt, Alexander 117, *118,* 120
vulnerability 48, 160, 204, 210, 215, 384, 394

Waldenfels, Bernhard 114, 290
Wallace, David Foster 336
walking 84, 254, 256, 324, 371, 398, 444
Warhol, Andy 175
Warner, Marina 57–58
Watzlawick, Paul 206
Weheliye, Alexander 155; concept of "humanity otherwise" 155; *Genres of the Human* conference 155
Weitz, Morris 77
West African dance: 'philosophies of beauty and ethics' 299
Western liberalism: concepts of the "human" 153
Western philosophy 13, 16n11; history of violence 142; rationalist thinking 141–142
whirling: act of 45; *axis mundae* 48; movement of rotation (like usul) 48
Whitehead, A.N. 389
Wilderson, Frank 56
Wilson, Robert: *The CIVIL warS* 176
wisdom: Agathon 26; condition of the soul 24; as knowledge of ignorance 22; the live love of wisdom 7–8; love of wisdom (philo-sophia) 130, 140–142; piece of wisdom *(sophia)* 26; transmission of knowledge and 26
Wittgenstein, Ludwig 77, 178; technology of text-montages 391
Wolfe, Patrick 56
Wollheim, Richard 79; *Art and its Objects* 78
women 16n10, 57, 58, 59n5, 91–95, 154, 260, 276, 278, 282, 305, 307, 333, 347, 349, 350, 397, 399, 400, 401, 403, 409, 412
wonder 74, 111, 112, 172, 175, 177, 196, 213, 296, 339, 372, 392, 393, 402, 419
Woolf, Virginia 254; anti-Cartesian readings 257; *Jacob's Room* 257; *To the Lighthouse* 257; *Mrs. Dalloway* 257; *Time Passes* 257–259; *The Waves* 257
World Philosophies 12, 140, 143–145, 147, 150
Wright, Jay 429, 430
Wylie, John 253
Wynter, Sylvia: critical dance studies 155; humanity, aesthetics, decoloniality, or feminism 154; knowledge must be rewritten 154; "No Humans Involved: An Open Letter to My Colleagues," 154; notion of deciphering practices 153–155; ontocentrism 155; reflections on the significance of 153–155; Renaissance and Enlightenment imaginary 154; scholarship 155

Xenophon: *Apology* 141

Yang, Wayne 58
Yeats, W.B. 63
yoga: Anusara Yoga system 265; ashrams and 264; Ashtanga Yoga 268; BKS Iyengar's 'Light on Yoga' 264; doubling of vision and visualisation 262; form and intention 262; gaze or *darśan* of guru 263; hagiography 267; Instagram and YouTube 266; modern postural yoga 263; *māyā and mokṣa* 268; neoliberalism 268; perfection and gaze 263–265; performance and practice 262–263; performance of immanent 268; physical and spiritual alignment 265; post-lineage 265; postural alignment 264; pre-modern yoga philosophers 263; schools of 264–265; sense of 'discipline' or 'deliberate connection' 262; shaktipat *(śaktipāta)* 267; social media 269; spaces of intimacy or isolation 264; Swami Sivananda 264; trade on aesthetic performance of unworldly practitioners 268
Yuk Hui 348

Zamir, Tzachi 130
Zea Aguilar, Leopoldo 90; Latin American identity 90
Zech, Paul 418
Zene, Cosimo 12
Zhang Zai 349
Ziehe, Thomas 210
Zupančič, Alenka 408–409